Simulation and Optimization in Finance

The Frank J. Fabozzi Series

Simulation and Optimization in Finance

Modeling with MATLAB, @RISK, or VBA

DESSISLAVA A. PACHAMANOVA
FRANK J. FABOZZI

WILEY

John Wiley & Sons, Inc.

Published by John Wiley & Sons, Inc., Hoboken, New Jersey.
Published simultaneously in Canada.

For general information on our other products and services or for technical support, please
contact our Customer Care Department within the United States at (800) 762-2974, outside
the United States at (317) 572-3993 or fax (317) 572-4002.

Wiley publishes in a variety of print and electronic formats and by print-on-demand. Some
material included with standard print versions of this book may not be included in e-books
or in print-on-demand. If this book refers to media such as a CD or DVD that is not included
in the version you purchased, you may download this material at http://booksupport.wiley.com.
For more information about Wiley products, visit www.wiley.com.

Library of Congress Cataloging-in-Publication Data:

Pachamanova, Dessislava A.
  Simulation and optimization in finance : modeling with MATLAB, @RISK, or VBA /
Dessislava A. Pachamanova, Frank J. Fabozzi.
      p. cm. – (Frank J. Fabozzi series ; 173)
  Includes index.
  ISBN 978-0-470-37189-3 (cloth); 978-0-470-88211-5 (ebk);
  978-0-470-88212-2 (ebk)
1. Finance–Mathematical models–Computer programs.   I. Fabozzi, Frank J.   II. Title.
HG106.P33 2010
332.0285′53–dc22   2010027038

10 9 8 7 6 5 4 3 2 1

Dessislava A. Pachamanova
To my husband, Christian, and my children,
Anna and Coleman

Frank J. Fabozzi
To my wife, Donna, and my children, Patricia,
Karly, and Francesco

Contents

Preface

Simulation and Optimization in Finance: Modeling with MATLAB, @RISK, or VBA is an introduction to two quantitative modeling tools—simulation and optimization—and their applications in financial risk management. In addition to laying a solid theoretical foundation and discussing the practical implications of applying simulation and optimization techniques, the book uses simulation and optimization as a means to clarify difficult concepts in traditional risk models in finance, and explains how to build financial models with software. The book covers a wide range of applications and is written in a theoretically rigorous way, which will make it of interest to both practitioners and academics. It can be used as a self-study aid by finance practitioners and students who have some fundamental background in calculus and statistics, or as a textbook in finance and quantitative methods courses. In addition, this book is accompanied by a web site where readers can go to download an array of supplementary materials. Please see the "Companion Web Site" section toward the end of this Preface for more details.

CENTRAL THEMES

Simulation and Optimization in Finance contains 18 chapters in five parts. Part One, Fundamental Concepts, provides background on the most important finance, simulation, optimization, and optimization under uncertainty concepts that are necessary to understand the financial applications in later parts of the book. Part Two, Portfolio Optimization and Risk Measures, reviews the theory and practice of equity and fixed income portfolio management, from classical frameworks, such as mean-variance optimization, to recent advances in the theory of risk measurement, such as value-at-risk and conditional value-at-risk estimation. Part Three, Asset Pricing Models, discusses classical static and dynamic models for asset pricing, such as factor models and different types of random walks. Part Four, Derivative Pricing and Use, introduces important types of financial derivatives, shows how their value can be determined by simulation, reviews advanced simulation methods for efficient implementation of pricing algorithms, and discusses how derivatives can be employed for portfolio risk management and return enhancement purposes. Part Five, Capital Budgeting Decisions, reviews capital budgeting decision models, including real options, and discusses applications of simulation and optimization in capital budgeting under uncertainty.

It is important to note that there often are multiple numerical methods that can be used to handle a particular problem in finance. Many of the topics listed here, especially asset and derivative pricing models, however, have traditionally been out of reach for readers without advanced degrees in mathematics because understanding the theory behind the models and the advanced methods for modeling requires years of training. Simulation and optimization formulations provide a framework within which very challenging concepts can be explained through simple visualization and hands-on implementation, which makes the material accessible to readers with little background in advanced mathematics.

SOFTWARE

In our experience, teaching and learning cannot be effective without examples and hands-on implementation. Most of the chapters in this book have "Software Hints" sections that explain how to use the applications under discussion. The examples themselves are posted on the companion web site discussed later in the Preface.

In *Simulation and Optimization in Finance,* we assume basic familiarity with spreadsheets and Microsoft Excel, and use two different platforms to implement concepts and algorithms: the Palisade Decision Tools Suite and other Excel-based software (@RISK[1], Solver[2], VBA[3]), and MATLAB[4]. Readers do not need to learn both; they can choose one or the other, depending on their level of familiarity and comfort with spreadsheet programs and their add-ins versus programming environments such as MATLAB. Specifically, users with finance and social science backgrounds typically prefer an Excel-based implementation, whereas users with engineering and quantitative backgrounds prefer MATLAB. Some tasks and implementations are easier in one environment than in the other, and students who have used this book in the form of lecture notes in the past have felt they benefitted from learning about both platforms. Basic introductions to the software used in the book are provided in Appendices B through D, which can be accessed at the companion web site.

Although Excel and other programs are used extensively in this book, we were wary of turning it into a software tutorial. Our goal was to combine concepts and tools for implementing them in an effective manner without necessarily covering every aspect of working in a specific software environment.

We have, of course, attempted to implement all examples correctly. That said, the code is provided "as is" and is intended only to illustrate the concepts in this book. Readers who use the code for financial decision making are doing so at their own risk. For full information on the terms of use of the code, please see the licensing information in each file on the companion web site.

The following web sites provide useful information about Palisade Decision Tools Suite and MATLAB. Readers can download trial versions or purchase the software.

- Palisade Decision Tools Suite, http://www.palisade.com
- MATLAB, http://www.mathworks.com

TEACHING

Simulation and Optimization in Finance: Modeling with MATLAB, @RISK, or VBA covers finance and applied quantitative methods theory, as well as a wide range of applications. It can be used as a textbook for upper-level undergraduate or lower-level graduate (such as MBA or Master's) courses in applied quantitative methods, operations research, decision sciences, or financial engineering, finance courses in derivatives, investments or corporate finance with an emphasis on modeling, or as a supplement in a special topics course in quantitative methods or finance. In addition, the book can be used as a self-study aid by students, or serve as a reference for student projects.

The book assumes that the reader has no background in finance or advanced quantitative methods except for basic calculus and statistics. Most quantitative concepts necessary for understanding the notation or applications are introduced and explained in endnotes, software hints, and online appendices. This makes the book suitable for readers with a wide range of backgrounds and particularly so as a textbook for classes with mixed audiences (such as engineering and business students). In fact, the idea for this book project matured after years of searching for an appropriate text for a course with a mixed audience that needed a good reference for both finance and quantitative methods topics.

Every chapter follows the same basic outline. The concepts are introduced in the main body of the chapter, and illustrations are provided. At the end of each chapter, there is a summary that contains the most important discussion points. A Software Hints section provides instructions and code for implementing the examples in the chapter with both Excel-based software and MATLAB.

On the companion web site, there are practice sections for selected chapters. These sections feature examples that complement those found in their respective chapters. Some practice sections contain cases as well. The cases are more in-depth exercises that focus on a particular practical application not necessarily covered in the chapter, but possible to address with the tools introduced in that chapter.

We recommend that before proceeding with the main body of this book, readers consult the four appendices on the companion web site, namely Appendix A, Basic Linear Algebra Concepts; Appendix B, Introduction to @RISK; Appendix C, Introduction to MATLAB; and Appendix D, Introduction to Visual Basic for Applications. They provide background on basic mathematical and programming concepts that enable readers to understand the implementation and the code provided in the Software Hints sections.

The chapters that introduce fundamental concepts all contain code that can be found on the companion web site. Some more advanced chapters do not; the idea is that at that point students are sufficiently familiar with the applications and models to put together examples on their own based on the code provided in previous chapters. The material in the advanced chapters can be used also as templates for student course projects.

A typical course may start with the material in Chapters 2 through 6. It can then cover the material in Chapters 7 through 9, which focus on applications of optimization for single-period optimal portfolio allocation and risk management. The course then proceeds with Chapters 11 through 14, which introduce static and dynamic asset pricing models through simulation as well as derivative pricing by simulation, and ends with Chapters 17 and 18, which discuss applications of simulation and optimization in capital budgeting. Chapters 10, 15, and 16 represent good assignments for final projects because they use concepts similar to other chapters, but in a different context and without as much implementation detail.

Depending on the nature of the course, only some of Chapters 2 through 6 will need to be covered explicitly; but the information in these chapters is useful in case the instructor would like to assign the chapters as reading for students who lack some of the necessary background for the course.

COMPANION WEB SITE

Additional material for *Simulation and Optimization in Finance* can be downloaded by visiting www.wiley.com/go/pachamanova. **Please log in to the web site using this password: finance123.** The files on this companion web site are organized in the following folders: Appendices, Code, and Practice. The Appendices directory contains Appendix A through D. The Practice directory contains practice problems and cases indexed by chapter. (Practice problems are present for Chapters 4–16, 18, and Appendix D, as a bonus to the content in the book. Please note, however, that only problems are offered without solutions.) The Code directory has Excel and MATLAB subdirectories that contain files for use with the corresponding software. The latter files are referenced in the main body of the book and the Software Hints sections for selected chapters.

The companion web site is a great resource for readers interested in actually implementing the concepts in the book. Such readers should begin by reading the applicable appendix on the companion web site with information about the software they intend to use, then read the main body of a chapter, the chapter's Software Hints, and, finally, the Excel model files or MATLAB code in the code directory on the companion web site.

NOTES

1. An Excel add-in for simulation.
2. An Excel add-in for optimization that comes standard with Excel.
3. Visual Basic for Applications—a programming language that can be used to automate tasks in Excel.
4. A programming environment for mathematical and engineering applications that provides users with tools for number array manipulation, statistical estimation, simulation, optimization, and others.

About the Authors

Dessislava A. Pachamanova is an Associate Professor of Operations Research at Babson College where she holds the Zwerling Term Chair. Her research interests lie in the areas of portfolio risk management, simulation, high-performance optimization, and financial engineering. She has published a number of articles in operations research, finance, and engineering journals, and coauthored the Wiley title *Robust Portfolio Optimization and Management* (2007). Dessislava's academic research is supplemented by consulting and previous work in the financial industry, including projects with quantitative strategy groups at WestLB and Goldman Sachs. She holds an AB in mathematics from Princeton University and a PhD in operations research from the Sloan School of Management at MIT.

Frank J. Fabozzi is Professor in the Practice of Finance in the School of Management at Yale University. Prior to joining the Yale faculty, he was a Visiting Professor of Finance in the Sloan School at MIT. Frank is a Fellow of the International Center for Finance at Yale University and on the Advisory Council for the Department of Operations Research and Financial Engineering at Princeton University. He is the editor of the *Journal of Portfolio Management* and an associate editor of the *Journal of Fixed Income*. He earned a doctorate in economics from the City University of New York in 1972. In 2002 was inducted into the Fixed Income Analysts Society's Hall of Fame and is the 2007 recipient of the C. Stewart Sheppard Award given by the CFA Institute. He earned the designation of Chartered Financial Analyst and Certified Public Accountant. He has authored and edited numerous books in finance.

Acknowledgments

In writing a book that covers such a wide range of topics in simulation, optimization, and finance, we were fortunate to have received valuable help from a number of individuals. The following people have commented on chapters or sections of chapters or provided helpful references and introductions:

- Anthony Corr, Brett McElwee, and Max Capetta of Continuum Capital Management
- Nalan Gulpinar of the University of Warwick Business School
- Craig Stephenson of Babson College
- Hugh Crowther of Crowther Investment, LLC
- Bruce Collins of Western Connecticut State University
- Pamela Drake of James Madison University

Zack Coburn implemented the VBA code for the Software Hints sections in Chapters 7 and 14. Christian Hicks helped with writing and testing some of the VBA code in the book, such as the VBA implementation of the American option pricing model with least squares in Chapter 14. Professor Mark Potter of Babson College allowed us to modify his case, "Reebok International: Strategic Asset Allocation," for use as an example in Chapter 17, and some of the ideas are based on case spreadsheet models further developed by Kathy Hevert and Richard Bliss of Babson College. Some of the cases and examples in the book are based on ideas and research by Thomas Malloy, Michael Allietta, Adam Bergenfield, Nick Kyprianou, Jason Aronson, and Rohan Duggal. The real estate valuation project example in section 18.6.3 in Chapter 18 is based on ideas by Matt Bujnicki, Matt Enright, and Alec Kyprianou.

We would also like to thank Wendy Gudgeon and Stan Brown from Palisade Software and Steve Wilcockson, Naomi Fernandes, Meg Vulliez, Chris Watson, and Srikanth Krishnamurthy of Mathworks for their help with obtaining most recent versions of the software used in the book and for additional materials useful for implementing some of the examples.

DESSISLAVA A. PACHAMANOVA
FRANK J. FABOZZI

CHAPTER 1

Introduction

Finance is the application of economic principles to decision making, and involves the allocation of money under conditions of uncertainty. Investors allocate their funds among financial assets in order to accomplish their objectives. Business entities and government at all levels raise funds by issuing claims in the form of debt (e.g., loans and bonds) or equity (e.g., common stock) and, in turn, invest those funds. Finance provides the framework for making decisions as to how those funds should be obtained and then invested.

The field of finance has three specialty areas: (1) capital markets and capital market theory, (2) financial management, and (3) portfolio management. The specialty field of *capital markets* and *capital market theory* focuses on the study of the financial system, the structure of interest rates, and the pricing of risky assets. *Financial management*, sometimes called *business finance*, is the specialty area of finance concerned with financial decision making within a business entity. Although we often refer to financial management as *corporate finance*, the principles of financial management also apply to other forms of business and to government entities. Moreover, not all nongovernment business enterprises are corporations. Financial managers are primarily concerned with investment decisions and financing decisions within business. Making investment decisions that involve long-term capital expenditures is called *capital budgeting*. *Portfolio management* deals with the management of individual or institutional funds. This specialty area of finance—also commonly referred to as *investment management, asset management*, and *money management*—involves selecting an investment strategy and then selecting the specific assets to be included in a portfolio.

A critical element common to all three specialty areas in finance is the concept of risk. Measuring and quantifying risk is critical for the fair valuation of an asset, the selection of capital budgeting projects in financial management, the selection of individual asset holdings, and portfolio construction in portfolio management. The field of *risk management* includes the identification, measurement, and control of risk in a business entity or a portfolio.

Sophisticated mathematical tools have been employed in order to deal with the risks associated with individual assets, capital budgeting projects, and selecting assets in portfolio construction. The use of such tools is now commonplace in the financial industry. For example, in portfolio management, practitioners run statistical routines to identify risk factors that drive asset returns, scenario analyses to evaluate the risk of their positions, and algorithms to find the optimal way to allocate assets or execute a trade.

This book focuses on two quantitative tools—optimization and simulation—and discusses their applications in finance. In this chapter, we briefly introduce these two techniques, and provide an overview of the structure of the book.

OPTIMIZATION

Optimization is an area in applied mathematics that, most generally, deals with efficient algorithms for finding an optimal solution among a set of solutions that satisfy given constraints. The first application of optimization in finance was suggested by Harry Markowitz in 1952, in a seminal paper that outlined his mean-variance optimization framework for optimal asset allocation. Some other classical problems in finance that can be solved by optimization algorithms include:

- Is there a possibility to make riskless profit given market prices of related securities? (This opportunity is called an *arbitrage opportunity* and is discussed in Chapter 13.)
- How should trades be executed so as to reach a target allocation with minimum transaction costs?
- Given a limited capital budget, which capital budgeting projects should be selected?
- Given estimates for the costs and benefits of a multistage capital budgeting project, at what stage should the project be expanded/abandoned?

Traditional optimization modeling assumes that the inputs to the algorithms are certain, but there is also a branch of optimization that studies the optimal decision under uncertainty about the parameters of the problem. Fast and reliable algorithms exist for many classes of optimization problems, and advances in computing power have made optimization techniques a viable and useful part of the standard toolset of the financial modeler.

SIMULATION

Simulation is a technique for replicating uncertain processes, and evaluating decisions under uncertain conditions. Perhaps the earliest application of simulation in finance was in financial management. Hertz (1964) argued that traditional valuation methods for investments omitted from consideration an important component: the fact that many of the inputs were inaccurate. He suggested modeling the uncertainty through probability-weighted scenarios, which would allow for obtaining a range of outcomes for the value of the investments and associated probabilities for each outcome. These ideas were forgotten for a while, but have experienced tremendous growth in the last two decades. Simulation is now used not only in financial management, but also in risk management and pricing of different financial instruments. In portfolio management, for example, the correlated behavior of different factors over time is simulated in order to estimate measures of portfolio risk. In pricing financial options or complex securities, such as mortgage-backed securities, paths for the underlying risk factors are simulated; and the fair price of the securities is estimated as the average of the discounted payoffs over those paths. We will see numerous examples of such simulation applications in this book.

Simulation bears some resemblance to an intuitive tool for modifying original assumptions in financial models—what-if analysis—which has been used for a long time in financial applications. In *what-if analysis*, each uncertain input in a model is assigned a range of possible values—typically, best, worst, and most likely value—and the modeler analyzes what happens to the decision under these scenarios. The important additional component in simulation modeling, however, is that there are probabilities associated with the different outcomes. This allows for obtaining an additional piece of information compared to what-if analysis: the probabilities that specific final outcomes will happen. Probability theory is so fundamental to understanding the nature of simulation analysis, that we include a chapter (Chapter 3) on the most important aspects of probability theory that are relevant for simulation modeling.

OUTLINE OF TOPICS

The book is organized as follows. Part One (Chapters 2 through 6) provides a background on the fundamental concepts used in the rest of the book. Part Two (Chapters 7 through 10) introduces the classical underpinnings of modern portfolio theory, and discusses the role of simulation and optimization in recent developments. Part Three (Chapters 11 and 12) summarizes important models for asset pricing and asset price dynamics. Understanding how to implement these models is a prerequisite for the material in Part Four (Chapters 13 through 16), which deals with the pricing of financial derivatives, mortgage-backed securities, advanced portfolio management, and advanced simulation methods. Part Five (Chapters 17 and 18) discusses applications of simulation and optimization in capital budgeting and real option valuation. The four appendices (on the companion web site) feature introductions to linear algebra concepts, @RISK, MATLAB, and Visual Basic for Applications in Microsoft Excel.

We begin by listing important finance terminology in Chapter 2. This includes basic theory of interest; terminology associated with equities, fixed income securities, and trading; calculation of rate of return; and useful concepts in fixed income, such as spot rates, forward rates, yield, duration, and convexity.

Chapter 3 is an introduction to probability theory, distributions, and basic statistics. We review important probability distributions, such as the normal distribution and the binomial distribution, measures of central tendency and variability, and measures of strength of codependence between random variables. Understanding these concepts is paramount to understanding the simulation models discussed in the book.

Chapter 4 introduces simulation as a methodology. We discuss determining inputs for and interpreting output from simulation models, and explain the methodology behind generating random numbers from different probability distributions. We also touch upon recent developments in efficient random number generation, which provides the foundation for the advanced simulation methods for financial derivative pricing discussed in Part Four of the book.

In Chapter 5 we provide a practical introduction to optimization. We discuss the most commonly encountered types of optimization problems in finance, and elaborate on the concept of "difficult" versus "easy" optimization problems. We introduce optimization duality and describe intuitively how optimization algorithms work. Illustrations of simple finance problems that can be handled with optimization techniques are provided, including examples of optimal portfolio allocation and cash flow matching from the field of portfolio management, and capital budgeting from the field of financial management. We also discuss dynamic programming—a technique for solving optimization problems over multiple stages. Multistage optimization is used in Chapters 13 and 18. Finally, we review available software for different types of optimization problems and portfolio optimization in particular.

Classical optimization methods treat the parameters in optimization problems as deterministic and accurate. In reality, however, these parameters are typically estimated through error-prone statistical procedures or based on subjective evaluation, resulting in estimates with significant estimation errors. The output of optimization routines based on poorly estimated inputs can be at best useless and at worst seriously misleading. It is important to know how to treat uncertainty in the estimates of input parameters in optimization problems. Chapter 6 provides a taxonomy of methods for optimization under uncertainty. We review the main ideas behind dynamic programming under uncertainty, stochastic programming, and robust optimization, and illustrate the methods with examples. We will encounter these methods in applications in Chapters 9, 13, 14, and 18.

Chapter 7 uses the concept of optimization to introduce the mean-variance framework that is the foundation of modern portfolio theory. We also present an alternative framework for optimal decision making in investments—expected utility maximization—and explain its relationship to mean-variance optimization.

Chapter 8 extends the classical mean-variance portfolio optimization theory to a more general mean-risk setting. We cover the most commonly used alternative risk measures that are generally better suited than variance for describing investor preferences when asset return distributions are skewed or fat-tailed. We focus on two popular portfolio risk measures—value-at-risk and conditional value-at-risk—and show how to estimate them using simulation. We also formulate the problems of optimal asset allocation under these risk measures using optimization.

Chapter 9 provides an overview of practical considerations in implementing portfolio optimization. We review constraints that are most commonly faced by portfolio managers, and show how to formulate them as part of optimization problems. We also show how the classical framework for portfolio allocation can be extended to include transaction costs, and discuss index tracking, optimization of trades across multiple client accounts, and robust portfolio optimization techniques to minimize estimation error.

While Chapter 9 focuses mostly on equity portfolio management, Chapter 10 discusses the specificities of fixed income (bond) portfolio management. Many of the same concepts are used in equity and fixed income portfolio management (which are defined in Chapter 2); however, fixed income securities have some fundamental differences from equities, so the concepts cannot always be applied in the same way in which they would be applied for stock portfolios. We review classical measures of bond portfolio risk, such as duration, key rate duration, and spread duration. We discuss bond portfolio optimization relative to a benchmark index. We also give examples of how optimization can be used in liability-driven bond portfolio strategies such as immunization and cash flow matching.

Chapter 11 transitions from the topic of portfolio management to the topic of asset pricing, and introduces standard financial models for explaining asset returns—the Capital Asset Pricing Model (CAPM), which is based on the mean-variance framework described in Chapter 7, the Arbitrage Pricing Theory (APT), and factor models. Such models are widely used in portfolio management—they not only help to model the processes that drive asset prices, but also substantially reduce the computational burden for statistical estimation and asset allocation optimization algorithms.

Chapter 12 focuses on dynamic asset pricing models, which are based on random processes. We examine the most commonly used types of random walks, and illustrate their behavior through simulation. The models discussed include arithmetic, geometric, different types of mean-reverting random walks, and more advanced hybrid models. In our presentation in the chapter, we assume that changes in asset prices happen at discrete time intervals. At the end of the chapter, we extend the concept of a random walk to a random process in continuous time.

The concepts introduced in Chapter 12 are reused multiple times when we discuss valuation of complex securities and multistage investments in Parts Four and Five of the book. The first chapter in Part Four, Chapter 13, is an introduction to the topic of financial derivatives. It lists the main classes of financial derivative contracts (futures and forwards, options, and swaps), explains the important concepts of arbitrage and hedging, and reviews classical methods for pricing derivatives, such as the Black-Scholes formula and binomial trees.

Chapter 14 builds on the material in Chapter 13, but focuses mainly on the use of simulation for pricing complex securities. Some of the closed-form formulas provided in Chapter 12 and the assumptions behind them become more intuitive when illustrated through simulation of the random processes followed by the underlying securities. A large part of the chapter is dedicated to variance reduction techniques, such as antithetic variables, stratified sampling, importance sampling, and control variates, as well as quasi–Monte Carlo methods. Such techniques are widely used today for efficient implementation of simulations for pricing securities and estimating sensitivity to different market factors. We provide specific examples of these techniques, and detailed VBA and MATLAB code to illustrate their implementation.

The numerical pricing methods in Chapter 15 are based on similar techniques to the ones discussed in Chapter 14, but the context is different. We introduce a complex type of fixed-income securities—mortgage-backed securities—and discuss in detail a part of the simulation that is specific to fixed-income securities—generating scenarios for future interest rates and the entire yield curve.

Chapter 16 builds on Chapters 7, 8, 9, 13, and 14, and contains a discussion of how derivatives can be used for portfolio risk management and return enhancement strategies. Simulation is essential for estimating the risk of a portfolio that contains complex financial instruments, but the process can be very slow in the case of large portfolios. We highlight some numerical issues, standard simulation algorithms, and review methods that have been suggested for reducing the computational burden.

Chapters 17 and 18 cover a different area of finance—financial management—but they provide useful illustrations for the difference applying simulation and optimization makes in classical finance decision-making frameworks. Chapter 17 begins with a review of so-called discounted cash flow (DCF) methodologies for evaluating company investment projects. It then discusses (through a case study) how simulation can be used to estimate stand-alone risk and enhance the analysis of such projects.

Chapter 18 introduces the real options framework, which advocates for accounting for existing options in project valuation. (The DCF analysis ignores the potential flexibility in projects—it assumes that there will be no changes once a decision is made.) While determining the inputs for valuation of real options presents significant challenges, the actual techniques for pricing these real options are based on the techniques for pricing financial options introduced in Chapters 13 and 14. Simulation and multistage optimization can again be used as valuable tools in this new context.

Fundamental Concepts

CHAPTER 2

Important Finance Concepts

This chapter reviews important finance concepts that are used throughout the book. We discuss the concepts of the time value of money, different asset classes, basic trading terminology, calculation of rate of return, valuation, and advanced concepts in fixed income, such as duration, convexity, key rate duration, and total return.

2.1 BASIC THEORY OF INTEREST

One of the most fundamental concepts in finance is the concept of the time value of money. A specific amount of money received today does not have the same nominal value in the future because of the possibility of investing the money today and earning interest. This section explains the rules for computing interest, and outlines the basic elements of dealing with cash flows obtained today and in the future. These concepts will reappear many times throughout the book—they are critical for pricing financial instruments and making investment decisions.

2.1.1 Compound Interest

Most bank accounts, loans, and investments interest calculations utilize some form of compounding. Simply put, *compound interest* involves interest on interest. Let us explain the concept with an example. If you deposit $100 in a bank deposit that pays 3% per year, at the end of the year you will have $103. Suppose you keep the money in the bank for a second year, again at 3% interest. Compound interest means that the interest during the second year will be accrued on the entire amount you have in the bank at the end of the first year—not only on your original deposit of $100, but also on the interest accrued during the first year. Therefore, at the end of the second year you will have

$$\$103 + 0.03 \cdot \$103 = \$106.09$$

If there was no compounding, you would have an additional $3 at the end of the first year, and again at the end of the second year, that is, the total amount in your account at the end of the second year would be $106.00. In general, the formula for computing the future value of an initial capital C invested for n years at interest rate r per year (compounded annually) is

$$C \cdot (1 + r)^n$$

In our example, computing the interest with and without compounding made a difference of 9 cents. The effect of compounding on the investment, however, can be substantial, especially over a long time horizon. For example, you can verify that if you invest $\$C$ at an interest rate of 7% per year with annual compounding, your investment will double in size in approximately 10 years. This increase is significantly larger than if interest is not compounded, that is, if you simply add the interest on the original investment over the 10 years. (The latter would be $10 \cdot 0.07 = 0.70$, or 70% increase in the original investment.)

Interest does not necessarily need to be compounded once per year—it can be compounded daily, monthly, quarterly, continuously. Usually, however, the interest rate r is still quoted as an annual rate. For example, with quarterly compounding, an interest of $r/4$ is accrued each quarter on the amount at the beginning of the quarter. At the end of the first quarter, the original amount C grows to $C \cdot (1 + r/4)$. At the end of the second quarter, the amount becomes $(C \cdot (1 + r/4) \cdot (1 + r/4))$. At the end of the first year, the total amount in the account is $C \cdot (1 + r/4)^4$. After n years, $\$C$ of initial capital grows to

$$C \cdot (1 + r/4)^{4 \cdot n}.$$

In general, if the frequency of compounding is m times per year at an annual (called *nominal*) rate r, the amount at the end of n years will be

$$C \cdot (1 + r/m)^{m \cdot n}.$$

The *effective* annual rate is the actual interest rate that is paid over the year, that is, the rate r_{eff} so that

$$C \cdot (1 + r/m)^m = C \cdot (1 + r_{\text{eff}}).$$

So, for example, if there is quarterly compounding and the nominal annual rate is 3%, the effective interest rate is

$$r_{\text{eff}} = (1 + 0.03/4)^4 - 1 = 0.0303 = 3.03\%.$$

Again, the difference between the nominal and the effective annual rate does not seem that large (only 0.03%); however, the difference increases with the frequency of compounding.

Suppose now that we divide the year into very, very small time intervals. You can think of compounding interest every millisecond. So, the number m in the expression for computing the compound interest rate becomes so large, it can be considered infinity. It turns out that when m tends to infinity, the expression $(1 + r/m)^m$ tends to a very specific number, e^r, where the number e has the value 2.7182 ... (it has infinitely many digits after the decimal point).[1]

Therefore, with continuous compounding, $C of initial capital becomes $C \cdot e^{r \cdot 1}$ at the end of the first year, $C \cdot e^{r \cdot 2}$ at the end of the second year, and $C \cdot e^{r \cdot n}$ after n years. If we are interested in the amount of capital after, say five months, and we are given the nominal interest rate r as an annual rate, we first convert five months to years (five months = 5/12 years), and then compute the future amount of capital as $C \cdot e^{r \cdot (5/12)}$.

Let us provide a concrete example. If the nominal interest rate is 3% per year and we invest $100, then with continuous compounding the amount at the end of the first year is $100 \cdot e^{0.03 \cdot 1} = \$103.05$. Therefore, the effective annual rate is 3.05%—higher than the effective annual rate of 3.03% with quarterly compounding we computed earlier. After five months, the amount in the account will be $100 \cdot e^{0.03 \cdot (5/12)} = \$101.26$.

2.1.2 Present Value and Future Value

In the previous section, we explained the concept of interest. Suppose you have $100 today, and you put it in a savings account paying 3% interest per year. At the end of the year, your $100 will become $103. Now suppose that somebody gives you a choice between receiving $100 today, or $100 one year from now. The two options would not be equivalent to you. Given the opportunity to invest the money at 3% interest, you would demand $103 one year from now to make you indifferent between the two options. In this example, the $103 received at the end of the year can be considered the future value of $100 received today, whereas $100 is the present value of $103 received one year from now. This is the important concept of the time value of money—money to be received in the future is less valuable than the same nominal amount of money received immediately.

Formally, the *present value* (sometimes also called the *discounted value*) of a single cash flow *CF* is the amount of money that must be invested today to generate the future cash flow. The present value of a cash flow depends on (1) the length of time until the cash flow will be received, and (2) the interest rate, which is called the *discount rate* in this context.

The present value (PV) of a cash flow CF received n years from now when the interest rate r is compounded annually is computed as

$$PV(CF) = \frac{CF}{(1 + r)^n}.$$

The expression

$$\frac{1}{(1 + r)^n}$$

is called the *discount factor*. The discount factor (let us call it d_n) is the number by which we need to multiply the future cash flow to obtain its present value. Note that the discount factor is a number less than 1—the present value of the cash flow is less than the future value in nominal terms because it is assumed that the interest accrued between the present and the future date will be a nonnegative amount.

The conversion between present and future value follow the interest calculation rules we introduced in the previous section. For example, if the annual interest rate r is continuously compounded, the present value of a cash flow CF received n years from now is

$$PV(CF) = \frac{CF}{e^{r \cdot n}} = CF \cdot e^{-r \cdot n}.$$

In this case, the discount factor is $d_n = e^{-r \cdot n}$.

It is easy to see how the concepts of present and future value extend when the "present" is not today's date. For example, suppose that we have invested \$100 today for three years in an account paying an annual rate of 3% compounded continuously. At the end of year 1, we will have \$100 $\cdot$ $e^{0.03 \cdot 1}$ = \$103.05 in the account. At the end of year 2, we will have \$100 $\cdot$ $e^{0.03 \cdot 2}$ = \$106.18 in the account. The amounts \$103.05 and \$106.18 are the future values of \$100 on hand today, in year 1 and year 2 dollars.

The present values of \$103.05 received at the end of year 1 and \$106.18 received at the end of year 2 are both \$100 (\$103.05 $\cdot$ $e^{-0.03 \cdot 1}$ and \$106.18 $\cdot$ $e^{-0.03 \cdot 2}$, respectively). Note that we can compute the present value of \$106.18 received at the end of year 2 in two ways. The first is to discount directly to the present, \$106.18 $\cdot$ $e^{-0.03 \cdot 2}$. The second is to discount \$106.18 first to its present value in year 1 dollars (\$106.18 $\cdot$ $e^{-0.03 \cdot 1}$ = \$103.05), and then discount the year 1 dollars to today dollars (\$103.05 $\cdot$ $e^{-0.03 \cdot 1}$ = \$100.00). The latter technique will be useful when pricing financial derivatives and real options are discussed in Chapters 13 through 16 and Chapter 18.

2.2 ASSET CLASSES

An *asset* is any possession that has value in an exchange. Assets can be classified as tangible or intangible. A tangible asset's value depends on particular physical properties of the asset. Buildings, land, and machinery are examples of tangible assets. Intangible assets, by contrast, represent legal claims to some future benefit and their value bears no relation to the form, physical or otherwise, in which the claims are recorded. Financial assets, financial instruments, or securities are intangible assets. For these instruments, the typical future benefit comes in the form of a claim to future cash.

In most developed countries, the four major asset classes are (1) common stocks, (2) bonds, (3) cash equivalents, and (4) real estate. An asset class is defined in terms of the investment attributes that the members of an asset class have in common. These investment characteristics include (1) the major economic factors that influence the value of the asset class and, as a result, correlate highly with the returns of each member included in the asset class; (2) have a similar risk and return characteristic; and (3) have a common legal or regulatory structure. Based on this way of defining an asset class, the correlation between the returns of different asset classes would be low.

The preceding four major asset classes can be extended to create other asset classes. From the perspective of a U.S. investor, for example, the four major asset classes listed earlier have been expanded as follows by separating foreign securities from U.S. securities: (1) U.S. common stocks, (2) non–U.S. (or foreign) common stocks, (3) U.S. bonds, (4) non-U.S. bonds, (5) cash equivalents, and (6) real estate.

Common stocks and bonds are further partitioned into more asset classes. For example, U.S. common stocks (also referred to as U.S. *equities*), are differentiated based on market capitalization. *Market capitalization* (or *market cap*) is computed as the number of shares outstanding times the market price per share. The term is often used as a proxy for the size of a company. Companies are usually classified as *large cap*, *medium cap (mid-cap)*, *small cap*, or *micro cap*, depending on their market capitalization. The division is somewhat arbitrary, but generally, micro-cap companies have a market capitalization of less than $250 million, small-cap companies have a market capitalization between $250 million and $1 billion, mid-cap companies have market capitalization between $1 billion and $5 billion, and large-cap companies have market capitalization of more than $5 billion. Companies that have market capitalization of more than $250 billion are sometimes referred to as *mega-caps*.

With the exception of real estate, all of the asset classes we have previously identified are referred to as *traditional asset classes*. Real estate and all other asset classes that are not in the preceding list are referred to as *nontraditional asset classes* or *alternative asset classes*. They include hedge funds, private equity, and commodities.

Along with the designation of asset classes comes a barometer to be able to quantify the performance of the asset class—the risk, return, and the correlation of the return of the asset class with that of another asset class. The barometer is called a *benchmark index*, *market index*, or simply *index*. An example would be the Standard & Poor's 500. We describe more indexes in later chapters. The indexes are also used by investors to evaluate the performance of professional managers whom they hire to manage their assets.

2.2.1 Equities

Most generally, *equity* means ownership in a corporation in the form of common stock. *Common stock* is securities that entitle the holder to a share of a company's success through dividends and/or capital appreciation, and provide voting rights in a company. The terms "equities" and "stocks" are often used interchangeably.

A *dividend* is a payment (usually, quarterly) disbursed by a company to its shareholders out of the company's current or retained earnings. Dividends can be given as cash (*cash dividends*), additional stock (*stock dividends*), or other property. Dividends are usually paid out by companies that have reached their growth potential, so they cannot benefit by reinvesting their earnings into further expansion.

Capital appreciation refers to the growth in a stock price. Because of capital appreciation, investors can make money by investing in a company that is still in its growth phase, even if the company does not pay dividends.

2.2.2 Fixed Income Securities

In its simplest form, a fixed income security is a financial obligation of an entity that promises to pay a specified sum of money at specified future dates. The entity that promises to make the payment is called the *issuer* of the security. Some examples of issuers are central governments such as the U.S. government and the French government, government-related agencies of a central government such as Fannie Mae and Freddie Mac in the United States, a municipal government such as the state of New York in the United States and the city of Rio de Janeiro in Brazil, a corporation such as Coca-Cola in the United States and Yorkshire Water in the United Kingdom, and supranational governments such as the World Bank.

Fixed income securities fall into two general categories: debt obligations and preferred stock. In the case of a debt obligation, the issuer is called the *borrower*. The investor who purchases such a fixed income security is said to be the *lender* or *creditor*. Debt obligations are virtually loans with interest, where the interest is paid over time in the form of coupons. The promised payments that the issuer agrees to make at the specified dates consist of two components: interest and principal payments. (The principal represents repayment of the funds borrowed at the end, that is, at the *maturity date* for the debt obligation.) Fixed income securities that are debt obligations include *bonds, asset-backed securities* (ABSs), and *bank loans.* Bonds are basically loans taken out by corporations, government entities, or municipalities. Bank loans are loans by banks to companies or individuals. ABSs are securities backed by pools of loans—mortgages or assets (e.g., cars). The assets in ABS pools are typically too small or illiquid to be sold individually. Pooling the assets allows them to be sold in pieces to investors, a process known as *securitization*. The largest number of ABSs by far are backed by pools of mortgages, and are referred to as *mortgage-backed securities* (MBSs). We will discuss MBSs, ABSs, and securitization in more detail in Chapter 15.

In contrast to a fixed income security that represents a debt obligation, *preferred stock* represents an ownership interest in a corporation. Dividend payments are made to the preferred stockholder and represent a distribution of the corporation's profit. Unlike investors who own a corporation's common stock, investors who own the preferred stock can only realize a contractually fixed dividend payment. Moreover, the payments that must be made to preferred stockholders have priority over the payments that a corporation pays to common stockholders. In the case of the bankruptcy of a corporation, preferred stockholders are given preference over common stockholders. Consequently, preferred stock is a form of equity that has characteristics similar to bonds.

Prior to the 1980s, fixed income securities were simple investment products. Holding aside default by the issuer, the investor knew how long interest would be received and when the amount borrowed would be repaid. Moreover, most investors purchased these securities with the intent of holding them to their maturity date. Beginning in the 1980s, the fixed income world changed. First, fixed income securities became more complex. There are features in many fixed income securities that make it difficult to determine when the amount borrowed will be repaid and for how long interest will be received. For some securities it is difficult to determine the amount of interest that will be received. Second, the hold-to-maturity investor was replaced by institutional investors who actively trade fixed income securities.

In this book, we will often use the terms "fixed income securities" and "bonds" interchangeably. Next, we introduce various features of fixed income securities, and explain how these features affect the risks associated with investing in fixed income securities. This introduction is only cursory. For an in-depth overview of fixed income products, we refer the reader to Fabozzi (2007).

The *term to maturity* of a bond is the number of years the debt is outstanding or the number of years remaining prior to final principal payment. The *maturity date* of a bond refers to the date that the debt will cease to exist, at which time the issuer will redeem the bond by paying the outstanding balance.

The *par value* of a bond is the amount that the issuer agrees to repay the bondholder at or by the maturity date. This amount is also referred to as the *principal value, face value, redemption value*, and *maturity value*.

Because bonds can have a different par value, the practice is to quote the price of a bond as a percentage of its par value. A value of 100 means "100% of par value." For example, if a bond has a par value of $1,000 and the issue is selling for $900, this bond would be said to be selling at 90. If a bond is quoted at 103 19/32 and has a par value of $1 million, then the dollar price is $(103.59375/100) \times \$1,000,000 = \$1,035,937.50$.

A bond may trade above or below its par value. When a bond trades below its par value, it is said to be *trading at a discount*. When a bond trades above its par value, it is said to be *trading at a premium*.

The *coupon rate*, which is also called the *nominal rate*, is the interest rate the issuer agrees to pay each year. The annual amount of the interest payment made to bondholders during the term of the bond is called the *coupon*. The coupon is calculated by multiplying the coupon rate by the par value of the bond. In other words,

$$\text{Coupon} = (\text{Coupon rate}) \cdot (\text{Par value})$$

For example, a bond with a 5% coupon rate and a par value of $1,000 will pay annual interest of $50 ($=0.05 \cdot \$1,000$).

In the United States, the usual practice is for the issuer to pay the coupon in two semiannual installments. Mortgage-backed securities and asset-backed securities typically pay interest monthly. For bonds issued in some markets outside the United States, coupon payments are made only once per year.

Not all bonds make periodic coupon payments. For example, *zero-coupon bonds* do not pay out coupons during the life of the bond. The holder of a zero-coupon bond realizes interest by buying the bond substantially below its par value (i.e., buying the bond at a discount). Interest is then paid at the maturity date, where the interest is the difference between the par value and the price paid for the bond.

In addition, the coupon rate on a bond need not be fixed over the bond's life. *Floating-rate securities*, sometimes also called *floaters* or *variable-rate securities*, have coupon payments that reset periodically according to some reference rate. The typical formula (called the *coupon formula*) on certain determination dates when the coupon rate is reset is as follows:

$$\text{Coupon rate} = (\text{Reference rate}) + (\text{Quoted margin})$$

The quoted margin is the additional amount that the issuer agrees to pay above the reference rate. For example, suppose that the reference rate is the 1-month London interbank offer rate (LIBOR).[2] Suppose that the quoted margin is 100 basis points.[3] Then the coupon formula is

$$\text{Coupon rate} = (\text{1-month LIBOR}) + (\text{100 basis points})$$

An example of a floating rate security is an *inflation-linked* (or *inflation-indexed*) bond. For example, in 1987, the U.S. Department of Treasury began issuing inflation-adjusted securities referred to as *Treasury Inflation Protection Securities* (TIPS). The reference rate for the coupon formula is the rate of inflation as measured by the Consumer Price Index for All Urban Consumers (called CPI-U). Corporations and agencies in the United States also issue inflation-linked bonds. For example, in February 1997, J.P. Morgan & Company issued a 15-year bond that pays the CPI plus 400 basis points.

A floater may have a restriction on the maximum or minimum coupon rate that will be paid at any reset date. The maximum (respectively, the minimum) coupon rate is called a *cap* (respectively, a *floor*).

Typically, the coupon formula for a floater is such that the coupon rate increases when the reference rate increases, and decreases when the reference rate decreases. However, there are issues whose coupon rate moves in the opposite direction from the change in the reference rate. Such issues are called *inverse floaters* or *reverse floaters*. Such securities give and investor who believes that interest rates will decline the opportunity to obtain a higher coupon interest rate.[4]

Accrued Interest   Bond issuers do not disburse coupon interest payments every day. Instead, payments are made at prespecified dates. (As we mentioned earlier, in the United States, for example, coupon interest is typically paid every six months.) Thus, if an investor sells a bond between coupon payments and the buyer holds it until the next coupon payment, then the entire coupon interest earned for the period will be paid to the buyer of the bond since the buyer will be the holder of record. The seller of the bond gives up the interest from the time of the last coupon payment to the time until the bond is sold. The amount of interest over this period that will be received by the buyer even though it was earned by the seller is called *accrued interest*.

In the United States and in many countries, the bond buyer must pay the bond seller the accrued interest. The amount that the buyer pays the seller is the agreed upon price for the bond plus accrued interest. This amount is called the *full price*. (Some market participants refer to this as the *dirty price*.) The agreed upon bond price without accrued interest is simply referred to as the *price*. (Some refer to it as the *clean price*.)

There are exceptions to the rule that the bond buyer must pay the bond seller accrued interest. The most important exception is when the issuer has not fulfilled their promise to make the periodic interest payments. In this case, the issuer is said to be *in default*. In such instances, the bond is sold without accrued interest and is said to be *traded flat*.

Provisions for Paying Off Bonds   The most common structure in the United States and Europe for paying off the principal for both corporate and government bonds is to pay the entire amount in one lump sum payment at the maturity date. Such bonds are said to have a *bullet maturity*.

Fixed income securities backed by pools of loans, such as MBSs and ABSs, often have a schedule of partial principal payments. Such fixed income securities are said to be *amortizing securities*. For many loans, the payments are structured so that when the last loan payment is made, the entire amount owed is fully paid.

An issue may have a *call provision* granting the issuer the option to retire (pay off) all or part of the issue prior to the stated maturity date. Some issues specify that the issuer must retire a predetermined amount of the issue periodically.

Conversion Privilege   A *convertible bond* is an issue that grants the bondholder the right to convert the bond for a specified number of shares of common stock. Such a feature allows the bondholder to take advantage of favorable movements in the price of the issuer's common stock. An *exchangeable bond* allows the bondholder to exchange the issue for a specified number of shares of common stock of a corporation different from the issuer of the bond.

Currency Denomination   The payments that the issuer makes to the bondholder can be in any currency. For example, an issue in which payments to bondholders are in U.S. dollars is called a *dollar-denominated issue*. However, nothing prevents the issuer from making payments in different currencies. In fact, there can be issues whose coupon payments are in one currency and whose principal payment is in another. Issues with this characteristic are called *dual-currency issues*.

Embedded Options Some bonds have embedded options granted to the issuers or the bondholders. Options granted to issuers may include, for example, the right to call the issue (i.e., to pay the issue in full before the maturity date). As we mentioned earlier in this section, such bonds are referred to as *callable bonds*. Options granted to bondholders may include a conversion privilege, or a right to put the issue (i.e., demand immediate payment of the remaining principal). The latter option has value when interest rates rise above the issue's coupon rate because the bondholder is better off investing his money elsewhere. We will discuss financial options in more detail in Chapters 13 through 16.

It is important to note whether a bond has embedded options because those options change a bond's characteristics and value. As we will see in section 2.5, estimating the fair price of a bond requires projecting its cash flows between now and its maturity. These cash flows and their timing are influenced by the existence of options.

Credit Risk Investing in fixed income securities exposes investors to *credit risk*. While investors commonly refer to credit risk as if it is one dimensional, there are actually three forms of this risk: default risk, credit spread risk, and downgrade risk.

Default risk is the risk that the issuer will fail to satisfy the terms of the obligation with respect to the timely payment of interest and repayment of the amount borrowed. To gauge credit default risk, investors rely on analysis performed by nationally recognized statistical rating organizations (that is, more popularly known as rating agencies) that perform credit analysis of bond issues and issuers and express their conclusions in the form of a *credit rating*. The three major rating agencies are Moody's, Standard & Poor's, and Fitch, and their bond rating systems are summarized in Exhibit 2.1. Bond issues that are assigned a rating in the top four categories in the exhibit are referred to as *investment-grade bonds*. Bond issues that carry a rating below the top four categories are referred to as *noninvestment-grade bonds*, or more popularly as *high-yield bonds* or *junk bonds*. Thus, the bond market can be divided into two sectors: the *investment-grade sector* and the *noninvestment-grade sector*. *Distressed debt* is a subcategory of noninvestment-grade bonds. These bonds may be in bankruptcy proceedings, may be in default of coupon payments, or may be in some other form of

EXHIBIT 2.1 Bond ratings systems of Moody's, Standard & Poor's, and Fitch credit rating agencies.

Moody's	S&P	Fitch	Summary Description
Investment Grade—High-Credit Worthiness			
Aaa	AAA	AAA	Prime, maximum safety
Aa1	AA+	AA+	
Aa2	AA	AA	High-grade, high-credit quality
Aa3	AA–	AA–	
A1	A+	A+	
A2	A	A	Upper-medium grade
A3	A–	A–	
Baa1	BBB+	BBB+	
Baa2	BBB	BBB	Lower-medium grade
Baa3	BBB–	BBB–	
Speculative—Lower-Credit Worthiness			
Ba1	BB+	BB+	
Ba2	BB	BB	Low-grade, speculative
Ba3	BB–	BB–	
B1		B+	
B2	B	B	Highly speculative
B3		B–	
Predominantly Speculative, Substantial Risk, or in Default			
Caa	CCC+	CCC+	Substantial risk, in poor standing
	CCC	CCC	
Ca	CC	CC	May be in default, very speculative
C	C	C	Extremely speculative
	CI		Income bonds, no interest being paid
		DDD	
	D	DD	Default
		D	

distress. Historically, U.S. Treasuries are not rated because they are viewed as default-free.

Credit spread is the premium over the government or risk-free rate required by the market for taking on a certain assumed credit exposure. The benchmark is often a U.S. Treasury issue for the given maturity. Typically, if all other factors are held constant, the higher the credit rating, the smaller the credit spread to the benchmark rate. *Credit spread risk*, the second type of credit risk, is the risk of financial loss resulting from changes in the level of credit spreads used in the marking-to-market of a debt instrument. Changes in market credit spreads affect the value of the portfolio and can lead to losses for traders or underperformance relative to a benchmark for portfolio managers.

As just explained, investors gauge the credit default risk of an issue by looking at the credit ratings assigned to issues by the rating agencies. Once a credit rating is assigned to a debt obligation, a rating agency monitors the credit quality of the issuer and can reassign a different credit rating. An improvement in the credit quality of an issue or issuer is rewarded with a better credit rating, referred to as an *upgrade*; a deterioration in the credit rating of an issue or issuer is penalized by the assignment of an inferior credit rating, referred to as a *downgrade*. The actual or anticipated downgrading of an issue or issuer increases the credit spread and results in a decline in the price of the issue or the issuer's bonds. This type of risk is called *downgrade risk*, and is closely related to credit spread risk. A rating agency may announce in advance that it is reviewing a particular credit rating, and may go further and state that the review is a precursor to a possible downgrade or upgrade. This announcement is referred to as *putting the issue under credit watch*. The rating agencies periodically publish, in the form of a table, information about how issues that they have rated have changed over time. This table is called a *rating migration table* or *rating transition table*. The table is useful for investors to assess potential downgrades and upgrades.

2.3 BASIC TRADING TERMINOLOGY

In this book, we use basic terminology associated with buying and selling securities. This section briefly explains some important trading terminology.

2.3.1 Borrowing Funds to Purchase Securities

Often, investors borrow funds to purchase securities. Such investment strategies are known as *leveraged strategies*. The expectation is that the money earned by investing in the securities purchased with the borrowed funds will exceed the borrowing cost. There are several sources of funds available to an investor when borrowing funds. When securities are purchased with borrowed funds, the most common practice is to use the securities as collateral for the loan. In such instances, the transaction is referred to as a *collateralized loan.* Two collateralized borrowing arrangements are used by investors: margin buying and repurchase agreements.

Margin Buying   In a margin buying arrangement, the funds borrowed to buy the securities are provided by the broker and the broker gets the money from a bank. The interest rate banks charge brokers for these transactions is called the *call money rate* (or *broker loan rate*). The broker charges the investor the call money rate plus a service charge. In the United States, the Securities and Exchange Act of 1934 prohibits brokers from lending more than a specified percentage of the market value of the securities.

Margin buying is the most common collateralized borrowing arrangement for common stock investors—both individual (retail) investors and institutional investors—and retail bond investors. It is not as common for bond institutional investors.

Repurchase Agreement   The collateralized borrowing arrangement used by institutional investors in the bond market is the repurchase agreement. A *repurchase agreement* is the sale of a security with a commitment by the seller to buy the same security back from the purchaser at a specified price at a designated future date. The *repurchase price* is the price at which the seller and the buyer agree that the seller will repurchase the security on a specified future date called the *repurchase date*. The difference between the repurchase price and the sale price is the dollar interest cost of the loan. Based on the dollar interest cost, the sales price, and the length of the repurchase agreement, and implied interest rate can be computed. This implied interest rate is called the *repo rate*. The advantage to the investor of using this borrowing arrangement is that the interest rate is less than the cost of bank financing. When the term of the loan is one day, it is called an *overnight repo* (or *overnight RP*); a loan for more than one day is called a *term repo* (or *term RP*). The repo rate varies from transaction to transaction depending on a variety of factors.

2.3.2 Long and Short Positions

When an investor takes a position in the market by buying a security, the investor is said to be in a *long position* in the security. Obviously, the investor gains from a long position if the security's price increases after the purchase.

When an investor borrows a security from a broker and sells it, with the understanding that the security must be returned later, the investor is said to be taking a *short position* in the security (or selling it short). Short-selling strategies are useful if the investor believes that the price of the security will fall. After borrowing the security from the broker today, the investor can sell the security in the market at today's price, buy the security back later at a (hopefully) lower price, and return the security to the broker while realizing a profit.

2.4 CALCULATING RATE OF RETURN

Section 2.2 discussed two asset classes in detail. In this section, we explain an important concept associated with assets—the rate of return—which in some ways bears characteristics of an interest rate.

The *simple rate of return* (usually called just *return*) on an asset is the percentage difference between the amount received from investing in the asset and the amount originally invested in the asset:

Return = (Amount received − Amount invested)/(Amount invested)

In order to compute the return, of course, we need to specify the investment horizon in advance.

Suppose we invest $\$C_t$ in an asset at time t, and the value of our investment is $\$C_T$ at time T. The return on the asset between time t and T, which we denote $r_{(t,T)}$,[5] is

$$r_{(t,T)} = \frac{C_T - C_t}{C_t}.$$

If we are given the return and the initial amount invested, and would like to compute the amount received from our investment, we would use the equality

$$C_T = C_t \cdot (1 + r_{(t,T)}).$$

In this sense, the rate of return acts similarly to the rate of interest. When the asset is a stock, the return can be calculated as

$$r_{(t,T)} = \frac{P_T - P_t + D_t}{P_t},$$

where P_t and P_T are the market prices of the stock at times t and T, respectively, and D_t is the amount of dividends paid between times t and T.

Returns are compounded much in the way compound interest is. Let us explain this with an example. Suppose that an initial capital of $C_0 = \$1,000$

in some investment has value $C_1 = \$1,300$ at the end of year 1, and value $C_2 = \$1,000$ at the end of year 2. What is the return on the investment over the two years?

We know, of course, the return should be 0 since the initial capital is identical to the capital at the end of two years:

$$r_{(0,2)} = (C_2 - C_0)/C_0 = (1,000 - 1,000)/1,000 = 0$$

If we compute the returns over the two years separately, we get a return of 30% ($r_{(0,1)} = (1,300 - 1,000)/1,000 = 0.30$) over year 1 and a return of approximately –23% ($r_{(1,2)} = (1,000 - 1,300)/1,300 = -0.23$) over year 2. If we add these two returns, we would obtain a return of 30% $-$ 23% $=$ 7%, which is intuitively wrong.

Instead, we compound the returns over the two time periods, and obtain the following for the return at the end of two years:

$$r_{(0,2)} = (1 + 0.30) \cdot (1 - 0.23) - 1 = 0.001$$

This number is 0 (there is some rounding error), which agrees with our intuition.[6]

In general, an investment of \$1 at time 0 will grow to $(1 + r_{(0,1)})(1 + r_{(1,2)}) \ldots (1 + r_{(t-1,t)})$ dollars at the end of year t, and the return $r_{(0,t)}$ from time 0 to time t equals

$$r_{(0,t)} = (1 + r_{(0,1)})(1 + r_{(1,2)}) \ldots (1 + r_{(t-1,t)}) - 1$$

The expression $(1 + r_{(t,T)})$ is called *gross return*. In the previous two-year example, the gross return over the two years is $(1 + r_{(0,2)}) = 1.00$. The gross return over year 1 is $(1 + r_{(0,1)}) = 1.30$, and the gross return over year 2 is $(1 + r_{(1,2)}) = 0.75$.

Returns can also be expressed in geometric (log) form. The *log return* between time t and T is defined as

$$\log(1 + r_{(t,T)})$$

where *log* is the natural logarithm, that is, the function so that $e^{\log(x)} = x$.[7,8] Note that when using log returns, the implicit assumption is that returns are accumulated continuously (think of the analogy with continuously compounded interest).

It is easy to see that

$$\log(1 + r_{(t,T)}) = \log\left(1 + \frac{C_T - C_t}{C_t}\right) = \log\left(\frac{C_T}{C_t}\right).$$

If the time interval (t, T) is small, the numerical value of the return $r_{(t,T)}$ will also be small. Therefore, $\log(1 + r_{(t,T)})$ will be approximately $r_{(t,T)}$ for short time periods.[9]

If we are dealing with a stock, then

$$\log(1 + r_{(t,T)}) = \log\left(1 + \frac{P_T - P_t + D_t}{P_t}\right) = \log\left(\frac{P_T + D_t}{P_t}\right).$$

There are several advantages to using log returns in financial modeling, whose applications will become clearer when financial derivative pricing models are discussed in Chapters 13 and 14. On an intuitive level, log returns are more economically meaningful because the asset price can never become negative regardless of how negative the returns may be. (This is not the case with the definition of return we introduced at the beginning of this section.) Furthermore, the log return over multiple time periods is simply the sum of the one-period log returns. Namely,

$$\begin{aligned}\log(1 + r_{(0,t)}) &= \log\left((1 + r_{(0,1)})(1 + r_{(1,2)}) \cdots (1 + r_{(t-1,t)})\right) \\ &= \log(1 + r_{(0,1)}) + \log(1 + r_{(1,2)}) + \cdots + \log(1 + r_{(t-1,t)})\end{aligned}$$

Finally, a widely used concept in bond portfolio management is *total return*. The total return is computed as

$$\text{Total return} = (\text{Amount received})/(\text{Amount invested})$$

where the amount received is comprised of three sources:

1. The coupon payments.
2. The change in the value of the bond.
3. Income from reinvestment of coupon payments and principal repayment (in the case of amortizing securities) from the time of receipt to the end of the investment horizon.

For example, suppose that an investor purchases a fixed income security for \$90 and expects a return over a 1-year investment horizon from the three sources equal to $5. Then the expected total return is 5.56% (= $5/$90). Total return is discussed in more detail in section 2.6.8.

2.5 VALUATION

Valuation is the process of determining the fair value of a financial asset. This process is also referred to as *valuing* or *pricing* a financial asset. The fundamental principle of financial asset valuation is that the value of an asset is equal to the present value of its expected cash flows. This principle applies regardless of the financial asset. Thus, the valuation of a financial asset involves the following three steps:

1. Estimate the expected cash flows.
2. Determine the appropriate interest rate or interest rates that should be used to discount the cash flows.
3. Calculate the present value of the expected cash flows found in Step 1 using the interest rate or interest rates determined in Step 2.

In this book, we introduce many different valuation models. Here we discuss classic valuation models for stocks and bonds.

2.5.1 Valuation Models for Equities

Common stock can be thought of as a perpetual security—the owner of the shares has the right to receive a portion of cash flows from the company paid out as dividends. The value of one share should equal the present value of all future cash flows (dividends) the owner of the stock expects to receive from that share. Hence, to value one share, the investor must forecast future dividends. This approach to the valuation of common stock is referred to as the *discounted cash flow approach*, and the first dividend discount model dates back to John Williams (1938).

The *theoretical* (also called *fair*) *value* of the stock price is

$$\frac{D_1}{(1+r)} + \frac{D_2}{(1+r)^2} + \frac{D_3}{(1+r)^3} + \cdots$$

where r is an appropriate discount rate. Note that this is an infinite sum.

Future dividends are not known with certainty, and whether a corporation pays out dividends is decided by its board of directors. If a company does not pay dividends (e.g., it retains earnings), however, the same principle applies, as the retained earnings should be paid out as dividends eventually.

In that case, the fair value of the stock is defined to be the present value of the discounted cash flow stream.

Later in the book, we will discuss optimal portfolio allocation. One of the inputs to such models is the expected return of a security. It is intuitive how an estimate of this return can be produced from cash flow discount models for the stock price—the expected return on a stock would be the value of r in the previous formula that makes the value calculated with the formula equal to the observed market price of the stock. Since the formula for the price contains an infinite sum, additional assumptions must be made in order to be able to compute the expected return. For example, one can attempt to forecast the price P_T of the stock at some future date T, in which case the formula becomes

$$P_0 = \frac{D_1}{(1+r)} + \frac{D_2}{(1+r)^2} + \frac{D_3}{(1+r)^3} + \cdots + \frac{P_T}{(1+r)^T}.$$

From here, the value of the expected return can be found by trial and error.

Alternatively, one can make the assumption that future dividends will grow at a constant rate g. This model was developed by Gordon (1962) and is therefore often referred to as the *Gordon model*. We have

$$D_{t+1} = D_t \cdot (1+g) = D_1 \cdot (1+g)^{t-1}.$$

Therefore, the infinite sum in the dividend discount model becomes

$$D_1 \cdot \frac{1}{(1+r)} \cdot \left(1 + \frac{(1+g)^1}{(1+r)^1} + \frac{(1+g)^2}{(1+r)^2} + \cdots \right).$$

The infinite sum inside the parentheses can now be computed in closed form because it is a sum of an infinite geometric series of the kind

$$1 + q + q^2 + q^3 + \cdots$$

(where q in this case is $(1+g)/(1+r)$), which equals

$$\frac{1}{1-q}$$

Therefore, the Gordon model results in a stock price of

$$\frac{D_1}{r - g}$$

Given the current market price of the stock and using the preceding formula, a value for the expected return r can be derived.

There are numerous other valuation models, and a complete review is beyond the scope of this book. It is important to keep in mind, however, that all of the parameters that go into these models need to be estimated, and if the various quantities are defined by different accounting practices or forecasting models, they can lead to significantly different valuations.

2.5.2 Valuation Models for Fixed Income Securities

The value of a bond is the discounted sum of its payments. In other words,

$$B_0 = \frac{C_1}{(1 + r)} + \frac{C_2}{(1 + r)^2} + \frac{C_3}{(1 + r)^3} + \cdots + \frac{C_T}{(1 + r)^T}$$

where C_t denotes the cash flow (coupons or coupon plus principal) paid at date t. While the concept is simple, the details of its implementation, including how to determine an appropriate discount rate, can lead to different valuations. The minimum interest rate r the investor should require is the prevalent discount rate in the marketplace on a default-free cash flow. In the United States, U.S. Treasuries are considered the norm for default-free securities. This is one of the reasons the Treasury market is closely watched.

Consider a bond with a $100 principal, a coupon rate of 10% paid annually, and a term to maturity of 3 years. Assume a discount rate of 6%. Today's value of the bond is

$$\frac{10}{(1 + 0.06)} + \frac{10}{(1 + 0.06)^2} + \frac{110}{(1 + 0.06)^3} = \$110.69.^{10}$$

If a 12% annual discount rate was used, the bond value today would have been

$$\frac{10}{(1 + 0.12)} + \frac{10}{(1 + 0.12)^2} + \frac{110}{(1 + 0.12)^3} = \$95.20.$$

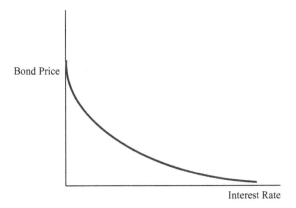

EXHIBIT 2.2   Relationship between bond price and discount rate.

Note that the value of the bond is lower when the interest rate is higher. This is an important property of bond prices: when interest rates go up, bond prices generally decline. The opposite is true as well—when interest rates go down, bond prices generally increase. (See Exhibit 2.2.) The relationship between bond prices and interest rates is actually nonlinear: the bond price is a *convex* function of interest rates.[11] You can observe this by computing the bond values for several different values of the discount rate. The shape of the relationship between bond prices and interest rates is important for risk management purposes. We will discuss it in more detail in the context of bond portfolio management in Chapter 10.

When one observes bond prices in the market, one can use the information about the bond and its market price to determine the interest rate that makes the present value of the stream of cash flows equal to the bond price. This implied interest rate is called *yield to maturity* (YTM), or simply *yield*. It is quoted on an annual basis. To find it, one would use an iterative trial-and-error procedure. In other words, different values for the yield will be tried until the computed present value of the bond cash flows equals the observed value.

Since the cash flows are every six months, the yield to maturity found by solving the equation for the bond price is a semiannual yield to maturity. This yield can be annualized by either (1) doubling the semiannual yield or (2) compounding the yield. The market convention is to annualize the semiannual yield by simply doubling its value. The yield to maturity computed on the basis of this market convention is called the *bond-equivalent yield*. It is also referred to as a *yield on a bond-equivalent basis*.

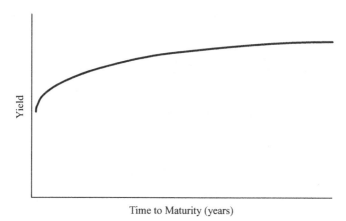

Time to Maturity (years)

EXHIBIT 2.3   Upward-sloping yield curve.

Observed bond yields tend to be different depending on the time to maturity. The plot of bond yields versus the length of time corresponding to these yields is referred to as the *yield curve*. An example of a yield curve is given in Exhibit 2.3. The usual shape of the yield curve is upward-sloping; however, the yield curve can have different shapes depending on market conditions. The reason why an upward-sloping curve is considered "normal" is because investors are assumed to demand more yield for long-term investments than for short-term investments. Long-term investments are subject to more uncertainty. However, sometimes long-term bonds have lower yields than short-term bonds. In the latter case, we refer to the yield curve as an *inverted yield curve*. If the yields for all maturities were the same, of course, the yield curve would simply be a flat horizontal line.

Knowledge of the yield curve is helpful because it allows us to position a particular bond with regard to other bonds in its class. It allows us to compute the required yield for a bond. The *required yield* reflects the yield for financial instruments with comparable risk to a bond we are trying to price. Given the required yield, we can determine the price of the bond by using the required yield as the interest rate r in the pricing formula shown earlier in this section.

In the previous bond value calculation examples, we assumed that the discount rate is the same for all cash flows. In reality, the discount rates are typically different, depending on the length of time until the cash flow will be received. The U.S. Treasury rates, which are the relevant reference rates for default-free cash flows, are followed particularly closely. To see how the value of the bond would be computed when the discount rates for the cash flows are different, consider again the example of the bond with \$100 principal, a coupon rate of 10% paid annually, and a term to maturity of 3 years. Assume that the discount rates for year 1, 2, and 3 are of 6.00%, 6.80%, and 7.20%, respectively. Today's value of the bond is

$$\frac{10}{(1+0.06)} + \frac{10}{(1+0.0680)^2} + \frac{110}{(1+0.0720)^3} = \$108.55.$$

2.6 IMPORTANT CONCEPTS IN FIXED INCOME

This section reviews important advanced concepts in fixed income.

2.6.1 Spot Rates

The spot rate is the interest rate charged for money held from the present time until a prespecified time t. The convention is to quote spot rates as yearly rates, but the specific characteristics of the compounding (yearly, m time periods per year, or continuous) vary. The interest rates we used in the section on valuation were all spot rates.

Sometimes, spot rates are referred to as *zero rates* (short for *zero-coupon rates*) because they are in fact the return on a zero-coupon bond that is bought today and paid out a certain number of years in the future. Suppose the 5-year Treasury spot (zero) rate with continuous compounding is quoted as 6% per annum. This means that if the price of a 5-year zero-coupon bond today is B_0, and the payout after five years is B_5, then the following holds:

$$B_5 = B_0 \cdot e^{0.06 \cdot 5}.$$

In general, let s_t denote the spot rate for time period t.[12] Then, if B_t denotes the price of a zero-coupon bond with maturity t, we have

$$B_t = B_0 \cdot e^{s_t \cdot t}.$$

2.6.2 The Term Structure

The term structure defines the relationship between time and interest rates, with spot rates as the underlying interest rates. It is usually presented as a graph, as the yield curve in Exhibit 2.3. The term structure in interest rates is in fact a yield curve, but its meaning is a bit more academic, as it focuses on pure interest rates for default-free securities rather than yields. Knowledge of the term structure is crucial for pricing and trading purposes.

The obvious way to find the term structure of interest rates is to compute the interest rates implied in the prices of a series of zero-coupon default-free bonds. However, it is difficult to find zero-coupon bonds that span all maturities, especially long maturities.[13] This does not diminish the importance or usefulness of constructing the term structure. The term structure can be constructed from coupon-bearing bonds by a procedure called *bootstrapping*.[14] The idea is to use several coupon-bearing bonds, determine the spot rates implied by the bonds with the shortest maturity, use that knowledge to compute the spot rate implied by the bond with the next-shortest maturity, and proceed in this manner until the whole term structure is constructed. The same method is used to construct other spot rate curves, such as the spot rate curve for LIBOR.[15] There will obviously be gaps in the term structure because we cannot necessarily determine every point on the curve from market prices. Interpolation and polynomial approximations are used to complete the term structure given a few points.

Given a term structure of interest rates, discount factors for securities of different maturities can be determined. For example, if a coupon bond pays coupons six months from now and a year from now, we can read the interest rates corresponding to six months and one year from the term structure, and use those rates to discount the cash flows from the bond's coupons when valuing the bond.

2.6.3 Forward Rates

Forward rates can be thought of as the current market consensus of future spot rates: they are interest rates for money to be invested between two dates in the future, but under terms agreed upon today. The concept of forward rates is very useful for pricing and investment purposes. Similarly to spot rates, forward rates are quoted as yearly rates.

Forward rates can be derived from the term structure of interest rates. Examples of forward rates that can be extrapolated from the Treasury yield curve include

- 6-month forward rate six months from now.
- 6-month forward rate three years from now.
- 1-year forward rate one year from now.
- 3-year forward rate two years from now.
- 5-year forward rate three years from now.

We will use the following notation to denote forward rates: $_t f_m$, where the subscript t indicates a t-year interest rate, and the subscript m indicates that the t years begin m years from now. For example, $_{0.5} f_3$ is the 6-month forward rate three years from now, and $_3f_2$ is the 3-year forward rate two years from now. When $m = 0$, the forward rate is the same as the spot rate; that is, $_tf_0 = s_t$.

How do we compute forward rates? Consider, for example, an investor with a 1-year investment horizon who is faced with the following two choices:

- Buy a 2-year Treasury note.
- Buy a 1-year Treasury bill and, when it matures in one year, buy another 1-year Treasury bill.

The investor would be indifferent between the two choices only if the return on the two is the same. If one of them offers a better return than the other, all investors will prefer that option, which will drive up its price, and hence reduce its return until it equals the return on the option that was less desirable at the beginning.[16] The value of an investment of $C with the first option after two years will be

$$C \cdot (1 + s_2)^2,$$

where s_2 is the 2-year spot rate. The return on a 2-year investment with the second option will be

$$C \cdot (1 + s_1) \cdot (1 + {_1f_1}),$$

where s_1 is the 1-year spot rate, and $_1f_1$ is the implied rate in a 1-year Treasury bill purchased one year from now, that is, the 1-year forward one year from now. Since the returns on the two investments must be equal, we get

$$(1 + s_2)^2 = (1 + s_1) \cdot (1 + {_1f_1}),$$

which allows us to compute the forward rate $_1f_1$ as

$$_1f_1 = \frac{(1 + s_2)^2}{(1 + s_1)} - 1.$$

For m time periods ahead, we have

$$_1f_m = \frac{(1 + s_{m+1})^{m+1}}{(1 + s_m)} - 1.$$

In general, if we are given the term structure, and hence have information about spot rates s_t and s_T for two times t and T, then we can estimate the forward rate between t and T, $_{(T-t)}f_t$, as

$$_{(T-t)}f_t = \frac{(1 + s_T)}{(1 + s_t)} - 1.$$

2.6.4 Credit Spreads

When cash flows are not default-free, the Treasury rates cannot be used to discount them for valuation purposes. This is because, technically, investors should require a higher yield from default-risky than from default-free securities to compensate for the risk they are taking. For pricing default-risky securities, a *term structure of credit spreads* is often used, where a credit spread is defined as the difference between the yield on a default-free bond and a default-risky bond with the same cash flow characteristics. Dealer firms typically estimate a term structure for credit spreads for each credit rating and market sector. Generally, the credit spread increases with time to maturity. In addition, the shape of the term structure is not the same for all credit ratings. Typically, the lower the credit rating, the steeper the term structure of credit spreads. This is because the risk of default is higher when the default-risky security is a longer-term investment.

2.6.5 Duration

The value of a bond investment is sensitive to changes in interest rates. This is because if the discount rates used to evaluate the different cash flows from the bond change, so will its price. All other things being equal, bonds with long maturities are more sensitive to changes in interest rates than bonds with short maturities. However, maturity alone is not sufficient for measuring the degree of interest rate sensitivity. Intuitively, the higher the bond's coupon rate, the more dependent the bond's total dollar return will be on the reinvestment of the coupon payments in order to produce the yield to maturity at the time of purchase. Hence, a change in interest rates during the life of the bond can have a substantial impact on the total return.

Duration is a measure of the sensitivity of a bond's price with respect to changes in interest rates which takes into consideration the issues previously discussed. In mathematical terms, it is the derivative of the bond price with respect to interest rates, that is, it measures *first-order sensitivity*. As Exhibit 2.2 showed, the relationship between the bond price and interest rates is in fact nonlinear, so the duration would not explain the exact change in bond prices for a given change in interest rates. Convexity, which we will describe in the next section, complements duration to provide a more accurate description of the sensitivity. It is important to note, however, that both duration and convexity describe the sensitivity of bond prices to interest rates when there is a *parallel shift in the yield curve*, that is, when the rates for all maturities move up or down simultaneously and by the same number of basis points. This clearly places a limitation on the usefulness of duration and convexity as measures of bond interest rate risk. Nevertheless, duration and convexity are very popular, fundamental tools in fixed income analysis.

Even though defining duration as the first derivative of the price/yield function is mathematically correct, it is not really used in practice because it is difficult to explain to clients what the relevance of such a mathematical concept is to measuring actual investment risk. Instead, duration is typically explained as the approximate price sensitivity of a bond to a 100-basis-point change in rates. Thus, a bond with a duration of 5 will change by approximately 5% for a 100-basis-point change in interest rates (that is, if the yield required for this bond changes by approximately 100 basis points). For a 50-basis-point change in interest rates, the bond's price will change by approximately 2.5%; for a 25 basis point change in interest rates, 1.25%, and so on.

Let us now define duration more rigorously. The exact formulation is

$$\frac{\text{Price if yields decline} - \text{Price if yields rise}}{2 \cdot (\text{Initial price}) \cdot (\text{Change in yield in decimal})}.$$

Let D denote duration, B_0 denote the initial price, Δy denote the change in yield, B_- denote the price if yields decrease by Δy, and B_+ denote the price if yields increase by Δy. We have

$$D = \frac{B_- - B_+}{2 \cdot B_0 \cdot \Delta y}.$$

It is important to understand that the two values in the numerator of the preceding equation, B_+ and B_-, are the estimated values obtained from a valuation model if interest rates change. Consequently, the duration measure is only as good as the valuation model employed to obtain these estimated values. The more difficult it is to estimate the value of a bond, the less confidence a portfolio manager may have in the estimated duration. We will see in Chapter 10 that the duration of a portfolio is nothing more than a market-weighted average of the duration of the bonds comprising the portfolio. Hence, a portfolio's duration is sensitive to the estimated duration of the individual bonds.

To illustrate the duration calculation, consider the following bond: a 6% coupon five-year bond trading at par value to yield 6%. The current price is $100. Suppose the yield is changed by 50 basis points. Thus, $\Delta y = 0.005$ and $B_0 = \$100$. This is simple bond to value if interest rates or yield is changed. If the yield is decreased to 5.5%, the value of this bond would be $102.1600. If the yield is increased to 6.5%, the value of this bond would be $97.8944. Therefore, $B_- = \$102.1600$ and $B_+ = \$97.8944$. Substituting into the equation for duration, we obtain

$$\text{Duration} = \frac{102.1600 - 97.8944}{2 \cdot (100) \cdot (0.005)} = 4.27.$$

Dollar Duration   In estimating the sensitivity of the price of bond to changes in interest rates, we looked at the percentage price change. However, for two bonds with the same duration but trading at different prices, the dollar price change will not be the same. To see this, suppose that we have two bonds, A and B, that both have durations of 5. Suppose further that the current price of A and B are $100 and $90, respectively. A 100-basis-point change for both bonds will change the price by approximately 5%. This means a price change of $5 (5% times $100) for A, and a price change of $4.5 (5% times $90) for B.

The dollar price change of a bond can be measured by multiplying duration by the full dollar price and the number of basis points (in decimal form) and is called the *dollar duration*. That is,

Dollar duration = (Duration) · (Dollar price) · (Change in rates in decimal)

The dollar duration for a 100-basis-point change in rates is

Dollar duration = (Duration) · (Dollar price) · 0.01

So, for bonds A and B, the dollar duration for a 100-basis-point change in rates is

For bond A: Dollar duration = 5 · $100 · 0.01 = $5.0

For bond B: Dollar duration = 5 · $90 · 0.01 = $4.5

Knowing the dollar duration allows a portfolio manager to neutralize the risk of bond position. For example, consider a position in bond B. If a trader wants to eliminate the interest rate risk exposure of this bond,[17] the trader will look for a position in one or more other financial instruments, such as an interest rate derivative,[18] whose value will change in the opposite direction to bond B's price by an amount equal to $4.5. So, if the trader has a long position in B, the position will decline in value by $4.5 for a 100-basis-point increase in interest rates. To eliminate this risk exposure, the trader can take a position in another financial instrument whose value increases by $4.5 if interest rates increase by 100 basis points.

The dollar duration can also be computed without knowing a bond's duration. This is done by simply looking at the average price change for a bond when interest rates are increased and decreased by the same number of basis points.

Modified Duration, Macaulay Duration, and Effective Duration   A popular form of duration that is used by practitioners is modified duration. *Modified duration* is the approximate percentage change in a bond's price for a 100-basis-point change in interest rates, assuming that the bond's cash flows do not change when interest rates change. What this means is that in calculating the values used in the numerator of the duration formula, the cash flows used to calculate the current price are assumed. Therefore, the change in the bond's value when interest rates change by a small number of basis points is due solely to discounting at the new yield level.

Modified duration is related to another measure commonly cited in the bond market: *Macaulay duration*. The formula for this measure, first used by Frederick Macaulay in 1938, is rarely used in practice, so it will not be produced here. For a bond that pays coupon interest semiannually, modified duration is related to Macaulay duration as follows:

$$\text{Modified duration} = \text{Macaulay duration}/(1 + \text{yield}/2),$$

where yield is the bond's yield to maturity in decimal form. Practically speaking, there is very little difference in the computed values for modified duration and Macaulay duration.

The assumption that the cash flows will not change when interest rates change makes sense for bonds because the payments by the issuer are not altered when interest rates change. This is not the case for bonds with embedded options, mortgage-backed securities, and certain types of asset-backed securities. For these securities, a change in interest rates may alter the expected cash flows.[19]

For such bonds, there are specific valuation models that take into account how changes in interest rates will affect cash flows. When the values used in the numerator of the equation for duration are obtained from a valuation model that takes into account both the discounting at different interest rates and how the cash flows can change, the resulting duration is referred to as *effective duration* or *option-adjusted duration*.

Spread Duration for Fixed Rate Bonds   Duration is a measure of the change in the value of a bond when rates change. The interest rate that is assumed to shift is the Treasury rate. However, for non-Treasury securities, the yield is equal to the Treasury yield plus a spread to the Treasury yield curve. The price of a bond exposed to credit risk can change even though Treasury yields are unchanged because the spread required by the market changes. A measure of how a non-Treasury issue's price will change if the spread sought by the market changes is called *spread duration* and is a measure of credit spread risk, which we described earlier in this chapter. For example, a spread duration of 2.2 for a security means that if the Treasury rate is unchanged but spreads change by 100 basis points, the security's price will change by approximately 2.2%.

2.6.6 Convexity

The duration measure indicates that regardless of whether interest rates increase or decrease, the approximate percentage price change is the same. However, while for small changes in yield the percentage price change will be the same for an increase or decrease in yield, for large changes in yield this is not true. This suggests that duration is only a good approximation of the percentage price change for a small change in yield.

The reason for this is that duration is in fact a first approximation for a small change in yield. The approximation can be improved by using a *second-order approximation*. This approximation is referred to as *convexity*. The use of this term in the industry is unfortunate since the term convexity is also used to describe the shape or curvature of the price/yield relationship. The convexity measure of a security can be used to approximate the change in price that is not explained by duration.

Convexity Measure   The convexity measure of a bond can be approximated using the following formula:

$$\text{Convexity measure} = \frac{B_+ + B_- - 2 \cdot B_0}{2 \cdot B_0 \cdot (\Delta y)^2}$$

where the notation is the same as used earlier for defining duration.

For a hypothetical 6%, 25-year bond selling to yield 9%, we can compute that for a 10-basis-point change in yield ($\Delta y = 0.001$), we have $B_0 = 70.3570$, $B_- = 71.1105$, and $B_+ = 69.6164$. Substituting these values into the convexity measure given by the preceding equation, we obtain

$$\text{Convexity measure} = \frac{69.6164 + 71.1105 - 2 \cdot 70.3570}{2 \cdot 70.3570 \cdot (0.001)^2} = 91.67$$

We will see how to use this convexity measure shortly. Before doing so, there are three points that should be noted. First, there is no simple interpretation of the convexity measure as there is for duration.[20] Second, it is more common for market participants to refer to the value computed in the previous equation as the "convexity of a bond" rather than the "convexity measure of a bond." Finally, the convexity measures reported by dealers and vendors will differ. The reason is that the convexity value obtained from the preceding equation will be scaled for the reason explained later.

Convexity Adjustment to Percentage Price Change Given the convexity measure, the approximate percentage price change adjustment due to the bond's convexity (that is, the percentage price change not explained by duration) is

$$\text{Convexity adjustment to percentage price change} = \text{Convexity measure} \cdot (\Delta y)^2 \cdot 100.$$

For example, for the 6%, 25-year bond selling to yield 9%, the convexity adjustment to the percentage price change based on duration if the yield increases from 9% to 11% is

$$91.67 \cdot (0.02)^2 \cdot 100 = 3.67.$$

If the yield decreases from 9% to 7%, the convexity adjustment to the approximate percentage price change based on duration would also be 3.67%.

The approximate percentage price change based on duration and the convexity adjustment is found by adding the two estimates. So, for example, if yields change from 9% to 11%, the estimated percentage price change would be:

$$
\begin{aligned}
\text{Estimated change approximated by duration} &= -21.20\% \\
\text{Convexity adjustment} &= -3.66\% \\
\text{Total estimated percentage price change} &= -17.54\%
\end{aligned}
$$

The actual percentage price change can be computed to be −18.03%. Hence, the approximation has improved compared to using only duration.

For a decrease of 200 basis points, from 9% to 7%, the approximate percentage price change would be as follows:

$$
\begin{aligned}
\text{Estimated change approximated by duration} &= +21.20\% \\
\text{Convexity adjustment} &= +3.66\% \\
\text{Total estimated percentage price change} &= +24.86\%
\end{aligned}
$$

The actual percentage price change can be computed to be +25.46%. Once again, we see that duration combined with the convexity adjustment does a good job of estimating the sensitivity of a bond's price change to large changes in yield.

The bond prices used to calculate the convexity measure can be obtained by either assuming that when the yield changes, the expected cash flows do not change, or that they do change. In the former case, the resulting convexity is referred to as standard convexity. (Actually, in the industry, convexity is not qualified by the adjective "standard.") *Effective convexity*, in contrast, assumes that the cash flows do change when yields change. The distinction is the same as the one made for duration.

As with duration, for bonds with embedded options there can be a large difference between the calculated standard convexity and effective convexity. In fact, for all option-free bonds, either convexity measure will have a positive value. For bonds with embedded options, the calculated effective convexity can be negative when the calculated modified convexity is positive.

2.6.7 Key Rate Duration

As explained earlier, duration assumes that when interest rates change, all yields on the yield curve change by the same amount. This is a problem when using duration for a portfolio that will typically have bonds with different maturities. Consequently, it is necessary to be able to measure the exposure of a bond or bond portfolio to shifts in the yield curve. There have been several approaches to measuring yield curve risk. The most commonly used measure is *key rate duration* introduced by Thomas Ho.[21]

The basic principle of key rate duration is to change the yield for a particular maturity of the yield curve and determine the sensitivity of either an individual bond or a portfolio to that change holding all other yields constant. The sensitivity of the change in the bond's value or portfolio's value to a particular change in yield is called *rate duration*. There is a rate duration for every point on the yield curve. Consequently, there is not just one rate duration. Rather, there is a set of durations representing each maturity on the yield curve. Note that the total change in the value of a bond or a portfolio if all rates change by the same number of basis points is in fact the standard duration of a bond or portfolio.

Ho's approach focuses on 11 key maturities of the Treasury yield curve. These rate durations are called key rate durations. The specific maturities on the spot rate curve for which a key rate duration is measured are 3 months, 1 year, 2 years, 3 years, 5 years, 7 years, 10 years, 15 years,

20 years, 25 years, and 30 years. Changes in rates between any two key rates are calculated using a linear approximation.

A key rate duration for a particular portfolio maturity should be interpreted as follows: Holding the yield for all other maturities constant, the key rate duration is the approximate percentage change in the value of a portfolio (or bond) for a 100-basis-point change in the yield for the maturity whose rate has been changed. Thus, a key rate duration is quantified by changing the yield of the maturity of interest and determining how the value or price changes. In fact, the equation we introduced for duration is used. The prices denoted by B_- and B_+ in the equation are the prices in the case of a bond and the portfolio values in the case of a bond portfolio found by holding all other interest rates constant and changing the yield for the maturity whose key rate duration is sought.

The concept of key rate durations is very important when evaluating portfolio risk. We will discuss this concept again in Chapter 16.

2.6.8 Total Return

An investor who purchases a bond can expect to receive a dollar return from one or more of these three sources:

- The periodic coupon interest payments made by the issuer.
- Income from reinvestment of the periodic interest payments (the *interest-on-interest component*).
- Any capital gain (or capital loss—negative dollar return) when the bond matures or is sold.

Any measure of a bond's potential yield should take into consideration each of these three potential sources of return. The yield to maturity takes into account coupon interest and any capital gain (or loss). It also considers the interest-on-interest component. Implicit in the yield-to-maturity computation, however, is the assumption that the coupon payments can be reinvested at the computed yield to maturity. Reinvesting the coupon interest payments at a rate of interest less than the yield to maturity, for example, will produce a lower yield than the yield to maturity. This risk is called *reinvestment risk*.

Rather than assuming that the coupon interest payments are reinvested at the yield to maturity, an investor can make an explicit assumption about the reinvestment rate based on expectations. The *total return* is a measure of yield that incorporates an explicit assumption about the reinvestment rate.

The total return measure allows a portfolio manager to project the performance of a bond on the basis of the planned investment horizon and expectations concerning reinvestment rates and future market yields. This permits the portfolio manager to evaluate which of several potential bonds considered for acquisition will perform the best over the planned investment horizon. As we have emphasized, this cannot be done using the yield to maturity. Using total return to assess performance over some investment horizon is called *horizon analysis*. When a total return is calculated over an investment horizon, it is referred to as a *horizon return*. Horizon return and total return are typically used interchangeably.

An often-cited objection to the total return measure is that it requires the portfolio manager to formulate assumptions about reinvestment rates and future yields, as well as to think in terms of an investment horizon. Unfortunately, some portfolio managers find comfort in measures such as the yield to maturity and yield to call simply because they do not require incorporating any particular expectations. The horizon analysis framework, however, enables the portfolio manager to analyze the performance of a bond under different interest rate scenarios for reinvestment rates and future market yields. This procedure is referred to as *scenario analysis*. Only by investigating multiple scenarios can the portfolio manager see how sensitive the bond's performance will be to each scenario.[22]

To illustrate scenario analysis, consider a portfolio manager who is deciding on whether to purchase a 20-year, 9% option-free bond selling at $109.896 per $100 of par value. The yield to maturity for this bond is 8%. Assume also that the portfolio manager's investment horizon is three years. The portfolio manager believes the reinvestment rate can vary from 3% to 6.5% and the projected yield at the end of the investment horizon can vary from 5% to 12%. Exhibit 2.4(A) shows different projected yields at the end of the three-year investment horizon, and Exhibit 2.4(B) gives the corresponding price for the bond at the end of the investment horizon. For example, consider the 10% projected yield at the end of the investment horizon. The price of a 17-year option-free bond with a coupon rate of 9% would be $91.9035. Exhibit 2.4(C) shows the total future dollars at the end of three years under various scenarios for the reinvestment rate and the projected yield at the end of the investment horizon. For example, with a reinvestment rate of 4% and a projected yield at the end of the investment horizon of 10%, the total future dollars would be $120.290. Exhibit 2.4(D) shows the total return on an effective rate basis for each scenario.

Exhibit 2.4 is useful for a portfolio manager in assessing the potential outcome of a bond (or a portfolio) over the investment horizon. For example, a portfolio manager knows that the maximum and minimum total return for the scenarios shown in the table will be 16.72% and –1.05%, respectively, and also knows the scenarios under which each will be realized.

EXHIBIT 2.4 Scenario analysis.

Bond A: 9% coupon, 20-year option-free bond
Price: $109.896
Yield to maturity: 8%
Investment horizon: Three years

A. Projected Yield at End of Investment Horizon

5.00%	6.00%	7.00%	8.00%	9.00%	10.00%	11.00%	12.00%

B. Projected Sale Price at End of Investment Horizon

145.448	131.698	119.701	109.206	100.000	91.9035	84.763	78.4478

C. Total Future Dollars

Reinv. Rate	5.00%	6.00%	7.00%	8.00%	9.00%	10.00%	11.00%	12.00%
3.0%	173.481	159.731	147.734	137.239	128.033	119.937	112.796	106.481
3.5%	173.657	159.907	147.910	137.415	128.209	120.113	112.972	106.657
4.0%	173.834	160.084	148.087	137.592	128.387	120.290	113.150	106.834
4.5%	174.013	160.263	148.266	137.771	128.565	120.469	113.328	107.013
5.0%	174.192	160.443	148.445	137.950	128.745	120.648	113.508	107.193
5.5%	174.373	160.623	148.626	138.131	128.926	120.829	113.689	107.374
6.0%	174.555	160.806	148.809	138.313	129.108	121.011	113.871	107.556
6.5%	174.739	160.989	148.992	138.497	129.291	121.195	114.054	107.739

D. Total Return (Effective Rate)

Reinv. Rate	5.00%	6.00%	7.00%	8.00%	9.00%	10.00%	11.00%	12.00%
3.0%	16.44	13.28	10.37	7.69	5.22	2.96	0.87	21.05
3.5%	16.48	13.32	10.41	7.73	5.27	3.01	0.92	20.99
4.0%	16.52	13.36	10.45	7.78	5.32	3.06	0.98	20.94
4.5%	16.56	13.40	10.50	7.83	5.37	3.11	1.03	20.88
5.0%	16.60	13.44	10.54	7.87	5.42	3.16	1.08	20.83
5.5%	16.64	13.49	10.59	7.92	5.47	3.21	1.14	20.77
6.0%	16.68	13.53	10.63	7.97	5.52	3.26	1.19	20.72
6.5%	16.72	13.57	10.68	8.02	5.57	3.32	1.25	20.66

Another way to use scenario analysis is in assessing the likelihood that an investment objective will not be realized. For example, suppose that a life insurance company has issued a three-year guaranteed investment contract in which it has guaranteed an effective annual interest rate of 7.02%. Suppose that the premiums are invested in the bond analyzed in Exhibit 2.4, and that the portfolio manager's investment objective is a minimum return of 7.02%

plus a spread of 100 basis points. The spread represents the profit that the life insurance company seeks to earn. Thus, the minimum return is 8.02%. From Exhibit 2.4, the portfolio manager can see that if the yield at the end of the investment horizon is 8% or greater, and that if the reinvestment rate over the three-year investment horizon is less than 6.5%, a total return on an effective rate basis will be less than the investment objective of a minimum return of 8.02%.

SUMMARY

- Compound interest involves earning interest on the interest from an investment.
- The present value of a future cash flow is the amount of money that must be invested today to generate the future cash flow.
- The discount factor is the number by which we need to multiply the future cash flow to obtain its present value.
- In portfolio management, the most important decision made is the allocation of funds among asset classes.
- Asset classes are classified as traditional and alternative asset classes.
- In most developed countries, the four major asset classes are (1) common stocks, (2) bonds, (3) cash equivalents, and (4) real estate.
- Borrowing funds to purchase securities is known as a leveraged strategy. Two borrowing arrangements used by investors are margin buying and repurchase agreements.
- When an investor takes a position in the market by buying a security, the investor is said to be in a long position in the security. When an investor borrows a security from a broker and sells it, with the understanding that the security must be returned later, the investor is said to be taking a short position in the security (or selling it short).
- The simple rate of return (usually called just return) on an asset is the percentage difference between the amount received from investing in the asset and the amount originally invested in the asset.
- The log return is computed as the natural logarithm of one plus the return (the latter is called the gross return). When using log returns, the implicit assumption is that returns are accumulated continuously.
- Investors in fixed income securities are exposed to credit risk, which includes default risk, credit spread risk, and downgrade risk.
- Default risk is gauged by credit ratings assigned by rating agencies.
- Valuation is the process of determining the fair value of a financial asset. The fundamental principle of financial asset valuation is that its value is equal to the present value of its expected cash flows.

- The implied interest rate that makes the present value of a stream of cash flows from a bond equal to the bond's market price is called yield to maturity or simply yield.
- The spot rate (also called zero rate) is the interest rate charged for money held from the present time until a prespecified time t.
- The term structure defines the relationship between time and interest rates, with spot rates as the underlying interest rates.
- Forward rates are the current market consensus of future spot rates: they are interest rates for money to be invested between two dates in the future, but under terms agreed upon today.
- For pricing default-risky securities, a term structure of credit spreads is often used, where a credit spread is defined as the difference between the yield on a default-free bond and a default-risky bond with the same cash flow characteristics.
- Duration is a measure of the sensitivity of a bond's price with respect to changes in interest rates. It is a first-order approximation to the change in bond price when interest rates change by a fixed amount.
- Convexity is a second-order approximation to the change in bond price when interest rates change by a fixed amount. It allows for estimating the curvature of the relationship between changes in bond price and changes in interest rates more accurately.
- Spread duration is a measure of the exposure of a fixed income security or portfolio to credit spread risk.
- Total return is a more complete measure of a bond's potential return than yield-to-maturity. It takes into consideration the periodic coupon interest payments made by the issuer, the income from reinvestment of the periodic interest payments (the interest-on-interest component) without assuming that they will be reinvested at the same rate, and any capital gain (or capital loss—negative dollar return) when the bond matures or is sold.

NOTES

1. The value for the number e is so often used in applications, that it can be computed with almost any software package. For example, in Excel, the expression =exp(1) returns the value of e^1, which is 2.7183 rounded to four digits after the decimal point. In MATLAB, exp(1) gives the same answer.
2. LIBOR is the interest rate which major international banks charge each other for loans (usually in Eurodollars, where a Eurodollar is an American dollar held by a foreign institution outside the United States). Such loans allow banks with liquidity requirements to borrow quickly from other banks with surpluses. The

LIBOR rate is used by banks for large loans made over a period of anywhere between one day and five years. The 1-month LIBOR rate is the rate charged on loans with maturity of one month. LIBOR is the primary benchmark for interest rates around the world. It is set daily by a group of banks, but varies throughout the day.

3. In the fixed income market, market participants refer to changes in interest rates of differences in interest rates in terms of basis points. A *basis point* (bp) is defined as 0.0001, or equivalently, 0.01%. Consequently, 100 basis points are equal to 1%. (In our example the coupon formula can be expressed as 1-month LIBOR + 1%.) A change in interest rates from, say, 5% to 6.2% means that there is a 1.2% change in rates, or 120 basis points.

4. Inverse floaters were behind the Orange County bankruptcy of 1994; at the time the largest municipality bankruptcy that had repercussions across the entire municipalities bond market, and raised the cost of capital for municipalities across the United States.

5. In general, we use the notation $r_{(t_1, t_2)}$ to denote the return between times t_1 and t_2.

6. To see this, note that the capital at the end of the second year is

$$C_2 = (1 + r_{(1,2)})C_1 = (1 + r_{(1,2)}) \left[(1 + r_{(0,1)})C_0 \right] = (1 + r_{(1,2)})(1 + r_{(0,1)})C_0.$$

Therefore, the return over the two years is

$$r_{(0,2)} = \frac{C_2 - C_0}{C_0} = \frac{(1 + r_{(1,2)})(1 + r_{(0,1)})C_0 - C_0}{C_0} = (1 + r_{(1,2)})(1 + r_{(0,1)}) - 1.$$

7. We introduced the number e in section 2.1.

8. In Excel, the natural logarithm function is ln. For example, =ln(5) returns 1.6094. The result 1.6094 is the number so that e raised to the power of that number equals 5, that is, $e^{1.6094} = 5$. In MATLAB, the natural logarithm function is log.

9. It is a mathematical property of the natural logarithm function that $\log(1 + x)$ when x is small is approximately equal to x. To see this, write out the Taylor expansion of $\log(1+x)$:

$$\log(1 + x) = x - \frac{1}{2}x^2 + \frac{1}{3}x^3 - \cdots$$

When x is "small," the terms involving squares, cubes, etc. are even smaller and can be ignored, so x remains the only term that is significant.

10. Most bonds traded in the United States pay coupons semiannually. To value them, one uses the same formula, but divides the annual coupon rate and the applicable discount rate by 2. For example, if the bond in this example paid a $10 coupon semiannually with term to maturity of three years, we would divide

the interest rate of 6% by two (it becomes 3%), and find the present value of six cash flows of $5 (=$10/2). The value of the bond would be

$$\frac{5}{(1+0.03)} + \frac{5}{(1+0.03)^2} + \frac{5}{(1+0.03)^3} + \frac{5}{(1+0.03)^4} + \frac{5}{(1+0.03)^5}$$
$$+ \frac{105}{(1+0.03)^6} = \$110.80.$$

Note that a semiannual interest rate of 3% is not equivalent to an annual rate of 6% because of the effects of compounding. However, the convention in the bond market is to quote annual interest rates that are just double the semiannual interest rates, so this bond value calculation is technically correct.

11. Convex functions are discussed in more detail in Chapter 5. See Exhibit 5.3 in Chapter 5 for a picture of a convex function.
12. As mentioned earlier, we assume that s_t is quoted as a yearly rate.
13. The 6-month and 1-year Treasury securities (called Treasury bills) are issued as zero-coupon instruments. The longest maturity for Treasury bonds is 30 years.
14. Bootstrapping can be a confusing term because it has completely different meanings in finance and simulation. We will discuss the statistical concept of bootstrapping in section 3.11.3.
15. See Chapter 6 in Fabozzi (2007) for an illustration of the bootstrapping procedure.
16. This is an example of a *no-arbitrage argument*: if two investments have the same cash flows and the same risk, they should have the same return; otherwise there would be an arbitrage opportunity. We will discuss the concept of arbitrage in Chapter 13.
17. A strategy that reduces or eliminates risk is called *hedging*. We will discuss hedging in more detail in section 13.2.2.
18. Interest rate derivatives are discussed in Chapters 13, 14, and 16.
19. Such securities are discussed in Chapter 15.
20. The intuition is mostly mathematical—convexity represents a quadratic approximation to the relative curvature at a given point of the price-yield curve, whereas duration represents a linear approximation. In effect, we are constructing the Taylor series of the bond price around a specific point of the price-yield curve, and considering the first two terms in the approximation.
21. See, for example, Ho (1999).
22. As we will see later, a more advanced form of scenario analysis is simulation, which will be the focus of this book. We will see applications of simulation in fixed income in particular in Chapters 14, 15, and 16.

CHAPTER 3

Random Variables, Probability Distributions, and Important Statistical Concepts

To deal with risk, we need a way to model the uncertainty in the world around us. Mathematically, information about uncertainty can be summarized in probability distributions. This chapter reviews the concepts of random variables, discrete and continuous probability distributions, distribution summary measures, and an important law in statistics called the Central Limit Theorem. We focus on probability distributions that are most widely used in financial applications.

3.1 WHAT IS A PROBABILITY DISTRIBUTION?

A natural way to think of uncertainty is in terms of *scenarios*. Scenarios represent the possible events that could happen. For example, the value of a stock you own but are contemplating selling may go up (one scenario) or down (another scenario) one year from now. To these scenarios, you could assign *probabilities*, which reflect your estimate of the likelihood that the scenarios will occur. For example, you estimate that the probability that the stock's value will go up is 0.30 (30%), and the probability that it will go down is 0.70 (70%).

The information contained in the scenarios and the probabilities can be summarized in probability distributions. Basically, probability distributions are listings of the possible uncertain values and their probabilities. This information is often presented in graphs—we will see examples later in this chapter. We will also see that in order to analyze and summarize insights from probability distributions, we need to have numbers (not categories) on the horizontal axis of the graph, popularly referred to as the "x-axis." Thus, it is not a good idea to create a probability distribution for which the random event mentioned in the previous paragraph—that the stock's value will go up or down—is plotted because "up" and "down" are not numerical quantities.

In order to create a probability distribution, we need to assign numerical values to the uncertain outcomes. Let us think of the outcome "up" as a 1, and of the outcome "down" as a 0. Such *mapping* of events to numerical values is called a *random variable*. The term is actually a misnomer because random variables are neither random nor variables. They are numerical representations, or, equivalently, function assignments, of the outcomes of uncertain events to numbers. Probability distributions are plots of distributions of random variables, and do not necessarily map one-to-one to a list of outcomes.

Note, by the way, that the two probabilities of the two scenarios for the movement of the value of the stock add up to 1 (100%). This is because we assume that only one of the two events can happen (so, for example, the stock's value cannot stay the same), which means that the two scenarios exhaust the possible states of the world, and thus should add up to 100%. This is a general feature of probability distributions—the probabilities of all the values of the random variable in the probability distribution must add up to 1, or 100%. We should not specify a probability distribution in which they do not add up to 1. For example, if we wanted to add a third scenario—say, that the value could of the stock stays the same—then we would need to reassign probabilities to the three scenarios in such a way that the total sum of the probabilities remains 1.

3.2 BERNOULLI PROBABILITY DISTRIBUTION AND PROBABILITY MASS FUNCTIONS

Exhibit 3.1 shows the probability distribution we described in the previous section when there are two scenarios. It is in fact a special kind of distribution, and has a name because it is used so often—the Bernoulli distribution. The random variable that follows this distribution (the random variable takes values 0 and 1) is called the *Bernoulli random variable*. Let us call this random variable $\tilde{X}$. Notice that a tilde sign ($\sim$) js placed over the X. The tilde sign is used to denote uncertainty and randomness.

We can describe one possible distribution of type Bernoulli as

$$P(\tilde{X} = 0) = 0.70,$$

$$P(\tilde{X} = 1) = 0.30.$$

We read a mathematical statement of this kind as "the probability that the random variable $\tilde{X}$ takes a value of 0 is 0.70 or 70%." This listing of

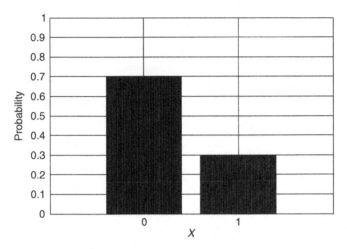

EXHIBIT 3.1   Bernoulli distribution with $p = 0.3$.

values of the random variable and the associated probabilities is called the *probability mass function* (PMF). It only exists for random variables that take *discrete* (countably many) values, that is, that have discrete probability distributions. More generally, given a probability p, the PMF for a Bernoulli distribution is

$$p(\tilde{X} = x) = \begin{cases} 1 - p, & x = 0 \\ p, & x = 1 \end{cases}.$$

We used x inside the parentheses to signal that this is the *realization* of the random variable $\tilde{X}$, not the random variable $\tilde{X}$ itself (which is a function). x is a specific value $\tilde{X}$ takes.

The graph in Exhibit 3.1 corresponds to the preceding probability listing as follows: there is a bar at each of the values the random variable can take (0 and 1), and the height of the bar equals the probability that the specific value for the random variable occurs. The heights of all bars in the graph add up to 1.

3.3 BINOMIAL PROBABILITY DISTRIBUTION AND DISCRETE DISTRIBUTIONS

Now suppose that you would like to model whether the value of the stock will be up or down in three years. Every year, it can go up with probability

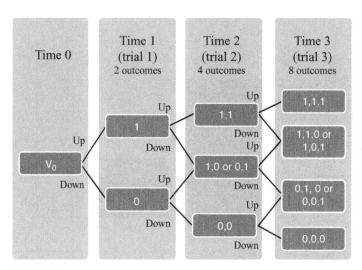

EXHIBIT 3.2 Movement of stock's value over three years: "1" = "success" (stock's value goes up). At the end of three years, we can have three successes in a row, two successes out of three, one success out of three, or no successes. The (0,1) combinations in the tree show the order of the successes or the failures up to that point in time.

0.30, and down with probability 0.70. Let the specific realizations of this Bernoulli random variable for each of the three years be X_1, X_2, and X_3.[1] We can visualize the movement of the stock value from the tree drawn in Exhibit 3.2. (Keep this picture in mind, as variations of it will appear again and again in financial instrument pricing applications.) For example, when $X_1 = 1$, $X_2 = 1$, and $X_3 = 1$, the movement in all three years is "up" and the stock's value will be at its highest.

Since you would like to sell the stock for as much money as you can, let us call the event of the value of the stock going up in any particular year a "success." Assume that the success in one year is independent of the success in another year, and let us count the number of successes out of the three possible times. This is going to be an uncertain quantity. The probability distribution of the number of successes in a prefixed number of trials is called the *binomial* distribution. In our example, the number of trials is three because in each of the three years there is a chance that the trial will be a "success" (the stock's value will go up) or a "failure" (the stock's value will go down). Note that the Bernoulli distribution is in fact a special case of the binomial distribution, in which the number of trials is 1.

The binomial distribution is very important and widely used in a variety of applications—from statistical analysis of polling results to modeling prices of financial securities and evaluating the economic prospects of a capital budgeting project.

To be mathematically specific, the binomial distribution can be used when the following four conditions are satisfied:

1. The number of trials is fixed in advance.
2. There can be only two outcomes (success and failure).
3. Success in each trial is independent of the result of the previous trial.
4. The probability of success remains the same from trial to trial.

Perhaps the easiest way to envision whether applying the binomial distribution is appropriate is to think of whether the situation under evaluation is equivalent to a sequence of coin flips with the same coin, in which we are interested in the probability that we get a given number (x) of tails in n flips.

Suppose we would like to plot the binomial distribution of the random variable describing the price movements of the stock over the next three years. What would be the values on the x-axis? The values for the random variable can be 0, 1, 2, or 3—the number of successes can be either 0 (the stock's value went down every year), 1 (the stock's value went down in one of the three years, but went up in the remaining two), and so on. We will denote the random variable by $\tilde{X}$, but note that this is not the same random variable as the random variable in section 3.2. In order to create the listing of probabilities, we compute:

$$P(\tilde{X} = 0) = (0.70) \cdot (0.70) \cdot (0.70) = 0.343 = 34.3\%$$

$$P(\tilde{X} = 1) = (0.30) \cdot (0.70) \cdot (0.70) + (0.70) \cdot (0.30) \cdot (0.70)$$

$$+(0.70) \cdot (0.70) \cdot (0.30) = .441 = 44.1\%$$

$$P(\tilde{X} = 2) = (0.30) \cdot (0.30) \cdot (0.70) + (0.70) \cdot (0.30) \cdot (0.30)$$

$$+(0.30) \cdot (0.70) \cdot (0.30) = .189 = 18.9\%$$

$$P(\tilde{X} = 3) = (0.30) \cdot (0.30) \cdot (0.30) = 0.027 = 2.70$$

Therefore, the distribution can be represented as the graph in Exhibit 3.3.

To clarify why the probabilities were computed in the way just illustrated, note that there is only one way to have three successes in three trials ($\tilde{X} = 3$): when every trial is a success. The probability of this event is the product of the probabilities that each of the three trials is a success. (The

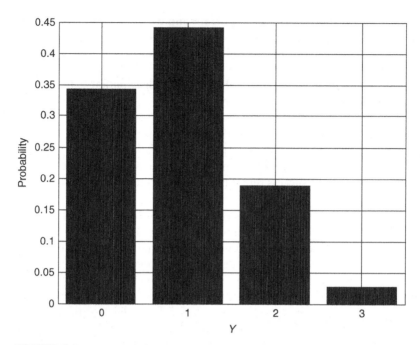

EXHIBIT 3.3   Binomial distribution with $n = 3$ trials and $p = 0.30$ probability of success.

multiplication of probabilities to obtain the total probability is permitted because the trials are assumed to be independent.) However, there are three ways to have one success in three trials: The success can be in the first, second, or third trial. To account for these different combinations, we can use the following well-known formula from the branch of mathematics called *combinatorics* (sometimes called the science of counting):

$$\frac{n!}{x!(n-x)!}.$$

The preceding formula computes the number of ways in which one can select x out of n objects. The symbol "$n!$" (pronounced "n factorial") stands for the expression $1 \cdot 2 \cdot \ldots \cdot n$. The exact formula for computing the probability of obtaining x successes in n trials when the probability of success is p (in our example, $p = 0.30$) is

$$P(\tilde{X} = x) = \frac{n!}{x!(n-x)!} p^x (1-p)^{n-x}, x = 0, \ldots, n$$

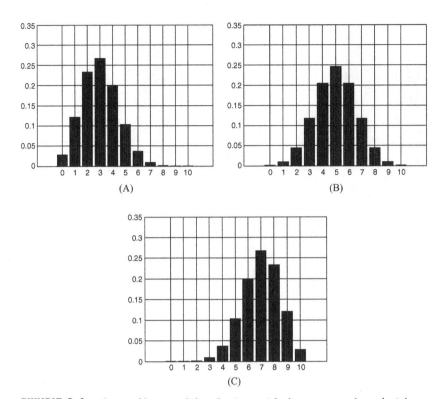

EXHIBIT 3.4   Shape of binomial distributions with the same number of trials ($n = 10$) and different values for the probability of success p: (A) $p = 0.3$; (B) $p = 0.5$; (C) $p = 0.7$.

This is the PMF of the binomial distribution, and is the formula software packages use to compute the binomial distribution probabilities. Note that depending on the magnitude of the probability of success, the binomial distribution can be shaped differently. Exhibit 3.4 illustrates the binomial distribution for three different values of the probability of success.

3.4   NORMAL DISTRIBUTION AND PROBABILITY DENSITY FUNCTIONS

The binomial distribution is a *discrete* probability distribution because the values the random variable can take are countable (0, 1, 2, etc.). Let us see what happens if we try to model the movements of the stock in 100 years.

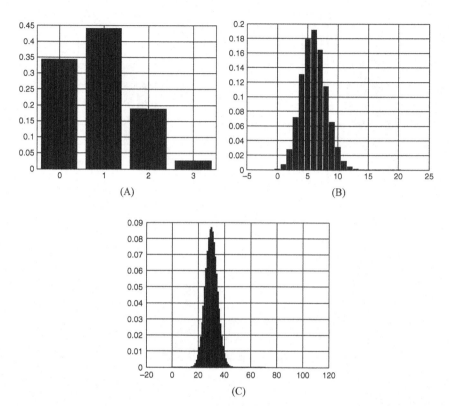

EXHIBIT 3.5　Shape of binomial distributions with the same probability of success $p = 0.3$ and an increasing number of trials n: (A) $n = 3$; (B) $n = 20$; (C) $n = 100$.

Exhibit 3.5 shows the binomial distribution for probability of success of 0.30 and number of trials $n = 3$, 20, and 100.

Note that the binomial distribution begins to look symmetric as the number of trials increases. Also, the range of values begins to look like a *continuum*. When the random variable takes values on a range, as opposed to at discrete points, the random variable is called *continuous*, and its probability distribution is called *continuous* as well. Continuous distributions are defined by their *probability density functions* (PDFs)—basically, functions that describe the shape of the curve on the graph. They are often denoted by the standard mathematical notation for functions, $f(x)$, where x represents the possible values the random variable can take.

A common mistake is to think of $f(x)$ as the probability that the random variable will take the value x, analogously to the way we defined the PMF

$p(x)$. This is incorrect. In fact, the value of $f(x)$ may be greater than 1, which a probability cannot be. Instead, we need to think about probabilities for continuous distributions in terms of *areas* under a curve that describes the probability distribution. Intuitively, the reason continuous distributions are associated with areas under the PDF $f(x)$ is that a continuum represents an infinite number of values that the random variable can take. If we try to assign a bar whose height equals a nonzero probability to each value the random variable can take, as we did in the case of the binomial distribution, the total sum of all bars (and, hence the total probability for that distribution) will be infinity. However, the total probability, added up over all possible values for the random variable, cannot be more than 1.

Consequently, a better way to think of the probability of each particular value of the random variable is as infinitely small (virtually, 0), but then realize that when many, many of these values are added together, they have a significant probability mass. This is the concept of *integration* in calculus. The area under a given curve can be computed by adding up an infinite number of tiny areas above intervals of length dx on the x-axis. The probability that a continuous random variable takes values between two constants a and b can be expressed as the integral

$$\int_a^b f(x)\,dx,$$

and the total probability (the area under the entire curve) should be 1:

$$\int_{-\infty}^{\infty} f(x)\,dx = 1.$$

It turns out that the binomial distribution approaches a very important continuous distribution, called the *normal distribution*, as the number of trials becomes large. The normal distribution is bell-shaped and is entirely defined by two parameters: its mean μ and standard deviation σ. This means that if we know them, we can draw the shape of the distribution. (We will introduce the concepts of mean and standard deviation shortly. For now, just think of μ and σ as inputs to the formula for the normal distribution PDF.) This is because the normal PDF is given by the formula

$$f(x) = \frac{1}{\sigma\sqrt{2\pi}} e^{-\frac{(x-\mu)^2}{2\sigma^2}}.$$

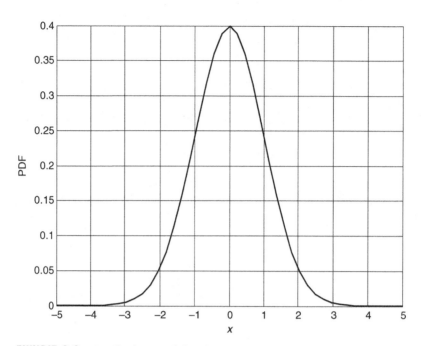

EXHIBIT 3.6 Standard normal distribution.

The standard normal distribution has $\mu = 0$ and $\sigma = 1$ (see Exhibit 3.6). You may also encounter the notation $f(x|\mu, \sigma)$, that is,

$$f(x|\mu, \sigma) = \frac{1}{\sigma\sqrt{2\pi}} e^{-\frac{(x-\mu)^2}{2\sigma^2}}.$$

The symbol | stands for "conditional on" or "given." In other words, given specific values for μ or σ, the PDF for the normal distribution is given by the preceding formula. The symbol | will be useful in other circumstances as well, such as stating the PDF of a random variable conditional on the realization of another random variable. For example, the probability distribution of asset returns in one time period may depend on ("be conditional on") the realization of asset returns in the previous time period. We will provide a more formal definition of conditioning in section 3.10.

The normal distribution appears surprisingly often in nature and was studied in detail well before its prominent use in finance. Modern day random process modeling in finance has borrowed a lot of findings from natural sciences such as physics and biology. For example, a classical assumption in modeling asset returns is that the changes in asset prices over small periods of time are normally distributed (despite the fact that the empirical evidence from real-world markets does not support the position that changes in asset returns follow a normal distribution). We will use the normal distribution extensively in this book.

The binomial and the normal distributions are famous representatives of the two classes of probability distributions: discrete and continuous. However, there are numerous other useful probability distributions that appear in practice. We will review some of these distributions later in this chapter. But first, let us introduce a couple of important concepts for describing probability distributions.

3.5 CONCEPT OF CUMULATIVE PROBABILITY

Cumulative probability is the probability that a random variable takes a value that is less than or equal to a given value. Cumulative probability is an important concept, and is available as a function from a number of software packages, including Excel and MATLAB. The *cumulative distribution function* (CDF) can be thought of as a listing of the cumulative probabilities up to every possible value the random variable can take. Examples of CDFs for a continuous and a discrete distribution are shown in Exhibit 3.7. The CDFs always start at 0 and end at 1, but the shape of the curve on the graph is determined by the PDF or PMF of the underlying random variable. (The CDF for a discrete random variable has a characteristic staircase-like shape—i.e., "step function" in mathematical jargon.)

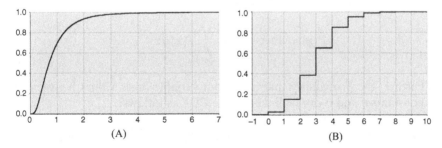

EXHIBIT 3.7 The CDF of (A) a continuous random variable (lognormal), and (B) a discrete random variable (binomial with 10 trials and probability of success 0.30). The values on the horizontal axis are the values the random variable takes.

To show how one would compute cumulative probability for a discrete distribution, let us consider the binomial distribution example from section 3.3, which is also the CDF plotted in Exhibit 3.7(B).

Suppose that the probability of success is 0.30, and we would like to compute the probability that the number of successes in 10 trials will be at most six. Intuitively, we are trying to estimate the total height of the first six bars in the first picture in Exhibit 3.4(B). We can write this expression as

$$P(\tilde{X} \leq 6) = P(\tilde{X} = 1) + \cdots + P(\tilde{X} = 6)$$

$$= \frac{10!}{1!(10-1)!} 0.30^1 (1 - 0.30)^{10-1} + \cdots$$

$$+ \frac{10!}{6!(10-6)!} 0.30^6 (1 - 0.30)^{10-6}$$

$$= \sum_{k=1}^{6} \frac{10!}{k!(10-k)!} 0.30^k (1 - 0.30)^{10-k}$$

where we have used the classical symbol Σ for sum.

To construct the entire CDF, we would perform the same calculation for all possible values of $\tilde{X}$, that is, compute $P(\tilde{X} \leq 0)$, $P(\tilde{X} \leq 1)$, ... , $P(\tilde{X} \leq 10)$. We would then plot $\tilde{X}$ on the x-axis, and the corresponding $P(\tilde{X} \leq x)$ on the vertical axis (by convention referred to as the y-axis).

For continuous distributions, we would replace the sum by an integral, and find the area under the PDF that is less than or equal to a given constant. For example, if $f(x)$ is the PDF of a continuous probability distribution (such as the normal distribution and other distributions such as t, chi-square, and exponential distributions that we describe later), then the CDF (usually denoted by $F(x)$) can be computed as

$$F(x) = P(\tilde{X} \leq x) = \int_{-\infty}^{x} f(x)\, dx.$$

Further, the probability that a random variable takes values between two constants a and b can be linked to the CDF as follows:

$$P(a \leq \tilde{X} \leq b) = \int_{a}^{b} f(x)\, dx = F(b) - F(a).$$

To illustrate this, let us look at the picture in Exhibit 3.8. Suppose we would like to compute the probability that the random variable takes a value

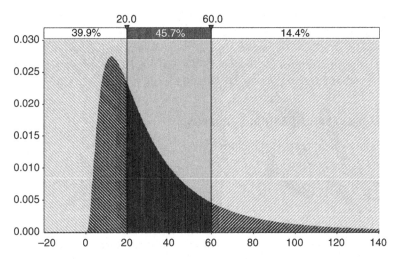

EXHIBIT 3.8   Calculation of the probability that the random variable falls between 20 and 60 as a difference of cumulative probabilities up to 20 and 60.

between 20 and 60 (which is the area under the PDF between 20 and 60, and is 45.7% according to the picture). To compute that probability, we can equivalently compute the cumulative probability (the area) up to 20 (which is 39.9% according to the picture) and subtract it from the cumulative probability (the area) up to 60 (which is $100\% - 14.4\% = 85.6\%$). We obtain $F(60) - F(20) = 85.6\% - 39.9\% = 45.7\%$, which is the same number.

3.6   DESCRIBING DISTRIBUTIONS

A probability distribution can be used to represent the uncertain outcomes of a project, or the possible future value of an investment in an asset. But what does the picture of this probability distributions tell us, and how can we convey the most important insights to others? This section introduces mathematical terminology for describing probability distributions. Specifically, the graph of a probability distribution gives us information about:

■ Where the most likely or most representative outcomes are (central tendency).
■ Whether we can be optimistic or pessimistic about the future (skew).
■ What the risk is (spread and tails of the distribution).

Finance practitioners are also often concerned with how "fat" the tails of the distribution are—which tells us how likely it is that "extreme" events, that is, events that are very far from the "representative" outcomes in the middle of the distribution, will occur. We will discuss a measure of this distribution characteristic (*kurtosis*) in section 3.6.4.

3.6.1 Measures of Central Tendency

Measures of central tendency include:

■ Mean
■ Median
■ Mode

The mean is by far the most commonly utilized measure in financial applications for theoretical reasons, despite the fact that it has some serious drawbacks, most notably sensitivity to extreme values. We discuss the mean in the most detail, and review briefly the other two measures.

Mean   On an intuitive level, the *mean* (also called the "expected value" or the "average") is the weighted average of all possible outcomes in the distribution, where the weights equal the probabilities that these values are taken. This is easier to imagine in the case of discrete distributions than in the case of continuous distributions, but the main idea is the same.

In mathematical jargon, the mean is called the *first moment* of a probability distribution.[2] It is denoted as $E[\tilde{X}]$ (for "expected value of the random variable $\tilde{X}$").

In the case of a discrete distribution,

$$E[\tilde{X}] = \sum_{\text{All values } x \text{ of the random variable}} x \cdot P(\tilde{X} = x).$$

In the case of a continuous distribution,

$$E[\tilde{X}] = \int_{-\infty}^{\infty} x \cdot f(x)\, dx.$$

For example, the mean of the Bernoulli distribution in section 3.2 is

$$0 \cdot 0.70 + 1 \cdot 0.30 = 0.30$$

The mean of a normal distribution can be computed as

$$E[\tilde{X}] = \int\limits_{-\infty}^{\infty} x \cdot \frac{1}{\sigma\sqrt{2\pi}} e^{-\frac{(x-\mu)^2}{2\sigma^2}} \, dx$$

In the case of the normal distribution, of course, this calculation is redundant since the parameter μ in the expression inside the integral is actually the mean. However, the mean is not a parameter in the PDF formulas for most probability distributions, and this is the calculation that would be used to compute it. To practice, you can compute the preceding integral, and verify that the calculation indeed gives μ as the answer.

As a final remark, we note that the mean is not always the "middle point" of the range of the distribution. (We will see ample examples in this book.) One outlier (that is, one value for the random variable that is very far from the others) can shift the mean significantly. Note also that the mean does not have to be one of the values of the probability distribution, as the previous Bernoulli example illustrated. (The mean for the Bernoulli distribution was 0.30, which is not 0 or 1.) The mean is merely the "center of gravity" of the probability distribution.

Median   The *median* is a more robust measure of the "middle" of the distribution. It is the value on the horizontal so that 50% of the distribution lies on each side of it. Since the median does not take into consideration where the values on each side of it lie (as opposed to the mean, which considers the actual values and their probabilities of occurrence), the median is not as influenced by the presence of extreme values (values that are very far from the center of the distribution) as the mean.

Mode   The *mode* of a distribution is the most likely outcome. One can think of it as the value at which the PDF/PMF of the distribution is at its highest. For example, in Exhibit 3.4, the mode of the first binomial distribution is 3, the mode of the second distribution is 5, and the mode of the third distribution is 7.

You may hear about "unimodal" or "bimodal" distributions. These terms basically just refer to how many "peaks" the distribution has. Almost all theoretical distributions used in financial modeling are unimodal, as their properties are easier to model mathematically. The distributions we have introduced so far, for example, are unimodal. Of course, real-world data do not always follow neat mathematical rules, and may present you with distributions that have more than one mode.

3.6.2 Measures of Risk

Variance and Standard Deviation When thinking of risk, one usually thinks of how far the actual realization of an uncertain variable will fall from what one *expects*. Therefore, a natural way to define a measure of uncertainty is as the *spread*, or *dispersion* of a distribution. Two measures that describe the spread of the distribution are *variance* and *standard deviation*. The two are strongly related: the standard deviation is the square root of the variance, and we usually need to compute the variance before computing the standard deviation. Exhibit 3.9 illustrates the relationship between variance/standard deviation and the spread of the distribution. Suppose we are considering investing in two assets, A and B. The probability distribution for B has a wider spread and higher variance/standard deviation than the probability distribution for A.

Mathematically, the variance of a random variable is related to the *second moment* of a probability distribution, and is computed as follows:

For discrete distributions:

$$Var(\tilde{X}) = \sum_{\text{All values } x \text{ of the random variable}} (x - \mu)^2 \cdot P(\tilde{X} = x)$$

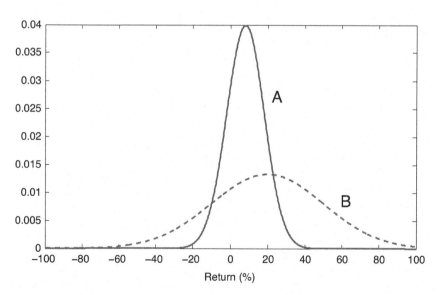

EXHIBIT 3.9 Comparison of two probability distributions in terms of risk and central tendency.

For continuous distributions:

$$Var(\tilde{X}) = \int_{-\infty}^{\infty} (x - \mu)^2 \cdot f(x)\, dx$$

In the preceding equations, μ denotes the mean of the distribution.

In words, the variance is the sum of the squared deviations of all values in the probability distribution from the mean (used as a measure for the center) of the distribution. The reason why squared deviations are used is so that deviations to the left of the mean do not cancel deviations to the right of the mean when added together.[3] Otherwise, a distribution that has many observations far from the center and, therefore, has a large "spread," may end up with the same variance as a distribution with values very close to the mean and a small spread. In fact, a distribution that has a very wide spread may end up with a variance of zero if all large positive deviations from the mean have corresponding large negative deviations. This would make variance useless as a measure of spread.

Sometimes, a more convenient (and equivalent) way of expressing the variance is through the equation

$$Var(\tilde{X}) = E[\tilde{X}^2] - \left(E[\tilde{X}] \right)^2$$

$$= \sum_{\text{All values } x} x^2 \cdot P(\tilde{X} = x) - \left(\sum_{\text{All values } x} x \cdot P(\tilde{X} = x) \right)^2 \quad \text{(in the discrete case)}$$

$$= \int_{-\infty}^{\infty} x^2 \cdot f(x)\, dx - \left(\int_{-\infty}^{\infty} x \cdot f(x)\, dx \right)^2 \quad \text{(in the continuous case)}$$

These expressions link the variance explicitly to the first and the second moments of the distribution.

The variance of a distribution measures the spread in square units of the random variable, and the number is difficult to interpret. The *standard deviation* is widely used instead. The standard deviation simply takes the square root of the variance ($\sigma_X = \sqrt{Var(\tilde{X})}$), and presents a measure of the average deviation of the values in the distribution from the mean that has the same units as the random variable, hence making it easier to interpret. In the financial context, standard deviation is often used interchangeably with the term "volatility."

Coefficient of Variation   Let us consider again the picture in Exhibit 3.9. We mentioned that the probability distribution for A has a smaller standard deviation than the probability distribution for B, but notice also that the mean of the distribution for A is lower than the mean for the distribution for B. If you had to invest in one of them, which one would you choose? This situation brings up the idea of measuring spread (the "risk" of the distribution) relative to the mean (the "representative" value of the distribution). This is the statistical concept of *coefficient of variation* (CV), which is reported in percentages, and is mathematically expressed as

$$CV = \frac{\sigma}{\mu} \times 100,$$

where μ is the mean and σ is the standard deviation of the distribution. The CV gives us a unit-free ratio that can be used to compare random variables. If the CV for investment A is 70% and the CV for investment B is 50%, we may decide that investment A is more "risky" than B relative to the average return we can expect, even though investment A has the smaller standard deviation.

CV represents the trade-off between expectation and risk from the statistical point of view. In finance, the inverse ratio is often used (that is, instead of the amount of risk per unit of expected reward, one looks at the expected reward per unit of risk). The financial measure became popular based on work by Sharpe (see, for example, Sharpe 1994). We will talk about the Sharpe ratio in the context of portfolio optimization in Chapter 7. The main idea behind using both measures, however, is the same.

Range   The *range* of a random variable is the difference between the maximum and the minimum value a random variable can take. It can sometimes be used as a measure of "riskiness"; however, be on alert that it is not applicable in many situations. For example, some important probability distributions, such as the normal distribution, have an infinite range, as the random variables can take values from negative infinity to positive infinity. You should also be extremely careful when using range in the context of simulation. We will discuss this issue further in Chapter 4.

Percentiles   Another useful term for describing distributions is the *percentile*. The α-percentile of a distribution is the number on the x-axis so that a percentage α of the total probability lies to the left of that number. Probability distributions can be compared by their percentiles: for example, if the 5th percentile of the distribution for investment B in Exhibit 3.9 is less than the 5th percentile of the distribution for investment A, we may argue that investment B is more risky than investment A because it will result in a lower outcome than investment A with 5% probability. We will use percentiles extensively in the context of analyzing simulation results (Chapter 4) and portfolio risk management (Chapter 8).

3.6.3 Skew

Distributions can be symmetric or asymmetric (skewed), depending on whether the "tails" at the two ends of the distribution are the same or different. Whether distributions are further classified as *left-skewed* (*negatively skewed*) or *right-skewed* (*positively skewed*) basically depends on where the mean is relative to the median. Symmetric distributions have the same mean and median, whereas left-skewed distributions have a longer left tail (which implies that the mean is to the left of the median, as it has been skewed by extreme values). There are several rather involved definitions that are used to represent skew mathematically, and it is beyond the scope of the book to present them here. The important thing to note is that all of the formulas for skew use the *third moment* of a probability distribution, and agree on the intuitive definition of skew: that left skew means longer left tail, whereas right skew means longer right tail. The normal distribution, which is symmetric, has a skew of 0.

3.6.4 Kurtosis

In finance, we are frequently interested in the behavior in the "tails" of a distribution. If the tails are "fat," this means that extreme observations are more likely to happen, and expected values are not as useful. *Kurtosis* measures the "fatness" of the tails of a distribution. The normal distribution, which is used as the standard for comparison, has a kurtosis of 3. A kurtosis of more than 3 (in general, high value for kurtosis) means that the probability distribution has fatter tails and a sharper peak than the normal distribution, whereas a low value for kurtosis means that the tails are "leaner" than the tails of the normal distribution.[4] The mathematical formula for kurtosis, just as the formula for skew, is rather involved, but the important thing to note is that kurtosis is related to the *fourth moment* of a probability distribution.

3.7 BRIEF OVERVIEW OF SOME IMPORTANT PROBABILITY DISTRIBUTIONS

This section lists some additional important probability distributions, their PMFs/PDFs, and summary measures. For an overview of these and other probability distributions and how they arise in practice, see, for example, Evans, Hastings, and Peacock (2000).

3.7.1 Discrete Distributions

We have already discussed two discrete distributions, the binomial distribution and the Bernoulli distribution. Next we discuss two other discrete distributions: the discrete uniform distribution and the Poisson distribution. Other interesting discrete distributions that will not be covered here are the geometric distribution, hypergeometric distribution, and negative binomial distribution.

Discrete Uniform Distribution   The *discrete uniform distribution* represents a situation in which a random variable can take a prespecified number of discrete values, and each value has an equal chance of occurring. A simple example of such distribution is a roll of a fair die: There are six possible outcomes, 1, 2, 3, 4, 5, 6, and each of them happens with the same probability (see Exhibit 3.10).

It can be easily seen that if the random variable can take N values and if the total probability needs to be 1, then the probability of each

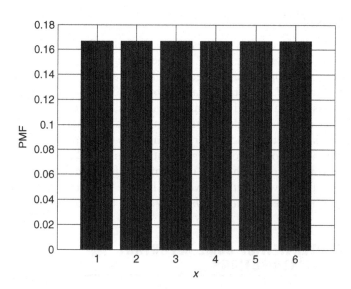

EXHIBIT 3.10   Discrete uniform distribution.

individual value should be 1/*N*. Therefore, the PMF of the discrete uniform distribution is

$$P(\tilde{X} = x) = \frac{1}{N}.$$

The discrete uniform distribution is very useful in a variety of applications, and we will encounter it again, for example, when learning about sampling by bootstrapping in Chapter 8.

Poisson Distribution   The *Poisson distribution* applies in situations in which one is concerned about the probability of having a given number of arrivals in a prespecified time interval, where these arrivals are assumed to be independent of one another. It is widely used for modeling jumps in electricity prices (referred to as "spikes," because prices typically return to their original levels), and in credit risk modeling because defaults or other credit-related events can be modeled as "arrivals" in a random process.[5] We will see applications in Chapter 12.

The Poisson PMF is given by

$$f(x) = \frac{\lambda^x}{x!} e^{-\lambda}.$$

It requires an input parameter, λ, that corresponds to the average number of arrivals during the time period.

A picture of a Poisson distribution with $\lambda = 5$ is shown in Exhibit 3.11. You can imagine incorporating the distribution into a model for the process followed by the price of electricity, in which the price spikes on average five times per day because of transmission constraints or unexpected outages. The Poisson distribution in the picture is slightly skewed, which means that the probability that fewer than five spikes occur in a day is slightly more than the probability that more than five spikes occur in a day.

The Poisson distribution has a number of interesting properties. Notably, it looks very much like a binomial distribution if the number of trials in the binomial distribution is large, and the probability of success at every trial is adjusted so that the probability of success remains constant as the number of trials grows large. More precisely, a binomial random variable with number of trials n and probability of success λ/n at every trial approaches a Poisson distribution with parameter λ as n grows large.

Furthermore, the Poisson distribution looks like the normal distribution if the parameter λ (mean arrivals per unit time) grows large. In fact, the effect is noticeable for λ as small as 20 arrivals. (Plot the distribution with

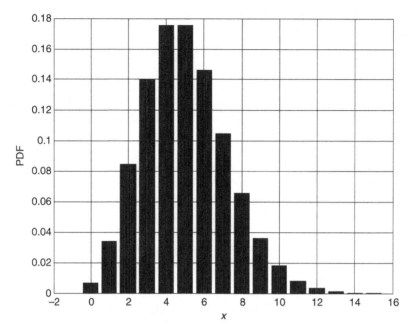

EXHIBIT 3.11   Poisson distribution with $\lambda = 5$.

@RISK or MATLAB to see its shape.) As λ increases, the Poisson distribution approaches a normal distribution with mean λ and standard deviation $\sqrt{\lambda}$.

3.7.2 Continuous Distributions

In addition to the normal distribution that we described earlier, the continuous distributions that we review are the

- Continuous uniform distribution
- Triangular distribution
- Student's t-distribution
- Lognormal distribution
- Exponential distribution
- Chi-square distribution
- Beta distribution

Other interesting continuous distributions that are not discussed here are gamma (Erlang) distribution, Cauchy distribution, and Gumbel (Extreme Value) distribution.

Continuous Uniform Distribution The *continuous uniform distribution* represents a situation in which a random variable can take a continuum of values on a *range* (say, between two numbers *a* and *b*) with equal probability. This distribution presents a simple example of why the value of the PDF $f(x)$ at a point x should not be treated as the probability of x. Since the total probability mass under the PDF needs to be 1, the height of the line on the graph of the uniform distribution (that is, the value of the PDF at each point on the range $[a,b]$) is $1/(b - a)$. This number can be greater than 1, depending on the values of *a* and *b*, which is not allowed for a probability. For example, if *a* is 3 and *b* is 3.5, then $(b - a) = 0.5$, and the PDF $f(x)$ at any point x between 3 and 3.5 is $1/0.5 = 2$ (see Exhibit 3.12(A)).

To summarize, the PDF of the continuous uniform distribution is

$$f(x) = \frac{1}{b - a}, \quad a \leq x \leq b.$$

The "standard" continuous uniform distribution on the interval $[0,1]$ (that is, when $a = 0$ and $b = 1$) plays a very important role in simulation. We will come back to it in Chapters 4 and 14.

Triangular Distribution The *triangular distribution* is a simple distribution with wide applications in capital budgeting, marketing, and decision analysis. It is often used when we do not have very much information about

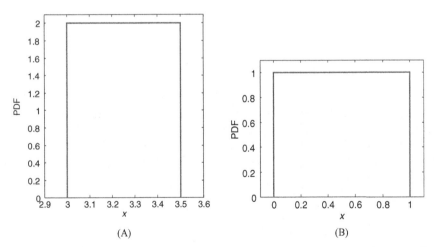

EXHIBIT 3.12 Examples of continuous uniform distributions: (A) on the interval [3, 3.5]; (B) on the interval [0, 1].

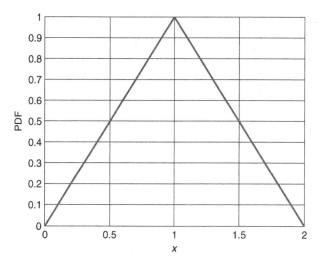

EXHIBIT 3.13 Triangular distribution.

the underlying distribution, but can specify a worst-case scenario (1), a best-case scenario (2), and a most likely scenario (3). Exhibit 3.13 shows an example of a triangular distribution. Its PDF outlines a triangle, and the triangle does not need to be symmetric. The PDF is given by

$$
f(x) = \begin{cases} \dfrac{2(x-a)}{(b-a)(c-a)} & \text{for } a \leq x \leq c \\[2mm] \dfrac{2(b-x)}{(b-a)(b-c)} & \text{for } c \leq x \leq b \\[2mm] 0 & \text{otherwise} \end{cases}
$$

Student's t-Distribution The *Student's t-distribution* (or simply *t*-distribution) looks very much like the normal distribution in shape, but the weight in the tails is determined by a parameter v (associated with degrees of freedom in statistics).[6] Examples t-distributions for different values of are given in Exhibit 3.14. The PDF for the t-distribution is

$$
f(x) = \frac{\Gamma\left(\dfrac{v+1}{2}\right)}{\Gamma\left(\dfrac{v}{2}\right)} \frac{1}{\sqrt{v\pi}} \frac{1}{\left(1+\dfrac{x^2}{v}\right)^{\frac{v+1}{2}}},
$$

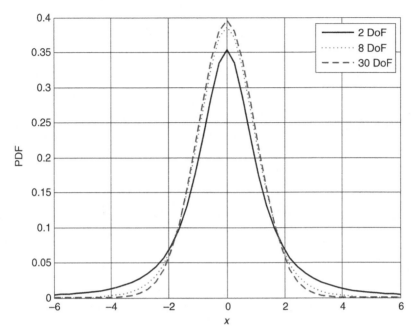

EXHIBIT 3.14 Examples of *t*-distributions for different degrees of freedom.

where $\Gamma(y)$ is the so-called *gamma function* $(\Gamma(y) = \int_0^\infty t^{y-1} e^{-t} dt)$.

The *t*-distribution arises in some very important applications in statistics, in particular, in calculating confidence interval estimates for the true mean of a distribution and hypothesis testing (see sections 3.11.2 and 3.11.4). Since simulation bears strong resemblance to statistical sampling, we will encounter the *t*-distribution when we discuss simulation in the next chapter.

Lognormal Distribution The *lognormal distribution* has one of the most prominent uses in modern finance. It arises when values for the random variable cannot be negative, and tend to be asymmetrically distributed, which has been observed for stock prices and real estate prices (see Exhibit 3.15). The PDF of the lognormal distribution is

$$f(x) = \frac{1}{x\sigma\sqrt{2\pi}} e^{-\frac{(\ln(x)-\mu)^2}{2\sigma^2}}, \quad x > 0$$

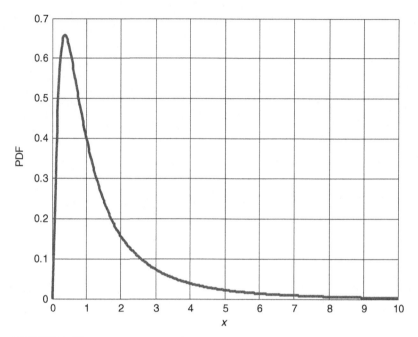

EXHIBIT 3.15 Lognormal distribution.

Note the resemblance to the PDF for the normal distribution from 3.4. In fact, there is a very direct relationship between a lognormal and a normal random variable. Specifically, if $\tilde{Y}$ is a normal random variable with mean μ and standard deviation σ, then the random variable $\tilde{X} = e^{\tilde{Y}}$ is lognormal with the PDF above.

Exponential Distribution The *exponential distribution* is related to the Poisson distribution. While the Poisson distribution measures the number of arrivals in a given period of time (assuming arrivals are independent), the exponential distribution measures the time between independent arrivals. The PDF of the exponential distribution is

$$f(x) = \lambda e^{-\lambda x}, \quad x \geq 0.$$

In fact, the parameter λ is the same parameter we saw in the definition of the Poisson distribution.

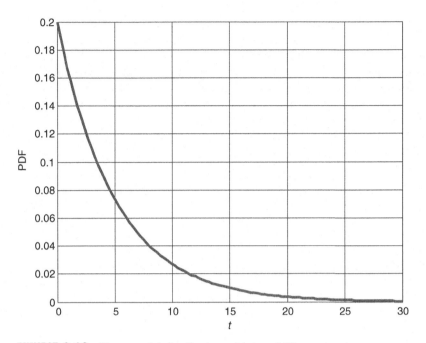

EXHIBIT 3.16   Exponential distribution with $\lambda = 0.02$.

If we expect an average of λ arrivals during a unit time period, then the average time we would expect between arrivals is $1/\lambda$ (which happens to be the mean of the exponential distribution). A picture of the exponential distribution is shown in Exhibit 3.16. Note that if we "slice" the distribution vertically and consider the piece of the curve to the right of the value at which we sliced, that piece has the same shape as the original distribution. This is the so-called "memoryless" property of the exponential distribution, which, counterintuitively, means that the distribution of the time until the next arrival does not depend on how long you have waited. Specifically, if 30 minutes have already elapsed, the probability that you will see an arrival after 10 minutes is the same as the probability you would have seen an arrival after 10 minutes at the beginning of the first time period of 30 minutes.

Similarly to the Poisson distribution, the exponential distribution is widely used in credit risk modeling and in high-frequency modeling of arrival time between orders in financial markets (referred to as "trade duration").

Chi-Square Distribution   The *chi-square distribution* (often denoted $\chi 2$ *distribution*) is used predominantly in hypothesis testing in statistics. The reason we list it here, given our focus on financial applications, is because it is the basis for goodness-of-fit tests that decide whether a particular distribution is appropriate for modeling an observed set of data. The sum of k independent squared normal random variables follows a chi-square distribution with k degrees of freedom. [7]

The PDF of the chi-square distribution is given by

$$f(x) = \frac{2^{-k/2}}{\Gamma(k/2)} x^{k/2-1} e^{-x/2}, \quad x > 0,$$

where Γ is the gamma function, as defined earlier in this section, and k is the "degrees of freedom." A picture of the distribution is shown in Exhibit 3.17.

Beta Distribution   The *beta distribution* is very flexible in terms of shape, and is useful for representing a variety of models of uncertainty. In contrast to other distributions that have a distinctive skew, the beta distribution is

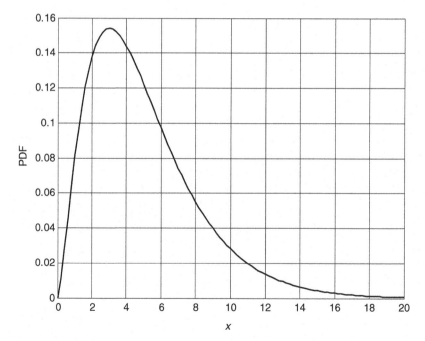

EXHIBIT 3.17   Chi-square distribution with five degrees of freedom.

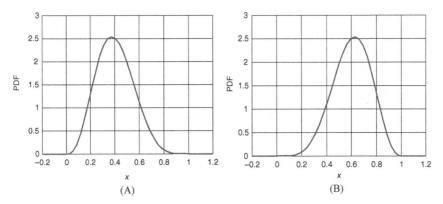

EXHIBIT 3.18 Examples of beta distributions: (A) A beta distribution with parameter values equal to 4 and 6; (B) A beta distribution with parameter values equal to 6 and 4.

defined by two parameters, α and β, which define the shape and the skew of the distribution. The precise formula for the PDF is

$$f(x) = \frac{x^{\alpha-1}(1-x)^{\beta-1}}{\dfrac{\Gamma(\alpha)\Gamma(\beta)}{\Gamma(\alpha+\beta)}}, \quad x > 0, \alpha > 0, \beta > 0.$$

Exhibit 3.18 illustrates the shape with parameter values equal to 4 and 6, and 6 and 4, respectively. You can observe that the skew of the beta distribution changes depending on the relative magnitudes of α and β.

3.8 DEPENDENCE BETWEEN TWO RANDOM VARIABLES: COVARIANCE AND CORRELATION

So far, we have shown how one can describe a single random variable. In finance, we often need to worry about the relationships between two or more variables. For example, in the context of investments, if the return investment A in Exhibit 3.9 goes up on average, does the return on investment B go up as well? In capital budgeting, if the value of one project we are considering goes down, will the value of other projects in the company's portfolio go up or down? If we can measure these kinds of relationships, we can, for example, protect ourselves against extreme situations in which all of our investments crash simultaneously.

Two commonly used measures of codependence between random variables are *covariance,* often denoted by *Cov,* and *correlation,* often denoted by the Greek letter rho (ρ). The two are strongly related.

The idea behind covariance is to measure simultaneous deviations from the means for two random variables, X and Y. If $\tilde{X}$ takes a value above its mean μ_X, does $\tilde{Y}$ take a value above its mean μ_Y as well? If it does, then we would like to increase our measure of covariation to reflect a higher degree of codependence. If the two random variables move in opposite directions (that is, when one of them takes a value above its mean, the other one takes a value below its mean), then we would like to subtract from our measure of covariation. Mathematically, this idea is expressed as

$$Cov(\tilde{X}, \tilde{Y}) = E\left[(\tilde{X} - \mu_X)(\tilde{Y} - \mu_Y)\right].$$

Recall that E stands for "expectation," or "average." Thus, the covariance measures whether the two random variables move together on average. If the covariance is 0, the two variables are independent.

The concept of covariance appears very often in modern portfolio theory, and we will come back to it in Chapter 8. However, sometimes it is more convenient to use a normalized form of the expression for covariance—the *correlation coefficient.* The problem with covariance is that its units are products of the original units of the two random variables, so the number for covariance is difficult to interpret. The correlation coefficient divides the covariance by the product of the standard deviations of the two random variables:

$$\rho = Corr(\tilde{X}, \tilde{Y}) = \frac{Cov(\tilde{X}, \tilde{Y})}{\sigma_X \sigma_Y}$$

The result is a value that is always between −1 and 1. If the correlation between two random variables is close to 1, they are strongly positively correlated; that is, if one of them takes a value above its mean, the other one is very likely to take a value above its mean as well. If the correlation is close to −1, they are strongly negatively correlated; that is, if one of them takes a value above its mean, the other one is very likely to take a value below its mean. If the correlation is 0, then the two variables are independent—meaning knowing whether one of them is above or below its mean value does not tell you anything about where the value of the other variable may be.

An important observation here is that covariance and correlation exist only for pairs of random variables. They are not computed for more than two variables at a time. Thus, if the situation calls for analysis of dependence between more than two random variables, the covariances and correlations are reported in a table (referred to as a "covariance matrix" and "correlation matrix", respectively). If there are N variables to analyze, the covariance and the correlation tables each have N rows and N columns. The entry in the ith row and jth column is the covariance/correlation of the ith variable and the jth variable. The values in the diagonal of these matrices (that is, entries in the ith row and ith column) are equal to the variance of the ith variable (in the case of covariance matrix) and 1 (in the case of the correlation matrix). Appendix A, Basic Linear Algebra Concepts, on the companion web site, briefly introduces matrix arrays. We will discuss covariance and correlation matrices in more detail in Chapter 7.

When dealing with financial data, we often need to be concerned with *autocorrelation*. Autocorrelation exists when the realizations of a random process over time (such as the movement of a stock price) depend on the history of the process, that is, when a random variable (such as the stock return) in one time period is correlated with itself (the return) during previous time periods. We will see examples in Chapters 12, 14 and 15.

It is worth noting that while covariance and correlation are very useful measures of dependence, and are widely used in financial applications, they do not paint a complete picture of how random variables are codependent, and can sometimes be misleading. This is particularly true in cases in which two variables are nonlinearly related.[8] Exhibit 3.19 contains one such illustration. Consider two random variables, $\tilde{X}$ and $\tilde{Y}$, where $\tilde{X}$ follows a continuous uniform distribution on the interval [0,20], and $\tilde{Y} = e^{\tilde{X}}$. One hundred observations from the probability distribution of $\tilde{X}$ are drawn, the corresponding values for $\tilde{Y}$ are computed, and the points are plotted in Exhibit 3.19. Note that $\tilde{X}$ and $\tilde{Y}$ are perfectly dependent—knowing the value of $\tilde{X}$, we can predict the exact value for $\tilde{Y}$. Yet, when we compute the correlation coefficient between $\tilde{X}$ and $\tilde{Y}$, we get a value of about 0.5. The latter shows relatively strong positive dependence, but is not 1, that is, it does not reflect the fact that $\tilde{X}$ and $\tilde{Y}$ are actually perfectly dependent. The correlation coefficient would measure the dependence correctly, however, if $\tilde{X}$ and $\tilde{Y}$ had a linear relationship, that is, if $\tilde{Y}$ were a linear function of $\tilde{X}$ of the kind $a\tilde{X} + b$ for some constants a and b.

3.9 SUMS OF RANDOM VARIABLES

As we mentioned in section 3.4, we often need to consider more than one uncertainty at a time, and thus we need tools to deal with sums of random variables, for example, the behavior of our total investments or overall return on multiple projects. Summarizing the joint probability distributions

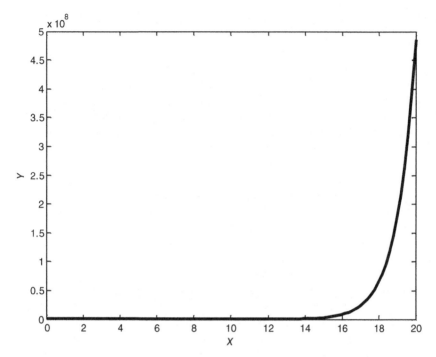

EXHIBIT 3.19   A connected graph of the realizations of $\tilde{X}$ versus the realizations of $\tilde{Y} = e^{\tilde{X}}$.

for sums of two or more random variables is not as easy as summing the two distributions. In this section, we review a few important facts about analyzing sums of random variables.

Suppose the return on investment A in Exhibit 3.9 is the random variable $\tilde{X}$, and the return on investment B is the random variable $\tilde{Y}$. Let $E[\tilde{X}]$ and $E[\tilde{Y}]$ be the expected returns of the two investments, and σ_X and σ_Y be their standard deviations. Suppose now we invest 0.40 (40%) of our funds in A, and 0.60 (60%) of our funds in B. Therefore, the return on the portfolio is $0.40 \cdot \tilde{X} + 0.60 \cdot \tilde{Y}$. What is the expected return on the portfolio, and what is the portfolio's standard deviation?

First, we need to ask what are the expected values of $0.40 \cdot \tilde{X}$ and $0.60 \cdot \tilde{Y}$. Note that even though 0.40 and 0.60 are numbers (constants), the products $0.40 \cdot \tilde{X}$ and $0.60 \cdot \tilde{Y}$ are random variables because they depend on random variables.

It turns out that for any random variable $\tilde{X}$,

$$E[a \cdot \tilde{X}] = a \cdot E[\tilde{X}]$$

if a is a constant.

Furthermore, it is always true that the expectation of the sum of two random variables is equal to the sum of the expectations:

$$E[\tilde{X} + \tilde{Y}] = E[\tilde{X}] + E[\tilde{Y}].$$

Therefore,

$$E[a \cdot \tilde{X} + b \cdot \tilde{Y}] = a \cdot E[\tilde{X}] + b \cdot E[\tilde{Y}].$$

This allows us to compute the expected value of our portfolio:

$$E[0.40 \cdot \tilde{X} + 0.60 \cdot \tilde{Y}] = 0.40 \cdot E[\tilde{X}] + 0.60 \cdot E[\tilde{Y}].$$

What about the risk of the portfolio? Most people would be tempted to extend the preceding reasoning to portfolio variance and standard deviation as well. However, variance and standard deviation are not nearly as "convenient" as the expectation operator. It turns out that

$$Var[a \cdot \tilde{X}] = a^2 \cdot Var[\tilde{X}],$$

$$Var(\tilde{X} + \tilde{Y}) = Var(\tilde{X}) + Var(\tilde{Y}) + 2 \cdot Cov(\tilde{X}, \tilde{Y}),$$

and

$$Var(a \cdot \tilde{X} + b \cdot \tilde{Y}) = a^2 \cdot Var(\tilde{X}) + b^2 \cdot Var(\tilde{Y}) + 2 \cdot a \cdot b \cdot Cov(\tilde{X}, \tilde{Y}).$$

There are no "nice" formulas for the standard deviation of a sum of random variables. We basically need to compute the variance of the sum (as we just did), and take the square root of the resulting expression to compute the standard deviation.[9]

There are two things to note. First, the constants a and b are squared once they are taken out of the expression inside the parentheses for the variance. Second, there is an additional term in the sum of the variances, which involves the covariance of the two random variables. Why does this hold at an intuitive level? We will provide some examples of this effect in Chapter 7, but the main idea is that if the random variables move in opposite directions of each other on average (this means that their covariance is negative), the variance of their sum (that is, the variance of the portfolio) is reduced. We are more likely to get extreme values for the combination of investments if they move in the same direction, that is, if they are strongly positively correlated. This was one of the great insights that came out of Harry Markowitz's theory on optimal portfolio allocation, which won him the 1990 Nobel Prize in Economic Science. It led to the proliferation of *diversification* as a strategy in managing assets.

So far, we reviewed what happens to the mean and the variance of a sum of two random variables. What about the actual probability distribution of a random variable that equals the sum of two random variables, for example, $\tilde{Z} = \tilde{X} + \tilde{Y}$?

It turns out that computing the distribution of $\tilde{Z}$ is not as easy as adding up the PMFs or PDFs of $\tilde{X}$ and $\tilde{Y}$. If it was, a total sum of probabilities for the distribution of $\tilde{Z}$ would be more than 1. Moreover, the distribution of the sum of the two random variables may look nothing like the distributions of the individual variables. For example, Exhibit 3.20 illustrates the distribution of the sum of two uniform random variables on [0,1]. The resulting distribution is the triangular distribution. Intuitively, this makes sense. For example, the mean values for both uniform distributions are in the middle—at 0.5. So, it appears logical that most of the mass for the sum of the probability distributions would be in the middle too—at the sum of the expected values, $0.5 + 0.5 = 1$. Also, the range for the new variable $\tilde{Z}$ should be [0,2]. This is because the ranges for $\tilde{X}$ and $\tilde{Y}$ are both [0,1], so the minimum value for their sum is $0 + 0 = 0$, and the maximum value for their sum is $1 + 1 = 2$.

Unfortunately, most sums of probability distributions are not as easy to visualize. The actual formula for computing the distribution of the sum of two random variables involves nontrivial integration, and is referred to as *convolution*. Let $f_X(x)$, $f_Y(y)$, and $f_Z(z)$ be the PDFs of the random variables $\tilde{X}$, $\tilde{Y}$ and $\tilde{Z}$ at points x, y, and z, respectively. Then the PDF for the sum $\tilde{Z}$ is

$$f_Z(z) = \int\limits_{-\infty}^{\infty} f_Y(z - x)\, f_X(x)\, dx.$$

As we learn more about simulation techniques in Chapter 4, the advantages of using simulation to evaluate such complex integrals will become evident.

3.10 JOINT PROBABILITY DISTRIBUTIONS AND CONDITIONAL PROBABILITY

The previous section reviewed important facts about sums of random variables. In this section, we introduce the concepts of joint probability distribution and conditional probability, which are also useful in situations in which we are dealing with more than one random variable.

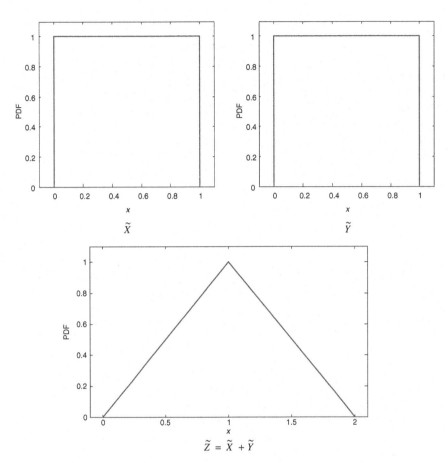

EXHIBIT 3.20 Sum (convolution) of two uniform random variables. The resulting probability distribution is triangular.

Joint probability is simply the probability that two random variables take two values at the same time. The joint PMF of two discrete random variables $\tilde{X}$ and $\tilde{Y}$ is denoted $p(\tilde{X}, \tilde{Y})$ or $p(\tilde{X} = x, \tilde{Y} = y)$. The joint PDF of two continuous random variables $\tilde{X}$ and $\tilde{Y}$ is denoted $f(\tilde{X}, \tilde{Y})$. When $\tilde{X}$ and $\tilde{Y}$ both follow a specific probability distribution, their joint probability distribution is typically referred to as a "multivariate" distribution. For example, if $\tilde{X}$ and $\tilde{Y}$ both follow normal distributions, their joint distribution is called *multivariate normal distribution*. If $\tilde{X}$ and $\tilde{Y}$ both follow binomial distributions, their joint distribution is called *multinomial distribution*.

In section 3.4, we briefly introduced the notation |, which means "conditional on." Conditioning on information has important applications in financial modeling, and we will see examples of it, for example, when we introduce variance reduction techniques in Chapter 14.

When two random variables are dependent, then knowing something about the realization of one of them should give us information about the likely realizations of the other one. (If it did not, then the two variables would be independent by definition.) The *conditional probability* that a random variable $\tilde{X}$ will take a value x given that a random variable $\tilde{Y}$ has taken value y is

$$P(\tilde{X} = x|\tilde{Y} = y) = \frac{P(\tilde{X} = x \text{ and } \tilde{Y} = y)}{P(\tilde{Y} = y)}.$$

Intuitively, the fact that $\tilde{Y}$ has taken the value y eliminates some of the possible outcomes for $\tilde{X}$, and the revised probability that $\tilde{X}$ will take a value x is computed as a percentage of all those instances in which $\tilde{X} = x$ given $\tilde{Y} = y$.

The *conditional PDF* of a continuous random variable $\tilde{X}$ given $\tilde{Y}$ is

$$f_{\tilde{X}|\tilde{Y}}(x|y) = \frac{f_{\tilde{X},\tilde{Y}}(x,y)}{f_{\tilde{Y}}(y)}.$$

This concept and notation extend to the summary measures for probability distributions as well. The *conditional expectation* of the random variable $\tilde{X}$ given that $\tilde{Y}$ has taken value y is simply the weighted average for the values of $\tilde{X}$ that are possible given the realization y of $\tilde{Y}$. The conditional expectation is denoted $E[\tilde{X}|\tilde{Y} = y]$, and the notation carries over to variance, covariance, and so on. The following facts hold:

$$E[\tilde{X}] = E_Y[E_X[\tilde{X}|\tilde{Y}]]$$
$$Var(\tilde{X}) = E_X[Var(\tilde{X}|\tilde{Y})] + Var(E_X[\tilde{X}|\tilde{Y}])$$
$$Cov(\tilde{X}, \tilde{Z}) = E_Y[Cov(\tilde{X}, \tilde{Z})|\tilde{Y}] + Cov(E_X[\tilde{X}|\tilde{Y}], E_Z[\tilde{Z}|\tilde{Y}])$$

For example, the first statement says that if we compute the mean of the possible values of a random variable $\tilde{X}$ when a specific realization of a random variable $\tilde{Y}$ has occurred, and then compute the sum (integral) of the means of the possible value of $\tilde{X}$ for all possible realizations of $\tilde{Y}$ (weighted by the probability of obtaining these realizations for $\tilde{Y}$), we should obtain the actual mean of $\tilde{X}$.

3.11 FROM PROBABILITY THEORY TO STATISTICAL MEASUREMENT: PROBABILITY DISTRIBUTIONS AND SAMPLING

More often than not, we are faced with data from which we try to deduce how uncertainty should be modeled, rather than knowing the exact probability distribution that these data should follow. Suppose you have collected a sample of N independent observations $X_1, \ldots, X_N$. You can imagine grouping similar observations together into "bins" (the bins can be as small as a single number), and creating a histogram of observed values. This histogram will be an *empirical* probability distribution. All of the concepts explained in section 3.6 (for describing central tendency, spread, skew, covariability, etc.) are valid for empirical distributions derived from samples of data. The difference is that when dealing with real-world data, we need to take into consideration the fact that there is inevitably some "noise." This noise may come from many sources, including inaccuracies in recording or handling the data, but a substantial source of imprecision in estimation is the limited number of observations. With financial data in particular, we can never observe or anticipate everything that can happen. We are not only limited in our ability to reconstruct a probability distribution from a fixed number of observations and forecasts, but also need to worry about rare events, which are difficult to observe, and thus are not necessarily a part of our sample. Hence, our estimates of the parameters of the "underlying" probability distribution for the empirical data are inherently inaccurate.

We refer to means, standard deviations, correlations, covariances, and other quantities estimated from data as *descriptive statistics* or simply *statistics*, while we refer to their "real" values (assumed to come from a specific underlying probability distribution that we cannot observe exactly because of the noise) as *parameters*. In fact, different notations are used to differentiate between the two concepts. Parameters are usually denoted by Greek letters such as μ (for mean), σ (for standard deviation), σ^2 (for variance), and ρ (for correlation). Statistics are usually denoted by Latin letters, such as $\overline{X}$ (for sample mean), s (for sample standard deviation), s^2 (for sample variance), and r (for sample correlation).

To compute these sample statistics, we use formulas very similar to the formulas for the corresponding parameters:

- Sample mean:

$$\overline{X} = \frac{1}{N} \cdot \sum_{n=1}^{N} X_n$$

■ Sample variance:

$$s^2 = \frac{1}{N-1} \cdot \sum_{n=1}^{N} (X_n - \overline{X})^2$$

■ Sample standard deviation:

$$s = \sqrt{\frac{1}{N-1} \cdot \sum_{n=1}^{N} (X_n - \overline{X})^2}$$

■ Sample covariance:

$$SCov(\tilde{X}, \tilde{Y}) = \frac{1}{N-1} \cdot \sum_{n=1}^{N} (X_n - \overline{X})(Y_n - \overline{Y})$$

■ Sample correlation:

$$r(\tilde{X}, \tilde{Y}) = \frac{SCov(\tilde{X}, \tilde{Y})}{s_X s_Y}$$

Note, for example, that the principle behind computing the sample mean is very similar to the principle behind computing the mean of a general distribution. The mean is still a weighted average of the possible values of the random variable. It is just that our sample contains N independent observations, so the probability of each of them must be $1/N$ (otherwise, the total probability would not add up to 1). Therefore, to compute the mean, we are weighing each observation by its probability of occurrence ($1/N$), and adding up the observations.

A substantial amount of research in statistics has been dedicated to finding ways to make the estimation of parameters through sampling accurate. For example, covariance and correlation estimates are widely used in forecasting the return on assets for portfolio management purposes, and are notoriously inaccurate because, as surprising as it seems, there are not actually enough data to estimate them reliably. (This is complicated by the fact that they vary over time.) The correlation coefficient we described in section 3.8 is the classical Pearson correlation coefficient. Another kind of correlation coefficient is the Spearman correlation. It does not incorporate as much information about the data as the Pearson correlation coefficient, but tends to be more stable than the Pearson correlation when there is noise in the data. The Spearman correlation is a *rank* correlation. In other words, instead of considering the *values* of the random variables, it computes the correlation between the ranks of the observations in a sample. The mean of the random variable is replaced by the mean of the rank.

Additionally, inferential statistics is concerned with evaluating the degree of accuracy of sample estimates. Some powerful and far-reaching concepts in this context include the Central Limit Theorem, confidence intervals estimates, bootstrapping, and hypothesis testing. These concepts are also widely used in simulation modeling.

3.11.1   Central Limit Theorem

Suppose that we have a sample of N independent observations $X_1, \ldots, X_N$ drawn from the same underlying distribution. (The shorthand for this statement is that $X_1, \ldots, X_N$ are IID, that is, independent and identically distributed.) Let us assume that the mean of the underlying distribution is μ_X and its standard deviation is σ_X. Let S_N denote the sum of the N observations, that is,

$$S_N = \sum_{n=1}^{N} X_n.$$

Then, as long as the sample size N is moderately large (greater than 30), and under some relatively mild technical conditions on the underlying probability distribution, the distribution of the sum S_N is normal with mean equal to $\mu_S = N \cdot \mu_X$ and standard deviation $\sigma_S = \sigma_X \cdot \sqrt{N}$. This means that if we are to take many, many samples (always of size N) from this distribution, compute the sums of the N observations for each of these samples, and plot these sums, we would obtain a graph that looks very much like the normal distribution.

The expressions for the mean and the standard deviation of the sum of IID random variables in the *Central Limit Theory* (CLT) follow easily from the rules in section 3.9. However, the fact that the distribution of the sum approaches normal is not at all obvious. It is one of the greatest demonstrated links between probability theory and applied statistics, and is to a large extent the reason for the popularity of the normal distribution in practice. The power of the CLT is the conclusion that many real-world phenomena should be well described by the normal distribution, even if the underlying random process that generates them is unknown.

The CLT result serves as the justification for many practitioners to use the normal distribution as an approximation when they analyze the risk of their investments. The argument is that as returns accumulate over time, "things become normal." The problem arises, however, if the assumptions behind the CLT are not satisfied in practice. For example, the underlying distributions from which samples are drawn change over time depending on market conditions, and there can be correlation across returns from different time periods, so the IID assumption does not necessarily hold. The nonnormality of returns is especially pronounced in high-frequency trading, as the time intervals between trades are too short to allow for "things to approach" the normal distribution. As we will see in Parts Two and Three, this kind of reasoning can lead to a gross underestimation of investment risk.

3.11.2 Confidence Intervals

One of the consequences of the CLT is that it allows us to make statements about the accuracy of our estimate of the sample mean. The sample mean $\overline{X}$ we introduced earlier in this section can be expressed as a sum of N IID variables, $X_1/N, \ldots, X_N/N$. Therefore, the CLT applies. Using the rules in section 3.9, it can be shown that the sample mean $\overline{X}$ follows an approximately normal distribution with mean $\mu_{\overline{X}} = \mu_X$ and standard deviation $\sigma_{\overline{X}} = \sigma_X/\sqrt{N}$.

Therefore, we know the variability of our sample mean estimate. The standard deviation of $\overline{X}$, also called *standard error* of the estimate, is inversely proportional to the square root of the number of observations in the sample. Not surprisingly, the more observations we have, the more accurate our estimate of the true average of the distribution will be. In practice, of course, we do not know the true standard deviation σ_X (if we knew it, we would know the mean as well, so we would not be trying to estimate mean). So, we need to make some adjustments—use the standard deviation s from the sample to approximate σ_X—and modify the estimation slightly to account for the additional inaccuracy that using a sample statistic in the formula brings.[10]

The concept of *confidence interval* (CI) estimates is to present not only a point estimate for the parameter of interest (in this case, one value for the sample mean $\overline{X}$), but also to state something about how far away this estimate will be from the true parameter (the true mean of the underlying distribution). This is achieved by stating an interval centered at $\overline{X}$ whose length depends on:

1. The variability of the estimate (the larger the standard error of $\overline{X}$, the less likely it is that we will get the correct estimate for the true mean from the sample).
2. The degree of confidence we have that this interval will cover the true mean.

Typical values for the confidence level include 90%, 95%, and 99%. The exact formula for a $(100 - \alpha)\%$ CI for the sample mean $\overline{X}$ is

$$\left[\overline{X} - t_{(100-\alpha/2), N-1} \frac{s}{\sqrt{N}}, \; \overline{X} + t_{(100-\alpha/2), N-1} \frac{s}{\sqrt{N}} \right],$$

where $t_{(100-\alpha/2), N-1}$ is $(100 - \alpha)^{\text{th}}$ percentile (the value on the x-axis) of a t-distribution with $N - 1$ degrees of freedom.[11] In words, the $(100 - \alpha)\%$ CI for the sample mean $\overline{X}$ states that the probability that the interval computed from the preceding formula covers the true mean μ is $(100 - \alpha)\%$.

As we saw in Exhibit 3.17, the t-distribution becomes very close to the normal distribution as the parameter for degrees of freedom v (which here equals $N - 1$) becomes large. In the context of simulation, where sample sizes would generally be large, replacing the value of the percentile from the t-distribution with the value of the percentile from the normal distribution will make no difference for all practical purposes.

3.11.3 Bootstrapping

The CI estimate for the mean is the confidence interval most widely used in practice. However, sometimes we need to evaluate the accuracy of other parameter estimates for one or more distributions. For example, we may be concerned about how accurate our estimates of the distribution percentile or skewness are. (This kind of application is relevant in portfolio risk management.) Alternatively, suppose that you have computed the correlation between historical returns on Investment A and Investment B from Exhibit 3.9, and have discovered that it is 0.6. Is this a strong correlation in the statistical sense, that is, does it appear to be strong just by chance (because we picked a good sample), or can we expect that will remain strong in other samples, given the overall variability in this sample's data?

The procedure of computing the CI estimate of the mean is a representative of classical methods in statistics, which relied on mathematical formulas to describe the accuracy of a sample statistic estimate. There are some theoretical results on confidence interval estimates for distribution parameters other than the mean, but in general, the results are not as easy to summarize as the closed-form expression for the CI estimate for the mean from section 3.2.

Bootstrapping[12] is a statistical technique that is useful in such situations. It involves drawing multiple samples of the same size (say, k samples) at random from the observations in the original sample of n observations. Each of the k samples is drawn with replacement—that is, every time an observation is drawn, it is placed back in the original sample, and is eligible to be drawn again, in the same sample or in future samples.

After drawing k samples from the original sample, the statistic corresponding to the parameter we are interested in estimating (whether it is percentile, skewness, correlation, or a general function of the random variable) is computed for each of the k samples. The so-obtained k values for the sample statistic are used to form an approximation for the parameter's *sampling distribution*. This sampling distribution can be used, for example, to determine what values of the sample statistic are most likely to occur, what is the variability of the estimate, and what the 5th and the 95th percentile of the approximate sampling distribution are. These percentiles provide an approximation for the confidence interval for the true parameter we are trying to estimate.

At first glance, this technique appears pointless. Why do we not collect k more samples instead of reusing the same data set k times? The reason is that it is expensive to collect data, and that sometimes additional data collection is not an option, especially with financial data.

Bootstrapping is used not only for evaluating the accuracy in the estimate of a probability distribution parameter, but also as a simple method for generating forecasts for uncertain quantities based on a set of historical observations for risk management purposes. The concept of simulation is necessary to understand how the bootstrap method is actually applied, as the random draws from the original sample need to be generated with a random number generator. (See Chapter 4 for a discussion of the simulation technique, and Practice 4.2 on the companion web site to see an application of the bootstrapping technique for evaluating the accuracy of the estimate of the 5th percentile of a portfolio's return.)

3.11.4 Hypothesis Testing

Hypothesis testing is a fundamental concept in statistics. The procedure is as follows. We start out by stating a hypothesis (the *null hypothesis*) about a parameter for the distribution that corresponds to a variable of interest. For example, we claim that the skew of the distribution for the returns of the S&P 500 index is zero. (As we will see later in this book, while often unjustified, making assumptions like these substantially simplifies risk measurement and derivative pricing.) Then we take a sample of S&P 500 returns, and estimate the skew for that sample. Suppose we get a skew of −0.11. The statistical hypothesis testing methodology allows us to test whether the value obtained from the sample (−0.11) is sufficiently "close" to the hypothesized value (0) to conclude that, in fact, the "real" skew could indeed be zero, and that the difference is only a consequence of sampling error.

To test whether the difference between the hypothesized and the observed value is *statistically significant*, that is, large enough to be considered a reason to reject the original hypothesis, we would compute a quantity called *test statistic*, which is a function of observed and hypothesized parameters. In some cases, this test statistic follows a known probability distribution. For example, if we are testing a hypothesis about the sample mean, then the test statistic is called the *t-statistic* because it follows a *t*-distribution with degrees of freedom equal to the sample size minus one. Knowing that the test statistic follows a specific distribution, we can see whether the test statistic obtained from the sample is "very far" from the center of the distribution, which tells us whether the sample estimate we obtained would be a rare occurrence if the hypothesized value were true.

There are different ways to measure the rarity of the observed statistic. Modern statistical software packages typically report a *p-value*, which is the probability that, if our null hypothesis were true, we would get a more extreme sample statistic than the one we observed. If the *p*-value is "small" (the actual cutoff is arbitrary, but the values typically used are 1%, 5%, or 10%), then we would reject the null hypothesis. This is because a small *p*-value means that there is very small probability that we would have obtained a sample statistic as extreme as the one we obtained if the hypothesis were true, that is, that the current test statistic is in the tails of the distribution.

The type of hypothesis tests we described so far are called *one-sample hypothesis tests* because they interpret the information only for one sample. There are *two-sample hypothesis tests* that compare observed statistics from two samples with the goal of testing whether two populations are statistically different. They could be used, for example, to compare whether the returns of one investment have been statistically better on average than the returns on another investment.

Finally, more sophisticated hypothesis tests are used in the background for a number of important applications in financial modeling. Multivariate regression analysis, which we will discuss in the context of factor model estimation in Chapter 11, uses hypothesis testing to determine whether a forecasting model is statistically significant. Goodness-of-fit tests, which are used in the context of fitting probability distributions to observed data, use statistical hypothesis testing to determine whether the observed data are statistically "significantly close" to a hypothesized probability distribution. Chi-square tests, which we mentioned in section 3.7.2, are a very popular type of goodness-of-fit tests. (See also the discussion on selecting probability distributions as inputs for simulation models in section 4.1.1 of the next chapter.)

SUMMARY

- Uncertainty can be represented by random variables with associated probability distributions.
- Probability distributions can be viewed as "listings" of all possible values that can happen and the corresponding probability of occurrence, and are conveniently represented in graphs (histograms and bar charts).
- Probability distributions can be discrete or continuous. Discrete distributions are defined over a countable number of values, whereas continuous distributions are defined over a range. Discrete distributions are described by probability mass functions (PMFs), whereas continuous distributions are described by probability density functions (PDFs).
- A continuous random variable can take an infinite number of values, and the probability of each individual value is 0. In the context of continuous distributions, we replace the concept of probability of a value with the concept of probability of an interval of values, and the probability is the area under the PDF.
- Probability distributions can be summarized in terms of central tendency (mean, median, and mode), variability (standard deviation, variance, coefficient of variance [CV], range, percentile, etc.), skewness, and kurtosis.
- The mean, variance, skew, and kurtosis of a probability distribution are related to the first, second, third, and fourth moment of the distribution. The moments of a probability distribution can be computed from its moment generating function. Inversely, if the moments of a probability distribution are known, most generally the distribution can be uniquely identified. However, sometimes the moments do not exist.
- Important discrete probability distributions include the binomial distribution, the Bernoulli distribution, the discrete uniform distribution, and the Poisson distribution.
- Important continuous probability distributions include the normal distribution, the continuous uniform distribution, the triangular distribution, the Student's t-distribution, the lognormal distribution, the exponential distribution, the chi-square distribution, and the beta distribution.
- Covariance and correlation are measures of average codependence of two random variables.
- Empirical distributions are derived from data. All summary measures for probability distributions apply to empirical distributions.
- The Central Limit Theorem states that the probability distribution a sum of N independent and identically distributed observations tends to a normal distribution with a specific mean and standard deviation.

- Confidence intervals allow us to state both our estimate of a parameter of an unknown probability distribution and our confidence in that estimate.
- Bootstrapping is a statistical technique for evaluating the accuracy of sample statistics based on one sample of observations. It involves drawing multiple samples from the original sample, calculating the sample statistic in each of them, and analyzing the resulting distribution of the sample statistic. Bootstrapping can also be used as a simple way to generate future forecasts for uncertain quantities based on a sample of past observations.
- Hypothesis testing is a statistical methodology for evaluating whether a statistic observed in a sample is significantly different from the expected value of a parameter of interest. It is used in many applications, including goodness-of-fit tests, multivariate regression analysis, and comparisons of two populations.

SOFTWARE HINTS

@RISK

@RISK has very convenient features for defining probability distributions. As explained in Appendix B, Introduction to @RISK (on the companion web site) you can see the distribution and how its shape changes immediately after entering the distribution parameters in the dialog box. It is also easy to compute probabilities and cumulative probabilities with @RISK by simply sliding the bar on the graph, as shown in Appendix B and Chapter 4. @RISK provides summary statistics for distributions automatically.

To calculate means, standard deviations, and other summary statistics for *empirical* distributions (that is, when you are given data in a sample, rather than data that have already been processed and organized to fit a probability distribution), you can use Excel's built-in functions as well:

- =AVERAGE(Array) computes the sample average value of Array.
- =STDEV(Array) computes the sample standard deviation of Array.
- =VAR(Array) computes the sample variance of Array.
- =PERCENTILE(k,Array) returns the value that represents the kth percentile in Array.
- =PERCENRANK(Array,x) returns the rank of the value x inside the data set Array.
- =COVAR(Array1,Array2) computes the sample covariance of Array1 and Array2.
- =CORREL(Array1,Array2) computes the sample correlation of Array1 and Array2.

	A	B	C	D	E
1	x	P(X=x)			
2	2	0.6			
3	5	0.1			
4	10	0.3			
5	Mean		4.7	=SUMPRODUCT(A2:A4,B2:B4)	

EXHIBIT 3.21 Example of calculation of the mean of a general discrete probability distribution with Excel.

Unfortunately, Excel has no built-in functions for computing descriptive statistics for general distributions. In other words, you cannot request that Excel compute the weighted average of distribution values. However, it is easy to do this manually. The function SUMPRODUCT(Array1, Array2) multiplies the corresponding values in Array1 and Array2, and adds them up. Exhibit 3.21 illustrates an example of its application. In this case, SUMPRODUCT computes the mean of a general discrete distribution by taking each of the values in the distribution (2, 5, and 10), multiplying it by its probability (0.6, 0.1, and 0.3), and adding up all the resulting products.

MATLAB

We provide the MATLAB commands for producing the probability distributions graphs in this chapter.

Bernoulli Distribution   Note that the Bernoulli distribution is just a binomial distribution with one trial, so we can use the MATLAB command for binomial PDF to plot the PDF of the Bernoulli distribution.

```
p = 0.3; % Probability of success for each trial
n = 1; % Number of trials
k = 0:n; % Outcomes
m = binopdf(k,n,p); % Probability mass vector
bar(k,m) % Create a bar chart
grid on
```

Binomial Distribution
```
p = 0.3; % Probability of success for each trial
n = 3; % Number of trials
k = 0:n; % Outcomes
```

```
m = binopdf(k,n,p); % Probability mass vector
bar(k,m) % Create a bar chart to visualize the probability
distribution
grid on
```

Normal Distribution

```
>> mu = 0; sigma = 1;
>> x=linspace(-5,5,45); y = normpdf(x,mu,sigma);
>> plot(x,y); grid on
```

Discrete Uniform Distribution

```
>> x = 1:6; y = (1/6)*ones(1,6);
>> bar(x,y); grid on
```

Continuous Uniform Distribution
To obtain the picture in Exhibit 3.12(A), use

```
>> x = 3:0.1:3.5; y = unifpdf(x,3,3.5);
>> plot([3 x 3.5],[0 y 0])
```

To obtain the picture in Exhibit 3.12(B), use

```
>> x = 0:0.1:1; y = unifpdf(x);
>> plot([0 x 1],[0 y 0])
```

Triangular Distribution
MATLAB has no function for computing the triangular PDF directly, but you can plot the function manually by using plot(x,y). For example, use

```
>> x = [0 1 2]; y = [0 1 0];
>> plot(x,y)
```

Student's *t*-Distribution
The function tpdf(x,n) computes the PDF of a *t*-distribution with n degrees of freedom. To obtain the family of *t*-distributions with varying degrees of freedom in Exhibit 3.14, use

```
>> x=linspace(-6,6,45);
>> y=tpdf(x,2); plot(x,y); grid on;
>> hold on
```

```
>> y=tpdf(x,8); plot(x,y,'r:');
>> y=tpdf(x,30); plot(x,y,'g—'); >> hold off
```

Lognormal Distribution
```
>> x = (0:0.02:10); y = lognpdf(x,0,1);
>> plot(x,y); grid on;
```

Exponential Distribution
```
>> lambda = 0.2; % Failure rate
t = 0:0.3:30; % Outcomes
f = exppdf(t,1/lambda); % Probability density vector
plot(t,f) % Visualize the probability distribution
grid on
```

Poisson Distribution
```
>> x = 0:15; y = poisspdf(x,5);
>> bar(x,y); grid on
```

Chi-Square Distribution
```
>> x = 0:0.2:20; y = chi2pdf(x,5); plot(x,y); grid on
```

Beta Distribution   To get the graph in Exhibit 3.18(A), use

```
>> x=linspace(-.2,1.2,45); y = betapdf(x,4,6);
>> plot(x,y); grid on;
```

To get the graph in Exhibit 3.18(B), use

```
>> x=linspace(-.2,1.2,45); y = betapdf(x,6,4);
>> plot(x,y); grid on;
```

MATLAB has a number of built-in functions for computing descriptive statistics of samples of data. These include mean (for calculating the mean of a sample), std (for calculating sample standard deviation), cov (for calculating sample covariance), corrcoef (for calculating sample correlation), and prctile (for calculating the kth percentile of a given set of data). See MATLAB's help for specific syntax and examples. Also, as explained in Appendix C, Introduction to MATLAB (on the companion web site) MATLAB's commands usually use as inputs multidimensional arrays, so you can compute summary statistics along different dimensions of the arrays. For example, suppose you have a set of data for the returns on 30 assets over 100 days, stored in a matrix DataMx with 100 rows and 30 columns. You can compute the mean return on a specific asset over the 100 days by computing the mean in that stock's column (mean(DataMx,2)), or compute the mean return on the 30 assets on a particular day by computing the mean in that day's row (mean(DataMx,1)), with a single command option in the mean command that specifies which dimension you are considering.

NOTES

1. The notation X_i, a capital letter corresponding to the name of the random variable, followed by an index, is a standard statistics notation to denote the ith observation in a sample of observations drawn from the distribution of the random variable $\tilde{X}$.

2. A complete review of probability theory is beyond the scope of this book, but the concept of moments of probability distributions is often mentioned in quantitative finance, so let us explain briefly what a moment generating function (MGF) is. The kth moment of a random variable is defined as

$$
m_k\left(\tilde{X}\right) = E\left[\tilde{X}^k\right] =
\begin{cases}
\displaystyle\sum_{\text{All values } x \text{ of the random variable}} x^k \cdot P(\tilde{X} = x) \\
\displaystyle\int_{-\infty}^{\infty} x^k \cdot f(x)\, dx
\end{cases}.
$$

For many useful cases (albeit not for all because for some distributions some moments may not exist), knowing these moments allows us to indentify uniquely the actual probability distribution. The MGF lets us generate these moments. It is defined as

$$
M_t\left(\tilde{X}\right) = E\left[e^{t\tilde{X}}\right] =
\begin{cases}
\displaystyle\sum_{\text{All values } x \text{ of the random variable}} e^{tx} \cdot P(\tilde{X} = x) \\
\displaystyle\int_{-\infty}^{\infty} e^{tx} \cdot f(x)\, dx
\end{cases}.
$$

By setting the value of the parameter t to different values (that is, 1,2,3, etc.), we can recover the first, second, third, and so on moment. While this construction looks rather awkward, it is very useful for proving theoretical results such as "The sum of two independent normal random variables is also a normal random variable." (The sum of two random variables does not necessarily have the same distribution as the random variables in the general case.) This is done by computing the MGF of the sum of two normal variables, and then checking if the resulting MGF is of the same type as the MGF of a normal random variable, which is computationally more convenient than computing the actual probability distribution of the sum of two random variables.

3. Recall that squaring a number always results in a nonnegative number, so the sum of squared terms is nonnegative.
4. Some software and simulation software packages report *excess kurtosis*, rather than kurtosis, as default. The excess kurtosis is computed as the value for kurtosis minus 3 (the kurtosis of the normal distribution), so that the normal distribution has kurtosis of 0. Make sure that you check the help file for the software package you are using before you interpret the value for kurtosis in statistical output.
5. The Poisson distribution is also widely used in operations management applications, such as queue management, revenue management, and call center staffing.
6. W. S. Gossett stumbled across this distribution while working for the Guinness brewery in Dublin. At the time, he was not allowed to publish his discovery under his own name, so he used the pseudonym *Student*, and this is how the distribution is known today.
7. The squared random variables arise when computing squared differences between observed values (which vary because the sample is random) and expected values. Chi-square goodness-of-fit tests consider the sum of the total squared differences between the observed frequencies of values in a sample and the expected frequencies if the sample came from a particular distribution. Whether the difference between what was observed and what was expected is statistically "large" depends on value of the difference relative to the critical value of the chi-square test statistic, which is computed from the chi-square distribution. See the brief introduction of hypothesis testing in section 3.11.4.
8. In other words, their relationship cannot be described by a straight line.
9. Note that this also eliminates the possibility that the standard deviation of the sum of two random variables is the sum of the standard deviations of the two variables. This is *never* true if the two random variables have different variances. If the two variables are independent (and the covariance is 0), we get

$$\sigma_{a \cdot \bar{X} + b \cdot \bar{Y}} = \sqrt{Var(a \cdot \bar{X} + b \cdot \bar{Y})} = \sqrt{a^2 \cdot Var(\bar{X}) + b^2 \cdot Var(\bar{Y})}$$
$$\neq a \cdot \sqrt{Var(\bar{X})} + b \cdot \sqrt{Var(\bar{Y})} = a \cdot \sigma_{\bar{X}} + b \cdot \sigma_{\bar{Y}}$$

10. This is where the discovery of Student's *t*-distribution made a substantial contribution to modern statistics.
11. A number of software packages have commands for computing the value of t, including Excel and MATLAB. For example, in MATLAB (and most statistical packages) one would use a command of the kind `tinv(100-α/2, degrees of freedom)`. Excel has a similar command (`=TINV(α, degrees of freedom)`), but it is a bit inconsistent. It takes in as an argument α, not 100-α/2, to compute the (100-α/2)th percentile of the *t*-distribution.
12. As explained in Chapter 2, there is a methodology commonly used in bond analysis to derive the term structure of interest rates that is referred to as bootstrapping. The statistical concept of bootstrapping described in this chapter has nothing to do with that methodology.

CHAPTER 4

Simulation Modeling

This chapter reviews the main idea behind Monte Carlo (MC) simulation, and discusses important issues in its application to business problems, such as number of scenarios to generate, interpretation of output, and efficient ways to simulate random numbers. Depending on which software you decide to use for simulation, you may read Appendix B for an introduction to @RISK or Appendix C for an introduction to MATLAB—both found on the companion web site.

4.1 MONTE CARLO SIMULATION: A SIMPLE EXAMPLE

As explained in Chapter 3, the analysis of risk is based on modeling uncertainty, and uncertainty can be represented mathematically by probability distributions. These probability distributions are the building blocks for simulation models. Namely, simulation models take probability distribution assumptions on the uncertainties as inputs, and generate scenarios (often referred to as *trials*) that happen with probabilities described by the probability distributions. They then record what happens to variables of interest (called *output variables*) over these scenarios, and let us analyze the characteristics of the output probability distributions (see Exhibit 4.1).

Let us start with a simple example. Suppose you want to invest $1,000 in the U.S. stock market for one year. To do so, you decide that you want to invest in a stock index that represents the performance of the stock market. Specifically, you invest in a mutual fund whose investment objective is to reproduce the return performance on the S&P 500. A mutual fund with such an objective is referred to as an *index fund*. We will denote the initial investment, or capital, invested in the index fund as C_0 (i.e., $C_0 = \$1,000$). How much money do you expect to have at the end of the year? Let us label the amount of capital at the end of the year by $\tilde{C}_1$.[1] Note that $\tilde{C}_1$ will be a

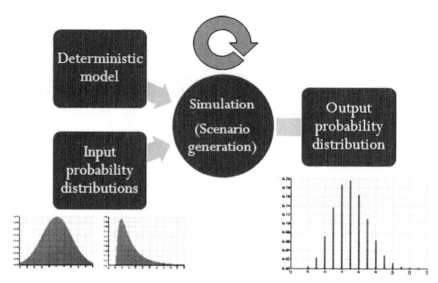

EXHIBIT 4.1 Typical Monte Carlo simulation system.

random variable because it will depend on how the market (i.e., S&P 500) performs over the year. In fact, if we let $\tilde{r}_{0,1}$ denote the market return over the time period $[0,1)$, then $\tilde{C}_1$ will equal

$$C_0 + \tilde{r}_{0,1} C_0$$

or, equivalently,

$$(1 + \tilde{r}_{0,1}) C_0$$

As explained in Chapter 2, the return $r_t, t + 1$ over a time period $[t, t + 1)$ can be computed as

$$\frac{P_{t+1} - P_t + D_t}{P_t}$$

where P_t and P_{t+1} are the values of the S&P 500 at times t and $t + 1$, respectively, and D_t is the amount of dividends paid over that time period. In this case, we can think of P_t and P_{t+1} as the S&P 500 index levels at the beginning $(t = 0)$ and at the end of the year $(t = 1)$, respectively, and assume that D_t is 0.

To estimate the end of year capital you would have, you can guess the return on the market, and compute the resulting value for $\tilde{C}_1$. However, this would give you only a point estimate of the possible values for your investment. A more sophisticated approach is to generate scenarios for the market return over the year, and compute $\tilde{C}_1$ in each of these scenarios. In other words, you can represent future returns by a probability distribution,[2] generate scenarios that are representative of this probability distribution, and then analyze the resulting distribution of your end-of-year capital. The resulting probability distribution of $\tilde{C}_1$ will be a set of scenarios itself. You can create a histogram of the outcomes, that is, collect the outcomes of the scenarios into nonoverlapping bins and draw bars above all bins with heights corresponding to the percentage of times outcomes in each bin were obtained in the simulation. This will allow you to visualize the *approximate* probability distribution of $\tilde{C}_1$, and analyze it with the statistical measures described in section 3.6 (central tendency, skew, variability, etc.) in the previous chapter. The distribution for $\tilde{C}_1$ from the simulation will be only an approximation because it will depend both on the *number* of scenarios and on the *set* of scenarios you generated for $\tilde{r}_{0,1}$. Intuitively, if you generate 1,000 scenarios that cover the possible values for $\tilde{r}_{0,1}$ well, you would expect to obtain a better representation of the distribution of $\tilde{C}_1$ than if you generated only two scenarios.

4.1.1 Selecting Probability Distributions for the Inputs

The first question you need to ask yourself when creating the simulation model about the future values of your funds is what distribution is appropriate for modeling the future market returns. One possible starting point is to look at a historical distribution of past returns, and assume that the future will behave in the same way. When creating scenarios for future realizations, then, you can draw randomly from historical scenarios. This is a very simple approach, which is based on the *bootstrapping* technique described in section 3.11.3.

Another possibility is to assume a particular probability distribution for future returns, and use historical data to estimate the *parameters* of this distribution, that is, the parameters that determine the specific shape of the distribution, such as the expected value (μ) and standard deviation (σ) for a normal distribution (see section 3.4), λ for a Poisson distribution (see section 3.7.1), or α and β for a beta distribution (see section 3.7.2). For example, if you assume a normal distribution for returns, then you can use the historical variability of returns as a measure of the standard deviation σ

of this normal distribution, and the historical average (mean) as the expected return μ of the normal distribution.

A third approach is not to start out with a particular distribution, but to use historical data to find a distribution for returns that provides the best *fit* to the data. As we mentioned in sections 3.7.2 and 3.11.4, the chi-square hypothesis test is one possible goodness-of-fit test. Other goodness-of-fit tests include the Kolmogorov-Smirnov (K-S) test, the Anderson-Darling (A-D) test, and root-mean-squared-error (RMSE).[3] Most simulation software packages, including MATLAB and @RISK, have commands that can test the goodness of fit for different probability distributions.[4]

Yet a fourth way is to ignore the past and look forward, constructing a probability distribution based on your subjective guess about how the uncertain variable in your model will behave. For example, using the beta distribution from Exhibit 3.18(A) to model the future market return will express a more pessimistic view about the market than using the beta distribution in Exhibit 3.18(B) or a normal distribution because most of the probability mass in the distribution in 3.18(A) is to the left, so low values for return will happen more often when scenarios are generated.

It is important to realize that none of these approaches will provide *the answer*. Simulation is a great tool for modeling uncertainty, but the outcome is only as good as the inputs we provide to our models. We discuss ways for defining input distributions in specific applications in the book. The art of simulation modeling is in providing good inputs and interpreting the results carefully.

4.1.2 Interpreting Monte Carlo Simulation Output

For purposes of our example, let us assume that the return on the market over the next year will follow a normal distribution. (This is a widely used assumption in practice, despite the fact that few empirical studies find evidence to support it.) Between 1977 and 2007, the S&P 500 returned 8.79% per annum on average, with a standard deviation of 14.65%. We will use these numbers as approximations for the average return and the standard deviation of the return on your investment in the stock market over the next year. Relying on historical data is flawed, but is a reasonable starting point.

This chapter's Software Hints section goes step-by-step through the actual implementation of our simple example with only Microsoft Excel functions, @RISK functions, and MATLAB functions. Here, we discuss the output one would obtain after generating 100 scenarios for the market return over the next year. Note that to generate these scenarios, we simply need to draw 100 numbers from a normal distribution with mean 8.79%

and standard deviation 14.65%. The input to the simulation would then be a sequence of 100 numbers such as

```
 0.0245
-0.1561
 0.1063
 0.1300
-0.0801
 0.2624
 0.2621
 0.0824
 0.1358
 0.1135
 0.0605
```

and so on.

The output graph would look like Exhibit 4.2. Summary statistics obtained based on the 100 values of the distribution are provided to the right of the graph.[5]

If historical trends hold, you would expect to have $1,087.90 on average at the end of the first year. The standard deviation of the end-year capital you would expect is $146.15, that is, on average, you would expect to be $146.15 off the mean value. With 5% probability, you will not be able to make more than $837.00 (the 5th percentile of the distribution), and with 95% probability you will make less than $1,324.00 (the 95th percentile of the distribution). The skewness is close to 0, and the kurtosis is close to 3, which means that the simulated distribution is close to normal. (In fact, the

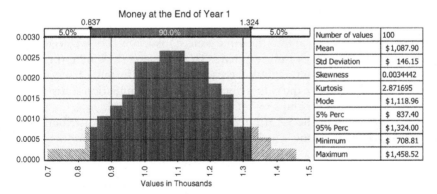

EXHIBIT 4.2 Histogram and summary statistics for the end-of-year distribution of 100 simulated values for $1,000 invested at the beginning of the year.

output distribution is normal because the input distribution we provided for the simulation of this simple relationship was normal, but the estimate from the simulation will never be perfectly accurate.)

Be careful with the interpretation of minima and maxima in a simulation. Theoretically, the minimum and maximum we could have obtained in this simulation are negative and positive infinity because the probability distribution for the return (the normal distribution) has an infinite range. We did not obtain a particularly small minimum or a particularly large maximum because we only simulated 100 values. An event in the tail of the distribution with probability of occurring of less than 1/100 would be unlikely to appear in this set of simulated values. The minimum and the maximum are highly sensitive to the number of simulated values and whether the simulated values in the tails of the distribution provide good representation for the tails of the distribution. There are smart ways to simulate scenarios so that the tails are well represented (we will talk about such methods later in this chapter), but the minimum and the maximum values obtained in a simulation should nevertheless be interpreted with care.

In section 3.11.2 in the previous chapter, we explained the statistical concept of confidence interval (CI) estimates. The main idea was the following: In statistics, when we want to estimate a specific parameter of a distribution, such as the mean, we take a sample and observe what the value of the parameter is in the sample (in technical terms, we record the value of the *sample statistic* for the mean). Instead of reporting a single value for our estimate for the mean, however, we could report an interval whose length is related to the probability that the true distribution parameter indeed lies in that interval.

Simulation is very similar to statistical sampling in that we try to represent the uncertainty by generating scenarios, that is, "sampling" values for the output parameter of interest from an underlying probability distribution. When we estimate the average (or any other parameter of interest) of the sample of scenarios, we run into the same issue statisticians do—we need to worry about the accuracy of our estimate. To compute a 95% CI estimate for the average end-of-year capital, we use the 95% CI formula from section 3.11.2, and substitute the values obtained from the simulation statistics: $N = 100$, $\overline{X} = 1,087.90$, and $s = 146.15$. The value for $t_{(100-\alpha/2)\%, N-1}$ for 95% CI is the value of the 97.5th percentile of the standard t-distribution with 99 degrees of freedom, which is 1.98. The 95% CI is therefore

$$\left(1,087.90 - 1.98 \cdot \frac{146.15}{\sqrt{100}}, 1,087.90 + 1.98 \cdot \frac{146.15}{\sqrt{100}}\right)$$
$$= (\$1,058.90, \$1,116.90).$$

Therefore, if the 100 scenarios were *independent* when generated, we can be 95% confident that the true average end-of-year capital will be between $1,058.90 and $1,116.90. It just happens that because of the simplicity of the example, we know exactly what the true mean is. It is $(1 + 0.0879) \cdot 1,000 = \$1,087.90$ because 8.79% was assumed to be the true mean of the distribution of returns (see section 3.9 for calculating means of functions of random variables), and it is indeed contained inside the 95% CI. In 5% of all possible collections of 100 scenarios, however, we will be unlucky to draw a very extreme sample of scenarios, and the true mean will not be contained in the confidence interval we obtain. Note that if we had calculated a 99% confidence interval, then this would happen in only 1% of the cases. If we generated $4N$ (instead of N) scenarios, then the 95% confidence interval's length would be half of the current length. (This is because the square root of the number of scenarios is contained in the denominator of the expression that determines the length of the confidence interval.) We will revisit the issue of confidence interval estimation and the implications for accuracy again later in this chapter when we talk about the number of scenarios needed in a simulation.

Also later in this chapter, we will explain how random numbers are actually generated. We will see that drawing "independent" samples from distributions is not the most efficient way to simulate random numbers that provide good representation of the underlying probability distribution. Most simulation engines nowadays (including the simulation engines in @RISK and MATLAB) use sophisticated methodology that estimates parameters from the distribution of output variables of interest a lot more accurately. The previous CI formula we used is in fact a conservative bound, rather than an exact estimate, for the actual accuracy in estimating the mean. Still, it is a useful benchmark to have.

4.2 WHY USE SIMULATION?

The example in the previous section illustrated a very basic MC simulation system. We started out with a deterministic model that involved a relationship between an input variable (market return $\tilde{r}_{0,1}$) and an output variable of interest (capital at the end of one year $\tilde{C}_1$). We modeled the input variable as a realization of a probability distribution (we assumed a normal distribution), generated scenarios for that input variable, and tracked what the value of the output variable was in every scenario by computing it through the formula that defines the relationship between $\tilde{C}_1$ and $\tilde{r}_{0,1}$. This is the general form of simulation models illustrated in Exhibit 4.1.

Despite its simplicity, this example allows us to point out one of the advantages of simulation modeling over pure mathematical modeling. Simulation enables us to evaluate (approximately) a *function* of a random variable. In this case, the function is very simple—the end-of-year capital, $\tilde{C}_1$, is dependent on the realization of the returns through the equation $(1 + \tilde{r}_{0,1})C_0$. If we are given a probability distribution for $\tilde{r}_{0,1}$, in some cases we can compute the probability distribution for $\tilde{C}_1$ in closed form. For example, if $\tilde{r}_{0,1}$ followed a normal distribution with mean $\mu_{0,1} = E[\tilde{r}_{0,1}]$ and standard deviation $\sigma_{0,1}$, then $\tilde{C}_1$ would follow a normal distribution too, with mean $(1 + \mu_{0,1})C_0$ and standard deviation $\sigma_{0,1}C_0$.

However, if $\tilde{r}_{0,1}$ did not follow a normal distribution, or if the output variable $\tilde{C}_1$ were a more complex function of the input variable $\tilde{r}_{0,1}$, it would be difficult and practically impossible to derive the probability distribution of $\tilde{C}_1$ from the probability distribution of $\tilde{r}_{0,1}$. Using simulation simplifies matters substantially.

There are three other important advantages of simulation that can only be appreciated in more complex situations. The first one is that simulation enables us to visualize the probability distribution resulting from compounding probability distributions for multiple input variables. The second is that it allows us to incorporate correlations between input variables. The third is that simulation is a low-cost tool for checking the effect of changing a strategy on an output variable of interest. Next, we extend the investment example to provide illustrations of such situations.

4.2.1 Multiple Input Variables and Compounding Distributions

Suppose now that you are planning for retirement and decide to invest in the market for the next 30 years (instead of only the next year). Suppose that your initial capital is still $1,000. You are interested in the return (and, ultimately, in the end-of-year capital, $\tilde{C}_{30}$) you will have after 30 years.

Let us assume that every year, your investment returns from investing in the S&P 500 will follow a normal distribution with the mean and standard deviation from the example in section 4.1.2. The final capital you have will depend on the realizations of 30 random variables—one for each year you are invested in the market.[6] We found through simulation in section 4.1.2 that the probability distribution of the capital at the end of the first year will be normal. What do you think the probability distributions for the total return and the capital at the end of the 30th year will look like? Will they be normal?

As explained in Chapter 2, an investment of $1 at time 0 will grow to $(1 + \tilde{r}_{0,1})(1 + \tilde{r}_{1,2}) \dots (1 + \tilde{r}_{t-1,t})$ dollars at the end of year t, and the total return $\tilde{r}_{0,t}$ from time 0 to time t equals

$$\tilde{r}_{0,t} = (1 + \tilde{r}_{0,1})(1 + \tilde{r}_{1,2}) \dots (1 + \tilde{r}_{t-1,t}) - 1.$$

Interestingly, the probability distribution of $\tilde{r}_{0,t}$ is not normal, and neither is the distribution of the capital at the end of 30 years. (The latter is basically a scaled version of the distribution of total return, since it can be obtained as $\tilde{C}_{0,t} = (1 + \tilde{r}_{0,t}) \cdot C_0$, and the initial capital C_0 is a constant [nonrandom] number). In general, here are some useful facts to keep in mind when dealing with multiple input probability distributions:

- When a constant is added to a random variable, as in 1 added to the random variable $\tilde{r}_{0,1}$, the distribution of $(1 + \tilde{r}_{0,1})$ has the same shape as the distribution of $\tilde{r}_{0,1}$; however, it is shifted to the right by 1.
- As we saw in section 3.9, when a random variable is added to another random variable (e.g., $\tilde{r}_{0,1} + \tilde{r}_{1,2}$), we cannot simply "add" the two probability distributions. In fact, even in cases when the two distributions have the same shape, the probability distribution of the sum of the random variables does not necessarily have the same shape. There are some exceptions—for instance, if we add two independent normal random variables, the probability distribution of the sum is normal. However, holding aside this case, this is not true in general.
- In our example, we are *multiplying* two random variables, $(1 + \tilde{r}_{0,1})$ and $(1 + \tilde{r}_{1,2})$ in order to obtain the total return. Products of random variables are even more difficult to visualize than sums of random variables. Again, it virtually never happens that a product of several random variables, even if the random variables all follow the same probability distributions, results in a random variable with that same probability distribution. The lognormal distribution, which we introduced in section 3.7.2 in the previous chapter, is a rare exception, and this is one of the reasons that the lognormal distribution is used so often in financial modeling. (Specific applications of the lognormal distribution are discussed in Chapter 12.)

Fortunately, simulation makes visualizing the probability distribution of the product easy. Exhibit 4.3 presents the output distributions for total return and capital at the end of 30 years. (For instructions in how to create the model, see Appendix B or C online, and then the summaries of instructions in this chapter's Software Hints.) We can observe (both from the graph and

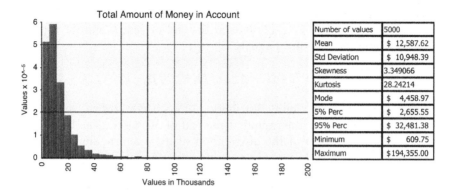

EXHIBIT 4.3   Output distribution for amount of capital after 30 years.

from the statistics for skewness and kurtosis) that the distribution is very skewed, even though the distributions for individual returns in each of the 30 years were symmetric.

4.2.2   Incorporating Correlations

Let us now complicate the situation more. Suppose that you have the opportunity to invest in stocks and Treasury bonds over the next 30 years. Suppose that today you allocate 50% of your capital to the stock market by investing in the index fund, and 50% in bonds. Furthermore, suppose over the 30 years you never rebalance your portfolio (i.e., you do not change the allocation between stocks and bonds). What will be the portfolio return after 30 years?

Historically, stock market and Treasury bond market returns have exhibited extremely low, but often statistically significant, negative correlation. This is because these two asset classes tend to move in opposite directions. When the stock market is performing poorly, investors tend to move their money to what they perceive to be safer investments such as bonds; conversely, when the stock market is performing well, investors tend to reallocate their portfolio increasing their allocation to the stock market and reducing their allocation to bonds.

Visualizing the impact of multiple input variables at the same time and incorporating correlations between these variables is very difficult to do in an analytical way. Simulation eliminates the need for complex mathematics, but preserves the benefits of creating richer and more accurate models. Correlations can be incorporated implicitly (by generating joint scenarios for realizations of input variables, e.g., by sampling from observed past data) or

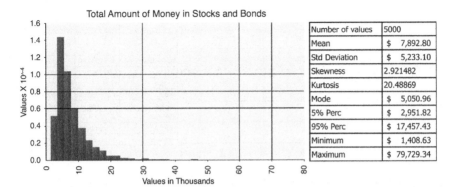

EXHIBIT 4.4 Histogram and summary statistics of the capital after 30 years from investing in the S&P 500 and Treasury bonds, taking into account the correlation between the returns on stocks and bonds.

explicitly, by specifying a correlations matrix as an input to the simulation. We will talk about incorporating the former technique further in Chapter 8. (See also Practice 4.2 on the companion web site.) Here, we give an example in which the correlations are specified as an input.

Let us assume that the correlation between the stock market and the Treasury bond market returns will be about –0.2. Let us also assume for the purposes of this exercise that the annualized return on the Treasury bonds in your portfolio will be normally distributed with mean 4% and standard deviation 7%. Therefore, the returns on the stock market and the bond market follow a multivariate normal distribution with correlation coefficient –0.2.

Exhibit 4.4 shows the output distribution after generating 5,000 scenarios for stock market (as measured by the S&P 500) returns and Treasury bond returns over 30 years. (See the end of this chapter for instructions on how to incorporate correlations in a simulation model with @RISK or MATLAB.) The shape of the distribution of the capital available after 30 years is similar to the shape of the distribution from Exhibit 4.3, but the variability is smaller. This issue is discussed further in the next section and in Chapter 7.

4.2.3 Evaluating Decisions

In the end, the goal of using simulation is to help us make decisions. Is a 50–50 portfolio allocation in stocks and bonds "better" than a 30–70 allocation? We will refer to the former allocation as Strategy A, and to the

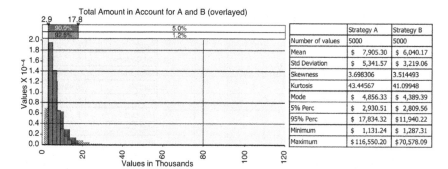

EXHIBIT 4.5 Comparison of Strategy A (equal allocation to stocks and bonds) and Strategy B (allocation of 30% to stocks and 70% to bonds).

latter as Strategy B. Let us evaluate the distribution of the capital at the end of 30 years for each allocation strategy, and use that knowledge to decide on the "better" allocation. Notice that it is unclear what "better" means in the context of uncertainty. We need to think about whether "better" for us means higher return on average, lower risk, acceptable trade-off between the two, and so on. Exhibit 4.5 contains the summary statistics of the simulated capital at the end of 30 years with each allocation over 5,000 scenarios.

We can observe that although Strategy A performs better than Strategy B as evaluated based on the mean capital at the end of 30 years, Strategy A's standard deviation is higher. In terms of risk–return trade-off, as measured by the coefficient of variation, Strategy A's CV is 67.57% (=\$5,341.57/\$7,905.30), whereas Strategy B's CV is 53.29% (=\$3,219.06/\$6,040.17), which makes Strategy A appear riskier than Strategy B. This is apparent also from the overlay chart shown in Exhibit 4.5—much of the mass of the histogram for Strategy B is contained within the histogram for Strategy A, which means that Strategy B has less variability and results in less extreme outcomes than Strategy A. One lesson here, however, is that the standard deviation may not be a good measure of risk when the underlying distributions are asymmetric. Strategy A's 5th percentile, for example, is higher than Strategy B's 5th percentile, meaning that if you are concerned with events that happen with 5% probability, Strategy A would be less risky. Strategy A also has a higher upside—its 95th percentile is higher than Strategy B's 95th percentile.[7] The fact that Strategy A has a high upside "penalizes" its standard deviation relative to the standard deviation of Strategy B because it results in more outcomes that are far away from the mean. A high standard deviation is not necessarily a bad thing if the largest deviations from the mean happen on the upside.

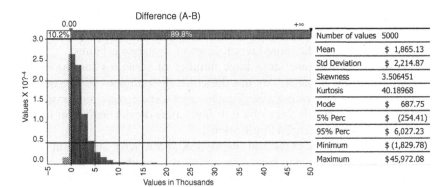

EXHIBIT 4.6 Histogram and summary statistics for the difference between the capital at the end of 30 years with Strategy A and with Strategy B.

It should be clear from the discussion so far that the summary statistics do not tell the whole story. It is important to look at the entire distribution of outcomes. Suppose now that we would like to compare Strategy A to Strategy B on a scenario-by-scenario basis. In what percentage of scenarios does Strategy B perform better than Strategy A? One efficient way to answer this question is to create an additional variable, Difference (A-B), that keeps track of the difference between the capital at the end of 30 years from Strategy A and from Strategy B during the simulation. Exhibit 4.6 shows a histogram of Difference (A-B) and presents its summary statistics.

It is interesting to observe that even though Strategy A appeared riskier than Strategy B based on the summary statistics in Exhibit 4.5 (Strategy A's standard deviation was almost twice the standard deviation of Strategy B), Strategy A results in lower realized outcomes than Strategy B in only 10.2% of the 5,000 generated scenarios. (As the graph in Exhibit 4.6 illustrates, 10.2% of the 5,000 scenarios for Difference (A-B) have values less than 0.) This perspective on the risk of one strategy versus the risk of another is valuable because it can substantially impact the final decision on which strategy to choose. For example, the problematic scenarios can be specifically identified, and in some situations, such as capital budgeting, managerial action can be taken to avoid them. A strategy that appears more risky may therefore be selected if it is desirable for other qualitative reasons.

When comparing two alternative decisions under uncertainty, it is technically correct (and fair) to evaluate them under the same set of scenarios. For example, when obtaining the summary statistics for Strategy A and Strategy B earlier, we should have used the same set of 5,000 scenarios for both. This would eliminate circumstances in which we happened to generate more favorable scenarios when evaluating one of the strategies than the other, which would have led us to conclude erroneously that the strategy evaluated over the more favorable set of scenarios is better.

In principle, if we generate a huge number of scenarios for the two strategies, even if the scenarios are not the same, the estimates will be quite accurate. However, generating a large number of scenarios is time consuming. Moreover, even a difference of a few digits after the decimal point may be significant in some financial applications.

The `RiskSimtable` command in @RISK does what we want by default—it generates the number of scenarios we specify, and then evaluates the values of the output variable over the same set of scenarios for each value of the parameters in the `RiskSimtable`. Thus, comparing summary statistics of several strategies when the `RiskSimtable` command is used is technically correct. However, `RiskSimtable` can be used only if one parameter changes at a time. (In our example, we varied one parameter: the percentage of capital to invest in stocks. The percentage to invest in bonds was determined automatically based on how much capital was left.) If we have a more complex situation with several parameters that can be tweaked, we would need to run every simulation separately. In that case, we would need to tell @RISK to simulate the same 5,000 scenarios even if we run the simulation with two separate calls. The way to do this is to specify the *seed* of the simulation under the **Sampling** tab of the dialog box that pops up after clicking on the **Settings Commands** button. We will explain what exactly the seed of the simulation is in section 4.4. For now, it is only important to understand that it determines how the random numbers are generated. By default, @RISK changes the seed every time it runs a simulation (as do other simulation packages). If we enter a particular number for the seed (depending on the software, different ranges for possible seed values are available), we will be fixing the scenarios that will be generated, which would enable @RISK to generate the same sequence of scenarios again next time it runs the simulation. MATLAB has similar options for setting the seed in a simulation.

If the program is not too long, the relationships are not overly complicated, and the intended number of scenarios is not too large, there is an easier alternative way to ensure that decisions are evaluated over the same set of scenarios. If we are evaluating the portfolio allocation example from this section in a spreadsheet, we can dedicate specific cells to the input variables (returns) that are common to all strategies we need to evaluate (see the models in this chapter's Software Hints). We can then reference the same cells during a simultaneous simulation for the capital at the end of the 30 years with each strategy, as is done in worksheet **Stock + Bond (2)** of the file **Ch4-ReturnSim.xlsx**. This will ensure that the same realizations of the input random variables in those cells are used for computing the output values for all strategies. In a programming language like MATLAB, we can dedicate variables in our program that store the generated scenarios, and then evaluate all the different strategies over that same set of scenarios. Storing 5,000 scenarios is not a problem, but if there are multiple variables and the number of scenarios increases substantially, we could run into memory problems.

4.3 IMPORTANT QUESTIONS IN SIMULATION MODELING

4.3.1 How Many Scenarios?

A simulation may not be able to capture all possible realizations of uncertainties in the model. For instance, think about the distribution of the end-of-year capital in section 4.1.1. As we explained in section 4.1.2., the possible number of values for the simulation output variable—the end-of-year capital—is technically infinite. Thus, we could never obtain the exact distribution of $\tilde{C}_1$ or the exact expected value $\tilde{C}_1$ by simulation. We can, however, get close. The accuracy of the estimation will depend on the number of generated scenarios. As discussed in section 4.1.2, if the scenario generation is truly random, then the variability (the standard error) of the estimate of the true expected value will be $s/\sqrt{N}$, where s is the standard deviation of the simulated values for the output variable, and n is the number of scenarios.

Hence, to double the accuracy of estimating the mean of the output distribution, we would need to quadruple (roughly) the number of scenarios. For instance, in the example in section 4.2, we generated 100 scenarios, and calculated that the average capital after one year is \$1,087.90, and that the 95% CI for the estimate of the average capital is (\$1,058.90, \$1,116.90). We concluded that we can be 95% confident that the true expected capital will be between \$1,058.90 and \$1,116.90, that is, that the true mean will not be further than \$29 from the mean estimated from the simulation (\$1,087.90). Now suppose that we had obtained the same numbers for sample mean (\$1,087.90) and sample standard deviation (\$146.15), but we had generated four times as many (400) scenarios. The 95% CI would have been

$$\left(1{,}087.90 - 1.97 \cdot \frac{146.15}{\sqrt{400}}, 1{,}087.90 + 1.97 \cdot \frac{146.15}{\sqrt{400}}\right)$$

$$= (\$1{,}073.53, \$1{,}102.27)[8]$$

This means that we could be 95% confident that the true mean would not be more than \$14.37 from the simulated mean of \$1,087.90, which is about half of the amount by which we could be off (\$29) when we generate 100 scenarios. Therefore, our accuracy has increased about twofold after quadrupling the number of generated scenarios.

Increasing the number of scenarios to improve accuracy can get expensive computationally, especially in more complicated multiperiod situations such as the simulation of a 30-year investment in section 4.2.1. Fortunately, there are modern methods for generation of random numbers and scenarios that can help reduce the computational burden.

While the average output from a simulation is important, it is often not the only quantity of interest, something that practitioners tend to forget when using simulation to value complex financial instruments. As we will see from the applications in this book, for example, in assessing the risk of a portfolio, a portfolio manager may be interested in the percentiles of the distribution of outputs, or the worst-case and best-case scenarios. Unfortunately, it is not as straightforward to determine the accuracy of estimates of percentiles and other sample statistics from a simulation. There are some useful results from probability theory that apply (see, for example, Chapter 9 in Glasserman 2004), and we can use bootstrapping, as described in section 3.11.3. However, in general, the question of how many scenarios we should generate to get a good representation of the output distribution does not have an easy answer. This issue is complicated further by the fact that results from probability theory do not necessarily apply to many of the scenario generating methods used in practice, which do not simulate "pure" random samples of observations, but instead use smarter simulation methods that reduce the number of scenarios needed to achieve good estimate accuracy. Some of these methods are discussed later in this chapter and in Chapter 14.

4.3.2 Estimator Bias

The statistical concept of *estimator bias* is important in simulation applications because it shows whether an estimator (a sample statistic) estimates the "right thing" on average (i.e., whether it approaches the true parameter one needs to estimate given a sufficient number of replications). For example, the average obtained from a sample of scenarios is an unbiased estimator of the true mean of a distribution because if we generate many samples and compute the sample averages, the average of these averages will approach the true mean. Depending on the way scenarios are generated, however, one may introduce a bias in the estimate of the parameter of interest. (This parameter does not need to be the mean of the distribution.) The magnitude of the bias is determined by the difference between the average value of the estimator that would be obtained if we generated many, many samples, and the true value of the parameter we are trying to estimate.

Let us go back to the multiperiod retirement planning example in section 4.2.1. We compounded the returns of the original capital of $1,000 every year to obtain the return distribution of over 30 years. Intuitively, though, returns should be compounded a lot more frequently to obtain a fair representation of a continuously compounded total return. The fact that we "discretized" the sample space by considering specific points of evaluation of the returns introduced an error, a bias, in our estimate of the total return. This issue is important in the evaluation of financial derivatives, which we will see in Part Four. Prices of financial instruments are typically assumed to follow continuous random processes, but time is often discretized when constructing simulation models. The average of the outcomes (the expected present value) is considered the fair price of the financial instrument; however, simulating asset prices in this manner generates a bias in the estimate of the expected present value because the simulated changes in the asset price along the way are not continuous or instantaneous, but happen over a fixed-length time interval. This kind of bias is referred to *discretization error bias*. In some cases, such as the case of geometric Brownian motion with fixed drift and volatility which is discussed in Chapter 12, we can obtain an unbiased estimator of the average financial derivative payoff by simulating future asset prices with a continuous-time formula. However, in many instances it is not possible to find such a closed-form expression for the future asset price. For example, such a formula does not exist when the volatilities for asset prices are time-dependent, or when one uses a mean-reversion process to describe the evolution of the underlying price. (Such random processes are discussed in Chapter 12.) In such cases, we can reduce the time interval length to reduce the bias, but it is important to keep in mind that reducing the time interval length increases the number of steps necessary to generate a random "path" for the future asset price, and becomes computationally expensive.

4.3.3 Estimator Efficiency

If there are two ways to obtain an estimate of a quantity of interest and the estimators are otherwise equivalent in terms of bias, which estimator should be preferred; that is, which estimator is more "efficient"? For example, consider two unbiased estimators of the mean, both of which are obtained as averages from a sample of independent replications. Their standard errors will be given by

$$\frac{s_1}{\sqrt{N_1}} \text{ and } \frac{s_2}{\sqrt{N_2}}$$

where s_1 and s_2 are the standard deviations from the samples of scenarios, and N_1 and N_2 are the number of scenarios for each of the estimators. Statistical theory states that one should prefer the estimator with the smaller standard deviation because it is more accurate.

In the case of simulation, however, such statistical concepts need to be extended to include numerical and computational considerations. For example, suppose that it takes longer to generate the scenarios for the estimator with the smaller standard deviation. Is that estimator still preferable, given that one can use the extra time to generate additional scenarios for the other estimator, thus reducing the latter estimator's standard error? It is natural (and theoretically justified) to modify the statistical measure of variability and efficiency so that it includes a concept of time. If τ_1 and τ_2 are the times it takes to generate one scenario for each of the two estimators, then one should select the estimator with the smaller of the time-adjusted standard errors $s_1\sqrt{\tau_1}, s_2\sqrt{\tau_2}$.

4.4 RANDOM NUMBER GENERATION

At the core of Monte Carlo simulation is the generation of random numbers. In fact, however, generating random numbers from a wide variety of distributions reduces to generating random numbers from the continuous uniform distribution on the unit interval [0,1], that is, to generating random numbers on the interval [0,1] in such a way that each value between 0 and 1 is equally likely to occur.[9] Many computer languages and software packages have a command for generating a random number between 0 and 1: `=RAND()` in Excel, `rand(1)` in MATLAB and FORTRAN, and ``rand()`` in C++.

4.4.1 Inverse Transform Method

A common method for converting a random number between 0 and 1 to a number from an arbitrary probability distribution is to evaluate the so-called "inverse" of the cumulative probability distribution function at the random number u generated from a continuous uniform distribution (denoted by $F^{-1}(u)$). The idea works because the total mass for a probability distribution is always 1, and the cumulative probability for any value of the distribution (defined as the probability that this particular value or any value below it will occur) is always between 0 and 1. In effect, you can imagine that by generating a random number between 0 and 1, you are picking a number on the horizontal axis of the CDF plots in Exhibit 3.7 in the previous chapter. As we mentioned in Chapter 3, the shape of the CDF depends on the specific probability distribution. To generate a random number from a probability distribution with a specific CDF, we can track the x-coordinate for the point on the CDF that has the random number between 0 and 1 as a y-coordinate. Note that if a particular value from the distribution of the random variable happens with high probability, the CDF evaluated at that point on the horizontal axis will contain a long vertical segment. A uniform random number generated on [0,1] will have a larger chance of falling in a segment that is long, and so the value from the distribution we would like to simulate will indeed happen with higher probability.

The Inverse Transform for Discrete Distributions To give a concrete example, let us see how "inverting" the cumulative probability distribution works for discrete distributions. Suppose that given a random number generator for numbers between 0 and 1, we would like to simulate values for a random variable that takes the value 5 with probability 50%, the value 15 with probability 30%, and the value 35 with probability 20%. Exhibit 4.7 illustrates the CDF of this probability distribution. Let us split the unit interval [0,1] on the vertical axis into three intervals based on the cumulative probabilities 50%, 80%, and 100% for obtaining the values 5, 15, and 35: [0,0.5], (0.5,0.8], and (0.8,1]. If the random number that is drawn from the uniform distribution falls in the interval [0,0.5] (which happens 50% of the time if the number generator is truly random), then we trace the value on the horizontal axis that corresponds to the point on the CDF with y coordinate equal to the generated random number, and record that value (which is 5) for that trial. If the random number is in the interval (0.05, 0.8] (which

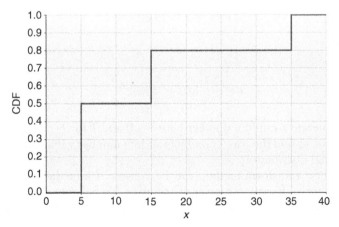

EXHIBIT 4.7 Graph of the CDF of a discrete distribution.

happens with probability 30%), then we record a value of 15 for that trial. Finally, if the random number is in the third interval (which happens with probability 20%), we record a value of 35. Thus, if many trials are run, the values 5, 15, and 35 are generated with the desired probabilities.[10]

The Inverse Transform for Continuous Distributions Some probability distributions have closed-form expressions for their inverse cumulative distributions. The exponential distribution is one such example. In section 3.7.2, we introduced the PDF of the exponential distribution:

$$f(x) = \lambda e^{-\lambda x}, \quad x \geq 0$$

The CDF of the exponential distribution can be computed as[11]

$$F(x) = P(X \leq x) = \int_0^x \lambda e^{-\lambda t} dt$$

$$= \left(-\frac{1}{\lambda} \lambda e^{-\lambda t} \right)\Big|_{t=x} - \left(-\frac{1}{\lambda} \lambda e^{-\lambda t} \right)\Big|_{t=0}$$

$$= -e^{-\lambda x} - (-e^{-\lambda \cdot 0})$$

$$= 1 - e^{-\lambda x}.$$

To compute the inverse function, we express x in terms of the CDF $F(x)$. We have

$$e^{-\lambda x} = 1 - F(x),$$

therefore,

$$x = -\frac{1}{\lambda} \ln(1 - F(x)).$$

If we generate a random number between 0 and 1 for $F(x)$, we can use this expression to find the corresponding random number x that comes from an exponential distribution.

The inverse transform method can be viewed as a method of picking *random percentiles* from a particular distribution. To build further intuition, let us generate a random number from a normal distribution with mean μ and standard deviation σ. Suppose we request a random number between 0 and 1, and the random number generator returns 0.975. To find the uniquely corresponding random number from a normal distribution with mean μ and standard deviation σ, we find the value on the horizontal axis for a normal distribution with mean μ and standard deviation σ so that 97.5% of the probability mass (the area under the PDF) is to the left of that value.[12] In contrast to the exponential distribution, however, the percentiles of the normal distribution cannot be calculated in closed form. A random number generator would *approximate* the inverse of the cumulative normal distribution function at a particular point.

While the inverse transform method is widely used, alternative methods exist for generating random numbers from distributions for which the inverse of the CDF is not easy to compute. Such methods include:

- The acceptance-rejection method.
- The composition method.
- The ratio of uniforms method.

Most of these methods, however, still rely on generating random numbers from the uniform distribution on [0,1]. For more details, see Fishman (2006) and Glasserman (2004).

Because the normal distribution is so widely used in practice, a number of methods have been developed specifically for efficient simulation of univariate and multivariate normal random variables. Such methods include the Box-Muller algorithm (Box and Muller 1958), and the Beasley-Springer-Moro methodology for approximating the inverse normal distribution (Beasley and Springer 1977; Moro 1995).

4.4.2 What Defines a "Good" Random Number Generator?

Given the discussion in the previous section, generating "good" uniform random numbers on [0,1] is critical for the performance of simulation algorithms. Interestingly, defining "good" random number generation is not as straightforward as it appears. Early random number generators tried to use "truly random" events for random number generation, such as the amount of background cosmic radiation. In practice, however, this kind of random number generation is time consuming and difficult. Moreover, it was realized that the ability to reproduce the random number sequence and to analyze the random number characteristics is actually a desirable property for random number generators. In particular, the ability to reproduce a sequence of random numbers allows for reducing the variance of estimates and for debugging computer code by rerunning experiments in the same conditions in which they were run in previous iterations of code development.

Most simulation software employs random number generation algorithms that produce streams of numbers that appear to be random, but in fact are a result of a clearly defined series of calculation steps in which the next "random number" x_n in the sequence is a function of the previous "random number" x_{n-1}, that is, $x_n = g(x_{n-1})$. The sequence starts with a number called the *seed*, and if the same seed is used in several simulations, each simulation sequence will contain exactly the same numbers, which is helpful for running fair comparisons between different strategies evaluated under uncertainty. It is quite an amazing statistical fact that some of these recursion formulas (named *pseudorandom number generators*) define sequences of numbers that imitate random behavior well and appear to obey (roughly) some major laws of probability, such as the the central limit theorem (section 3.11.1) and the Glivenko-Cantelli Theorem.[13]

In general, a pseudorandom number generator is considered "good" if it satisfies the following conditions:

- The numbers in the generated sequence are uniformly distributed between 0 and 1. This can be tested by running a chi-square or a Kolmogorov-Smirnov test.
- The sequence has a long cycle (i.e., it takes many iterations before the sequence begins repeating itself).[14]
- The numbers in the sequence are not autocorrelated.[15] This can be verified by running a Durbin-Watson test on the sequence of numbers. The Durbin-Watson test is widely used in statistics for identifying autocorrelation in time series of observations.

Next, some important types of pseudorandom number generators are surveyed. The goal is not to provide comprehensive coverage of random number generators, but rather to give you a flavor of the main ideas behind the method of producing apparently random numbers with deterministic algorithms.

4.4.3 Pseudorandom Number Generators

One of the earliest pseudorandom number generators is called the *midsquare technique*. It takes a number (the seed), squares it, and uses the set of middle digits as the next random number. For example, suppose that the seed is 5381. (It can be any number.) The members of the sequence of random numbers between 0 and 1 are then generated as

$$5381^2 = 28\underline{9551}61; \text{ middle four digits} = 9551; \text{ random number} = 0.9551,$$

$$9551^2 = 91\underline{2216}01; \text{ middle four digits} = 2216; \text{ random number} = 0.2216,$$

and so forth.

It is easy to predict when such an approach may run into difficulties. As soon as the "middle digits" become a small number such as 1 or 0, the sequence ends with the same numbers generated over and over again, that is, the sequence converges to a constant value such as 0 or to a very short cycle of values.

A better, commonly used type of pseudorandom number generator is *congruential* pseudorandom number generators. They generate a sequence of numbers of the form

$$x_n = g(x_{n-1}) \mod m,$$

where mod m stands for "*modulus m.*" $g(x_{n-1}) \mod m$ is the remainder after dividing $g(x_{n-1})$ by m. For example, 5 mod 3 = 2, 15 mod 5 = 0, and so on. The remainder is then scaled by another number, for example, divided by m, and the resulting number is used as the uniform random number on the interval [0,1]. Note that $g(x_{n-1}) \mod m$ will always be an integer between 0 and $m-1$. Thus, to create a good representation of randomness, one would want to make the range for the modulus as large as possible. For a 32-bit computer, for example, the maximum integer that can be stored is $2^{31} - 1$, which is large enough for practical purposes.

As an example, consider a simple *linear congruential pseudorandom generator* of the form

$$x_n = Ax_{n-1} \mod m.$$

(It is called linear because Ax_{n-1} is a linear function of x_{n-1}.) The first number in the sequence, x_0, is the seed. Algebraically, the expression for generating x_n above can be written as[16]

$$x_n = Ax_{n-1} - m \left\lfloor \frac{Ax_{n-1}}{m} \right\rfloor.$$

(The lower brackets notation is standard for "largest integer less than or equal to Ax_{n-1}/m.) Then, the sequence of fractions x_n/m is used as a sequence of pseudorandom numbers on the interval [0,1].

Suppose $A = 3$, m = 10, and the seed $x_0 = 1052$. We have the following sequence of random numbers:

$$x_1 = 3 \cdot 1052 - 10 \cdot \left\lfloor \frac{3 \cdot 1052}{10} \right\rfloor = 3 \cdot 1052 - 10 \cdot \lfloor 315.6 \rfloor$$

$$= 3 \cdot 1052 - 10 \cdot 315 = 6.$$

Therefore, the random number is 6/10, or **0.6**.

$$x_2 = 3 \cdot 6 - 10 \cdot \left\lfloor \frac{3 \cdot 6}{10} \right\rfloor = 3 \cdot 6 - 10 \cdot \lfloor 1.8 \rfloor = 3 \cdot 6 - 10 \cdot 1 = 8$$

Therefore, the next random number is 8/10, or **0.8**, and so on.

More generally, advanced random number generators include:

- Linear congruential generators (LCGs).
- Multiplicative recursive generators (MRGs).
- Feedback shift registers (FSRs).
- Generalized feedback shift registers (GFSRs).
- Combined multiplicative recursive generators (CMRGs).
- Twisted generalized feedback shift registers (TGFSRs).
- Add-with-carry (AWC) and subtract-with-borrow (SWB) generators.
- Inversive generators (IG).

FSRs, GFSRs, and TGFSRs generate new numbers by operating recursively on *bits* of previously generated random numbers. LCGs, MRGs, CMRGs, AWC/SWB and IGs operate recursively on previously generated random numbers. For more details, see, for example, McLeish (2005) and Fishman (2006). Most pseudorandom number generators used in popular software products nowadays have been thoroughly tested and are quite good, but it is important to keep in mind that pseudorandom number generators in software packages that are not explicitly built for simulation purposes (such as Excel) are usually not as good as random number generators in specialized simulation/mathematical software (such as @RISK and MATLAB).

4.4.4 Quasirandom (Low-Discrepancy) Sequences

A truly random number generator may produce clustered observations (see Exhibit 4.8(A)), which necessitates generating many scenarios in order to obtain a good representation of the output distribution of interest. Quasirandom sequences instead ensure a smooth representation of the range by continuously "filling in" gaps on the unit interval [0,1] left by previously generated random numbers (see an example of 1,000 generated values of a quasirandom sequence in Exhibit 4.8(B)). The term "quasirandom" is actually a misnomer because, unlike pseudorandom number sequences, quasirandom number sequences do not pretend to be random. They are deterministic on purpose, and their roots can be found in real analysis and abstract algebra rather than in simulation or probability theory. The term *low discrepancy*

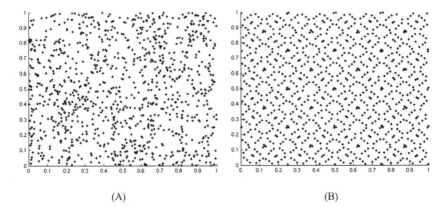

(A)   (B)

EXHIBIT 4.8 One thousand simulated number values for two uniform random variables on the interval [0,1]: (A) Pseudorandom number generator; (B) Sobol quasirandom sequence.

sequences is often used interchangeably with the term *quasirandom sequences*, and is more accurate.

Famous quasirandom sequences include Sobol (1967), Faure (1982), Halton (1960), and Hammersley (1960). These sequences build on a family of so-called Van der Corput sequences.[17] For example, the Van der Corput sequence of base 2 is

$$\frac{1}{2}, \frac{1}{4}, \frac{3}{4}, \frac{1}{8}, \frac{5}{8}, \frac{3}{8}, \frac{7}{8}, \cdots$$

The actual generation of Van der Corput sequences is somewhat technical, but the outcome is intuitive. Note that as new points are added to the sequence, they appear on alternate sides of $\frac{1}{2}$ in a balanced way. The main idea is that as the number of generated values increases, the sequence covers uniformly the unit interval.

The values generated with quasirandom sequences are treated as "random" numbers for the purposes of simulation modeling. In particular, instead of generating random numbers between 0 and 1 and "inverting" them to obtain an arbitrary probability distribution, we would "invert" the numbers in the quasirandom sequence. Different sequences have different advantages for specific financial applications, but the Faure and Sobol sequences in particular have been proven to generate very accurate estimates for derivative pricing in tests.[18] We will see applications of quasirandom sequences when the pricing of mortgage-backed securities and other financial derivatives are discussed in Chapters 14 and 15.

4.4.5 Stratified Sampling

A variety of so-called *variance reduction techniques* are used to speed up execution and improve accuracy in simulations. We discuss some of them in the context of financial derivative pricing in Chapter 14. Here, we will introduce one kind of random number generation—stratified sampling—that is now the default method of sampling in some simulation software packages such as @RISK. The term *stratified sampling* is used because of the analogy with the statistical methodology of collecting a representative sample by dividing the population into groups, or *strata*, of similar characteristics, and collecting information about each strata. This technique ensures that all important groups are represented in the final sample.

Similar to quasirandom number generation, stratified sampling tries to address the problem of "clustering observations" we mentioned in section 4.4.4. In contrast to quasirandom number generator techniques, however, which are deliberately nonrandom, stratified sampling preserves some degree of randomness. It just tries to "distribute" the randomness along the entire range of the probability distribution by dividing the ranges of possible values for every input random variable into a fixed number of strata, and simulating values over these ranges.

Stratified sampling is valuable not only because it improves accuracy, but also because it helps include extreme observations into the simulation. Observations in the tails of input distributions that are typically less likely to be generated may never occur in a simulation because the probability of their occurrence is small. Such observations, however, contain important information about extreme events that are of particular interest in financial applications. In order to ensure that they appear in the simulation, one would have to generate a huge number of scenarios.

A simple example of stratifying the numbers in the [0,1] interval is to divide the [0,1] interval into k smaller intervals of equal length:

$$\left[0, \frac{1}{k}\right], \left(\frac{1}{k}, \frac{2}{k}\right], \ldots, \left(\frac{k-1}{k}, 1\right].$$

Random numbers can then be drawn sequentially from each small interval. Therefore, values from the tails of the distribution of interest (which will be generated when uniform random numbers from the intervals $[0, \frac{1}{k}]$ and $(\frac{k-1}{k}, 1]$ are drawn) obtain better representation.

In multiple dimensions (i.e., when simulating several random variables), this method extends to dividing a hypercube (as opposed to an interval) into smaller hypercubes, and drawing an observation along each dimension of the smaller hypercubes. The sample size required to cover all strata, however,

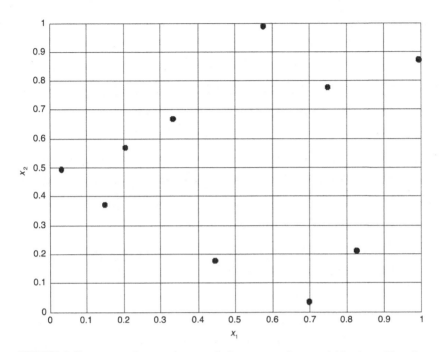

EXHIBIT 4.9 A Latin hypercube sample for two random variables ($p = 2$) and 10 strata along each dimension ($k = 10$).

may become prohibitive. Suppose, for example, that you have k intervals (strata) for each of p dimensions (each of p random variables). This means that there are k^p hypercubes, that is, we need to simulate at least k^p random numbers in order to have a number in each stratum. Generating random numbers, however, is computationally expensive. An enhanced extension to the basic stratified sampling method is *Latin Hypercube Sampling* (an option in many advanced simulation software products, including @RISK and MATLAB), which permutes the coordinates of an initially generated random vector of observations—one observation within each small hypercube—to reduce the number of times an actual random number is generated while ensuring that all strata are sufficiently well-represented (see Exhibit 4.9).

The method works as follows. First, we generate a random number within each small interval along each dimension. In the example in Exhibit 4.9, where we have two random variables (i.e., two dimensions), we would generate random numbers

$$x_1^{(1)}, \ldots, x_1^{(k)}$$

along the first dimension, and numbers

$$x_2^{(1)}, \ldots, x_2^{(k)}$$

along the second dimension. If we consider points with coordinates

$$(x_1^{(1)}, x_2^{(1)}), \ldots, (x_1^{(k)}, x_2^{(k)})$$

we would have random points in all of the little squares along the diagonal of the large [0,1] square. The first point is a point in the little square $[0, \frac{1}{k}]^2$, the second point is a point in the little square $(\frac{1}{k}, \frac{2}{k}]^2$, and so on. (In multiple dimensions, combining the random numbers for the corresponding small intervals to create random points with p coordinates would create random points in the little *hypercubes* along the main diagonal of the [0,1] hypercube.)

Now permute the coordinates of the points along each dimension.[19] For example, consider the points

$$(x_1^{(10)}, x_2^{(3)}), (x_1^{(2)}, x_2^{(1)}) \ldots, (x_1^{(k-3)}, x_2^{(2)}).$$

In other words, the first coordinates are still the random numbers we generated along the first dimension, and the second coordinates are still the random numbers we generated along the second dimension, but the order of the random numbers within each dimension has changed. The new points are not all in the hypercubes around the diagonal, and, as Exhibit 4.9 illustrates, exactly one random point falls in each of the k small intervals into which each axis is partitioned. If we consider all possible permutations of these coordinates, we will fill all small hypercubes. Thus, we would perform stratified sampling by generating only $k \cdot p$ random numbers (and permuting them), rather than generating k^p random numbers.[20]

SUMMARY

- Monte Carlo (MC) simulation is a valuable tool for evaluating functional relationships between variables, visualizing the effect of multiple-correlated variables, and testing strategies.
- MC simulation involves creating scenarios for output variables of interest by generating scenarios for input variables for which we have more information. The art of MC simulation modeling is in selecting input probability distributions wisely and interpreting output distributions carefully.

■ The distributions of output variables can be analyzed by statistical techniques. Statistics of interest include measures of central tendency (average, mode), measures of volatility (standard deviation, percentiles), skewness, and kurtosis. Minima and maxima from simulations should be interpreted with care because they often depend on the input assumptions and are very sensitive to the number of trials in the simulation.

■ The accuracy of estimation through simulation is related to the number of generated scenarios. Unfortunately, the relationship is nonlinear—in order to double the accuracy, we need to more than quadruple the number of scenarios.

■ Generating a random number from an arbitrary probability distribution in many cases reduces to generating a random number from the uniform distribution on the interval [0,1].

■ Random number generation is not trivial, and simulation software packages do not produce truly "random" numbers. There is value, however, in generating random number sequences that are replicable, and thus not completely random.

■ Pseudorandom number generators attempt to imitate random behavior by creating sequences of random numbers that obey statistical laws.

■ Quasirandom number generators do not pretend to generate random numbers—they try to address the "clustering" problem observed in truly random number generation, and ensure a smooth representation of the range of the distribution by continuously "filling in" gaps on the unit interval [0,1] left by previously generated random numbers. Quasirandom sequences that have been particularly successful in financial applications include the Faure and Sobol sequences.

■ Stratified sampling, of which Latin Hypercube Sampling is an advanced example, aims to provide good representation of a probability distribution by dividing the range of the random variable into smaller ranges or "strata," and generating random numbers within each stratum. This method "disperses" simulated values more evenly over the range of the distribution, addresses the clustering problem of random number generation, and provides better representation for the tails of the distribution.

SOFTWARE HINTS

There is a variety of software packages for simulation. Appendixes B and C, contain introductions to @RISK and MATLAB. Next, we review the implementation of the examples in Chapter 4 with @RISK and MATLAB.

@RISK

The implementation of the models in sections 4.1 and 4.2 is in the file **Ch4-ReturnSim.xlsx**. We use yellow background to indicate input cells, and red background to indicate output cells in the models. Instructors who would like to use this example in class can clear the contents of all of the yellow and red cells, distribute the rest of the file as a template to the students, and walk the class through the @RISK commands and the construction of the spreadsheet during lecture.

Example from Section 4.1.2 Worksheet 1 Year contains the simulation of the amount of money available at the end of the first year after investing at the stock market. Exhibit 4.10 is a screenshot of the spreadsheet with the formulas in each cell. Cell B11 contains the @RISK formula for normal distribution with mean stored in cell B7 and standard deviation stored in cell C7. Cell D11 is the output cell—it stores the values for the amount of money in the account at the end of one year as @RISK simulates scenarios for the return in cell B11.

Example from Section 4.2.1 Worksheet 30 Years contains the simulation of the amount of money available after investing in the stock market at the end of 30 years. It is filled out in the same way as worksheet **1 Year,** but there are 30 rows of data. (The implicit assumption in this model was that stock returns were not correlated across years.) Exhibit 4.11 is a screenshot of the spreadsheet with the formulas filled out. (Note that rows 13–38 are hidden. To unhide them, highlight rows 2 through 39, right-click and select **Unhide** from the shortcut menu.) Start by filling out the @RISK formula for normal distribution in cell B11. Copy and paste the formula down to include cell B40. Then, fill out the amount of money available at the end of each year as a product of the amount of money available in the previous

	A	B	C	D
1	Stock market investment			
2				
3	Initial investment	1000		
4	Time horizon (years)	1		
5				
6	Return	μ	σ	
7	Stock market	0.0879	0.1465	
8				
9				
10		Return	1+Return	Money in account
11	Year 1	=RiskNormal(B7,C7)	=1+B11	=RiskOutput("Money at the end of Year 1")+C11*B3
12				

EXHIBIT 4.10 Worksheet 1 Year in file Ch4-ReturnSim.xlsx.

	A	B	C	D
1	Stock market investment over 30 years			
2				
3	Initial investment	1000		
4	Time horizon (years)	30		
5				
6	Return	μ	σ	
7	Stock market	0.0879	0.1465	
8				
9				
10	Year	Return	1 + Return	Money in account
11	1	=RiskNormal($B$7,$C$7)	=1+B11	=C11*B3
12	2	=RiskNormal($B$7,$C$7)	=1+B12	=C12*D11
39	29	=RiskNormal($B$7,$C$7)	=1+B39	=C39*D38
40	30	=RiskNormal($B$7,$C$7)	=1+B40	=C40*D39
41	Total		=PRODUCT(C11:C40)	=RiskOutput("Total money in account")+D40

EXHIBIT 4.11   Worksheet 30 Years in file Ch4-ReturnSim.xlsx.

year times (1 + the return realized over the year). Cell D41 is the @RISK output cell that will keep track of the money at the end of 30 years.

Example from Section 4.2.2   Worksheet **Stock + Bond** contains the simulation model for the portfolio of stocks and bonds with portfolio weights of 50% in each investment. Exhibit 4.12 is a screenshot of the spreadsheet with a specific scenario generated for stock and bond returns over the 30-year period. (Note that rows 13–18 are hidden.) Important formulas to note are:

- Columns B and E contain returns as before. Column B contains returns for the stock market with the same probability distribution (normal) and the same parameters from cells B7 and C7. Column E contains input cells for the simulation of bond returns with the mean and the standard deviation from cells B8 and C8.
- To incorporate the effect of correlations, we need an additional argument in the @RISK formula for distribution assumptions. For example, instead of

```
= RiskNormal($B$7,$C$7)
```

to simulate a normal random variable for the stock return in cell B11, we would enter

```
= RiskNormal($B$7,$C$7,RiskCorrmat($D$7:$E$8,1,A11)),
```

instead of

```
= RiskNormal($B$8,$C$8)
```

to simulate a normal random variable for the bond return in cell E11, we would enter

```
= RiskNormal($B$8,$C$8,RiskCorrmat($D$7:$E$8,2,A11)).
```

The additional argument `RiskCorrmat(Array,Position,Instance)` refers to a correlation matrix stored in `Array` in which the variable we are simulating corresponds to row (and column) `Position`. (For example, Stocks were in the first row/column of the correlation matrix, and Bonds were in the second row/column; hence the `Position` argument for simulating stock return realizations was 1, and the `Position` argument for simulating bond return realizations was 2.) `Instance` is an optional argument which is used when multiple groups of inputs reference the same correlation matrix. It basically tells @RISK whether the correlated values it generates should be correlated within all groups, or only within a particular group. In our example, we assumed that stock and bond returns are correlated at each time period, but not across time periods, so we specified a separate instance for each time period (which we made equal to the index of the corresponding time period).

Instead of specifying an extra argument in the @RISK probability distribution formula for the input variables, we can incorporate correlations also by clicking on the **Define Correlations** button in the @RISK ribbon. There we have the option also to request that correlations are specified for a time series, and @RISK automatically assigns a new instance to each row of inputs to be correlated.

	A	B	C	D	E	F	G	H
1	Stock market and bond market investment over 30 years							
2								
3	Initial investment	$1,000.00						
4	Time horizon (years)	30						
5								
6	Return	μ	σ	Correlation matrix		weight		
7	Stock market	8.79%	14.65%	1	-0.2	0.5		
8	Bonds	4.00%	7.00%	-0.2	1	0.5		
9								
10	Year	Stock market return	1 + stock mkt return	Money in stocks	Bond return	1 + bond return	Money in bonds	Total amount in account
11		1	-0.18%	99.82%	$ 499.11	-2.36%	97.64%	$ 488.18	$ 987.28
12		2	1.74%	101.74%	$ 507.81	5.54%	105.54%	$ 515.20	$1,023.01
39		29	-3.61%	96.39%	$5,976.46	-6.42%	93.58%	$ 1,179.08	$7,155.54
40		30	0.50%	100.50%	$6,006.29	1.80%	101.80%	$ 1,200.29	$7,206.58
41	Total		1201.26%	$6,006.29		240.06%	$ 1,200.29	$7,206.58

EXHIBIT 4.12 Worksheet Stock + Bond in file Ch4-ReturnSim.xlsx.

Example from Section 4.2.3 Worksheet Stock + Bond (2) contains the simulation model for the portfolio of stocks and bonds with portfolio weights of (50%, 50%) or (30%, 70%) in each investment. Exhibit 4.13 is a screenshot of the spreadsheet with a specific scenario generated for stock and bond returns over the 30-year period. Cell H41 contains the output variable for Strategy A. Cell L41 contains the output variable for Strategy B. Cell I45 contains an output variable for the difference between the outcomes of Strategy A and Strategy B to enable the scenario-by-scenario analysis in section 4.2.3. An important fact to note is that the calculations of the Money in stocks and Money in Bonds for Strategy B in each time period (columns J and K) refer to the realization of stock and bond returns in columns B and E (implicitly by referring to columns C and F)—columns that are also referenced in the calculations of the Money in stocks and Money in Bonds for Strategy A in each time period (columns D and G).

To illustrate how RiskSimtable can be used to check different strategies and ensure that we evaluate the strategies over the same set of scenarios, we have created a worksheet **Stock + Bond (3)** in the same file. The spreadsheet is the same as the spreadsheet used in Exhibit 4.12), but cell F7 now contains the formula =RiskSimtable({0.5,0.3}). In order for this to work correctly, you need to also make sure that the portfolio weight for bonds in cell F8 is linked to the portfolio weight for stocks through the formula =1-F7, so that when @RISK ends the first simulation and changes the weight for stocks from 0.5 to 0.3, the weight for bonds is modified automatically in such a way that the portfolio weights still add up to 1. Finally, as explained in Appendix B, make sure that the number of simulations in the @RISK main ribbon is set to 2 before running the simulation—this will ensure that @RISK runs through the two values for stock portfolio weights specified in RiskSimtable.

	A	B	C	D	E	F	G	H	I	J	K	L
1	Stock market and bond market investment over 30 years with different portfolio weights											
2												
3	Initial investment	$ 1,000.00										
4	Time horizon (years)	30										
5												
6	Return	μ	σ	Correlation matrix		weights (A)	weights (B)					
7	Stock market	8.79%	14.65%	1	-0.2	0.5	0.3					
8	Bonds	4.00%	7.00%	-0.2	1	0.5	0.7					
9												
10	Year	Stock market return	1+stock mkt return	Money in stocks	Bond return	1+bond return	Money in bonds	Total amount in account		Money in stocks	Money in bonds	Total amount in account
11	1	16.22%	116.22%	$ 581.12	0.95%	100.95%	$ 504.76	$ 1,085.88		$ 348.67	$ 706.66	$ 1,055.33
12	2	-2.35%	97.65%	$ 567.49	8.55%	108.55%	$ 547.92	$ 1,115.41		$ 340.50	$ 767.09	$ 1,107.59
39	29	3.99%	103.99%	$ 4,515.02	-5.11%	94.89%	$ 2,098.40	$ 6,613.42		$ 2,709.01	$ 2,937.76	$ 5,646.77
40	30	6.29%	106.29%	$ 4,798.90	4.05%	104.05%	$ 2,183.46	$ 6,982.37		$ 2,879.34	$ 3,056.85	$ 5,936.19
41	Total		959.78%	$ 4,798.90		436.69%	$ 2,183.46	$ 6,982.37		$ 2,879.34	$ 3,056.85	$ 5,936.19
42								Total amount				Total amount
43								Strategy A				Strategy B
44												
45						Difference (A-B)		$1,046.18				

EXHIBIT 4.13 Worksheet Stock + Bond (2) in file Ch4-ReturnSim.xlsx.

MATLAB

Example from Section 4.1.2 Let us explain how to obtain the output in section 4.1.2 in MATLAB. First, we store the initial capital in the variable C0:

```
>> C0 = 1000;
```

MATLAB has commands for generating the most commonly used random numbers directly. For example, a normal random variable can be simulated with

```
>> normrnd(mean,stdev,numRows,numColumns)
```

In the previous expression, `mean` and `stdev` are the mean and the standard deviation of the normal random variables. `numRows` and `numColumns` specify the dimension of the array of random numbers we would like to generate. For example in section 4.1.2, use the command

```
>> return01 = normrnd(.0879,.1465,100,1)
```

to generate 100 values for the return over the next year and assign them to a vector array `return01` of dimension (100 rows, 1 column). Then, compute the distribution of your money at the end of the first year by entering the command

```
>> C1 = (1 + return01)*C0
```

This will create a vector array of 100 values for the capital at the end of year 1. We can then use this array to create graphs and compute descriptive statistics. The mean, standard deviation and 5th percentile of the distribution for `C1` can be found with the commands

```
>> mean(C1)
>> std(C1)
>> prctile(C1,5)
```

We can also ask for a list of percentile values by passing an array of percentiles as an argument to the `prctile` function.

```
>> prctile(C1,[5 50 95])
```

This gives us the 5th percentile, the 50th percentile (the median), and the 95th percentile of the distribution of `C1`.

To plot a histogram of the distribution of outcomes for C1, use the MATLAB hist function. The command

```
>>[frequencyCounts,binLocations] = hist(C1,numBins);
```

will return the frequency counts and the bin locations for the number of bins (numBins) you have specified.[21] You can then use the command bar to plot the histogram. In this particular case, the sequence of commands

```
>>[frequencyCounts,binLocations] = hist(C1,10);
>> bar(binLocations,frequencyCounts)
```

produce the graph in Exhibit 4.14.[22]

Technically speaking, bar plots are not the correct representation for continuous random variables. There should not be any gaps between the bars on the graph because the possible values for C1 in this case should happen in a continuum. (This is because the distribution for returns is normal, i.e., continuous.) So, instead, we can use the command directly (without specifying output variables [frequencyCounts,binLocations]) to produce a histogram. (See Exhibit 4.15.)

To learn about commands for generating different random distributions and to see an overview of methods for random number generators,

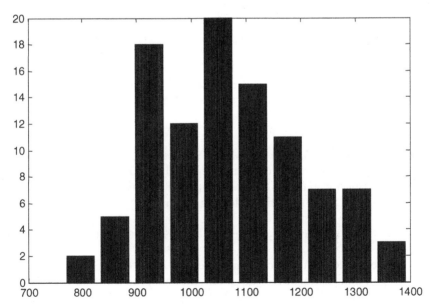

EXHIBIT 4.14 Bar plot of the distribution of the simulation output variable C1.

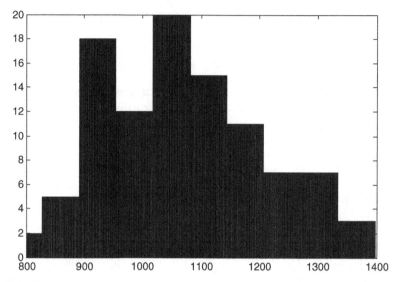

EXHIBIT 4.15 Histogram of the distribution of the output variable C1.

type "random number generation" in MATLAB's help window. Also, try typing

```
>> lookfor rnd
```

at the MATLAB command prompt. This will produce a list of all functions in MATLAB that contain the string "rnd" in their title. Aside from a couple of unrelated hits, these are the functions that directly generate random numbers from different probability distributions.

Example from Section 4.2.1 Now let us generate the distribution of the total return after 30 years. We can simulate 30 columns of 100 observations each of single-period returns. (Hence, column k contains the 100 returns simulated for year k.) We use the following command:

```
>> singlePeriodReturns30 = normrnd(.0879,.1465,100,30)
```

Now we can compute the cumulative returns at the end of 30 years and the corresponding capital at the end of 30 years with the command

```
>> capital30 = 1000*prod(1+singlePeriodReturns30,2)
```

Let us break up this command and explain each piece.

```
1+singlePeriodReturns30
```

returns the original matrix (of 100 rows and 30 columns) of simulated single-period returns, but it adds 1 to each entry in the matrix. (So, we obtain an array with entries $(1 + r_{0,1})$, $(1 + r_{1,2})$, ..., $(1 + r_{29,30})$ for the first row (the first generated scenario), and similarly for the remaining 99 rows (the remaining 99 scenarios.)

The function prod(X,DIM) computes the product of the elements of a matrix array along the specified dimension DIM. In this case, we specified dimension 2, which means prod will work with the entries in the columns of the array. In other words,

```
prod(1+singlePeriodReturns30,2)
```

will return an array with 100 rows and 1 column, and the column will contain the products of $(1 + r_{0,1})$, $(1 + r_{1,2})$, ..., $(1 + r_{29,30})$ for each row (i.e., for each of the 100 scenarios for 30 years of returns).

Finally, multiplying this array by 1,000 computes the amount of capital after 30 years (starting with initial capital of \$1,000) in each of the 100 scenarios for returns. We name the variable for the amount of capital after 30 years capital30. We can then analyze it by plotting the histogram of its 100 simulated values, computing the descriptive statistics, and so on, as we showed in the previous section.

Example from Section 4.2.2   To generate scenarios for the joint realizations of returns for stocks and bonds from a multivariate normal distribution, we will use the MATLAB function mvnrnd(MU,SIGMA,cases). It takes as inputs a vector array of means MU and a covariance matrix SIGMA, and generates as many scenarios as are specified in cases.

In our example, the vector of means MU is [0.0879,0.04]. The standard deviations of stock and bond returns are 0.1465 and 0.07, respectively, and the correlation coefficient is –0.02. Therefore, the covariance matrix SIGMA is

$$
\begin{bmatrix} 0.1465^2 & -0.2 \cdot (0.1465) \cdot (0.07) \\ -0.2 \cdot (0.1465) \cdot (0.07) & 0.07^2 \end{bmatrix} = \begin{bmatrix} 0.0215 & -0.0002 \\ -0.0002 & 0.49 \end{bmatrix}.
$$

At the MATLAB prompt, we enter

```
>> MU = [0.0879,0.04];
>> SIGMA = [0.0215,-0.0002;-0.0002,0.49];
```

If you then type

```
>> mvnrnd(MU,SIGMA,5000),
```

MATLAB will return 5000 rows (scenarios) of pairs of observations that are correlated with correlation coefficient -0.2:

```
     ans =
 0.0245   -0.0901
-0.1563    0.5503
 0.1063   -0.3720
 0.1301    1.5678
-0.0802   -0.0539
 0.2625    0.1181
 0.2623    0.7851
 0.0824    0.0815
 0.1359   -0.0274
 0.1135   -0.5429
```

and so on.

These are the returns on the stock market and the Treasury bond market for year 1 of your investment. To compute the amount of capital at the end of the first year in each of these 5,000 scenarios (remembering that we invested 50% of the initial $1,000, that is, $500 in stocks and 50% in bonds), we would compute

```
>> capital1 = sum(500*(1+mvnrnd(MU,SIGMA,5000)),2)
```

The sum function, like the prod function we explained in the previous section, takes a first argument which is an array, and sums the corresponding elements in the dimension specified by the second argument. Here the command

```
500*(1+mvnrnd(MU,SIGMA,5000))
```

creates a matrix with two columns, the first one of which represents the amount invested in stocks at the end of the first year, and the second one of which represents the amount invested in bonds at the end of the first year. When we sum the corresponding elements in the two columns, we obtain a $5,000 \times 1$ array of values for the capital at the end of the first year. We could use this information to compute the descriptive statistics of the investment at the end of the first year.

If we want to analyze the investment at the end of 30 years, we need to repeat this process 30 times. The following script computes the distribution of the value of the capital at the end of 30 years (assuming we invest an equal amount of the original capital in stocks and bonds):

```
>> stocksRet = ones(5000,1); bondsRet = ones(5000,1);
>> for iYear = 1:30
scenarios = mvnrnd(MU,SIGMA,5000);
stocksRet = stocksRet.*(1+scenarios(:,1));
bondsRet = bondsRet.*(1+scenarios(:,2));
end
>> capital30 = 500*stocksRet + 500*bondsRet;
```

We can then analyze the distribution of the capital at the end of 30 years. For example, to compute its mean, we type

```
>> mean(capital30)
ans =
    7.9882e+003
```

Example from Section 4.2.3 To evaluate different investment strategies, we just need to loop over a range of weights for our stock investment. (The weights for the bond investment will be determined by the difference between 1 and the weight for the stock investment.) To ensure that the strategies are evaluated over the same set of scenarios, first we generate the scenarios for the returns on the stock and the bond market over 30 years as in the previous section:

```
>> stocksRet = ones(5000,1); bondsRet = ones(5000,1);
>> for iYear = 1:30
scenarios = mvnrnd(MU,SIGMA,5000);
stocksRet = stocksRet.*(1+scenarios(:,1));
bondsRet = bondsRet.*(1+scenarios(:,2));
end
```

Then, we iterate through different weights, storing the 5,000 scenarios for the capital after 30 years (given initial capital of $1,000) for each of these combinations of weights:

```
>> counter = 1;
>> for iWeight = 0.2:0.2:1
capital30(:,counter) = iWeight*1000*stocksRet + (1-
iWeight)*1000*bondsRet;
counter = counter + 1;
end
```

So, for example, the first column of the matrix array `capital30` contains the 5,000 scenarios for the capital after 30 years when stocks are 20% of the initial $1,000 investment, and bonds are 80%. Each of the columns of `capital30` can be analyzed and the descriptive statistics for the different investment strategies can be compared.

NOTES

1. Recall from Chapter 3 that we use tilde ($\sim$) to denote uncertain quantities and random variables.
2. Note that there are an infinite number of values a return can take, since a return is expressed as a percentage. So, while you can certainly input a discrete set of possible scenarios for return, it is not unnatural to assume that the actual realization of the return is drawn from a *continuous* probability distribution.
3. There is no rule for which goodness-of-fit test is "best." Each of them has advantages and disadvantages. The chi-square test is the most general one, and can be used for data that come from both continuous and discrete distributions; however, to calculate the chi-square test statistic, one needs to divide the data into "bins," and the results depend strongly on how the bins are determined. The K-S and the A-D tests apply only for continuous distributions. They do not depend on dividing the data into bins, so their results are less arbitrary. The K-S statistic is concerned primarily with whether the *centers* of the empirical and the expected distribution are "close," whereas A-D focuses on the discrepancy between the *tails* of the observed and the expected distribution. For all three tests, the smaller the value of the test statistic, the closer the fit is. (As we mentioned in section 3.11.4, most statistical software packages report a p-value, that is, a "probability," in addition to a test statistic. The larger the p-value, the closer the fit.) Finally, the RMSE measures the squared error of the differences between observed and the expected values. The smaller the number, the better, but the actual magnitude of the RMSE depends on the distribution and data at hand.
4. @RISK has a **Distribution Fitting** button in its ribbon in Excel that allows the user to (1) specify whether the distribution to be fitted is continuous or discrete (which narrows down the type of goodness-of-fit tests); (2) check a list of distributions that need to be checked for goodness-of-fit; and (3) tweak options in the computation of the chi-square goodness-of-fit statistic. @RISK then lists, in order of goodness-of-fit, the possible probability distributions and their parameters.

   MATLAB's Statistics Toolbox contains a **Distribution Fitting** tool as well. It allows the user to enter a possible distribution for a set of data, and provides estimates of the parameters of the distribution. To check for goodness-of-fit, one can use the MATLAB function `[h,p]=chi2gof(...)` from the command line, which provides the value of the chi-square statistic for the fit of a particular distribution. The higher the value of the statistic h, the less evidence there is that the data come from the tested distribution. Alternatively, one can look at p—the *p*-value of the chi-square test. The *p*-value measures the probability that one can have chi-square statistic computed from the data that is more extreme than the current chi-square statistic. The higher the value for p, the less likely this is the case. Therefore, a high value of p (e.g., 75%) suggests that the data fit the chosen distribution quite well.

5. Note that, depending on the specific set of 100 scenarios we have generated, the graph will look different. Therefore, the descriptive statistics and the look of the graph we present here will only be close to what you would obtain if you try to repeat this experiment.

6. We do not discuss the possibility that returns in different years may be correlated here. We will learn how to create more sophisticated models for asset returns in Chapter 12.

7. We could be looking at the minimum and maximum realized outcomes as measures of the "riskiness" of Strategy A and Strategy B as well, but recall that those are very sensitive to the number of trials in the simulation, and should be interpreted with care.

8. Note that the value for $t_{(100-\alpha/2)\%,n-1}$ has decreased slightly as well—this is because we now have more observations, that is, more degrees of freedom, so the *t*-distribution is less spread out and is closer to the normal distribution.

9. Recall that the continuous uniform distribution looks like a simple rectangle (Exhibit 3.12), and it is very easy to compute probabilities and cumulative probabilities for the values for the continuous uniform random variable. Because the length of the interval is 1 and the total area under the PDF must be 1, the height of the curve should be 1 as well. Therefore, the probability that the continuous uniform random variable takes a value between two numbers *a* and *b* (the area under the PDF between *a* and *b*) is simply $(b - a) \cdot 1$, that is, $b - a$.

10. To understand better how this works, you can practice generating values from a general discrete probability distribution in Excel. For example, we can simulate these values with the corresponding probabilities by creating a table with the interval ranges in the first two columns, and the corresponding values (5, 15, and 35) in the third column, and using the Excel function

```
VLOOKUP(lookup_value,table_array,col_index_num)
```

to look up the range in which a number generated with RAND() falls.

Fortunately, @RISK contains direct commands for specifying general discrete distributions. MATLAB does not have as many different distribution options, but many of the most widely used distributions are in its library.

11. We present the calculation here because the exponential distribution is widely used in modeling the arrival time of credit risky events when pricing credit derivatives and managing bond portfolio risk (see Chapter 16).

12. In Excel, the function =NORMINV(RAND(), mean, standard deviation) can be used to find that random number on the *x*-axis (the *x*-percentile) of a normal distribution with the specified mean and standard deviation.

Specialized simulation software packages use such algorithms to generate a random variable from any distribution. @RISK does it behind the scenes when the user specifies directly the probability distribution to be generated by clicking on the button **Define Distribution**. In MATLAB, one can use both the direct and the indirect approach. For example, to generate a single number from a normal distribution, one can enter `norminv(rand(1), mean, standard deviation)`. More recent versions of MATLAB's Statistics Toolbox contain direct commands for generating random numbers from a variety of distributions, for example, `normrnd` for normal random variables, `poissrnd` for Poisson random variables, and so on. Type `lookfor rnd` at the MATLAB prompt for a listing of available distributions, and see the end of this chapter for how such commands are used.

13. The Glivenko-Cantelli Theorem is a statement about the behavior of an empirical CDF as the number of independent and identically distribution (IID) observations recorded from the underlying distribution grows. Glivenko and Cantelli showed that as the number of observations grows, the empirical CDF approaches the true CDF uniformly.

14. A long cycle is desirable because if the random number generator converges to only a small set of values for the random number, we cannot obtain a good representation of the probability distribution we are trying to sample.

15. See section 3.8 in the previous chapter for a definition of autocorrelation.

16. The intuition is that the remainder after division with m is the difference between the number Ax_{n-1} and the largest number that is divisible by m but is still less than Ax_{n-1}.

17. Such sequences are discussed in detail in Chapter 14.

18. See the survey in Boyle, Broadie, and Glasserman (1997).

19. To permute, you can first draw one of the coordinates at random, then draw one coordinate from the remaining ones, and so on until only one is left.

20. The Latin Hypercube method works well for generating independent random variables, but complications occur when we need to generate correlated random variables. See Chapter 4 in Glasserman (2004) for further discussion and examples.

21. The number of bins you specify for the histogram will make a difference for how the histogram appears. For example, it is intuitively undesirable for a histogram to have only two bins. One rule of thumb used in statistics is to compute the number of bins by taking the square root of the number of observations, and rounding up.

22. Please note that your graph may look slightly different because the random numbers you generated will not necessarily be the same as the random numbers generated to create the picture. They will vary from trial to trial.

CHAPTER 5

Optimization Modeling

This chapter introduces optimization—a methodology for selecting an optimal strategy given an objective and a set of constraints. Optimization appears in a variety of financial applications, including portfolio allocation, trading strategies, identifying arbitrage opportunities, and pricing financial derivatives. We will encounter it in Chapters 7, 8, 9, 14, and 18, among others. In this chapter, we motivate the discussion by a simple example and describe how optimization problems are formulated and solved.

Let us recall the retirement example from section 4.2.2. We showed how to compute the realized return on the portfolio of stocks and bonds if we allocate 50% of our capital in each of the two investments. Can we obtain a "better" portfolio return with a different allocation? (As discussed in section 4.2.3 of the previous chapter, a "better" return is not well-defined in the context of uncertainty, so for the sake of argument, let us assume that "better" means higher *expected* return.) We found that if the allocation is (100%, 0%) instead of (50%, 50%), we end up with a higher portfolio expected return, but also higher portfolio standard deviation. What about an allocation of (30%, 70%)? It turned out that the portfolio expected return is lower, and so is the standard deviation. What about an allocation of (20%, 80%)?

In this example, we are dealing with only two investments, and we have no additional requirements on the portfolio structure. It is, however, still difficult to enumerate all the possibilities and find those that provide the optimal trade-off of return and risk. In practice, portfolio managers are handling thousands of investments and need to worry about transaction costs, requirements on the portfolio composition, and trading constraints, which makes it impossible to find the "best" portfolio allocation by trial-and-error. The optimization methodology provides a disciplined way to approach the problem of optimal asset allocation.

5.1   OPTIMIZATION FORMULATIONS

The increase in computational power and the tremendous pace of developments in the operations research field in the past 15 to 20 years has led to highly efficient algorithms and user-friendly software for solving optimization problems of many different kinds. The art of optimization modeling is therefore in framing a situation so that the formulation fits within recognized frameworks for problem specifications, and can be passed to optimization solvers. It is important to understand the main building blocks of optimization formulations, as well as the limitations of the software and the insights that can be gained from the output of optimization solvers.

An optimization problem formulation consists of three parts:[1]

1. A set of *decision variables* (usually represented as an $N \times 1$ − dimensional vector array[2] $\mathbf{x}$).
2. An *objective function*, which is a function of the decision variables ($f(\mathbf{x})$).
3. A set of *constraints* defined by functions ($g_i(\mathbf{x})$, $h_j(\mathbf{x})$), $i = 1,\ldots,I$, $j = 1,\ldots,J$ of the general form $g_i(\mathbf{x}) \leq 0$ (inequality constraints) and $h_j(\mathbf{x}) = 0$ (equality constraints).

The decision variables are numerical quantities that represent the decisions to be made. In the portfolio example, the decision variables could be the portfolio weights (alternatively, they could be the amounts to allocate to each asset class). The objective function is a mathematical expression of the goal, and the constraints are mathematical expressions of the limitations in the business situation. In our example, the objective function could be an expression to compute the expected portfolio return, and the constraints could include an expression that computes total portfolio risk. We can then maximize the expression of the objective function subject to an upper limit on the risk we are willing to tolerate. (We will derive actual formulations in Chapters 7 through 10.)

Optimization software expects users to specify all three components of an optimization problem, although it is sometimes possible to have optimization problems with no constraints. The latter kind of optimization problems is referred to as *unconstrained* optimization. Unconstrained optimization problems are typically solved with standard techniques from calculus,[3] and the optimal solution is selected from all possible points in the N-dimensional space of the decision variables $\mathbf{x}$. When there are constraints, only some points in that space will be *feasible*, that is, will satisfy the constraints. The values of the decision variables that are feasible and result in the best value for the objective function are called the *optimal solution*. Optimization solvers typically return only one optimal solution. However, it is possible to have multiple optimal solutions, that is, multiple feasible solutions **x** that produce the same optimal value for the objective function.[4]

When formulating optimization problems, it is important to realize that the decision variables need to participate in the mathematical expressions for the objective function and the constraints that are passed to an optimization solver because the whole idea of optimization algorithms is that they can tweak the values of the decision variables in these expressions in a smart, computationally efficient way, in order to produce the best value for the objective function with values for the decision variables that satisfy all of the constraints. In other words, we cannot simply pass the expression

$$\text{Maximize} \quad \text{Portfolio expected return}$$

to an optimization solver, unless the portfolio expected return is expressed as a function of the decision variables (the portfolio weights). As we will derive in Chapter 7, the expected portfolio return can be expressed in terms of the portfolio weights as $\mathbf{w}'\boldsymbol{\mu}$, where $\mathbf{w} = (w_1, \ldots, w_N)'$ and $\boldsymbol{\mu} = (\mu_1, \ldots, \mu_N)'$ are N-dimensional arrays containing the weights and the expected returns of the N assets in the portfolio, respectively. So, the objective function would be written as

$$\max_{\mathbf{w}} \quad \mathbf{w}'\boldsymbol{\mu}$$

which is interpreted as "maximize the value of $\mathbf{w}'\boldsymbol{\mu}$ over the possible values for $\mathbf{w}$."

In addition, the input data in a classical optimization problem formulation need to be fixed numbers, not random variables. For example, the objective function of an optimization problem cannot be passed to a solver as

$$\text{Maximize} \quad \text{Portfolio return}$$

where portfolio return $= \mathbf{w}'\tilde{\mathbf{r}}$, and $\tilde{\mathbf{r}} = (\tilde{r}_1, \ldots, \tilde{r}_N)'$ is the N-dimensional array with (uncertain) asset returns with some probability distributions. Some areas in optimization, such as robust optimization and stochastic programming, study methodologies for solving optimization problems in which the input data are subject to uncertainty and follow theoretical or empirical probability distributions. However, in the end, the methods for solving such problems reduce to specifying the coefficients in the optimization problem as *fixed* numbers that are representative of the underlying probability distributions in a particular way.

5.1.1 Minimization vs. Maximization

Most generally, optimization solvers require an optimization problem formulation to be of the kind

$$\min_{\mathbf{x}} \quad f(\mathbf{x})$$

$$\text{subject to} \quad g_i(\mathbf{x}) \leq 0 \quad i = 1, \ldots, I$$

$$h_j(\mathbf{x}) = 0 \quad j = 1, \ldots, J$$

There are variations on this formulation, and some have to do with whether the optimization problem falls in a specific class. (Different categories of optimization problems based on the form of their objective function and the shape of their feasible set are discussed in section 5.2.) Some optimization software syntax, such as the MATLAB Optimization Toolbox syntax, allows for specifying only minimization problems, while other optimization software packages are more flexible, and accept both minimization and maximization problems. Standard formulation requirements, however, are not as restrictive as they appear at first sight. For example, an optimization problem that involves finding the maximum of a function $f(\mathbf{x})$ can be recast as a minimization problem by minimizing the expression $-f(\mathbf{x})$, and vice versa—an optimization problem that involves finding the minimum of a function $f(\mathbf{x})$ can be recast as a maximization problem by maximizing the expression $-f(\mathbf{x})$. To obtain the actual value of the objective function, one then flips the sign of the optimal value. Exhibit 5.1 illustrates the situation for a quadratic function of one variable x. The optimal value for max $f(x)$ is obtained at the optimal solution x^*. The optimal value for $\min - f(x)$ is obtained at x^* as well. Notice also that

$$\max_{x} f(x) = -\min_{x} -f(x)$$

For the previous portfolio expected return maximization example, stating the objective function as

$$\max_{\mathbf{w}} \mathbf{w}'\mu$$

or

$$\min_{\mathbf{w}} -\mathbf{w}'\mu$$

will produce the same optimal values for the decision variables $\mathbf{w}$. To get the actual optimal objective function value for $\max_{\mathbf{w}} \mathbf{w}'\mu$, we would flip the sign of the optimal objective function value obtained after minimizing $-\mathbf{w}'\mu$.

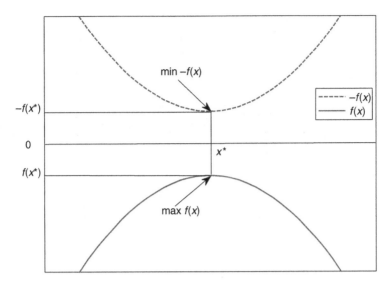

EXHIBIT 5.1 Example of the optimal objective function values for a quadratic objective function $f(x)$ of a single decision variable x.

5.1.2 Local vs. Global Optima

In optimization, we distinguish between two types of optimal solutions: *global* and *local* optimal solutions. A global optimal solution is the "best" solution for any value of the decision variables vector **x** in the set of *all* feasible solutions. A local optimal solution is the best solution in a *neighborhood* of feasible solutions. In other words, the objective function value at any point "close" to a local optimal solution is worse than the objective function value at the local optimal solution. Exhibit 5.2 illustrates the global (point A) and local (point B) optimal solution for the unconstrained minimization of a function of two variables.

Most classical optimization algorithms can only find local optima. They start at a point, and go through solutions in a direction in which the objective function value improves. Their performance has an element of luck that has to do with picking a "good" starting point for the algorithm. For example, if a nonlinear optimization algorithm starts at point C in Exhibit 5.2, it may find the local minimum B first, and never get to the global minimum A. In the general case, finding the global optimal solution can be difficult and time consuming, and involves finding all local optimal solutions first, and then picking the best one among them.

The good news is that in some cases, optimization algorithms can explore the special structure of the objective function and the constraints to

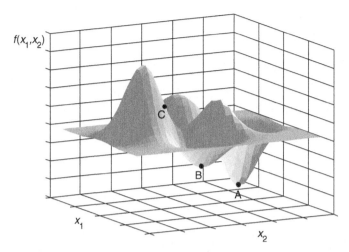

EXHIBIT 5.2 Global (point A) versus local (point B) minimum for a function of two variables x_1 and x_2.

deliver stronger results. In addition, for some categories of optimization problems, a local optimal solution is in fact guaranteed to be the global optimal solution, and many optimization problems in finance have that property. (We review the most important kinds of such "nice" optimization problems in section 5.2.) This makes recognizing the type of optimization problem in a given situation and formulating the optimization problem in a way that enables optimization algorithms to take advantage of the special problem structure even more critical.

5.1.3 Multiple Objectives

In practice, we often encounter situations in which we would like to optimize several objectives at the same time. For example, a portfolio manager may want to maximize the portfolio expected return and skew, while minimizing the variance and the kurtosis. There is no straightforward way to pass several objectives to an optimization solver. A multiple-objective optimization problem needs to be reformulated as an optimization problem with a single objective. There are a couple of commonly used methods to do this. We can assign weights to the different objectives, and optimize the weighted sum of objectives as a single-objective function. Alternatively, we can optimize the most important objective, and include the other objectives as constraints, after assigning to each of them a bound on the value we are willing to tolerate.

5.2 IMPORTANT TYPES OF OPTIMIZATION PROBLEMS

Optimization problems can be categorized based on the form of their objective function and constraints, and the kind of decision variables. The type of optimization problem with which we are faced a particular situation determines what software is appropriate, the efficiency of the algorithm for solving the problem, and the degree to which the optimal solution returned by the optimization solver is trustworthy and useful. Awareness of this fact is particularly helpful in situations in which there are multiple ways to formulate the optimization problem. The way in which we state the formulation will determine whether the optimization solver will be able to exploit any special structure in the problem, and whether it can achieve stronger results.

5.2.1 Convex Programming

As mentioned in section 5.1.2, some general optimization problems have a "nice" structure in the sense that a local optimal solution is guaranteed to be the global optimal solution. *Convex optimization problems* have that property. A general convex optimization problem is of the form

$$\min_{\mathbf{x}} \quad f(\mathbf{x})$$
$$\text{subject to} \quad g_i(\mathbf{x}) \leq 0 \quad i = 1, \ldots, I$$
$$\mathbf{Ax} = \mathbf{b}$$

where both $f(\mathbf{x})$ and $g_i(\mathbf{x})$ are convex functions, and $\mathbf{Ax} = \mathbf{b}$ is a system of linear equalities. A *convex function* of a single variable x has the shape showed in Exhibit 5.3(A). For a convex function, a line that connects any two points on the curve is always above the curve. The "opposite" of a convex function is a *concave function* (see Exhibit 5.3(B)), which looks like

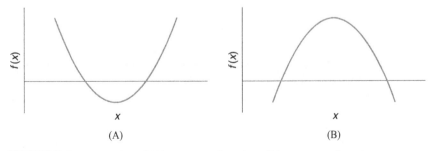

EXHIBIT 5.3 Examples of (A) a convex function; (B) a concave function.

a "cave." For a concave function, a line that connects any two points on the curve is always below the curve.

Convex programming problems encompass several classes of problems with special structure, including *linear programming* (LP), some *quadratic programming* (QP), *second-order cone programming* (SOCP), and *semidefinite programming* (SDP). Algorithms for solving convex optimization problems are more efficient than algorithms for solving general nonlinear problems, but it is important to keep in mind that even within the class of convex problems, some convex problems are computationally more challenging than others. LP problems are best studied and easiest to solve with commercial solvers, followed by convex QP problems, SOCP problems and SDP problems.

We introduce LP, QP, and SOCP in more detail next. Many classical problems in finance involve linear and quadratic programming, including asset-liability problems, portfolio allocation problems, and some financial derivative pricing applications. SDP problems are advanced formulations that have become more widely used in financial applications with recent advances in the field of robust optimization. They are beyond the scope of this book, but we refer interested readers to Fabozzi, Kolm, Pachamanova, and Focardi (2007) for a detailed overview of robust optimization formulations.

5.2.2 Linear Programming

Linear programming refers to optimization problems in which both the objective function and the constraints are linear expressions in the decision variables.[5] The standard formulation statement for linear optimization problems is

$$
\begin{aligned}
\min_{\mathbf{x}} \quad & \mathbf{c}'\mathbf{x} \\
\text{subject to} \quad & \mathbf{A}\mathbf{x} = \mathbf{b} \\
& \mathbf{x} \geq 0
\end{aligned}
$$

All optimization problems involving linear expressions for the objective function and the decision variables can be converted to this standard form. Section 5.3.1 will present an example.

Linear optimization problems are the easiest kind of problems to solve. Modern specialized optimization software can handle LP formulations with hundreds of thousands of decision variables and constraints in a matter of seconds. In addition, linear optimization problems belong to the class of convex problems for which a local optimal solution is guaranteed to be the global optimal solution. (This is discussed in more detail in section 5.4.2.) LPs arise in a number of finance applications, such as asset allocation and identification of arbitrage opportunities. The sample optimization problem formulations in section 5.3.1 and 5.3.2 are linear optimization problems.

5.2.3 Quadratic Programming

Quadratic programming problems have an objective function that is a quadratic expression in the decision variables, and constraints that are linear expressions in the decision variables. The standard form of a quadratic optimization problem is

$$
\min_{\mathbf{x}} \quad \frac{1}{2}\mathbf{x}'\mathbf{Q}\mathbf{x} + \mathbf{c}'\mathbf{x}
$$
$$
\text{subject to} \quad \mathbf{A}\mathbf{x} = \mathbf{b}
$$
$$
\mathbf{x} \geq 0
$$

where $\mathbf{x}$ is an N-dimensional vector of decision vectors as before, and the other arrays are input data:

$\mathbf{Q}$ is an $N \times N$ matrix.

$\mathbf{c}$ is an N-dimensional vector.

$\mathbf{A}$ is a $J \times N$ matrix.

$\mathbf{b}$ is an J-dimensional vector.

When the matrix $\mathbf{Q}$ is positive semidefinite,[6] then the objective function is convex. (It is a sum of a convex quadratic term and a linear function, and a linear function is both convex and concave.) Since the objective function is convex and the constraints are linear expressions, we have a convex optimization problem. The problem can be solved by efficient algorithms, and we can trust that any local optimum they find is in fact the global optimum. When $\mathbf{Q}$ is not positive semidefinite, however, the quadratic problem can have several local optimal solutions and stationary points, and is therefore more difficult to solve.

The most prominent use of quadratic programming in finance is for asset allocation and trading models. We will see examples in Chapters 7 through 10.

5.2.4 Second-Order Cone Programming

Second-order cone programs (SOCPs) have the general form

$$\min_{\mathbf{x}} \quad \mathbf{c}'\mathbf{x}$$

$$\text{subject to} \quad \mathbf{A}\mathbf{x} = \mathbf{b}$$

$$||\mathbf{C}_i\mathbf{x} + \mathbf{d}_i|| \leq \mathbf{c}_i'\mathbf{x} + e_i, \quad i = 1, \ldots, I$$

where $\mathbf{x}$ is an N-dimensional vector of decision vectors as before, and the other arrays are input data:

$\mathbf{c}$ is an N-dimensional vector.

$\mathbf{A}$ is a $J \times N$ matrix.

$\mathbf{b}$ is a J-dimensional vector.

$\mathbf{C}_i$ are an $I_i \times N$ matrix.

$\mathbf{d}_i$ are I_i-dimensional vectors.

e_i are scalars.

The notation $||.||$ stands for second norm, or Euclidean norm. (It is sometimes denoted $||.||_2$ to differentiate it from other types of norms.) The Euclidean norm of an N-dimensional vector $\mathbf{x}$ is defined as

$$||\mathbf{x}|| = \sqrt{x_1^2 + \cdots + x_N^2}$$

The SOCP class of problems is more general than the classes covered in sections 5.2.2 and 5.2.3. LPs, convex QPs, and convex problems with quadratic objective function and quadratic constraints can be reformulated as SOCPs with some algebra.

It turns out that SOCP problems share many nice properties with linear programs, so algorithms for their optimization are very efficient. SOCP formulations arise mostly in robust optimization applications. Such formulations are discussed in section 6.3.

5.2.5 Integer and Mixed Integer Programming

So far, we have classified optimization problems according to the form of the objective function and the constraints. Optimization problems can be classified also according to the type of decision variables $\mathbf{x}$. Namely, when the decision variables are restricted to be integer (or, more generally, discrete) values, we refer to the corresponding optimization problem as an *integer programming* (IP) or a *discrete problem*. When some decision variables are discrete and some are continuous, we refer to the optimization problem as a *mixed integer programming* (MIP) problem. In special cases of integer problems in which the decision variables can only take values 0 or 1, we refer to the optimization problem as a *binary optimization problem*.

Integer and mixed integer optimization formulations are useful for formulating extensions to classical portfolio allocation problems. Index-tracking formulations and many constraints on portfolio structure faced by managers in practice require modeling with discrete decision variables. Examples of constraints include maximum number of assets to be held in the portfolio (so-called *cardinality constraints*), maximum number of trades, round lot constraints (constraints on the size of the orders in which assets can be traded in the market),[7] and fixed transaction costs. Simple illustrations of integer modeling are provided in the next section and are further discussed in Chapter 9.

5.3 OPTIMIZATION PROBLEM FORMULATION EXAMPLES

To provide better intuition for how optimization problems are formulated, we give a few simplified examples of financial problem formulations. We will see more advanced nonlinear problems formulations in the context of portfolio applications in Chapters 7 through 9.

The first example in this section is explained in detail, so that the process of optimization problem formulation can be explicitly outlined. The problem formulation is the crucial step—once we are able to define a business situation as one of the optimization problem types reviewed in the previous section, we can find the optimal solution with optimization software. Later in this chapter, we explain how optimization formulations can be input into solvers, and how the output can be retrieved and interpreted.

5.3.1 Portfolio Allocation

The portfolio manager at a large university in the United States is tasked with investing a $10 million donation to the university endowment. He has decided to invest these funds only in mutual funds[8] and is considering the following four: an aggressive growth fund (Fund 1), an index fund (Fund 2), a corporate bond fund (Fund 3), and a money market fund (Fund 4), each with a different expected annual return and risk level.[9] The investment

EXHIBIT 5.4 Data for the portfolio manager's problem.

Fund Type	Growth	Index	Bond	Money Market
Fund number	1	2	3	4
Expected return	20.69%	5.87%	10.52%	2.43%
Risk level	4	2	2	1
Max. investment	40%	40%	40%	40%

guidelines established by the Board of Trustees limit the percentage of the money that can be allocated to any single type of investment to 40% of the total amount. The data for the portfolio manager's task are provided in Exhibit 5.4. In addition, in order to contain the risk of the investment to an acceptable level, the amount of money allocated to the aggressive growth and the corporate bond funds cannot exceed 60% of the portfolio, and the aggregate average risk level of the portfolio cannot exceed 2. What is the optimal portfolio allocation for achieving the maximum expected return at the end of the year, if no short selling is allowed?[10]

To formulate the optimization problem, the first thing we need to ask ourselves is what the objective is. In this case, the logical objective is to maximize the expected portfolio return. The second step is to think of how to define the decision variables. The decision variables need to be specified in such a way as to allow for expressing the objective as a mathematical expression of the quantities the manager can control to achieve his objective. The latter point is obvious, but sometimes missed when formulating optimization problems for the first time. For example, while the market return on the assets is a variable and increasing market returns will increase the portfolio's return, changing the behavior of the market is not under the manager's control. The manager, however, can change the amounts he invests in different assets in order to achieve his objective.[11] Thus, the vector of **decision variables** can be defined as

$\mathbf{x} = (x_1, x_2, x_3, x_4)$: amounts (in $) invested in Fund 1, 2, 3, and 4, respectively

Let the vector of expected returns be $\mu = (20.69\%, 5.87\%, 10.52\%, 2.43\%)$. Then, the objective function can be written as

$$f(x) = \mu'\mathbf{x} = (20.69\%) \cdot x_1 + (5.87\%) \cdot x_2 + (10.52\%) \cdot x_3 + (2.43\%) \cdot x_4.$$

It is always a good idea to write down the actual description and the units for the decision variables, the objective function and the constraints. For example, the units of the objective function value in this example are dollars.

Finally, we have several constraints:

- The total amount invested should be $10 million. This can be formulated as $x_1 + x_2 + x_3 + x_4 = 10,000,000$.
- The total amount invested in Fund 1 and Fund 3 cannot be more than 60% of the total investment ($6 million). This can be written as $x_1 + x_3 \leq 6,000,000$.
- The average risk level of the portfolio cannot be more than 2. This constraint can be expressed as 4*(proportion of investment with risk level 4) + 2*(proportion of investment with risk level 2) + 1*(proportion of investment with risk level 1) $\leq$ 2 or, mathematically,

$$\frac{4 \cdot x_1 + 2 \cdot x_2 + 2 \cdot x_3 + 1 \cdot x_4}{x_1 + x_2 + x_3 + x_4} \leq 2.$$

Note that this is not a linear constraint. (We are dividing decision variables by decision variables.) Based on the discussion in section 5.2.2, from a computational perspective, it is better to have linear constraints whenever we can. There are a couple of different ways to convert this particular constraint into a linear constraint. For example, we can multiply both sides of the inequality by $x_1 + x_2 + x_3 + x_4$, which is a nonnegative number and will preserve the sign of the inequality as is. In addition, in this particular example we know that the total amount $x_1 + x_2 + x_3 + x_4 = 10,000,000$, so the constraint can be formulated as

$$4 \cdot x_1 + 2 \cdot x_2 + 2 \cdot x_3 + 1 \cdot x_4 \leq 2 \cdot 10,000,000.$$

The maximum investment in each fund cannot be more than 40% of the total amount ($4,000,000). These constraints can be written as

$$x_1 \leq 4,000,000, \ x_2 \leq 4,000,000, \ x_3 \leq 4,000,000, \ x_4 \leq 4,000,000$$

Finally, given the no short selling requirement, the amounts invested in each fund cannot be negative. (Note we are assuming that the portfolio manager can invest only the \$10,000,000, and cannot borrow more.)

$$x_1 \geq 0, \; x_2 \geq 0, \; x_3 \geq 0, \; x_4 \geq 0.$$

These are *nonnegativity constraints*. Even though they seem obvious in this example, they still need to be specified explicitly for the optimization solver.

The final optimization formulation can be written in matrix form. The objective function is

$$\max_{x_1,x_2,x_3,x_4} \begin{bmatrix} 0.2069 & 0.0587 & 0.1052 & 0.0243 \end{bmatrix} \cdot \begin{bmatrix} x_1 \\ x_2 \\ x_3 \\ x_4 \end{bmatrix}.$$

Let us organize the constraints together into groups according to their signs. (This will be useful when solving the problem with optimization software is discussed later.)

$$\text{Equality}(=): \begin{bmatrix} 1 & 1 & 1 & 1 \end{bmatrix} \cdot \begin{bmatrix} x_1 \\ x_2 \\ x_3 \\ x_4 \end{bmatrix} = 10{,}000{,}000$$

$$\text{Inequality}(\leq): \begin{bmatrix} 1 & 0 & 1 & 0 \\ 4 & 2 & 2 & 1 \\ 1 & 0 & 0 & 0 \\ 0 & 1 & 0 & 0 \\ 0 & 0 & 1 & 0 \\ 0 & 0 & 0 & 1 \end{bmatrix} \cdot \begin{bmatrix} x_1 \\ x_2 \\ x_3 \\ x_4 \end{bmatrix} \leq \begin{bmatrix} 6{,}000{,}000 \\ 20{,}000{,}000 \\ 4{,}000{,}000 \\ 4{,}000{,}000 \\ 4{,}000{,}000 \\ 4{,}000{,}000 \end{bmatrix}.$$

$$\text{Nonnegativity}(\geq): \begin{bmatrix} x_1 \\ x_2 \\ x_3 \\ x_4 \end{bmatrix} \geq \begin{bmatrix} 0 \\ 0 \\ 0 \\ 0 \end{bmatrix}.$$

This problem is an LP. It would look like the standard form in section 5.2.2, except for the inequality ($\leq$) constraints. We can rewrite the LP in standard form by converting them to equality constraints. We introduce six additional nonnegative variables $\mathbf{s} = (s_1, \ldots, s_6)$ (called *slack variables*), one for each constraint in the group Inequality ($\leq$):

$$
\begin{bmatrix}
1 & 0 & 1 & 0 & 1 & 0 & 0 & 0 & 0 & 0 \\
4 & 2 & 2 & 1 & 0 & 1 & 0 & 0 & 0 & 0 \\
1 & 0 & 0 & 0 & 0 & 0 & 1 & 0 & 0 & 0 \\
0 & 1 & 0 & 0 & 0 & 0 & 0 & 1 & 0 & 0 \\
0 & 0 & 1 & 0 & 0 & 0 & 0 & 0 & 1 & 0 \\
0 & 0 & 0 & 1 & 0 & 0 & 0 & 0 & 0 & 1
\end{bmatrix}
\cdot
\begin{bmatrix}
x_1 \\ x_2 \\ x_3 \\ x_4 \\ s_1 \\ s_2 \\ s_3 \\ s_4 \\ s_5 \\ s_6
\end{bmatrix}
=
\begin{bmatrix}
6{,}000{,}000 \\
20{,}000{,}000 \\
4{,}000{,}000 \\
4{,}000{,}000 \\
4{,}000{,}000 \\
4{,}000{,}000
\end{bmatrix}.
$$

Then, we add the nonnegativity constraints on the slack variables to the problem formulation:

$$[x_1, x_2, x_3, x_4, s_1, s_2, s_3, s_4, s_5, s_6]' \geq 0.$$

Optimization solvers in the past required that the problem be passed in standard form; however, solvers and optimization languages are much more flexible today, and do their own conversion to standard form. In any case, as this example illustrates, it is easy to go from a general linear problem formulation to the standard form. The optimization software we will use in this book—Excel's Solver, Palisade's Evolver, and MATLAB's Optimization Toolbox—have their own problem input specifications, but these specifications are straightforward to handle. We explain how to solve this problem with software in this chapter's Software Hints.

5.3.2 Cash Flow Matching

Consider an asset manager who is managing funds for the corporate sponsor of a defined benefit pension plan that needs to ensure a particular stream of semiannual cash payments over the next four years for retiring plan participants.[12] For example, the pension plan may have semiannual obligations representing annuity payments. Let the cash obligations for the eight payment dates of the next four years be represented by a vector $\mathbf{m} = (m_1, \ldots, m_8)$.

The asset manager on behalf of its client, the pension plan, is considering investing in five different high investment-grade quality bonds. Over the next eight payment dates (i.e., semiannually), bond i pays out coupons $\mathbf{c}_i = (c_{i1}, \ldots, c_{i8})$. If the bond matures at date t, the corresponding c_{it} equals

EXHIBIT 5.5 Cash flow matching example data.

Current Bond Price (p_i)	$102.36	$110.83	$96.94	$114.65	$96.63	
Cash Flows (c_{it})						Obligations (m_t)
$t = 1$	$ 2.50	$ 5.00	$ 3.00	$ 4.00	$ 3.50	$ 100,000.00
$t = 2$	$ 2.50	$ 5.00	$ 3.00	$ 4.00	$ 3.50	$ 200,000.00
$t = 3$	$ 2.50	$ 5.00	$ 3.00	$ 4.00	$ 3.50	$ 100,000.00
$t = 4$	$ 2.50	$ 5.00	$ 3.00	$ 4.00	$ 3.50	$ 200,000.00
$t = 5$	$102.50	$ 5.00	$ 3.00	$ 4.00	$ 3.50	$ 800,000.00
$t = 6$		$105.00	$ 3.00	$ 4.00	$ 3.50	$1,200,000.00
$t = 7$			$103.00	$ 4.00	$ 3.50	$ 400,000.00
$t = 8$				$104.00	$103.50	$1,000,000.00

the coupon rate plus the principal. The bonds currently trade at ask prices $\mathbf{p} = (p_1, \ldots, p_5)$. The relevant data are provided in Exhibit 5.5. The asset manager would like to ensure that the coupon payments from the bonds cover the pension plan's obligations.[13]

To formulate this problem, we must, again, ask ourselves what the objective of the fund is. Although it is not stated explicitly in the problem, it makes sense for the objective to be to minimize the cost of acquiring the bonds today while still meeting all expected future obligations.

The decision variables can be defined as the amounts $\mathbf{x} = (x_1, x_2, x_3, x_4, x_5)$ to invest in each of the five bonds. The cost of acquiring the bonds today is

$$\sum_{i=1}^{5} p_i \cdot x_i = \mathbf{p}'\mathbf{x}.$$

The constraints are that at each payment date, the cash flows from the coupons of all the bonds are at least as large as the liabilities. Therefore, the optimization problem can be stated as

$$\min_{x_1, \ldots, x_5} \quad \sum_{i=1}^{5} p_i \cdot x_i$$

$$\text{subject to} \quad \sum_{i=1}^{5} c_{it} \cdot x_i \geq m_t, \quad t = 1, \ldots, 8$$

$$x_i \geq 0, \quad i = 1, \ldots, 5.$$

Again, this formulation is an LP because both the objective function and the constraints are linear functions of the decision variables x_1, x_2, x_3, x_4, x_5.

In practice, the amounts for the bond investments may need to be presented as *round lots*. This can be achieved by using integer variables. We can introduce new integer variables $z = (z_1, z_2, z_3, z_4, z_5)$ that correspond to the number of lots to buy of each bond. Suppose that a lot for bond i is l_i. To obtain the optimal number of lots of each bond to purchase, we rewrite the problem formulation above as

$$\min_{x_1,\ldots,x_5,z_1,\ldots,z_5} \sum_{i=1}^{5} p_i \cdot x_i$$

$$\text{subject to} \quad \sum_{i=1}^{5} c_{it} \cdot x_i \geq m_t, \quad t = 1, \ldots, 8$$

$$x_i \geq 0, \quad i = 1, \ldots, 5$$

$$x_i = z_i \cdot l_i, \quad i = 1, \ldots, 5$$

$$z_i \text{ integer}, \quad i = 1, \ldots, 5$$

Since some of the variables are continuous $(x_1, x_2, x_3, x_4, x_5)$ and some are discrete $(z_1, z_2, z_3, z_4, z_5)$, the LP formulation becomes an MIP, which is computationally harder to solve.

For implementation of this example of cash flow matching, see this chapter's Software Hints and the files **Ch5-CashFlowMatching.xlsx** and **CashFlowMatching.m**. Note, however, that while the LP formulation can be solved with any solver, both Excel Solver and MATLAB's Optimization Toolbox will have trouble solving the MIP. To solve the MIP problem, we would need a more advanced solver such as ILOG's CPLEX.[14]

5.3.3 Capital Budgeting

The operating manager at a pharmaceutical company is considering funding proposals for eight different research and development (R&D) projects, but she has limited funds C ($C = \$1,000,000$). The cost of investing in Project i is c_i, and the present value of Project i's estimated benefit is b_i. Specific numbers c_i and b_i are shown in Exhibit 5.6. (We will explain how projects are valued in Chapters 17 and 18.) Each project is on a "take it or leave it" basis, that is, it is not possible to fund a project partially. Which projects should the operating manager fund in order to maximize the present value of the expected total benefit?

EXHIBIT 5.6 Costs, present value (PV) of project benefits, and benefit/cost ratios for each of the eight R&D projects. All numbers are in thousands of dollars.

Project	1	2	3	4	5	6	7	8
Project cost	$400.00	$350.00	$200.00	$100.00	$300.00	$250.00	$300.00	$350.00
Project benefits (PV)	$950.00	$780.00	$440.00	$215.00	$630.00	$490.00	$560.00	$600.00
Benefit/cost ratio	2.38	2.23	2.20	2.15	2.10	1.96	1.87	1.71

If we did not know about optimization problem formulations, a logical approach is to rank the projects according to their benefit to cost ratios, and to pick as many (in order of decreasing benefit to cost ratios) as can be funded with the $1 million budget.

Going from left to right in the table in Exhibit 5.6, we select Projects 1, 2, and 3. The total cost is

$$\$400,000 + \$350,000 + \$200,000 = \$950,000,$$

so we stop after selecting Project 3. The present value of the total benefits is

$$\$950,000 + \$780,000 + \$440,000 = \$2,170,000.$$

Is this the best we can do? Notice that we were left with a budget of about $50,000 we could have invested. There is no project that can be had for $50,000, but suppose that we replaced Project 3 with Project 6, which had an outlay of $250,000, and would have exhausted the budget of $1 million. The total benefit from investing in Projects 1, 2, and 6 is

$$\$950,000 + \$780,000 + \$490,000 = \$2,220,000,$$

which is higher than the number we found with the first approach. In fact, there is a combination of projects that results in an even higher expected benefit: Projects 1, 3, 4, and 5. The total benefit is

$$\$950,000 + \$440,000 + \$215,000 + \$630,000 = \$2,235,000,$$

and it turns out that this is the maximum benefit we can get for an investment budget of $1 million.

It is not easy to see immediately that the combination of Projects 1, 3, 4, and 5 gave the optimal solution, and this was a simple problem, in which the manager was faced with no additional constraints. It is even harder to identify the optimal solution once further conditions on the projects are imposed.

This situation is a good example of how binary optimization can be useful for financial applications. Let us introduce decision variables $x_1, \ldots, x_8$ (one corresponding to each project) that equal 1 if the project is selected, and 0 otherwise. The total benefit then can be computed as

$$\$950{,}000 \cdot x_1 + \$780{,}000 \cdot x_2 + \$440{,}000 \cdot x_3 + \$215{,}000 \cdot x_4$$
$$+ \$630{,}000 \cdot x_5 + \$490{,}000 \cdot x_6 + \$560.000 \cdot x_7 + \$600{,}000 \cdot x_8$$

Note that if the decision is not to invest in Project i, then the benefit of that project is not counted towards the total benefit. The total cost of funding the selected projects can be computed in a similar manner.

We can now formulate the optimization problem:

$$\min_{x_1, \ldots, x_8} \quad \sum_{i=1}^{8} b_i \cdot x_i$$

$$\text{subject to} \quad \sum_{i=1}^{8} c_i \cdot x_i \leq C$$

$$x_i \text{ binary}, \quad i = 1, \ldots, 8$$

Solving this problem will produce the optimal solution we mentioned above:

$$(x_1, x_2, x_3, x_4, x_5, x_6, x_7, x_8) = (1, 0, 1, 1, 1, 0, 0, 0).$$

Now suppose that the manager is facing additional constraints:

(a) If he funds Project 1, he must fund Project 8 as well.
(b) Projects 4 and 5 are mutually exclusive since their goals are virtually the same, that is, if the manager funds Project 4, he will not fund Project 5, and vice versa.

Let us first formulate the problem with constraint (a). The condition needs to be formulated mathematically, that is, classical optimization solvers do not understand "If–then" statements.[15] We can express the condition as the additional constraint

$$x_1 \leq x_8$$

or, equivalently, as

$$x_1 - x_8 \leq 0.$$

To gain some intuition, note that if the manager finds that it is optimal to invest in Project 1, that is, $x_1 = 1$, then the constraint above will force x_8 to be 1 as well, that is, the optimal solution will contain investments in both Project 1 and Project 8. However, if the manager does not invest in Project 1, that is, $x_1 = 0$, then x_8 is free to be 0 or 1, that is, the manager may or may not invest in Project 8.

The optimal solution with additional constraint (a) turns out to be to invest in Projects 2, 4, 5, and 6, for a total estimated benefit of $2,115,000.

Now let us formulate constraint (b). Again, we need to express it mathematically. We can state the condition as

$$x_4 + x_5 \leq 1.$$

This will work because in order for the constraint to be satisfied, only one of the variables x_4, x_5 can be 1. (They may both be 0, of course.) Therefore, the manager would be able to invest in at most one of Project 4 or 5. The optimal solution when both constraints (a) and (b) are added to the original optimization problem is

$$(x_1, x_2, x_3, x_4, x_5, x_6, x_7, x_8) = (0, 1, 0, 1, 0, 1, 1, 0)$$

for a total benefit of $2,045,000, and a total cost of $1,000,000. In other words, the manager should invest in Projects 2, 4, 6, and 7.

5.4 OPTIMIZATION ALGORITHMS

How do optimization solvers actually find the optimal solution for a problem? As a general rule, optimization algorithms are of iterative nature. They start with an initial solution and generate a sequence of intermediate solutions until they get "close" to the optimal solution. The degree of "closeness" is determined by a parameter called *tolerance*, which usually has some default value, but can often be modified by the user. Frequently, the tolerance parameter is linked to a measure of the distance between the current and the subsequent solution, or to the incremental progress made by subsequent iterations of the algorithm in improving the objective function value. If subsequent iterations of the algorithm bring very little change relative to the status quo, the algorithm is terminated.

The algorithms for optimization in today's optimization software are rather sophisticated, and an extensive introduction to these algorithms is beyond the scope of this book. However, many optimization solvers let the user select which optimization algorithm to apply to a specific problem, and some basic knowledge of what algorithms are used for different classes of optimization solvers is helpful for deciding what optimization software to use and what options to select for the problem at hand.

5.4.1 Linear Optimization: The Simplex Algorithm and Interior Point Methods

The first optimization algorithm, called the *simplex algorithm*, was developed by George Dantzig in 1947. It solves linear optimization problems by iteratively solving systems of linear equations to find intermediate feasible solutions in a way that continually improves the value of the objective function. The name of the algorithm refers to the geometric term *simplex*. A 2-dimensional simplex is a triangle—a set of points that lie between the lines that can be drawn between 2 + 1 points in the 2-dimensional space. In N-dimensional space, a simplex is a collection of all the points that can be enclosed by hyperplanes connecting the outermost points in the set.[16] (See Exhibit 5.7.) It turns out that the feasible sets for the decision variables in linear optimization problems are simplexes, and a pretty amazing fact about linear optimization problems is that at least one possible optimal solution must lie at the "corner" of the simplex. (It is possible that other optimal solutions lie on the "edge" of the set, however.) The simplex algorithm takes advantage of this fact. It visits the corners of the simplex that contains the feasible solutions to the linear optimization problem iteratively in order to find the corner solution that results in the best possible value for the objective function, which it then reports as the optimal solution. Despite its age, the simplex algorithm is still widely used for linear optimization, and is remarkably efficient in practice.

In the 1980s, another class of efficient algorithms called *interior point methods* was developed, inspired by a new algorithm Narendra Karmakar created for linear programming problems. In contrast to the simplex method, which traverses the simplex of feasible points along the edges and only considers the corners, interior point methods reach the optimal solution from

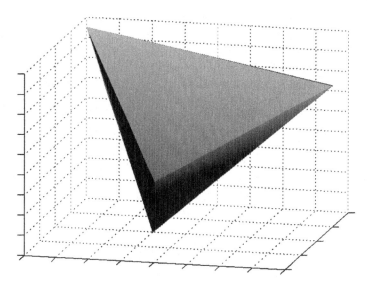

EXHIBIT 5.7   Simplex in 3-dimensional space.

the inside of the feasible set. If there are multiple optimal solutions, interior point algorithms may not find the corner one. Thus, if a linear optimization problem has multiple optimal solutions, solving the problem with a solver that uses the simplex algorithm versus a solver that uses an interior point algorithm may result in different optimal solutions. The advantage of interior point methods is that they can be applied not only to linear optimization problems, but also to a wider class of convex optimization problems.

5.4.2   Constrained Nonlinear Optimization: The KKT Conditions and Lagrange Multipliers

Many nonlinear optimization algorithms are based on using information from a special set of equations that represent necessary conditions that a solution x is optimal. These conditions are the Karush-Kuhn-Tucker (KKT) conditions for optimality. We explain the intuition behind them next.

When an optimization problem is unconstrained and the objective function is differentiable, the optimum can be found using standard techniques from calculus. If we are minimizing a function $f(x)$ of a single variable x, then the derivative of $f(x)$, $f'(x)$, must be 0 at the optimal point x^* (see Exhibit 5.7). To see this, recall that the derivative represents the amount the function will change when x changes by a small amount. If $f'(x^*)$ is less than 0, then we can move a small distance from x^* in the positive direction, and achieve a smaller value for $f(x)$, so $f(x^*)$ is not in fact the minimum. Similarly, if $f'(x^*)$ is greater than 0, then we can move a small distance from x^* in the negative direction, and achieve a smaller value for $f(x)$.

When there are constraints $g_i(x)$ and $h_j(x)$, a parallel condition for x^* to be the minimum holds, but it involves the derivatives of the constraint functions as well. Namely, at the optimum x^*, the following equality must hold:

$$f'(x^*) + \sum_{i=1}^{I} u_i \cdot g_i'(x^*) + \sum_{j=1}^{J} v_j \cdot h_j'(x^*) = 0.$$

Here u_i and v_j are special numbers called *Lagrange multipliers*, and u_i need to be nonnegative. In addition, of course, for a point x^* to be the optimum, it needs to be feasible as well, that is, it must satisfy all constraints in the optimization problem. The Lagrange multipliers are not known in advance, but in some cases can be computed from the equality above and the conditions on feasibility.

The KKT conditions are a generalization of the statements above when there are multiple decision variables. If f, $g_i(x)$ and $h_j(x)$ are functions of an N-dimensional vector of variables $\mathbf{x}$, then we need to consider the *gradients* of the objective function and the constraint functions.[17] Then, the KKT necessary conditions for a point $\mathbf{x}^*$ to be a minimum can be expressed as

$$\nabla f(\mathbf{x}^*) + \sum_{i=1}^{I} u_i \cdot \nabla g_i(\mathbf{x}^*) + \sum_{j=1}^{J} v_j \cdot \nabla h_j(\mathbf{x}^*) = 0$$

$$u_i \geq 0, i = 1, \dots, I$$

$$u_i \cdot g_i(\mathbf{x}^*) = 0, i = 1, \dots, I$$

$$h_j(\mathbf{x}^*) = 0, j = 1, \dots, J$$

$$g_i(\mathbf{x}^*) \leq 0, i = 1, \dots, I$$

The last two conditions simply require that the point $\mathbf{x}^*$ must satisfy all the constraints, that is, be a feasible solution, in order to be considered a candidate for the global minimum.

Note that it is not easy to find a point $\mathbf{x}$ that satisfies the KKT conditions because, depending on the expressions for the objective function and the constraint functions, some of the equations in the system may be nonlinear. Even if a point that satisfies the KKT conditions is found, it may not be the

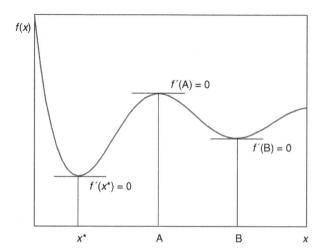

EXHIBIT 5.8 The condition that the derivative of a
function $f(x)$ is equal to 0 is satisfied at (A) the global
minimum x^*, (B) a local maximum (point A), and (c) a
local minimum (point B).

global optimum, since the KKT conditions are necessary, but not sufficient
for optimality. In other words, if a point $\mathbf{x}^*$ is the global optimal solution,
it must satisfy these conditions, but if a point $\mathbf{x}$ satisfies these conditions, it
is not necessarily the global optimal solution. This reasoning is easiest to visualize in the simple case in which we have the unconstrained minimization
problem in Exhibit 5.8. The derivative of $f(x)$ is 0 not only at the global
minimum (x^*), but also at point A (local maximum), and point B (local minimum). The derivative can also be 0 at so-called *inflection* points (or *saddle*
points), which are neither minima, nor maxima, but points at which the
function changes curvature. The KKT conditions are, fortunately, necessary
and sufficient for optimality in the case of convex optimization problems.
They take a special form in the case of linear optimization problems and
some other classes of convex problems, which is exploited in interior point
algorithms for finding the optimal solution.

The importance of the KKT conditions for general nonlinear optimization is that they enable a nonlinear optimization problem to be reduced to a
system of nonlinear equations, whose solution can be attained by using successive approximations. Widely used algorithms for nonlinear optimization
include barrier methods, primal–dual interior point methods, and sequential
quadratic programming methods. The latter try to solve the KKT conditions
for the original nonlinear problem by optimizing a quadratic approximation

to a function derived from the objective function and the constraints of the original problem. For more details, we refer the reader to Bazaraa, Sharali, and Shetty (1993) and Freund (2004).

5.4.3 Integer Programming Algorithms

At first glance, integer and mixed integer optimization problems appear to be easier than standard optimization problems because the number of feasible values for the decision variables to be explored appears smaller than the feasible values for optimization problems with continuous variables. In fact, however, integer programming problems as a general rule are more difficult and take longer to solve. Enumeration of all possible solutions for problems of realistic size is prohibitively expensive computationally, so we still need to resort to algorithms that search for the optimal solution in a smart way. Such algorithms are easier to create for problems with continuous variables than for problems with integer variables.

IP optimization problems are typically solved by branch-and-bound algorithms, branch-and-cut routines, and heuristics[18] that exploit the special structure of the problem.[19] The main idea behind many of these algorithms is to start by solving a *relaxation* of the optimization problem in which the decision variables are not restricted to be integer numbers. The algorithms then begin with the solution found in the initial stage, and narrow down the choices of integer solutions. In practice, a simple rounding of the initial fractional optimal solution is sometimes good enough. However, it is important to understand that simple rounding of the initial solution can lead to an integer solution that is very far from the actual optimal solution, and this problem is even more pronounced when the number of integer decision variables is large.

There are some good commercial optimization solvers that can handle linear and convex quadratic mixed-integer optimization problems, but there are virtually no solvers that can handle more general nonlinear mixed integer problems efficiently.

5.4.4 Randomized Search Algorithms

In this chapter, we referred several times to the difficulty of finding the global optimal solution when there are multiple local optima. Classical nonlinear optimization algorithms typically stop when they have found a solution that is the best in its "neighborhood," and if they come across a local optimum first, they may never reach the global optimum. A number of algorithms try to avoid these pitfalls by incorporating an element of randomness in their search. In other words, they allow moves to feasible solutions with worse value of the objective function to happen with some probability, rather than pursuing always a direction in which the objective function improves. The hope is that this will avoid getting stuck in a local optimum.

Randomized search algorithms fall into several classes, including *simulated annealing, tabu search*, and *genetic algorithms*. Genetic algorithms in particular have become an option in several popular software packages for optimization, such as Premium Solver and Palisade's Evolver, which is discussed shortly. MATLAB also has a Genetic Algorithms and Direct Search Toolbox, which contains simulated annealing and genetic algorithms. We explain simulated annealing and genetic algorithms in more detail, so that the available options in these software packages become more intuitive.

At every step, the simulated annealing algorithm generates a new feasible solution to the optimization problem, and generally accepts it as the next solution if the solution improves the value of the objective function. However, even if the solution does not improve the value of the objective function, the simulated annealing algorithm accepts it with some probability. The magnitude of the probability of accepting a seemingly inferior solution as the next point in the search is determined by a positive parameter T (called the *temperature*) that is an input to the algorithm. If the temperature is small, the simulated annealing algorithm is less likely to deviate substantially from a path in which the objective function value is improving; if the temperature is large, the simulated annealing is more adventurous in picking solutions that can be very different. At an intuitive level, when the algorithm is close to the optimum, we want the temperature to be small, so that the algorithm stays in that neighborhood and eventually finds the optimal solution. However, at the initial stages of the algorithm, we may be better off if the temperature is large because the algorithm will scout more areas with solutions faster, and will not spend time in a particular neighborhood. In advanced solvers, the default value of the parameter T is usually set to a value that works reasonably well for a wide variety of difficult, highly nonlinear problems.

Like simulate annealing, genetic algorithms are useful in cases in which the objective function or the constraints are highly nonlinear or have discontinuities. However, genetic algorithms tend to be slower than classical optimization algorithms and simulated annealing because they tend to require more objective function evaluations. Despite this drawback, genetic algorithms can be more efficient than other randomized algorithms in cases in which some of the decision variables are integer numbers, or in cases in which the optimization problem has a special structure.

Before a genetic algorithm starts, a way must be found for any potential solution to the optimization problem to be encoded as a string of integers, or binary bits. This string is referred to as a *chromosome*. It looks something like

$$1101 \quad 0000 \quad 1111 \quad 0010$$

The chromosome may be composed of *genes*, which could be individual bits or groups of bits. In the preceding example, we may treat groups of four bits as genes.

At the beginning of the algorithm, a fixed number of such chromosomes are generated. (This is the initial *population*.) Each of them is assigned a *fitness score*, which evaluates how good the solution represented by that chromosome is. (The fitness score is related to the objective function value evaluated at that solution.) Then, two members from the population are selected at random. (The probability of being selected is typically related to the fitness score of a particular chromosome.) You can think of them as the "parents." The *crossover rate*, specified by the user, determines how the genes of the parents are swapped. It is often specified to be about 0.7. The *mutation rate*, also specified by the user, determines what percentage of the bits on average flip from 1 to 0 and from 0 to 1 randomly. It is usually something small (e.g., 0.001). After going through a number of iterations specified by the user, the algorithm stops, and returns the best solution found so far.

To summarize, randomized search algorithms for optimization have their drawbacks—they can be slow, and provide no guarantee that they will find the global optimum. However, they are appropriate for handling difficult integer problems, nonlinear problems and problems with discontinuities, when traditional optimization solvers fail.

5.4.5 Algorithm Efficiency

Thus far we have been using the word "efficient" to describe an optimization algorithm. While the term is intuitive and generally means "fast," in some cases it is important to differentiate between different ways to measure the efficiency of an algorithm. Established conventions estimate the efficiency of an algorithm by the number of steps, or elementary operations it takes to solve a problem of a given size. (The "size" of a problem is determined by the number of operations need to solve the problem, which is related to the number of decision variables and the number of constraints.[20]) However, such bounds typically estimate the worst-case performance. A large number of steps does not necessarily mean worse performance in practice. For most practical purposes, we care only whether a given algorithm performs well on typical instances of the problems, not whether the algorithm is slow for some pathological examples. The simplex method for linear optimization, for example, provides no guarantees on how many steps it may take to come up with the optimal solution. Yet, the algorithm works remarkably well in practice.

Still, a theoretical superiority of one algorithm over another does often lead to better performance in practice as well. Thus, algorithms that run in *polynomial time* in the problem size are generally preferable to algorithms that take *exponential time*. An algorithm is said to run in polynomial time if it requires $O(n^k)$ operations to solve, where n is the problem size and k is a positive integer.[21] An algorithm is said to run in exponential time if it requires $O(k^n)$ operations to solve the problem. As an example, if $k = 10$ and $n = 80$ (the problem size can easily be 80 for real-life problems), we will need more operations to solve the optimization problem than there are, arguably, atoms in the universe. No matter how much technology has improved, algorithms that run in exponential time are very hard to handle for large problems.

5.5 OPTIMIZATION DUALITY

The Lagrange multipliers **u** and **v** from the KKT conditions in section 5.4.2 have a special role in optimization theory and practice. They are in fact variables in a certain *dual* optimization problem that is related to the original, or *primal*, optimization problem in very specific ways. If the primal problem is a minimization problem, then the dual problem is a maximization problem, and vice versa. The number of variables in the dual problem is equal to the number of constraints in the primal problem, and vice versa. Moreover, there is a relationship between the optimal objective function values of the primal and the dual problem that can frequently be exploited. *Optimization duality theory* has numerous critical applications, including, but not restricted to the following:

- A good dual problem solution can be used to compute a bound for the value of the objective function of the primal problem, and so can be used to identify when a primal solution is near-optimal.
- For some types of convex optimization problems, it can be verified that an optimal solution to the primal problem has been found by constructing a dual problem solution with the same objective function value.
- Often, the dual problem has better mathematical or computational structure than the primal problem. This fact can be used to compute optimal solutions for both the primal and the dual optimization problems. In addition, computation of dual variables is part of a number of

efficient optimization algorithms. The primal-dual interior point method (mentioned in section 5.4.2) is one such algorithm.

▪ We can use dual variables to perform sensitivity analysis on the primal optimization problem. The dual variable corresponding to a particular constraint in the primal problem represents the incremental change in the optimal solution value per unit increase in the value on the right hand side of the constraint equality or inequality.

Duality theory is not as widely used in specific financial applications as some other aspects of optimization, but has been used in the context of finding arbitrage opportunities (see Chapter 13), and it plays a major part in the methodology for deriving robust optimization problem formulations for portfolio optimization problems (see section 6.3 in the next chapter). It is therefore helpful to explain how dual problems are constructed and interpreted for some important classes of optimization problems.

Consider again the general optimization problem P (the primal problem):

$$
\text{P:} \quad
\begin{aligned}
&\min_{\mathbf{x}} && f(\mathbf{x}) \\
&s.t. && g_i(\mathbf{x}) \le 0, && i = 1, \ldots, I \\
& && h_j(\mathbf{x}) = 0, && j = 1, \ldots, J
\end{aligned}
$$

The dual problem D is constructed in three steps:

▪ Place the constraints in the objective function by using I nonnegative multipliers u_i and J multipliers v_j to form the so-called *Lagrangian function*

$$
L(\mathbf{x}, \mathbf{u}) := f(\mathbf{x}) + \mathbf{u}'g(\mathbf{x}) + \mathbf{v}'h(\mathbf{x}) = f(\mathbf{x}) + \sum_{i=1}^{I} u_i g_i(\mathbf{x}) + \sum_{j=1}^{J} v_j h_j(\mathbf{x})
$$

▪ Create the dual function

$$
L^*(\mathbf{u}) := \min_{\mathbf{x}} \left\{ f(\mathbf{x}) + \mathbf{u}'g(\mathbf{x}) + \mathbf{v}'h(\mathbf{x}) \right\}.
$$

▪ Write the dual problem

$$
\text{D:} \quad
\begin{aligned}
&\max_{\mathbf{u}} && L^*(\mathbf{u}) \\
&s.t. && \mathbf{u} \ge 0
\end{aligned}
$$

EXHIBIT 5.9 Primal and dual formulations for important types of convex optimization problems.

	Primal Problem	Dual Problem
LPs	$\min_{x}$ $c'x$ s.t. $Ax = b$ $x \geq 0$	$\max_{u}$ $u'b$ s.t. $A'u \leq c'$
	$\min_{x}$ $c'x$ s.t. $Ax \geq b$	$\max_{u}$ $u'b$ s.t. $A'u = c$ $u \geq 0$
QPs	$\min_{x}$ $\frac{1}{2}x'Qx + c'x$ s.t. $Ax \geq b$	$\max_{u}$ $u'b - \frac{1}{2}(c - A'u)'Q^{-1}(c - A'u)$ s.t. $u \geq 0$
SOCPs	$\min_{x}$ $c'x$ s.t. $\|C_i x + d_i\| \leq c_i'x + e_i,$ $i = 1, \ldots, I$	$\max_{u,v}$ $-\sum_{i=1}^{I} u_i'd_i + v_i e_i$ s.t. $\sum_{i=1}^{I} u_i C_i + v_i c_i = c$ $\|u_i\| \leq v_i, i = 1, \ldots, I$

Usually, we construct the dual problem in the hope that computing the optimal solution will be an easy task.

Examples of primal and dual problems for linear and quadratic problems are summarized in Exhibit 5.9. The dual of the dual problem is the primal problem.

Note that the type of problem (LP, QP, SOCP) in the primal is preserved in the dual problem for all of these examples of convex problems. (This is not the case in general nonlinear optimization.) Moreover, it can be shown that for all of these types of convex problems, the objective function value of the primal problem for a feasible primal problem solution is at least as large as the objective function value of the dual problem for a feasible dual problem. In fact, for these types of convex optimization problems, it is guaranteed that if the primal problem has an optimal solution, then so does the dual, and the respective objective function values are the same. This has important implications for optimization algorithm applications.

5.6 MULTISTAGE OPTIMIZATION

Financial planning and pricing decisions often involve finding optimal strategies over multiple time periods ahead. For example, a firm may be considering a sequence of operational decisions over the next few years. It is often possible to capture this multistage framework through standard optimization formulations, but it can be difficult, and it does not always allow for employing the most efficient algorithms for solving the problem. Models of dynamic choice in finance typically involve representation of future cash flow streams, and are perhaps best visualized by a graph. On the horizontal axis, one denotes the time periods at which the cash flows occur. At each time period, nodes are used to represent different possible *states* or conditions of the dynamic system at that point in time. The collection of all states is called the *state space*. Our actions influence which state is reached at the next point in time. States that are reachable from a particular state are linked to that state.

5.6.1 Finite State Space

Examples of two simple dynamical systems are illustrated in Exhibit 5.10(A) and (B). Each node in the graphs represents a state. The graphs are called *binomial trees*, or *binomial lattices*, because there are exactly two branches emanating from each node. The number of branches corresponds to the number of options available to the decision maker at each particular state. If there were three available choices, the number of branches emanating from each node would be three. There can also be dynamical systems with an infinite number of branches emanating from each node. We will see an example later in this section. Note that the branches in Exhibit 5.10(A)

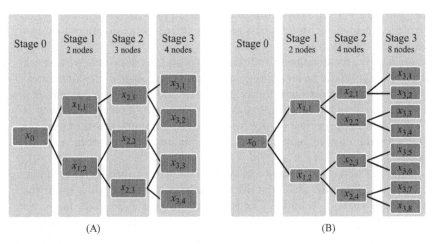

(A)   (B)

EXHIBIT 5.10 (A) Recombining binomial tree; (B) nonrecombining binomial tree.

recombine, whereas the branches in Exhibit 5.10(B) do not. Graphs with recombining branches are referred to as *recombining trees* or *recombining lattices*.

Let us consider a very simple example. Suppose you have purchased a 3-year lease for an oil well. The estimated reserves of the well are 600,000 barrels. Every year, you can either pump oil normally (Strategy 1), in which case you pump 100,000 barrels, or use an enhanced pumping method which allows you to pump 200,000 barrels (Strategy 2). The increased production capacity through the enhanced pumping method comes at a price: to extract u_t barrels at time t with the enhanced method costs you $20 \cdot u_t^2/x_t$ dollars, where x_t is the amount of available reserves at time t. In contrast, the cost of extracting u_t barrels with the normal pumping method is u_t^2/x_t dollars. Note that in both cases, as the amount of available oil x_t decreases, the cost of pumping increases. This expression incorporates the implicit assumption that it becomes harder to pump the oil as the reserves are depleted.

The expected price of a barrel of oil over the first, second, and third year of your lease is \$45, \$30, and \$40, respectively, and the discount factor per year is 0.9. Assuming that you can pump either 100,000 barrels or 200,000 barrels each year, what is the optimal strategy to maximize the present value (PV) of your profit from the lease?

One approach to finding the optimal solution would be to look at the price of oil in each of the three years, compute the revenue and cost from each strategy each year, and then pick the strategy that results in the best profit during that year. Unfortunately, however, the profit every year depends on the level of current oil reserves. To see this, suppose that the current reserves are x_t and the current price is p_t. The profit of Strategy 1 is $p_t \cdot 100{,}000 - u_t^2/x_t$. The profit of Strategy 2 is $p_t \cdot 200{,}000 - 20 \cdot u_t^2/x_t$. Therefore, optimal decisions across years are interdependent, and we cannot treat every year separately.

To describe the dynamics of the cash flows and the decisions, we first ask ourselves what would be an appropriate definition of *state* in this dynamical system. The state must incorporate all information about the system at a particular point in time. In our example, the amount of current reserves at time t, x_t, is an appropriate choice for state. The amount of current reserves determines the cost of pumping oil, and that impacts the profit and our decision.

The evolution of our dynamical system can be described by the graph in Exhibit 5.11. (See also file **Ch5-OilExample.xlsx**.) We can pump oil at the beginning of years 0, 1, and 2. The lease ends in year 3. At every node, we can make the decision to pump 100,000 or 200,000 barrels of oil, which takes us to one of the nodes at the next time period. For example, at time 0

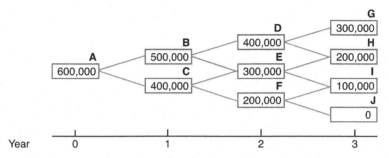

EXHIBIT 5.11 Binomial tree representing the state space for the oil well multistage optimization problem. (See file **Ch5-OilExample.xlsx.**)

(node A), we start out with $x_0 = 600,000$ barrels of oil. If we pump using the normal method, that is, our decision $u_0 = 100,000$, the oil reserves decrease by 100,000, and the system is at node B at time 1. If we pump using the enhanced method, then the oil reserves decrease by 200,000, and the system is at node C at time 1. Depending on the node at which we are in year 1 (node B or node C), we can again decide whether to use the normal or the enhanced method ($u_1 = 100,000$ or $u_1 = 200,000$, respectively). If we are at node B at time 1, our decision will take us either to node D (if we use the normal method) or to node E (if we use the enhanced method). If we are at node C, our decision will take us either to node E (if we use the normal method) or to node F (if we use the enhanced method). Note that this tree is recombining because, for example, we can get to node E (have reserves of 300,000 barrels) either by following the path A-B-E (pumping 100,000 in the first year and 200,000 in the second year) or the path A-C-E (pumping 200,000 in the first year and 100,000 in the second year).

There are 8 "paths" in the graph: A-B-D-G, A-B-D-H, A-B-E-H, A-B-E-I, A-C-E-H, A-C-E-I, A-C-F-I, and A-C-F-J. Each path represents a particular strategy. To find the optimal path to take, we could evaluate the present value of the profit along each path, and select the path that gives us the maximum present value of profit. The calculation can be done for this example. However, in practice we may encounter situations in which there are many more time periods, and many more possible states. The problem quickly becomes computationally intractable. For example, if we expand the number of time periods in a binomial tree to 20, the number of paths to be evaluated becomes 2^{20}, which is 1,048,576. For each of these paths, we need to store information at each time period in order to add it up and obtain the present value of the profit obtained from selecting that path. Not only is the number of paths large, but it also seems superfluous to recalculate the profit at each node several times, given that some paths share nodes.

The trick to solving the problem with minimum number of calculations and minimum amount of storage required is to work backwards starting from the final nodes on the right. At each node, we can store only the information about the best path so far, and forget about all other paths. This sequential optimization method is called *dynamic programming*. Dynamic programming is based on Bellman's (1957) *Principle of Optimality*, which states that to achieve total optimality in a sequential decision process, all future decisions after reaching a particular state must be optimal with respect to that state. In other words, it is impossible to have a suboptimal decision at some intermediate state, and still reach the overall optimum. Therefore, we only need to keep track of the optimal decision at each state reachable from the current state, and can use recursive relationships to describe the optimal decision at any particular state in terms of the optimal decisions in future states. We explain the dynamic programming algorithm as it applies to the oil well problem next.

There is no profit realized at nodes G, H, I, and J because the lease has expired by then. (We assume that all profit is obtained at the beginning of the year.) So, we can ignore them in our calculation. At the beginning of year 2, we can be at nodes D, E or F. Suppose we are at D, that is, the current level of oil reserves is 400,000 barrels. The profit that can be realized using the normal method is

$$40 \cdot 100,000 - 100,000^2/400,000 = \$3,975,000.$$

The profit realized using the enhanced method is

$$40 \cdot 200,000 - 20 \cdot 200,000^2/400,000 = \$6,000,000.$$

Obviously, $6,000,000 is the higher profit, so we should use the enhanced method if we are at node D.

Similarly, we can compute the highest profit at nodes E and F. If we are at E, the optimal strategy is to use the enhanced method, and the profit we can realize is $5,333,333.33. If we are at F, the optimal strategy is again to use the enhanced method, and the realized profit will be $4,000,000.

Next, we consider the previous time period. At the beginning of year 1, we can be either at node B or at node C.

Suppose we are at node B, that is, the oil reserves are 500,000. If we select the normal method, we will realize a current profit of $30 \cdot 100,000 - 100,000^2/500,000 = \$2,980,000$, and will move to node D, which will realize an additional profit of $5,400,000, which is the present value of $6,000,000 in year 1 dollars ($= 0.9 \cdot \$6,000,000$). The total profit from employing the normal method in year 1 is therefore $2,980,000 + $5,400,000 = $8,380,000.

Suppose now that we select the enhanced method if we are at node B. This means that in the next year, we will be at node E. The current profit is $4,400,000, and the best profit we can realize at node E is $5,333,333.33, so the total profit in year 1 dollars is $4,400,000 + 0.9 \cdot \$5,333,333.33 = $9,200,000.00.

Clearly, selecting the enhanced method at node B results in a higher total profit from year 1 onward (accounting for both the profit in year 1 and the best profit that can be realized in year 2 if we are at node B in year 1).

We proceed in a similar manner to compute the profits at nodes C and A. At each node, we only record the present value of the optimal profit from that node onward, and the best strategy from that point onward. The optimal path and the profit from the best strategy at each node (from that node onward) are shown in Exhibit 5.12. The optimal path, that is, the path that leads to the highest present value of total profit ($14,664,166.67), is A-C-E-I. This means that the optimal strategy is to use the enhanced method for the first year, the normal method for the second year, and the enhanced method again for the third year.

Note that the strategies at some nodes are not obvious. For example, if we are at node A, and we look at the optimal profit realized at nodes B and C, we may be tempted to use the normal method over the first year, ending up at node B. This is because the optimal profit at node B going

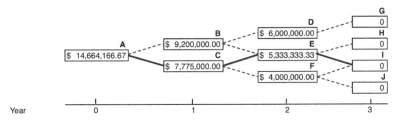

Year

EXHIBIT 5.12 Optimal profit from each state onward and optimal decision path (marked by bold line segments) for the oil well problem. The nodes in the tree match the states in Exhibit 5.10.

forward ($9,200,000.00) is higher than the optimal profit at node C going forward ($7,775,000.00). However, the price of oil over the first year is high enough that it turns out that, overall, is it optimal to pump more oil (using the enhanced method) during the first year and then end up in node C, even though the optimal profit going forward from node C is less than the optimal profit going forward from B.

Standard Notation Used in Dynamic Programming   Let us summarize the dynamic programming approach by introducing some standard notation. The variable that summarizes all necessary information at each state is referred to as a *state variable*. In our example, it was x_t, the amount of oil available at time t. Our decisions (the amount of oil to pump) were represented by a variable $u_t = \{100,000, 200,000\}$, which is referred to as a *control*, or *policy*, *variable*. The state variable was a function of the control variable and the state at which we were in the previous period, and was updated at every stage by the transition equation

$$x_{t+1} = x_t - u_t.$$

In the general case, we write $x_{t+1} = g(x_t, u_t)$.

The total number of stages in our problem was $T = 3$. Our goal was to optimize an *objective function*, the present value of the total profit, which was a sum of the present values of the profits at each stage, and was a function of the state and the control variable at each stage. We can write the objective function as

$$\sum_{t=0}^{T-1} f_t(x_t, u_t).$$

In order to compute the optimal value of the objective function (the optimal total profit), at each node of the dynamic programming algorithm, we computed the optimal profit from that stage onward. The reward (or cost, depending on the problem) *from a specific node onward* is referred to as the *value function*. It is usually denoted by V. The dynamic programming algorithm maximizes the sum of the immediate reward of the current step (say, cash flow $c(u_t)$) and the optimal reward from the steps that follow. The value function recursion can be written as

$$V_t(x_t) = \max_{u_t} \left\{ c(u_t) + d \cdot V_{t+1}^*(u_t) \right\}$$

where $V_{t+1}^*(u_t)$ is the optimal value of the value function at stage $t + 1$ over all possible values for the control u_t, and d is the discount factor over one stage. In our oil well example, we had

$$
V_t(x_t) = \max \left\{
\begin{array}{l}
p_t \cdot 100{,}000 - 100{,}000^2/x_t + 0.9 \cdot V_{t+1}^*(x_t - 100{,}000), \\
p_t \cdot 200{,}000 - 20 \cdot 200{,}000^2/x_t + 0.9 \cdot V_{t+1}^*(x_t - 200{,}000)
\end{array}
\right\}
$$

where p_t was the price of oil at time t.

In order to compute the actual values of the value function, a dynamic programming algorithm requires a *boundary condition*. As its name implies, a boundary condition gives information about values at the extremes. In the oil well example, we knew that the profit that can be realized at the beginning of year 3 was 0 (because the lease expires in three years). This allowed us to compute the value function at the beginning of time period 3. From there, we could compute the optimal values at the previous stages.

On the Relationship between Dynamic Programming and Classical Optimization Formulations   At the beginning of this section, we mentioned that many dynamic programming formulations can be stated in a standard optimization form, although often this is not the easiest or most efficient way to approach the problem. To illustrate the relationship between dynamic programming and the classical optimization formulations discussed in section 5.2 and 5.3, we formulate the oil well example in this section as a standard optimization problem.

First, we introduce decision variables x_0, x_1, and x_2 that will store the optimal amount of reserves at each stage. Technically, x_0 is not a variable (we are given the initial amount of reserves), but we keep the notation for consistency.

Second, we introduce decision variables u_0, u_1, and u_2 that will store our optimal decision about the amount of oil to pump at each stage.

Next, we note that our decision choices u_0, u_1, and u_2 are discrete—we can only pump 100,000 or 200,000 barrels each year. The situation is reminiscent of the cash flow matching problem in section 5.3.2, and more specifically of the modification of the problem in which we restricted the bonds that are purchased to be in round lots by introducing binary variables. We can approach the oil well problem formulation in a similar way. Let z_0, z_1, and z_2 be binary variables, with the following interpretation: z_t is 1 if we choose the normal method, that is, we pump 100,000 barrels of oil, and z_t is 0 if we choose the enhanced method, that is, we pump 200,000 barrels of oil. Then, we can link the policy decision variables u_0, u_1, and u_2 to the binary decision variables z_0, z_1, and z_2 as

$$u_t = 100{,}000 \cdot z_t + 200{,}000 \cdot (1 - z_t), \quad t = 0, 1, 2.$$

This equality states the correct relationship because one of the terms in the sum is always 0. If $z_t = 1$, that is, we use the normal method, the second term is 0, and u_t is 100,000. If $z_t = 0$, that is, we use the enhanced method, the first term is 0, and u_t is 200,000.

We also need to state explicitly the relationships between the oil reserves at each stage x_0, x_1, and x_2, and the policy variables u_0, u_1, and u_2. It is easy to see that we have

$$x_t = x_{t-1} - u_{t-1}, \quad t = 1, 2,$$

that is, to obtain the optimal amount of reserves to have at each stage, we subtract the optimal amount that was pumped at the previous stage from the amount available at the previous stage.

The objective is, of course, to maximize the profit over all three stages, and we need to discount the profit received at future dates properly to compute the correct total present value. The optimization problem formulation is therefore

$$
\begin{aligned}
\max_{x,u,z} \quad & p_0 \cdot u_0 - z_0 \cdot u_0^2/x_0 - (1 - z_0) \cdot 20 \cdot u_0^2/x_0 \\
& + 0.9 \cdot \left(p_1 \cdot u_1 - z_1 \cdot u_1^2/x_1 - (1 - z_1) \cdot 20 \cdot u_1^2/x_1 \right) \\
& + 0.9^2 \cdot \left(p_2 \cdot u_2 - z_2 \cdot u_2^2/x_2 - (1 - z_2) \cdot 20 \cdot u_2^2/x_2 \right) \\
\text{s.t.} \quad & u_0 = 100{,}000 \cdot z_0 + 200{,}000 \cdot (1 - z_0) \\
& u_1 = 100{,}000 \cdot z_1 + 200{,}000 \cdot (1 - z_1) \\
& u_2 = 100{,}000 \cdot z_2 + 200{,}000 \cdot (1 - z_2) \\
& x_0 = 600{,}000 \\
& x_1 = x_0 - u_0 \\
& x_2 = x_1 - u_1 \\
& u_0, u_1, u_2, x_1, x_2 \geq 0 \\
& z_0, z_1, z_2 \text{ binary}
\end{aligned}
$$

Note that we used a trick in the formulation of the objective function because the expression for the cost is different depending on the method we use. We subtracted the cost "twice": once for the normal method and once for the enhanced method. However, we multiplied the expression for the cost of each method by an expression containing the binary variable z_t, so that only the cost for the method that is selected is subtracted from the profit; the cost for the method that is not selected is 0 in the objective function.

An implementation of the problem is presented in worksheet **Classical Formulation** in file **Ch5-OilExample.xlsx**. The optimal solution and optimal strategy at each stage are the same as the solution we would obtain by using the dynamic programming algorithm:

$z_0 = 0$ (use the enhanced method at stage 0)

$z_1 = 1$ (use the normal method at stage 1)

$z_2 = 0$ (use the enhanced method at stage 2)

$u_0 = 200,000$ (pump 200,000 barrels of oil at stage 0)

$u_1 = 100,000$ (pump 100,000 barrels of oil at stage 1)

$u_2 = 200,000$ (pump 200,000 barrels of oil at stage 2)

$x_0 = 600,000$ (amount of reserves at stage 0 is 600,000 barrels)

$x_1 = 400,000$ (amount of reserves at stage 1 is 400,000 barrels)

$x_2 = 300,000$ (amount of reserves at stage 2 is 300,000 barrels)

5.6.2 Infinite State Space

As we mentioned earlier in this section, in some financial applications we need to deal with dynamical systems with an infinite state space. Think, for example, of investments that are managed over multiple time periods. If the state of the system is determined by our current holdings and the percentage invested in assets represents our policy, then technically, we could have an infinite number of possible states—the possible combinations of weights of assets in the portfolio at each point in time can be infinite. In such cases, we cannot easily visualize the dynamic system, and we cannot compute the optimal strategy at every state as we did in the example above. The best we can do is to hope to find an expression that describes the optimal strategy in each state in terms of the information in that state. This is not always possible, and sometimes approximations are used. Next, we show an example in which the optimal strategy in each of an infinite number of states can actually be computed in closed form.

Let us consider a modification of the oil well problem from the previous subsection. As before, suppose that you have purchased a 3-year lease for the oil well. The estimated reserves of the well are 600,000 barrels. You can use an enhanced method to pump oil that allows you to pump as much oil as you want during the year at a cost of $20 \cdot u_t^2/x_t$, where u_t is the amount of oil that was pumped, and x_t is the amount of available reserves at time t. As before, the expected price of a barrel of oil over the first, second, and third year of your lease is \$45, \$30, and \$40, respectively, and the discount factor per year is 0.9. How much oil should you pump in each year to maximize your profit over the three years?

Given the similarities with the example in section 5.6.1, it is easy to see that the most appropriate choice of state for the dynamical system is the amount of oil reserves available at time t. However, we can no longer draw a binomial tree like the one in Exhibit 5.10—there are an infinite number of states at each stage.

Fortunately, we can still solve the problem by using the dynamic programming recursion. Suppose that we are at the beginning of year 2, with one year left on the lease. The profit at the beginning of year 2 (again, assuming that all cash flows from the oil pumped in that year are received at that time) is $p_2 \cdot u_2 - 20 \cdot u_2^2/x_2$. The value function at any state at the beginning of year 2, $V_2(x_2)$, can be written as

$$V_2(x_2) = \max_{u_2} \left\{ p_2 \cdot u_2 - 20 \cdot u_2^2/x_2 \right\}.$$

This is an actual unconstrained optimization problem. The expression to maximize, $p_2 \cdot u_2 - 20 \cdot u_2^2/x_2$, is a quadratic function in u_2, and has the shape in Exhibit 5.3(B). It is easy to see that the maximum is given at the point where the derivative is equal to 0. The derivative with respect to u_2 is

$$p_2 - 40 \cdot u_2/x_2.$$

Setting the derivative to 0 yields

$$u_2^* = p_2 \cdot x_2/40.$$

Technically, there is one constraint in this optimization problem that we did not include in the calculation. We should make sure that $u_2 \leq x_2$, that is, that we do not pump more oil than we have available. It is easy to see that this will indeed be the case. Given that $p_2 = \$40$, we actually get $u_2^* = x_2$, that is, we should pump all oil available at time 2.

Next, we try to find the optimal amount of oil to pump one time period back—at time 1. The dynamic programming recursion tells us that u_1 will be the solution to the following optimization problem:

$$V_1(x_1) = \max_{u_1} \left\{ \underbrace{p_1 \cdot u_1 - 20 \cdot u_1^2/x_1}_{\text{current cash flow (at time 1)}} + \underbrace{0.9}_{\text{discount factor}} \cdot \underbrace{V_2^*(u_1)}_{\text{optimal profit from next step onward}} \right\}$$

To solve this problem, we need to know $V_2^*(u_1)$. We can find it by plugging the optimal value u_2^* (which we already found) into the expression for profit at time 2, $V_2(x_2)$. We get

$$\begin{aligned}
V_2^*(x_2) &= p_2 \cdot u_2^* - 20 \cdot \left(u_2^*\right)^2/x_2 \\
&= p_2^2 \cdot x_2/40 - 20 \cdot p_2^2 \cdot x_2^2/(40^2 \cdot x_2) \\
&= p_2^2 \cdot x_2/80
\end{aligned}$$

Therefore, the optimal value of the profit in year 1 is

$$V_1(x_1) = \max_{u_1} \left\{ p_1 \cdot u_1 - 20 \cdot u_1^2/x_1 + 0.9 \cdot p_2^2 \cdot x_2/80 \right\}$$

As we mentioned at the end of section 5.6.1, the state variable is updated as

$$x_{t+1} = x_t - u_t$$

because the value of the available oil reserves is equal to the value of the oil reserves from the previous time period reduced by the amount we pumped over the previous time period. Therefore, we can substitute x_2 in the expression for $V_1(x_1)$ with $x_1 - u_1$. We obtain

$$V_1(x_1) = \max_{u_1} \left\{ -20 \cdot u_1^2/x_1 + u_1 \cdot (p_1 - 0.9 \cdot p_2^2/80) + 0.9 \cdot p_2^2 \cdot x_1/80 \right\}$$

The quadratic function to be maximized looks like the function in Exhibit 5.3(B). We can find the maximum by taking the derivative with respect to u_1, and setting it to 0. The value of u_1 at which the maximum is attained is

$$u_1^* = (p_1 - 0.9 \cdot p_2^2/80) \cdot x_1/40$$

Substituting $p_1 = \$30$ and $p_2 = \$40$, we get

$$u_1^* = (12/40) \cdot x_1 = 0.3 \cdot x_1.$$

Therefore, the optimal strategy at time 1 is to pump 30% of the available reserves. The value function is estimated as

$$V_1(x_1) = -20 \cdot 0.3^2 \cdot x_1^2/x_1 + 0.3 \cdot x_1 \cdot (30 - 0.9 \cdot 40^2/80) + 0.9 \cdot 40^2 \cdot x_1/80$$
$$= 19.8 \cdot x_1$$

We proceed in a similar manner to evaluate the optimal strategy at time 0. The value function can be written as

$$V_0(x_0) = \max_{u_0} \left\{ \underbrace{p_0 \cdot u_0 - 20 \cdot u_0^2/x_0}_{\text{current cash flow (at time 0)}} + \underbrace{0.9}_{\text{discount factor}} \cdot \underbrace{V_1^*(u_0)}_{\text{optimal profit from next step onward}} \right\}.$$

Again, we have

$$x_1 = x_0 - u_0$$

and so

$$V_1^*(u_0) = 19.8 \cdot (x_0 - u_0).$$

Therefore,

$$V_0(x_0) = \max_{u_0} \left\{ -20 \cdot u_0^2/x_0 + 27.18 \cdot u_0 + 17.82 \cdot x_0 \right\}.$$

(Here we used the fact that the current price of oil is $p_0 = \$45$.) The maximum is attained at

$$u_0^* = (27.18/40) \cdot x_0 = 0.6795 \cdot x_0.$$

Hence, the optimal strategy at time 0 is to pump 67.95% of the available reserves. We actually know the reserves at time 0: $x_0 = 600{,}000$. Therefore, we can compute the actual amount to pump at time 0:

$$u_0^* = 0.6795 \cdot 600{,}000 = 407{,}700.$$

We can now trace the complete optimal strategy over the three years of the lease. At time 0, pump 67.95% of the optimal reserves, which is 407,700 barrels. At time 1, pump 30% of the remaining reserves, which is $0.30 \cdot (600,000 - 407,700) = 57,690$ barrels. At time 2, pump all remaining reserves, which is $600,000 - 407,700 - 57,690 = 134,610$ barrels. The optimal profit over the three years is given by

$$V_0(x_0) = -20 \cdot 407,700^2/600,000 + 27.18 \cdot 407,700 + 17.82 \cdot 600,000$$
$$= \$16,232,643$$

5.6.3 Steps in Formulating Multistage Optimization Problems

The dynamic programming examples in sections 5.6.1 and 5.6.2 give us some insights as to the general steps we may want to take in constructing a dynamic programming algorithm:

- Think of the solution as a sequence of decisions that occur in multiple stages, and represent the total cost (alternatively, reward) as a sum of the costs (rewards) of the individual decisions.
- Define the states in the dynamical system in such a way that they summarize all relevant past information.
- Determine which state transitions are possible, and link those states. The cost/reward of moving to a state should equal the cost/reward of the decision that forces that transition.
- Write an expression that computes the optimal cost/reward recursively starting from the last state and going backward to the state of origin.

While this framework is helpful, in general, it is not straightforward to describe a given dynamical system in such a way as to allow for finding the solution through a dynamic programming recursion. The issue is similar to the issue of how to consider a business situation and formulate an optimization problem in such a way that it can be passed to a solver. In the case of dynamic programming, the main step to ensure a successful formulation is to find a good definition of the state space—in other words, to define the state variables in such a way that the rewards/costs of the transitions to the next state variables and the value function depend solely on the current state and decision variables. It takes practice and skill, and sometimes, it is not possible to do. However, the dynamic optimization idea in general is useful, and has many variations in finance. We will see more examples of multistage optimization problems in Chapters 6, 13, 14, and 18.

5.7 OPTIMIZATION SOFTWARE

When selecting an optimization software product, it is important to differentiate between optimization *solvers* and optimization *modeling languages*.

An optimization solver is software that implements numerical routines for finding the optimal solution of an optimization problem. Well-known commercial optimization solvers include MOSEK[22] and ILOG's CPLEX[23] for linear, mixed-integer, and quadratic problems, and MINOS, SNOPT, and CONOPT for general nonlinear problems,[24] but there are a number of other commercial and free solvers available.

Optimization modeling languages have emerged as user-friendly platforms that allow the user to specify optimization problems in a more intuitive generic fashion, independently of the specific algorithmic and input requirements of optimization routines. Typically, optimization language software automates the underlying mathematical details of the optimization model formulation, but does not actually solve the problem. It passes the formulation to a solver, and retrieves the results from the solver in a convenient format. Popular optimization languages include AMPL[25] and GAMS.[26]

Optimization solvers and modeling languages are often part of *modeling environments* that handle not only the optimization, but also the input and output processing, statistical analysis, and perform other functions a user may need for a comprehensive analysis of a situation. MATLAB is an example of a high-level technical computing and interactive environment for model development that also enables data visualization, data analysis, and numerical simulation. The optimization solvers in MATLAB's Optimization Toolbox can solve a variety of constrained and unconstrained optimization problems for linear programming, quadratic programming, nonlinear optimization, and binary integer programming. Other examples of modeling environments include ILOG's OPL Studio, which allows users to build optimization models that are then accessed from a subroutine library using VBA, Java, or C/C++. Thus, a user can connect optimization systems directly to data sources, and make calls to optimization subroutines repeatedly. Palisade's Decision Tools Suite[27] also contains a number of software add-ins for optimization, statistical analysis, and sensitivity analysis that use a spreadsheet program—Microsoft Excel—as the underlying platform.

Excel's inherent capabilities for optimization are rather limited. Excel Solver, which ships with Excel, can handle only optimization problems of small size, up to a few hundred variables and constraints. It is a perfectly acceptable solver for linear optimization problems, but its performance (and the output one would obtain from it) is unreliable for more complex problems of the general nonlinear or integer programming type. Premium Solver

Platform,[28] which is sold by the developers of Excel Solver, is an extended and improved version of the standard Excel Solver, and can handle linear, integer, and quadratic problems of larger size. It employs efficient interior point methods for solving classical optimization formulations, and genetic algorithms for arbitrary Excel optimization models that contain spreadsheet functions such as IF, INDEX, and COUNTIF (such functions are not recognized in traditional optimization problem formulations). Palisade's Evolver is another add-in for Excel that uses genetic algorithms to solve optimization problems. The Palisade Decision Tools Suite also contains RiskOptimizer, which is a tool for optimization given possible scenarios for the uncertain parameters in the problem.

It is useful to mention that there are numerous optimization software packages that target financial applications in particular, especially portfolio management applications. Established vendors of portfolio management software include Axioma,[29] MSCI Barra,[30] ITG,[31] and Northfield Information Services.[32]

SUMMARY

- An optimization formulation consists of three parts: (1) an objective function, (2) a set of decision variables, and (3) a set of constraints.
- A solution is feasible if it satisfies all constraints. A solution is optimal if it is feasible and produces the best value of the objective function among all feasible solutions.
- A solution is a local optimum if it produces the best value of the objective function among all feasible solutions in its neighborhood. There may be multiple local optima, depending on the type of optimization problem.
- Optimization problems are categorized according to: (1) the form of the objective function and the constraints, and (2) the type of decision variables (discrete or continuous). Important classes of optimization problems include linear programming, quadratic programming, convex programming, integer programming, and mixed integer programming.
- For convex optimization problems, a local optimal solution is also the global optimal solution.
- Using optimization duality theory, we can construct a dual problem for a given optimization problem. The dual problem may have better computational properties, and may help solve the primal problem or bound the optimal objective function values of the primal problem.
- The Karush-Kuhn-Tucker (KKT) conditions are necessary conditions for local optima of constrained optimization problems. Their structure

is exploited by numerous algorithms for convex and general nonlinear optimization.

- Most optimization algorithms are iterative in nature. The number of iterations taken by the algorithm is determined by the stopping criteria specified by the user, such as the tolerance level.

- Important types of optimization algorithms include the simplex algorithm (for linear problems), interior point methods (for linear and convex problems), branch-and-bound or branch-and-cut algorithms (for integer programs), and randomized search algorithms (for all types of optimization problems).

- Randomized search algorithms, such as genetic algorithms, simulated annealing, and tabu search, do not guarantee the optimality of the solution they return. Neither do general optimization algorithms when applied to nonlinear optimization problems that do not have special structure.

- Linear problems are the "easiest" class of optimization problems in the sense that today, linear problems with hundreds of thousands of decision variables and constraints can be solved efficiently. Convex problems (which include linear programs) have nice structure, and are typically more efficient to solve than general nonlinear programming. Integer and mixed-integer problems are challenging, and require specialized optimization software.

- Dynamic programming is a method for optimization over multiple stages. It solves the problem sequentially, by starting at the last stage and keeping track only of the best solution from the current stage onward.

- An optimization solver is software that implements numerical routines for finding the optimal solution of an optimization problem. Different solvers handle different kinds of optimization problems.

- An optimization modeling language automates the underlying mathematical details of the optimization model formulation, but typically does not actually solve the problem. It passes the formulation to a solver, and retrieves the results from the solver in a convenient format. The advantage of using optimization languages is that the user can formulate the problem only once, and use different options for solvers.

SOFTWARE HINTS

In this book, we will support optimization solvers that come standard with Excel and Palisade's Decision Tools Suite, as well as MATLAB's Optimization Toolbox. On a philosophical level, the solvers employ very different approaches. The best way to illustrate their use is through examples, so we explain how to implement the linear programming formulation of the portfolio allocation example in section 5.3.1 and the binary programming formulation of the capital budgeting example in section 5.3.3. The solution to the third example, the cash flow matching exercise (section 5.3.2) is contained in the file **Ch5-CashFlowMatching.xlsx** (respectively, **CashFlowMatching.m**). Please note that both Excel Solver and MATLAB's Optimization Toolbox cannot handle IPs well, so the cash flow matching example in section 5.3.2 is solved without the round lot constraints.

Excel Solver

Excel Solver comes prepackaged with Excel. It should be available under the **Data** tab. If you do not see it there, go to the main Excel button, click on **Excel Options** at the bottom, click **Add-Ins**, select **Solver Add-In,** then click **Go.** Solver should appear under the **Data** tab.

The Solver dialog box is shown in Exhibit 5.13. Solver expects users to input a target cell, changing cells, and constraints, and specify whether the optimization problem is a maximization or minimization problem.

The entry for the *target cell* should be a reference to a cell that contains a formula for the objective function of the optimization problem. This formula should link the target cell and the *changing cells*. The changing cells are cells dedicated to the decision variables—they can be left empty, or have some initial values that the solver will eventually replace with the optimal values. The initial values of the changing cells are used by Solver as the starting point of the algorithm. They do not always matter when the optimization

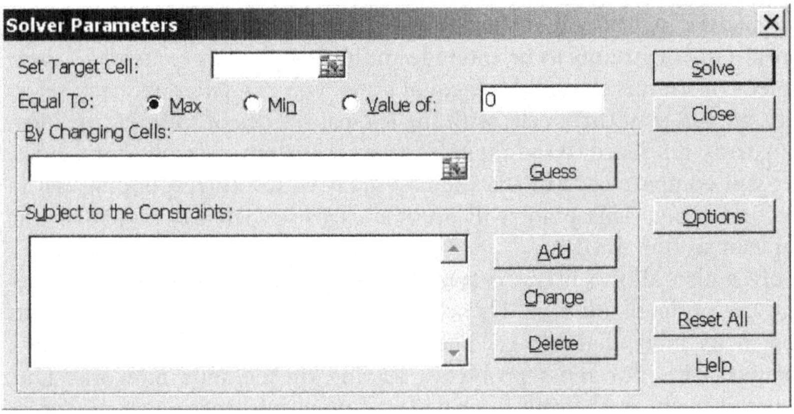

EXHIBIT 5.13 Solver dialog box.

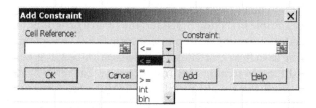

EXHIBIT 5.14   Add Constraint dialog box.

problem is linear, but they can cause Solver to find very different solutions if the problem is nonlinear or contains integer variables.

The constraints can be entered by clicking on the **Add** button, then entering the left-hand side and the right-hand side of a constraint, as well as the sign of the constraint. The constraint dialog box is shown in Exhibit 5.14. By clicking on the middle button, the user can specify inequality constraints ($\leq$ or $\geq$) or equality constraints (=). Solver also lets the user specify whether a set of decision variables is integer (int) or binary (bin). To do that, the user must have designated the cells corresponding to these decision variables as changing cells, and then add the int or bin constraint through the Add Constraint dialog box.

An important fact to remember is that Solver expects constraints to be entered as cell comparisons, that is, it can compare the value of one cell to the value of another cell in the spreadsheet. You cannot type a formula directly into the Add Constraint dialog box—the formula needs to be already contained in the cell that is referenced. A good way to organize your optimization formulation in Excel is to create a column of cells containing the formulas on the left-hand side of all constraints, and a column of cells containing the right-hand sides (the limits) of all constraints. That allows for groups of constraints to be entered simultaneously. For example, if there are three constraints that all have equal signs, you can enter an array reference to the range of three cells with the left-hand sides of these constraints, and an array reference to the range of three cells with the right-hand sides. Solver will compare each cell in the first array to the corresponding cell in the second array. This point will become clearer when we implement the example in section 5.3.1.

Solver also allows users to specify options for the algorithms it uses to find the optimal solution. This can be done by clicking on the **Options** button in its main dialog box. The Solver **Options** dialog box is shown in Exhibit 5.15. For most problems, leaving the defaults in works fine; however, it is always helpful to provide as much information to the solver as possible to ensure optimal performance. For example, if we know that

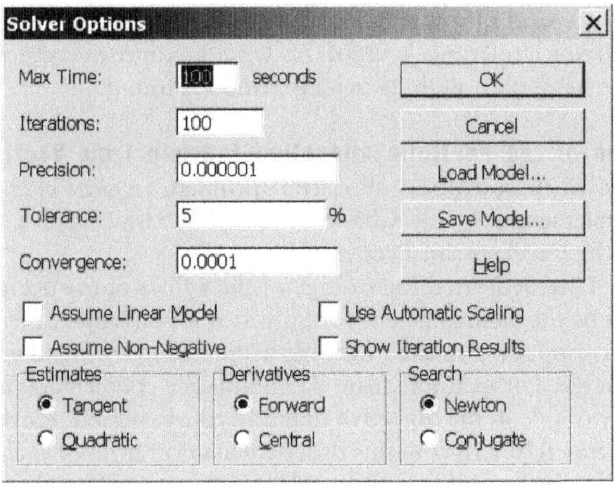

EXHIBIT 5.15 Solver Options dialog box.

the optimization problem is linear, we can check **Assume Linear Model**. The **Assume Non-Negative** option is a shortcut to declaring all decision variables nonnegative (rather than entering separate constraints for each decision variable). The **Show Iteration Results** option lets the user step through the search for the optimal solution. The **Use Automatic Scaling** option is helpful when there is big difference between the magnitudes of decision variables and input data because sometimes that leads to problems due to *poor scaling*. An optimization problem is poorly scaled if changes in the decision variables produce large changes in the objective or constraint functions for some components of the vector of decision variables than for others. (For example, if we are trying to find the optimal percentages to invest, but the rest of the data in the problem is in the millions, the solver may run into numerical difficulties because a small change in a value measured in percentages will have a very different magnitude than a small change in a value measured in millions.) Some optimization techniques are very sensitive to poor scaling. In that case, checking the **Use Automatic Scaling** option instructs it to scale the data so the effect can be minimized.

The options at the bottom of the Solver **Options** dialog box have to do with the numerical details of the algorithm used, and can be left at their default values. The remaining options—**Max Time, Iterations, Precision, Tolerance,** and **Convergence,** let the user specify the tolerance levels in the search for the optimal value of the objective function—that is, how close we want to get to the optimal solution. The default for the tolerance level is 5% because optimization algorithms frequently find a near-optimal solution quickly, but then spend a lot of time checking whether this is the best possible solution. Specifying a tolerance level of 0% would require that the algorithm stops when the best solution in its neighborhood is found.

Implementation of the Portfolio Allocation Example from Section 5.3.1

Let us now solve the portfolio allocation problem in section 5.3.1. The solution is implemented in file **Ch5-PortfolioAlloc.xlsx**. Exhibit 5.16 is a screenshot of the Excel spreadsheet with the model.

Cells B4:E4 are dedicated for storage of the values of the decision variables, and will be the changing cells for Solver. It is convenient then to keep the column corresponding to each variable dedicated to storing data for that particular variable. For example, row 7 contains the coefficients in front of each decision variable in the objective function (the expected returns). Similarly, the cell array B10:E16 contains the coefficients in front of each variable in each constraint in the problem. Cells H10:H16 contain the right-hand side limits of all constraints. (In fact, we are entering the data in matrix form.)

In cell F7, we enter the formula for calculating the objective function value in terms of the decision variables:

```
= SUMPRODUCT($B$4:$E$4,B7:E7)
```

The SUMPRODUCT function in Excel takes as inputs two arrays, and returns the sum of the products of the corresponding elements in each array. In this case, the SUMPRODUCT formula is equivalent to the formula

```
= B7*B4+C7*C4+D7*D4+E7*E4
```

but the SUMPRODUCT formula is clearly a lot more efficient to enter, especially when there are more decision variables.

	A	B	C	D	E	F	G	H
1	Portfolio allocation problem							
2								
3	Decision variables	Fund 1	Fund 2	Fund 3	Fund 4			
4	amounts	$2,000,000.00	$ 0.00	$4,000,000.00	$4,000,000.00			
5								
6	Objective function							
7	Maximize expected return ($)	20.69%	5.87%	10.52%	2.43%	$ 931,800.00		
8								
9	Constraints							Limits
10	Total investment	1	1	1	1	$ 10,000,000.00	=	$ 10,000,000.00
11	Fund 1 + Fund 3 <= 60%	1	0	1	0	$ 6,000,000.00	<=	$ 6,000,000.00
12	Max average risk level	4	2	2	1	$ 20,000,000.00	<=	$ 20,000,000.00
13	Max investment Fund 1	1				$ 2,000,000.00	<=	$ 4,000,000.00
14	Max investment Fund 2		1			$ 0.00	<=	$ 4,000,000.00
15	Max investment Fund 3			1		$ 4,000,000.00	<=	$ 4,000,000.00
16	Max investment Fund 4				1	$ 4,000,000.00	<=	$ 4,000,000.00

EXHIBIT 5.16   Excel model of the portfolio allocation example from section 5.3.1.

Cells F10:F16 contain the formulas for the left-hand sides of the seven constraints. For example, cell F10 contains the formula

```
= SUMPRODUCT($B$4:$E$4,B10:E10)
```

Now the advantage of organizing the data in this array form in the spreadsheet is apparent. When creating the optimization model, we can copy the formula in cell F10 down to all cells until cell F16. Thus, we can enter the information for multiple constraints very quickly.

Click the **Data** tab, click **Solver** in the Analysis group, and enter the information in Exhibit 5.17.

Our goal is to maximize the expression stored in cell F7 by changing the values in cells B4:E4, subject to a set of constraints. Note that since all constraints in rows 11–16 have the same sign ($\geq$), we can pass them to Solver as one entry. Solver interprets the constraint

```
$F$11:$F$16 < = $H$11:$H$16
```

equivalently to the set of constraints

```
$F$11< = $H$11
$F$12< = $H$12
$F$13< = $H$13
$F$14< = $H$14
$F$15< = $H$15
$F$16< = $H$16
```

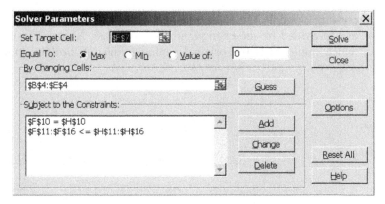

EXHIBIT 5.17 Solver inputs for the portfolio allocation problem.

We also check the **Assume Linear Model** and the **Assume Nonnegative** options. The optimal solution is contained in the spreadsheet screenshot in Exhibit 5.15. To attain the optimal return of $931,800 while satisfying all required constraints, the manager should invest $2,000,000 in Fund 1, $0 in Fund 2, $4,000,000 in Fund 3, and $4,000,000 in Fund 4.

Implementation of the Capital Budgeting Example from Section 5.3.3
Next, we briefly show an example of implementing a binary programming problem with Solver. See file **Ch5-CapitalBudgeting.xlsx**. Worksheet **Model** contains the implementation of the original model, without constraints (a) and (b). (See a screenshot of the model in Exhibit 5.18.) Worksheet **Model 2** contains the original model plus constraint (a). Worksheet **Model 3** contains the original model plus constraints (a) and (b).

The spreadsheet setup of the problem in worksheet **Model** is very similar to the setup of the portfolio allocation model from section 5.3.1. Cells B4:I4 are dedicated to storing the values of the binary decision variables $x_1, \ldots, x_8$, and will become the changing cells for Solver. Cells B7:I8 contain the coefficients of the objective function (the estimated benefit from each project), and cell J7 contains the formula = SUMPRODUCT(B7:I7,$B$4:$I$4), which calculates the total benefit, and will become the target cell for Solver. Cells B10:I10 contain the coefficients of the total budget constraint, and cell J10 contains the formula = SUMPRODUCT(B10:I10,$B$4:$I$4), which calculates the total cost of the selected projects. Cell L10 contains the total budget limit, which is part of the input data.

The Solver dialog box is shown in Exhibit 5.19. Note that one special set of constraints that is specified in the **Constraints** window is $B$4:$I$4 = binary. This instructs Solver to choose only 0–1 values for the changing cells B4:I4. The suboptimal solution after running Solver is illustrated in Exhibit 5.20.

An interesting example of the difference the **Options** specifications in Solver make is provided by the example in the worksheet **Model 2** in the same file, which implements the original capital budgeting problem plus

	A	B	C	D	E	F	G	H	I	J	K	L
1	Capital budgeting problem											
2												
3	Decision variables											
4	Invest or not?	1	0	1	1	1	0	0	0			
5												
6	Objective function											
7	Maximize PV of benefits	$950.00	$780.00	$440.00	$215.00	$630.00	$490.00	$560.00	$600.00	$2,235.00		
8												
9	Constraints									Total cost		Limit
10	Total budget	$400.00	$350.00	$200.00	$100.00	$300.00	$250.00	$300.00	$350.00	$1,000.00	<=	$1,000.00

EXHIBIT 5.18 The capital budgeting optimization model in Excel.

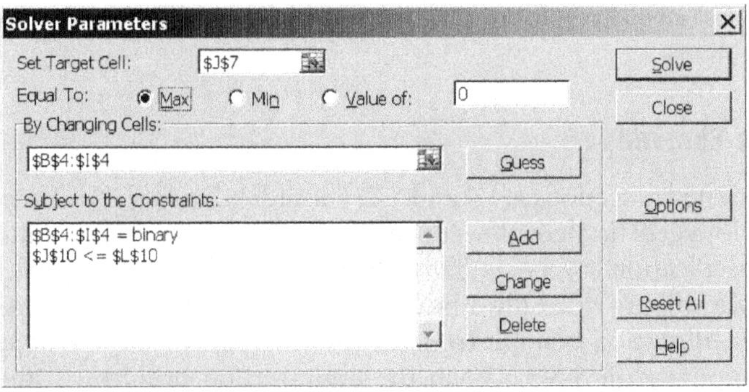

EXHIBIT 5.19 Solver dialog box for the capital budgeting optimization model.

constraint (a) (see section 5.3.3 for the formulation of constraint (a)). If we start with no entries in cells B7:I7 (the decision variables) and leave the Solver **Options** defaults when we run the optimization, Solver returns the solution in Exhibit 5.20, which has an objective function value of $2,065,000. The optimal solution is actually different: the objective function value is $2,115,000, and the optimal values for the binary variables are as follows: (0,1,0,1,1,1,0,0). We can reach the optimal solution if we tighten our tolerance, that is, if we set the **Tolerance** parameter in the Solver **Options** dialog box to 0% (instead of the default of 5%). Then, Solver will search until it finds the absolute optimal solution, rather than accept a solution that has an objective function that can be within 5% of the optimal objective function value.

Changing the defaults does not make much difference in the case of linear problems, but can be very important when solving difficult nonlinear or integer problems. Even when the defaults are changed, however, Solver

EXHIBIT 5.20 Suboptimal solution returned by Solver for the model in worksheet **Model 2** when the starting point is 0 for all changing cells, and the options (including the tolerance level) are left at their default values.

may return erroneous or suboptimal solutions when called on nonlinear and integer problems.

Palisade's Evolver

As we mentioned in sections 5.4.4 and 5.7, Palisade's Evolver is an Excel add-in that employs genetic algorithms to come up with the optimal solution. The problem specification is very similar to the problem specification with Excel Solver, so we will provide only a brief discussion for the implementation of the portfolio allocation example from section 5.3.1 and the capital budgeting example from section 5.3.3. When the optimization problem is linear, it is not really worthwhile to employ genetic algorithms—linear optimization algorithms in classical solvers are very efficient. However, when the problem contains integer variables, or nonlinear functions, genetic algorithms may find a better solution than classical algorithms, and may find it faster.

Palisade's Evolver tab in the Excel ribbon contains the commands displayed in Exhibit 5.21.

The model is entered by clicking the **Model Definition** button. The **Settings** button allows for changing the settings of the genetic algorithm and the length of the search, such as the initial population size, the number of trials to be run, the maximum time to run the algorithm, and so on. Once the model and the settings are specified, the user clicks the **Start** button to begin the algorithm.

Implementation of the Portfolio Allocation Example from Section 5.3.1

The spreadsheet setup of the model in Excel is the same as in Exhibit 5.16. (see also worksheet **Model (Evolver)** in the file **Ch5-PortfolioAlloc.xlsx**.) It is helpful to dedicate cells in the spreadsheet to the formula for the objective function, the left and the right hand side of the constraints, and the decision variables. The Evolver dialog box is then filled out as follows (Exhibit 5.22). The objective function value is entered under **Cell**, and the user specifies whether the value should be is maximized or minimized. The **Adjustable Cell Ranges** fields are equivalent to the **Changing cells** range in

EXHIBIT 5.21 Palisade's Evolver tab.

Excel Solver, and are filled with references to the cells that store the values of the decision variables. Evolver also allows for specifying the ranges for the decision variables. These ranges are entered under **Minimum** and **Maximum** in the **Adjustable Cell Ranges** fields. Under **Values**, one can specify whether the decision variables are continuous (choose **Any**, which is the entry in Exhibit 5.22) or discrete (choose **Integer**).

An additional option under **Adjustable Cell Ranges** is to specify whether the **Budget** rule should be used when trying different solutions (the current selection in Exhibit 5.22). This option speeds up calculations if the decision variables in the problem need to add up to a specific number, which is the case in many portfolio allocation models, as the portfolio weights often need to add up to 1. In our example, the amounts invested need to add up to the amount available for investment, $10,000,000. We can speed up the search for the optimal solution by entering initial values in all decision variable cells (cells B4:E4 in Exhibit 5.16) so that they add up to $10 million. Evolver will then assume that this is the "budget" to which it needs to adhere while searching for the optimal solution. If no such budget is required,

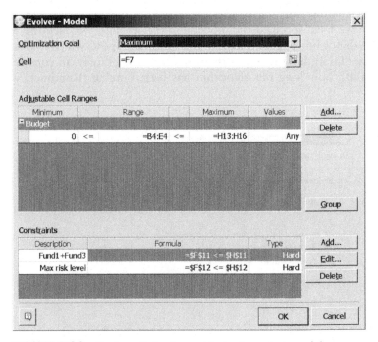

EXHIBIT 5.22 Evolver dialog box with the formulation of the portfolio allocation problem.

then the **Budget** option can be changed to **Recipe,** which is a more generic specification, or some other options. (Click **Group** and then **Edit** to see a list of all options.) If there are different groups of variables, that is, some of them have to add up to a specific "budget," while others do not, or some are continuous, while other are integer, then separate groups of decision variables can be entered by clicking **Group** and then **New** and specifying a method with every new group.

Finally, constraints can be entered or edited in the **Constraints** field by clicking **Add** or **Edit.** In contrast to classical solvers such as Excel Solver, constraints can be specified as "soft" or "hard." Hard constraints are ones that must be satisfied, while soft constraints can be violated, and Evolver will report if they are. Classical optimization solvers treat constraints only as "hard." It is useful to enter a description of the constraint, as we have done in the first column of the **Constraints** field.

A screenshot of the Evolver Optimization Settings dialog box is provided in Exhibit 5.23. It is generally better to leave the general settings at their defaults, but control the running time of the algorithm. For example, we can specify the maximum number of trials to run by checking **Trials** and entering a value, or the maximum amount of time by checking **Time,** both under the **Runtime** tab.

Once we have specified the model and the settings, we click the **Start** button. A dialog box appears (see Exhibit 5.24) that reports which trial is run right now (**Trial**), how many of the solutions so far satisfy all constraints (**Trial/Valid**), how long the algorithm has been running (**Runtime**), what

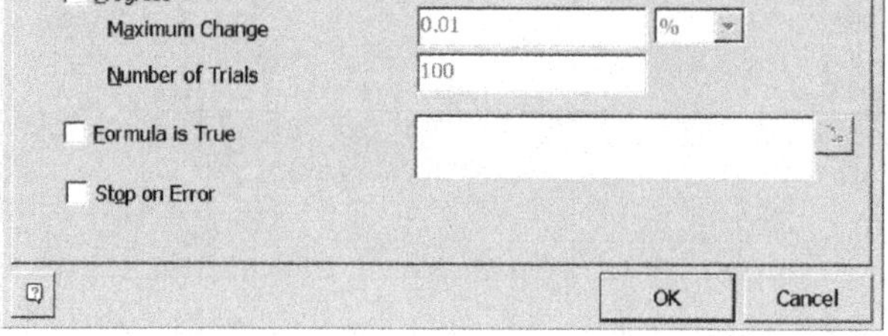

EXHIBIT 5.23   Evolver Optimization Settings dialog box.

Evolver Progress

Trial:	18739 (3444 Valid)
Runtime:	00:00:33
Original:	931626.3051
Best:	931798.6892

EXHIBIT 5.24 Evolver
Progress dialog box.

was the original value of the objective function which, in our case, is the dollar return on the portfolio (**Original**), and what is the best value of the objective function in all iterations of the algorithm so far (**Best**). We can stop the algorithm by clicking on the red button in the lower right corner of the Evolver Progress dialog box, and see a more detailed report of the optimization results.

As we mentioned before, even after running Evolver for many trials, it may not find the optimal solution. However, in most practical instances, it will get to a solution that is close to the optimal relatively quickly.

Implementation of the Capital Budgeting Example from Section 5.3.3 We briefly show the implementation of the capital budgeting example from section 5.3.3 in order to illustrate some differences in variable specification in Evolver for linear and integer programming optimization problems.

The spreadsheet setup for the model is the same as in Exhibit 5.18 (see also worksheet **Model 3 (Evolver)** in file **Ch5-CapitalBudgeting.xlsx**.) Exhibit 5.25 illustrates the dialog box for Evolver for that example. The main ideas are the same as the implementation of the portfolio allocation example in the previous section, but we would like to draw attention to a couple of differences. First, the decision variables in this problem (cells B4:I4) are binary. To enter that information in Evolver, we specify bounds of 0 and 1 for the **Adjustable Cell Ranges**, and change the entry under **Values** to **Integer**. Second, we do not have restrictions on the number of projects that can be funded. Therefore, the budget method does not apply here. Instead, we select **Recipe** as the method for this group of decision variables. We do have a total budget, but the budget refers to the total funding costs that we are allowed to assume, not to the values of the decision variables

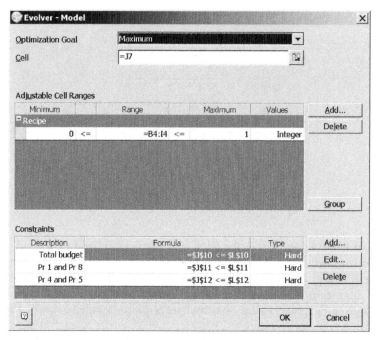

EXHIBIT 5.25   Evolver dialog box for the implementation of the capital budgeting example.

themselves. Therefore, we specify the total budget as a separate constraint under **Constraints**.

MATLAB's Optimization Toolbox

MATLAB's Optimization Toolbox has a very different approach and syntax for formulating optimization problems. As explained in Appendix C, MATLAB is an array-based mathematical language. It expects optimization formulations to be passed to its solvers in an array form, and it contains functions that call specific solvers for specific types of optimization problems. (See Exhibit 5.26 for a quick overview. See also MATLAB's help for a complete listing.) If the Genetic Algorithms and Direct Search Toolbox is available, the range of solvers is expanded to include randomized search algorithms.

The most often used solver in MATLAB is `fmincon`, which is the solver for general nonlinear optimization. However, if we know the type of problem we are trying to solve, we are always better off giving the optimization software as much information as we can in order to make the optimization

EXHIBIT 5.26 MATLAB Optimization Toolbox functions/solvers appropriate for specific types of optimization problems. Asterisk (*) is used to denote solvers that are available only through the Genetic Algorithms and Direct Search Toolbox. Blank entries mean that there is currently no solver available. Technically, the Genetic Algorithms and Direct Search Toolbox can be used for solving discrete problems as well; however, this requires additional programming.

			Objective		
Constraints	Linear	Quadrtic	Least Squares	Smooth Nonlinear	Nonsmooth
None	N/A	quadprog	lsqcurvefit, lsqnonlin	fminsearch, fminunc	fminseach,*
Bound	linprog	quadprog	lsqucurvefit, lsqlin, lsqnonlin, lsqnonneg	fminbnd, fmincon, fseminf	*
Linear	linprog	quadprog	lsqlin	fmincon, fseminf	*
Smooth nonlinear	fmincon	fmincom	fmincom	fmincon, fseminf	*
Discrete	bintprog				

process more accurate and efficient. In financial applications, we are most likely to encounter situations in which we will need linprog (an LP solver), quadprog (a quadratic programming solver), bintprog (a binary programming solver), and randomized search algorithms, such as simulannealbnd and ga.

We will use linprog and bintprog to solve the portfolio allocation and capital budgeting examples in sections 5.3.1 and 5.3.3. Before we show the actual implementation, we need to explain how solvers are actually called in MATLAB. There are two ways to call the solvers: as functions directly from the command prompt (equivalently, from within M-files) or through the *optimization tool*.

To solve an LP, we would call linprog(f,A,b,Aeq,beq,lb,ub). The function arguments f,A,b,Aeq,beq,lb,ub are supposed to correspond to the following LP formulation:

$$\min_{x} \quad f'x$$
$$s.t. \quad Ax \leq b$$
$$Aeq \cdot x = beq$$
$$lb \leq x \leq ub$$

Therefore, before we call `linprog`, we need to write our LP in this particular form. We will show how this is done shortly.

The MATLAB optimization tool provides an interface between the solvers and the user. While using such an interface may not be optimal when solving sequences of optimization problems, as in the case of dynamic programming or stochastic programming, it is quite convenient when solving a single optimization problem because it lists all available solvers, prompts the user for the different inputs that the optimization solvers expect, and allows for easy manipulation of the options. Options can be specified directly when a solver is called from the command prompt as well, but it is more clumsy.

The optimization tool is called by typing `optimtool` at the MATLAB command prompt. The optimization tool dialog box is shown in Exhibit 5.27. The panel on the left-hand side is dedicated to the specification of the inputs: the type of solver that needs to be called, the arrays with the problem data, the starting point, and so on. The panel in the middle allows for changing the level of tolerance in the search for the optimal solution. For example, the Function tolerance is currently set at the default value of 1e-06, which is 10^{-6}. This means that the selected algorithm will continue to iterate through solutions until the improvement in successive objective function values becomes smaller than 10^{-6}. Sometimes, such level of accuracy is unnecessary. For example, if our objective function is measured in dollars and cents (e.g., the optimal revenue in the portfolio allocation

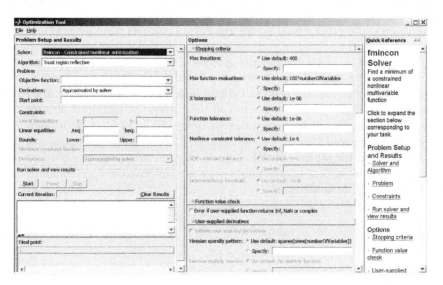

EXHIBIT 5.27 The optimization tool interface in MATLAB.

example in section 5.3.1), then technically we do not need precision beyond 2–3 points after the decimal point. Therefore, we can speed up the algorithm by relaxing the requirements on tolerance. Other useful options include level of display (whether to show iterations of the optimization algorithm or not), and function plots at intermediate stages.

Implementation of the Portfolio Allocation Example from Section 5.3.1

The file **PortfolioAlloc.m** contains code for computing the optimal portfolio allocation for the portfolio allocation example in section 5.3.1, which is an LP problem.

The process for formulating the optimization problem is as follows. First, we ask ourselves what corresponds to the vector of decision variables x in the linprog formulation. In our example, x maps directly to the vector of amounts to invest in each asset. We then enter problem data, such as the expected returns vector expReturnsVec. We allocate empty arrays to store the values of the optimal solution amountsVec and the optimal value of the objective function optReturn after collecting the information from the solver.

Next, we create the input data for the linprog solver. The solver expects a vector of objective function coefficients f, which in our case is the vector of expected returns on the different assets. Note, however (line 12) that we specify f as -expReturnsVec. This is because expects a minimization problem, and our objective function is to maximize expected revenue, so we need to convert our problem to the required form by minimizing the negative of the expression for the maximization objective. (See section 5.1.1.) At the end (line 48), we take the negative of the optimal value for expected return found by the solver, so that we arrive at the actual optimal value for the maximization problem. The optimal values of the decision variables, which in this case are the amounts to invest, amountsVec, do not need to be modified after the optimization results are returned by the solver.

Lines 14–40 contain the specification of the other inputs in the problem. Note that we are in fact using the matrices of coefficients for the groups of constraints (inequality, equality, and nonnegativity) that we defined in section 5.3.1. Namely, A (lines 15–20) is the matrix of left-hand-side inequality constraint coefficients; Aeq (line 28) is the matrix of left-hand-side equality constraint coefficients, b (line 23) is the vector of right-hand-side coefficients of the inequality constraints, and beq (line 32) is the vector of right-hand-side coefficients of the equality constraints (in our example, we have only one equality constraint). The lower bounds, lb (line 36), are the zeros from the right-hand side of the nonnegativity constraints on the decision variables, so we create a vector array with size equal to the number of decision variables that contains only zeros. We have explicit upper bounds of $4,000,000 on each decision variable since we cannot invest more than that amount in each individual fund, so we could have stated those bounds as the input vector ub. However, these bounds have already been included in the matrix A, so we do not need to state them again. Instead, we state the individual upper bounds as infinity, that is, as the product of the number inf (in MATLAB, that denotes infinity) and a vector of ones. (See line 40 of the previous code.)

An equivalent formulation of the constraints from MATLAB's perspective would have been to specify the arrays A, beq, and ub as

```
A =  [1 0 1 0;
      4 2 2 1]
b = [6000000 20000000]'
ub = 4000000*ones(numAssets,1)
```

with all other input arrays remaining the same.

After all inputs have been specified, the linprog solver is called (line 42). The syntax in line 42 outputs requests that the output from the optimization be stored in the arrays we specified at the beginning, amountsVec and optReturn. The results are then printed to screen, and are formatted according to format('bank') (line 44), which basically rounds numbers to two decimal places.

After running the M-file, we obtain the following output:

```
amountsVec =
    2000000.00
          0.00
    4000000.00
    4000000.00

optReturn =
     931800.00
```

If you prefer to solve the problem by using the optimization tool, you need to fill out the dialog box as shown in Exhibit 5.28. Select linprog as the solver from the drop-down menu at the top. Under **Algorithm**, you can either leave the default (**Large Scale**), or select **Medium scale—simplex**, which is appropriate because our problem is quite small. We entered the names of the arrays that correspond to the objective function coefficients and the constraint coefficients in the corresponding fields in the left panel of the dialog box. Note that these arrays must be prefilled, that is, they must be entered from the command prompt, or read from a file before the problem

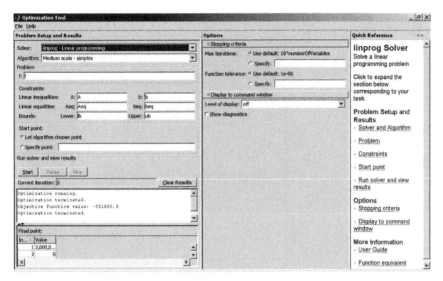

EXHIBIT 5.28   The optimization tool dialog box for the portfolio allocation problem.

is solved through the optimization tool; otherwise the solver will complain that these arrays are empty. You can make sure that the arrays f, A, b, Aeq, beq, lb, and ub are filled in by checking first whether they are listed in the **Workspace** window at the upper left corner of the MATLAB desktop. Once all the input data are specified, click on the **Start** button in the left panel to solve the problem. The solution appears in the field below the **Start** button.

The optimization model can be saved as script in an M-file by selecting **File I Generate M-file** from the main menu in the optimization tool. In addition, the optimization results can be exported to the workspace and further manipulated by selecting **File I Export to Workspace**. To export only the results, as opposed to the entire model, check **Export results to a MATLAB structure named:** optimresults. This creates a structure of results, optimresults, that shows up in the **Workspace**. So, for example, the optimal solution (the portfolio allocation) can be called by typing optimresults.x at the command prompt. (See Exhibit 5.29.) Similarly, the optimal value of the objective function can be retrieved by typing optimresults.fval at the command prompt.

Implementation of the Capital Budgeting Example from Section 5.3.3   The file **CapitalBudgeting.m** contains code for finding the best combination of projects to fund from the capital budgeting example in section 5.3.3, which is

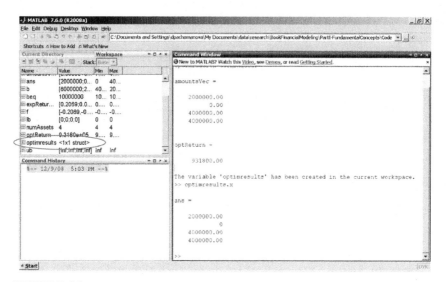

EXHIBIT 5.29   Handling the structure of optimization results exported from
MATLAB's optimization tool.

a binary integer problem. We use the `bintprog` solver in MATLAB to solve
the optimization problem. The main ideas of the formulation are very similar
to the ones from the portfolio allocation example. The solver `bintprog`
assumes that all decision variables in the optimization problem are binary,
and requires that the formulation be in the following form:

$$\min_{\mathbf{x}} \quad \mathbf{f}'\mathbf{x}$$
$$s.t. \quad \mathbf{Ax} \leq \mathbf{b}$$
$$\mathbf{Aeq} \cdot \mathbf{x} = \mathbf{beq}$$
$$\mathbf{x} \quad \text{binary}$$

The code in file **CapitalBudgeting.m** solves the original optimization
problem; then solves the original problem with the additional constraint (a),
and then solves the original problem with two additional constraints, (a)
and (b). (See section 5.3.3 for the constraint specification.)

The formulation of the original capital budgeting problem is in lines
6–32. Similarly to the portfolio allocation example, in lines 11–12, we create arrays in which the optimal values of the objective function (`optBene-`
`fits`) and the decision variables (`fundBin`) will be stored. Again, we have a
maximization problem, so we convert it to the minimization problem

required by `bintprog` by considering the negative of the objective function. We have only one constraint: that the sum of all costs cannot be more than the allocated budget of $1,000,000, so the matrix A (line 20) and the vector of right-hand-side constraint limits b (line 23) are small. We have no additional equality constraints, so we create empty arrays for the input matrices Aeq and beq (lines 26 and 27, respectively). We solve the problem by calling the solver, storing the optimal results in the arrays dedicated to them, reverting the sign of the optimal value of the objective function, and printing the output to screen (lines 29–32).

Next, we implement the original capital budgeting problem plus constraint (a). Recall from section 5.3.3 that the formulation of the constraint was

$$x_1 - x_8 \leq 0,$$

so we add a second row to the matrix of inequality constraint coefficients A, with 1 in the position corresponding to the first binary variable, –1 in the eighth position, and 0s everywhere else (lines 38–39). We also add an entry of 0 to the vector of right-hand side limits of the inequality constraints, b (line 40). All other problem specifications remain the same. We are now ready to call the solver again, and print the results to screen.

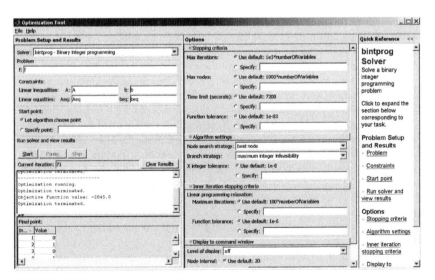

EXHIBIT 5.30 Formulation of the capital budgeting problem with constraints (a) and (b) with MATLAB's optimization tool.

The addition of constraint (b) happens in a similar manner. The problem formulation is updated and passed to the solver in lines 50–55. When the M-file is run, the optimization results from all three formulations are printed to screen.

The formulation of the capital budgeting problem with the MATLAB optimization tool is very similar to the formulation of the portfolio allocation problem, but the Solver field contains a reference to the `bintprog` solver, rather than the `linprog` solver. Again, the data arrays that are input in the problem need to be specified before the **Start** button is pressed. (See Exhibit 5.30.)

NOTES

1. See Appendix A on the companion web site for a review of the matrix-vector notation.
2. Optimization formulations can handle decision variables that are matrix arrays as well, but these types of problems are too advanced for the purposes of this book. This area of optimization is called semidefinite programming. See Fabozzi, Kolm, Pachamanova, and Focardi (2007) for a discussion of its applications in finance.
3. In other words, by setting the derivative of the objective function to zero.
4. Unfortunately, there is no straightforward way to request that all optimal solutions be listed in optimization software output. If we are interested in checking whether there is another optimal solution, we need to modify the optimization problem formulation to exclude the current optimal solution, and rerun the optimization solver again. If a second optimal solution exists, it will be found by the solver when the first optimal solution is no longer a feasible option.
5. Linear expressions involve sums and differences of terms of the kind (*constant · decision variable*), and exclude expressions like (*constant · decision variable²*), (*decision variable 1 · decision variable 2*), (*decision variable 1 / decision variable 2*), log(*decision variable*), and so on. Note that an expression of the kind (*constant² · decision variable*) is still a linear expression in the decision variable, even if it is not a linear expression in the constant. Linear optimization formulations are concerned only with whether the expressions in the objective function and constraints are linear expressions in the decision variables.
6. See Appendix A on the companion web site for a definition of positive semidefinite matrix.
7. In the stock market, a round lot is 100 shares. In the bond market, a round lot varies with the type of bond.
8. A mutual fund, more specifically an open-end investment company, uses proceeds from the sale of shares to the public to invest in various securities. The value of one share of a mutual fund is computed by dividing the difference between the mutual fund's asset and liabilities by the number of shares

outstanding. This value is called the net asset value (NAV). Mutual funds have different investment objectives. In the case of a money market fund, the fund manager can only invest in short-term high quality investments (money market instruments). This type of mutual fund has the lowest risk and therefore the lowest expected return (see Exhibit 5.4).

9. This is just a simplified example of portfolio allocation with risk considerations. Definitions of risk and more sophisticated portfolio allocation schemes are discussed in detail in Chapters 7 through 9.

10. See Chapter 2 for a definition of short selling.

11. As we mentioned earlier, there are often different ways to formulate an optimization problem for the same business situation. For example, the decision variables for this example can be defined as the percentages invested (rather than the dollar amounts invested) in each fund. The problem formulation will be very similar, and the optimal solution will qualitatively be the same.

12. In a defined benefit pension plan, the sponsor of the plan, such as corporation or a municipality, has contractually agreed to make payments to the plan participants of a specified amount after the participant retires. In contrast, in a defined contribution retirement plan, the employer agrees only to set aside prior to the employee's retirement a certain amount of money each year but it is the responsibility of the employee to invest those funds.

13. Note that in our illustration, we are assuming high investment-grade quality bonds. This means that the issuers of these bonds have a low probability of failing to meet their obligation to make the coupon payments.

14. See http://www.ilog.com/products/cplex/. We will discuss optimization solvers and software later in this chapter.

15. Some randomized search solvers accept such conditions, see sections 5.4.4 and 5.7. However, such algorithms do not guarantee that they will find the optimal solution.

16. In mathematical terms, a simplex is the convex hull of a set of $N + 1$ points in N-dimensional space, that is, the minimum set that contains all the points, and any line drawn between points in the set stays within the set.

17. Recall that the gradient of a function f of N variables $x_1, x_2, \ldots, x_N$ is defined as the partial derivative with respect to each individual variable,

$$\nabla f(\mathbf{x}) = \left(\frac{\partial}{\partial x_1} f(\mathbf{x}), \ldots, \frac{\partial}{\partial x_N} f(\mathbf{x}) \right)$$

18. A heuristic is a logical, approximate way to solve an optimization problem that, however, is not necessarily guaranteed to produce the optimal result. The initial selection of projects based on the ranking of their benefit/cost ratios in the capital budgeting example in section 5.3.3 of this chapter was an example of a greedy heuristic—our simple investment algorithm selected each subsequent project as the project with the highest ranking among the projects not already selected. As we saw, this algorithm did not give us the optimal solution, although it did produce a good solution.

19. For an intuitive overview of some of these algorithms, see Chapter 9 in Fabozzi, Kolm, Pachamanova, and Focardi (2007). For complete mathematical treatment of the subject, see, for example, Bertsimas and Tsitsiklis (1997) or Nemhauser and Wolsey (1999).

20. For more rigorous discussion, see Bertsimas and Tsitsiklis (1997).

21. Order notation ($O(.)$) allows us to represent the idea that an expression or a quantity is "about the same size as" another expression or quantity. A function $f(x)$ is "of the order of" a function $g(x)$ if $f(x)$ does not exceed $g(x)$ in magnitude (up to a scaling factor c) around any specific point of interest. If the specification of the point is omitted, it is usually assumed that the statement is valid for all points on the real line.

22. See MOSEK ApS, *The MOSEK Optimization Software*, http://www.mosek.com/.

23. See *IBM ILOG CPLEX Optimizer: High Performance Mathematical Programming Engine*, http://www.ilog.com/products/cplex/. At the time of writing of this book, ILOG became part of IBM. See also http://www-01.ibm.com/software/integration/optimization/cplex-optimizer.

24. See AIMMS, *Optimization Software for Operations Research Applications*, http://www.aimms.com.

25. See AMPL, *A Modeling Language for Mathematical Programming*, http://www.ampl.com/.

26. See GAMS, *The GAMS System*, http://www.gams.com/.

27. See Palisade, *The Decision Tools Suite: Integrated Decision Making in Excel*, http://www.palisade.com/.

28. See Frontline Systems, http://www.solver.com/.

29. See Axioma, *Axioma Portfolio Optimizer*, http://www.axiomainc.com/.

30. See MSCI Barra, *Barra Optimizer*, http://www.barra.com/.

31. See ITG, *ITG Opt*, http://www.itginc.com/.

32. See Northfield, *Optimizer Service: Risk Analysis and Portfolio Construction*, http://www.northinfo.com/.

CHAPTER 6

Optimization under Uncertainty

The optimization formulations presented in Chapter 5 have numerous applications in finance and other fields. However, that discussion omitted an important aspect of realistic optimization modeling. We assumed that the input data, such as the coefficients in front of the decision variables in the objective function and the constraints, or the cash flows that happen in a multistage system, are certain. In practice, however, optimization often needs to be performed under conditions in which the input data are random, or represent statistical estimates and subjective guesses. Models in which all input data are fixed or nonrandom are often referred to as *deterministic*. By contrast, models that contain parameters that vary are referred to as *nondeterministic*, *probabilistic*, or *stochastic*.

Concepts from probability theory, statistics, and simulation (Chapters 3 and 4) can be used to extend the basic framework of deterministic optimization (Chapter 5) and to deal with uncertainty. It is important to keep in mind, however, that randomness adds a high level of complexity to optimization formulations, and that the output of the resulting models needs to be interpreted carefully.

There are three general approaches for incorporating considerations for uncertainty in optimization problems: dynamic programming, stochastic programming, and robust optimization. As we mentioned in section 5.6 in the previous chapter, dynamic programming methods are specifically designed to deal with stochastic uncertain systems over multiple stages. The optimization problem is solved recursively, going backward from the last state, and computing the optimal solution for each possible state of the system at a particular stage. In finance, dynamic programming is used in the context of pricing of some derivative instruments, investment strategies such as statistical arbitrage, and long-term corporate financial planning.

Stochastic programming methods can be used in both single-period and multiperiod settings. They rely on representing the uncertain data by scenarios, and focus on finding the strategy so that, for example, the *expected* value of the objective function over all scenarios (sometimes, penalized for some measure of risk) is optimal. Stochastic algorithms have been successfully applied in a variety of financial contexts, such as management of portfolios of fixed income securities, corporate risk management, security selection, and asset/liability management for individuals as well as for financial entities such as banks, pension funds, and insurance companies.[1] They are particularly useful in situations in which modeling complicated dependencies in a number of uncertain parameters over multiple time periods is essential. This kind of situations often arise, for example, in managing callable bond portfolios or international asset portfolios, where the callable feature of the bonds, interest rate risk, default risk, or currency risk need to be taken into consideration.

Robust optimization is a technique whose applications in finance have been explored more recently. It can be used to address the same type of problems as dynamic programming and stochastic programming do; however, it takes a worst-case approach to optimization formulations. In addition, in robust optimization one typically makes relatively general assumptions on the probability distributions of the uncertain parameters in order to work with problem formulations that are more tractable computationally.

The fields of dynamic programming, stochastic programming, and robust optimization have some overlap, but historically, they have evolved independently of each other. This chapter explains the three techniques for optimization under uncertainty in detail.

6.1 DYNAMIC PROGRAMMING

As explained in section 5.6, dynamic programming solves a large multistage optimization problem sequentially, starting at the last stage and proceeding backward, thus keeping track only of the optimal paths from any given time period onward.

Dynamic programming under uncertainty is sometimes also called *stochastic control*.[2] It shares the main elements of dynamic programming models we considered in section 5.6: There is an underlying dynamic system and an objective function (called a *reward* or a *cost* function depending on whether the problem is a maximization or a minimization) that is additive over time. The dynamic system at any point in time t is described by a vector of state variables $\mathbf{x}_t$ that summarizes all past information about the system. However, while the state variable in the deterministic dynamic programming problems we considered in section 5.6 evolved according to the relationship

$$\mathbf{x}_{t+1} = g_t(\mathbf{x}_t, \mathbf{u}_t)$$

where $\mathbf{u}_t$ is a vector of *control*, or *policy*, variables to be selected by the decision-maker, when there is uncertainty in the system, we have

$$\mathbf{x}_{t+1} = g_t(\mathbf{x}_t, \mathbf{u}_t, \xi_t),$$

where ξ_t is a *random variable* (also called disturbance or noise depending on the context). The reward at time t, which we will denote by

$$f_t(\mathbf{x}_t, \mathbf{u}_t, \xi_t),$$

accumulates over time, as it did in the case of deterministic dynamic programming problems.

Dynamic programming problems can be defined over a *finite horizon*, for example, over a period of time T, or over an *infinite horizon*. In most financial applications, we encounter finite horizon dynamic programming systems, so we will assume that the horizon is finite and time is discrete. The total reward/cost can then be written as

$$\sum_{t=0}^{T} f_t(\mathbf{x}_t, \mathbf{u}_t, \xi_t).$$

At the end of section 5.6.1, we presented the expression for the dynamic programming recursion. In the general case, assuming that we would like to maximize the total reward, at every state our goal was to find a policy vector $\mathbf{u}_t$ so that

$$V_t(\mathbf{x}_t) = \max_{\mathbf{u}_t} \left\{ c(\mathbf{u}_t) + d \cdot V_{t+1}^*(\mathbf{u}_t) \right\}.$$

In other words, we selected $\mathbf{u}_t$ so that the value of the reward from this stage forward is highest. Suppose now that there is uncertainty, that is, our actions do not determine the exact outcome, but instead there is some probabilistic component in the realization of future rewards. In that case, a natural goal is to select $\mathbf{u}_t$ so that the *expected* value of the reward from this stage forward is highest, where the term "expected value" is used in the sense of Chapter 3, that is, it is the weighted average of possible outcomes from some probability distribution on the future values. In other words, we write

$$V_t(\mathbf{x}_t) = \max_{\mathbf{u}_t} \left\{ c(\mathbf{u}_t) + d \cdot E[V_{t+1}^*(\mathbf{u}_t)|\mathbf{x}_t] \right\}$$

where $E[V_{t+1}^*(\mathbf{u}_t)|\mathbf{x}_t]$ is the expected value of the optimal reward from this stage forward, given that we are currently at state $\mathbf{x}_t$.

To build some intuition, let us go back to the oil well example from section 5.6. You have purchased a 3-year lease for an oil well. The estimated reserves of the well are 600,000 barrels. Every year, you can either pump oil normally (Strategy 1), in which case you pump 100,000 barrels, or use an enhanced pumping method which allows you to pump 200,000 barrels (Strategy 2). To extract u_t barrels at time t with the enhanced method costs you $20 \cdot u_t^2/x_t$ dollars, where x_t is the amount of available reserves at time t. To extract u_t barrels with the normal pumping method is u_t^2/x_t dollars. The discount factor per year is 0.9.

The implicit assumption in that example was that we knew exactly what oil prices would be in each of the three years of the lease. Suppose instead that the evolution of oil prices in each year of the lease is described by the tree in Exhibit 6.1, where the numbers above the branches denote the probabilities of ending up in that node starting from the node at the previous stage. (Note that the probabilities on all branches emanating from the same node add up to 1.) In other words, every year the price can be 20% (1.2 times) higher than the price in the previous year with probability 0.40, or be 20% (0.8 times) lower than the price in the previous year with probability 0.60.

Assuming that you can pump either 100,000 barrels or 200,000 barrels each year, what is the optimal strategy to maximize the *expected* present value (PV) of your profit from the lease? Note that we can no longer know the exact value, since the total profit from each node forward (except the nodes at the third stage) has an element of uncertainty. Note also that the tree in Exhibit 6.1 does not represent the state space of the problem. The state space should incorporate all information necessary to make a decision going forward. To make a decision, we need to know (1) the level of remaining reserves x_t, and (2) the price p_t. (In the deterministic version of this problem in section 5.6.1, the price p_t was the same for all nodes at the same stage.) So, in a sense we have a two-dimensional tree: every state is determined by

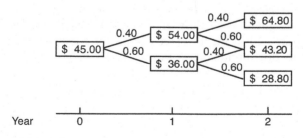

EXHIBIT 6.1 Price process for the oil well problem.

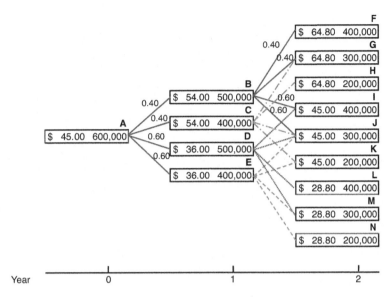

Year 0 1 2

EXHIBIT 6.2 State space for the oil well problem.

the pair (x_t, p_t). Exhibit 6.2 illustrates the state space. Note how much larger the state space is compared to the state space in section 5.6.1.

To solve the problem, we use a sequential optimization algorithm similar to the algorithm described in section 5.6.1. (See file **Ch6-OilExample.xlsx**.) First, we compute the value function at the last-stage nodes. For example, the profit at state F is the maximum of the profits obtained using the normal or the enhanced methods at the price realized and the reserves available at node F:

$$V(F) = \max \left\{ \begin{array}{l} 64.80 \cdot 100,000 - 100,000^2/400,000, \\ 64.80 \cdot 200,000 - 20 \cdot 200,000^2/400,000 \end{array} \right\}$$

$$= \max \{\$6,455,000, \$10,960,000\}$$

$$= \$10,960,000$$

Therefore, if we are in state F in year 3 (i.e., if the price per barrel is $64.80 and we have 400,000 barrels left), the optimal strategy is to use the enhanced method.

The values at nodes G, H, I, J, K, L, M, and N are computed similarly (Exhibit 6.3). To compute the values at nodes B, C, D, and E at the previous stage, we use the recursive relation for the value function. The value function at all states at stages other than the last stage is the sum of the profit obtained at that stage and the expected (probability-weighted) discounted profit from states at the next stage that can be reached from the current state:

$$V_t(x_t, p_t) = \max \begin{cases} p_t \cdot 100{,}000 - 100{,}000^2/x_t \\ \quad + 0.9 \cdot (0.4 \cdot V_{t+1}^*(x_t - 100{,}000, 1.2 \cdot p_t) \\ \quad + 0.6 \cdot V_{t+1}^*(x_t - 100{,}000, 0.8 \cdot p_t)), \\ p_t \cdot 200{,}000 - 20 \cdot 200{,}000^2/x_t + \\ \quad + 0.9 \cdot (0.4 \cdot V_{t+1}^*(x_t - 200{,}000, 1.2 \cdot p_t) \\ \quad + 0.6 \cdot V_{t+1}^*(x_t - 200{,}000, 0.8 \cdot p_t)) \end{cases}$$

For example, the profit at state B is calculated as

$$V(B) = \max \begin{cases} p_B \cdot 100{,}000.00 - 100{,}000.00^2/x_B \\ \quad + 0.90 \cdot (0.40 \cdot V(F) + 0.60 \cdot V(I)), \\ p_B \cdot 200{,}000.00 - 20 \cdot 200{,}000.00^2/x_B \\ \quad + 0.90 \cdot (0.40 \cdot V(G) + 0.60 \cdot V(J)) \end{cases}$$

This is because if we use the normal method if we are at B, we will reduce our reserves by 100,000 to 400,000. This means that we will reach F with probability 0.40 or I with probability 0.60. By contrast, if we use the enhanced method, we will reach G with probability 0.40 or J with probability 0.60. Keeping track of the different states is quite challenging, and needs to be done with care.

The optimal expected profit from state B onwards is calculated to be:

$$V(B) = \max \begin{cases} 54.00 \cdot 100{,}000.00 - 100{,}000.00^2/500{,}000.00 \\ \quad + 0.90 \cdot (0.40 \cdot 10{,}960{,}000.00 + 0.60 \cdot 7{,}000{,}000.00), \\ 54.00 \cdot 200{,}000.00 - 20 \cdot 200{,}000.00^2/500{,}000.00 \\ \quad + 0.90 \cdot (0.40 \cdot 10{,}293{,}333.33 + 0.60 \cdot 6{,}333{,}333.33) \end{cases}$$

$$= \max\{\$13{,}105{,}600.00, \$16{,}325{,}600.00\}$$

$$= \$16{,}325{,}600.00$$

Therefore, if we are at state B in year 2, we should choose to pump oil with the enhanced method.

We proceed in the same manner to compute the best method to use and the expected profit at nodes C, D, E, and A, in that order. We can now trace the optimal strategy over the three years (see Exhibit 6.3). We start out with 600,000 barrels as reserves, and a price of $45 per barrel. The optimal strategy at node A is to use the enhanced method. That takes us either to state C (with probability 0.40) or to state E (with probability 0.60).

If we are in state C, the optimal strategy is to use the enhanced method again, which will take us either to state H or to state K. In both states H and K, it is optimal to use the enhanced method again.

If we are in state E, it is optimal to use the enhanced method, which takes us to state K (with probability 0.40) or N (with probability 0.60). If we are at state K, it is optimal to use the enhanced method. However, if we end up at state N, it is optimal to use the normal method.

The expected total profit from the oil well over the three years is the value function at node A: $17,573,110.67.

As this example showed, the extension of dynamic programming methods to incorporate uncertainty is logical, but can substantially increase the level of complexity of already computationally intensive dynamic programming algorithms. In practice, approximation algorithms are often used in order to reduce the size and complexity of dynamic programming problems. In particular, we would try to come up with a good estimate of the form of the optimal policy as a function of the state in which we are, rather than evaluate the exact optimal policy in every state of the world.[3] We will see

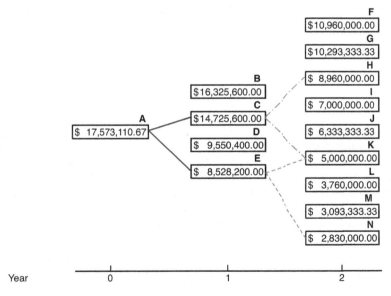

EXHIBIT 6.3 Optimal strategy and profit at each state.

some examples when we talk about derivative pricing in Chapter 14, but in general, there is no recipe for how we might select the approximation.

6.2 STOCHASTIC PROGRAMMING

Perhaps the easiest way to think of a stochastic programming formulation is to imagine writing an optimization problem formulation of the kind described in section 5.2 of Chapter 5, and searching for an optimal solution over *scenarios* for the input data.

Consider a general stochastic optimization (say, maximization) problem, in which we have an objective function $F(\mathbf{x}, \xi)$ that depends on a decision vector $\mathbf{x}$ of dimension N and a vector of uncertain parameters ξ of dimension d. Such optimization problems are not well-defined since the objective depends on the unknown value of ξ. Namely, every realization of the vector of random variables ξ corresponds to a different realization of the objective function. Thus, we have a different probability distribution of objective function values for every feasible solution $\mathbf{x}$. It is wrong to say that one probability distribution is "better" than another unless we specify what "better" means. Hence, it is impossible to state what the optimal solution $\mathbf{x}^*$ is, since by definition the optimal solution is the one that gives the "best" value of the objective function.

The simplest way to make the objective well-defined is to optimize it on average:

$$\max_{\mathbf{x}} \ f(\mathbf{x}) = E[F(\mathbf{x}, \xi)],$$

where the expectation is taken over scenarios for ξ.[4] This means that we define the optimal solution $\mathbf{x}^*$ as the solution that results in a probability distribution for the objective function value with the highest mean of all probability distributions of objective function values.

What if uncertainty is present in the constraints? In some cases we can formulate such problems by introducing penalties for violating the constraints, thus defining a *mean-risk objective function*.[5] An alternative approach is to require that the constraints be satisfied for all possible (in particular, the worst-case) values of the uncertain parameters. This is a stochastic programming method whose philosophy overlaps with the philosophy of *robust optimization*, which we will explain in the next section. Finally, we may impose the requirement that the constraints be satisfied with a high probability. This leads to a stochastic programming formulation with *chance constraints*.

In summary, stochastic programming can be used to address the presence of uncertain input data in three types of optimization problems:

1. Expected value for one- and multistage models.
2. Models involving risk measures.
3. Chance-constrained models.

Each model type is discussed next.

6.2.1 Multistage Models

In *multistage stochastic programming models*, decision variables and constraints are divided into groups corresponding to time periods, or stages $t = 1, \ldots, T$. The information structure of the model (i.e., what is known at each stage) is specified in advance. The standard form of a multistage stochastic linear program is[6]

$$
\min_{\mathbf{x}} \quad \tilde{\mathbf{c}}_0' \mathbf{x}_0 + E_{\xi_1}[(\tilde{\mathbf{c}}_1^{\xi_1})' \mathbf{x}_1^{\xi_1} + \cdots + E_{\xi_{T-1}|\xi_{T-2}}[(\tilde{\mathbf{c}}_{T-1}^{\xi_1, \ldots, \xi_{T-1}})' \mathbf{x}_{T-1}^{\xi_1, \ldots, \xi_{T-1}}
$$
$$
+ E_{\xi_T|\xi_{T-1}}[(\tilde{\mathbf{c}}_T^{\xi_1, \ldots, \xi_T})' \mathbf{x}_T^{\xi_1, \ldots, \xi_T}]]]
$$

s.t.

$$
\begin{array}{rcl}
\mathbf{A}_0 \mathbf{x}_0 & = & \mathbf{b}_0 \\
\mathbf{B}_0^{\xi_1} \mathbf{x}_0 + \quad \mathbf{A}_1^{\xi_1} \mathbf{x}_1^{\xi_1} & = & \mathbf{b}_1^{\xi_1} \\
\ddots \qquad\qquad \vdots \\
\mathbf{B}_{T-1}^{\xi_T} \mathbf{x}_{T-1}^{\xi_1, \ldots, \xi_{T-1}} + \mathbf{A}_T^{\xi_T} \mathbf{x}_T^{\xi_1, \ldots, \xi_T} & = & \mathbf{b}_T^{\xi_T} \\
\mathbf{x}_0, \mathbf{x}_1^{\xi_1}, \ldots, \mathbf{x}_{T-1}^{\xi_1, \ldots, \xi_{T-1}}, \mathbf{x}_T^{\xi_1, \ldots, \xi_T} & \geq & 0
\end{array}
$$

Here the array $\xi = \{\xi_1, \ldots, \xi_T\}$ represents the realizations of an underlying process that drives the uncertainty in the coefficients of the objective function, and $\mathbf{A}$ and $\mathbf{B}$ are matrices with data. Note that the vectors of solutions $\mathbf{x}$ are indexed off the vectors of uncertainty ξ_t at each stage t, except at the beginning (stage 0). In stochastic programming, decision variables can be divided into two categories: anticipative and adaptive. *Anticipative decision variables* (such as $\mathbf{x}_0$ in the above formulation) correspond to decisions that must be made at that particular stage, and all information for making the decision is available. *Adaptive decision variables* (such as $\mathbf{x}_t^{\xi_1, \ldots, \xi_t}$ in the previous formulation) depend on future realizations of the random parameters.

A large number of financial applications—asset-liability management, index tracking, active investment management—can be treated as a sequence of decisions and observations, and represented in this form. The "block" formulation of the stochastic optimization problem is preferable because specialized software (stochastic optimization packages in particular) can take advantage of the structure when applying decomposition algorithms for solving the problem. In order to complete the multistage stochastic programming model, we need to specify the structure of the random process for the uncertain coefficients, which is typically reduced to a set of scenarios. The scenarios are organized in an event tree which at each stage describes the unfolding of the uncertainties with respect to possible values of the uncertain parameters. The values of these realizations (denoted ξ previously) are then plugged into the preceding problem formulation.

Exhibit 6.4 shows an example of such a tree if only one uncertain parameter is modeled. There are three time periods, and two optimization stages. The nodes represent points in time at which the information about the realizations of the uncertain parameter is updated. They are numbered for each stage t. The numbers in bold above the nodes denote the specific realizations of the uncertain parameter. At time 0, its value is known and unique (it is 33 in this example). At that time, there is only one node (node 0), which is called the *root* of the tree. At the last stage, there are $S_T = 5$ possible scenarios, represented by the paths from the root to the *leaves* of the tree, that is, the last-stage nodes. The numbers above the arcs of the tree represent the probabilities of moving to the next node *conditional* on having reached its ancestor node. Note that the probabilities on all branches emanating from the same node add up to 1.

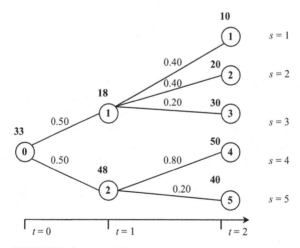

EXHIBIT 6.4 Simplified example of a scenario tree.

Given this scenario tree, we can create the block stochastic programming formulation as follows:

- Define decision variables $x_t^{(s)}$ for each possible scenario s at each time period t. There are different ways to define a set of decision variables, but one possibility is to have eight of them: $x_0^{(0)}$ for stage 0; $x_1^{(1)}$ and $x_1^{(2)}$ for stage 1; and $x_2^{(1)}$, $x_2^{(2)}$, $x_2^{(3)}$, $x_2^{(4)}$, $x_2^{(5)}$ for stage 2. In this example, the number of scenarios at each stage is equal to the number of nodes at that stage because the tree does not recombine.

- Write out the objective as a function of these decision variables and the uncertain data:

$$\max_{\mathbf{x}} (\mathbf{c}_0)' \mathbf{x}_0 + \pi_1^{(1)} \left(\mathbf{c}_1^{(1)}\right)' \mathbf{x}_1^{(1)} + \pi_1^{(2)} \left(\mathbf{c}_1^{(2)}\right)' \mathbf{x}_1^{(2)} + \pi_2^{(1)} \left(\mathbf{c}_2^{(1)}\right)' \mathbf{x}_2^{(1)}$$
$$+ \pi_2^{(2)} \left(\mathbf{c}_2^{(2)}\right)' \mathbf{x}_2^{(2)} + \pi_2^{(3)} \left(\mathbf{c}_2^{(3)}\right)' \mathbf{x}_2^{(3)} + \pi_2^{(4)} \left(\mathbf{c}_2^{(4)}\right)' \mathbf{x}_2^{(4)}$$
$$+ \pi_2^{(4)} \left(\mathbf{c}_2^{(4)}\right)' \mathbf{x}_2^{(4)} + \pi_2^{(5)} \left(\mathbf{c}_2^{(5)}\right)' \mathbf{x}_2^{(5)}$$

The objective is a sum of the reward at the initial node and the expected rewards at all remaining nodes. In the expression above, $\pi_t^{(s)}$ denotes the probability of scenario s at time t. For example, $\pi_1^{(1)} = 0.50$ and $\pi_2^{(4)} = (0.50)(0.80) = 0.40$.

- Write a set of constraints for each stage and each scenario:

$$\begin{aligned}
\text{Stage 0:} \quad & \mathbf{A}_0^{(0)} \mathbf{x}_0^{(0)} = \mathbf{b}_0^{(0)} \\
\text{Stage 1:} \quad & \mathbf{B}_0^{(1)} \mathbf{x}_0^{(0)} + \mathbf{A}_1^{(1)} \mathbf{x}_1^{(1)} = \mathbf{b}_1^{(1)} \\
& \mathbf{B}_0^{(2)} \mathbf{x}_0^{(0)} + \mathbf{A}_1^{(2)} \mathbf{x}_1^{(2)} = \mathbf{b}_1^{(2)} \\
\text{Stage 2:} \quad & \mathbf{B}_1^{(1)} \mathbf{x}_1^{(1)} + \mathbf{A}_2^{(1)} \mathbf{x}_2^{(1)} = \mathbf{b}_2^{(1)} \\
& \mathbf{B}_1^{(2)} \mathbf{x}_1^{(1)} + \mathbf{A}_2^{(2)} \mathbf{x}_2^{(2)} = \mathbf{b}_2^{(2)} \\
& \mathbf{B}_1^{(3)} \mathbf{x}_1^{(1)} + \mathbf{A}_2^{(3)} \mathbf{x}_2^{(3)} = \mathbf{b}_2^{(3)} \\
& \mathbf{B}_1^{(4)} \mathbf{x}_1^{(2)} + \mathbf{A}_2^{(4)} \mathbf{x}_2^{(4)} = \mathbf{b}_2^{(4)} \\
& \mathbf{B}_1^{(5)} \mathbf{x}_1^{(2)} + \mathbf{A}_2^{(5)} \mathbf{x}_2^{(5)} = \mathbf{b}_2^{(5)}
\end{aligned}$$

Note that the constraints keep track of the ancestor of each node. For example, nodes 1, 2, and 3 at stage 2 have a common ancestor: node 1 from stage 1. So, the decision variables associated with the scenarios ending at those nodes ($x_2^{(1)}$, $x_2^{(2)}$, and $x_2^{(3)}$) are linked to the decision variable associated with node 1 from stage 1 ($x_1^{(1)}$) via the first three constraints from Stage 2.

■ Write the so-called *nonanticipativity conditions*, if applicable. Nonanticipativity conditions make sure that scenarios with the same past have identical decisions up to the stage at which they have the same history. In this case, the nonanticipativity conditions are incorporated implicitly by our choice of decision variables and the fact that only one scenario corresponds to each node. Some formulations that involve alternative definitions of the decision variables, such as the original nonblock formulation of the portfolio problem, require stating the nonanticipativity constraints explicitly.[7]

Four common ways to create scenario trees for the uncertain parameters are:[8]

1. Bootstrapping historical data.
2. Using parametric models in which one assumes specific probability distributions and then estimates their parameters from data.
3. Generating simple discrete distributions whose moments are then matched to moments of real data distributions.
4. Constructing vector autoregressive models.

We need to use caution when creating the tree. Its dimension becomes unmanageable very quickly, and, as the previous simple example illustrated, the number of decision variables and constraints in the optimization problem is directly related to the number of scenarios. If, for example, you are managing a portfolio, and you allow the possible returns for the N assets in the portfolio to have just two possible realizations at each stage, the total number of scenarios at the last stage is 2^{NT}. If your portfolio consists of only 10 assets, and is rebalanced monthly over one year, you would need to work with 2^{120} scenarios for the possible asset returns. Needless to say, optimization problems of such dimension are impossible to solve. Since the size of the problem tends to grow exponentially with the number of nodes, it is important to represent the underlying stochastic process with as few nodes as possible. However, it is also important to take into consideration the trade-off between the dimension of the problem and the accuracy of approximation of the underlying stochastic process, otherwise little insight is gained from solving the optimization problem.

Let us now formulate a simple stochastic optimization problem explicitly. Consider again the oil well example from section 6.1. The scenario tree for the price of oil over the three years of the lease was presented in Exhibit 6.1. We reproduce it in Exhibit 6.5, with the scenarios explicitly

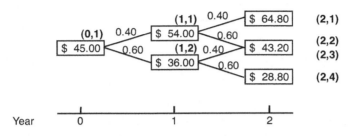

EXHIBIT 6.5 Scenario tree for the oil well problem with scenario labels for each stage.

labeled above or next to each node. The first number in the node labels is the time period, and the second number in the label is the scenario at that stage. Note that even though there are only 3 nodes at the last stage (year 2), there are 4 scenarios. Namely, a price of $43.20 can be reached in two ways: the price in year 0 can go up to $54.00 in year 1 and then down to $43.20 in year 2, or go down to $36.00 in year 1 and then up to $43.20 in year 2.

We use the optimization formulation from the end of section 5.6.1 of the previous chapter as a basis for the formulation of the multistage stochastic programming problem. Let us introduce decision variables $x_0^{(1)}$ for stage 0; $x_1^{(1)}$ and $x_1^{(2)}$ for stage 1; and $x_2^{(1)}$, $x_2^{(2)}$, $x_2^{(3)}$, $x_2^{(4)}$ for stage 2 to denote the available oil reserves in each scenario at each stage. Let us also introduce variables $u_0^{(1)}$ for stage 0; $u_1^{(1)}$ and $u_1^{(2)}$ for stage 1; and $u_2^{(1)}$, $u_2^{(2)}$, $u_2^{(3)}$, $u_2^{(4)}$ to denote the amounts of oil to pump in each scenario at each stage, as well as binary variables $z_0^{(1)}$ for stage 0; $z_1^{(1)}$ and $z_1^{(2)}$ for stage 1; and $z_2^{(1)}$, $z_2^{(2)}$, $z_2^{(3)}$, $z_2^{(4)}$ to denote the decision of whether to pump or not in each scenario and at each stage.

As in the original problem formulation, we have the following relationship between $u_0^{(1)}$ and $z_0^{(0)}$:

$$u_t^{(s)} = 100{,}000 \cdot z_t^{(s)} + 200{,}000 \cdot (1 - z_t^{(s)}), t = 0, 1, 2; s = 1, \ldots, S_t$$

We also have the relationship between the amount of oil at each stage, the amount of oil pumped at that stage, and the available reserves at the next stage. However, we need to be careful to link only variables that are associated with a specific scenario, and so we need to keep track of the "ancestors" of the node at which we are, that is, we need to know how we reached a particular node. For example, let us consider the node at stage 3 in the tree that corresponds to a price of $43.20. Since we have two ways of getting to that node, we need to write a separate equality for each scenario:

$$x_2^{(2)} = x_1^{(1)} - u_1^{(1)}$$
$$x_2^{(3)} = x_1^{(2)} - u_1^{(2)}$$

The first equality is associated with scenario 2 at stage 3: we got to the price of \$43.20 by going through node 1 at stage 1 (a price of \$54.00) first. The second equality is associated with scenario 3 at stage 3: we got to the price of \$43.20 by going through node 2 at stage 1 (a price of \$36.00) first.

The final step in the formulation is to figure out the probability of each scenario. Let us denote those by $\pi_0^{(1)}$ for stage 0; $\pi_1^{(1)}$ and $\pi_1^{(2)}$ for stage 1; and $\pi_2^{(1)}, \pi_2^{(2)}, \pi_2^{(3)}, \pi_2^{(4)}$ for stage 2. We have

$\pi_0^{(1)} = 1$ (we start out at that node, so we can ignore this probability)

$\pi_1^{(1)} = 0.40$ (probability of price going up)

$\pi_1^{(2)} = 0.60$ (probability of price going down)

$\pi_2^{(1)} = 0.40 \cdot 0.40 = 0.16$ (probability of price going up twice)

$\pi_2^{(2)} = 0.40 \cdot 0.60 = 0.24$ (probability of price going up and then down)

$\pi_2^{(3)} = 0.60 \cdot 0.40 = 0.24$ (probability of price going down and then up)

$\pi_2^{(4)} = 0.60 \cdot 0.60 = 0.36$ (probability of price going down twice)

The complete stochastic programming formulation of the oil well example is as follows:

$$
\begin{aligned}
\max_{\mathbf{x,u,z}} \quad & p_0^{(1)} \cdot u_0^{(1)} - z_0^{(1)} \cdot \left(u_0^{(1)}\right)^2 / x_0^{(1)} - (1 - z_0^{(1)}) \cdot 20 \cdot \left(u_0^{(1)}\right)^2 / x_0^{(1)} \\
& + 0.9 \cdot \pi_1^{(1)} \cdot \left(p_1^{(1)} \cdot u_1^{(1)} - z_1^{(1)} \cdot \left(u_1^{(1)}\right)^2 / x_1^{(1)} - (1 - z_1^{(1)}) \cdot 20 \cdot \left(u_1^{(1)}\right)^2 / x_1^{(1)} \right) \\
& + 0.9 \cdot \pi_1^{(2)} \cdot \left(p_1^{(2)} \cdot u_1^{(2)} - z_1^{(2)} \cdot \left(u_1^{(2)}\right)^2 / x_1^{(2)} - (1 - z_1^{(2)}) \cdot 20 \cdot \left(u_1^{(2)}\right)^2 / x_1^{(2)} \right) \\
& + 0.9^2 \cdot \pi_2^{(1)} \cdot \left(p_2^{(1)} \cdot u_2^{(1)} - z_2^{(1)} \cdot \left(u_2^{(1)}\right)^2 / x_2^{(1)} - (1 - z_2^{(1)}) \cdot 20 \cdot \left(u_2^{(1)}\right)^2 / x_2^{(1)} \right) \\
& + 0.9^2 \cdot \pi_2^{(2)} \cdot \left(p_2^{(2)} \cdot u_2^{(2)} - z_2^{(2)} \cdot \left(u_2^{(2)}\right)^2 / x_2^{(2)} - (1 - z_2^{(2)}) \cdot 20 \cdot \left(u_2^{(2)}\right)^2 / x_2^{(2)} \right) \\
& + 0.9^2 \cdot \pi_2^{(3)} \cdot \left(p_2^{(3)} \cdot u_2^{(3)} - z_2^{(3)} \cdot \left(u_2^{(3)}\right)^2 / x_2^{(3)} - (1 - z_2^{(3)}) \cdot 20 \cdot \left(u_2^{(3)}\right)^2 / x_2^{(3)} \right) \\
& + 0.9^2 \cdot \pi_2^{(4)} \cdot \left(p_2^{(4)} \cdot u_2^{(4)} - z_2^{(4)} \cdot \left(u_2^{(4)}\right)^2 / x_2^{(4)} - (1 - z_2^{(4)}) \cdot 20 \cdot \left(u_2^{(4)}\right)^2 / x_2^{(4)} \right)
\end{aligned}
$$

s.t. $u_0^{(1)} = 100{,}000 \cdot z_0^{(1)} + 200{,}000 \cdot (1 - z_0^{(1)})$

$\quad u_1^{(1)} = 100{,}000 \cdot z_1^{(1)} + 200{,}000 \cdot (1 - z_1^{(1)})$

$\quad u_1^{(2)} = 100{,}000 \cdot z_1^{(2)} + 200{,}000 \cdot (1 - z_1^{(2)})$

$\quad u_2^{(1)} = 100{,}000 \cdot z_2^{(1)} + 200{,}000 \cdot (1 - z_2^{(1)})$

$\quad u_2^{(2)} = 100{,}000 \cdot z_2^{(2)} + 200{,}000 \cdot (1 - z_2^{(2)})$

$\quad u_2^{(3)} = 100{,}000 \cdot z_2^{(3)} + 200{,}000 \cdot (1 - z_2^{(3)})$

$\quad u_2^{(4)} = 100{,}000 \cdot z_2^{(4)} + 200{,}000 \cdot (1 - z_2^{(4)})$

$\quad x_1^{(1)} = 600{,}000$

$\quad x_1^{(1)} = x_0^{(1)} - u_0^{(1)}$

$\quad x_1^{(2)} = x_0^{(1)} - u_0^{(1)}$

$\quad x_2^{(1)} = x_1^{(1)} - u_1^{(1)}$

$\quad x_2^{(2)} = x_1^{(1)} - u_1^{(1)}$

$\quad x_2^{(3)} = x_1^{(2)} - u_1^{(2)}$

$\quad x_2^{(4)} = x_1^{(2)} - u_1^{(2)}$

$\quad u_0^{(1)}, u_1^{(1)}, u_1^{(2)}, u_2^{(1)}, u_2^{(2)}, u_2^{(3)}, u_2^{(4)}, x_0^{(1)}, x_1^{(1)}, x_1^{(2)}, x_2^{(1)}, x_2^{(2)}, x_2^{(3)}, x_2^{(4)} \geq 0$

$\quad z_0^{(1)}, z_1^{(1)}, z_1^{(2)}, z_2^{(1)}, z_2^{(2)}, z_2^{(3)}, z_2^{(4)}$ binary

In the preceding formulation, $p_t^{(s)}$ denotes the price in scenario s at stage t. We have

$$p_0^{(1)} = \$45.00$$
$$p_1^{(1)} = \$54.00$$
$$p_1^{(2)} = \$36.00$$
$$p_2^{(1)} = \$64.80$$
$$p_2^{(2)} = \$43.20$$
$$p_2^{(3)} = \$43.20$$
$$p_2^{(4)} = \$28.80$$

The dimension of realistic multistage stochastic programming problems is typically very large, and optimization is challenging even with today's advanced technology. For certain types of stochastic problems, and linear optimization problems in particular, techniques such as nested *Benders decomposition*[9] and *importance sampling* can be used. The idea behind

Benders decomposition is to split the multistage problem into a series of two-stage relations. Subproblems of much smaller size than the original problem are solved at each stage and scenario—these subproblems receive a trial solution from their ancestors, and communicate a trial solution to their successors. Some stochastic programming software packages contain subroutines for decomposition of large stochastic programming problems that can be called directly.[10] However, if we want to use standard optimization solvers, we need to implement the decomposition ourselves by calling the optimization solver repeatedly for each different subproblem.

Because the number of scenarios substantially impacts the speed with which multistage stochastic optimization problems can be solved, a substantial amount of research has been dedicated to developing methodologies for effective scenario generation. The main idea is that scenario generation should not try to approximate well the probability distributions of the uncertain parameters, but rather approximate well the optimal value of the optimization problem. It has been shown that stochastic programming problems with two stages can be solved very efficiently, and with proven accuracy, by employing Monte Carlo simulation methods.[11] However, little is known about the computational complexity and the quality of approximation of Monte Carlo sampling methods for multistage problems. In the financial modeling context, factor models and bundling of similar sample paths (as opposed to building entire scenario trees) have been used in order to reduce the dimension of such multistage problems.[12] Factor models are discussed in more detail in Chapter 11.

6.2.2 Mean-Risk Stochastic Models

Mean-risk stochastic models use an objective function that is composed of two parts: the expectation and some measure of risk.[13] As explained earlier in this section, when there is uncertainty in the coefficients in the optimization formulation, finding the optimal solution reduces to finding the solution that results in the "best" probability distribution of objective function values. We mentioned one definition of "best" probability distribution—the probability distribution with the highest mean. There are other plausible definitions, however. In particular, if we are also concerned about the degree of variability in the probability distribution of the objective function values, we can include a term in the objective function that penalizes for risk.

For example, suppose there are N assets with random returns $\tilde{r}_1, \tilde{r}_2, \ldots, \tilde{r}_N$ in the next year. We would like to invest percentages $w_1, w_2, \ldots, w_N$ of our capital so as to maximize the portfolio expected return and penalize for the variance of the distribution of possible portfolio returns. (Portfolio risk measures are discussed in more detail in Chapter 8.) Suppose we are given a set of S possible scenarios for returns, and μ_i are the average returns for assets $i = 1, \ldots, N$ over the scenarios. Let r_i^s be the realization of the return of security i in scenario s. The return of the portfolio in scenario s is simply the sum of the individual asset returns multiplied by their weights in the portfolio, that is,

$$\sum_{i=1}^{N} r_i^s w_i$$

Let us denote the probabilities of the S scenarios by $\pi_1, \ldots, \pi_S$, where

$$\sum_{s=1}^{S} \pi_s = 1$$

The expected return on a portfolio with weights $w_1, w_2, \ldots, w_N$ over the N scenarios equals

$$\sum_{i=1}^{N} \mu_i w_i$$

and the variance of the portfolio return over the S scenarios is[14]

$$\sum_{s=1}^{S} \pi_s \left(\underbrace{\sum_{i=1}^{N} r_i^s w_i}_{\text{portfolio return in scenario } s} - \underbrace{\sum_{i=1}^{N} \mu_i w_i}_{\text{expected portfolio return}} \right)^2$$

Therefore, we can define the following objective for our portfolio optimization problem under uncertainty:

$$\max_{\mathbf{w}} \sum_{i=1}^{N} \mu_i w_i - \kappa \left[\sum_{s=1}^{S} \pi_s \left(\underbrace{\sum_{i=1}^{N} r_i^s w_i}_{\text{portfolio return in scenario } s} - \underbrace{\sum_{i=1}^{N} \mu_i w_i}_{\text{expected portfolio return}} \right)^2 \right].$$

EXHIBIT 6.6   Scenarios for the returns of the four funds.

Fund #	1	2	3	4
Scenario 1	50.39%	15.69%	23.29%	2.50%
Scenario 2	−9.02%	−3.96%	−2.25%	2.36%
Mean return	20.69%	5.87%	10.52%	2.43%

Here, κ is a penalty coefficient that is determined by the user—the more tolerance we have for uncertainty, the smaller the coefficient is. If we only cared about the expected portfolio return over the S scenarios, we would set κ to 0. We can specify additional constraints, as we would do in any optimization problem.

To gain some additional intuition, let us consider a simplified extension of the portfolio allocation example in section 5.3.1. Suppose that the expected returns of the four funds are the same, but we believe that their returns could end up in one of two scenarios: a "good" scenario, Scenario 1, or a "bad" scenario, Scenario 2 (see Exhibit 6.6). Suppose also that we believe that the probability of Scenario 1 is 0.30, and the probability of Scenario 2 is 0.70.

The stochastic programming mean-risk formulation of this problem is

$$
\begin{aligned}
\max_{\mathbf{w}} \quad & 20.69 \cdot w_1 + 5.87 \cdot w_2 + 10.52 \cdot w_3 + 2.43 \cdot w_4 \\
& - \kappa \cdot 0.3 \cdot (50.39 \cdot w_1 + 15.69 \cdot w_2 + 23.29 \cdot w_3 + 2.50 \cdot w_4 \\
& - (20.69 \cdot w_1 + 5.87 \cdot w_2 + 10.52 \cdot w_3 + 2.43 \cdot w_4))^2 \\
& - \kappa \cdot 0.7 \cdot (-9.02 \cdot w_1 - 3.96 \cdot w_2 - 2.25 \cdot w_3 + 2.36 \cdot w_4 \\
& - (20.69 \cdot w_1 + 5.87 \cdot w_2 + 10.52 \cdot w_3 + 2.43 \cdot w_4))^2
\end{aligned}
$$

subject to the remaining constraints in the problem.

Different risk measures can, of course, be defined. We will return to mean-risk models in Chapters 7 through 9.

6.2.3 Chance-Constrained Models

Chance-constrained stochastic optimization problems contain requirements on the probability that the solution will satisfy the constraints for all realizations of the random parameters in the problem. If the original constraint is

$$\tilde{\mathbf{a}}'\mathbf{x} \leq b$$

where $\mathbf{x}$ is the vector of decision variables and $\tilde{\mathbf{a}}$ is a vector of uncertain coefficients, then the general form of the chance constraint is

$$P(\tilde{\mathbf{a}}'\mathbf{x} > b) \leq \varepsilon$$

where P denotes *probability*, and ε is some small number, such as 0.05 (5%). In order for the probabilistic constraint above to be satisfied, we need to find such a solution $\mathbf{x}$ such that the original constraint $\tilde{\mathbf{a}}'\mathbf{x} \leq b$ is violated for at most $\varepsilon\%$ of all possible values for the uncertain coefficients. An important example of a chance-constrained stochastic programming problem in the portfolio management context is portfolio value-at-risk (VaR) optimization, which we will see in Chapter 8.

Based on our introduction to optimization models in Chapter 5, it is clear that a probabilistic constraint is not part of any of the standard optimization formulations. We need to apply different tricks to convert the constraint into a form that can be passed to an optimization solver, and this involves making different assumptions. In the case in which we are given S scenarios for vector of uncertain coefficients $\tilde{\mathbf{a}}$, we would need to replace this probabilistic constraint with an equivalent group of constraints:

$$(\mathbf{a}^{(s)})'\mathbf{x} \leq b + M \cdot y_s, \qquad s = 1, \ldots, S$$

$$\sum_{s=1}^{S} y_s \leq \lfloor \varepsilon \cdot S \rfloor$$

$$y_s \in \{0, 1\}, \qquad s = 1, \ldots, S$$

In the preceding formulation, M is some "large" constant relative to the size of the problem that is specified by the user. Note that we have introduced S new binary decision variables y_s, and have $S+1$ constraints instead of the original one probabilistic constraint. If $y_s = 0$, this forces the constraint

$$(\mathbf{a}^{(s)})'\mathbf{x} \leq b$$

to be satisfied, that is, for $\tilde{\mathbf{a}}'\mathbf{x} \leq b$ to be satisfied in scenario s. However, if $y_s = 1$, the term $M \cdot y_s$ is "large," that is, the right-hand side of the constraint is no longer restrictive, and the constraint no longer needs to be satisfied. The additional constraint

$$\sum_{s=1}^{S} y_s \leq \lfloor \varepsilon \cdot S \rfloor$$

limits the number of binary variables that are 1 to not more than $\lfloor \varepsilon \cdot S \rfloor$ (which is the integer part of $\varepsilon \cdot S$). For example, if we are given 115 scenarios for $\tilde{a}$, and $\varepsilon = 5\%$, we guarantee that not more than 5 ($= \lfloor 0.05 \cdot 115 \rfloor = \lfloor 5.75 \rfloor$) of the y's are 1, that is, the constraint is not violated in more than 95% of the scenarios.

The introduction of binary variables and additional constraints increases the size and complexity of the original optimization problem significantly, and can overwhelm even the best solvers when the number of scenarios (and, hence the number of binary variables) is large. Moreover, the problem type becomes nonconvex, which means that if the solver returns a solution, we cannot be confident that it is the optimal one. Therefore, probabilistic constraints need to be handled with care.

Note that a chance constraint basically requires that the $100(1 - \varepsilon)$th percentile of the distribution of the random variable $\tilde{a}'x$ be less than the right-hand-side limit b. Therefore, in rare cases in which we know the distribution of $\tilde{a}'x$ and can compute a closed-form expression for its $100(1 - \varepsilon)$th percentile, we can convert a probabilistic constraint directly into a single nonprobabilistic constraint.

This is the case when all uncertain coefficients $\tilde{a}_1, \ldots, \tilde{a}_N$ in the chance constraint are assumed to come from a multivariate normal distribution. We can compute the exact $100(1 - \varepsilon)$th percentile of the probability distribution $\tilde{a}'x$ in terms of the means of the uncertain coefficients $\tilde{a}$, the standard deviations and the covariance structure of the uncertain coefficients $\tilde{a}$, and the solution vector $\mathbf{x}$.

The $100(1 - \varepsilon)$th percentile of the distribution of a normal random variable $\tilde{z}$ with a mean μ and standard deviation σ is given by $\mu + \Phi^{-1}(1 - \varepsilon) \cdot \sigma$, where $\Phi^{-1}(.)$ denotes the inverse of the cumulative standard normal distribution. (In other words, $\Phi^{-1}(1 - \varepsilon)$ is the $100(1 - \varepsilon)$th percentile of a standard normal distribution.[15]) We often encounter the notation $z_{(1-\varepsilon)}$ for the same concept. From the equations for expectation and variance of a sum of random variables, we can compute the mean of the normal random variable $\tilde{a}'x$ as $\hat{a}'x$, and its standard deviation—as $\sqrt{x'\Sigma x}$.[16] Therefore, the deterministic constraint equivalent of the chance constraint under the assumption of normally distributed uncertain coefficients is

$$\hat{a}'x + z_{(1-\varepsilon)} \cdot \sqrt{x'\Sigma x} \leq b.$$

This is an SOCP constraint (see section 5.2.4), which is easier to handle than a large set of constraints involving mixed-integer decision variables if you have the right solver. Recently, robust optimization techniques have been successfully applied for approximating the optimal solutions of problems with chance constraints in stochastic programming.[17] We will come back to this problem in Chapter 9.

6.3 ROBUST OPTIMIZATION

A major problem with dynamic and stochastic programming formulations is that in practice it is often difficult to obtain detailed information on the probability distributions of the uncertainties in the model. At the same time, depending on the number of scenarios involved, dynamic and stochastic programming methods can be prohibitively costly computationally. *Robust optimization* makes optimization models robust with respect to uncertainty in the input data of optimization problems by solving so-called *robust counterparts* of these problems for appropriately defined *uncertainty sets* for the random parameters. The robust counterparts contain no uncertain coefficients, that is, they are deterministic optimization problems. In fact, the robust counterparts are worst-case formulations of the original optimization problems, where the worst-case is computed over the possible values the input parameters could take within their uncertainty sets. Typically, the uncertainty sets are defined in smart ways that do not lead to overly conservative or computationally challenging formulations. If the uncertainty sets are defined as a set of scenarios for the uncertain coefficients, robust optimization shares some features of stochastic programming. However, classical robust optimization focuses on the worst-case, while classical stochastic programming focuses on the average over these scenarios.

6.3.1 Uncertainty Sets and Robust Counterparts

To provide some intuition for the robust optimization philosophy, let us consider a linear constraint of the kind

$$\tilde{a}'x \le b.$$

Let us assume that we use a statistical procedure to estimate some kind of "nominal," or expected, values for the elements of the vector of coefficients $\tilde{a}$. We obtain estimates (let us denote them by $\hat{a} = (\hat{a}_1, \ldots, \hat{a}_N)$), and 95% confidence intervals for the true parameter values, $(\hat{a}_i - \delta_i, \hat{a}_i + \delta_i)$ for $i = 1, \ldots, N$.[18] A natural choice for uncertainty set for $\tilde{a}$ is the collection of confidence intervals, which can be written as

$$U_\delta(\hat{a}) = \left\{ a \mid |a_i - \hat{a}_i| \le \delta_i, i = 1, \ldots, N \right\}.$$

This mathematical expression states that coefficient a_i can take any value between $\hat{a}_i - \delta_i$ and $\hat{a}_i + \delta_i$, where δ_i is the nonnegative number representing the half-length of the confidence interval formed around the estimate $\hat{a}_i$.

The robust counterpart of the preceding linear constraint is the following expression:

$$\max_{\mathbf{a} \in U_\delta(\hat{\mathbf{a}})} \left\{ \mathbf{a}'\mathbf{x} \right\} \leq b$$

In other words, we require that the constraint be satisfied even for the worst-case value of the expression $\mathbf{a}'\mathbf{x}$ when $\mathbf{a}$ varies in the specified uncertainty set. In this case, the worst-case value is obtained at the maximum because if the maximum value of $\mathbf{a}'\mathbf{x}$ is less than or equal to b, then the constraint is clearly satisfied for all smaller values of $\mathbf{a}'\mathbf{x}$. If the inequality were in the opposite direction, that is,

$$\tilde{\mathbf{a}}'\mathbf{x} \geq b$$

then the worst case would happen at the minimum of the expression $\mathbf{a}'\mathbf{x}$, that is, the robust counterpart would be

$$\min_{\mathbf{a} \in U_\delta(\hat{\mathbf{a}})} \left\{ \mathbf{a}'\mathbf{x} \right\} \geq b$$

We can easily write the robust counterpart of the constraint in a form that can be passed to an optimization solver. The maximum of the expression $\mathbf{a}'\mathbf{x}$ when $\mathbf{a}$ varies in $U_\delta(\hat{\mathbf{a}})$ is given by

$$\hat{\mathbf{a}}'\mathbf{x} + \delta'|\mathbf{x}|$$

This can be seen without any advanced mathematics. If the value of a particular decision variable x_i is nonnegative, then $|x_i| = x_i$, and the maximum value of $a_i \cdot x_i$ is obtained by multiplying the maximum possible value of a_i in the uncertainty set, $\hat{a}_i + \delta_i$, by x_i. If the value of x_i is negative, then $|x_i| = -x_i$, which is a positive number, and the maximum value of $a_i \cdot x_i$ is obtained by multiplying the maximum possible value of a_i in the uncertainty set, $\hat{a}_i + \delta_i$, by $-x_i$.

The uncertainty set we considered previously, $U_\delta(\hat{\mathbf{a}})$, is extremely simple, and in fact its applications in finance have been very limited because it is too conservative. The shape of the uncertainty set is a rectangle in two dimensions, and looks like a box in more dimensions (see Exhibit 6.7(A)). The robust optimization approach finds the optimal solution when $\mathbf{a}$ is at one of the corners of the "box"—the corner in which all elements of $\mathbf{a}$ are at their "worst" values in terms of constraint violation, and result in the maximum value for the expression $\mathbf{a}'\mathbf{x}$.

Instead, it may be realistic to be less conservative, and assume that all uncertain coefficients will not take their worst-case values at the same time. In addition, we may have information about the standard deviations

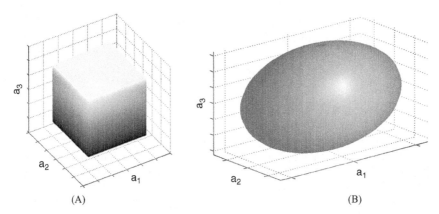

EXHIBIT 6.7 (A) "Box" uncertainty set in 3 dimensions; (B) ellipsoidal uncertainty set in 3 dimensions.

and the covariance structure of the uncertain coefficients. More advanced uncertainty sets can be specified to capture this information. A classical uncertainty set in robust optimization is the ellipsoidal uncertainty set (see Exhibit 6.7(B)), which mathematically can be represented as

$$U_\delta(\hat{\mathbf{a}}) = \left\{ \mathbf{a} \mid (\mathbf{a} - \hat{\mathbf{a}})' \, \Sigma_{\mathbf{a}}^{-1} \, (\mathbf{a} - \hat{\mathbf{a}}) \leq \delta^2 \right\}$$

Here, $\Sigma_{\mathbf{a}}$ is the covariance matrix of the uncertain coefficients $\tilde{\mathbf{a}}$, and δ is some tolerance for robustness that is specified by the user. This uncertainty set states that the constraint should be satisfied for all values of **a** whose total squared distances from their nominal estimated values $\hat{\mathbf{a}}$ (scaled by their variability) are less than or equal to δ^2. Often, this uncertainty set is seen in the literature as

$$U_\delta(\hat{\mathbf{a}}) = \left\{ \mathbf{a} \mid \left\| \Sigma_{\mathbf{a}}^{-1/2}(\mathbf{a} - \hat{\mathbf{a}}) \right\| \leq \delta \right\}$$

where $\|.\|$ stands for second, or Euclidean norm.[19] The two expressions for the ellipsoidal uncertainty set are equivalent.

Let us now find the robust counterpart of the constraint

$$\tilde{\mathbf{a}}'\mathbf{x} \leq b$$

when the vector of uncertain coefficients $\tilde{\mathbf{a}}$ varies in the ellipsoidal uncertainty set. To obtain it, we need to find the maximum value of the expression on the left hand side of the constraint when $\tilde{a}$ is in the uncertainty set. This reduces to solving the optimization problem

$$\max_{a} \quad a'x$$
$$\text{s.t.} \quad \left\| \Sigma_a^{-1/2}(a - \hat{a}) \right\| \leq \kappa$$

This is a second-order cone problem (SOCP),[20] and for the moment we are treating the original decision variables x as fixed (known). Instead, we will try to find the maximum value of the expression $a'x$ when a are the decision variables.

Let us write the dual of the problem above (see Exhibit 5.9 in Chapter 5). We obtain

$$\min_{u,v} \quad \left(-u'\Sigma_a^{-1/2}\hat{a} \right) + \kappa v$$
$$\text{s.t.} \quad \Sigma_a^{-1/2}u + 0 \cdot v = x$$
$$\|u\| \leq v$$

Note that one of the constraints allows us to express u in terms of v and w:

$$u = \Sigma_a^{1/2}x.$$

Therefore, the dual problem is equivalent to

$$\min_{v} \quad x'\Sigma_a^{1/2}\Sigma_a^{-1/2}\hat{a} + \kappa v$$
$$\text{s.t.} \quad \left\| \Sigma_a^{1/2}x \right\| \leq v,$$

which can be rewritten as

$$\min_{v} \quad x'\hat{a} + \kappa v$$
$$\text{s.t.} \quad \left\| \Sigma_a^{1/2}x \right\| \leq v.$$

Note that the minimum will be obtained when the constrained is satisfied with equality, that is, when

$$v = \left\| \Sigma_a^{1/2}x \right\|.$$

and, therefore, the minimum will be

$$\hat{a}'x + \kappa \cdot \left\| \Sigma_a^{1/2} x \right\|.$$

Since this is an SOCP, duality theory states that the optimal objective function value will be the same as the value of the primal (maximization) problem. Therefore, the worst-case value for $a'x$ will be given by the same expression,

$$\hat{a}'x + \kappa \cdot \left\| \Sigma_a^{1/2} x \right\|$$

for any fixed values of the decision variables vector x. Note that the preceding expression does not contain the uncertain coefficients $\tilde{a}$, but instead computes the worst-case value in terms of parameters that are known, such as the nominal values of the uncertain coefficients $\hat{a}$ and the covariance matrix of the uncertain coefficients Σ_a. The final step is to replace the expression in the original constraint, and optimize with x as decision variables again:

$$\hat{a}'x + \kappa \cdot \left\| \Sigma_a^{1/2} x \right\| \le b$$

This constraint formulation is equivalent to the constraint in the original problem we wanted to solve. However, now the formulation is in a form that can be passed to an optimization solver because all coefficients are certain. Nonlinear solvers such as MINOS can handle it. Alternatively, since it is an SOCP, a solver such as SeDuMi[21] or SDPT3[22] would be able to take advantage of its structure and solve it more efficiently.

To summarize, the methodology for creating a single optimization problem to represent the robust counterpart of a constraint is based on a trick from optimization duality. Namely, we first formulate a problem in which the original variables x are treated as fixed, and we try to find the worst-case value for the expression containing the vector of uncertain parameters $\tilde{a}$. We then use optimization duality to convert the expression with uncertain coefficients into a constraint that does not contain uncertain parameters, and plug it into the original constraint. Finally, we solve the original optimization problem with the modified constraint and with x as decision variables. While a certain amount of preprocessing is involved in formulating the robust problem, there is only one call to an optimization solver once the robust counterpart problem is formulated correctly.

The shape of the uncertainty set and the calibration of the different parameters that enter its specification play an important part in the performance of the robust counterpart in practice. The uncertainty sets we saw in these examples were symmetric, that is, we assumed that the uncertain coefficients could deviate from their nominal values by the same amount in each direction. In theory, we could select uncertainty sets that represent better the probability distributions of the uncertain coefficients when these probability distributions are skewed.[23] Recently, there has also been interest in developing "structured" uncertainty sets, that is, uncertainty sets that are intersections of elementary uncertainty sets, or are constructed for a specific purpose.[24]

6.3.2 Multistage Robust Optimization

Robust optimization formulations can be used in multistage settings to replace dynamic programming or stochastic programming algorithms. Namely, instead of considering scenarios with realizations of the different uncertain parameters in a multistage problem, robust optimization formulations specify uncertainty sets around these parameters at each stage.

To provide an illustration, let us go back to the oil well example from Section 1 in this chapter. Recall that in section 5.6.1, we derived the classical optimization problem formulation for the oil problem if we knew the oil prices for each time period in advance. In a robust optimization framework, we would treat the future prices $\bar{p}_1$ and $\bar{p}_2$ as uncertain coefficients in the optimization problem. The robust counterpart statement of the problem would be as follows: Find the optimal strategy when oil prices in each time period take their "worst" within some prespecified uncertainty sets. The robust counterpart is then the following modification of the optimization formulation of the problem in section 5.6.1:

$$\max_{x,u,z} \quad p_0 \cdot u_0 - z_0 \cdot u_0^2/x_0 - (1 - z_0) \cdot 20 \cdot u_0^2/x_0$$

$$+ 0.9 \cdot \min_{p_1 \in U(p_1)} \left\{ p_1 \cdot u_1 - z_1 \cdot u_1^2/x_1 - (1 - z_1) \cdot 20 \cdot u_1^2/x_1 \right\}$$

$$+ 0.9^2 \cdot \min_{p_2 \in U(p_2)} \left\{ p_2 \cdot u_2 - z_2 \cdot u_2^2/x_2 - (1 - z_2) \cdot 20 \cdot u_2^2/x_2 \right\}$$

$$\text{s.t.} \quad u_0 = 100{,}000 \cdot z_0 + 200{,}000 \cdot (1 - z_0)$$

$$u_1 = 100{,}000 \cdot z_1 + 200{,}000 \cdot (1 - z_1)$$

$$u_2 = 100{,}000 \cdot z_2 + 200{,}000 \cdot (1 - z_2)$$

$$x_0 = 600{,}000$$

$$x_1 = x_0 - u_0$$

$$x_2 = x_1 - u_1$$

$$u_0, u_1, u_2, x_1, x_2 \geq 0$$

$$z_0, z_1, z_2 \text{ binary}$$

Here, $U(p_1)$ and $U(p_2)$ are some uncertainty sets for the parameters $\tilde{p}_1$ and $\tilde{p}_2$. For example, if they are confidence intervals of the kind

$$[\hat{p}_1 - \delta_1, \hat{p}_1 - \delta_2]$$

and

$$[\hat{p}_2 - \delta_2, \hat{p}_2 - \delta_2]$$

then the robust counterpart is very simple—we only need to replace the expression for the objective function with

$$\max_{x,u,z} \quad p_0 \cdot u_0 - z_0 \cdot u_0^2/x_0 - (1 - z_0) \cdot 20 \cdot u_0^2/x_0$$
$$+ 0.9 \cdot \left((\hat{p}_1 - \delta_1) \cdot |u_1| - z_1 \cdot u_1^2/x_1 - (1 - z_1) \cdot 20 \cdot u_1^2/x_1\right)$$
$$+ 0.9^2 \cdot \left((\hat{p}_2 - \delta_2) \cdot |u_2| - z_2 \cdot u_2^2/x_2 - (1 - z_2) \cdot 20 \cdot u_2^2/x_2\right)$$

The logic behind the derivation of the preceding expression is the same as the logic behind our derivation of the robust counterpart of a constraint at the beginning of this section, when the uncertain parameters vary in a box uncertainty set.[25] In fact, since u_1 and u_2 are restricted to be nonnegative, we can remove their absolute value signs, which will make the optimization formulation more solver-friendly.

Suppose that we consider the following intervals for the uncertainty sets for $\tilde{p}_1$ and $\tilde{p}_2$: [\$36.00, \$54.00] and [\$28.80, \$64.80], which are the minimum and the maximum values for the oil prices from the tree in Exhibit 6.1. To solve the robust counterpart formulation above, we plug $\hat{p}_1 - \delta_1 = 36.00$ and $\hat{p}_2 - \delta_2 = 28.80$. We obtain the following optimal solution:

$z_0 = 0$ (use the enhanced method at stage 0)

$z_1 = 0$ (use the enhanced method at stage 1)

$z_2 = 1$ (use the normal method at stage 2)

$u_0 = 200,000$ (pump 200,000 barrels of oil at stage 0)

$u_1 = 200,000$ (pump 200,000 barrels of oil at stage 1)

$u_2 = 100,000$ (pump 100,000 barrels of oil at stage 2)

$x_0 = 600,000$ (amount of reserves at stage 0 is 600,000 barrels)

$x_1 = 400,000$ (amount of reserves at stage 1 is 400,000 barrels)

$x_2 = 200,000$ (amount of reserves at stage 2 is 300,000 barrels)

The present value of the total profit from this strategy is \$14,638,966.67. Recall that when we optimized the expected (average) total profit in section 6.1, the optimal expected profit was $17,573,110.67. The optimal profit with the robust optimization strategy is lower because it is the profit obtained under the worst case scenario.

The optimal strategy found with the dynamic programming algorithm was to use the enhanced method in year 0 and 1, which is the same as the optimal strategy found by the robust optimization formulation for the first two years. In year 2, if the price in year 2 was $28.80, the optimal strategy of the dynamic programming algorithm also agreed with the year 2 strategy in the robust optimization solution (to use the normal method). However, the dynamic programming solution was to use the enhanced method if the price was higher ($43.30). The multistage robust optimization method does not give us information about strategies under scenarios other than the worst-case scenario in the uncertainty set we specify.

Given that the dynamic programming method provided us with a more detailed solution than the robust optimization worst-case analysis, why would we want to use robust optimization? The answer is that in most realistic situations, dynamic programming algorithms suffer from the "curse of dimensionality"—the dimensions of the state space and the number of value function estimations and other calculations that need to be performed are so large, that they can overwhelm even the most state-of-the-art software. Robust optimization keeps the dimension of the problem low even as the number of stages and the number of states increase, but still allows us to incorporate considerations for uncertainty when searching for the optimal strategy. Furthermore, the uncertainty sets for the uncertain parameters can be specified in clever ways, so that the formulation is not overly conservative. Whether or not using robust optimization for a particular multistage problem is a good idea has to do with the trade-off between the amount of time or memory it will take to solve the problem over multiple scenarios, and the required degree of accuracy of the solution.

The robust multistage example in which the uncertain parameters are restricted to fall within intervals is quite simplistic. In practice, we can specify more sophisticated uncertainty sets. (See Practice 6.4 on the companion web site for an example of a multistage robust formulation with an ellipsoidal uncertainty set for the uncertain coefficients.)

SUMMARY

- Dynamic programming, stochastic programming, and robust optimization are all methodologies for optimization under uncertainty. Although there is overlap among the three approaches, historically they have evolved independently of each other.

- The dynamic programming approach is used for optimization over multiple stages. Its main idea is to break up the large multistage problem into a sequence of smaller optimization problems, starting from the last stage and proceeding backwards.
- The stochastic programming approach most generally deals with optimization problems in which scenarios are generated for the values of the uncertain parameters. The optimization may be performed so that the objective function is optimized on average, or may include penalties for constraint violation and risk considerations. Stochastic programming can be applied to both single- and multistage optimization problems.
- In most real-world applications, the dimensions of dynamic and stochastic programming methods are too large to handle computationally. Often, approximation algorithms are used; some such algorithms employ Monte Carlo simulation and sample the state space efficiently.
- Robust optimization handles uncertainty in the coefficients of optimization problems by solving so-called robust counterparts of these problems. The robust counterparts are optimization problems that are formulated in terms of the worst-case realizations of the uncertain parameters within prespecified uncertainty sets.
- The robust optimization methodology can be applied in both single- and multistage problems, and can be a computationally attractive alternative to dynamic and stochastic programming methods.

NOTES

1. See, for example, Ziemba and Mulvey (1998), Consigli and Dempster (1996), Zenios and Kang (1993), Carino and Ziemba (1998), Bogentoft, Romeijn and Uryasev (2001), Ziemba (2003), and Hillier and Eckstein (1993).
2. As explained in section 5.6, this technique dates back to Bellman (1957). Modern treatment of the area with applications in engineering, finance, and operations research is provided in Bertsekas (1995). Applications of dynamic programming to optimal consumption and portfolio selection are discussed, for example, in Merton (1995), and Ingersoll (1987).
3. See, for example, Chryssikou (1998) for a development of approximate dynamic programming approaches that characterize the optimal investment policy for multistage portfolio optimization problems.
4. In other words, we maximize a weighted average of objective functions, where each weight is the probability that the scenario that results in that particular objective function will occur.
5. See, for example, Mulvey et al. (1995) and Ruszczynski and Shapiro (2003).

6. The notation $E_{\xi_t|\xi_{t-1}}[\cdot]$ means "expectation of the expression inside the brackets over realizations of the uncertain variable ξ_t at time t conditional on the realizations of ξ_{t-1} at time $t-1$."

7. For example, in an alternative formulation we could associate two variables with every given node: one variable at stage t, and a copy of that decision variable for each particular "child" of that node. This kind of representation may be convenient for formulating the problem in a modeling language, depending on how the scenario data are stored. For instance, in the scenario tree in Exhibit 6.4, we could have two copies of the variable $x_1^{(2)}$ (associated with node 2 at stage 1): $x_1^{(2,4)}$ for its "child" node 4 at stage 2, and $x_1^{(2,5)}$ for its "child" node 5 at stage 2. Then, the constraints

$$B_1^{(4)}x_1^{(2)} + A_2^{(4)}x_2^{(4)} = b_2^{(4)}$$

and

$$B_1^{(5)}x_1^{(2)} + A_2^{(5)}x_2^{(5)} = b_2^{(5)}$$

should be written as

$$B_1^{(4)}x_1^{(2,4)} + A_2^{(4)}x_2^{(4)} = b_2^{(4)}$$

and

$$B_1^{(5)}x_1^{(2,5)} + A_2^{(5)}x_2^{(5)} = b_2^{(5)}$$

We must specify explicitly that $x_1^{(2,4)} = x_1^{(2,5)}$ to make sure that the nonanticipativity condition is satisfied. For further details, see, for example, Fragniere and Gondzio (2005).

8. For a survey of stochastic programming applications in financial optimization and scenario generation techniques, see Yu, Ji, and Wang (2003), and Gulpinar, Rustem, and Settergren (2004). For a description of the different econometric techniques used in scenario generation, see Fabozzi, Focardi, and Kolm (2006).

9. See Birge (1985).

10. For example, OSL/SE by IBM and SPInE by the CHARISMA research center at Brunel University.

11. A good overview of recent developments in stochastic programming and importance sampling in particular is available in Ruszczynski and Shapiro (2003).

12. See Bogentoft et al. (2001) and Mulvey et al. (2000).

13. See Chapter 3.6.2 for an introduction to risk measures in the context of probability distributions. We will discuss risk measures in the context of portfolio allocation in Part Two of the book.

14. The definition of variance of a discrete probability distribution is provided in section 3.6.2.

15. See section 3.4.
16. To verify that this is the case, see Appendix A at the companion web site and write out the expressions for expected values and variances of sums of random variables when the random variables are given in a vector/matrix form. We will discuss this in more detail in Chapters 7 and 9.
17. See Chen, Sim, and Sun (2007) and Natarajan, Pachamanova, and Sim (2008).
18. See Chapter 3.11.2 for a definition of confidence intervals, and Chapter 4.1.2 for their use in simulation.
19. See section 5.2.4.
20. See section 5.2.4.
21. See Computational Research at Lehigh, *SeDuMi*, http://sedumi.ie.lehigh.edu/.
22. See Kim-Chuan Toh, Michael J. Todd, and Reha H. Tutuncu, "SDPT3 version 4.0—a MATLAB software for semidefinite-quadratic-linear programming," http://www.math.nus.edu.sg/~mattohkc/sdpt3.html.
23. See, for example, Natarajan, Pachamanova and Sim (2008).
24. For more details, see Chapters 10 and 12 in Fabozzi, Kolm, Pachamanova, and Focardi (2007).
25. Note that the expression in the objective function can be treated as a constraint. Namely, we can introduce a new decision variable, and maximize that variable subject to an additional constraint that the new variable be less than the expression for the objective function. (See Practice 6.3 on the companion web site.) Therefore, if we have a method for determining the robust counterpart of a constraint, we can apply it to find the robust counterpart of the objective function as well.

Portfolio Optimization and Risk Measures

Asset Diversification and Efficient Frontiers

The concepts of portfolio risk management and diversification have been instrumental in the development of modern financial decision making. These breakthrough ideas originated in an article by Harry Markowitz that appeared in the *Journal of Finance* in 1952. Before Markowitz's publication, the focus in the investment industry was on identifying and investing in "winners"—stocks that appeared undervalued relative to some measure of their potential, or promised sustainable growth, that is, stocks that had high *expected returns*. Markowitz reasoned that investors should decide based on both the expected return from their investment, and on the *risk* from that investment. He defined risk as the variance of future returns. The idea of incorporating risk in investment decisions and applying a disciplined quantitative framework to investment management was novel at the time.[1]

Originally, this investment philosophy generated little interest, but eventually, the finance community adopted it. Over the years, the theory of portfolio selection formulated by Markowitz has been extended and reinvented based on a modification of the assumptions made in the original model that limited its application. It has also introduced a whole new terminology, which is now the norm in the investment management community. Markowitz's investment theory is popularly referred to as *mean-variance analysis*, *mean-variance portfolio optimization*, and *Modern Portfolio Theory* (MPT). In 1990, Markowitz was awarded the Nobel Memorial Prize in Economic Sciences in recognition of his seminal work.

As we will see in this chapter, the definition of risk as the variance of returns leads to the conclusion that *diversification* is preferable as an investment strategy. In essence, Markowitz's framework quantified the conventional wisdom of "not putting all of your eggs in one basket." Mathematically, the portfolio variance is a sum of terms including both the variances of the returns of the individual assets and the covariances (equivalently, the correlations) between those returns. Investing all of your money in assets that are strongly correlated is not considered a prudent strategy, even if individually each of the stocks appears to be a "winner" based on preliminary analysis. If any single asset performs worse than expectations, it is likely, due to its high correlation with the other assets, that the other assets will also perform poorly, decreasing substantially the value of the entire portfolio.

It is worth mentioning that Markowitz's theory of portfolio selection is a *normative* theory. A normative theory is one that describes a standard or norm of behavior that investors should pursue in constructing a portfolio, in contrast to a theory that is actually followed. Asset pricing theory, which discussed in detail in Part Three of the book, goes on to formalize the relationship that should exist between asset returns and risk if investors construct and select portfolios according to mean-variance analysis. In contrast to a normative theory, asset pricing theory is a *positive theory*—a theory that derives the implications of hypothesized investor behavior. An example of a positive theory is the Capital Asset Pricing Model, which we will introduce in Chapter 11.

In this chapter, we explain the basic assumptions in Markowitz's model, and show how the model can be implemented in practice. We also show that the mean-variance approach is consistent with two different frameworks: expected utility maximization under certain conditions, and the assumption that future security returns are jointly normally distributed.

7.1 THE CASE FOR DIVERSIFICATION

Consider an investor who is evaluating an investment in two stocks over the next year. The stocks' expected returns are $E[\tilde{r}_1] = \mu_1 = 9.1\%$ and $E[\tilde{r}_2] = \mu_2 = 12.1\%$, and their standard deviations are $\sigma_1 = 16.5\%$ and $\sigma_2 = 15.8\%$.

At first glance, Stock 2 is the clear winner. Its expected return is higher than Stock 1's, and its standard deviation is lower than Stock 1's. Thus, by investing 100% of his wealth in Stock 2, the investor could achieve better return for less risk, if risk is defined as the standard deviation of possible outcomes.

Now suppose the investor is given the additional information that the correlation coefficient between the two stocks' returns is $\rho_{12} = -0.22$. Let us denote the weight of Stock 1 in the portfolio by w_1, and the weight of Stock 2 by w_2. Note that the sum of the weights of the two stocks must be 100%, that is, $w_2 = 1 - w_1$.

The portfolio return (which is a random variable and denoted by a tilde ($\sim$) over the return variable r) can be expressed as

$$\tilde{r}_p = w_1\tilde{r}_1 + w_2\tilde{r}_2$$

The portfolio expected return and the variance can be computed from the rules listed in section 3.9 of Chapter 3. In particular, the portfolio expected return is

$$E[\tilde{r}_p] = E[w_1\tilde{r}_1 + w_2\tilde{r}_2] = E[w_1\tilde{r}_1] + E[w_2\tilde{r}_2] = w_1 E[\tilde{r}_1] + w_2 E[\tilde{r}_2]$$
$$= w_1\mu_1 + w_2\mu_2$$

The portfolio variance is

$$\sigma_p^2 = Var(w_1\tilde{r}_1 + w_2\tilde{r}_2) = Var(w_1\tilde{r}_1) + Var(w_2\tilde{r}_2) + 2Covar(w_1\tilde{r}_1, w_2\tilde{r}_2)$$
$$= w_1^2\sigma_1^2 + w_1^2\sigma_1^2 + 2w_1 w_2\sigma_{12}.$$

Since we are given the correlation coefficient instead of the covariance, we can express the portfolio variance through the correlation coefficient (see the definition of correlation coefficient in section 3.8)

$$\sigma_p^2 = w_1^2\sigma_1^2 + w_2^2\sigma_2^2 + 2w_1 w_2\sigma_1\sigma_2\rho_{12}.$$

The portfolio standard deviation is, of course, simply the square root of the portfolio variance computed above.

Exhibit 7.1(A) and (B) illustrate how the portfolio return and standard deviation change with the fraction of the portfolio invested in Stock 1. (All of the calculations are contained in the worksheet **Diversification** in the file **Ch7-Diversification2Stocks.xlsm**.) We can observe that while the portfolio expected return is highest when 0% is invested in Stock 1, the portfolio standard deviation when the weight of Stock 1 is 0% is not the lowest possible. By investing in both Stock 1 and Stock 2, the investor can reduce the portfolio standard deviation to a level that is lower than the level of any of the individual stocks.

In the previous two-stock example, the fact that the stocks were negatively correlated made the effect of diversification particularly dramatic in terms of reducing the overall portfolio standard deviation. It turns out, actually, that the same conclusions—that diversification decreases the portfolio standard deviation—hold when stock returns are uncorrelated, or exhibit weak correlations. The conclusion holds true in observed

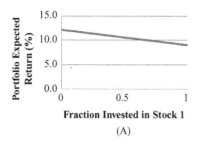 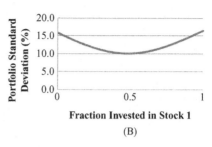

(A)   (B)

EXHIBIT 7.1   (A) Change in portfolio expected return as the fraction invested in Stock 1 increases from 0 to 1; (B) change in portfolio standard deviation as the fraction invested in Stock 1 increases from 0 to 1.

stock return behavior as well. Exhibit 7.2 is a screenshot of the file **Ch7-Diversification30Stocks.xlsx**. The file contains monthly returns over a four-year period for 30 randomly selected stocks from the S&P 500. (The time period was specifically selected to include both upturns and downturns in the market.) The average correlation of these stocks is slightly positive. Yet, as the graph in Exhibit 7.2 illustrates, the standard deviation of a portfolio obtained by weighting equally a selected number of stocks decreases as the number of stocks grows larger. Diversification in this case is beneficial even for a portfolio whose weights were determined casually—by weighting each stock equally. We can do even better by selecting the portfolio weights in a more targeted way—by calculating the weights that will minimize the portfolio risk as measured by its variance.

A fact worth noting here is that diversification cannot necessarily eliminate risk completely. For example, as the graph in Exhibit 7.2 shows, we reach a point (about 13 stocks in this particular example) beyond which adding more stocks does not reduce the standard deviation of the portfolio. A study by Evans and Archer (1968), the first of its kind, suggested that the major benefits of diversification can be obtained with 10 to 20 stocks. More recent studies by Campbell, Lettau, Malkiel, and Xu (2001) and Malkiel (2002) show that the volatility of individual stocks has increased between the 1960s and the 1990s. On the other hand, the correlations between individual stocks have decreased over the same time period. Together, these two effects have canceled each other out, leaving the overall market volatility the same. However, Malkiel's study suggests that it now takes almost 200 individual equities to obtain the same amount of diversification that was historically possible with as few as 10 individual equities.

Several studies have suggested that real-world asset returns behavior can be mapped to a probability distribution known as *the stable Paretian*

	A	B	C	D	E	AG	AH	AI	AJ	AK	AL	AM	AN	AO	AP
1	Mret	ORCL	DUK	AIR	AMD	1 stock	3 stocks	5 stocks	7 stocks	10 stocks	13 stocks	15 stocks	20 stocks	25 stocks	30 stocks
2	20000131	-10.85%	15.21%	-0.92%	24.4	-10.85%	1.15%	4.16%	4.54%	1.33%	2.09%	-0.08%	0.21%	-0.91%	-1.16%
3	20000229	48.64%	-15.06%	34.28%	8.6	48.64%	22.62%	13.30%	5.18%	2.82%	0.62%	0.38%	0.34%	0.67%	2.28%
4	20000331	5.13%	8.25%	-29.74%	45.8	5.13%	-5.45%	6.02%	4.83%	4.42%	4.62%	3.84%	5.45%	5.67%	6.29%
5	20000428	2.40%	9.52%	-9.23%	53.3	2.40%	0.90%	12.70%	8.47%	3.88%	4.22%	4.12%	4.16%	2.11%	1.96%
57	20040831	-5.14%	4.26%	2.88%	-8.4	-5.14%	0.67%	-0.65%	0.52%	0.28%	1.11%	0.89%	-0.89%	-0.66%	-0.82%
58	20040930	13.14%	3.39%	16.36%	13.7	13.14%	10.96%	10.49%	7.46%	6.41%	5.29%	4.33%	3.24%	1.86%	1.90%
59	20041029	12.23%	7.16%	-5.62%	29.3	12.23%	4.59%	7.13%	4.47%	0.43%	0.20%	0.02%	0.38%	-0.09%	1.56%
60	20041130	0.63%	4.18%	16.34%	26.5	0.63%	7.05%	8.94%	7.54%	7.20%	7.03%	6.63%	5.97%	5.62%	5.89%
61	20041231	7.69%	0.20%	-0.37%	3.4	7.69%	2.51%	2.65%	2.70%	2.82%	2.41%	2.64%	3.41%	3.00%	2.83%
62															
63	average	-0.30%	-4.72%	-2.10%	-4.6	-0.04%	0.78%	1.19%	0.88%	0.72%	0.81%	0.67%	0.60%	0.48%	0.37%
64	std dev	19.56%	10.88%	24.09%	23.4	15.19%	9.18%	8.88%	7.11%	6.14%	5.37%	5.47%	5.78%	5.87%	6.00%

Portfolio Average Return and Standard Deviation

— average
— std dev

Number of Stocks

EXHIBIT 7.2 A screenshot of file Ch7-Diversification30Stocks.xlsx. The file contains monthly returns on 30 randomly selected stocks from the S&P 500 between January 2000 and December 2004. The graph illustrates the decrease in the realized standard deviation of an equally-weighted portfolio as the number of stocks in the portfolio increases.

distribution. Mandelbrot (1963) was the first to make this observation. The variance of a random variable following a stable Paretian distribution is not bounded (that is, it is infinite and therefore does not exist). This fact calls into question the principle of diversification. Adding assets with very large or infinite variances to a portfolio cannot reduce the overall portfolio standard deviation. In particular, Fama (1965) demonstrated that if asset returns behave like a stable Paretian distribution, diversification may no longer be meaningful. Most practitioners agree, however, that a certain degree of diversification is preferable and attainable in the markets.

7.2 THE CLASSICAL MEAN-VARIANCE OPTIMIZATION FRAMEWORK

Suppose that an investor would like to invest in N risky assets. The investor's choice can be represented as an $N \times 1$ vector array $\mathbf{w} = (w_1, \ldots, w_N)'$ of asset weights.[2] Each weight w_i represents the proportion of asset i held in the portfolio, and the total portfolio weight needs to be 100%, that is,

$$\sum_{i=1}^{N} w_i = 1.$$

In vector notation, the above requirement can be written as[3]

$$\mathbf{w}' \iota = 1,$$

where ι is an $N \times 1$ vector array of ones. If short selling is allowed,[4] then the weights can be negative.

Markowitz's framework assumes that the investor is making a decision for his investment over one time period of a prespecified length. The investor is concerned with the return on his portfolio *at the end* of that time period, but not during it or after the end of it. The returns of the N assets in the portfolio during that time period can be represented as a vector array of random variables: $\tilde{\mathbf{r}} = (\tilde{r}_1, \ldots, \tilde{r}_N)'$. Suppose the expected returns on the N assets are $\boldsymbol{\mu} = (\mu_1, \ldots, \mu_N)'$, and the covariance matrix of returns is

$$\boldsymbol{\Sigma} = \begin{bmatrix} \sigma_{11} & \cdots & \sigma_{1N} \\ \vdots & \ddots & \vdots \\ \sigma_{N1} & \cdots & \sigma_{NN} \end{bmatrix}$$

where σ_{ij} denotes the covariance between asset i and asset j, and the diagonal element σ_{ii} is the variance of asset i, that is, $\sigma_{ii} = \sigma_i^2$. (Note that $\sigma_{ij} = \sigma_{ji}$, that is, the covariance matrix is symmetric because the covariance between i and j is the same as the covariance between j and i.) Then, the expected return on a portfolio that has allocations of $\mathbf{w} = (w_1, \ldots, w_N)'$ is

$$\mu_p = \sum_{i=1}^{N} \mu_i \cdot w_i = \mu' \mathbf{w}$$

and the portfolio variance σ_p^2 is

$$\sigma_p^2 = \mathbf{w}' \Sigma \mathbf{w}.$$

If, instead of the covariance matrix, we know the correlation matrix

$$\mathbf{K} = \begin{bmatrix} 1 & \cdots & \rho_{1N} \\ \vdots & \ddots & \vdots \\ \rho_{N1} & \cdots & 1 \end{bmatrix}$$

and the standard deviations of the individual assets, we can either convert the correlation matrix into a covariance matrix element-by-element by using the relationship[5]

$$\rho_{ij} = \frac{\sigma_{ij}}{\sigma_i \sigma_j},$$

or we can use directly the correlation matrix in the expression for portfolio variance. To do that, we need to construct a vector $\mathbf{w}^s$ of products of the weights of the assets and the corresponding standard deviations, $\mathbf{w}^s = (w_1 \sigma_1, \ldots, w_N \sigma_N)'$. Then, the portfolio variance can be computed as

$$\sigma_p^2 = (\mathbf{w}^s)' \mathbf{K} \mathbf{w}^s$$

To provide some intuition, let us go back to the case of two assets with weights w_1 and w_2. The portfolio return can be written in vector notation as

$$\tilde{r}_p = [\, w_1 \quad w_1 \,] \cdot \begin{bmatrix} \tilde{r}_1 \\ \tilde{r}_2 \end{bmatrix} = \mathbf{w}' \tilde{\mathbf{r}}.$$

The portfolio expected return in matrix notation is

$$E[\tilde{r}_p] = E[\mathbf{w}'\tilde{\mathbf{r}}] = \mathbf{w}'E[\tilde{\mathbf{r}}] = [\, w_1 \quad w_1 \,] \cdot \begin{bmatrix} E[\tilde{r}_1] \\ E[\tilde{r}_2] \end{bmatrix} = \mathbf{w}'\boldsymbol{\mu}.$$

The portfolio variance in matrix notation is

$$\sigma_p^2 = \mathbf{w}'\boldsymbol{\Sigma}\mathbf{w} = [\, w_1 \quad w_2 \,] \cdot \begin{bmatrix} \sigma_1^2 & \sigma_{12} \\ \sigma_{21} & \sigma_2^2 \end{bmatrix} \cdot \begin{bmatrix} w_1 \\ w_2 \end{bmatrix}$$

$$= [\, w_1\sigma_1^2 + w_2\sigma_{21} \quad w_1\sigma_{12} + w_2\sigma_2^2 \,] \cdot \begin{bmatrix} w_1 \\ w_2 \end{bmatrix}.$$

Note that the last expression equals

$$w_1^2\sigma_1^2 + w_2^2\sigma_2^2 + 2w_1w_2\sigma_{12}$$

which is the same expression as the expression for variance we derived in section 7.1.

If we are given the correlation matrix rather than the covariance matrix, then we can compute the portfolio variance as

$$\sigma_p^2 = [\, w_1\sigma_1 \quad w_2\sigma_2 \,] \cdot \begin{bmatrix} 1 & \rho_{12} \\ \rho_{21} & 1 \end{bmatrix} \cdot \begin{bmatrix} w_1\sigma_1 \\ w_2\sigma_2 \end{bmatrix}$$

$$= [\, w_1\sigma_1 + w_2\sigma_2\rho_{21} \quad w_1\sigma_1\rho_{12} + w_2\sigma_2 \,] \cdot \begin{bmatrix} w_1\sigma_1 \\ w_2\sigma_2 \end{bmatrix}$$

$$= w_1^2\sigma_1^2 + w_2^2\sigma_2^2 + 2w_1w_2\sigma_1\sigma_2\rho_{12},$$

which again is equivalent to the expression for variance we derived in section 7.1 because $\sigma_1\sigma_2\rho_{12} = \sigma_{12}$.

The classical mean-variance portfolio allocation problem is formulated as follows:

$$\min_{\mathbf{w}} \quad \mathbf{w}'\boldsymbol{\Sigma}\mathbf{w}$$

$$\text{s.t.} \quad \mathbf{w}'\boldsymbol{\mu} = r_{\text{target}}$$

$$\mathbf{w}'\boldsymbol{\iota} = 1$$

Note that the objective function of this optimization problem is quadratic in the decision variables $\mathbf{w}$.[6] It turns out that this minimization problem is *convex* because the objective function is convex and all the constraints are linear functions of the decision variables.[7] To see that the objective function is a convex function of the decision variables w, consider the portfolio of two assets. The weight of the second asset, w_2, can be expressed through the weight of the first asset, w_1, as $w_2 = 1 - w_1$. Plugging into the expression for the portfolio variance, we obtain

$$\sigma_p^2 = w_1^2\sigma_1^2 + (1 - w_1)^2\sigma_2^2 + 2w_1(1 - w_1)\rho_{12}\sigma_1\sigma_2$$
$$= w_1^2(\sigma_1^2 + \sigma_2^2 - 2\rho_{12}\sigma_1\sigma_2) + w_1(-2\sigma_2^2 + 2\rho_{12}\sigma_1\sigma_2) + \sigma_2^2.$$

The sign of the coefficient in front of the decision variable w_1^2 determines whether the quadratic objective function will be concave or convex (see Exhibit 5.3 in Chapter 5). Note that the coefficient can be written as

$$\sigma_1^2 + \sigma_2^2 - 2\sigma_1\sigma_2 + 2\sigma_1\sigma_2 - 2\rho_{12}\sigma_1\sigma_2$$
$$= (\sigma_1^2 + \sigma_2^2 - 2\sigma_1\sigma_2) + 2\sigma_1\sigma_2(1 - \rho_{12})$$
$$= \underbrace{(\sigma_1 - \sigma_2)^2}_{\geq 0 \text{ (squared term)}} + \underbrace{2\sigma_1\sigma_2(1 - \rho_{12})}_{\geq 0 \text{ (because } -1 \leq \rho_{12} \leq 1)}$$

so it is always nonnegative. Therefore, the objective function has the shape in Exhibit 5.3(A) and, as a result, minimization will bring us to the global minimum at the tip of the curve.[8]

The optimal solution for the classical mean-variance portfolio allocation problem can be found in closed form by using Lagrange multipliers. The optimal weights are

$$\mathbf{w}^* = \mathbf{g} + \mathbf{h} \cdot r_{\text{target}},$$

where

$$\mathbf{g} = \frac{1}{ac - b^2} \cdot \mathbf{\Sigma}^{-1} \cdot [c \cdot \iota - b \cdot \mathbf{\mu}],$$

$$\mathbf{h} = \frac{1}{ac - b^2} \cdot \mathbf{\Sigma}^{-1} \cdot [a \cdot \mathbf{\mu} - b \cdot \iota]$$

and

$$a = \iota'\mathbf{\Sigma}^{-1}\iota.$$
$$b = \iota'\mathbf{\Sigma}^{-1}\mathbf{\mu}.$$
$$c = \mathbf{\mu}'\mathbf{\Sigma}^{-1}\mathbf{\mu}.$$

Typically, however, the classical mean-variance optimization is modified to include additional constraints or to express the objective in a different way, so no closed-form solution exists, and an optimization solver must be used to solve for the optimal weights. We provide instructions and code for the implementation of the mean-variance problem with Excel Solver and MATLAB's Optimization Toolbox in this chapter's Software Hints.

It is important to note that the problem of minimizing the portfolio variance is equivalent to the problem of minimizing the portfolio standard deviation (which is the square root of the portfolio variance) in the sense that the optimal weights will be the same. Minimizing the portfolio variance, however, is more solver-friendly. It is preferable that the minimum variance formulation is implemented with optimization software. The optimal portfolio standard deviation can then be easily derived from the optimal portfolio variance.

7.3 EFFICIENT FRONTIERS

Let us consider again the two-stock example from section 7.1, which is illustrated in worksheet **Diversification** in the file **Ch7-Diversification2Stocks .xlsm**. As the weight of Stock 1 in the portfolio increases, the portfolio expected return and risk trace out the solid curve in Exhibit 7.2(A). Each point on this curve is obtained for a different combination of stock weights. The point at the top right part of the curve is the portfolio obtained if 100% is invested in Stock 2. Note that that portfolio's expected return is 12.1% (the expected return of Stock 2) and its standard deviation is 15.8% (the standard deviation of Stock 2). At the other end (the point at the bottom right part of the curve) is a portfolio in which 100% is invested in Stock 1. As we trace the curve between its top rightmost point and its bottom rightmost point, we obtain different portfolio risk-return characteristics. It is difficult to say which risk-return combination is "optimal"—it will depend on the individual's risk tolerance. What we can say, however, is that no rational investor would prefer portfolios located on the lower part of the curve, such as Portfolio B in Exhibit 7.3(A). For the same level of portfolio risk (standard deviation of 13.0%), the investor could obtain a higher expected return—that of Portfolio A. Therefore, Portfolio A dominates Portfolio B. Exhibit 7.3(B) illustrates the *efficient frontier*—the upper part of the curve, which contains the set of portfolios that dominate all other portfolios given a specific tolerance for the level of risk or the level of expected return.

Consider now a portfolio of N assets, where N is greater than two. The set of all portfolio risk-return pairs obtained when varying the weights of the

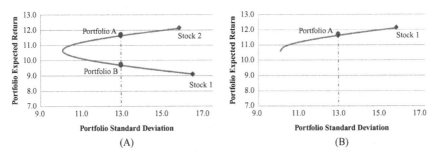

EXHIBIT 7.3 (A) Possible pairings of portfolio expected return and standard deviation as the weights of the two stocks vary between 0 and 1; (B) portfolio efficient frontier.

individual assets fills the shaded area in Exhibit 7.4. The Markowitz mean-variance formulation explained in section 7.2 helps us find the portfolios along the upper part of the curve (between Portfolio D and Portfolio E on the graph)—that is, the portfolios along the efficient frontier. Those portfolios offer the lowest standard deviation for a given level of expected return, and provide the best possible trade-off between return and risk. All portfolios in the shaded area (such as Portfolio C) and along the lower part of the curve (such as Portfolio B) are dominated by the portfolios on the efficient frontier. All portfolios above the efficient frontier (higher on the graph than the curve defined by Portfolios A, D, and E) are unattainable. Portfolio D has the lowest possible standard deviation among all combinations of weights for the assets in the portfolio. It is called the *minimum variance portfolio*.

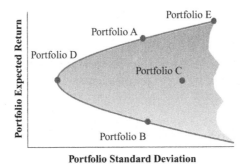

EXHIBIT 7.4 Feasible and mean-variance efficient portfolios.

If more assets are added to the portfolio, there is obviously a higher number of possible combinations of weights for these assets in the portfolio. The feasible set in Exhibit 7.4 widens and the efficient frontier gets pushed outward to reflect the fact that there are now more possibilities for diversification.

To construct the efficient frontier, we simply solve the portfolio optimization problem from section 7.2 in this chapter, and plot the optimal standard deviation obtained for any level of target expected return. Code for calculating the efficient frontier with Excel (using VBA) and MATLAB is provided on the companion web site, and an explanation of the implementation is given in this chapter's Software Hints.

7.4 ALTERNATIVE FORMULATIONS OF THE CLASSICAL MEAN-VARIANCE OPTIMIZATION PROBLEM

The mean-variance optimization problem we introduced in section 7.2 has a couple of alternative but equivalent formulations that are used in practice.

7.4.1 Expected Return Formulation

Instead of imposing a constraint on the expected return and minimizing the portfolio variance, we could impose a constraint on the portfolio variance and maximize the expected return. The optimization formulation is then

$$
\begin{aligned}
\max_{\mathbf{w}} \quad & \mathbf{w}'\boldsymbol{\mu} \\
\text{s.t.} \quad & \mathbf{w}'\boldsymbol{\Sigma}\mathbf{w} = \sigma_{\text{target}}^2 \\
& \mathbf{w}'\boldsymbol{\iota} = 1
\end{aligned}
$$

This formulation, which we will refer to as the *expected return maximization formulation* of the classical mean-variance optimization problem, is particularly widely used by portfolio managers whose goal is to limit their risk relative to a benchmark. Such applications are discussed in Chapter 9.

7.4.2 Risk Aversion Formulation

Another possible formulation is to model the trade-off between risk and return directly through the objective function. This can be accomplished by assigning a penalty term for high portfolio variance, that is, a risk-aversion coefficient λ. The *risk aversion mean-variance formulation* is stated as follows:

$$\max_{\mathbf{w}} \quad \mathbf{w}'\mu - \lambda \cdot \mathbf{w}'\Sigma\mathbf{w}$$
$$\text{s.t.} \quad \mathbf{w}'\iota = 1$$

The risk aversion coefficient λ is referred to as the *Arrow-Pratt risk aversion coefficient*. When λ is small, the aversion to risk is also small, leading to more risky portfolios because the portfolio variance is not penalized as much in the objective of the optimization problem. If we gradually increase λ starting from 0, and we solve the optimization problem for each value of λ, we in fact calculate every portfolio along the efficient frontier. It is a common practice to calibrate λ so that the portfolio has the desired risk-return characteristics ("risk profile"). The calibration is often performed via backtests with historical data. For most portfolio allocation decisions in practice, the risk aversion coefficient is somewhere between 2 and 4.

7.5 THE CAPITAL MARKET LINE

So far, we described Markowitz's framework for selecting an optimal portfolio of risky assets. As demonstrated by Sharpe (1964), Lintner (1965) and Tobin (1958), however, the efficient set of portfolios available to investors who can in addition invest in a risk-free asset (think of it as borrowing or lending money), is superior to the efficient set of portfolios available to investors who can only invest in risky assets.

Let us assume that there is a risk-free asset, with a risk-free return denoted by r_f, and that the investor can borrow and lend at this rate.[9] The investor still needs to select weights $\mathbf{w} = (w_1, \ldots, w_N)$ for the N risky assets, but the weights for the risky assets no longer need to add up to 1 because the remainder can be absorbed by the riskless asset. Therefore, the total portfolio return is

$$\mathbf{w}'\mathbf{r} + (1 - \mathbf{w}'\iota) \cdot r_f.$$

Since the return on the risk-free asset is assumed to be known and fixed, the total expected portfolio return is

$$\mathbf{w}'\mu + (1 + \mathbf{w}'\iota) \cdot r_f$$

and the portfolio variance is

$$\mathbf{w}'\boldsymbol{\Sigma}\mathbf{w}.$$

Note that the portfolio variance is the same as in the case of a portfolio of all risky assets because the risk-free asset does not contribute to the total portfolio risk.

The minimum variance portfolio optimization problem can therefore be formulated as

$$\min_{\mathbf{w}} \quad \mathbf{w}'\boldsymbol{\Sigma}\mathbf{w}$$
$$\text{s.t.} \quad \mathbf{w}'\boldsymbol{\mu} + r_f \cdot (1 - \mathbf{w}'\boldsymbol{\iota}) = r_{\text{target}}$$

and, similarly to the case with no risk-free asset, the optimal solution can be found by using an optimizer or computed in closed form. It turns out that the optimal portfolio weights are given by the formula

$$\mathbf{w} = C \cdot \boldsymbol{\Sigma}^{-1} \cdot (\boldsymbol{\mu} - r_f \cdot \boldsymbol{\iota})$$

where

$$C = \frac{r_{\text{target}} - r_f}{(\boldsymbol{\mu} - r_f \cdot \boldsymbol{\iota})'\boldsymbol{\Sigma}^{-1}(\boldsymbol{\mu} - r_f \cdot \boldsymbol{\iota})}$$

This formula suggests that the weights of the risky assets are proportional to the vector $\boldsymbol{\Sigma}^{-1} \cdot (\boldsymbol{\mu} - r_f \cdot \boldsymbol{\iota})$, with a proportionality constant C. Therefore, with a risk-free asset, all minimum variance portfolios are a combination of the risk-free asset and a given risky portfolio. This risky portfolio is called the *tangency portfolio*. Under certain assumptions, it can be shown that the tangency portfolio must consist of all assets available to investors, and each asset must be held in proportion to its market value relative to the total market value of all assets.[10] Hence, the tangency portfolio is often referred to as the *market portfolio*, or simply *the market*.

The composition of the market portfolio, $\mathbf{w}^M$ can be computed explicitly as[11]

$$\mathbf{w}^M = \frac{1}{\boldsymbol{\iota}'\boldsymbol{\Sigma}(\boldsymbol{\mu} - r_f \cdot \boldsymbol{\iota})} \cdot \boldsymbol{\Sigma}^{-1}(\boldsymbol{\mu} - r_f \cdot \boldsymbol{\iota})$$

It turns out, actually, that the market portfolio is also the optimal solution for the following optimization problem:

$$\max_{\mathbf{w}} \quad \frac{\mathbf{w}'\boldsymbol{\mu} - r_f}{\sqrt{\mathbf{w}'\boldsymbol{\Sigma}\mathbf{w}}}$$
$$\text{s.t.} \quad \mathbf{w}'\boldsymbol{\iota} = 1$$

The expression in the objective function is called the *Sharpe ratio*.[12] It is the ratio of the portfolio excess return (relative to the risk-free asset) to the portfolio standard deviation, that is, it represents the trade-off between return ($\mathbf{w}'\boldsymbol{\mu} - r_f$) and risk ($\sqrt{\mathbf{w}'\boldsymbol{\Sigma}\mathbf{w}}$). The Sharpe ratio is widely used in the context of evaluating portfolio performance.

The fact that all risky portfolios available to the investor are linear combinations of the market portfolio and the risk free rate means that they all lie on a line (see Exhibit 7.5). This line is called the *Capital Market Line* (CML). Observe that all portfolios that lie on the Markowitz efficient frontier are inferior to the portfolios on the CML in the sense that they result in a lower expected return for the same amount of risk. For example, in Exhibit 7.5, Portfolio A, which is on the Markowitz efficient frontier, has a lower expected return than Portfolio B, which is on the CML. The only portfolio on the Markowitz efficient frontier that is not dominated by portfolios on the CML is the tangency portfolio.

If we assume that all investors use the mean-variance framework, then every investor will select a portfolio on the CML that represents a combination of the market portfolio, and borrowing or lending at the risk-free rate.

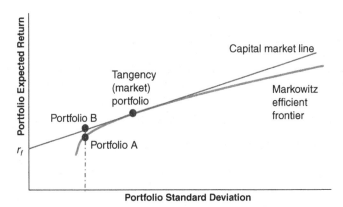

EXHIBIT 7.5 Capital market line.

This important property of the mean-variance framework is called *separation*. Portfolios on the CML to the left of the market portfolio represent combinations of risky assets and the risk-free asset. Portfolios on the CML to the right of the market portfolio represent purchases of risky assets made with funds borrowed at the risk-free rate.

The separation property also has important implications in practice. Practical portfolio construction usually reduces to the following two steps:

1. Asset allocation: Decide how to allocate the investor's wealth between the risk-free security and the set of risky securities.
2. Risky portfolio construction: Decide how to distribute the risky portion of the investment among the set of risky securities.

We can derive a formula for the CML algebraically. The reason for going though this exercise will become clear in Chapter 11, when we link the CML to an important modeling tool used in practical portfolio management: risk factor models.

If all investors invest a portion w_{rf} of their portfolio in the risk free asset, and a portion w_M in the market portfolio, then their expected portfolio returns, $E[r_p]$, are equal to the weighted averages of the expected returns of the two assets:

$$E[r_p] = w_{rf} \cdot r_f + w_M \cdot E[r_M].$$

Since the two portfolio weights must add up to 1, we can rewrite the preceding equality as

$$E[r_p] = r_f + w_M \cdot (E[r_M] - r_f).$$

The return on the risk-free asset and the return on the market portfolio are uncorrelated and the variance of the risk-free asset is equal to zero. Therefore, the variance of the portfolio consisting of the risk-free asset and the market portfolio is given by (see section 7.1 in this chapter):

$$\sigma_p^2 = w_{rf}^2 \sigma_{rf}^2 + w_M^2 \sigma_M^2 + 2 w_{rf} w_M \sigma_{rf} \sigma_M \rho_{(rf,M)}$$
$$= w_M^2 \sigma_M^2$$

Since the standard deviation is the square root of the variance, we can write

$$\sigma_p = w_M \sigma_M$$

Hence, the weight of the market portfolio can be expressed as

$$w_M = \frac{\sigma_p}{\sigma_M}.$$

If we substitute the previous result and rearrange terms, we get an explicit line equation for the CML:

$$E[r_p] = r_f + \left(\frac{E[r_M] - r_f}{\sigma_M} \right) \cdot \sigma_p.$$

The bracketed expression in the second term in the equation for the CML,

$$\left(\frac{E[r_M] - r_f}{\sigma_M} \right),$$

is referred to as the *risk premium*. It is also referred to as the *equilibrium market price of risk* because it, being the slope of the CML, determines the additional expected return needed to compensate for a unit change in risk (standard deviation).

7.6 EXPECTED UTILITY THEORY

In the classical Markowitz framework, the investor chooses a desired trade-off between risk and return, and solves an optimization problem to find the portfolio weights that result in a portfolio with the desired risk profile. Alternatively, risk preferences can be expressed through *utility functions*. An investor's utility function assigns values to levels of wealth. The *expected utility framework* is based on the idea that a rational investor would choose his portfolio allocation **w** so as to maximize his expected utility one time period ahead. More formally, let the investor's utility function be denoted by u, and let $\tilde{W}$ denote his end-of-period wealth. The investor's goal is to maximize $E[u(\tilde{W})]$, the "weighted average" of the values for the investor's utility evaluated at the possible outcomes for his wealth at the end of the time period. If his wealth at time 0 is W_0, then his expected utility optimization problem can be formulated as

$$\max_{\mathbf{w}} \quad E\left[u(W_0 \cdot (1 + \mathbf{w}'\tilde{\mathbf{r}})) \right]$$

$$\text{s.t.} \quad \mathbf{w}'\iota = 1$$

The Markowitz framework is consistent with expected utility theory in two cases. The first case is when asset returns are assumed to follow normal distributions. When returns follow a multivariate normal distribution, randomness is completely described by the returns' means, variances, and covariances. Therefore, $\mathbf{w}'\tilde{\mathbf{r}}$ can be written as a function of means, variances, and covariances, so $u(W_0 \cdot (1 + \mathbf{w}'\tilde{\mathbf{r}}))$ is also an expression that depends entirely on the means, variances and covariances, and so does its expected value E. This is consistent with the mean-variance optimization philosophy.

The second case is when investors are assumed to have quadratic utility functions. We explain the quadratic utility function in more detail next.

Quadratic Utility Function

A quadratic utility function has the form

$$u(x) = x - \frac{b}{2}x^2, \quad b > 0.$$

If we plug in $x = W_0 \cdot (1 + \mathbf{w}'\tilde{\mathbf{r}})$, we get the following expression for expected utility:

$$
\begin{aligned}
E\left[u(W_0 \cdot (1 + \mathbf{w}'\tilde{\mathbf{r}}))\right] &= \\
&= E[W_0 \cdot (1 + \mathbf{w}'\tilde{\mathbf{r}}) - \frac{b}{2} \cdot W_0^2 \cdot (1 + \mathbf{w}'\tilde{\mathbf{r}})^2] \\
&= E[W_0 + W_0 \cdot \mathbf{w}'\tilde{\mathbf{r}} - \frac{b}{2} \cdot W_0^2 - \frac{b}{2} \cdot W_0^2 \cdot (\mathbf{w}'\tilde{\mathbf{r}})^2 - \frac{b}{2} \cdot 2 \cdot W_0^2 \cdot \mathbf{w}'\tilde{\mathbf{r}}] \\
&= W_0 + W_0 \cdot E[\mathbf{w}'\tilde{\mathbf{r}}] - \frac{b}{2} \cdot W_0^2 - \frac{b}{2} \cdot W_0^2 \cdot E[(\mathbf{w}'\tilde{\mathbf{r}})^2] - \frac{b}{2} \cdot 2 \cdot W_0^2 \cdot E[\mathbf{w}'\tilde{\mathbf{r}}] \\
&= W_0 - \frac{b}{2} \cdot W_0^2 + W_0 \cdot E[\mathbf{w}'\tilde{\mathbf{r}}] - \frac{b}{2} \cdot W_0^2 \cdot \left(E[(\mathbf{w}'\tilde{\mathbf{r}})^2] + 2 \cdot E[\mathbf{w}'\tilde{\mathbf{r}}]\right) \\
&= u(W_0) + W_0 \cdot \mu_p - \frac{b}{2} \cdot W_0^2 \cdot \left(E[(\mathbf{w}'\tilde{\mathbf{r}})^2] + 2 \cdot \mu_p\right) \\
&= u(W_0) + W_0 \cdot \mu_p - \frac{b}{2} \cdot W_0^2 \cdot 2 \cdot \mu_p - \frac{b}{2} \cdot W_0^2 \cdot \left(\underbrace{E[(\mathbf{w}'\tilde{\mathbf{r}})^2] + \mu_p^2}_{\sigma_p^2} - \mu_p^2]\right) \\
&= u(W_0) + W_0 \cdot \mu_p \cdot (1 - b \cdot W_0) - \frac{b}{2} \cdot W_0^2 \cdot (\sigma_p^2 - \mu_p^2)
\end{aligned}
$$

Here μ_p and σ_p^2 denote the mean and the variance of the end-of-period portfolio return, respectively. The preceding expression illustrates that the portfolio mean and variance are sufficient for describing the expected utility of an investor with a quadratic utility function. Moreover, increasing the expected return of the portfolio increases the investor's expected utility, and decreasing the portfolio standard deviation decreases the investor's expected utility, which is consistent with the mean-variance optimization framework.

The general shape of the quadratic utility function is illustrated in Exhibit 7.6. As the graph shows, the quadratic utility function makes some unrealistic assumptions on investor behavior. The function is not monotonically increasing. At some level of wealth (specifically, at values greater than $1/b$), the utility of investors decreases as their wealth increases, which is a fairly unnatural assumption. A justification for the use of Markowitz's model, however, has been the assumption that asset returns follow normal distributions, even though many studies indicate otherwise. As we explained at the beginning of this section, in the case of normal distributions for returns, a mean-variance approach makes sense independently of the shape of the investors' utility functions.

The Markowitz model is useful also because it provides an approximation to other utility functions. Before we discuss approximating general utility functions, let us introduce a few more examples of utility functions. As a general rule, the shapes of widely used utility functions assume that investors are risk averse. A risk-averse investor is somebody who is indifferent or unwilling to accept a risky payoff at its expected value. Instead, a risk-averse investor requires additional compensation for accepting a risky payoff instead of a certain payoff, even if the expected values of the two payoffs are the same. In other words, the expected utility from an uncertain payoff of a risk-averse person is always less than or equal to the utility of the expected payoff. Mathematically, it turns out that risk-averseness translates into concave utility function shapes.[13] A "straight-line" utility function corresponds to indifference to risk, or *risk neutrality* because it represents a situation in which the expected utility of the uncertain payoff equals the utility of the expected payoff. The more "curved" (the less "flat") the utility functions are, the more risk-averse investors are assumed to be. The quadratic utility function (explained above) and the exponential, power, logarithmic utility functions (explained later) all assume risk averseness.

Linear Utility Function

The linear utility function is the simplest kind of utility function. It has the form

$$u(x) = a + b \cdot x$$

for some parameters a and b. As we mentioned previously, the linear utility function assumes that investors are *risk-neutral*, that is, that they are concerned only with expected return, not with risk. Recall from section 3.9 in Chapter 3 that the expected value of a linear function of a random variable is a linear function of the expected value of a random variable. The expected utility of the end-of-period wealth is

$$E[u(\tilde{W})] = E[a + b \cdot \tilde{W}] = a + b \cdot E[\tilde{W}]$$

whereas the utility of the expected end-of-period wealth is

$$u(E[\tilde{W}]) = a + b \cdot E[\tilde{W}].$$

Therefore, $E[u(\tilde{W})] = u(E[\tilde{W}])$. An investor with a linear utility function is indifferent between receiving a certain outcome of $E[\tilde{W}]$ and an uncertain outcome that is "on average" equal to $E[\tilde{W}]$. See Exhibit 7.6. for an illustration of the shape of the linear utility function.

Exponential Utility Function

The exponential utility function has the form

$$u(x) = -\frac{1}{a}e^{-ax}, \quad a > 0$$

Note that the exponential utility has negative values; however, this does not matter because the function is monotonically increasing (see Exhibit 7.6), and it is possible to compare the relative utilities for different levels of wealth.

Power Utility Function

The power utility function is of the form

$$u(x) = ax^a, \quad 0 < a \leq 1$$

(see Exhibit 7.6).

Logarithmic Utility Function

The logarithmic utility function has the form

$$u(x) = \ln(x)$$

Note that this function is only defined for $x > 0$ (see Exhibit 7.6).

In practice, it is very difficult to determine the utility function of an investor, and the situation is further complicated by the fact that the investor's utility function type and the degree of risk averseness may change depending on circumstances. The choice of utility function for portfolio allocation depends on the application, as well as computational considerations. For example, the exponential utility function is widely used because it is generally easier to optimize than some of the other utility functions.

The problem of expected utility optimization is not as intractable as it used to be, given the advances in computational power today. However,

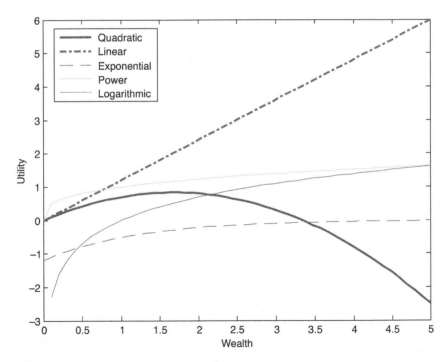

EXHIBIT 7.6 Examples of different utility functions.

virtually no practitioners rely on a full-scale utility optimization approach. Typically, practitioners work with a mean-variance approximation of a chosen utility function that best represents their investors' preferences. A general utility function can be approximated by mean-variance optimization by expanding the expression for expected utility using Taylor series around the expected end-of-period wealth.[14] Jean (1971) was the first to suggest this approach. Later, more general and rigorous discussion was provided by several authors. The main idea is as follows.

Let us denote the expected end-of-period wealth by $\hat{W}$. Note that

$$\hat{W} = E[W_0 \cdot (1 + \mathbf{w}'\tilde{\mathbf{r}})] = E[W_0] + E[W_0 \cdot (\mathbf{w}'\tilde{\mathbf{r}})] = W_0 + W_0 \cdot \mathbf{w}'\boldsymbol{\mu}$$

The end-of-period expected utility can be expanded in a Taylor series around the expected end-of-period wealth $\hat{W}$:

$$E[u(\tilde{W})] = u(\hat{W}) + u'(\hat{W}) \cdot E[\tilde{W} - \hat{W}] + \frac{1}{2!} \cdot u''(\hat{W}) \cdot E[(\tilde{W} - \hat{W})^2]$$

$$+ \frac{1}{3!} \cdot u'''(\hat{W}) \cdot E[(\tilde{W} - \hat{W})^3] + \frac{1}{4!} \cdot u''''(\hat{W}) \cdot E[(\tilde{W} - \hat{W})^4]$$

$$+ O((\tilde{W} - \hat{W})^5)$$

The functions $E[(\tilde{W} - \hat{W})^k]$, $k = 1, 2, 3, \ldots$ are called the *central moments* of the random variable $\tilde{W}$. They are related to the moments of the distribution of the random variable $\tilde{W}$.[15] It is easy to see that the second central moment, $E[(\tilde{W} - \hat{W})^2]$, is actually the variance of the random variable $\tilde{W}$.[16] Since $E[W - \hat{W}] = E[W] - \hat{W} = 0$, we can write

$$E[u(\tilde{W})] = u(\hat{W}) + \frac{1}{2!} \cdot u''(\hat{W}) \cdot E[(\tilde{W} - \hat{W})^2]$$

$$+ \frac{1}{3!} \cdot u'''(\hat{W}) \cdot E[(\tilde{W} - \hat{W})^3] + \frac{1}{4!} \cdot u''''(\hat{W}) \cdot E[(\tilde{W} - \hat{W})^4]$$

$$+ O((\tilde{W} - \hat{W})^5)$$

An approximation for the problem of maximizing the expected utility of an investor can be achieved by using only the first two terms of the preceding expression. These expressions involve the expected end-of-period wealth and the variance of the expected end-of-period wealth in a way consistent with the classical mean-variance framework. A complete formulation of the optimization problem would, of course, involve the third term (which is related to skewness), the fourth term (which is related to kurtosis), and all other higher-order central moment terms.

Levy and Markowitz (1979) compared the performance of portfolio allocations obtained by maximizing expected power utility with that of portfolio allocations obtained with standard mean-variance optimization, and found that the mean-variance approximation worked quite well. Cremers, Kritzman, and Page (2003, 2005) showed empirically that the log and the power utility functions are fairly insensitive to higher moments, and, therefore, mean-variance optimization performs quite well for investors with logarithmic or power utility. However, for discontinuous or S-shaped utility functions, this result no longer holds, and mean-variance optimization leads to a significant loss in utility compared to an optimization of the full utility function.[17]

SUMMARY

- The basic principle of modern portfolio theory, which originated in Harry Markowitz's work from 1952, is that for a given level of expected return, a rational investor would select the portfolio with the minimum variance among all possible portfolios. This chapter introduced three equivalent formulations of this principle: (1) the portfolio variance minimization formulation; (2) the expected return maximization formulation; and (3) the risk-aversion formulation.
- Markowitz's mean-variance framework in effect quantified the idea of diversification as a prudent strategy. Mathematically, the portfolio variance is a sum of terms including both the variances of the returns of the individual assets and the covariances (equivalently, the correlations) between those returns. In a well-diversified portfolio, the weak performance of a single asset will be compensated by the performance of other assets that are not strongly correlated with that asset.
- Portfolio allocations obtained by minimizing the portfolio variance are called mean-variance efficient portfolios. The set of all mean-variance efficient portfolios is called the efficient frontier.
- The portfolio on the efficient frontier with the smallest variance is called the global minimum variance portfolio.
- A utility function assigns a value to all possible outcomes faced by an investor. The expected utility is the weighted average of these values over all possible outcomes, where the weights correspond to the probabilities of these outcomes. The concept of expected utility maximization allows us to generalize the framework of optimal portfolio choice.

- While it is difficult to produce the utility function for a specific investor, commonly used types of utility functions include exponential, logarithmic, power, and quadratic. These functions all incorporate risk averseness. The *linear* utility function represents the preferences of an investor who is risk neutral, that is, who is concerned only with expected outcome, and not with the risk associated with that outcome.
- The Markowitz mean-variance portfolio optimization framework is consistent with the expected utility maximization framework in two cases: when future asset returns are assumed to follow normal distributions, or when investors are assumed to have quadratic utility functions. In addition, the Markowitz framework works well as an approximation to expected utility maximization for several important types of utility functions.

SOFTWARE HINTS

We illustrate how to implement the mean-variance optimization problem with Excel Solver and MATLAB's Optimization Toolbox for the example with two stocks from section 7.1. Before implementing the code, it would be helpful to review Chapter 5. Excel Solver cannot handle large problems, and we recommend that readers switch to a different optimization package, such as Premium Solver[18] and Palisade's Evolver[19] if their problem is of a larger size. Alternatively, readers can use MATLAB's or ILOG CPLEX's optimization engine from within Excel.

Excel

An example of the implementation of the mean-variance optimization problem with two stocks from Chapter 7.1 is provided in file **Ch7-Diversification2Stocks.xlsm**. Worksheet **Optimization** illustrates the implementation of the mean-variance optimization problem using the long-hand formulas from Chapter 7.2, whereas worksheet **Optimization (Mx)** illustrates the implementation using the array manipulation function MMULT in Excel, which is useful for portfolios with more than two assets.

Worksheet Setup We start out with worksheet **Optimization**. (See a screenshot in Exhibit 7.7.) The input data for the problem is stored as follows: the assets' expected returns (cells B2:C2), the assets' standard deviations (cells B3:C3), and their correlation coefficient (cell B5). The worksheet is set up to enable computing the minimum portfolio variance by considering

	A	B	C	D	E	F
1		Stock 1	Stock 2			
2	Expected returns	9.10	12.10			
3	Standard deviations	16.50	15.80			
4						
5	Correlation coefficient	-0.22		Covariance	-57.35	
6	**Target return**	**11.00**				
7						
8	**Optimization problem formulation:**					
9						
10	Decision Variables	Stock 1	Stock 2			
11	weights	0.37	0.63			
12						
13	**Objective Function**	Using covariance			Using correlation	
14	Minimize portfolio variance	110.10			110.10	
15						
16	Constraints					
17	Expected portfolio return	13.79 >=		11.00		
18	Sum of weights	1.00 =		1.00		
19						
20						
21						

| ⏮ ◀ ▶ ⏭ | Diversification | **Optimization** | Optimization (Mx) | Efficient Frontier | ⟲ |

EXHIBIT 7.7 Setup for the mean-variance portfolio optimization problem in Excel.

either the correlation or the covariance between the two assets. The covariance is computed in cell E5 as =B5*B3*C3 (the correlation coefficient times the two standard deviations; see section 3.8 in Chapter 3). The portfolio target return can be specified in cell B6.

The three building blocks of the optimization model (decision variables, objective function and constraints; see Chapter 5) are specifically outlined in the worksheet for clarity.

Cells B11:C11 will contain the optimal weights. They can be left blank at the beginning, or some arbitrary values can be entered to make sure that the formulas for calculating the portfolio mean and variance are correct.

Cell B14 will contain the optimal portfolio variance, and is linked to the asset weights via the formula

=($B$3^2)*($B$11^2)+($C$3^2)*($C$11^2)+2*$B$11*$C$11*$E$5

(The portfolio standard deviation can be computed by simply taking a square root, SQRT, of the portfolio variance. See also section 7.2 for an explanation of the computation of the portfolio standard variance.)

Alternatively, we can compute the portfolio variance by using the correlation between the two assets. The formula is stored in cell E14:

```
=($B$3^2)*($B$11^2)+($C$3^2)*($C$11^2)+2*$B$5*$B$3*$C$3*$B$
11*$C$11
```

Rows 17 and 18 contain the two standard constraints: the constraint that the portfolio expected return should be greater than or equal to the target return specified in cell B6, and the "budget" constraint that requires that the sum of the portfolio weights should be 1. Since Excel Solver requires that the constraints are specified in a specific format: a cell representing the left hand side is compared to a cell representing the right hand side, cells B17 and B18, dedicated to the "left-hand sides" of the two constraints contain the formulas

```
=$B$2*$B$11+$C$2*$C$11
```

and

```
=$B$11+$C$11
```

whereas cells D17 and D18, dedicated to the "right-hand sides" of the two constraints, contain the bounds: the target return (the number from cell B6) and 1, respectively.

Using Excel Solver   To solve the problem, we call Excel Solver (click the **Data tab** and then click **Solver** in the Analysis group), and enter the values for the target cell (the objective function), the changing cells (the decision variables), and the constraints as shown in Exhibit 7.8.

The optimal portfolio variance for target expected return of 11% is 110.10, for portfolio weights 36.67% and 63.33%. The optimal portfolio standard deviation for that level of target return is therefore $\sqrt{110.10} = 10.49\%$.

When the portfolio consists of more than two stocks, it is convenient to reference inputs as arrays (rather than individual cells) and use Excel array functions such as SUMPRODUCT and MMULT. Worksheet **Optimization (Mx)** contains an example of the implementation of the portfolio problem using Excel's array functions (see Exhibit 7.7).

Applying Array Functions   As explained in Chapter 5, SUMPRODUCT (Array1, Array2) returns the sum of the products of the corresponding individual elements of two arrays. In the portfolio optimization context, we

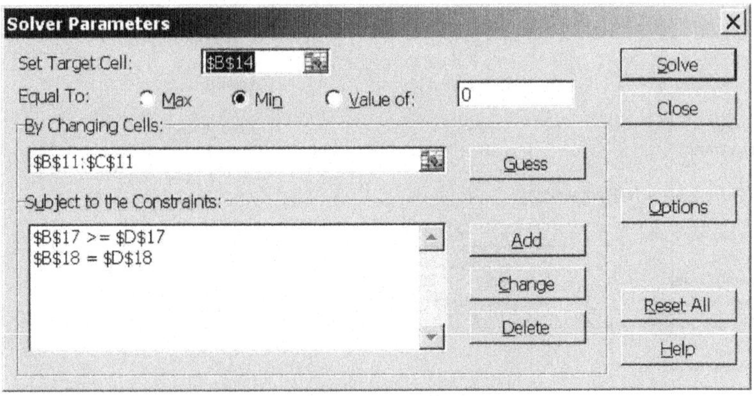

EXHIBIT 7.8 Excel Solver inputs for solving the minimum portfolio standard deviation optimization problem.

can express the expected portfolio return as a "sumproduct" of the individual stocks' returns and their weights. Thus, the formula for portfolio expected return in cell B17 of worksheet **Optimization (Mx)** can be written as

=SUMPRODUCT($B$2:$C$2,$B$11:$C$11)

Alternatively, we can use the MMULT function. MMULT(Array1, Array2) returns the matrix product of two arrays. This implies that the dimensions of the arrays must agree. In other words, while SUMPRODUCT(Array1, Array2) requires that Array1 and Array2 have the same dimensions, MMULT requires that the number of columns of Array1 is the same as the number of rows of Array2. Therefore, to perform the same expected return calculation we performed with SUMPRODUCT, we would need to enter the formula

=MMULT(B11:C11,TRANSPOSE(B2:C2))

in cell B17. In addition, to complete the calculation, it is not sufficient to press simply Enter. After entering the MMULT formula, while the cursor is still active in the formula bar, press Ctrl-Shift-Enter simultaneously.[20] The value of the portfolio variance in cell B14 can be computed similarly. We create the covariance matrix of the two stock returns in cells G6:H7, and reference it in the formula in cell B14 as follows:[21]

=MMULT(MMULT(B11:C11,G6:H7),TRANSPOSE(B11:C11))

	A	B	C	D	E	F	G	H
1		Stock 1	Stock 2			Correlation matrix		
2	Expected returns	9.10	12.10			Stock 1	1	-0.22
3	Standard deviations	16.50	15.80			Stock 2	-0.22	1
4								
5	Correlation	-0.22				Covariance matrix		
6	**Target return**	**11**				Stock 1	272.25	-57.354
7						Stock 2	-57.354	249.64
8	**Optimization problem formulation:**							
9								
10	Decision Variables	Stock 1	Stock 2					
11	weights	0.37	0.63					
12	weights*stdev	6.05	10.01					
13	Objective Function	Using covariance		Using correlation				
14	Minimize portfolio variance	110.10		110.10				
15								
16	Constraints							
17	Expected portfolio return	11.00 >=		11.00				
18	Sum of weights	1.00 =		1.00				
19								
20								
21								

⊢ ◄ ► ⊣   Diversification   Optimization   **Optimization (Mx)**   Efficient Frontier

EXHIBIT 7.9   Setup for the mean-variance portfolio optimization problem with array functions in Excel.

If, instead of the covariance matrix, we would like to use the correlation matrix (cells G2:H2), then we can compute the portfolio variance by first creating an array of products of the weights and the standard deviations for each stock (cells B12:C12 in worksheet **Optimization (Mx)**; see Exhibit 7.9), and then using these products in the formula for the variance in cell D14 as follows:

```
=MMULT(MMULT(B12:C12,G2:H3),TRANSPOSE(B12:C12))
```

Calling Excel Solver happens in the same way as before.

Calculating the Efficient Frontier with VBA   To calculate the efficient frontier, we would need to make multiple calls to Solver. Worksheet Efficient Frontier illustrates the result. The VBA code for creating the efficient frontier can be seen after opening the VBE in the file **Ch7-Diversification2 Stocks.xlsm**.

The code takes the inputs in cells named min_return, increment, and iterations in worksheet **Efficient Frontier**, which happen to be cells N4, N5, and N6, respectively. It starts at the value for min_return, and runs Solver on the optimization problem in worksheet **Optimization (Mx)** with min_return as the expected return. It records the minimum value for the portfolio variance (actually, the optimal portfolio standard deviation, since it takes the square root of the variance), and increases min_return by the amount of the increment. This new value becomes the new expected return, Solver is called, and the optimal solution for the portfolio optimization problem in worksheet **Optimization (Mx)** is recorded. The process continues for a number of times determined by the number of iterations specified by the user in cell N6. At the end, the pairs of expected portfolio returns and optimal portfolio standard deviations are plotted in a graph to obtain the efficient frontier.

To run the script, we can select the Efficient Frontier macro from the list of macros, or click on the button **Generate efficient frontier** in worksheet **Efficient Frontier**. For instructions on how to associate a button with a macro, see section 2.4 in Appendix D on the companion web site.

MATLAB

As explained in Chapter 5, MATLAB's Optimization Toolbox has a number of functions that can be called to solve particular types of optimization problems. To obtain the optimal portfolio allocation, we need to transform the minimum variance problem into one of the standard forms supported by MATLAB, and then call the appropriate function with the correct arguments. The minimum variance portfolio allocation problem is a quadratic optimization problem with linear constraints. The quadprog function in MATLAB solves exactly problems of this kind:

$$\min_{\mathbf{x}} \quad \frac{1}{2}\mathbf{x}'\mathbf{H}\mathbf{x} + \mathbf{f}'\mathbf{x}$$
$$\text{s.t.} \quad \mathbf{A}\mathbf{x} \leq \mathbf{b}$$
$$\mathbf{Aeq} \cdot \mathbf{x} = \mathbf{beq}$$
$$\mathbf{lb} \leq \mathbf{x} \leq \mathbf{ub}$$

and is called with the command

```
quadprog(H,f,A,b,Aeq,beq,lb,ub)
```

A MATLAB script that generates the input data and then calls the optimization solver is contained in the file **EfficientFrontier.m**.

Lines 10–36 in the code solve a single instance of the minimum variance optimization problem, while lines 38–56 repeat the optimization for several values of the target expected return, and use the results to plot the efficient frontier.

Note that the function arguments are specified in terms of the available data. For example, to map the objective function of the mean-variance optimization problem

$$\min_{\mathbf{w}} \quad \mathbf{w}' \Sigma \mathbf{w}$$

into the MATLAB objective function expression

$$\min_{\mathbf{x}} \quad \frac{1}{2} \mathbf{x}' \mathbf{H} \mathbf{x} + \mathbf{f}' \mathbf{x},$$

we set $\mathbf{H} = 2\Sigma$ and create an input vector $\mathbf{f}$ whose entries are all zeros (lines 12–16 in the code).

We need to be careful in specifying the dimensions of the arrays when calling the `quadprog` function in order for the matrix and vector operations to work out correctly. We also need to be careful in specifying the inequalities in the optimization formulation in the correct way. For example, the mean-variance optimization problem formulation has an inequality constraint of the kind

$$\mathbf{w}' \mu \geq r_{\text{target}}.$$

However, the inequality constraint assumed by the `quadprog` function is of the general form

$$\mathbf{A} \mathbf{x} \leq \mathbf{b}$$

that is, the inequality sign points the opposite way. Therefore, we need to specify the required target return constraint in MATLAB as

$$-\mathbf{w}' \mu \leq -r_{\text{target}}.$$

Lines 19 and 20 in the code above create a matrix $\mathbf{A}$ of dimension $1 \times$ `numAssets` equal to the negative of the transpose of the column vector of weights $\mathbf{w}$, and a scalar b equal to the negative of the target return r_{target} so that the above constraint can be passed to the solver.

The command

```
[weights,variance] = quadprog(H,f,A,b,Aeq,beq,lb,ub);
```

on line 32 ensures that the optimal solution to the optimization problem will be stored in a vector called `weights`, and the optimal objective function value (the minimum portfolio variance) will be stored in the scalar `variance`.

Lines 35 and 36 print the values of the optimal standard deviation and the optimal weights to screen.

The MATLAB output from running the previous code is as follows:

```
stdDev =
    10.4928
weights =
    0.3667
    0.6333
```

Lines 44–50 contain a `for` loop that runs the optimization problem for values of the target return between 9.5 and 12, increasing the target return by 0.5 at each iteration. The expected portfolio return and the optimal standard deviation obtained from the optimization output are stored in vectors x and y. Lines 52–56 plot the efficient frontier using the values stored in x and y, and label the graph.

NOTES

1. We need to clarify here that *utility theory*, which was developed in the economics literature before Markowitz's publication, allowed for incorporating risk implicitly by considering special kinds of investor utility functions that described risk averseness. However, Markowitz's publication suggested the first tangible and practical quantitative framework that defined investment decision making explicitly as a trade-off between risk and return. See section 7.6 in this chapter for a brief introduction to utility theory.
2. See Appendix A at the companion web site for a review of matrix notation and definition of matrix transpose (').
3. See Appendix A at the companion web site for a review of matrix array multiplication.
4. See Chapter 2 for a definition of the term short selling.
5. See section 3.8.
6. See Chapter 5 for a review of optimization problem formulations, classification, and terminology.
7. See Chapter 5 for use of convex functions in optimization.
8. This statement is a bit simplified because the function plotted in Exhibit 5.3 is a function of a single variable x, whereas here we have a function of two variables, so the picture would be three-dimensional. The general conclusion, however, is the same.
9. In practice, this assumption is not valid for most investors. Specifically, an investor may not be able to borrow and lend at the same interest rate, or may only be permitted to lend. If there are no short selling restrictions on the risky

assets, however, the theoretical conclusions under such conditions are similar to the results presented in this section. See, for example, Black (1972) and Ingersoll (1987).

10. See Fama (1970).
11. See Chapter 2 in Fabozzi, Kolm, Pachamanova, and Focardi (2007), p. 37.
12. See, for example, Sharpe (1994).
13. See, for example, Chapter 1 in Huang and Litzenberger (1988).
14. The Taylor series is a representation of a function as an infinite sum of terms calculated from the values of its derivatives at a single point. The Taylor series expansion of a function $f(x)$ around a point a is given by

$$f(a) + \frac{f'(a)}{1!} \cdot (x - a) + \frac{f''(a)}{2!} \cdot (x - a)^2 + \cdots$$

where $f'(a), f''(a), \ldots$ are the first, second, $\ldots$ derivatives of the function f evaluated at the point a, and $n! = 1 \cdot 2 \cdot 3 \cdot \ldots \cdot n$.

15. See section 3.6 of Chapter 3.
16. See section 3.6 of Chapter 3.
17. See Kahneman and Tversky (1979).
18. See Frontline Systems, "Our Premium Upgrade for the Excel Solve," *Solver.com,* http://www.solver.com/xlspremsolv.htm.
19. See Palisade, *Evolver,* http://www.palisade.com/evolver/.
20. Note that to obtain the complete output of the MMULT function in Excel, the array of cells that will contain the output needs to be highlighted before the formula is typed and Ctrl-Shift-Enter is pressed. In this example, we did not need to worry about it because the product of two vectors is an array of dimension one. The output will be contained in the active cell. If, however, the expected output array was of dimensions 2×3, and we did not highlight a cell range of size 2×3 cells, then only the first entry of the output 2×3 array would be calculated and returned in the active cell.
21. Note that in this worksheet example, the array of cells containing the portfolio weights is horizontal, rather than vertical. So, we compute the portfolio variance as $w\Sigma w'$ rather than $w'\Sigma w$, which was the standard form for portfolio variance used in this chapter.

CHAPTER 8

Advances in the Theory of Portfolio Risk Measures

Portfolio risk managers either use their experience in stock picking or rely on quantitative modeling techniques in the portfolio selection process. Generally speaking, however, the main objective of portfolio selection is the construction of a portfolio that maximizes expected returns given a certain tolerance for risk. We already introduced one such measure of risk, portfolio variance, in Chapter 7.

As explained in Chapter 7, mean-variance portfolio allocation is optimal in two cases: when investors have quadratic utility functions, or when returns follow a multivariate normal distribution. The former condition is difficult to verify empirically, and it is likely that the utility functions of individuals will vary with market conditions. With respect to the latter condition, although there might be exceptions, the overwhelming empirical evidence suggests that the return distribution for financial assets throughout the world are not normal distributed. This is particularly true of complex derivative securities' returns, as we will see in Chapters 14 through 16, and observable during financial crises such as the 1997 Asian financial crisis, the 1998 Russian financial crisis, and the 2007 subprime mortgage crisis.

In addition to these theoretical reasons, there is an intuitive problem with the portfolio variance as a measure of risk. As we saw in section 3.6.2 of Chapter 3, the variance of a probability distribution is a measure of the spread, or dispersion of the distribution. Using the variance in the portfolio optimization context means that outcomes that are above the expected portfolio returned are deemed as risky as outcomes that are below the expected portfolio return. This is counterintuitive to many, as investors are more likely to be concerned about outcomes that fall short of expectations, rather than outcomes that exceed expectations.

Using the portfolio variance as a risk measure has been a subject of considerable debate in both academic circles and in practice. The goal of this chapter is to discuss the issue in more detail, and present alternative risk measures that have been proposed. Since about the mid-1990s, considerable thought and innovation in the financial industry have been directed toward creating a better understanding of risk and its measurement, and toward improving the management of risk in financial portfolios. There has been an even greater sense of urgency to establish better risk management practices after the collapse of the financial markets in the fall of 2008. We review some important types of risk measures, such as semivariance, Roy's safety-first criterion, and quantile-based risk measures. Also discussed in detail is the history of, estimation of, and portfolio allocation under value-at-risk and conditional value-at-risk—two important risk measures that are widely used in practice.

It is worth noting that Markowitz's portfolio theory and the Capital Asset Pricing Model (CAPM),[1] which builds upon it, still provide a useful framework for incorporating multiple risk sources into a joint portfolio risk measure, and are widely used by asset managers and risk managers. Their use, however, has been mostly restricted to equity portfolio management. It was realized early on that it is difficult to apply the mean-variance framework for fixed-income portfolio management, hedge fund management, or for aggregating risk at the firm level at major financial institutions.

8.1 CLASSES OF RISK MEASURES

Most generally, risk measures can be divided into two classes: *dispersion* and *downside* risk measures. This section provides examples of risk measures from the two categories.

8.1.1 Dispersion Risk Measures

Dispersion risk measures measure the amount of dispersion of the returns around the expected portfolio return. Hence, they are measures of uncertainty in the estimate of the expected portfolio return. Uncertainty, however, does not necessarily quantify risk. Dispersion measures consider both positive and negative deviations from the mean, and treat those deviations as equally risky. In other words, outperformance relative to the mean is penalized as much as underperformance.

Variance and Standard Deviation Because of the key role it plays in the theory of portfolio selection as set forth by Markowitz more than 55 years ago, the portfolio *variance* (or, equivalently, *standard deviation*) is the most well-known dispersion measure. The portfolio variance is defined as

$$\sigma_p^2 = E\left[\left(\tilde{r}_p - E[\tilde{r}_p]\right)^2\right] = E\left[\left(\sum_{i=1}^{N} w_i \tilde{r}_i - \sum_{i=1}^{N} w_i \mu_i\right)^2\right]$$

and the portfolio standard deviation is defined as

$$\sigma_p = \left(E\left[\left(\tilde{r}_p - E[\tilde{r}_p]\right)^2\right]\right)^{1/2} = \left(E\left[\left(\sum_{i=1}^{N} w_i \tilde{r}_i - \sum_{i=1}^{N} w_i \mu_i\right)^2\right]\right)^{1/2}$$

where $\tilde{r}_i$ are the returns of the N individual assets in the portfolio, μ_i are their means, and

$$\tilde{r}_p = \sum_{i=1}^{N} w_i \tilde{r}_i$$

is the return of the portfolio.

As explained in Chapter 7, the expressions for the portfolio variance and standard deviation can be written using matrix notation as

$$\sigma_p^2 = \mathbf{w'\Sigma w}$$

and

$$\sigma_p = \sqrt{\mathbf{w'\Sigma w}}$$

respectively, where $\mathbf{\Sigma}$ is the covariance matrix of the portfolio.

Absolute Deviation Konno and Yamazaki (1991) introduced the *absolute deviation* (AD) portfolio risk measure. Instead of the portfolio standard deviation, which is the average of the squared deviations of the possible realizations of portfolio returns from the expected portfolio return, the absolute deviation measures the average absolute value of the deviations of the possible realizations of portfolio returns from the expected portfolio return. Formally, the absolute deviation risk measure can be written as

$$AD(\tilde{r}_p) = E\left[\left|\tilde{r}_p - E[\tilde{r}_p]\right|\right] = E\left[\left|\sum_{i=1}^{N} w_i \tilde{r}_i - \sum_{i=1}^{N} w_i \mu_i\right|\right]$$

where $\tilde{r}_i$ are the returns of the N individual assets in the portfolio, μ_i are their means, and $\tilde{r}_p$ is the return on the portfolio, as before.[2]

The computation of the optimal mean-absolute deviation portfolio is substantially simplified because the resulting optimization problem is linear and can be solved by standard linear programming algorithms.[3] Another advantage of estimating the portfolio absolute deviation compared to the portfolio standard deviation is that there is no need to estimate the covariance matrix of the assets in the portfolio. Finding a reliable and stable estimate of the covariance matrix is a challenging task in practice.

It can also be shown that if the individual asset returns are multivariate normally distributed, the AD is a multiple of the standard deviation of the portfolio (σ_p). Namely,

$$AD(\tilde{r}_p) = \sqrt{\frac{2}{\pi}} \cdot \sigma_p$$

Hence, if asset returns are multivariate normally distributed, mean-variance and mean-absolute deviation portfolio optimization result in equivalent allocations.

Absolute Moment   The *absolute moment risk measure* of order q is defined as[4]

$$AM_q(\tilde{r}_p) = \left(E\left[|\tilde{r}_p - E[\tilde{r}_p]|^q\right]\right)^{1/q} = \left(E\left[\left|\sum_{i=1}^{N} w_i\tilde{r}_i - \sum_{i=1}^{N} w_i\mu_i\right|^q\right]\right)^{1/q}, \quad q \geq 1$$

It is basically a generalization of the standard deviation $(q = 2)$ and the absolute deviation $(q = 1)$ portfolio risk measures.

8.1.2 Downside Risk Measures

As we mentioned in the introduction to this chapter, most investors are concerned about the outcomes that fall short of expectations, rather than the outcomes that exceed expectations. This fact cannot be accurately represented by the portfolio variance and other dispersion measures. Markowitz (1959) himself acknowledged this shortcoming of his model, and suggested a downside dispersion risk measure, semivariance, as an alternative way of measuring portfolio risk. The same realization prompted research into a number of other *downside dispersion risk measures*, many of which are special cases of the lower-partial moment risk measure (also called the Fishburn risk measure). This section describes several such risk measures.

Lower-Partial Moment   The lower-partial moment risk measure is defined as

$$\left(E\left[\left(\min\left\{\tilde{r}_p - t, 0\right\}\right)^q\right]\right)^{1/q} = \left(E\left[\left(\min\left\{\sum_{i=1}^N w_i \tilde{r}_i - \sum_{i=1}^N w_i \mu_i, 0\right\}\right)^q\right]\right)^{1/q}$$

In the case of a continuous probability distribution for the portfolio return, the expression above is equivalent to

$$\int_{-\infty}^{t} (t - r)^k f(r)\, dr$$

whereas in the case of a discrete probability distribution for the portfolio return, it is equivalent to[5]

$$\sum (t - r)^k \cdot P(\tilde{r} = r)$$

where the sum is over all values of the random variable less than or equal to t.

The constant t represents a cutoff point between the downside of concern to the investor, and the upside that is not of concern. In practice, the value of t is often selected to be the short-term interest rate, the expected return, or a minimum required return. The notation $\tilde{r}$ stands for the random variable representing portfolio return.

On an intuitive level, you can think of the lower partial moment as the "weighted average" of the portfolio return deviations from the threshold (raised to a specific power k) when the return is less than the threshold t. Fishburn (1977) showed that $q = 1$ corresponds to a risk-neutral investor, $0 < q \leq 1$ corresponds to a risk-seeking investor, and $q > 1$ corresponds to a risk-averse investor.

Semivariance   *Semivariance* is defined as the average of the squared deviations from the mean of all values that are below the mean. Thus, it is a special case of the lower partial moment risk measure when $k = 2$ and t

equals the mean of the probability distribution for the portfolio return. The portfolio semivariance can be written as

$$E\left[\min\left\{\left(\sum_{i=1}^{N}w_i\tilde{r}_i - \sum_{i=1}^{N}w_i\mu_i\right)^2, 0\right\}\right]$$

Roy's Safety-First Criterion The theory behind *Roy's safety-first criterion* is that rather than thinking in terms of overall portfolio risk, the investor first makes sure that a certain amount of the invested principal is preserved, so the investor tries to minimize the probability that the return earned is less than or equal to the threshold t.[6] Mathematically, it can be expressed as an optimization problem:

$$\min_{\mathbf{w}} P(\tilde{r}_p \le t)$$

that is,

$$\min_{\mathbf{w}} P\left(\sum_{i=1}^{N}w_i\tilde{r}_i \le t\right)$$

Note that Roy's safety-first criterion is actually a special case of the lower-partial moment formula when $k = 0$.

In the financial industry, Roy's safety-first criterion is often referred to as *shortfall risk*. When the threshold t is zero, the shortfall risk is called the *risk of loss*.

Quantile-Based Risk Measures The theory of stochastic dominance, which gained popularity in the 1970s, provided new tools for comparing probability distributions, and drew attention to so-called quantile-based risk measures. *Quantile-based risk measures* evaluate volatility in terms of the percentiles of a distribution, and are justified from a theoretical point of view in the sense that they are consistent with the preferences of risk-averse investors. The most widely used quantile-based risk measure in practice is *value-at-risk*. More recently, a related risk measure, *conditional value-at-risk* (also encountered as *expected shortfall*), has gained popularity because of its desirable theoretical and computational properties. Conditional value-at-risk is in fact a multiple of the lower-partial moment formula with $k = 1$.

Value-at-risk and conditional value-at-risk are two very important developments in the theory of risk measures. In the remainder of this chapter, we elaborate on the history, estimation, and portfolio allocation under these two risk measures.

8.2 VALUE-AT-RISK

Value-at-risk (VaR) is related to the percentiles of probability distributions, and measures the predicted maximum portfolio loss at a specified probability level over a certain time horizon. Commonly used probability levels include 0.95 and 0.99, and the corresponding VaR is referred to as 95% VaR or 99% VaR (in other words, the probability is stated as a percentage). Typical time horizons include 1 day and 10 days. The portfolio loss is defined as the difference between the initial value of the portfolio at the current time t, V_t, and the future value of the portfolio at time $t + 1$, V_{t+1}.[7]

VaR can be used for individual assets, trading positions, and portfolios. Mathematically, VaR at a probability level $100(1 - \varepsilon)\%$ is defined as the value γ such that the probability that the negative of the portfolio return will exceed γ is not more than some small number ε:

$$\text{VaR}_{(1-\varepsilon)}(\tilde{r}) = \min\{\gamma \,|\, P(-\tilde{r} > \gamma) \le \varepsilon\}$$

(In the preceding expression, $\tilde{r}$ denotes the random variable representing the portfolio return, and $-\tilde{r}$ is associated with the portfolio loss, as we will see shortly.) For example, when $\varepsilon = 0.05$, then $(1 - \varepsilon) = 0.95$, $100(1 - \varepsilon)\% = 95\%$, and we are interested in the 95% VaR, which is the level of the portfolio losses that will not be exceeded with probability of more than 5%.

Asset managers often use a modified version of VaR, which measures the loss relative to a benchmark.[8] The formula for VaR above still stands, but $\tilde{r}$ is the *excess return* relative to the benchmark, that is, the difference between the return on the portfolio and the return on the benchmark.

VaR is reported as a *dollar amount of losses*. Let us see how the definition of VaR in terms of the return can be stated in dollar terms.

Suppose that $\tilde{r}$ is the arithmetic portfolio return.[9] It is easy to see that if we know the value γ and would like to obtain VaR as a dollar amount for possible losses, we simply need to multiply γ by the portfolio value at the beginning of the time period of interest. In particular, the negative of the arithmetic return over time period t, $-\tilde{r}_{t,t+1}$, is

$$-\tilde{r}_{t,t+1} = \frac{V_t - \tilde{V}_{t+1}}{V_t}$$

where V_t is the portfolio value at time t. The numerator in this expression is the loss over time period t, $V_t - \tilde{V}_{t+1}$. Hence, the loss over time period t can be written as

$$V_t - \tilde{V}_{t+1} = -\tilde{r}_{t,t+1} \cdot V_t$$

The portfolio value at time t, V_t, is known; it can be treated as a constant. Therefore, the probability distribution of the loss is the same as the probability distribution of the negative of the return $-\tilde{r}_{t,t+1}$, scaled by a constant. If we know γ, the $100(1 - \varepsilon)$th percentile of the latter distribution, the $100(1 - \varepsilon)$th percentile of the former can be computed as $\gamma \cdot V_t$.

Let us now compute VaR in dollar terms if we are working with geometric returns $\tilde{r}$. We have

$$-\tilde{r}_{t,t+1} = -\ln\left(\frac{\tilde{V}_{t+1}}{V_t}\right) = -\left(\ln\left(\tilde{V}_{t+1}\right) - \ln\left(V_t\right)\right) = \ln\left(V_t\right) - \ln\left(\tilde{V}_{t+1}\right)$$

Just as before, the portfolio value at time t, V_t, can be treated as a constant. Therefore, the probability distribution of $\ln(\tilde{V}_{t+1})$ is the same as the probability distribution of $\tilde{r}$. We can rewrite the previous equality as

$$\ln\left(\tilde{V}_{t+1}\right) = \tilde{r}_{t,t+1} + \ln\left(V_t\right)$$

or, equivalently, as

$$\tilde{V}_{t+1} = e^{\tilde{r}_{t,t+1} + \ln(V_t)} = e^{\tilde{r}_{t,t+1}} \cdot V_t$$

and, therefore, the loss $(V_t - \tilde{V}_{t+1})$ can be expressed as

$$V_t - \tilde{V}_{t+1} = \left(1 - e^{\tilde{r}_{t,t+1}}\right) \cdot V_t$$

So, if we know the value of γ, we can compute the VaR as

$$\left(1 - e^{-\gamma}\right) \cdot V_t$$

The difference in estimating VaR from the two different assumptions for returns is not very large for short holding periods and realistic return parameters. For example, suppose that we computed $\gamma = 0.004000$. (We will explain how to obtain an estimate of γ later.) Then, $\left(1 - e^{-\gamma}\right) = \left(1 - e^{-0.004000}\right) = 0.003992$. For an initial portfolio value of \$100 million, we have VaR = \$400,000 for arithmetic returns, and VaR = \$399,201.07 for geometric returns.

In practice, VaR is often computed directly as a dollar amount because historical data are available in a cash flow form. More specifically, it is in either profit/loss (P/L) or loss/profit (L/P) form.

The P/L generated by an asset or a portfolio of assets is the value of the asset (or portfolio) at the end of time period t plus any interim cash flows (dividends, interest, realized capital gain or loss on disposal of assets) and minus the asset value at the beginning of period t:

$$(P/L)_{t+1} = V_{t+1} + D_{t+1} - V_t$$

(As a general rule, the amounts should be properly discounted, so that all dollar amounts are commensurate, but if the time periods themselves are short, the adjustment will be small.) When the data are in P/L form, positive values indicate profits and negative values indicate losses. The $100(1 - \varepsilon)\%$ VaR is then the εth percentile of the distribution of the P/L values. (See Exhibit 8.1(A).)

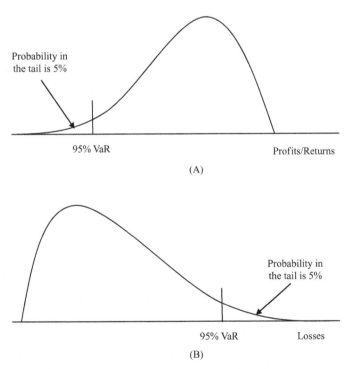

EXHIBIT 8.1 (A) 95% VaR computed from P/L data; (B) 95% VaR computed from L/P data.

The loss/profit (L/P) form is basically the negative of the profit/loss (P/L) data:

$$(L/P)_t = -(P/L)_t$$

In that case, the $100(1 - \varepsilon)\%$ VaR is the $100(1 - \varepsilon)$th percentile of the distribution of the L/P values. (See Exhibit 8.1(B).)

8.2.1 The History of the Value-at-Risk Metric

Among banks, the consensus to use the maximum likely loss as a way to look at risk evolved gradually, and was established formally in 1996, when the Basel Committee on Banking Supervision of the Bank for International Settlements (BIS) proposed several amendments to the original 1988 Basel Accord for minimal capital requirements for banks of its member countries. While the original accord covered only credit risk (deposits and lending), the new proposal that took effect in 1998 also covered market risk, including organization-wide commodities exposures (measured by the 10-day 95% VaR).

The deliberate effort among the central banks that were members of the Basel Committee to come up with better risk management schemes at the firm level, however, had started almost two decades earlier. The impetus for this effort was the realization that there was little connection between the limits that were imposed on trading positions and the risk that was being taken by banks. Good trades were passed over because of arbitrary trading limits, and good capital allocation was missed for the same reason. In addition, banks, whose primary business had been loans, were beginning to meld with investment banks, whose primary business was trading stocks, bonds, and complex financial instruments, and with asset management companies whose focus was investments. There was a need for an integrated approach to risk management that allowed banks to evaluate their exposure across divisions and for increasingly complex positions. Hence, a number of banks began developing internal systems for measuring firmwide risk.

J.P. Morgan was one of the early leaders in this endeavor. Industry legend has it that J.P. Morgan's integrated risk management system was started when Dennis Weatherstone, the then-chairman of J.P. Morgan, asked his staff to give him a daily one-page report describing the firmwide risk over the next 24 hours, taking into consideration the bank's entire trading portfolio. The "4:15" report, as the report became widely known because it was to be delivered at the close of trading every day, used VaR to estimate the maximum loss with a given probability over the next trading day. The fact that VaR was quoted as a dollar amount, rather than a percentage, or a probability, made it convenient for reporting results to management, and eliminated the need to explain complex mathematics.

The original calculation of VaR was based on a normal approximation to the distribution of the firm's profits over the next day, similar to the calculation of VaR under a normal distribution we will show in section 8.2.2. While, theoretically, the calculation was straightforward, its practical implementation was immensely time consuming and complicated, as it involved compiling data and estimating a number of statistical parameters, such as expected returns, variances, and covariances among different complex trading positions. Still, the system was completed by 1990. In 1993, J.P. Morgan presented the system at its research conference, and witnessed a great deal of interest from potential clients. Instead of leasing it or attempting to generate fees from consulting, however, in 1994 J.P. Morgan decided to make a simplified version of their internal system, RiskMetrics, available online, along with the data necessary for the statistical estimation of VaR. This move generated a huge amount of publicity for J.P. Morgan, and accelerated the adoption of VaR as a risk measure across financial institutions. By the mid-1990s, VaR had established itself as the dominant measure of risk. As computer equipment became cheaper and faster and developers more experienced, VaR systems continued to spread and became more elaborate, including not only measures of market risks, but also credit risks, liquidity risks, and operational risks.

Unfortunately, as we will see later, VaR was not understood well, and the simplicity of its risk estimate as a single dollar amount could be very misleading. Complicating matters, while all banks reported and monitored their VaR, there was no established regulation on how to compute it. Some banks used the original RiskMetrics approach, incorporating estimates of standard deviations and correlations between the returns of different traded instruments. Others opted for historical simulation approaches that estimated VaR from histograms of past P/L data. Yet others used forward-looking Monte Carlo simulation, generating future scenarios for the underlying drives of uncertainty in their company's positions. We explain these methods for estimating VaR in more detail in sections 8.2.2 and 8.2.3. A higher-level discussion of applications of VaR in portfolio risk management with complex financial instruments is provided in Chapter 16.

8.2.2 Calculation of Value-at-Risk for a Normal Distribution

Let us assume that our P/L data follow a normal distribution. To estimate $100(1 - \varepsilon)\%$ VaR, we need to find the value of the $100(1 - \varepsilon)$th percentile of the distribution. In the case of the normal distribution, there is a closed-form expression for the percentiles. Every percentile can be expressed as a sum of the mean of the distribution and the standard deviation scaled by a multiplier—namely,

$$\text{VaR}_{(1-\varepsilon)} = -\mu_{P/L} + z_{(1-\varepsilon)} \cdot \sigma_{P/L}$$

where $\mu_{P/L}$ is the mean, and $\sigma_{P/L}$ is the standard deviation of the P/L distribution, respectively. The number $z_{(1-\varepsilon)}$ is the $100(1-\varepsilon)$th percentile of a standard normal distribution. A widely used notation for the same expression is $\Phi^{-1}(1-\varepsilon)$, which we introduced in section 6.2.3.[10] The concept is used in so many applications, that most spreadsheet and statistical software packages contain a function for computing it. As we mentioned in Chapter 4, in Excel $z_{(1-\varepsilon)}$ is computed with the formula NORMSINV $(1-\varepsilon)$. (So, for example, $z_{0.95}$ corresponding to the 95th percentile is computed as NORMSINV(0.95), which is 1.6445.) In MATLAB, $z_{(1-\varepsilon)}$ can be computed with a similar command: norminv $(1-\varepsilon)$.

If, instead, we have normally distributed L/P data, then we would use the formula

$$\text{VaR}_{(1-\varepsilon)} = \mu_{L/P} + z_{(1-\varepsilon)} \cdot \sigma_{L/P}$$

If we are given data on asset returns and assume arithmetic returns, the formula for VaR would be

$$\text{VaR}_{(1-\varepsilon)} = \left(-\mu_r + z_{(1-\varepsilon)} \cdot \sigma_r\right) \cdot V_t$$

where V_t is the portfolio value at the beginning of the period over which VaR is estimated.

If, instead, we assume geometric returns, then it can be easily shown (see the derivation at the beginning of section 8.2) that

$$\text{VaR}_{(1-\varepsilon)} = \left(1 - e^{\mu_r - z_{(1-\varepsilon)} \cdot \sigma_r}\right) \cdot V_t$$

If we are trying to estimate the VaR for a portfolio, the μ and the σ in the formulas above would be the portfolio mean and standard deviation. (Depending on the data, they may be reported as dollar amounts or percentage returns.) You can now see why we need information on the covariance structure of the different assets in the portfolio if the VaR is to be computed this way: as we showed in Chapter 7, the covariances are an input to the computation of the portfolio variance, which is then used to compute the portfolio standard deviation.

There are some severe problems with the assumption of normality in the VaR estimation context:

- Using normal-distribution-based VaR is technically correct for elliptical distributions for returns, of which the normal distribution is an example. This is because such distributions are entirely described by their means and variances. Most real-world data, however, exhibit "fat tails" and are not normally distributed. When a distribution has fatter tails than the normal distribution, the VaR computed with the normal approximation can grossly underestimate the real VaR.
- Even when returns are assumed to be normally distributed, inaccuracies in the estimation of the input parameters to the model can render the risk evaluation process meaningless. Accurate estimation of the covariance structure even for equities—the "simplest" assets—is challenging because the covariance structure varies over time.
- Recall from section 3.8 that covariance and correlation measure only the strength of *linear* dependence between random variables. A bank may have thousands of positions in complex types of financial securities with payoffs that are not linearly correlated. (This is discussed in more detail in Part Three.) Thus, estimating the risk of a firm's portfolio by using only the correlation structure and the mean for estimating the risk leaves out important information about the actual distribution of returns for the entire portfolio.

Despite the fact that the normal-distribution-based VaR suffers from a number of problems, it is unfortunately widely used. It was the model underlying the RiskMetrics system when it became freely available, and many financial companies adopted it, not understanding (or choosing to ignore) its drawbacks. The whole point of using a risk estimation framework that is different from the traditional mean-variance framework, however, is that it should enable financial institutions to evaluate risk in highly nonnormal situations. Thus, it is not satisfactory to measure tail risk as a multiple of the standard deviation, as the normal approximation to the VaR does.

8.2.3 Calculation of Value-at-Risk Using Historical and Simulated Data Scenarios

A more realistic way to estimate VaR is to use scenarios for the possible realizations of the uncertainties underlying the prices of the different securities in the portfolio. The scenario approach allows us to incorporate dependencies between uncertainties implicitly, and to estimate the actual percentile of the probability distribution of future portfolio losses, eliminating strong assumptions such as normality.

Suppose we have S scenarios for the possible losses (L/P) over the time period of interest stored in an array `LossData`. The $100(1 - \varepsilon)\%$ VaR is found by sorting the data (in an increasing order), and selecting scenario with index $(S - \lfloor \varepsilon \cdot S \rfloor + 1)$ in the sorted data array.[11] Intuitively, we select the scenario that results in the highest magnitude of loss so that the total number of scenarios in which the loss is greater is not more than $\lfloor \varepsilon \cdot S \rfloor$.

In Excel 2007, the data can be sorted by clicking on the **Data** tab, selecting **Sort**, and referencing the array where the data are stored. In MATLAB, the data can be sorted with the command `SortedLossData = sort(LossData)`. The default for the MATLAB command `sort` is to order the elements of the array that is passed to it in increasing order, so the $100(1 - \varepsilon)\%$ VaR is the $(S - \lfloor \varepsilon \cdot S \rfloor + 1)$st element of the array `SortedLossData`. Requesting that element is accomplished with the command `SortedLossData(S-floor(`ε`*S)+1))`.

For example, if we have 1000 L/P scenarios, then the 95% VaR will be the 951st highest scenario $((1000 - \lfloor 0.05 \cdot 1000 \rfloor + 1) = 951)$. If we have 1005 L/P scenarios, then the 95% VaR will be the 956th highest scenario $((1005 - \lfloor 0.05 \cdot 1005 \rfloor + 1) = 956)$.[12]

How do we actually decide on the set of scenarios to consider for the VaR estimation procedure? The simplest approach is to use historical scenarios over a given window (e.g., 1000 observations), updating the most recent scenarios and dropping scenarios that happened before the most recent 1000 observations. Such scenarios may be bootstrapped; that is, simulation techniques may be used to sample from the set of scenarios and generate a new set with the same general risk profile.[13] The advantage of using bootstrapping is that the bootstrapped data sets are also useful for gauging the accuracy of the VaR estimate.[14]

The obvious drawback of this approach is that important insights from scenarios that happened outside the window may be lost. For example, the VaR computed from scenarios for market performance over the year 2006 would be quite low because the market generally rose during that time period. However, including scenarios from previous financial crises would have enabled us to obtain a better estimate for what was to come in 2008.

Even when such extreme scenarios are included in the data set, an important cause for concern is that some events, such as the market crash of October 1987, are single events that will not impact the VaR unless the confidence level is set very high. One way in which this situation can be mended is by assigning weights to different historical observations, and preserving a longer-term memory of possible events. The weights can be determined in different ways. One possible assignment is to do it based on age, that is, to discount older observations relative to newer ones. Another possible assignment of weights is based on the current volatility forecast. Namely, if recent market volatility has been 1% and the forecasted volatility over the time horizon of risk estimation is higher, then we can adjust all historical returns by a coefficient to reflect the greater anticipated market volatility. Other approaches for determining scenario weights include incorporating considerations for the correlations between different assets and so-called semiparametric bootstrap approaches.[15] In practice, a thoughtful approach to risk estimation would combine two sets of scenarios: a "moderate" set of scenarios based on the current situation in the market and recent history, and an "extreme" set of scenarios that repeats major stock, bond and currency market crises, weighing scenarios in a sensible way. To smooth the gaps in the VaR estimates obtained from historical data, especially in the tails of the distribution, practitioners also often fit a probability distribution to observed historical data, so that the tails of the distribution can be explicitly modeled when VaR is simulated.[16]

There are multiple advantages to using historical observations to generate scenarios for the purposes of risk evaluation. First, the fact that these scenarios have actually occurred gives them plausibility. Second, they are easy to understand and generate. A statement like "If a market crash similar to the crash in October 2008 happens, our portfolio stands to lose $X" is easy to communicate and conceptualize. However, this approach is inherently backward-looking. Simulation of random processes can instead be used to generate forward-looking risk models based on modeling the uncertainty in a set of underlying market risk factors. Such approaches are discussed in more detail in Chapter 16, after introducing random processes and financial derivatives in Chapters 11 through 15. Unfortunately, traditional Monte Carlo simulation approaches can be very time consuming. In Chapters 14 and 16, we will introduce some methodologies for reducing the number of scenarios while still achieving an accurate risk estimate.

8.2.4 VaR Calculation Example

To illustrate how VaR can be calculated under the assumptions in sections 8.2.2 and 8.2.3, let us consider two sets of P/L data in column D in worksheets **VaR 1** and **VaR 2**, respectively, in the file **Ch8-VaRCalculation.xlsx**.

The P/L distribution for the set of data in worksheet VaR 1 is shown in Exhibit 8.2. The data in this sample are symmetrically distributed (the mean and the median are approximately the same, and the skewness is close to 0), with a distribution that is not as peaked as (i.e., is "flatter" than)

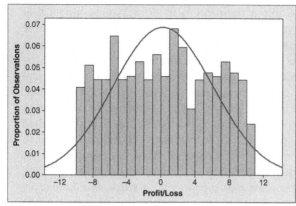

Mean: 0.20
Standard deviation: 5.79
Skewness: 0.03
Kurtosis: −1.17
Minimum: −9.57
Maximum: 10.39
Median: 0.19

EXHIBIT 8.2 P/L distribution of the data in worksheet **VaR 1** of the file Ch8-VaRCalculation.xlsx.

the normal distribution. The VaR calculation directly from historical data is presented in cells F32:F33 in the worksheet **VaR 1**. The 99% VaR from historical data is $9.50 (cell F32), whereas the normal approximation to the 99% VaR based on the estimate of the mean and the standard deviation of the P/L data is $13.27 (cell F33). In this case, the normal approximation to the 99% VaR overestimates the "true" 99% VaR computed as a percentile of the P/L historical data.

More often than not, however, historical P/L graphs look like the graph in Exhibit 8.3. This historical distribution was obtained from the daily stock prices of a major financial institution (Citigroup) between the beginning of 2005 and the end of 2008, after the major financial crisis in the fall of 2008, and is stored in worksheet **VaR 2** of the file **Ch8-VaRCalculation.xlsx**. While the distribution still appears symmetric (the skewness is close to 0), the distribution has "fat tails"—it has a lot more observations in the tails than a normal distribution would have. This is confirmed also by the high positive value for the kurtosis. In this case, the normal approximation to the 99% VaR severely underestimates the 99% VaR obtained as a percentile of the historical data. The normal approximation 99% VaR is $1.67 (cell F33), whereas the VaR computed directly from historical data is $2.12 (cell F32).

Worksheets **VaR 1** and **VaR 2** also contain a calculation of the 99% VaR based on a bootstrapping procedure and simulating portfolio losses (rather than P/L). There are 500 realizations for L/P (which is the negative of P/L) that are drawn randomly from the set of historical data (column D in

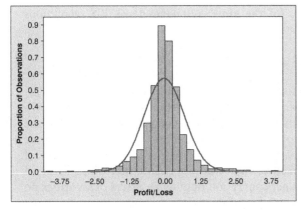

Mean: −0.04
Standard deviation: 0.70
Skewness: 0.01
Kurtosis: 4.89
Minimum: −4.15
Maximum: 4.00
Median: −0.04

EXHIBIT 8.3 P/L distribution of the data in worksheet **VaR 1** of the file **Ch8-VaRCalculation.xlsx.**

both worksheets), and are sorted in an increasing order in column O in both worksheets. The 99% VaR is the 496th observation in each data set. The bootstrapped 99% VaR in **VaR 1** is $9.50, whereas the bootstrapped 99% VaR in **VaR 2** is $2.12. (See this chapter's Software Hints for an explanation of how the random scenarios can be drawn from historical data with @RISK and MATLAB.)

8.2.5 Selection of Value-at-Risk Parameters and Regulatory Requirements

The calculation of VaR requires two input parameters that appear arbitrary: the confidence level $(1 - \varepsilon)$ and the time horizon. How are these parameters selected?

Theoretically, the best length to use for the time horizon is the amount of time it would take to liquidate all positions in the portfolio in an orderly fashion.[17] It is typically assumed that a time period of two weeks (10 business days) is sufficient, and this is the holding period specified by regulation. (BIS capital requirements state a holding period of 10 days.) The time horizons used by financial institutions for internal purposes may be one trading day or one month, and there are some financial institutions that operate on longer holding periods (e.g., a quarter). However, shorter time periods are more likely to be used for backtesting and validation of VaR models because robust validation can only be performed with sufficiently large data sets, and the latter are more available for short time periods. To convert VaR estimates for a short time period (e.g., a day) into a VaR estimate for a long time period (e.g., 10 days) for the same confidence level, BIS regulations sanction the use of the approximation

$$\text{VaR}_{(1-\varepsilon),10} = \text{VaR}_{(1-\varepsilon),1} \sqrt{10}$$

The mathematics behind this conversion will become clearer in Part Three, but the intuitive reasoning is that for certain types of random processes used to model security prices, variability over time increases with the square root of the length of the time period. Thus, the VaR over T time periods should be larger than the VaR over one time period by a factor of square root of $\sqrt{T}$. (In practice, this is an approximation rather than an exact conversion; it is an exact conversion only when prices of securities do indeed follow the specific type of random process.)

Banks can use any confidence level for estimating VaR for internal purposes, but when they report VaR externally, they typically use a confidence level that is consistent with other banks (typically, a number in the range 95% to 99%). A very useful technique for setting the VaR parameters for internal risk management purposes is to analyze the value of VaR for pairs of values of the confidence level parameter and the length of the time horizon. Thus, a VaR surface rather that a single value of VaR is examined to determine if the risk is acceptable for any values of the two parameters. As the confidence level increases (i.e., ε becomes smaller), the estimation of VaR becomes more challenging because there are fewer historical observations in the "tail" that can be used to calibrate VaR models accurately.

The official capital adequacy standards for banks prescribed by the 1996 Amendment to the 1988 Basel Accord include the following:

- Banks in the G-10 countries[18] should report a 10-day VaR at the 99% level.
- Banks are free to calculate their VaR using their own models under certain conditions:
  - The models used for internal risk management should be the same as the ones used for reporting to regulators.
  - The models must be approved by the regulating body.
  - The models must meet certain technical conditions on computing the risks of relatively complex positions.
- Banks must calibrate their daily VaR measures to daily P/L observations. They must perform backtesting daily, and must identify the number of trading days in which losses exceed the VaR.
- The results of these backtests are used to assess VaR models and to determine a value for a so-called *hysteria factor*, or a *multiplier* to apply to standard VaR estimation results. In particular, the VaR value

reported for regulatory purposes should be always the greater of the standard VaR value and the average of the VaR values over the last 60 days, multiplied by the hysteria factor, which is a number between 3 and 4. For example, if there are fewer than five exceptions to the VaR models over the last 250 days, then the multiplier is 3; if there are five exceptions, the multiplier is 3.40, and so on.

The more recent Basel Accord, Basel II, which was published in 2004, retained these main features, but also included new provisions on credit risk and operational risk models.

It is important to note that while the point of these regulations is to improve bank solvency, these capital requirements do little to achieve this goal. Not only are some of the rules arbitrary, but there is also a lot of leeway given to the individual banks in backtesting and reporting VaR, which can make the whole process of reporting VaR for regulatory purposes meaningless.

8.2.6 Optimization of Value-at-Risk

In addition to risk management, VaR can be used in making decisions for portfolio allocation purposes.

The portfolio VaR optimization problem is in fact a problem with chance constraints, which we introduced in section 6.2.3. To see this, note that we can state the VaR minimization problem as

$$
\begin{aligned}
\min_{\gamma, \mathbf{w}} \quad & \gamma \\
\text{s.t.} \quad & P(-\tilde{\mathbf{r}}'\mathbf{w} > \gamma) \leq \varepsilon \\
& \mathbf{w}'\iota = 1
\end{aligned}
$$

where $\tilde{\mathbf{r}}$ is the N-dimensional vector of (uncertain) asset returns over the time horizon for portfolio optimization, and $\mathbf{w}$ is the N-dimensional vector of asset weights in the portfolio. In words, this optimization formulation states that we would like to minimize a number γ (which is a decision variable) so that the probability that the portfolio losses exceed γ is less than or equal to a small number ε. We also have the standard budget constraint that the portfolio weights must add up to 1, or 100%.[19]

Given our discussion about optimization problems with chance constraints in section 6.2.3, optimizing a portfolio allocation so that the resulting VaR is the lowest among all possible distributions is nontrivial. Suppose, for example, that we are given data on S possible scenarios for vectors of individual asset returns $\mathbf{r}^{(1)}, \ldots, \mathbf{r}^{(S)}$. The VaR optimization problem can be written as[20]

$$
\begin{aligned}
\min_{\gamma, \mathbf{w}} \quad & \gamma \\
\text{s.t.} \quad & (-\mathbf{r}^{(s)})'\mathbf{w} \leq \gamma + M \cdot y_s, \quad s = 1, \ldots, S \\
& \sum_{s=1}^{S} y_s \leq \lfloor \varepsilon \cdot S \rfloor \\
& \mathbf{w}'\iota = 1 \\
& y_s \in \{0, 1\}, \quad s = 1, \ldots, S
\end{aligned}
$$

where M is a "large" constant. Since the input data in the formulation are asset returns (which are small in magnitude), a value of 100 for M is large enough for all practical purposes. The optimal value of γ returned by the solver will be the minimum value for the VaR.

Note that for a data set consisting of 1,000 scenarios, this problem formulation involves solving a mixed integer optimization problem[21] with 1,000 binary variables, which can take a very long time. In practice, the optimization of VaR can be done with approximations, or with additional assumptions. For example, if we assume that the asset returns follow a multivariate normal distribution with a vector of means μ and a covariance matrix Σ, then the portfolio VaR optimization problem can be written as[22]

$$
\begin{aligned}
\min_{\gamma, \mathbf{w}} \quad & \gamma \\
\text{s.t.} \quad & -\mu'\mathbf{w} + z_{(1-\varepsilon)} \cdot \sqrt{\mathbf{w}'\Sigma\mathbf{w}} \leq \gamma \\
& \mathbf{w}'\iota = 1
\end{aligned}
$$

where $z_{(1-\varepsilon)}$ is the $100(1 - \varepsilon)$th percentile of a standard normal distribution, as explained in section 8.2.2 of this chapter and section 6.2.3 of Chapter 6. Notice that this formulation is equivalent to the optimization formulation

$$
\begin{aligned}
\min_{\mathbf{w}} \quad & -\mu'\mathbf{w} + z_{(1-\varepsilon)} \cdot \sqrt{\mathbf{w}'\Sigma\mathbf{w}} \\
\text{s.t.} \quad & \mathbf{w}'\iota = 1
\end{aligned}
$$

which can also be written as

$$
\begin{aligned}
\max_{\mathbf{w}} \quad & \mu'\mathbf{w} - z_{(1-\varepsilon)} \cdot \sqrt{\mathbf{w}'\Sigma\mathbf{w}} \\
\text{s.t.} \quad & \mathbf{w}'\iota = 1
\end{aligned}
$$

This formulation involves optimizing the portfolio allocation using only the portfolio mean ($\mu'\mathbf{w}$) and the portfolio standard deviation $\sqrt{\mathbf{w}'\Sigma\mathbf{w}}$. Thus, the portfolio allocations resulting from solving this will suffer from the same drawbacks as allocations obtained with mean-variance formulations.

8.2.7 Arguments For and Against Value-at-Risk

At its introduction, VaR was hailed as an advanced and comprehensive way to handle portfolio risk. Its appeal was due to several features not shared by basic measures used to estimate risk before VaR and its ultimate endorsement by the Basel Committee:

- As we mentioned earlier, VaR is expressed as a dollar amount, making it easier to convey information about risk exposure to a wide range of decision makers.
- VaR estimates downside risk rather than dispersion, and it is a probabilistic measure of risk in the sense that implicit in the number reported for VaR is an estimate of the probability that the loss will exceed that amount. This is not the case with other measures of risk, such as variance.
- Before VaR, measures of the risk of trading and portfolio positions included duration (see Chapter 2), option Greeks (discussed in Chapters 13 and 14) and others. Those risk measures, however, do not give a sense of the entire distribution of possible outcomes; in a sense they are based on a "what-if" analysis.
- VaR could be applied to any type of asset and position. This is not the case for variance (which is meaningful mostly for equity and commodity positions and portfolios and not for complex financial securities with highly non-normal distributions of possible returns), duration (which is applicable only to fixed income portfolios), or Greeks (which are applicable to financial option positions). Thus, VaR provides a consistent way to compare risks of equity, fixed income, and other positions, and can be used to aggregate risks across the entire firm.

Even early on, however, many criticisms of VaR surfaced. Two of the most vocal early critics of VaR included Nassim Taleb (1997a,b), who summarized many of his arguments in his best-selling book *The Black Swan* (Taleb 2007), and Richard Hoppe (1998). They criticized the literal transfer of techniques from the mathematical and the physical sciences to model social systems in which processes are not stationary, and depend on the complex dynamic interactions of rational and irrational market agents. Taleb (1997a) said:

> *You are worse off relying on misleading information than on not having any information at all. If you give a pilot an altimeter that is sometimes defective he will crash the plane. Give him nothing and he will look out the window.*

Such criticisms are valid for all risk management systems—indeed, risk estimates are subject to errors, model risk (i.e., making wrong assumptions about the underlying processes), and implementation risk (i.e., risk of errors because of the way systems are implemented). However, VaR suffers of some unique disadvantages that should be understood before it is used as a risk measure.

First, as has become clear by now, VaR does not tell us *how much* we could lose if a low-risk tail event occurs. A trading strategy that has the loss distribution in Exhibit 8.4(A) appears just as risky as the trading strategy in Exhibit 8.4(B) in terms of VaR. It is clear, however, that we stand to lose more, and more often, with trading strategy in Exhibit 8.4(B). Thus, using VaR as the "threshold" for approving an investment strategy can leave investors exposed to extreme losses.

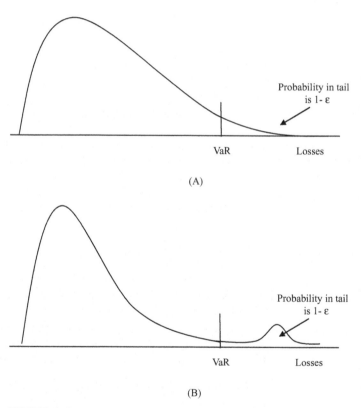

EXHIBIT 8.4 Two trading strategies (A) and (B) with the same VaR and different losses in the tail. In (B), the VaR is the same, but the potential losses in the tail are larger on average.

Second, VaR's reporting of the loss at a certain percentile of the distribution without consideration for the size of the losses in the tail of the distribution encourages traders to take more low-probability, high-impact bets. Such risks do not show up in the VaR estimates, but can have a devastating effect on the firm and, in fact, can destabilize the entire financial system, as the financial system collapse in the fall of 2008 demonstrated. Taleb (1997a) actually predicted this long before it was a reality. He pointed out that if everybody uses VaR as a risk measure, taking on low-probability risks in the tail, then the events in the tail become highly correlated, and are no longer low-probability risk events if the financial system is considered as a whole. Danielsson and Zigrand (2001) also showed that VaR regulatory constraints on financial institutions can actually aggravate financial crises and even cause them because the markets cannot clear properly.

Third, VaR computation and optimization is difficult. It does not make sense to use a mean-variance framework to estimate or optimize VaR because that eliminates the whole purpose of using a tail-risk measure. However, estimating VaR by simulation and optimizing VaR can be very computationally intensive. VaR optimization based on scenarios in particular has nonsmooth and nonconvex constraints, which means that we cannot trust the solutions from the optimization solver even if the solver takes a long time to search for the optimal solution.

Finally, problems exist with the theoretical foundation of VaR as well. In a seminal article, Artzner, Delbaen, Eber, and Heath (1999) pointed out that use of VaR actually discourages diversification, which goes against intuition and established portfolio management practices. Let us consider a simple example to illustrate this fact.

Suppose we can invest in two zero-coupon bonds, A and B, both with $100 face value.[23] Bond A costs $97.00 today and will pay $111.55 one year from now. Bond B costs $90.00 today and will pay $103.50 one year from now. Both bonds, however, have a 4% probability of default. If a particular bond defaults, we will lose our entire original investment in that bond, and therefore will not receive any payment.

The original value of the individual bonds, the distribution of the individual bond's losses, and the 95% VaR for the position in each bond are shown in Exhibit 8.5.

Let us show the calculations for Bond A. The loss on Bond A is computed as ($97.00 – Final payment), and is therefore −$14.55 (a profit) if the bond pays as promised, and $97.00 (an actual loss) if the bond defaults. Since the loss of $97.00 happens with probability of 4%, which is in the tail of the distribution, the 95% VaR does not account for it, and hence the 95% VaR equals −$14.55. The interpretation is that we will realize a profit of $14.55 on our position in Bond A with probability no less than 5%. Similarly, we

EXHIBIT 8.5 Calculation of the VaRs of two individual positions in zero-coupon bonds with 4% probability of default.

	Position Today	End Payment	Distribution of Losses		95% VaR
			Probability	Amount of Loss	
Bond A	$97.00	$111.55	0.96	$(14.55)	$(14.55)
			0.04	$ 97.00	
Bond B	$90.00	$103.50	0.96	$(13.50)	$(13.50)
			0.04	$ 90.00	

can obtain the 95% VaR of the individual position in Bond B—it is again a profit (a loss of −$13.50).

The sum of the VaRs of the two positions is therefore −$14.55 (−$13.50) = −$28.05, that is, it is a profit of $28.05.

Now let us compute the probability distribution of the losses on a portfolio that consists of a long position in Bond A and a long position in Bond B.

- With probability 92.16% (= 0.96^2), both Bond A and Bond B will make their final payments, in which case the loss on the portfolio will be −$14.55 + (−$13.50) = −$28.05; that is, there will be a profit of $28.05.
- With probability 3.84% (= 0.96·0.04), Bond B will default and Bond A will pay, in which case the loss on the portfolio will be (−$14.55) + $90.00 = $75.45.
- With probability 3.84% (= 0.04·0.96), Bond A will default and Bond B will pay, in which case the loss on the portfolio will be $97.00 + (−$13.50) = $83.50.
- With probability 0.16% (= 0.04^2), both bonds will default, in which case the loss will be $97.00 + $90.00 = $187.00.

The probability distribution of the portfolio losses is illustrated in Exhibit 8.6. Note that the cumulative probability becomes 95% at a value of $75.45 for losses, which determines the value of the 95% VaR.

Hence, in this example the 95% VaR of the portfolio, $75.45, is higher than the sum of the individual 95% VaRs (−$28.05). In fact, a risk manager who uses the 95% VaR portfolio as a risk measure for this portfolio would prefer to increase the portfolio's holdings in one of these bonds rather than diversify and invest in both at the same time. Ironically, VaR, which gained popularity because of its ability to summarize firmwide risk based on

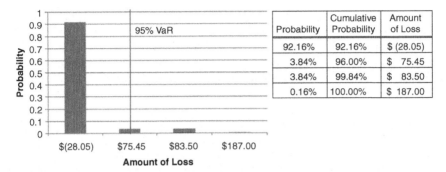

EXHIBIT 8.6   Probability distribution of portfolio losses and 95% VaR.

compounding risk reports from different parts of the firm, is actually ill-suited for calculating compounded risks!

8.3 CONDITIONAL VALUE-AT-RISK AND THE CONCEPT OF COHERENT RISK MEASURES

In view of the conceptual difficulties associated with classical measures of risk, Artzner, Delbaen, Eber, and Heath (2001) suggested a new class of risk measures they called *coherent risk measures*. A risk measure ρ is a coherent measure of risk if it satisfies the following conditions for any two random variables $\tilde{x}$ and $\tilde{y}$:

1. *Monotonicity.* If $\tilde{x} \geq 0$, then $\rho(\tilde{x}) \leq 0$.
2. *Subadditivity.* $\rho(\tilde{x} + \tilde{y}) \leq \rho(\tilde{x}) + \rho(\tilde{y})$.
3. *Positive homogeneity.* For any positive real number c, $\rho(c \cdot \tilde{x}) = c \cdot \rho(\tilde{x})$.
4. *Translational invariance.* For any real number c, $\rho(\tilde{x} + c) \leq \rho(\tilde{x}) - c$.

In words, these properties can be interpreted as follows:

1. If there are only positive returns, then the risk should be nonpositive.
2. The risk of a portfolio of two assets should be less than or equal to the sum of the risks of the individual assets.
3. If the amount of assets in the portfolio is increased c times, the risk becomes c times larger.
4. Cash or another risk-free asset does not contribute to portfolio risk.

Conditions (1), (3), and (4) are rather technical, and arguments have been presented in the literature that not all of them need to be satisfied for a risk measure to be considered acceptable in practice. Condition (2), however, is worth noting. It expresses the principle of diversification: aggregating different risks should diversify them away, not increase the overall risk.

As we saw in the example at the end of the previous section, VaR violates the second condition. In particular, there are instances in which the sum of the risks of two individual investments as represented by their VaRs is less than the risk (as represented by the VaR) of the portfolio of the two investments.

Taken together, the four conditions for coherence are rather restrictive. The standard deviation does not satisfy them either—it violates the monotonicity property. Artzner, Delbaen, Eber, and Heath (2001) suggested a tail-based risk measure that we mentioned earlier, conditional value-at-risk (CVaR), which satisfies all four conditions, and is related to the popular risk measure VaR. The intuitive explanation behind CVaR and the easy way in which the portfolio allocation problem could be solved rapidly increased its popularity in practice.

While $100(1 - \varepsilon)\%$ VaR only considers the maximum loss with a given probability ε, the $100(1 - \varepsilon)\%$ CVaR asks what happens on average if the losses exceed the $100(1 - \varepsilon)\%$ VaR; that is, what is the *expected loss in the tail*. Thus, CVaR addresses a major problem associated with VaR, which is that VaR ignores losses that may happen with low probability.

The formal definition of the $100(1 - \varepsilon)\%$ CVaR is

$$\mathrm{CVaR}_{(1-\varepsilon)}(\tilde{r}) = E\left[\,-\tilde{r}\,|\,-\tilde{r} \geq \mathrm{VaR}_{(1-\varepsilon)}(\tilde{r})\,\right]$$

Note that this definition implies that the $100(1 - \varepsilon)\%$ CVaR is always greater than or equal to the $100(1 - \varepsilon)\%$ VaR. In other words, if we manage our portfolio risk using CVaR, we will be implicitly minimizing our portfolio VaR as well.[24]

It is difficult to estimate the CVaR for a general distribution but, similarly to VaR, there are methods for estimating CVaR in special cases, such as the case in which we assume that future losses are normally distributed, or when we are given a set of scenarios for possible realizations of the portfolio returns.

8.3.1 Estimation of Conditional Value-at-Risk from a Normal Distribution

Let us first illustrate the calculation of CVaR for a normal distribution when the data is in P/L format, and is assumed to follow a normal distribution. In this case, the $100(1 - \varepsilon)\%$ CVaR is given by the expression[25]

$$\mathrm{CVaR}_{(1-\varepsilon)} = -\mu_{P/L} + \frac{\varphi(z_{(1-\varepsilon)})}{\varepsilon} \cdot \sigma_{P/L}$$

where

$\mu_{P/L}$ is the mean of the P/L distribution
$\sigma_{P/L}$ is the standard deviation of the P/L distribution

The number $z_{(1-\varepsilon)}$ is the $100(1 - \varepsilon)$th percentile of a standard normal distribution, as before, and we use $\varphi(z_{(1-\varepsilon)})$ to denote the value of the normal probability density at the point $z_{(1-\varepsilon)}$. For any z, the value of $\varphi(z)$ can be found with the command `NORMDIST(z,0,1,0)` in Excel, or `normpdf(z)` in MATLAB. For example, let $\varepsilon = 0.05$. Therefore, $1 - \varepsilon = 0.95$ and $z_{(1-\varepsilon)} = $ `norminv(0.95)` $= 1.6448$. The value of $\varphi(z_{(1-\varepsilon)})$ is then 0.1031 (computed as `NORMDIST(1.6448,0,1,0)` in Excel or `normpdf(1.6448)` in MATLAB).

If, instead, we have normally distributed L/P data, then we would use the formula

$$\mathrm{CVaR}_{(1-\varepsilon)} = \mu_{L/P} + \frac{\varphi(z_{(1-\varepsilon)})}{\varepsilon} \cdot \sigma_{L/P}$$

Finally, if we are given data on asset returns and assume arithmetic returns, the formula for CVaR would be

$$\mathrm{CVaR}_{(1-\varepsilon)} = \left(-\mu_r + \frac{\varphi(z_{(1-\varepsilon)})}{\varepsilon} \cdot \sigma_r \right) \cdot V_t$$

where V_t is the portfolio value at the beginning of the period over which CVaR is estimated.

8.3.2 Estimation of Conditional Value-at-Risk from a Discrete Distribution

Suppose we have a discrete distribution of scenarios for portfolio losses, and a loss amount of l_j occurs with probability p_j. The $100(1 - \varepsilon)\%$ CVaR is given by

$$\mathrm{CVaR}_{(1-\varepsilon)} = \frac{1}{\varepsilon} \cdot \sum_{j \text{ such that } l_j \geq \mathrm{VaR}_{(1-\varepsilon)}} p_j \cdot l_j$$

One special case of a discrete distribution that is encountered often in practice is a discrete uniform distribution, in which every scenario in a set of S scenarios could happen with the same probability $1/S$. This happens, for example, when we use historical scenarios as a basis for our CVaR calculations. In this case, CVaR is the average of all scenarios that exceed the VaR, or, equivalently, the average of the highest $\lfloor \varepsilon \cdot S \rfloor$ scenarios. For simplicity, suppose that we have sorted the S scenarios for losses in increasing order (i.e., scenario S is the scenario with the highest loss). We can compute the $100(1 - \varepsilon)\%$ CVaR as

$$\text{CVaR}_{(1-\varepsilon)} = \frac{1}{\lfloor \varepsilon \cdot S \rfloor} \cdot \sum_{s=S-\lfloor \varepsilon \cdot S \rfloor+1}^{S} l_s$$

For example, if there are 215 scenarios and $\varepsilon = 0.05$, then $\lfloor \varepsilon \cdot S \rfloor = \lfloor 0.05 \cdot 215 \rfloor = \lfloor 10.75 \rfloor = 10$. The 95% CVaR is the average of the 10 scenarios with highest losses. If the scenarios are sorted in increasing order, we take the average of the losses in scenarios $206, 207, \ldots, 215$.

If the data are in the form of arithmetic returns, we can compute the CVaR by using the same expression as above, but replacing the loss with the negative of the return in each scenario, and multiplying the resulting amount by the portfolio value at the beginning of the time period under consideration.

8.3.3 Optimization of Conditional Value-at-Risk

The CVaR of a portfolio of N assets is a function of both the uncertain returns of the different assets in the portfolio (the N-dimensional vector $\tilde{\mathbf{r}}$), and the weights $\mathbf{w}$ these assets have in the portfolio. For any given set of weights $\mathbf{w}$, the portfolio return is given by $\tilde{r}_p = \tilde{\mathbf{r}}'\mathbf{w}$. Suppose the portfolio return $\tilde{r}_p$ follows a probability distribution with density function f. Then, we can express the $100(1 - \varepsilon)\%$ CVaR mathematically as

$$\text{CVaR}_{(1-\varepsilon)} = \frac{1}{\varepsilon} \cdot \int_{-r \geq \text{VaR}_{(1-\varepsilon)}} (-r) \cdot f(r) \, dr.$$

We can recognize the term inside the integral as the expected value of the portfolio loss (as a percentage of amount invested) in the tail of the distribution.

In fact, CVaR is a function of the portfolio weights for the different assets $\mathbf{w}$, which determine the probability distribution of $\tilde{r}_p$. The existence of expected value in the definition of CVaR suggests the possibility of using stochastic programming methods if we want to find the asset allocation that results in the minimum portfolio CVaR.[26] Unfortunately, the definition of CVaR in terms of VaR makes it hard to optimize the CVaR because we need to go through the VaR, which itself suffers from computational difficulties when it comes to optimization. Rockafellar and Uryasev (2000) suggested using an auxiliary objective function instead of CVaR that has better computational properties. Namely, consider the function

$$F_{1-\varepsilon}(\mathbf{w}, \xi) = \xi + \frac{1}{\varepsilon} \cdot \int_{-r \geq \xi} (-r - \xi) \cdot f(r) \, dr$$

which can be equivalently written as

$$F_{1-\varepsilon}(\mathbf{w}, \xi) = \xi + \frac{1}{\varepsilon} \cdot \int_{-\infty}^{\infty} \max\{-r - \xi, 0\} \cdot f(r) \, dr$$

It turns out that if we try to minimize this function by varying $\mathbf{w}$ and ξ, the minimum value of the function will in fact equal the $100(1 - \varepsilon)\%$ CVaR. Mathematically, this is expressed as

$$\min_{\mathbf{w}} \text{CVaR}_{1-\varepsilon} = \min_{\mathbf{w}, \xi} F_{1-\varepsilon}(\mathbf{w}, \xi)$$

Hence, we can find the minimum value of CVaR without finding VaR first.[27] The value of ξ in the optimal solution will actually equal the VaR of the optimal portfolio found by optimizing the CVaR. However, the weights for the portfolio that minimizes CVaR will not necessarily be the weights for the portfolio that minimizes VaR. An example is shown in this chapter's Software Hints.

Note that the integral in the expression for $F_{1-\varepsilon}(\mathbf{w}, \xi)$ is multidimensional, and its calculation depends on knowing the joint probability density function of the returns of all assets in the portfolio. This is not only difficult to estimate, but is often undesirable to use, as multidimensional integration is very time consuming. There is a specific case in which the minimization of CVaR is a tractable optimization problem: when the joint probability density function of the returns for the assets in the portfolio is represented in a set of scenarios. This is typically the kind of data we have in practice: we can use historical data, or generate scenarios by simulation. Suppose also that each scenario in the set is equally likely. In that case, the function can be written as

$$F_{(1-\varepsilon)}(\mathbf{w}, \xi) = \xi + \frac{1}{\lfloor \varepsilon \cdot S \rfloor} \cdot \sum_{s=1}^{S} \max\left\{-(\mathbf{r}^{(s)})'\mathbf{w} - \xi, 0\right\}$$

where the N-dimensional vector $\mathbf{r}^{(s)}$ is the vector of returns on the N assets in the sth scenario. (Note here that $(\mathbf{r}^{(s)})'\mathbf{w}$ is the portfolio return in the sth scenario.)

To make this function more optimization-solver friendly, we get rid of the expression

$$\max\left\{-(\mathbf{r}^{(s)})'\mathbf{w} - \xi, 0\right\}$$

by introducing auxiliary decision variables $y_1, \ldots, y_S$, one for each scenario. We write the portfolio CVaR minimization problem as

$$\min_{\mathbf{w}, \xi, \mathbf{y}} \quad \xi + \frac{1}{\lfloor \varepsilon \cdot S \rfloor} \cdot \sum_{s=1}^{S} y_s$$

$$\text{s.t.} \quad y_s \geq -(\mathbf{r}^{(s)})'\mathbf{w} - \xi, \quad s = 1, \ldots, S$$

$$y_s \geq 0, \quad s = 1, \ldots, S$$

$$\mathbf{w}'\iota = 1$$

To understand the meaning of the first two sets of constraints, note that the objective function contains a minimization of the sum of the variables y_s. The optimization solver will try to make the values of these variables as small as possible. The first two sets of constraints, however, restrict the auxiliary variables y_s to be greater than both $-(\mathbf{r}^{(s)})'\mathbf{w} - \xi$ and 0. Thus, in order to satisfy both sets of constraints, the solver will set them equal to the larger of the two values, that is, to the maximum of $-(\mathbf{r}^{(s)})'\mathbf{w} - \xi$ and 0, which is the expression in $F_{(1-\varepsilon)}(\mathbf{w}, \xi)$. See Practice 8.5 on the companion web site for an alternative derivation of the optimization formulation using optimization duality theory instead of the auxiliary function $F_{(1-\varepsilon)}(\mathbf{w}, \xi)$.

The previous formulation is a linear optimization problem, which makes sample CVaR optimization a particularly attractive option from a computational perspective. Adding portfolio constraints encountered in practice, such as number of positions, trading costs, and so on. (see Chapter 9) generally results in equally tractable (linear or mixed-integer) optimization formulations. For example, we can formulate an optimization problem of maximizing the expected portfolio return subject to a constraint on the portfolio CVaR by rewriting the previous problem as

$$\max_{\mathbf{w},\xi,y} \quad \mu'\mathbf{w}$$

$$\text{s.t.} \quad \xi + \frac{1}{\lfloor \varepsilon \cdot S \rfloor} \cdot \sum_{s=1}^{S} y_s \leq b_{1-\varepsilon}$$

$$y_s \geq -(\mathbf{r}^{(s)})'\mathbf{w} - \xi, \quad s = 1, \ldots, S$$

$$y_s \geq 0, \quad s = 1, \ldots, S$$

$$\mathbf{w}'\iota = 1$$

where μ is the N-dimensional vector of expected returns on the N assets, and $b_{1-\varepsilon}$ is the average loss in the tail the portfolio manager is willing to tolerate.

This chapter's Software Hints contains examples of the implementation of sample portfolio CVaR optimization with Excel Solver and MATLAB's Optimization Toolbox.

SUMMARY

- The mean-variance portfolio optimization framework takes into consideration only the first two moments of the distribution of portfolio returns, the mean and the variance, and does not take into consideration higher moments. Thus, it omits important information about the skewness, kurtosis, and higher moments of the distribution.
- A number of advanced risk measures have been suggested to incorporate such considerations better. In particular, many advanced portfolio risk measures look at the potential for downside risk. Such risk measures include semivariance, Roy's safety first, and quantile-based risk measures such as value-at-risk (VaR) and conditional value-at-risk (CVaR).
- VaR measures the maximum portfolio loss at a specified probability level over a given time horizon. Specifically, it is defined as the value such that the probability that the portfolio loss will exceed it is not more than some small number.
- The position or portfolio VaR can be estimated via three methods: (1) based on an approximation by the normal distribution; (2) via historical simulation; (3) via Monte Carlo (forward-looking) simulation.
- Despite its advantages as a comprehensive measure of risk that can be applied to any type of asset and position, VaR suffers from a number of

drawbacks. From a practical perspective, VaR does not convey information about the size of the possible extreme losses. Moreover, employing it as a risk management tool in an institution may encourage undesirable behavior, as traders have an incentive to take low-probability, high-impact bets that do not show up on the VaR radar screen. From a theoretical perspective, VaR does not support the principle of diversification.

■ CVaR corrects some of the undesirable properties of VaR in that CVaR is concerned with measuring extreme losses, and supports the principle of diversification. CVaR is defined as the expected loss in the tail of the probability distribution of portfolio losses, that is, it reports the expected loss if the losses exceed the VaR.

■ CVaR can be estimated similarly to VaR: (1) based on an approximation by the normal distribution; (2) via historical simulation; (3) via Monte Carlo (forward-looking) simulation.

■ Portfolio allocation with the goal of minimizing VaR is a difficult stochastic optimization problem with chance constraints. It is generally very computationally intensive to solve, and the solution returned by the solver is not guaranteed to be optimal.

■ The portfolio CVaR optimization problem is a difficult problem except in a case which is widely the context in practice: when the data for the problem are in the form of scenarios for the possible realizations of asset returns. In the latter case, the portfolio CVaR minimization problem has a tractable linear programming formulation.

SOFTWARE HINTS

Excel/Palisade Decision Tools Suite

VaR Estimation First, we explain how to bootstrap a given random number of scenarios (say, 500) from a list of historical observations. Let us consider the example of VaR estimation from section 8.2.4. We focus on worksheet VaR 1 in the file **Ch8-VaRCalculation.xlsx**. In cell P3, we use the formula

```
= RiskOutput("Boostrapped P/L")+−RiskDuniform(D3:D589)
```

to create a random variable that draws a number from the array D3:D589 with equal probability (Duniform stands for "discrete uniform distribution"), and records the negative of that number. Therefore, the value that is recorded for that cell when the simulation is run is an observation for L/P (which is the negative of P/L). The first part of the preceding expression makes the cell an output cell for @RISK, so that @RISK can keep track of the values generated during the simulation.

Column O contains 500 scenarios that were generated from the simulation. They can be saved into a spreadsheet by clicking on the **Excel Reports** button in the @RISK tab, and checking **Simulation Data**. The 99% VaR is the 496th of these scenarios (0.99·500), that is, it is $9.50. The value is marked in yellow (cell O498) in the spreadsheet.

An alternative way to estimate the 99th percentile of a simulated output distribution from @RISK is to use the `RiskPercentile` command. For example, to find the 99% VaR as the 99th percentile of the L/P distribution simulated by @RISK in cell P3, we write

```
= RiskPercentile(P3,0.99)
```

The `RiskPercentile` formula is a shortcut—it is equivalent to looking at the output from the simulation, and making a note of the 99th percentile. It is important to note, however, that the value obtained with `RiskPercentile` may not be exactly the same as the value of the 496th sorted scenario for losses.

CVaR Estimation To estimate CVaR from a historical or simulated data, first we need to sort the scenarios in increasing order. (In Excel, click the **Data** tab, and then **Sort** in the Sort & Filter group.) The procedure is illustrated in the file **Ch8-CVaRCalculation.xlsx**. Column N in the worksheets **CVaR 1** and **CVaR 2** contains the P/L data from column D, sorted in increasing order. The 99% CVaR is the negative of the average of the lowest 1% of the P/L observations, that is, of the observations in cells N3:N7 in worksheet **CVaR 1** (respectively, cells N3:N12 in worksheet **CVaR2**).

VaR Optimization File **Ch8-VaRCVaROpt.xlsx** contains 60 scenarios for return realizations of three stocks. We will use the data to implement the scenario optimization formulation of the VaR minimization problem from section 8.3.3.

Exhibit 8.7 contains a partial snapshot of the worksheet with the optimization setup from worksheet **VaR** in the file **Ch8-VaRCVaROpt.xlsx**. Cells B3:D3 contain the values of the decision variables (the weights for the three stocks). Cell G3, the target cell, will be minimized by Solver, but it contains no formula. It will be specified as a decision variable (changing cell) itself as part of the optimization problem (see the Solver dialog box in Exhibit 8.8). Cells G10:G69 are changing cells as well—they correspond to the variables y in the formulation in section 8.2.5. Cells I10:I69 contain the formulas that correspond to the first set of constraints in the VaR

	A	B	C	D	E	F	G	H	I
1	VaR optimization					Objective function			
2		Stock 1	Stock 2	Stock 3			4.02%		
3	Asset weights	47.81%	32.38%	19.81%					
4	Expected returns	0.11%	2.09%	1.98%		Constraints			
5	epsilon	0.05				budget	100.00% =		100%
6	number scenarios (S)	60				total number of ys	3 <=		3.00
7	int(epsilon*S)	3.00							
8	large constant M	10.00							
9	Month No.	Stock 1	Stock 2	Stock 3		Variables y			
10	1	-7.03%	20.14%	-15.43%			0 >=		-0.47%
11	2	-10.03%	-10.03%	-5.74%			1 >=		0.46%
12	3	0.62%	-1.17%	17.84%			0 >=		-0.81%
13	4	7.47%	13.05%	21.71%			0 >=		-1.67%
14	5	-6.67%	6.00%	-0.31%			0 >=		-0.33%
15	6	10.03%	-8.25%	0.51%			0 >=		-0.68%
16	7	-19.18%	5.89%	13.35%			0 >=		0.00%
17	8	-0.35%	13.47%	1.28%			0 >=		-0.91%
18	9	-13.72%	25.68%	16.05%			0 >=		-0.96%
19	10	8.89%	-0.46%	8.87%			0 >=		-1.05%
20	11	8.91%	10.19%	-4.57%			0 >=		-1.13%
21	12	0.32%	5.98%	-0.44%			0 >=		-0.66%
22	13	-1.19%	-13.82%	2.15%			0 >=		0.00%
23	14	-2.25%	8.94%	8.02%			0 >=		-0.80%
24	15	1.70%	0.35%	4.54%			0 >=		0.22%

EXHIBIT 8.7 Solver setup for portfolio VaR optimization based on scenarios for possible asset returns.

optimization formulation with scenarios for the returns. For example, cell I10 contains the formula

$$= (-\text{SUMPRODUCT}(\text{B10}:\text{D10},\$\text{B}\$3:\$\text{D}\$3)-\$\text{G}\$2)/\$\text{B}\$8$$

Note that we picked the value of the "large constant" M to be 10, rather than some extremely large number. M = 10 is large relative to the other coefficients in the problem, so this is sufficient.

EXHIBIT 8.8 Excel Solver setup for the sample VaR optimization problem.

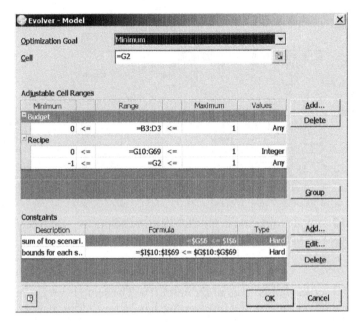

EXHIBIT 8.9 Evolver dialog box for the VaR optimization problem.

There are also a couple of additional constraints, the budget constraint (cells G5:I5), and the constraint on the total number of observations to be considered in the tail (cells G6:I6).

Solving the problem with Excel Solver produces an optimal value for the VaR of 4.62%, and optimal asset weights of 47.81%, 32.38%, and 19.81%, respectively. This problem is challenging for many optimization solvers.

The same spreadsheet setup can be used also to solve the problem with Palisade's Evolver (see worksheet **VaR(Evolver)** in the same file). A screenshot of the Evolver dialog box is shown in Exhibit 8.9. Because of the fact that Evolver uses genetic algorithms, the performance of the solver is extremely influenced by the starting point, that is, the initial values for the changing cells. It may take many iterations to reach a reasonably good solution.

CVaR Optimization The worksheet **CVaR** in the file **Ch8-VaRCVaROpt .xlsx** contains scenarios for return realizations of three stocks, and the setup for the CVaR optimization problem from section 8.3.3 with Excel Solver. Since the problem is linear, Excel Solver can handle it easily, and it is not necessary to use advanced solvers like Evolver.

	A	B	C	D	E	F	G	H	I
1	CVaR optimization					Objective function			
2		Stock 1	Stock 2	Stock 3	Auxiliary variable xi		6.87%		
3	Asset weights	18.03%	44.14%	37.82%	5.83%				
4	Expected returns	0.11%	2.09%	1.98%		Constraints			
5	epsilon	0.05				budget	100.00% =		100%
6	number scenarios (S)	60							
7	int(epsilon*S)	3.00							
8									
9	Month No.	Stock 1	Stock 2	Stock 3			Variables y		
10	1	-7.03%	20.14%	-15.43%			0 >=		-0.076201902
11	2	-10.03%	-10.03%	-5.74%			0.02576037 >=		0.02576037
12	3	0.62%	-1.17%	17.84%			0 >=		-0.121714932
13	4	7.47%	13.05%	21.71%			0 >=		-0.211527212
14	5	-6.67%	6.00%	-0.31%			0 >=		-0.071590216
15	6	10.03%	-8.25%	0.51%			0 >=		-0.041902992
16	7	-19.18%	5.89%	13.35%			0 >=		-0.100233074
17	8	-0.35%	13.47%	1.28%			0 >=		-0.121997327
18	9	-13.72%	25.68%	16.05%			0 >=		-0.207660511
19	10	8.89%	-0.46%	8.87%			0 >=		-0.105860854

EXHIBIT 8.10 CVaR worksheet in file **Ch8-VaRCVaROpt.xlsx,** which contains the setup for CVaR optimization with Excel Solver.

A partial screenshot is given in Exhibit 8.10. The setup is very similar to the one for VaR optimization. However, we have a few additional variables and constraints.

Cells B3:D3 contain the values of the decision variables (the weights for the three stocks). We also have the changing cell E3, which will contain the value of ξ in the formulation for the CVaR optimization objective function. Finally, we will have the changing cells G10:G69, which will correspond to the variables y in the formulation in section 8.3.3. The formulas for the right-hand sides of the constraints in which they participate are in cells I10:I69. For example, cell I10 contains the formula

```
=-SUMPRODUCT(B10:D10,$B$3:$D$3)-$E$3
```

Cell G3, the target cell, will be minimized by Solver, and contains the formula

```
=E3+(1/B7)*SUM(G10:G69)
```

As in the case of VaR optimization, there is also the budget constraint (cells G5:I5), and the constraint that the variables y need to be nonnegative. (The latter constraint is imposed directly in the Solver dialog box; see Exhibit 8.11.)

The optimal solution is in Exhibit 8.10. The optimal value for the portfolio CVaR is 6.87% (cell G2), and the optimal portfolio weights are 18.03%, 44.14%, and 37.82% (cells B3:D3). The value for the auxiliary decision

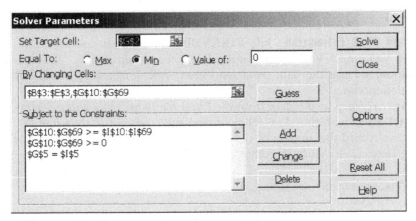

EXHIBIT 8.11 Excel Solver dialog box for the CVaR optimization problem.

variable ξ (cell E3) is 5.83%. The value for ξ is actually the portfolio VaR value. To see that this is the case, consider the simulation output from 10,000 bootstrapped returns for the optimal portfolios obtained with VaR and CVaR optimization. The portfolio returns were obtained by running the simulation in spreadsheet Data (cells E4 and E5 record the portfolio return with the optimal weights for VaR and CVaR, respectively). The output is stored in worksheet **Simulation Output Data**.

The realized 95% VaR obtained for the portfolio with optimal weights in terms of VaR (47.81%, 32.38%, and 19.81%) is 4.62%, as the optimization problem forecasted. The realized 95% VaR obtained for the portfolio with optimal weights in terms of CVaR (18.03%, 44.14%, and 37.82%) is 5.83% – higher than 4.62%, which is to be expected because the optimization problems had different objective functions. In fact, 5.83% is the optimal value of ξ (cell E3) that we obtained after the CVaR portfolio optimization. But note that the optimal value of ξ is not actually the best VaR that we could get for a portfolio consisting of these three stocks.

You can also observe that the realized 95% CVaR obtained for the portfolio with optimal weights in terms of VaR (47.81%, 32.38%, and 19.81%) is 8.40%, while the realized 95% CVaR obtained for the portfolio with optimal weights in terms of CVaR (18.03%, 44.14%, and 37.82%) is 6.87%, as the CVaR optimization forecasted. Again, the simulated portfolio CVaR for a portfolio with weights obtained by minimizing CVaR is better than the simulated portfolio CVaR for a portfolio with weights obtained by minimizing a different objective function, such as VaR.

MATLAB

VaR and CVaR Estimation File VaRCVaREst.m contains code for computing VaR and CVaR from historical and boostrapped data. As an illustration, we use the data from worksheet **VaR 1** in the file **Ch8-VaR Calculation.xlsx**.

After reading in the data from the Excel file (which is a column array with P/L data) with the `xlsread` command and storing it in the array `PLData`, we record the number of observations in the data set in the variable `numObservations` with the command

```
[numObservations,numColumns] = size(PLData);
```

Let us use $\varepsilon = 1\%$ for the VaR and CVaR computation. First, we sort the array of data in an increasing order:

```
sortedPLData = sort(PLData);
```

Since we are given the data in P/L form, we need to find the index of the observation so that 1% of the observations are to the left of it. Let the name of the variable in which we save this index be `obsIndex`. We have

```
obsIndex = floor(epsilon*numObservations);
```

(The command `floor` in MATLAB rounds down a fractional value.) If the data were in L/P form and were sorted in increasing order in the array sortedLPData, we would have used instead the formula

```
obsIndex = numObservations - floor(epsilon*numObservations)
+ 1
```

to find the index of the observation so that 1% of the observations are to the right of it.

The actual computation of VaR involves simply requesting the observation with index `obsIndex` from the sorted data array `sortedPLData`:

```
VaR = -sortedPLData(obsIndex)
```

In the case of L/P data, we would have used the formula

```
VaR = sortedLPData(obsIndex).
```

To find the CVaR from the sorted P/L data array, we use the formula

```
CVaR = -mean(sortedPLData(1:obsIndex))
```

If the data were in L/P form, we would use

```
CVaR = mean(sortedLPData(obsIndex:end))
```

After running the code in MATLAB, we see the output

```
VaR =
    9.5044
CVaR =
    9.5384
```

The estimate of VaR and CVaR from a list of bootstrapped scenarios is found in an analogous way, and the code is available in the file **VaRC-VaREst.m**. The command

```
randomIndices = unidrnd(numObservations,1,numScenarios);
```

generates `numScenarios` random numbers between 1 and `numObserva-tions`, drawing each number between 1 and `numObservations` with equal probability. We treat these random numbers as random indices, and use them to pick a set of `numScenarios` random scenarios from the array with P/L data. We use the command

```
boostrappedData = PLData(randomIndices);
```

to accomplish that. (Note that when a vector array of indices is passed as an argument to an array, as in `PLData(randomIndices)`, the result is an array which only contains the observations with indices in the array `randomIndices`).

Next, we sort the array with boostrapped data, determine the observation number so that 1% of the observations are to the left of it (in the case of P/L data), and use it to compute the actual values of VaR and CVaR. The MATLAB code is presented below.

```
%generate random numScenarios from original data
boostrappedData = PLData(randomIndices);
```

```
%sort data to compute VaR and CVaR
sortedBoostrappedData = sort(boostrappedData);

%compute VaR and CVaR
scenarioIndex = floor(epsilon*numScenarios);
boostrappedVaR = -sortedBoostrappedData(scenarioIndex)
boostrappedCVaR = -
mean(sortedBoostrappedData(1:scenarioIndex))
```

VaR and CVaR Optimization At present, MATLAB cannot be used to find the optimal portfolio allocation for VaR over scenarios because the optimization problem is of the mixed-integer kind, which cannot be handled by MATLAB's optimization solvers. Instead, one may want to use good mixed-integer solvers such as CPLEX, and if necessary, link them to MATLAB code through modeling languages like TOMLAB[28] and ROME.[29]

It is also difficult to optimize the normal approximation formulation to the portfolio VaR because of the presence of the square root in the objective function. However, as we mentioned in Chapter 8, the normal approximation to the portfolio VaR is basically analogous to using mean-standard deviation portfolio allocation, so classical mean-variance allocation schemes can be used instead.

The formulation for the CVaR optimization problem when the uncertain data are presented as scenarios (section 8.3.3) can be solved directly with MATLAB because the optimization problem formulation is linear. The MATLAB code is in the file **CVaROpt.m**. We use the data set from the file **Ch8-VaRCVaROpt.xlsx**, worksheet **CVaR**.

In the code, we use the MATLAB function for solving linear optimization problems, `linprog` (see the introduction to MATLAB's Optimization Toolbox in the Software Hints for Chapter 5). To prepare the inputs to the function, we need to write the problem formulation from section 8.3.3 in a matrix form. First, we rewrite the formulation in the following way:

$$\min_{\mathbf{w},\xi,\mathbf{y}} \quad \xi + \frac{1}{\lfloor \varepsilon \cdot S \rfloor} \cdot \sum_{s=1}^{S} y_s$$

$$\text{s.t.} \quad -(\mathbf{r}^{(s)})'\mathbf{w} - \xi - y_s \leq 0, \quad s = 1, \ldots, S$$

$$\mathbf{w}'\iota = 1$$

$$y_s \geq 0, \quad s = 1, \ldots, S$$

Since the `linprog` formulation requires a single vector **x** of decision variables, we merge all decision variables into it: the weights **w**, the auxiliary variable ξ, and the auxiliary variables **y**. Thus, **x** is an $N + 1 + S$ dimensional vector, where N is the number of assets in the portfolio, and S is the number of scenarios (observations) in the data set.

To represent the objective function vector **f**, we concatenate three vectors: an N-dimensional vector of zeros (that part of **f** will correspond to the **weights** part of the decision variables vector **x**), a single-element array with 1 as an entry (that part of **f** will correspond to the variable ξ in the decision variables vector **x**), and an S-dimensional vector of coefficients $1/\lfloor \varepsilon \cdot S \rfloor$, which will correspond to the **y** part of the decision variables vector **x**). It is easy to concatenate vector and matrix arrays in MATLAB; as shown in the code, the vector **f** can be represented as

```
f = [zeros(numAssets,1); 1; (1/K)*ones(numObservations,1)]
```

You can observe that multiplying the vector array for **f**,

$$
\mathbf{f} = \left[\underbrace{\begin{matrix} 0 & \cdots & 0 \end{matrix}}_{N} \quad 1 \quad \underbrace{\frac{1}{\lfloor \varepsilon \cdot S \rfloor} \quad \cdots \quad \frac{1}{\lfloor \varepsilon \cdot S \rfloor}}_{S} \right]
$$

by the decision variables array **x**,

$$
\mathbf{x} = \left[\underbrace{\begin{matrix} w_1 & \cdots & w_N \end{matrix}}_{N} \quad \xi \quad \underbrace{\begin{matrix} y_1 & \cdots & y_S \end{matrix}}_{S} \right]
$$

will result in the objective function in the preceding optimization problem formulation.

To represent the set of constraints

$$
\mathbf{Ax} \le \mathbf{b},
$$

we create the matrix **A** as a concatenation of three arrays: an $S \times N$ array corresponding to the negatives of the return realizations in each scenario (those will be multiplied by the **weights** portion of the vector of decision variables **x**), an $S \times 1$ array corresponding to the coefficients of -1 in front of the auxiliary variable ξ, and an $S \times S$ array corresponding to the coefficients of -1 in front of the auxiliary variable y_s in the scenario s in each row. The latter array is in fact the negative of an identity matrix[30] of dimension

$S \times S$, which in MATLAB can be declared with the command `eye(S,S)`. The vector **b** is simply an S-dimensional column array of zeros.

The set of equalities $\mathbf{w}'\iota = 1$ in the CVaR problem formulation can be written in the standard $\mathbf{Aeq \cdot x = b}$ form of the MATLAB `linprog` function by declaring a matrix (in fact, a single row vector) of dimension $N + 1 + S$, which contains ones in its first N entries, and zeros everywhere else.

Finally, we declare the bounds on the different variables. The upper bounds on all decision variables are infinity, which can be represented by the vector

```
ub = inf*ones(1, numAssets + 1 + numObservations).
```

The lower bounds are different for the different parts of the decision variable vector **x**. The weights are unrestricted in this case, and so is the auxiliary variable ξ. However, the variables **y** are restricted to be nonnegative. Thus, the vector of lower bounds `lb` is a concatenation of three different vectors:

```
lb = [-inf*ones(numAssets,1); -inf;
zeros(numObservations,1)]
```

The last three lines of the CVaR optimization code call the MATLAB linear optimization solver, and print the relevant results. The optimal **weights** for the different assets in the portfolio are retrieved as the first N entries of the optimal vector **x**, and the value of the portfolio CVaR is the optimal value of the objective function, `fval`.

NOTES

1. The CAPM is discussed in Chapter 11.
2. |.| is simply the standard notation for absolute value.
3. See section 5.2.2 of Chapter 5.
4. See section 3.6.1 of Chapter 3 for a brief definition of the moments of a probability distribution.
5. See sections 3.6.1 and 3.6.2 of Chapter 3 for an introduction to the notation in these expressions. Section 3.6.1 introduced briefly the concept of moments of a probability distribution.
6. See Roy (1952).
7. Note that the difference $V_t - V_{t+1}$ is a positive number if there is a loss, and a negative number if there is a profit.
8. A benchmark is a hypothetical portfolio of assets that functions as a performance standard against which portfolio management is measured. See Siegel (2003) for a review of benchmarks and their uses.

9. See Chapter 2 for a definition of geometric returns.

10. See section 3.4 of Chapter 3 for a definition of the standard normal distribution, section 3.11.2 for the use of a similar notation of percentile in the context of confidence interval estimation, and section 6.2.3 of Chapter 6 for use in stochastic programming.

11. As explained in section 6.2.3 of Chapter 6, the notation $\lfloor a \rfloor$ stands for the integer part of the number a, i.e., for the nearest integer less than or equal to a.

12. Note that the value for the VaR computed with the described method of sorting the data first may be different from the value returned by the commands for computing percentiles in Excel (PERCENTILE) or MATLAB (prctile). While for continuous data, the value of the percentile is the value of the VaR, for discrete data, conventions for computing VaR may vary. The approach for estimation of VaR from discrete data described in this chapter picks a conservative estimate of VaR—it considers the value of the smallest loss that is greater than the value for the percentile.

13. See section 3.11.3 of Chapter 3 for an introduction to the bootstrapping technique.

14. See section 3.11.3 of Chapter 3 and Practice 4.3 on the companion web site for an illustration of the technique for estimating the accuracy of the VaR estimate.

15. See Chapter 4 in Dowd (2005).

16. Some software packages have functions for fitting probability distributions to data. For example, in @RISK one can request the software to suggest a list of distributions that fit the data most closely, in order of relevance. See section 4.1.1 of Chapter 4 and section 3.11.4 of Chapter 3.

17. A quick liquidation of positions may have an effect on the current market prices of the different securities, which will change the estimate of the VaR. Therefore, the estimation of VaR is done assuming that markets behave as usual, that is, positions are liquidated in an orderly fashion.

18. Today, the G-10 countries actually include 11 industrial countries. They are Belgium, Canada, France, Germany, Italy, Japan, the Netherlands, Sweden, Switzerland, the United Kingdom, and the United States.

19. See Chapter 7.

20. See section 6.2.3 of Chapter 6.

21. See section 5.4.3 of Chapter 5.

22. See section 6.2.3 of Chapter 6.

23. See Chapter 2 for a definition of zero-coupon bond.

24. The latter fact can be proved more formally; see, for example, Rockafellar and Uryasev (2002).

25. See practice problem Practice 8.4 on the companion web site for a derivation of this expression.

26. See section 6.2 of Chapter 6 for an introduction to stochastic programming.

27. The $100(1 - \varepsilon)\%$ VaR is a minimizer of the function $F_{1-\varepsilon}(\mathbf{w}, \xi)$. In other words, in some cases the value of ξ that results in the minimum of the function $F_{1-\varepsilon}(\mathbf{w}, \xi)$ will in fact be the $100(1 - \varepsilon)\%$ VaR, and so VaR will be computed as a by-product of computing CVaR. However, there is additional nontrivial

amount of work involved in verifying that the value of ξ obtained in the optimization is indeed the $100(1 - \varepsilon)\%$ VaR, and hence it cannot be assumed that CVaR optimization would provide a computationally efficient way of computing VaR. (For more details, see Rockafellar and Uryasev [2000].) Still, knowing that CVaR minimization implies VaR minimization is useful when making portfolio allocation decisions (rather than computing the actual value of VaR).

28. See TOMLAB Optimization, *The TOMLAB Optimization Environment*, http://tomopt.com/tomlab/.

29. Robust Optimization, ROME, ROME is currently being developed at the National University of Singapore Business School. See Robust Optimization, *ROME*, http://robustopt.com/resources.html.

30. The identity matrix is an array with 1s in the diagonal, and 0s everywhere else.

CHAPTER 9

Equity Portfolio Selection
in Practice

As we saw in Chapters 7 and 8, quantitative investment management can be formulated as a question of determining a probability distribution of portfolio returns and engineering the optimal trade-off between risk and return as a function of individual preferences. From a statistical point of view, a key innovation is the attention paid to the ratio between the bulk of the risk and the risk in the tails. However, for many quantitative asset management firms the starting point for portfolio allocation models is still the mean-variance framework introduced in Chapter 7. Practitioners have customized the framework to include practical approaches for parameter estimation through factor models (which are covered in Chapter 11), considerations for transaction costs and taxes, and other constraints, such as maximum exposure to an industry, or maximum tracking error relative to an index.

In investment management, an important decision is the allocation of funds among asset classes. The funds are then managed within the asset classes. As explained in Chapter 2, the two major asset classes are equities and fixed income securities. Equity portfolio management differs from fixed income portfolio management in substantive ways, and fixed income portfolio management is discussed separately in Chapter 10. Regardless of the asset class being managed, however, the investment process follows the same integrated activities. These activities can be defined as follows:[1]

- An investor's objectives, preferences, and constraints are identified and specified to develop explicit investment policies.
- Strategies are developed and implemented through the choice of optimal combinations of financial and real assets in the marketplace.
- Market conditions, relative asset values, and the investor's circumstances are monitored.
- Portfolio adjustments are made as appropriate to reflect significant changes in any or all of the relevant variables.

It is important to note that banks and financial entities engage in financial operations other than pure investing. Many of these operations are profitable but risky, and their risk must be managed or eliminated. This is accomplished by utilizing financial instruments that allow firms to transfer the risk to the market, rather than keeping it on their balance sheets. Such strategies are discussed in a more comprehensive portfolio risk management context in Chapter 16, after introducing financial derivatives in Chapters 13 and 14.

In this chapter, we focus on the second activity of the investment process, developing and implementing a portfolio strategy. We introduce quantitative formulations of portfolio allocation problems widely used in equity portfolio management. Quantitative equity portfolio selection often involves extending the classical Markowitz framework (Chapter 7) or the more advanced tail-risk portfolio allocation frameworks (Chapter 8) to include different constraints that take specific investment guidelines and institutional features into account.

We begin by discussing the activities involved in the investment process in more detail, so that we can provide context for the rest of the discussion. We then provide a classification of the most common portfolio constraints used in practice, and discuss extensions such as index tracking formulations, the inclusion of transaction costs, optimization of trades across multiple client accounts, tax-aware strategies, and incorporating robustness in portfolio allocation procedures by using robust statistics, simulation, and robust optimization techniques.

9.1 THE INVESTMENT PROCESS

As outlined in the introduction to this chapter, portfolio management in practice consists of four activities, which can be summarized as follows:[2]

1. Setting the investment objectives.
2. Developing and implementing a portfolio strategy.
3. Monitoring the portfolio.
4. Adjusting the portfolio.

This section discusses each of these activities in more detail.

9.1.1 Setting Investment Objectives

Investment objectives vary by the type of financial institutions, and are essentially dictated by the nature of an institution's liabilities. For banks, the objective is to earn a return on invested funds that is higher than the cost of acquiring those funds. For defined benefit pension plans, the investment objective is to generate sufficient cash flow from the investment portfolio to satisfy the plan's pension obligations. Life insurance companies sell a variety of products guaranteeing a dollar payment or a stream of dollar payments at some time in the future. They charge policyholders premiums that depend on the interest rate the company can earn on its investments. To realize a profit, the company must earn a higher return on the premium it invests than the implicit (or explicit) interest rate it has guaranteed policyholders. Finally, for regulated investment companies (i.e., mutual funds and closed-end funds), hedge funds, and managed accounts by trust departments, the main objective of portfolio selection is often to maximize expected returns at a certain level of risk. The target return and risk level can be defined as absolute, or relative to a benchmark, where a benchmark is a collection of securities against which the portfolio manager's performance can be evaluated.

We can therefore divide investors into two general categories based on the characteristics of their benchmark. The first category of investor specifies the benchmark as a function of its liability structure. The investment objective is to generate a cash flow from their portfolio that, at a minimum, satisfies the liability structure. This is often referred to as asset-liability management. The second category of investor specifies the benchmark as a target level of return, or as an index such the S&P 500 or the Russell 1000. The investment objective is then to outperform the target. In this chapter, we will focus on investors in the second category, but provide some background on fixed income liability-driven portfolio management in Chapter 10.

9.1.2 Developing and Implementing a Portfolio Strategy

Typically, an investment policy is developed by the investor in conjunction with a consultant. Given the investment policy, investment guidelines are established for individual managers hired by the investor. The portfolio allocation among different asset classes (bonds, stocks, etc.) is usually decided in advance, and then each portfolio manager is hired to manage a specific asset class, or a subset of an asset class. In this chapter as well as Chapter 10, we discuss the actual implementation of portfolio strategies for two specific asset classes—equities and fixed income securities.

The implementation of the portfolio strategy can be divided into the following tasks:

- Selecting the type of investment strategy.
- Formulating the inputs for portfolio construction.
- Constructing the portfolio.

We explain each task next.

Selecting the Type of Investment Strategy   In the broadest terms, portfolio strategies can be classified either as *active strategies* or *passive strategies*. Active strategies utilize information provided by manager intuition or quantitative *risk factor models*[3] to come up with strategies that select the most attractive investment opportunities in the portfolio manager's opinion. Passive strategies require minimal management. One popular type of passive strategy is *indexing*, whose objective is to replicate the performance of a designated equity market index. Quantitative formulations of the portfolio indexing problem are discussed in section 9.3.

Formulating the Inputs for Portfolio Construction   Formulating the inputs for portfolio construction in an active quantitative portfolio strategy involves forecasting the inputs that are expected to impact the performance of a security and the portfolio as a whole. In the case of mean-variance analysis, for example, of interest are the factors that determine the expected returns of the assets in the portfolio and the covariance structure of the portfolio. Some of these inputs are extrapolated from past market data, others reflect the market's "expectations" that are priced into observed security prices in the market today.[4] In the end, quantitatively generated forecasts are combined with the manager's subjective evaluation to form the inputs to the portfolio allocation framework.

Constructing the Portfolio   Given the manager's forecasts and the market-derived information, the manager identifies attractive investments, and assembles the portfolio. The exact portfolio allocation can be determined based on the optimization problem formulations introduced later in this chapter, but the ultimate decision is made after careful human evaluation of the portfolio strategy.

9.1.3 Monitoring the Portfolio

Once the portfolio has been constructed, it must be monitored. Monitoring involves two activities. The first is to assess whether there have been changes in the market that might suggest that any of the key inputs used in constructing the portfolio may not be realized. The second task is to monitor the performance of the portfolio.

The portfolio performance is monitored in two phases. The first phase is *performance measurement*, which involves the calculation of the return realized by the manager over a specified time interval (the *evaluation period*). The second phase is performance evaluation, which determines whether the manager has added value, and how the manager achieved the observed return. The decomposition of the performance results to explain why those results were achieved is called *return attribution analysis*. Performance evaluation is discussed in more detail in Chapter 11.

9.1.4 Adjusting the Portfolio

Investment management is an ongoing process, and portfolio strategies are in fact performed in a multiperiod context. Portfolio selection strategies are designed to take advantage of market conditions, but those conditions exist temporarily, and as the conditions change, the portfolio manager must perform *portfolio rebalancing*. In doing so, the portfolio manager typically takes the steps discussed in the following sections.

By monitoring developments in the capital market, the portfolio manager determines whether to revise the inputs used in the portfolio construction process. Based on the new inputs, the manager then constructs a new portfolio. In constructing a new portfolio, the costs of trading are often evaluated against the benefits of rebalancing. Such costs include transaction costs and taxes, and are discussed in more detail in sections 9.4 and 9.5.

9.2 PORTFOLIO CONSTRAINTS COMMONLY USED IN PRACTICE

Institutional features and investment policy specifications often lead to more complicated requirements than simple minimization of risk (whatever the definition of risk may be) or maximization of expected portfolio return. For example, as we mentioned earlier, there can be constraints that limit the number of trades, the exposure to a specific industry, or the number of stocks to be kept in the portfolio. Some of these constraints are imposed by the clients, while others are imposed by regulators. For example, in the case of regulated investment companies, restrictions on asset allocation are set forth in the prospectus and may be changed only with the approval of the fund's board of directors. Pension funds must comply with Employee Retirement Income Security Act (ERISA) requirements.[5] The objective of the portfolio optimization problem can also be modified to consider specifically the trade-off between risk and return, transactions costs, or taxes.

In this section, we will take a single-period view of investing, in the sense that the goal of the portfolio allocation procedure will be to invest optimally over a single predetermined period of interest, such as one month.[6] We will use w_0 to denote the vector array of stock weights in the portfolio at the beginning of the period, and w to denote the weights at the end of the period (to be determined).

Many investment companies, especially institutional investors, have a long investment horizon. However, in reality, they treat that horizon as a sequence of shorter period horizons. Risk budgets are often stated over a time period of a year, and return performance is monitored quarterly or monthly.

9.2.1 Long-Only (No-Short-Selling) Constraints

Many funds and institutional investors face restrictions or outright prohibitions on the amount of short selling they can do. When short selling is not allowed, the portfolio allocation optimization model contains the constraints $\mathbf{w} \geq 0$.

9.2.2 Holding Constraints

Diversification principles argue against investing a large proportion of the portfolio in a single asset, or having a large concentration of assets in a specific industry, sector, or country. Limits on the holdings of a specific stock can be imposed with the constraints

$$\mathbf{l} \leq \mathbf{w} \leq \mathbf{u}$$

where $\mathbf{l}$ and $\mathbf{u}$ are vectors of lower and upper bounds of the holdings of each stock in the portfolio.

Consider now a portfolio of 10 stocks. Suppose that the issuers of assets 1, 3, and 5 are in the same industry, and that we would like to limit the portfolio exposure to that industry to be at least 20% but at most 40%. To limit exposure to that industry, we add the constraint

$$0.20 \leq w_1 + w_3 + w_5 \leq 0.40$$

to the portfolio allocation optimization problem.

More generally, if we have a specific set of stocks Ij out of the investment universe I consisting of stocks in the same category (such as industry or country), we can write the constraint

$$L_j \leq \sum_{j \in I_j} w_j \leq U_j$$

In words, this constraint requires that the sum of all stock weights in the particular category of investments with indices I_j is greater than or equal to a lower bound L_j and less than a maximum exposure of U_j.

9.2.3 Turnover Constraints

High portfolio turnover can result in large transaction costs that make portfolio rebalancing inefficient and costly. Thus, some portfolio managers limit the amount of turnover allowed when trading their portfolio. (Another way to control for transaction costs is to minimize them explicitly, and the appropriate formulations are discussed later in this chapter.)

Most commonly, turnover constraints are imposed for each stock:

$$|w_i - w_{0,i}| \leq u_i$$

that is, the absolute magnitude of the difference between the final and the initial weight of stock i in the portfolio is restricted to be less than some upper bound u_i. Sometimes, a constraint is imposed to minimize the portfolio turnover as a whole:

$$\sum_{j \in I_j} |w_j - w_{0,j}| \leq U_j$$

that is, the total absolute difference between the initial and the final weights of the stocks in the portfolio is restricted to be less than or equal to an upper bound U_j. Under this constraint, some stock weights may deviate a lot more than others from their initial weights, but the total deviation is limited.

Turnover constraints are often imposed relative to the *average daily volume* (ADV) of a stock.[7] For example, we may want to restrict turnover to be no more than 5% of the ADV. (In the latter case, the upper bound u_i is set to a value equal to 5% of the ADV.) Modifications of these constraints, such as limiting turnover in a specific industry or sector, are also frequently applied.

9.2.4 Risk Factor Constraints

In practice, it is very common for quantitatively oriented portfolio managers to use *factor models* to control for risk exposures to different risk factors. Such risk factors could include the market return, size, and style.[8] Let us assume that the return on stock i has a factor structure with K risk factors, that is, can be expressed through the equality

$$r_i = \alpha_i + \sum_{k=1}^{K} \beta_{ik} \cdot f_k + \varepsilon_i$$

The factors f_k are common to all securities. The coefficient β_{ik} in front of each factor f_k shows the sensitivity of the return on stock i to factor k. The value of α_i shows the expected excess return of the return on stock i, and ε_i is the idiosyncratic (called *nonsystematic*) part of the return of stock i. The coefficients α_i and β_{ik} are typically estimated by multiple regression analysis.[9]

To limit the exposure of a portfolio of N stocks to the kth risk factor, we impose the constraint

$$\sum_{i=1}^{N} \beta_{ik} \cdot w_i \leq U_k.$$

The mathematics behind risk factor models will become more intuitive in Chapter 11, but this constraint formulation is easy to understand at this stage as well. The total return on the portfolio can be written as

$$\sum_{i=1}^{N} w_i \cdot r_i = \sum_{i=1}^{N} w_i \cdot \left(\alpha_i + \sum_{k=1}^{K} \beta_{ik} \cdot f_k + \varepsilon_i \right)$$

$$= \sum_{i=1}^{N} w_i \cdot \alpha_i + \sum_{i=1}^{N} \left(w_i \cdot \left(\sum_{k=1}^{K} \beta_{ik} \cdot f_k \right) \right) + \sum_{i=1}^{N} w_i \cdot \varepsilon_i.$$

The sensitivity of the portfolio to the different factors is represented by the second term, which can also be written as

$$\sum_{k=1}^{K} \left(\left(\sum_{i=1}^{N} w_i \cdot \beta_{ik} \right) \cdot f_k \right).$$

Therefore, the exposure to a particular factor k is the coefficient in front of f_k, that is,

$$\sum_{i=1}^{N} \beta_{ik} \cdot w_i.$$

On an intuitive level, the sensitivity of the portfolio to a factor k will be larger the larger the presence of factor k in the portfolio through the exposure of the individual stocks. Thus, when we compute the total exposure of the portfolio to factor k, we need to take into consideration both how important this factor is for determining the return on each of the securities in the portfolio, and how much of each security we have in the portfolio.

A commonly used version of the maximum factor exposure constraint is

$$\sum_{i=1}^{N} \beta_{ik} \cdot w_i = 0.$$

This constraint forces the portfolio optimization algorithm to find portfolio weights so that the overall risk exposure to factor k is 0, that is, so that the portfolio is neutral with respect to changes in factor k. Portfolio allocation strategies that claim to be "market-neutral" typically employ this constraint, and the factor is in fact the return on the market.

9.2.5 Cardinality Constraints

Depending on the portfolio allocation model used, sometimes the optimization subroutine recommends holding small amounts of a large number of stocks, which can be costly when one takes into consideration the transaction costs incurred when acquiring these positions. Alternatively, a portfolio manager may be interested in limiting the number of stocks used to track a particular index. (Index tracking is discussed in section 9.3.) Mathematically, modeling the constraint of a limited number of stocks to be held in the portfolio is actually very similar to modeling the number of projects to be selected in the capital budgeting example discussed in section 5.3.3 of Chapter 5. To formulate the constraint on the number of stocks to be held in the portfolio (called *cardinality constraint*), we introduce binary variables, one for each of the N stocks in the portfolio. Let us call these binary variables $\delta_1, \ldots, \delta_N$. Variable δ_i will take value 1 if stock i is included in the portfolio, and 0 otherwise.

Suppose that out of the N stocks in the investment universe, we would like to include a maximum of K stocks in the final portfolio. K here is a positive integer, and is less than N. This constraint can be formulated as

$$\sum_{i=1}^{N} \delta_i \leq K$$

$$\delta_i \text{ binary}, i = 1, \ldots, N.$$

We need to make sure, however, that if an stock is not selected in the portfolio, then the binary variable that corresponds to that stock is set to 0, so that the stock is not counted as one of the K stocks left in the portfolio. When the portfolio weights are restricted to be nonnegative, this can be achieved by imposing the additional constraints

$$0 \leq w_i \leq \delta_i, \ i = 1, \ldots, N.$$

If the optimal weight for stock i turns out to be different from 0, then the binary variable δ_i associated with stock i is forced to take value 1, and stock i will be counted as one of the K stocks to be kept in the portfolio. If the optimal weight for stock i is 0, then the binary variable δ_i associated with stock i can be either 0 or 1, but that will not matter for all practical purposes because the solver will set it to 0 if there are too many other attractive stocks that will be counted as the K stocks to be kept in the portfolio. At the same time, since the portfolio weights w_i are between 0 and 1, and δ_i is 0 or 1, the constraint $w_i \leq \delta_i$ does not restrict the values that the stock weight w_i can take.

The constraints are a little different if short sales are allowed, in which case the weights may be negative. We have

$$-M \cdot \delta_i \leq w_i \leq M \cdot \delta_i, \ i = 1, \ldots, N,$$

where M is a "large" constant (large relative to the size of the inputs in the problem; so in this portfolio optimization application $M = 10$ can be considered "large"). You can observe that if the weight w_i is anything but 0, the value of the binary variable δ_i will be forced to be different from 0, that is, δ_i will need to be 1, since it can only take values 0 or 1.

9.2.6 Minimum Holding and Transaction Size Constraints

Cardinality constraints are often used in conjunction with minimum holding/trading constraints. The latter set a minimum limit on the amount of a stock that can be held in the portfolio, or the amount of a stock that can be traded, effectively eliminating small trades. Both cardinality and minimum holding/trading constraints aim to reduce the amount of transaction costs.

Threshold constraints on the amount of stock i to be held in the portfolio can be imposed with the constraint

$$|w_i| \geq L_i \cdot \delta_i$$

where L_i is the smallest holding size allowed for stock i, and δ_i is a binary variable, analogous to the binary variables δ_i defined in the previous section—it equals 1 if stock i is included in the portfolio, and 0 otherwise. (All additional constraints relating to δ_i and w_i described in the previous section still apply.)

Similarly, constraints can be imposed on the minimum trading amount for stock i. As we explained earlier in this section, the size of the trade for stock i is determined by the absolute value of the difference between the current weight of the stock, $w_{0,i}$, and the new weight w_i that will be found by the solver: $|w_i - w_{0,i}|$. The minimum trading size constraint formulation is

$$|w_i - w_{0,i}| \geq L_i^{\text{trade}} \cdot \delta_i$$

where L_i^{trade} is the smallest trading size allowed for stock i.

As we explained in section 5.2.5 of Chapter 5, adding binary variables to an optimization problem makes the problem more difficult for the solver, and can increase the computation time substantially. That is why in practice, portfolio managers often omit minimum holding and transaction size constraints from the optimization problem formulation, electing instead to eliminate weights and trades that appear too small manually, after the optimal portfolio is determined by the optimization solver. It is important to realize, however, that modifying the optimal solution for the simpler portfolio allocation problem (the optimal solution in this case is the weights/trades for the different stocks) by eliminating small positions manually does not necessarily produce the optimal solution to an optimization problem that contained the minimum holding and transaction size constraints from the beginning. In fact, there can be pathological cases in which the solution is very different from the true optimal solution. However, for most cases in practice, the small manual adjustments to the optimal portfolio allocation do not cause tremendous discrepancies or inconsistencies.

9.2.7 Round Lot Constraints

So far, we have assumed that stocks are infinitely divisible, that is, that we can trade and invest in fractions of stocks, bonds, and the like. This is, of course, not true—in reality, securities are traded in multiples of minimum transaction lots, or *rounds* (e.g., 100 or 500 shares).

In order to represent the condition that securities should be traded in rounds, we need to introduce additional decision variables (let us call them z_i, $i = 1, \ldots, N$) that are integer and will correspond to the number of lots of a particular security that will be purchased. Each z_i will then be linked to the corresponding portfolio weight w_i through the equality

$$w_i = z_i \cdot f_i, \ i = 1, \ldots, N$$

where f_i is measured in dollars, and is a fraction of the total amount to be invested. For example, suppose there are a total of $100 million to be invested, and stock i trades at $50 in round lots of 100. Then

$$f_i = \frac{50 \cdot 100}{100,000,000} = 5 \cdot 10^{-7}.$$

All remaining constraints in the portfolio allocation can be expressed through the weights w_i, as usual. However, we also need to specify for the solver that the decision variables z_i are integer.

An issue with imposing round lot constraints is that the budget constraint

$$\mathbf{w}'\iota = 1,$$

which is in fact

$$\sum_{i=1}^{N} z_i \cdot f_i = 1,$$

may not be satisfied exactly. To understand this better, recall the capital budgeting example from section 5.3.3, which illustrated a similar situation in a different context—when projects with different budgets were added up without the ability to adjust their budgets up or down, they did not necessarily use the entire available budget (or could end up over budget).

One possibility to handle this problem is to relax the budget constraint. For example, we can state the constraint as

$$\mathbf{w}'\iota \leq 1,$$

or, equivalently,

$$\sum_{i=1}^{N} z_i \cdot f_i \leq 1.$$

This will ensure that we do not go over budget.

If our objective is stated as expected return maximization, the optimization solver will attempt to make this constraint as tight as possible, that is, we will end up using up as much of the budget as we can. Depending on the objective function and the other constraints in the formulation, however, this may not always happen. We can try to force the solver to minimize the slack in the budget constraint by introducing a pair of nonnegative decision variables (let us call them ε^+ and ε^-) that account for the amount that is "overinvested" or "underinvested." These variables will pick up the slack left over because of the inability to round the amounts for the different investments. Namely, we impose the constraints

$$\sum_{i=1}^{N} z_i \cdot f_i + \varepsilon^- - \varepsilon^+ = 1$$
$$\varepsilon^- \geq 0, \varepsilon^+ \geq 0$$

and subtract the following term from the objective function,

$$\lambda_{rl} \cdot (\varepsilon^- + \varepsilon^+),$$

where λ_{rl} is a penalty term associated with the amount of over- or underinvestment the portfolio manager is willing to tolerate (selected by the portfolio manager). In the final solution, the violation of the budget constraint will be minimized. Note, however, that this formulation technically allows for the budget to be overinvested.

Note that the optimal portfolio allocation we obtain after solving this optimization problem will not be the same as the allocation we would obtain if we solve an optimization problem without round lot constraints, and then round the amounts to fit the lots that can be traded in the market.

Cardinality constraints, minimum holding/trading constraints, and especially round lot constraints, require more sophisticated binary and integer programming solvers, and are difficult problems to solve in the case of large portfolios.

9.3 BENCHMARK EXPOSURE AND TRACKING ERROR MINIMIZATION

Expected portfolio return maximization under the mean-variance framework or other risk measure minimization are examples of active investment strategies, that is, strategies that identify a universe of attractive investments, and ignore inferior investments opportunities. As we explained in section 9.1.2, a different approach, referred to as a passive investment strategy, argues that in the absence of any superior forecasting ability, investors might as well resign themselves to the fact that they cannot beat the market. From a theoretical perspective, the analytics of portfolio theory tell them to hold a broadly diversified portfolio anyway. Many mutual funds are managed relative to a particular benchmark or stock universe, such as the S&P 500 or the Russell 1000. The portfolio allocation models are then formulated in such a way that the tracking error relative to the benchmark is kept small.

9.3.1 Standard Definition of Tracking Error

To incorporate a passive investment strategy, we can change the objective function of the portfolio allocation problem so that instead of minimizing a portfolio risk measure, we minimize the tracking error with respect to a benchmark that represents the market, such as the Russell 3000, or the S&P 500. Such strategies are often referred to as *indexing*. The *tracking error* can be defined in different ways. However, practitioners typically mean a specific definition: the variance (or standard deviation) of the difference between the portfolio return, $\mathbf{w}'\tilde{\mathbf{r}}$, and the return on the benchmark, $\mathbf{w}_b'\tilde{\mathbf{r}}$. Mathematically, the tracking error (TE) can be expressed as

$$
\begin{aligned}
\text{TE} &= Var(\mathbf{w}'\tilde{\mathbf{r}} - \mathbf{w}_b'\tilde{\mathbf{r}}) \\
&= Var\left((\mathbf{w} - \mathbf{w}_b)'\tilde{\mathbf{r}}\right) \\
&= (\mathbf{w} - \mathbf{w}_b)'\, Var\,(\tilde{\mathbf{r}})\,(\mathbf{w} - \mathbf{w}_b) \\
&= (\mathbf{w} - \mathbf{w}_b)'\,\boldsymbol{\Sigma}\,(\mathbf{w} - \mathbf{w}_b)
\end{aligned}
$$

where $\boldsymbol{\Sigma}$ is the covariance matrix of the stock returns. You can observe that the formula is very similar to the formula for the portfolio variance we derived in Chapter 7; however, the portfolio weights in the formula from Chapter 7 are replaced by differences between the weights of the stocks in the portfolio and the weights of the stocks in the index.

A question that may be on some readers' minds is why we need to optimize portfolio weights in order to track a benchmark, when technically the most effective way to track a benchmark is by investing the portfolio in the stocks in the benchmark portfolio in the same proportions as the proportions of these securities in the benchmark. The problem with this approach is that, especially with large benchmarks such as the Russell 3000, the transaction costs of a proportional investment and the subsequent rebalancing of the portfolio can be prohibitive (i.e., dramatically adversely impact the performance of the portfolio relative to the benchmark). Furthermore, in practice, securities are not infinitely divisible, so investing a portfolio of a limited size in the same proportions as the composition of the benchmark will still not achieve zero tracking error. Thus, the optimal formulation is to require that the portfolio follows the benchmark as closely as possible.

While indexing has become an essential part of many portfolio strategies, most portfolio managers cannot resist the temptation to identify at least some securities that will outperform others. Hence, restrictions on the tracking error are often imposed as a constraint, while the objective function is something different than minimizing the tracking error. The tracking error constraint takes the form

$$
(\mathbf{w} - \mathbf{w}_b)'\,\boldsymbol{\Sigma}\,(\mathbf{w} - \mathbf{w}_b) \leq \sigma_{\text{TE}}^2
$$

where σ_{TE}^2 is a limit (imposed by the investor) on the amount of tracking error the investor is willing to tolerate. This is a quadratic constraint, which is convex and computationally tractable, but requires specialized optimization software.

9.3.2 Alternative Ways of Defining Tracking Error

There are alternative ways in which tracking-error type constraints can be imposed.

For example, we may require that the absolute deviations of the portfolio weights (**w**) from the index weights (**w**$_b$) are less than or equal to a given vector array of upper bounds **u**:

$$|\mathbf{w} - \mathbf{w}_b| \leq \mathbf{u}$$

where the absolute values |.| for the vector differences are taken component-wise, that is, for pairs of corresponding elements from the two vector arrays. These constraints can be stated as linear constraints by rewriting them as

$$\mathbf{w} - \mathbf{w}_b \leq \mathbf{u}$$

$$-(\mathbf{w} - \mathbf{w}_b) \leq \mathbf{u}.$$

Similarly, we can require that for stocks within a specific industry (whose indices in the portfolio belong to a subset I_j of the investment universe I), the total tracking error is less than a given upper bound U_j:

$$\sum_{j \in I_j} (w_j - w_{b,j}) \leq U_j.$$

Finally, tracking error can be expressed through risk measures other than the absolute deviations or the variance of the deviations from the benchmark. Rockafellar and Uryasev (2002) suggest using CVaR[10] to manage the tracking error. (As we know from Chapter 8, CVaR is a computationally tractable risk measure as long as the data are presented in the form of scenarios.[11]) We provide below a formulation that is somewhat different from Rockafellar and Uryasev (2002), but preserves the main idea.

Suppose that we are given S scenarios for the return of a benchmark portfolio (or an instrument we are trying to replicate), $b_s, s = 1, \ldots, S$. These scenarios can be generated by simulation, or taken from historical data. We also have N stocks with returns $r_i^{(s)}(i = 1, \ldots, N, s = 1, \ldots, S)$ in each scenario. The value of the portfolio in scenario s is

$$\sum_{i=1}^{N} r_i^{(s)} \cdot w_i,$$

or, equivalently, $(\mathbf{r}^{(s)})'\mathbf{w}$, where $\mathbf{r}^{(s)}$ is the vector of returns for the N stocks in scenario s. Consider the differences between the return on the benchmark and the return on the portfolio,

$$b_s - (\mathbf{r}^{(s)})'\mathbf{w} = -((\mathbf{r}^{(s)})'\mathbf{w} - b_s).$$

If this difference is positive, we have a loss; if the difference is negative, we have a gain; both gains and losses are computed relative to the benchmark. Rationally, the portfolio manager should not worry about differences that are negative; the only cause for concern would be if the portfolio underperforms the benchmark, which would result in a positive difference. Thus, it is not necessarily to limit the variance of the deviations of the portfolio returns from the benchmark, which penalizes for positive and negative deviations equally. Instead, we can treat these differences in the same way as we treated absolute portfolio losses in section 8.3 of Chapter 8, and impose a limit on the amount of loss we are willing to tolerate in terms of the CVaR of the distribution of losses relative to the benchmark.

From the formulation of the CVaR optimization problem from section 8.3, it is easy to see that the tracking error constraint in terms of the CVaR can be stated as the following set of constraints:

$$\xi + \frac{1}{\lfloor \varepsilon \cdot S \rfloor} \cdot \sum_{s=1}^{S} y_s \leq U_{TE}$$

$$y_s \geq - \left((\mathbf{r}^{(s)})' \mathbf{w} - b_s \right) - \xi, \quad s = 1, \ldots, S$$

$$y_s \geq 0, s = 1, \ldots, S$$

where U_{TE} is the upper bound on the negative deviations.

This formulation of tracking error is appealing in two ways. First, it treats positive and negative deviations relative to the benchmark differently, which agrees with the strategy of an investor seeking to maximize returns overall. Second, it results in a linear set of constraints, which are easy to handle computationally, in contrast to the first formulation of the tracking error constraint in this section, which results in a quadratic constraint.

9.3.3 Actual vs. Predicted Tracking Error

The tracking error calculation in practice is often backward-looking. For example, in computing the covariance matrix Σ in the standard tracking error definition in section 9.3.1, or in selecting the scenarios used in the CVaR-type tracking error constraint in section 9.3.2, we may use historical data. The tracking error calculated in this manner is called the ex post tracking error, backward-looking error, or actual tracking error.

The problem with using the actual tracking error for assessing future performance relative to a benchmark is that the actual tracking error does not reflect the effect of the portfolio manager's current decisions on the future active returns and hence the tracking error that may be realized in the future. The actual tracking error has little predictive value and can be misleading regarding portfolio risk.

Portfolio managers need forward-looking estimates of tracking error to reflect future portfolio performance more accurately. In practice, this is accomplished by using the services of a commercial vendor that has a *multi-factor risk model*[12] that has identified and defined the risks associated with the benchmark, or by building such a model in-house. Statistical analysis of historical return data for the stocks in the benchmark are used to obtain the risk factors and to quantify the risks. Using the manager's current portfolio holdings, the portfolio's current exposure to the various risk factors can be calculated and compared to the benchmark's exposures to the risk factors. From the differential factor exposures and the risks of the factors, a *forward-looking tracking error* for the portfolio can be computed. This tracking error is also referred to as *ex ante tracking error* or *predicted tracking error*.

There is no guarantee that the predicted tracking error will match exactly the tracking error realized over the future time period of interest. However, this calculation of the tracking error has its use in risk control and portfolio construction. By performing a simulation analysis on the factors that enter the calculation, the manager can evaluate the potential performance of portfolio strategies relative to the benchmark, and eliminate those that result in tracking errors beyond the client-imposed tolerance for risk. The actual tracking error, on the other hand, is useful for assessing actual performance relative to a benchmark.

9.4 INCORPORATING TRANSACTION COSTS

Transaction costs can be generally divided into two categories: explicit (such as bid-ask spreads, commissions and fees), and implicit (such as price movement risk costs[13] and market impact costs[14]).

The typical portfolio allocation models are built on top of one or several forecasting models for expected returns and risk. Small changes in these forecasts can result in reallocations that would not occur if transaction costs are taken into account. In practice, the effect of transaction costs on portfolio performance is far from insignificant. If transaction costs are not taken into consideration in allocation and rebalancing decisions, they can lead to poor portfolio performance.

This section describes some common transaction cost models for portfolio rebalancing. We use the mean-variance framework as the basis for describing the different approaches. However, it is straightforward to extend the transaction cost models into other portfolio allocation frameworks.

The earliest, and most widely used, model for transaction costs is the mean-variance risk-aversion formulation with transaction costs.[15] The optimization problem has the following objective function:

$$\max_{\mathbf{w}} \quad \mathbf{w}'\boldsymbol{\mu} - \lambda \cdot \mathbf{w}'\boldsymbol{\Sigma}\mathbf{w} - \lambda_{TC} \cdot TC$$

where TC is a transaction cost penalty function, and λ_{TC} is the transaction cost aversion parameter. In other words, the objective is to maximize the expected portfolio return less the cost of risk and transaction costs. We can imagine that as the transaction costs increase, at some point it becomes optimal to keep the current portfolio rather than to rebalance. Variations of this formulation exist. For example, it is common to maximize expected portfolio return minus transaction costs, and impose limits on the risk as a constraint (i.e., to move the second term in the objective function in the constraints).

Transaction costs models can involve complicated nonlinear functions. Although software exists for general nonlinear optimization problems, the computational time required for solving such problems is often too long for realistic investment applications, and, as we explained in Chapter 5, the quality of the solution is not guaranteed. In practice, an observed complicated nonlinear transaction costs function is often approximated with a computationally tractable function that is assumed to be separable in the portfolio weights, that is, it is often assumed that the transaction costs for each individual stock are independent of the transaction costs for another stock. For the rest of this section, we will denote the individual cost function for stock i by TC_i.

Next, we explain several widely used models for the transaction cost function.

9.4.1 Linear Transaction Costs

Let us start simple. Suppose that the transaction costs are proportional, that is, they are a percentage c_i of the transaction size $|t| = |w_i - w_{0,i}|$.[16] Then, the portfolio allocation problem with transaction costs can be written simply as

$$\max_{\mathbf{w}} \quad \mathbf{w}'\boldsymbol{\mu} - \lambda \cdot \mathbf{w}'\boldsymbol{\Sigma}\mathbf{w} - \lambda_{TC} \cdot \sum_{i=1}^{N} c_i \cdot |w_i - w_{0,i}|.$$

The problem can be made solver-friendly by replacing the absolute value terms with new decision variables y_i, and adding two sets of constraints. Hence, we rewrite the objective function as

$$\max_{\mathbf{w},\mathbf{y}} \quad \mathbf{w}'\boldsymbol{\mu} - \lambda \cdot \mathbf{w}'\boldsymbol{\Sigma}\mathbf{w} - \lambda_{TC} \cdot \sum_{i=1}^{N} c_i \cdot y_i$$

and add the constraints

$$y_i \geq w_i - w_{0,i},$$
$$y_i \geq -(w_i - w_{0,i}).$$

This preserves the quadratic optimization problem formulation, a formulation that can be passed to quadratic optimization solvers such as Excel Solver and MATLAB's `quadprog` function because the constraints are linear expressions, and the objective function contains only linear and quadratic terms.

In the optimal solution, the optimization solver will in fact set the value for y_i to $|w_i - w_{0,i}|$. This is because this is a maximization problem and y_i occurs with a negative sign in the objective function, so the solver will try to set y_i to the minimum value possible. That minimum value will be the maximum of $(w_i - w_{0,i})$ or $-(w_i - w_{0,i})$, which is in fact the absolute value $|w_i - w_{0,i}|$.

9.4.2 Piecewise-Linear Transaction Costs

Taking the model in the previous section a step further, we can introduce piecewise-linear approximations to transaction cost function models. This kind of function is more realistic than the linear cost function, especially for large trades. As the trading size increases, it becomes increasingly more costly to trade because of the market impact of the trade.

An example of a piecewise-linear function of transaction costs for a trade of size t of a particular security is illustrated in Exhibit 9.1. The transaction cost function illustrated in the graph assumes that the rate of increase of transaction costs (reflected in the slope of the function) changes at certain threshold points. For example, it is smaller in the range 0 to 15% of daily volume than in the range 15% to 40% of daily volume (or some other trading volume index). Mathematically, the transaction cost function in Exhibit 9.1 can be expressed as

$$\text{TC}(t) = \begin{cases} s_1 t, & 0 \leq t \leq 0.15 \cdot \text{Vol} \\ s_1(0.15 \cdot \text{Vol}) + s_2(t - 0.15 \cdot \text{Vol}), & 0.15 \cdot \text{Vol} \leq t \leq 0.40 \cdot \text{Vol} \\ s_1(0.15 \cdot \text{Vol}) + s_2(0.25 \cdot \text{Vol}) & 0.40 \cdot \text{Vol} \leq t \leq 0.50 \cdot \text{Vol} \\ \quad + s_3(t - 0.40 \cdot \text{Vol}), & \end{cases}$$

where s_1, s_2, s_3 are the slopes of the three linear segments on the graph. (They are given data.)

To include piecewise-linear functions for transaction costs in the objective function of a mean-variance (or any general mean-risk) portfolio optimization problem, we need to introduce new decision variables that correspond to the number of pieces in the piecewise-linear approximation

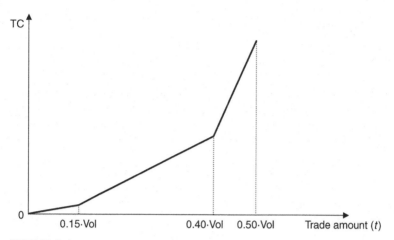

EXHIBIT 9.1 Example of modeling transaction costs (TC) as a piecewise-linear function of trade size t.

of the transaction cost function (in this case, there are 3 linear segments, so we introduce variables z_1, z_2, z_3). We write the penalty term in the objective function for an individual stock as[17]

$$\lambda_{TC} \cdot (s_1 \cdot z_1 + s_2 \cdot z_2 + s_3 \cdot z_3).$$

If there are N stocks in the portfolio, the total transaction cost will be the sum of the transaction costs for each individual stock, that is, the penalty term that involves transaction costs in the objective function becomes

$$-\lambda_{TC} \sum_{i=1}^{N} (s_{1,i} \cdot z_{1,i} + s_{2,i} \cdot z_{2,i} + s_{3,i} \cdot z_{3,i}).$$

In addition, we specify the following constraints on the new decision variables:

$$0 \leq z_{1,i} \leq 0.15 \cdot \text{Vol}_i$$
$$0 \leq z_{2,i} \leq 0.25 \cdot \text{Vol}_i$$
$$0 \leq z_{3,i} \leq 0.10 \cdot \text{Vol}_i$$

Note that because of the increasing slopes of the linear segments and the goal of making that term as small as possible in the objective function, the optimizer will never set the decision variable corresponding to the second segment, $z_{2,i}$, to a number greater than 0 unless the decision variable corresponding to the first segment, $z_{1,i}$, is at its upper bound. Similarly, the optimizer would never set $z_{3,i}$ to a number greater than 0 unless both $z_{1,i}$ and $z_{2,i}$ are at their upper bounds. So, this set of constraints allows us to compute the amount of transaction costs incurred in the trading of stock i as $z_{1,i} + z_{2,i} + z_{3,i}$.

Of course, we also need to link the amount of transaction costs incurred in the trading of stock i to the optimal portfolio allocation. This can be done by adding a few more variables and constraints. We introduce variables y_i, one for each stock in the portfolio, that would represent the amount traded (but not the direction of the trade), and would be nonnegative. Then, we require that

$$y_i = z_{1,i} + z_{2,i} + z_{3,i}$$

for each stock i, and also that y_i equals the change in the portfolio position of stock i. The latter condition can be imposed by writing the constraint

$$y_i = |w_i - w_{0,i}|$$

where $w_{0,i}$ and w_i are the initial and the final amount of stock i in the portfolio, respectively.[18]

Despite their apparent complexity, piecewise-linear approximations for transaction costs are very solver-friendly, and save time (relative to nonlinear models) in the actual portfolio optimization. Although modeling transaction costs this way requires introducing new decision variables and constraints, the increase in the dimension of the portfolio optimization problem does not affect significantly the running time or the performance of the optimization software because the problem formulation is easy from a computational perspective.

9.4.3 Quadratic Transaction Costs

The transaction cost function is often parameterized as a quadratic function of the form

$$\mathrm{TC}_i(t) = c_i \cdot |t| + d_i \cdot |t|^2.$$

The coefficients c_i and d_i are calibrated from data, such as by fitting a quadratic function to an observed pattern of transaction costs realized for trading a particular stock under normal conditions.[19]

Including this function in the objective function of the portfolio optimization problem results in a quadratic program that can be solved with widely available quadratic optimization software.

9.4.4 Fixed Transaction Costs

In some cases, we need to model fixed transaction costs. Those are costs that are incurred independently of the amount traded. To include such costs in the portfolio optimization problem, we need to introduce binary variables $\delta_1, \ldots, \delta_N$ corresponding to each stock, where δ_i equals 0 if the amount traded of stock i is 0, and 1 otherwise. The idea is similar to the idea we used to model the requirement that only a given number of stocks can be included in the portfolio.

Suppose the fixed transaction cost is a_i for stock i. Then, the transaction cost function is

$$\mathrm{TC}_i = a_i \cdot \delta_i$$

The objective function formulation is then

$$\max_{\mathbf{w}, \boldsymbol{\delta}} \quad \mathbf{w}'\boldsymbol{\mu} - \lambda \cdot \mathbf{w}'\boldsymbol{\Sigma}\mathbf{w} - \lambda_{\mathrm{TC}} \cdot \sum_{i=1}^{N} a_i \cdot \delta_i,$$

and we need to add the following constraints to make sure that the binary variables are linked to the trades $|w_i - w_{0,i}|$:

$$|w_i - w_{0,i}| \leq M \cdot \delta_i, \quad i = 1, \ldots, N,$$

$$\delta_i \text{ binary}$$

where M is a "large" constant. When the trading size $|w_i - w_{0,i}|$ is nonzero, δ_i will be forced to be 1. When the trading size is 0, then δ_i can be either 0 or 1, but the optimizer will set it to 0, since it will try to make its value the minimum possible in the objective function.

Of course, combinations of different trading cost models can be used in practice. For example, if the trade involves both a fixed and a variable quadratic transaction cost, then we could use a transaction cost function of the kind

$$\mathrm{TC}_i(t) = a_i \cdot \delta_i + c_i \cdot |t| + d_i \cdot |t|^2.$$

The important thing to take away from this section is that when transaction costs are included in the portfolio rebalancing problem, the result is a reduced amount of trading and rebalancing, and a different portfolio allocation than the one that would be obtained if transaction costs are not taken into consideration.

9.5 INCORPORATING TAXES

When stocks in a portfolio appreciate or depreciate in value, *capital gains* (respectively, *losses*) accumulate. When stocks are sold, investors pay taxes on the *realized* net capital gains. The taxes are computed as a percentage of the difference between the current market value of the stocks and their tax basis, where the *tax basis* is the price at which the stocks were bought originally.[20] The percentage is less for long-term capital gains (when stocks have been held for more than a year) than it is for short-term capital gains (when stocks have been held for less than a year).[21] Since shares of the same stock could have been bought at different points in time (in different *lots*), selling one lot of the stock as opposed to another could incur a different amount of tax. In addition to capital gains taxes, investors who are not exempt from taxes owe taxes on the dividends paid on stocks in their portfolios. Those dividends are historically taxed at a higher rate than capital gains, and after 2010 will be taxed as income, that is, at the investor's personal tax rate. The tax liability of a particular portfolio therefore depends on the timing of the execution of trades, on the tax basis of the portfolio, on the accumulated short-term and long-term capital gains, and on the tax bracket of the investor.

Over two-thirds of marketable portfolio assets in the United States are held by individuals, insurance, and holding companies who pay taxes on their returns. (Exceptions are, for example, pension funds, which do not pay taxes year-to-year.) Studies have indicated that taxes are the greatest expense investors face—greater than commissions and investment management fees. To gain some intuition about the effect of taxes on the income of an investor over the investor's lifetime, consider a portfolio that has a capital appreciation of 6.00% per year. After 30 years, $1,000 invested in that portfolio will turn into $1,000 \cdot (1 + 0.06)^{30} = \$5,743.49$. Now suppose that the capital gains are realized each year, and a tax of 35% is paid on the gains (the remainder is reinvested). After 30 years, $1,000 invested in the portfolio will turn into $1,000 \cdot (1 + (1 - 0.35) \cdot 0.06)^{30} = \$3,151.13$, about half of the amount without taxes even when the tax is about one-third of the capital gains. In fact, in order to provide the same return as the portfolio with no taxes, the portfolio with annual realized capital gains would need to generate a capital appreciation of 9.23% per year! You can imagine that the same logic would make benchmark tracking and performance measurement very difficult on an after-tax basis.

As investors have become more aware of the dramatic impact of taxes on their returns, there is increasing pressure on portfolio managers to include tax considerations in their portfolio rebalancing decisions and to report after-tax performance. Consequently, the demand for computationally efficient and quantitatively rigorous methods for taking taxes into consideration in portfolio allocation decisions has grown in recent years. The complexity of the problem of incorporating taxes, however, is considerable, both from a theoretical and practical perspective:

- The presence of tax liabilities changes the interpretation of even fundamental portfolio performance summary measures such as market value and risk. Thus, well-established methods for evaluating portfolio performance on a pretax basis do not work well in the case of tax-aware portfolio optimization. For example, in traditional portfolio management a loss is associated with risk, and is therefore minimized whenever possible. However, in the presence of taxes, losses may be less damaging because they can be used to offset capital gains and reduce the tax burden of portfolio rebalancing strategies. Benchmarking is also not obvious in the presence of taxes: two portfolios that have exactly the same current holdings are not equivalent if the holdings have a different tax basis.[22]

- Tax considerations are too complex to implement in a nonautomated fashion; at the same time, their automatic inclusion in portfolio rebalancing algorithms requires the ability to solve very difficult, large-scale optimization problems.

- The best approach for portfolio management with tax considerations is optimization problem formulations that look at return forecasts over several time periods (e.g., until the end of the year) before recommending new portfolio weights. However, the latter *multiperiod view* of the portfolio optimization problem is very difficult to handle computationally—the dimension of the optimization problem, that is, the number of variables and constraints, increases exponentially with the number of time periods under considerations.

We need to emphasize that while many of the techniques described in the previous sections of this chapter are widely known, there are no standard practices for tax-aware portfolio management that appear to be established. Different asset management firms interpret tax-aware portfolio allocation and approach the problem differently. To some firms, minimizing turnover,[23] such as by investing in index funds, or selecting strategies that minimize the portfolio dividend yield[24] qualify as tax-aware portfolio strategies. Other asset management firms employ complex optimization algorithms that incorporate tax considerations directly in portfolio rebalancing decisions, so that they can keep up with the considerable burden of keeping track of thousands of managed accounts and their tax preferences. The fact is, even using simple rules of thumb, such as always selling stocks from the oldest lots after rebalancing the portfolio with classical portfolio optimization routines, can have a positive effect on after-tax portfolio returns. The latter strategy minimizes the likelihood that short-term gains will be incurred, which in turn reduces taxes because short-term capital gains are taxed at a higher rate than long-term capital gains.

Apelfeld, Fowler, and Gordon (1996) suggested a tax-aware portfolio rebalancing framework that incorporates taxes directly into the portfolio optimization process. The main idea of their approach is to treat different lots of the same stock as different securities, and then penalize for taxes as if they were different transaction costs associated with the sale of each lot. (This means, for example, that Microsoft stock bought on Date 1 is treated as a different security from Microsoft stock bought on Date 2.) Many tax-aware quantitative investment strategies employ versions of this approach, but there are a few issues to beware when using it in practice:

- The first one is a general problem for all tax-aware approaches when they are used in the context of active portfolio management. For a portfolio manager who handles thousands of different accounts with different tax exposures, it is virtually impossible to pay attention to the tax cost incurred by each individual investor. While the tax-aware method described above minimizes the overall tax burden by reducing the amount of realized short-term sales, it has no provisions for differentiating between investors in different tax brackets because it is difficult to think of each trade as divided between all investors, and adjusted for each individual investor's tax circumstances. This issue is so intractable, that in practice it is not really brought under consideration.
- The dimension of the problem can become unmanageable very quickly. For example, a portfolio of 1,000 securities, each of which has 10 different lots, is equivalent to a portfolio of 10,000 securities when each lot is treated as a different security. Every time a new purchase is realized, a new security is added to the portfolio, since a new lot is created. One needs to exercise care and "clean up" lots that have been sold and therefore have holdings of zero each time the portfolio is rebalanced.

■ As we explained in section 9.2, practitioners typically use factor models for forecasting returns and estimating risk. We will explain factor models in more detail in Chapter 11, but here we will mention that one of the assumptions when measuring portfolio risk through factor models is that the specific risk of a particular security is uncorrelated with the specific risk of other securities. (The only risk they share is the risk expressed through the factors in the factor model.) This assumption clearly does not hold when different "securities" are in fact different lots of the same stock.

DiBartolomeo (2000) describes a modification to the model used by Northfield Information Service's portfolio management software that eliminates the last two problems. Instead of treating each lot as a separate security, the software imposes a piecewise linear transaction costs (see section 9.4 and Exhibit 9.1) where the break points on the horizontal axis correspond to the current size of different lots of the same security. The portfolio rebalancing algorithm goes through several iterations for the portfolio weights, and at each iteration, only the shares in the highest cost basis tax lot can be traded. Other shares of the same stock can be traded in subsequent iterations of the algorithm, with their appropriate tax costs attached.

The approaches we described so far take into consideration the short-term or long-term nature of capital gains, but do not incorporate the ability the offset capital gains and losses accumulated over the year. This is an inherent limitation of single-period portfolio rebalancing approaches, and is a strong argument in favor of adopting more realistic multiperiod portfolio optimization approaches. The rebalancing the portfolio at each point in time should be made not only by considering the immediate consequences for the market value of the portfolio, but also the opportunity to correct for tax liabilities by realizing other capital gains or losses by the end of the taxable year. The scarce theoretical literature on multiperiod tax-aware portfolio optimization contains some characterizations of optimal portfolio strategies under numerous simplifying assumptions.[25] However, even under such simplifying assumptions, the dimension of the problem grows exponentially with the number of stocks in a portfolio, and it is difficult to come up with computationally viable algorithms for portfolios of realistic size.

9.6 MULTIACCOUNT OPTIMIZATION

Portfolio managers who handle multiple accounts face an important practical issue. When individual clients' portfolios are managed, portfolio managers incorporate their clients' preferences and constraints. However, on any given trading day, the necessary trades for multiple diverse accounts are pooled and executed simultaneously. Moreover, typically trades may not be crossed, that is, it is not simply permissible to transfer an asset that should be sold on behalf of one client into the account of another client for whom the asset should be bought.[26] The trades should be executed in the market. Thus, each client's trades implicitly impact the results for the other clients: the *market impact* of the combined trades may be such that the benefits sought for individual accounts through trading are lost due to increased overall transaction costs. A robust, multiaccount management process should ensure accurate accounting and fair distribution of transaction costs among the individual accounts.

One possibility to handle the effect of trading in multiple accounts is to use an iterative process in which the market impact of the trades in previous iterations is taken into account at each iteration.[27] More precisely, single clients' accounts are optimized as usual, and once the optimal allocations are obtained, the portfolio manager aggregates the trades and computes the actual marginal transaction costs based on the aggregate level of trading. The portfolio manager then reoptimizes individual accounts using these marginal transaction costs, and aggregates the resulting trades again to compute new marginal transaction costs, and so on. The advantage of this approach is that little needs to be changed in the way individual accounts are typically handled, so the existing single-account optimization and management infrastructure can be reused. The disadvantage is that most generally this iterative approach does not guarantee a convergence (or its convergence may be slow) to a "fair equilibrium" in which clients' portfolios receive an unbiased treatment with respect to the size and the constraint structure of their accounts.[28] The latter equilibrium is the one that would be attained if all clients traded independently and competitively in the market for liquidity, and is thus the correct and fair solution to the aggregate trading problem.

An alternative, more comprehensive approach is to optimize trades across all accounts simultaneously. O'Cinneide, Scherer, and Xu (2006) describe such a model, and show that it attains the fair equilibrium we mentioned previously.[29] Assume that client k's utility function is given by u_k, and is in the form of a dollar return penalized for risk. Assume also that a transaction cost model τ gives the cost of trading in dollars, and that τ is a convex increasing function.[30] Its exact form will depend on the details of how trading is implemented. Let t be the vector of trades. It will typically have the form $(t_1^+, \ldots, t_N^+, t_1^-, \ldots, t_N^-)$, that is, it will specify the aggregate buys t_i^+ and the aggregate sells t_i^- for each asset $i = 1, \ldots, N$, but it may also incorporate information about how the trade could be carried out.[31]

The multiaccount optimization problem can be formulated as

$$\max_{\mathbf{w}_1,\ldots,\mathbf{w}_K,\mathbf{t}} \quad E[u_1(\mathbf{w}_1)] + \cdots + E[u_K(\mathbf{w}_K)] - \tau(\mathbf{t})$$
$$s.t. \quad \mathbf{w}_k \in C_k, k = 1, \ldots, K$$

where $\mathbf{w}_k$ is the N-dimensional vector of asset holdings (or weights) of client k, and C_k is the collection of constraints on the portfolio structure of client k. The objective can be interpreted as maximization of net expected utility, that is, as maximization of the expected dollar return penalized for risk and net of transaction costs.

The problem can be simplified by making some reasonable assumptions. For example, it can be assumed that the transaction cost function τ is additive across different assets, that is, trades in one asset do not influence trading costs in another. In such a case, the trading cost function can be split into more manageable terms:

$$\tau(\mathbf{t}) = \sum_{i=1}^{N} \tau_i(t_i^+, t_i^-)$$

where $\tau_i(t_i^+, t_i^-)$ is the cost of trading asset i as a function of the aggregate buys and sells of that asset. Splitting the terms $\tau_i(t_i^+, t_i^-)$ further into separate costs of buying and selling, however, is not a reasonable assumption because simultaneous buying and selling of an asset tends to have an offsetting effect on its price.

To formulate the problem completely, let $\mathbf{w}_k^0$ be the vector of original holdings (or weights) of client k's portfolio, $\mathbf{w}_k$ be the vector of decision variables for the optimal holdings (or weights) of client k's portfolio, and $\eta_{k,i}$ be constants that convert the holdings (or weight) of each asset i in client i's portfolio $w_{k,i}$ to dollars, i.e., $\eta_{k,i}w_{k,i}$ is client k's dollar holdings of asset i.[32] We also introduce new variables $\mathbf{w}_k^+$ to represent the an upper bound on the weight of each asset client k will buy:

$$w_{k,i} - w_{k,i}^0 \leq w_{k,i}^+, \quad i = 1, \ldots, N, k = 1, \ldots, K.$$

The aggregate amount of asset i bought for all clients can then be computed as

$$t_i^+ = \sum_{k=1}^{K} \eta_{k,i} \cdot w_{k,i}^+.$$

The aggregate amount of asset i sold for all clients can be easily expressed by noticing that the difference between the amounts bought and sold of each asset is exactly equal to the total amount of trades needed to get from the original position $w_{k,i}^0$ to the final position $w_{k,i}$ of that asset:[33]

$$t_i^+ - t_i^- = \sum_{k=1}^{K} \eta_{k,i} \cdot \left(w_{k,i} - w_{k,i}^0 \right).$$

Here t_i^+ and t_i^- are nonnegative variables.

The multiaccount optimization problem then takes the following form:

$$\max_{\mathbf{w}_1,\ldots,\mathbf{w}_K,\mathbf{t}^+,\mathbf{t}^-} E[u_1(\mathbf{w}_1)] + \cdots + E[u_K(\mathbf{w}_K)] - \sum_{i=1}^{N} \tau_i(t_i^+, t_i^-)$$

$$s.t. \quad \mathbf{w}_k \in C_k, k = 1, \ldots, K$$

$$w_{k,i} - w_{k,i}^0 \leq w_{k,i}^+, \quad i = 1, \ldots, N, k = 1, \ldots, K$$

$$t_i^+ = \sum_{k=1}^{K} \eta_{k,i} w_{k,i}^+, \quad i = 1, \ldots, N$$

$$t_i^+ - t_i^- = \sum_{k=1}^{K} \eta_{k,i} \cdot \left(w_{k,i} - w_{k,i}^0 \right), \quad i = 1, \ldots, N$$

$$t_i^+ \geq 0, t_i^- \geq 0, w_{k,i}^+ \geq 0, \quad i = 1, \ldots, N, k = 1, \ldots, K$$

O'Cinneide, Scherer, and Xu (2006) studied the behavior of the model in simulated experiments with a simple model for the transaction cost function, namely one in which

$$\tau(t) = \theta \cdot t^\gamma,$$

where t is the trade size, and θ and γ are constants satisfying $\theta \geq 0$ and $\gamma \geq 1$.[34] θ and γ are specified in advance and calibrated to fit observed trading costs in the market. The transaction costs for each client k can therefore be expressed as

$$\tau_k = \theta \sum_{i=1}^{N} \left| w_{k,i} - w_{k,i}^0 \right|^\gamma.$$

O'Cinneide, Scherer, and Xu observed that key portfolio performance measures, such as the information ratio (IR),[35] turnover, and total transaction costs, change under this model relative to the traditional approach. Not surprisingly, the turnover and the net information ratios of the portfolios obtained with multiaccount optimization are lower than those obtained with single-account optimization under the assumption that accounts are traded separately, while transaction costs are higher. These results are in fact more realistic, and are a better representation of the post-optimization performance of multiple client accounts in practice.

9.7 ROBUST PARAMETER ESTIMATION

The most commonly used approach for estimating security expected returns, covariances, and other parameters that are inputs to portfolio optimization models is to calculate the sample analogues from historical data.[36] These are sample estimates for the parameters we need. It is important to remember that when we rely on historical data for estimation purposes, we in fact assume that the past provides a good representation of the future.

It is well-known, however, that expected returns exhibit significant time variation (referred to as *nonstationarity*). They are impacted by changes in markets and economic conditions, such as interest rates, the political environment, consumer confidence, and the business cycles of different industry sectors and geographical regions. Consequently, extrapolated historical returns are often poor forecasts of future returns.

Similarly, the covariance matrix is unstable over time. Moreover, sample estimates of covariances for portfolios with thousands stocks are notoriously unreliable because we need large data sets to estimate them, and such large data sets of relevant data are difficult to procure. Estimates of the covariance matrix based on *factor models* are often used to reduce the number of statistical estimates needed from a limited set of data. We return to this issue after discussing factor models in Chapter 11.

In practice, portfolio managers often alter historical estimates of different parameters subjectively or objectively, based on their expectations and forecasting models for future trends. They also use statistical methods for finding estimators that are less sensitive to outliers and other sampling errors, such as Bayesian and shrinkage estimators. A complete review of advanced statistical estimation topics is beyond the scope of this book. We provide a brief overview of the most widely used concepts, and refer readers to Chapters 6 and 8 in Fabozzi, Kolm, Pachamanova, and Focardi (2007) for further details.

Shrinkage is a form of averaging different estimators. The shrinkage estimator typically consists of three components: (1) an estimator with little or no structure (like the sample mean); (2) an estimator with a lot of structure (the shrinkage target); and (3) a coefficient that reflects the shrinkage intensity. Probably the most well-known estimator for expected returns in the financial literature was proposed by Jorion (1986). The shrinkage target in Jorion's model is a vector array with the return on the minimum variance portfolio,[37] and the shrinkage intensity is determined from a specific formula.[38] Shrinkage estimators are used for estimates of the covariance matrix of returns as well (see, for example, Ledoit and Wolf 2003), although equally weighted *portfolios of covariance matrix estimators* have been shown to be equally effective as shrinkage estimators as well.[39]

Bayesian estimation approaches, named after the English mathematician Thomas Bayes, are based on subjective interpretations of the probability that a particular event will occur. A probability distribution, called the *prior distribution,* is used to represent the investor's knowledge about the probability before any data are observed. After more information is gathered (e.g., data are observed), a formula (known as Bayes' rule) is used to compute the new probability distribution, called the *posterior distribution.*

In the portfolio parameter estimation context, a posterior distribution of expected returns is derived by combining the forecast from the empirical data with a prior distribution. One of the most well-known examples of the application of the Bayesian framework in this context is the *Black-Litterman model,*[40] which produces an estimate of future expected returns by combining the market equilibrium returns (i.e., returns that are derived from pricing models and observable data) with the investor's subjective views. The investor's views are expressed as absolute or relative deviations from the equilibrium together with confidence levels of the views (as measured by the standard deviation of the views).

The ability to incorporate exogenous insight, such as a portfolio manager's opinion, into quantitative forecasting models is important; this insight may be the most valuable input to the model. The Bayesian framework provides a mechanism for forecasting systems to use both important traditional information sources such as proprietary market data, and subjective external information sources such as analyst's forecasts.

It is important to realize that regardless of how sophisticated the estimation and forecasting methods are, they are always subject to estimation error. What makes matters worse, however, is that different estimation errors can accumulate over the different activities of the portfolio management process, resulting in large aggregate errors at the final stage. It is therefore critical that the inputs evaluated at each stage are reliable and robust, so that the aggregate impact of estimation errors is minimized.

9.8 PORTFOLIO RESAMPLING

Robust parameter estimation is only one part of ensuring that the quantitative portfolio management process as a whole is reliable. It has been observed that portfolio allocation schemes are very sensitive to small changes in the inputs that go into the optimizer. In particular, a well-known study by Black and Litterman (1992) demonstrated that in the case of mean-variance optimization, small changes in the inputs for expected returns had a substantial impact on the portfolio composition. "Optimal" portfolios constructed under conditions of uncertainty can have extreme or nonintuitive weights for some stocks.

With advances in computational capabilities and new research in the area of optimization under uncertainty, practitioners in recent years have been able to incorporate considerations for uncertainty not only at the estimation, but also at the portfolio optimization stage. Methods for taking into consideration inaccuracies in the inputs to the portfolio optimization problem include simulation (resampling) and robust optimization. We explain portfolio resampling in this section, and robust portfolio optimization in the following section.

A logical approach to making portfolio allocation more robust with respect to changes in the input parameters is to generate different scenarios for the values these parameters can take, and find weights that remain stable for small changes in the input parameters. Simulation is therefore a natural technique to use in this context. In the literature, using simulation to generate robust portfolio weights has been referred to as *portfolio resampling*.[41] To illustrate the resampling technique, we explain how it is applied to portfolio mean-variance optimization as an example.

Suppose that we have initial estimates for the expected stock returns, $\hat{\mu}$, and covariance matrix $\hat{\Sigma}$, for the N stocks in the portfolio. (As before, we use "hat" to denote a statistical estimate.)

- We simulate S samples of N returns from a multivariate normal distribution with mean $\hat{\mu}$ and covariance matrix $\hat{\Sigma}$.
- We use the S samples we generated in the previous step to compute S new estimates of vectors of expected returns $\hat{\mu}_1, \ldots, \hat{\mu}_S$ and covariance matrices $\hat{\Sigma}_1, \ldots, \hat{\Sigma}_S$.
- We solve S portfolio optimization problems, one for each estimated pair of expected returns and covariances $(\hat{\mu}_s, \hat{\Sigma}_s)$, and save the weights for the N stocks in a vector array $\mathbf{w}^{(s)}$, where $s = 1, \ldots, S$. (The optimization problem itself could be any of the standard mean-variance formulations: maximize expected return subject to constraints on risk, minimize risk

subject to constraints on the expected return, or maximize the utility function.[42])

■ To find the final portfolio weights, we average out the weight for each stock over the S weights found for that stock in each of the S optimization problems. In other words,

$$\mathbf{w} = \frac{1}{S} \sum_{s=1}^{S} \mathbf{w}^{(s)}.$$

For example, stock i in the portfolio has final weight

$$w_i = \frac{w_i^{(1)} + \cdots + w_i^{(S)}}{S}.$$

Perhaps even more valuable than the average estimate of the weights obtained from the simulation and optimization iterations is the probability distribution we obtain for the portfolio weights. If we plot the weights for each stock obtained over the S iterations, $w_i^{(1)}, \ldots, w_i^{(S)}$, we can get a sense for how variable this stock weight is in the portfolio. A large standard deviation computed from the distribution of portfolio weight i will be an indication that the original portfolio weight was not very precise due to estimation error.

An important question, of course, is how large is "large enough." Do we have evidence that the portfolios we obtained through resampling are statistically different from one another? We can evaluate that by using a test statistic.[43] For example, it can be shown that the test statistic

$$d(\mathbf{w}^*, \mathbf{w}) = (\mathbf{w}^* - \mathbf{w})' \mathbf{\Sigma} (\mathbf{w}^* - \mathbf{w})$$

follows a chi-square (χ^2) distribution[44] with degrees of freedom equal to the number of securities in the portfolio. If the value of this statistic is statistically "large," then there will be evidence that the portfolio weights $\mathbf{w}^*$ and $\mathbf{w}$ are statistically different. This is an important insight for the portfolio manager, and its applications extend beyond just resampling. Let us provide some intuition as to why.

Suppose that we are considering rebalancing our current portfolio. Given our forecasts of expected returns and risk, we could calculate a set of new portfolios through the resampling procedure. Using the previous test statistic, we determine whether the new set of portfolio weights are statistically different from our current weights and, therefore, whether it would be worthwhile to rebalance. If we decide that it is worthwhile to rebalance, we could choose any of the resampled portfolios that are statistically different from our current portfolio. Which one should we choose? A natural choice would be to select the portfolio that would lead to the lowest transaction costs. The idea of determining statistically equivalent portfolios, therefore, has much wider implications than the ones illustrated in the context of resampling.

Resampling has its drawbacks:

- Since the resampled portfolio is calculated through a simulation procedure in which a portfolio optimization problem needs to be solved at each step, the approach is computationally cumbersome, especially for large portfolios. There is a trade-off between the number of resampling steps and the accuracy of estimation of the effect of errors on the portfolio composition.
- Due to the averaging in the calculation of the final portfolio weights, it is highly likely that all stocks will end up with nonzero weights. This has implications for the amount of transaction costs that will be incurred if the final portfolio is to be attained. One possibility is to include constraints that limit both the turnover and the number of stocks with nonzero weights. As we saw in section 9.2, however, the formulation of such constraints adds another level of complexity to the optimization problem, and will slow down the resampling procedure.
- Since the averaging process happens *after* the optimization problems are solved, the final weights may not actually satisfy some of the constraints in the optimization formulation. In general, only convex (e.g., linear) constraints are guaranteed to be satisfied by the averaged final weights. Turnover constraints, for example, may not be satisfied. This is a serious limitation of the resampling approach for practical applications.

Despite these limitations, resampling has advantages, and presents a good alternative to using only point estimates of inputs to the optimization problem.

9.9 ROBUST PORTFOLIO OPTIMIZATION

Another way in which uncertainty about the inputs can be modeled is by incorporating it directly into the optimization process. Robust optimization, the technique we introduced in section 6.3 of Chapter 6, is an intuitive and efficient way to deal with uncertainty. Robust portfolio optimization does not use the traditional forecasts, such as expected returns and stock covariances, but rather uncertainty sets containing these point estimates.

An example of such an uncertainty set is a confidence interval around the forecast for expected returns, but we can also formulate advanced uncertainty sets that incorporate more knowledge about the estimation error. For example, as we explained in section 6.3.1, a widely used uncertainty set is the ellipsoidal uncertainty set, which takes into consideration the covariance structure of the estimation errors.

Let us give a specific example of how the robust optimization framework can be applied in the portfolio optimization context. Consider the utility function formulation of the classical mean-variance portfolio allocation problem from section 7.4.2 of Chapter 7:

$$\max_{\mathbf{w}} \quad \mathbf{w}'\boldsymbol{\mu} - \lambda \cdot \mathbf{w}'\boldsymbol{\Sigma}\mathbf{w}$$

$$\text{s.t.} \quad \mathbf{w}'\boldsymbol{\iota} = 1$$

Suppose that we have estimates $\hat{\boldsymbol{\mu}}$ and $\hat{\boldsymbol{\Sigma}}$ of the vector of expected returns and the covariance matrix. Instead of the estimate $\hat{\boldsymbol{\mu}}$, however, we will consider a set of vectors $\boldsymbol{\mu}$ that are "close" to $\hat{\boldsymbol{\mu}}$. We define the "box" uncertainty set[45]

$$U_\delta(\hat{\boldsymbol{\mu}}) = \left\{ \boldsymbol{\mu} \mid |\mu_i - \hat{\mu}_i| \le \delta_i, i = 1, \ldots, N \right\}$$

In words, the set $U_\delta(\hat{\boldsymbol{\mu}})$ contains all vectors $\boldsymbol{\mu} = (\mu_1, \ldots, \mu_N)$ such that each component μ_i is in the interval $[\hat{\mu}_i - \delta_i, \hat{\mu}_i + \delta_i]$. The robust counterpart of the classical mean-variance problem with this uncertainty set can be found using the techniques described in section 6.3.1. To see the analogy, however, we can introduce an auxiliary variable v, and express the expression in the objective function as a constraint:

$$\max_{\mathbf{w}} \quad v$$

$$\text{s.t.} \quad \mathbf{w}'\boldsymbol{\mu} - \lambda \cdot \mathbf{w}'\boldsymbol{\Sigma}\mathbf{w} \ge v$$

$$\mathbf{w}'\boldsymbol{\iota} = 1$$

This is a standard trick in optimization: The value of the decision variable v is to be maximized, but is constrained from above by the expression $\mathbf{w}'\boldsymbol{\mu} - \lambda \cdot \mathbf{w}'\boldsymbol{\Sigma}\mathbf{w}$, so the optimizer will try to make $\mathbf{w}'\boldsymbol{\mu} - \lambda \cdot \mathbf{w}'\boldsymbol{\Sigma}\mathbf{w}$ as large as possible (i.e., maximize it) as well. The optimal solution to the problem does not change, but now we can compute the robust counterpart of the constraint

$$\mathbf{w}'\boldsymbol{\mu} - \lambda \cdot \mathbf{w}'\boldsymbol{\Sigma}\mathbf{w} \ge v$$

in the same way as we did for a constraint of the general type

$$\tilde{a}'x \leq b$$

in section 6.3.1 of Chapter 6. Namely, we first solve an optimization problem of the kind

$$\max_{\mu \in U_\delta(\hat{\mu})} \left\{ -w'\mu + \lambda \cdot w'\Sigma w \right\} \leq -v.$$

(Note here that we multiplied both sides of the constraint by -1, which reversed the sign of the constraint. This is just to demonstrate that we can bring the constraint exactly into the general form $\tilde{a}'x \leq b$.) This problem is actually equivalent to

$$\max_{\mu \in U_\delta(\hat{\mu})} \left\{ -w'\mu \right\} \leq -v - \lambda \cdot w'\Sigma w,$$

and since there is no μ in the expression at the right-hand side of the constraint, we can treat the whole expression as if it was a constant (with respect to μ). In other words, we have the constraint $\tilde{a}'x \leq b$, where $\tilde{a} = \mu$, $x = w$, and $b = -v - \lambda \cdot w'\Sigma w$.[46]

The robust counterpart of the mean-variance optimization problem under the box uncertainty set for expected returns is therefore

$$\max_{w} \quad w'\mu - \delta'|w| - \lambda \cdot w'\Sigma w$$

$$\text{s.t.} \quad w'\iota = 1$$

where $|w|$ denotes the absolute value of the entries of the vector of weights w. To gain some intuition, notice that if the weight of stock i in the portfolio is negative, the worst-case expected return for stock i is $\mu_i + \delta_i$ (we lose the largest amount possible). If the weight of stock i in the portfolio is positive, then the worst-case expected return for stock i is $\mu_i - \delta_i$ (we gain the smallest amount possible). Observe that $\mu_i w_i - \delta_i |w_i|$ equals $(\mu_i - \delta_i) w_i$ if the weight w_i is positive and $(\mu_i + \delta_i) w_i$ if the weight w_i is negative. Hence, the mathematical expression in the objective agrees with our intuition: it minimizes the worst-case expected portfolio return. In this robust version of the mean-variance formulation, stocks whose mean return estimates are less accurate (i.e., have a larger estimation error δ_i) are therefore penalized in the objective function, and will tend to have a smaller weight in the optimal portfolio allocation.

This optimization problem has the same computational complexity as the nonrobust mean-variance formulation—namely, it can be stated as a quadratic optimization problem. The latter can be achieved by using a standard trick that allows us to get rid of the absolute values for the weights. The idea is to introduce an N-dimensional vector of additional variables ψ to replace the absolute values $|\mathbf{w}|$, and to write an equivalent version of the optimization problem,

$$\max_{\mathbf{w},\psi} \quad \mathbf{w}'\hat{\mu} - \delta'\psi - \lambda\mathbf{w}'\Sigma\mathbf{w}$$

$$\text{s.t.} \quad \mathbf{w}'\iota = 1$$

$$\psi_i \geq w_i; \psi_i \geq -w_i, i = 1, \ldots, N$$

Therefore, incorporating considerations about the uncertainty in the estimates of the expected returns in this example has virtually no computational cost.

We can view the effect of this particular "robustification" of the mean-variance portfolio optimization formulation in two different ways. On the one hand, we can see that the values of the expected returns for the different stocks have been adjusted downward in the objective function of the optimization problem. In other words, the robust optimization model "shrinks" the expected return of stocks with large estimation error, meaning, in this case the robust formulation is related to statistical shrinkage methods.[47] On the other hand, we can interpret the additional term in the objective function as a "risk-like" term that represents penalty for estimation error. The size of the penalty is determined by the investor's aversion to estimation risk, and is reflected in the magnitude of the deltas.

More complicated specifications for uncertainty sets have more involved mathematical representations, but can still be selected so that they preserve an easy computational structure for the robust optimization problem. For example, a commonly used uncertainty set is the ellipsoidal uncertainty set[48]

$$U_\delta(\hat{\mu}) = \left\{ \mu |\, (\mu - \hat{\mu})'\, \Sigma_\mu^{-1}\, (\mu - \hat{\mu}) \leq \delta^2 \right\}$$

where Σ_μ is the covariance matrix of estimation errors for the vector of expected returns μ. This uncertainty set represents the requirement that the scaled sum of squares (scaled by the inverse of the covariance matrix of estimation errors) between all elements in the set and the point estimates $\hat{\mu}_1, \hat{\mu}_2, \ldots, \hat{\mu}_N$ can be no larger than δ^2. We note that this uncertainty set cannot be interpreted as individual confidence intervals around each point estimate. Instead, it captures the idea of a joint confidence region. In practical applications, the covariance matrix of estimation errors is often assumed to be diagonal. For this particular case, the set contains all vectors of expected returns that are within a certain number of standard deviations from the point estimate of the vector of expected returns, and the resulting robust portfolio optimization problem would protect the investor if the vector of expected returns is within that range.

It can be shown (see Practice 9.3 on the companion web site) that the robust counterpart of the mean-variance portfolio optimization problem with an ellipsoidal uncertainty set for the expected return estimates is the following optimization problem formulation:

$$\max_{\mathbf{w}} \quad \mathbf{w}'\boldsymbol{\mu} - \lambda \cdot \mathbf{w}'\boldsymbol{\Sigma}\mathbf{w} - \delta\sqrt{\mathbf{w}'\boldsymbol{\Sigma}_{\boldsymbol{\mu}}\mathbf{w}}$$

$$\text{s.t.} \quad \mathbf{w}'\iota = 1$$

This is a second-order cone problem, and requires specialized software to solve, but the methods for solving it are very efficient (see section 5.2.4 of Chapter 5).

Just as in the robust counterpart with a box uncertainty set, we can interpret the extra term in the objective function ($\delta\sqrt{\mathbf{w}'\boldsymbol{\Sigma}_{\boldsymbol{\mu}}\mathbf{w}}$) as the penalty for estimation risk, where δ incorporates the degree of the investor's aversion to estimation risk. Note, by the way, that the covariance matrix in the estimation error penalty term, $\boldsymbol{\Sigma}_{\boldsymbol{\mu}}$, is not necessarily the same as the covariance matrix of returns $\boldsymbol{\Sigma}$. In fact, it is not immediately obvious how $\boldsymbol{\Sigma}_{\boldsymbol{\mu}}$ can be estimated from data. $\boldsymbol{\Sigma}_{\boldsymbol{\mu}}$ it is the covariance matrix of the errors in the estimation of the expected (average) returns. Thus, if a portfolio manager forecasts 5% active return over the next time period, but gets 1%, he cannot argue that there was a 4% error in his expected return—the actual error would consist of both an estimation error in the expected return and the inherent volatility in actual realized returns. In fact, critics of the approach have argued that the realized returns typically have large stochastic components that dwarf the expected returns, and hence estimating $\boldsymbol{\Sigma}_{\boldsymbol{\mu}}$ from data is very hard, if not impossible.[49]

Several approximate methods for estimating $\boldsymbol{\Sigma}_{\boldsymbol{\mu}}$ have been found to work well in practice. For example, it has been observed that simpler estimation approaches, such as using just the diagonal matrix containing the variances of the estimates (as opposed to the complete error covariance matrix), often provide most of the benefit in robust portfolio optimization.[50] In addition, standard approaches for estimating expected returns, such as Bayesian statistics and regression-based methods, can produce estimates for the estimation error covariance matrix in the process of generating the estimates themselves.[51]

Among practitioners, the notion of robust portfolio optimization is often equated with the robust mean-variance model discussed in this section, with the box or the ellipsoidal uncertainty sets for the expected stock returns. While robust optimization applications often involve one form or another of this model, the actual scope of robust optimization can be much broader. We note that the term *robust optimization* refers to the technique of incorporating information about uncertainty sets for the parameters in the optimization model, and not to the specific definitions of uncertainty sets or the choice of parameters to model as uncertain. For example, we can use the robust optimization methodology to incorporate considerations for uncertainty in the estimate of the covariance matrix in addition to the uncertainty in expected returns, and obtain a different robust portfolio allocation formulation. Robust optimization can be applied also to portfolio allocation models that are different from the mean-variance framework, such as Sharpe ratio optimization and value-at-risk optimization.[52] Finally, robust optimization has the potential to provide a computationally efficient way to handle portfolio optimization over multiple stages—a problem for which so far there have been few satisfactory solutions.[53] There are numerous useful robust formulations, but a complete review is beyond the scope of this book. We refer interested readers to Fabozzi, Kolm, Pachamanova, and Focardi (2007) for further details.

Is implementing robust optimization formulations worthwhile? Some tests with simulated and real market data indicate that robust optimization, when inaccuracy is assumed in the expected return estimates, outperforms classical mean-variance optimization in terms of total excess return a large percentage (70%–80%) of the time.[54] Other tests have not been as conclusive (Lee, Stefek, and Zhelenyak [2006]). The factor that accounts for much of the difference is how the uncertainty in parameters is modeled. Therefore, finding a suitable degree of robustness and appropriate definitions of uncertainty sets can have a significant impact on portfolio performance. (See Practice 9.4 on the companion web site for an example of an alternative formulation of an uncertainty set for expected returns in the traditional mean-variance formulation.)

Independent tests by practitioners and academics using both simulated and market data appear to confirm that robust optimization generally results in more stable portfolio weights, that is, it eliminates the extreme corner solutions resulting from traditional mean-variance optimization. This fact has implications for portfolio rebalancing in the presence of transaction costs and taxes, as transaction costs and taxes can add substantial expenses when the portfolio is rebalanced. Depending on the particular robust formulations employed, robust mean-variance optimization also appears to improve worst-case portfolio performance, and results in smoother and more consistent portfolio returns. Finally, by preventing large swings in positions, robust optimization typically makes better use of the turnover budget and risk constraints.

Robust optimization, however, is not a panacea. By using robust portfolio optimization formulations, investors are likely to trade off the optimality of their portfolio allocation in cases in which nature behaves as they predicted for protection against the risk of inaccurate estimation. Therefore, investors using the technique should not expect to do better than classical portfolio optimization when estimation errors have little impact, or when typical scenarios occur. They should, however, expect insurance in scenarios in which their estimates deviate from the actual realized values by up to the amount they have prespecified in the modeling process.

SUMMARY

- The portfolio management process consists of four activities: (1) setting the investment objectives; (2) developing and implementing a portfolio strategy; (3) monitoring the portfolio; and (4) adjusting the portfolio.
- Portfolio strategies can be active or passive. Active strategies utilize information provided by manager intuition or quantitative models to come up with strategies that select the most attractive investment opportunities in the portfolio manager's opinion. Passive strategies require minimal management. One popular type of passive strategy is indexing, whose objective is to replicate the performance of a designated market index.
- Commonly used constraints in practice include long-only (no short-selling) constraints, turnover constraints, holding constraints, risk factor constraints, and tracking error constraints. These constraints can be handled in a straightforward way by the same type of optimization algorithms used for solving the classical mean-variance portfolio allocation problem.
- Minimum holding constraints, transaction size constraints, cardinality constraints, and round-lot constraints are also widely used in practice, but their nature is such that they require binary and integer modeling, which necessitates the use of mixed-integer and other specialized optimization solvers.
- Transaction costs can easily be incorporated in standard portfolio allocation models. Typical functions for representing transaction costs include linear, piecewise linear, and quadratic.
- Taxes can have a dramatic effect on portfolio returns; however, it is difficult to incorporate them into the classical portfolio optimization

framework. Their importance to the individual investor is a strong argument for taking a multiperiod view of investments, but the computational burden of multiperiod portfolio optimization formulations with taxes is extremely high.

- For investment managers who handle multiple accounts, increased transaction costs because of the market impact of simultaneous trades can be an important practical issue, and should be taken into consideration when individual clients' portfolio allocation decisions are made to ensure fairness across accounts.

- As the use of quantitative techniques has become widespread in the investment industry, the consideration of estimation risk and model risk has grown in importance. Methods for robust statistical estimation of parameters include shrinkage and Bayesian techniques.

- Portfolio resampling is a technique that uses simulation to generate multiple scenarios for possible values of the input parameters in the portfolio optimization problem, and aims to determine portfolio weights that remain stable with respect to small changes in model parameters.

- Robust portfolio optimization incorporates uncertainty directly into the optimization process. The uncertain parameters in the optimization problem are assumed to vary in prespecified uncertainty sets that are selected subjectively or based on data.

SOFTWARE HINTS

Excel Solver

Limiting the Number of Stocks in the Portfolio Let us give an example of implementing an optimal portfolio allocation problem with a constraint on the number of stocks to include. Consider the example in file **Ch9-Cardinality.xlsx**. (A screenshot of the worksheet **MV** is provided in Exhibit 9.2.) We have a portfolio of three stocks, and would like to maximize the expected return (cell B7) subject to the budget constraint (row 10), the constraint on the total number of stocks to have in the portfolio (row 11), and a constraint on the portfolio variance (row 13). Often, the total portfolio variance constraint is instead expressed as a tracking error constraint, that is, the variance of the deviations from a predetermined benchmark is considered. (See section 9.3.1.)

Cells B3:D3 are changing cells, where Excel Solver will store the optimal portfolio weights. The difference with the classical mean-variance optimization problem is that now we have another set of changing cells, B4:D4, which will be binary and will detect whether a stock is included in the portfolio or not. (These are the variables δ_i from the formulation in section 9.2.5.)

	A	B	C	D	E	F	G
1	Decision variables					Inputs	
2		Stock 1	Stock 2	Stock 3		large constant M	10
3	Asset weights	-31.80%	131.80%	0.00%			
4	Binary variables delta	1	1	0			
5							
6	Objective function	(maximize expected return)					
7		2.72%					
8							
9	Constraints						
10	budget	100.00% =		100%			
11	total number of stocks	2 <=		2			
12	portfolio variance	0.01 <=		1.00%			
13	binary constraints						
14	(bounds on weights)	-10	-10	0			
15		10	10	0			
16							

EXHIBIT 9.2 Worksheet **MV** in the file **Ch9-Cardinality.xlsx.**

The formula for the objective function (cell B7) is

$$= \text{SUMPRODUCT}(\text{B3}:\text{D3},\text{Data}!\text{G9}:\text{I9})$$

(The expected returns for each stock are approximated by simply taking the averages of time series in the worksheet **Data** in the same file, and are stored in cells G9:I9 in the worksheet **Data**.)

The formula for the budget constraint (in cell B10) is

$$= \text{SUM}(\text{B3}:\text{D3})$$

The formula for the constraint on the number of stocks (in cell B11) is

$$= \text{SUM}(\text{B4}:\text{D4})$$

(We are adding the binary variables δ_i for each stock, and restricting the sum to be less than or equal to 2.)

The formula for the portfolio variance (in cell B12) is

$$= \text{MMULT}(\text{B3}:\text{D3},\text{MMULT}(\text{Data}!\text{G3}:\text{I5},\text{TRANSPOSE}(\text{B3}:\text{D3})))$$

(The covariance matrix for the stock returns are approximated by simply taking the sample covariance matrix of the time series in the worksheet **Data** in the same file, and are stored in cells G3:I5 in the worksheet **Data**.)

There are also additional constraints to ensure that a binary variable is not set to 0 if the corresponding weight of a stock in the portfolio is different from 0. They are stored in rows 14 and 15. We have selected the value for the "large" constant M from the formulation in section 9.2.5 to be 10. (This is a large number relative to the size of the other inputs in this problem.) Cells B14:D14 contain the lower limits on the portfolio weights in terms of M and the corresponding binary variable δ_i. Cells B15:D15 contain the upper limits on the portfolio weights in terms of M and the corresponding binary variable δ_i. For example, cell B14 corresponding to the lower limit on the weight of Stock 1 contains the formula

$$= -\$G\$2*B4$$

and cell B15 corresponding to the upper limit on the weight of Stock 1 contains the formula

$$= \$G\$2*B4$$

(The value for the constant M is stored in cell G2.)

The Excel Solver dialog window is shown in Exhibit 9.3. Note that the options `Assume Linear Model` and `Assume Non-Negative` should not be checked in this particular example. (This problem is nonlinear because it has a quadratic constraint [the portfolio variance], and the weights are not restricted to be nonnegative.) Both the portfolio weights (cells B3:B5) and the binary variables (cells B4:D4) are specified as changing cells, and a constraint is also imposed on B4:D4 to be binary.

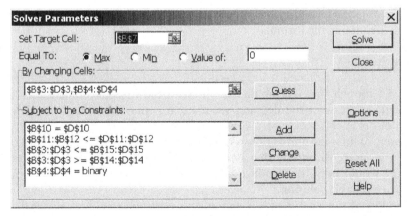

EXHIBIT 9.3 Solver dialog box for the optimal portfolio allocation problem with a constraint on the number of stocks to be included.

The optimal solution is shown in Exhibit 9.2. If we are limited to two stocks, it is optimal to invest in Stock 1 and Stock 2, with −31% in Stock 1 and 131% in Stock 2.

We deliberately chose a very small example to illustrate the setup of the model in Excel. Excel Solver would have a lot of trouble, and most likely not produce the correct result, if the portfolio contains a large number of stocks.

Index Tracking Let us examine the formulation of another problem that is easy to do with Solver. Suppose we would like to replicate the performance of the Dow Jones Composite Index (DJA) with 10 stocks from different industries (tickers AA, AXP, BAC, DD, GE, HD, INTC, CSCO, MRK, WMT). We have decided on these stocks in advance, and would like to determine their weights so as to minimize the tracking error as determined by the square difference between the portfolio return and the return on the DJA. The problem is formulated for Solver in the spreadsheet **Ch9-IndexTracking.xlsx**. A snapshot of the spreadsheet is provided in Exhibit 9.4. The data on returns are weekly, over the last six months before the current date. The data can also be generated by simulating possible scenarios for future stock returns.

The decision variables (changing cells) are B2:K2. They will contain the optimal portfolio weights. In column M, we compute the square difference between the portfolio return and the return on the DJA for every scenario. For example, cell M4 contains the formula

```
= (SUMPRODUCT($B$1:$K$1,B4:K4)-L4)^2
```

The objective function is simply the sum of all the squared differences, that is, it contains the formula

```
= SUM(M4:M28)
```

Even though this is a nonlinear problem, the objective function is a quadratic expression, the decision variables are continuous, and the only constraint is linear. Solver solves the problem without difficulty. However, if we were to limit the number of stocks to include in the replicating portfolio (e.g., if we were to require that only 5 out of the 10 stocks be included), then we would need to introduce integer variables, and Solver would not produce a reliable solution.

A more advanced example of minimizing portfolio tracking error is described in the following section. Such advanced optimization formulations, including portfolio allocation with the goal of minimizing probability of

	AA	AXP	BAC	DD	GE	HD	INTC	CSCO	MRK	WMT	DOW	Square difference
Weight	0.10844427	0.08241537	0	0.07932592	0.04730616	0.09631161	0	0.14660657	0.13895516	0.30267336		
	9.60%	0.84%	15.68%	0.00%	-0.22%	-0.08%	2.45%	0.20%	0.04%	-2.41%	1.07%	0.00%
	18.66%	0.40%	5.24%	-5.16%	0.45%	4.36%	1.27%	7.41%	-5.47%	2.67%	3.13%	0.00%
	4.06%	6.20%	1.8%	2.52%	2.90%	1.31%	4.45%	3.41%	5.39%	0.99%	3.97%	0.01%
	-1.88%	-3.43%	3.75%	3.12%	1.87%	-6.31%	-0.92%	-0.17%	2.75%	2.28%	-0.43%	0.01%
	-9.79%	-14.68%	-24.70%	-5.11%	-11.43%	-4.31%	-0.65%	-4.32%	2.62%	-3.97%	-5.64%	0.00%
	3.30%	16.92%	62.87%	1.83%	14.50%	-1.05%	-3.29%	-4.68%	2.14%	0.18%	4.51%	0.06%
	6.02%	-3.99%	-4.40%	-3.16%	4.79%	-2.05%	1.22%	6.68%	3.62%	4.55%	1.97%	0.01%
	-1.30%	16.00%	-14.15%	1.27%	-2.26%	0.80%	0.13%	2.39%	-8.86%	-4.64%	-0.29%	0.01%
	4.63%	15.83%	10.99%	7.33%	9.36%	0.77%	-2.38%	0.95%	-2.17%	-0.91%	1.08%	0.02%
	8.32%	22.83%	25.66%	1.96%	3.56%	3.60%	0.19%	-1.87%	-0.60%	-5.84%	0.48%	0.01%
	4.74%	6.09%	3.54%	14.41%	1.48%	5.80%	3.44%	7.14%	-2.58%	2.34%	3.98%	0.00%
	19.27%	17.86%	18.58%	9.87%	13.00%	6.63%	5.26%	6.54%	1.65%	6.01%	6.52%	0.04%
	14.14%	-6.34%	7.47%	6.00%	-0.83%	7.00%	-0.34%	2.58%	-1.29%	0.81%	3.13%	0.00%
	9.77%	27.58%	83.44%	15.53%	36.26%	15.06%	18.45%	9.38%	19.04%	0.57%	7.83%	0.17%
	-16.21%	-14.93%	-20.51%	-10.07%	-17.04%	-13.83%	-2.59%	-2.68%	-6.03%	-0.67%	-8.31%	0.01%
	-0.95%	-7.02%	4.22%	-7.95%	-9.28%	7.35%	-0.31%	-3.38%	-13.88%	-1.56%	-4.91%	0.01%
	-15.91%	-17.60%	-31.96%	-9.02%	-18.01%	-8.29%	-7.93%	-6.34%	-2.26%	7.50%	-7.33%	0.08%
	-10.95%	-12.21%	-9.14%	-8.83%	3.06%	-9.82%	-5.77%	-5.52%	-6.56%	-6.25%	-5.89%	0.02%
	7.83%	7.17%	-6.84%	7.01%	-8.49%	9.29%	14.19%	13.83%	7.83%	5.33%	4.91%	0.05%
	-6.48%	4.56%	5.45%	-4.97%	0.83%	-0.87%	-1.68%	-5.79%	1.24%	-2.54%	-0.26%	0.04%
	-11.66%	-5.94%	-13.09%	-3.24%	-13.83%	-6.38%	-4.51%	0.44%	0.04%	-6.23%	-3.09%	0.04%
	-12.77%	-11.54%	-44.73%	-1.73%	-12.75%	-2.77%	-2.90%	-5.27%	-1.88%	-0.04%	-4.61%	0.00%
	-10.73%	-0.52%	-9.35%	-2.94%	-6.27%	-1.12%	-6.91%	-1.53%	-7.32%	-9.79%	-4.39%	0.03%
	23.82%	7.93%	7.26%	4.80%	6.89%	2.42%	7.19%	4.24%	6.90%	3.31%	6.63%	0.00%
	0.82%	-7.82%	-3.19%	-2.42%	-3.21%	-2.73%	-1.80%	-2.22%	1.54%	-0.70%	-0.81%	0.00%

Objective function: 0.61%

Constraints
budget   1.00 = 1

EXHIBIT 9.4 Excel worksheet with the formulation of an index tracking problem.

loss, minimizing the Sharpe ratio of a portfolio, and others can be formulated with Solver, but the quality of the final solutions returned by Solver is unsatisfactory, so we should formulate them with Evolver instead.

Palisades Decision Tools Suite (Evolver)

We go over several examples of implementation of several portfolio allocation problems with Evolver.

Limiting the Number of Stocks in the Portfolio   We begin with the portfolio allocation problem with a constraint on the number of stocks to be contained in the portfolio. The setup for solving the problem in Evolver is the same as for Excel Solver. (See worksheet **MV (Evolver)** in the file **Ch9-Cardinality.xlsx.**) The dialog box for Evolver is shown in Exhibit 9.5.

    The optimal solution is the same as the solution obtained with Excel Solver. (See Exhibit 9.2.)

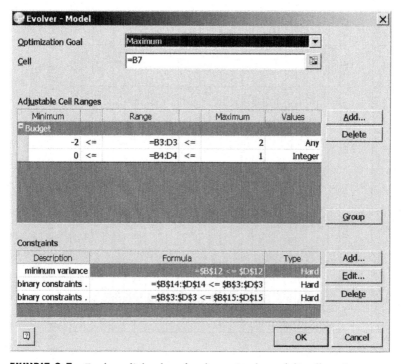

EXHIBIT 9.5   Evolver dialog box for the optimal portfolio allocation problem with a constraint on the number of stocks to be included.

Index Tracking As we saw in the Excel Solver section of the Software Hints, the formulation of the limited index tracking problem with Solver is easy to do. The problem is implemented with Evolver in worksheet Index Tracking (Evolver) in the same file, **Ch9-IndexTracking.xlsx**. The Evolver dialog box is shown in Exhibit 9.6. The only difference is that we do not need to specify the budget constraint explicitly because it is implicitly followed when we restrict the values for the decision variables (the weights) to be selected according to the "budget" method (see the second window in the Evolver dialog box). The budget method makes sure that if you start out with weights that add up to 1, all subsequent weights Evolver picks will add up to 1, that is, the budget constraint will be satisfied.

Limited Index Tracking Now consider the problem of tracking an index with a limited number of stocks. We will work with the data in the file **Ch9-IndexTrackingLim.xlsx**. As in the case of limiting the number of stocks in a mean-variance portfolio, we need to introduce binary variables—one

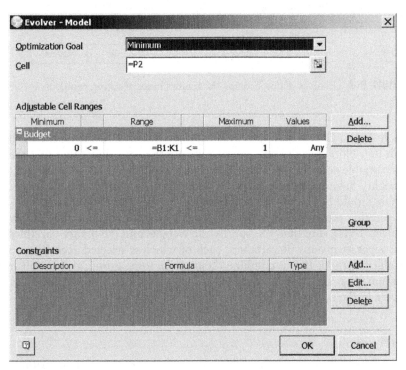

EXHIBIT 9.6 Evolver dialog box for the index tracking problem.

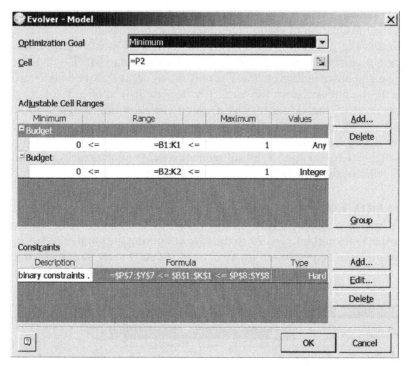

EXHIBIT 9.7   Evolver dialog box for the limited index tracking problem.

for each stock. The formulation of the problem with Evolver is shown in
Exhibit 9.7. Note that the only constraints are the constraints that link the
binary variables and the weights. The remaining constraints (the fact that
the weights have to add up to 1, and that the number of stocks in the
portfolio should be limited) can be imposed by specifying those conditions
when entering the variables (called adjustable cells) in the middle window
in Evolver. Make sure that you specify the weights and the binary variables
as two separate groups of variables, each of which is selected according to
the budget method. If you combine them in the same group, then Evolver
will assume that their total sum needs to be equal to the sum of the values
that were in the cells at the beginning of the algorithm.

MATLAB

As we saw in Chapter 9, many of the real portfolio optimization algorithms
require quadratic constraints or constraints with integer variables. At the

time of writing of this book, MATLAB's capabilities for solving such problems directly are limited. It is possible, however, to put together scripts that take advantage of the Genetic Algorithms Toolbox in MATLAB to solve such more complex problems. For example, the problem of finding a portfolio of a given number of stocks that tracks an index most closely can be constructed in this manner. The code for implementing the index tracking problem is quite involved, and is available from MATLAB's online file depository.[55]

NOTES

1. See pp. 1–3 and 1–5, Chapter 1, in J. L. Maginn and D. L. Tuttle (1990).
2. See Fabozzi (2007).
3. Risk factor models are discussed in more detail in Chapter 11.
4. Such asset pricing models are discussed in Chapter 11.
5. ERISA was enacted in 1974 as a federal regulatory scheme for private sector employee benefit plans, including health care plans. It sets forth requirements for benefit plan participation, funding, and vesting of benefits.
6. Multiperiod portfolio optimization models are still rarely used in practice, not because the value of multiperiod modeling is questioned, but because such models are often too intractable from a computational perspective.
7. As the term intuitively implies, the ADV measures the total amount of a given asset traded in a day on average, where the average is taken over a prespecified time period.
8. Risk factors and factor models are discussed in more detail in Chapter 11.
9. See Chapter 11.
10. See section 8.3 of Chapter 8 for an introduction to CVaR.
11. As explained in Chapter 8, another computationally tractable situation is when the data are normally distributed. In that case, minimizing CVaR is equivalent to minimizing the standard deviation
12. Such models are discussed in Chapter 11.
13. Price movement risk costs are the costs resulting from the potential for a change in market price between the time the decision to trade is made and the time the trade is actually executed.
14. Market impact is the effect a trader has on the market price of an asset when it sells or buys the asset. It is the extent to which the price moves up or down in response to the trader's actions. For example, a trader who tries to sell a large number of shares of a particular stock may drive down the stock's market price.
15. Versions of this model have been suggested in Pogue (1970), Schreiner (1980), Adcock and Meade (1994), Lobo, Fazel, and Boyd (2007), and Mitchell and Braun (2004).
16. Here we are thinking of w_i as the portfolio weights, but in fact it may be more intuitive to think of the transaction costs as a percentage of amount traded. It

is easy to go back and forth between portfolio weights and portfolio amounts by simply multiplying w_i by the total amount in the portfolio. In fact, we can switch the whole portfolio optimization formulation around, and write it in terms of allocation of dollars, instead of weights. We just need to replace the vector of weights $\mathbf{w}$ by a vector $\mathbf{x}$ of dollar holdings.

17. See, for example, Bertsimas, Darnell, and Soucy (1999).
18. As we explained earlier, this constraint can be written in an equivalent, more optimization solver-friendly form, namely,

$$y_i \geq w_i - w_{0,i},$$
$$y_i \geq -(w_i - w_{0,i})$$

19. Both MATLAB and Excel have tools for fitting quadratic functions to data.
20. The computation of the tax basis is different for stocks and bonds. For bonds, there are special tax rules, and the original price is not the tax basis.
21. The exact rates vary depending on the current version of the tax code, but the main idea behind the preferential treatment of long-term gains to short-term gains is to encourage long-term capital investments and fund entrepreneurial activity.
22. See Stein (1998).
23. Apelfeld, Fowler, and Gordon (1996) showed that a manager can outperform on an after-tax basis with high turnover as well, as long as the turnover does not result in net capital gains taxes. (There are other issues with high turnover, however, such as higher transaction costs that may result in a lower overall portfolio return.)
24. Dividends are taxed as regular income, that is, at a higher rate than capital gains, so minimizing the portfolio dividend yield should theoretically result in a lower tax burden for the investor.
25. See Constantinides (1984), Dammon and Spatt (1996), and Dammon, Spatt, and Zhang (2001, 2004).
26. The SEC in general prohibits cross-trading but does provide exemptions if prior to the execution of the cross-trade the asset manager can demonstrate to the SEC that a particular cross-trade benefits both parties. Similarly, Section 406(b)(3) of the Employee Retirement Income Security Act of 1974 (ERISA) forbids cross-trading, but there is a new cross-trading exemption in Section 408(b)(19) adopted in the Pension Protection Act of 2006.
27. See Khodadadi, Tutuncu, and Zangari (2006).
28. The iterative procedure is known to converge to the equilibrium, however, under special conditions; see O'Cinneide, Scherer and Xu (2006).
29. The issue of considering transaction costs in multiaccount optimization has been discussed by others as well. See, for example, Bertsimas, Darnell, and Soucy (1999).
30. As mentioned in section 9.4, realistic transaction costs are in fact described by nonlinear functions because costs per share traded typically increase with the size of the trade due to market impact.

31. For example, if asset i is a euro-pound forward, then a trade in that asset can also be implemented as a euro-dollar forward plus a dollar-forward, so there will be two additional assets in the aggregate trade vector $\mathbf{t}$. Such concepts will become more intuitive after introducing financial derivatives in Chapters 13 and 14.

32. Note that $\eta_{k,i}$ equals 1 if $w_{k,i}$ is the actual dollar holdings.

33. Note that, similarly to $\mathbf{w}_k^+$, we could introduce additional sell variables $\mathbf{w}_k^-$, but this is not necessary. By expressing aggregate sales through aggregate buys and total trades, we reduce the dimension of the optimization problem because there are fewer decision variables. This would make a difference for the speed of obtaining a solution, especially in the case of large portfolios and complicated representation of transaction costs.

34. Note that $\gamma = 1$ defines linear transaction costs. For linear transaction costs, multiaccount optimization produces the same allocation as single-account optimization because linear transaction costs assume that an increased aggregate amount of trading does not have an impact on prices.

35. The information ratio is the ratio of (annualized) portfolio residual return (alpha) to (annualized) portfolio residual risk, where risk is defined as standard deviation. The concept of alpha is discussed in Chapter 11.

36. See sections 3.6 and 3.11 of Chapter 3 for how to obtain sample estimates, and sections 8.2.3 and 8.3.2 for how to use historical data to estimate VaR and CVaR, respectively.

37. See section 7.3 of Chapter 7 for a definition of the minimum variance portfolio.

38. See Fabozzi, Kolm, Pachamanova, and Focardi (2007, 217).

39. See Disatnik and Benninga (2007) for an overview of such models.

40. See Chapter 8 in Fabozzi, Kolm, Pachamanova, and Focardi (2007) for a step-by-step description of the Black-Litterman model.

41. See Michaud (1998), Jorion (1992), and Scherer (2002).

42. See Chapter 7.

43. See section 3.11.4 of Chapter 3 for a brief introduction to statistical hypothesis testing.

44. See section 3.7.2 of Chapter 3.

45. See Exhibit 6.7(A) in Chapter 6.

46. Observe that this model incorporates the notion of aversion to estimation error in the following sense. When the interval $[\hat{\mu}_i - \delta_i, \ \hat{\mu}_i + \delta_i]$ for the expected return of the ith asset is large, meaning that the expected return has been estimated with large estimation error, then the minimization problem over μ is less constrained. Consequently, the minimum is smaller than it would be in situations when the interval for the expected return is smaller. Obviously, when the interval is small enough, the minimization problem will be so tightly constrained that it would deliver a solution that is close to the optimal solution of the classical portfolio optimization problem in which estimation errors are ignored. In other words, it is the size of the intervals (in general, the size of the uncertainty set) that controls the aversion to the uncertainty that comes from estimation errors.

47. See section 9.7 for a definition of statistical shrinkage.

48. See Exhibit 6.7(B) in Chapter 6.

49. See Lee, Stefek, and Zhelenyak (2006).

50. See Stubbs and Vance (2005).

51. See Chapter 12 in Fabozzi, Kolm, Pachamanova, and Focardi (2007) for a more in-depth coverage of the topic of estimating input parameters for robust optimization formulations.

52. See, for example, Goldfarb and Iyengar (2003) and Natarajan, Pachamanova, and Sim (2008).

53. See Ben-Tal, Margalit, and Nemirovski (2000) and Bertsimas and Pachamanova (2008).

54. See Ceria and Stubbs (2006).

55. See the collection of files at Mathworks Inc., *MATLAB Central,* http://www.mathworks.com/matlabcentral/fileexchange/authors/30003.

CHAPTER 10

Fixed Income Portfolio
Management in Practice

Chapters 7, 8, and 9 introduced fundamental concepts in risk measurement and quantitative equity portfolio management. We discussed risk measures such as variance, tracking error relative to an index, value-at-risk (VaR), and conditional value-at-risk (CVaR), as well as portfolio management strategies and formulations. Many of these concepts are used in fixed income portfolio management as well; however, fixed income securities have some fundamental differences from equities, so the concepts cannot always be applied in the same way in which they would be applied for stock portfolios. Furthermore, fixed income securities are strongly influenced by changes in interest rates and credit quality, which adds another dimension to portfolio analysis.

This chapter focuses on the basics of fixed income portfolio management in practice. We begin by reviewing measures of bond portfolio risk. Many bond portfolio strategies can be understood in terms of the risk and return relative to a benchmark, so we provide an overview of bond market indices and a classification of bond index strategies. We then proceed with a discussion of asset-liability portfolio strategies such as cash flow matching and immunization. We give examples of how optimization and simulation can be applied in bond portfolio allocation and risk management.

10.1 MEASURING BOND PORTFOLIO RISK

As just mentioned, many of the risk measures we discussed in the context of risk management of equity portfolios in Chapter 8 hold in the case of bond portfolios: we can evaluate a bond portfolio's standard deviation, tracking error, VaR, and CVaR similarly to the way we evaluated these risk measures by considering the portfolio returns in the case of equity portfolios. However, there are some additional measures of bond portfolio risk that are not really used in equity portfolio management. To appreciate these measures, we next discuss sources of bond portfolio risk, starting with classical measures of bond portfolio risk and moving on to more recent ways to look at risk, such as VaR and CVaR.

10.1.1 Interest Rate Risk

A portfolio's *duration* is the measure used to quantify the portfolio's exposure to changes in the level of interest rates. This risk measure is valid only if we make the assumption of a parallel shift in the yield curve. As we explained in Chapter 2, the duration of an individual bond is the approximate percentage change in market value for a 100 basis points change in interest rates. The interpretation of the duration of a portfolio is the same. A portfolio duration of 4, for example, means that the portfolio's market value will change by approximately 4% for a 100 basis point change in the interest rate for all maturities.

As explained in Chapter 2, three different versions of the duration measure are modified duration, Macaulay duration, and effective duration. *Modified duration* assumes that, when interest rates change, the cash flows do not change. This is a limitation when measuring the exposure of bonds with embedded options (e. g., callable bonds, mortgage-backed securities, and some asset-backed securities).[1] *Macaulay duration* is related to modified duration and suffers from the same failure to consider changes in cash flows when interest rates change. In contrast, *effective duration* takes these changes in cash flows into account and thus is the appropriate measure for bonds with embedded options. Effective duration is also referred to as *option-adjusted duration* or *adjusted duration.*[2]

The calculation of a portfolio's duration begins with the calculation of the duration for each of the individual bonds comprising the portfolio. This calculation requires the use of a valuation model. Duration is found by shocking (i.e., changing) interest rates up and down, computing the new value of the bond in both cases, and then computing the average percentage price change for the change in interest rates used. Consequently, the duration measure is only as good as the valuation model.

A portfolio's duration is obtained by calculating the weighted average of the durations of the bonds in the portfolio. The weight for a bond is the proportion of the market value of the portfolio represented by the bond. Mathematically, we have

$$D_p = w_1 \cdot D_1 + w_2 \cdot D_2 + \cdots + w_N \cdot D_N,$$

where N is the number of bonds in the portfolio, w_i is the weight of the ith bond, D_i is the duration of the ith bond, and D_p is the duration of the portfolio.

The duration of a bond index is computed in the same way since an index is simply a portfolio with particular weights.

A measure of the portfolio exposure to an individual issue or sector is given by its *contribution to portfolio duration*. This contribution is found by multiplying the percentage of the market value of the portfolio represented by the individual issue or sector ties the duration of the individual issue or sector. That is,

Contribution to portfolio duration =

(Weight of issue or sector in portfolio) · (Duration of issue or sector)

In Chapter 2, we explained that convexity helps to improve the estimate of interest rate risk provided by the duration of an individual bond. Convexity is used for measuring the interest risk of portfolios as well.

10.1.2 Yield Curve Risk

Duration provides a measure of the exposure of a portfolio or a benchmark index to changes in the level of interest rates. However, duration does not indicate the exposure of a portfolio or a benchmark index to changes in the shape of the yield curve.

One way to get a feel for the risk exposure resulting from yield curve shifts is to analyze the distribution of the present values of the cash flows for the portfolio under different scenarios for the yield curve. Another way is to compute the key rate durations of the portfolio and the benchmark. *Key rate duration*, which was described in Chapter 2, is the sensitivity of a portfolio's value to the change in a particular key spot rate. The specific maturities on the spot rate curve for which key rate durations are measured vary from firm to firm.

10.1.3 Spread Risk

For non-Treasury securities, the yield is equal to the Treasury yield plus a spread to the Treasury yield curve. Non-Treasury securities are referred to as *spread products*. The risk that the price of a bond changes due to changes in spreads is referred to as *spread risk*. A measure of how a spread product's price changes if the spread sought by the market changes is called *spread duration*.

Spread duration measures are typically used to capture the spread risk. There are three spread duration measures: nominal spread, zero-volatility spread, and option-adjusted spread.

The *nominal spread* is the traditional spread measure. That is, it is the difference between the yield on a spread product and the yield on a comparable maturity Treasury issue. Thus, when spread is defined as the nominal spread, spread duration indicates the approximate percentage change in price for a 100 basis points change in the nominal spread, holding the Treasury yield constant. It is important to note that, for any spread product, spread duration is the same as duration if the nominal spread is used. For example, suppose that the duration of a corporate bond is 5. This means that, for a 100 basis point change in interest rates, the value of the corporate bond changes by approximately 5%. It does not matter whether the change in rates is due to a change in the level of rates (i.e., a change in the Treasury rate) or a change in the nominal spread.

The *zero-volatility spread*, or *static spread*, is the spread that, when added to the Treasury spot rate curve, makes the present value of the cash flows (when discounted at the spot rates plus the spread) equal to the price of the bond plus accrued interest. It is a measure of the spread over the Treasury spot rate curve. When spread is defined in this way, spread duration is the approximate percentage change in price for a 100 basis point change in the zero-volatility spread, holding the Treasury spot rate curve constant.

The *option-adjusted spread* (OAS) is another spread measure that can be interpreted as the approximate percentage change in price of a spread product for a 100 basis point change in the OAS, holding Treasury rates constant. So, for example, if a corporate bond has a spread duration of 3, this means that if the OAS changes by 20 basis points, then the price of this corporate bond will change by approximately 0.6% ($= 0.03 \cdot 0.02 \cdot 100$). We will encounter OAS again in Chapter 15, when we discuss mortgage-backed securities.

The spread duration for a portfolio or a bond index is computed as a market weighted average of the spread duration for each sector.

10.1.4 Credit Risk

The credit risk of a portfolio on a stand-alone basis or relative to a benchmark index can be gauged by the portfolio allocation to each credit rating.[3] However, a better gauge is the contribution to duration by credit rating. Basically, the portfolio is divided into groups of bonds with the same credit rating, and the contribution to duration for each group is computed.

10.1.5   Estimating Value-at-Risk for Fixed Income Securities

Even though the measures described in the previous sections in this chapter are classical measures in bond portfolio management, many bond portfolio managers use additional measures, such as VaR and CVaR,[4] to obtain a fuller picture of portfolio risk.

To estimate the VaR or the CVaR of a bond portfolio, we need to simulate the distribution of possible values for the portfolio (or the total return of the portfolio[5]) at the end of the holding period. This requires the simulation of the term structure of interest rates. As we will explain in Chapter 15, there is a large literature on interest rate models. We will need the material in Chapters 12 and 15 to explain how term structure scenarios can be generated. However, we can understand the intuition behind the simulation now as well. Consider a simple example: Suppose that we are trying to estimate the VaR of a $1 position in a bond with 10 years to maturity after a one-year investment. We do the following:

- We calculate the initial price of the bond (given the yield curve observable today).
- We generate scenarios for the future values of interest rates, and estimate the price of the bond (given those future interest rates) after one year. Let us call this price the "terminal price," because it is at the end of the investment horizon.
- In each interest rate scenario, we calculate the losses from the position as the difference between the initial price and the terminal price (plus any coupon payments, appropriately discounted, that happened between today and one year from now).
- We now have a series of observations from losses for the bond position. The VaR or the CVaR can be estimated using the techniques described in Chapter 8.

Suppose we would like to incorporate not only interest rate risk, but also credit risk, in our VaR or CVaR estimate. To do that, we would need to take into consideration the following additional factors:

- *The default process.* A default is a binary event, and the cash flows associated with default are distributed far from normal. The only time we can make the assumption of normality is if we have a lot of small independent default events, in which case the Central Limit Theorem applies.[6]

- *The recovery rate.* The recovery rate is the amount recovered in the event of default. (The exact specification of recovery rate depends on the credit risk model used. For example, it could be measured as a percentage of the expected cash flows.)
- *The dependence between market and default risk.* Even though the two are often assumed to be independent in many pricing models, the reality is that the price difference between credit risky and riskless bonds will depend on both types of risks in a complex way. In addition, the default probability may change over time.
- *The complicated nature of credit enhancement agreements that often accompany credit risky positions.* Such agreements include collateral requirements, credit triggers, credit guarantee arrangements, and the like. In practice, these agreements help the institution manage its credit risk, but they make it more complicated to assess the actual impact of a credit event on a bond portfolio.

These complications actually make simulation a good way to approach the modeling of credit-risky positions. The procedure for evaluating the VaR or CVaR of a credit risky bond is similar to the procedure for a nondefaultable bond described earlier in this section. However, to evaluate future cash flows, we simulate the realizations of binary variables that tell us whether the cash flows are actually received. (Once a bond has defaulted, we make sure that no future cash flows are received.)

Estimating the VaR or the CVaR of a portfolio of credit risky bonds (as opposed to a position in a single bond) is more complicated because we need to simulate the dependencies between the defaults of the different bonds. Such dependencies have been often modeled through different types of copula functions.[7] Through transformations of the original variables, *copula functions* allow for modeling dependence between the random variables in a tractable way. The Gaussian copula is one such example.[8] Gaussian copula dependency models in particular, however, have received bad press after their failure to account for the high tail losses observed during the financial crisis of the fall of 2008. In addition, calibrating (i.e., finding the input parameters for) such models is very difficult in practice, because historically there have been few observations of multiple defaults happening simultaneously.

Let us now consider an example that takes advantage of both simulation and optimization to manage the credit risk of a bond portfolio. Anderson, Mausser, Rosen, and Uryasev (2001) describe an approach to optimizing bond portfolios so as to minimize the losses stemming from credit risk exposure. They consider a portfolio of 197 bonds from 29 different countries with a market value of $8.8 billion and duration of approximately 5. The goal is to rebalance the portfolio in order to minimize credit risk over a one-year horizon, that is, to minimize losses resulting from default and from a decline in market value because of downgrades in credit ratings.

To address the problem, they first generate scenarios for the future values of the losses due to credit migration (i.e., changes in the credit rating of obligors). This is done by simulation. They simulate 20,000 scenarios of joint credit states for bond issuers and the related losses. Based on these scenarios, they can evaluate the total losses on all bonds in the portfolio, equal to the sum of the differences between the value of each bond without credit migration and the value of that bond with credit migration. Then, they solve a CVaR minimization problem using the optimization formulation that we presented in section 8.3.3 of Chapter 8.

10.2 THE SPECTRUM OF BOND PORTFOLIO MANAGEMENT STRATEGIES

As in equity portfolio management, there is a spectrum of bond portfolio management strategies that ranges from passive (pure index matching) to active (completely at the portfolio manager's discretion). This spectrum is illustrated in Exhibit 10.1. The figure, developed by Volpert (1997) of the Vanguard Group, shows the risk and return of a bond strategy versus a benchmark. Volpert classifies bond management strategies as follows:

- Pure bond index matching.
- Enhanced indexing/matching primary risk factor approach.
- Enhanced indexing/minor risk factor mismatches.
- Active management/larger risk factor mismatches.
- Active management/full-blown active.

The difference between indexing and active management is the extent to which the portfolio can deviate from the primary risk factors that impact the performance of an index. The primary risk factors associated with an index are:

- The duration of the index
- The present value distribution of the cash flows
- Percent in sector and quality
- Duration contribution of sector
- Duration contribution of credit quality
- Sector/coupon/maturity cell weights
- Issuer exposure control

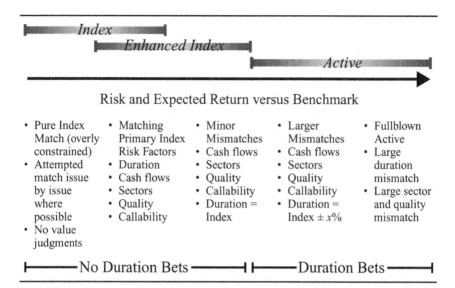

EXHIBIT 10.1 Bond management spectrum.
Source: Exhibit 1 in Volpert (1997, 192).

The first primary risk factor deals with the sensitivity of the value of the index to a parallel shift in interest rates. The second factor is important for controlling the yield curve[9] risk associated with an index. We discuss the different strategies and associated risk factors in more detail. Before we do that, however, we provide some information on the most frequently used bond indices.

10.2.1 Bond Market Indices

There is a wide range of bond market indices. They can be classified as broad-based bond market indices, specialized bond market indices, and international bond indices.

Broad-Based Bond Market Indices The three broad-based bond market indices most commonly used by institutional investors are the Barclays Capital U.S. Aggregate Index (previously the Lehman Brothers U.S. Aggregate Index), the Salomon Smith Barney Broad Investment-Grade Bond Index (SSBBIG), and the Merrill Lynch Domestic Market Index. There are more than 5,500 issues in each index, and a strong correlation (of the order of 98%) between the three indices.

The three broad-based indices are computed daily and are market-value weighted. This means that for each issue, the ratio of the market value of an issue relative to the market value of all issues in the index is used as the weight of the issue in all calculations. The securities in the SSBBIG index are all trader-priced. For the two other indices, the securities are either trader-priced or model-priced. Each index has a different way in which it handles intramonth cash flows that must be reinvested. For the SSBBIG index, these cash flows are assumed to be reinvested at the one-month Treasury bill rate, while for the Merrill Lynch index, they are assumed to be reinvested in the specific issue. There is no reinvestment of intramonth cash flows for the Barclays Capital index.

Each index is broken into sectors. The Barclays Capital index, for example, is divided into the following six sectors: (1) Treasury, (2) agency, (3) mortgage, (4) commercial mortgage-backed securities, (5) asset-backed securities, and (6) credit.

The nature of sectors (3), (4), and (5) will become clearer in Chapter 15. The credit sector includes domestic corporate issues and U.S.-dollar-denominated bonds of European issuers. The four sectors within the credit sector are (1) financial, (2) utility, (3) industrial, and (4) noncorporates.

All three indices exclude issues that are non-investment grade (i.e., below BBB) and issues that have a maturity of one year or less. To be included in the Barclays Capital index, the size of the issue must be more than $150 million; for the Merrill Lynch and SSB indices, the issue size needs to be $50 million. Only taxable issues are included in the broad-based bond market indices.

Specialized Bond Market Indices The specialized bond market indices focus on a sector or a subsector of the bond market. Indices on sectors of the market are published by the three firms that produce the broad-based bond market indices, as well as other brokerage firms and non-brokerage firms. Moreover, there is a family of U.S. bond municipal indices. The Barclays Capital municipal bond indices are the ones most commonly used. There are specialized indices such as the *managed money* and *insurance industry* tax-exempt indices to serve the benchmark needs of investor groups whose permissible investments in the tax-exempt municipal bond market are not likely to be met by the Barclays Capital Municipal Bond Index.

International Bond Indices Indices that comprise international (i.e., not only U.S.) bonds fall into three categories. The first category is indices that includes both U.S. and non-U.S. bonds. Such indices are referred to as *global bond indices* or *world bond indices*. The Barclays Capital Global Aggregate Bond Index is one such example.

The second category of international indices includes only non-U.S. bonds. Such indices are commonly referred to as *international bond indices* or *ex-U.S. bond indices.*

The third category includes specialized bond indices for particular non-U.S. bond sectors. Two examples of this type of index are Barclays Capital's Pan-European Aggregate Index and the Asian-Pacific Aggregate Index.

10.2.2 Pure Bond Indexing Strategy

In terms of risk and return, a pure bond index matching strategy minimizes the risk of underperforming an index. The factors that explain the popularity of bond indexing are similar to those for equity index strategies. First, the empirical evidence suggests that historically the overall performance of active bond managers has been worse than for passive managers. Second, the advisory management fees charged for an indexed portfolio are lower compared to active management advisory fees. Advisory fees charged by active managers typically range from 15 to 50 basis points. The range for indexed portfolios, in contrast, is 1 to 20 basis points (with the upper range representing the fees for enhanced indexing discussed later).

Critics of indexing point out that while an indexing strategy matches the performance of some index, the performance of that index does not necessarily represent optimal performance. Moreover, matching an index does not mean that the manager will satisfy a client's return requirement objective. For example, if the objective of a life insurance company or a pension fund is to have sufficient funds to satisfy a predetermined liability, indexing only reduces the likelihood that performance will not be materially worse than the index. The return on the index is not necessarily related to the liability.

Similarly to equities index strategies, pure bond indexing strategies involve creating a portfolio so as to replicate the performance of the index. And, similarly to equities index strategies, exact replication is too costly or impossible. First, the prices for each issue used by the organization that publishes the index may not be the execution prices available to the portfolio manager. Second, the prices used by organizations reporting the value of indices are based on bid prices. However, portfolio managers must transact at ask prices when constructing or rebalancing the indexed portfolio. Third, there are logistical problems unique to certain sectors in the bond market. For example, consider the corporate bond market. There are typically about 5,000 issues in the corporate bond sector of a broad-based market index. Because of the illiquidity for many of the issues, not only may the prices used by the organization that publishes the index be unreliable, but many of the issues may not even be available. Finally, recall that the total return[10] depends on the reinvestment rate available on interim cash flows received prior to month end. If the organization publishing the index regularly overestimates the reinvestment rate, then the indexed portfolio could underperform the index.

10.2.3 Enhanced Indexing/Matching Primary Risk Factors Approach

An enhanced indexing strategy can be pursued so as to construct a portfolio to match the primary risk factors without acquiring each issue in the index. Smaller funds often use this strategy because of the difficulties of acquiring all of the issues comprising the index. Generally speaking, the fewer the number of issues used to replicate the index, the smaller the tracking error due to transaction costs but the greater the tracking error risk because of the difficulties of matching the primary risk factors perfectly. In contrast, the more issues purchased to replicate the index, the greater the tracking error due to transaction costs, but the smaller the tracking error risk due to the mismatch of the primary factors between the indexed portfolio and the index.

10.2.4 Enhanced Indexing/Minor Risk Factor Mismatches

Another enhanced strategy is one where the portfolio is constructed so as to have minor deviations from the risk factors that affect the performance of the index. For example, there might be a slight overweighting of issues or sectors if the manager believes there is relative value. However, it is important to point out that the duration of the constructed portfolio is matched to the duration of the index. As Exhibit 10.1 shows, there are no duration bets (i.e., duration is matched exactly) for the pure index match strategy and the two enhanced index strategies.

10.2.5 Active Management/Larger Risk Factor Mismatches

Active bond strategies attempt to outperform the market by intentionally constructing a portfolio that will have a greater index mismatch than in the case of enhanced indexing. The decision to pursue an active strategy or to engage a client to request a portfolio manager to pursue an active strategy must be based on the belief that there is some type of gain from such costly efforts; for there to be a gain, pricing inefficiencies must exist. The particular strategy chosen depends on why the portfolio manager believes this is the case.

Volpert (1997) classifies two types of active strategies. In the more conservative of the two active strategies, the portfolio manager makes large mismatches relative to the index in terms of risk factors. This includes minor mismatches of duration. Typically, there will be a limitation as to the degree of duration mismatch. For example, the portfolio manager may be constrained to be within ±1 of the duration of the index. So, if the duration of the index is 4, the portfolio manager may have a duration that is between 3 and 5. Alternatively, if the manager believes that he can take advantage of an anticipated reshaping of the yield curve, there can be significant differences in the cash flow distribution between the index and the portfolio constructed by the manager. As another example, if the portfolio manager believes that issues rated A will outperform issues rated AA within the corporate sector, the portfolio manager may overweight the issues rated A and underweight issues rated AA.

10.2.6 Active Management/Full-Blown Active

In the full-blown active management case, the portfolio manager is permitted to make a significant duration bet without any constraint. The portfolio manager can have a duration of zero (i.e., be all in cash) or can leverage the portfolio to a high multiple of the duration of the index. The portfolio manager can decide not to invest in only one or more of the major sectors of the broad-based bond market indices. The portfolio manager can make a significant allocation to sectors not included in the index. For example, there can be a substantial allocation to nonagency mortgage-backed securities.[11]

Active portfolio strategies and enhanced indexing/minor risk factor mismatch strategies seek to generate additional return after adjusting for risk. This additional return is popularly referred to as *alpha*.[12] These strategies are referred to as *value added strategies* and can be classified as strategic strategies and tactical strategies.

Strategic strategies, sometimes referred to as *top-down value added strategies*, involve the following:

- Interest rate expectations strategies.
- Yield curve strategies.
- Inter- and intrasector allocation strategies.

Tactical strategies, sometimes referred to as *relative value strategies*, are short-term trading strategies. They include:

- Strategies based on rich/cheap analysis.
- Yield curve trading strategies.
- Return enhancing strategies employing futures and options.

Next, we discuss these strategies in more detail.

Interest Rate Expectations Strategies A portfolio manager who believes that he or she can accurately forecast the future level of interest rates will alter the portfolio's duration based on the forecast. Because duration is a measure of interest rate sensitivity, this involves increasing a portfolio's duration if interest rates are expected to fall and reducing duration if interest rates are expected to rise. For those portfolio managers whose benchmark is a bond market index, this means increasing the portfolio duration relative to the benchmark index if interest rates are expected to fall and reducing it if interest rates are expected to rise. The degree to which the duration of the managed portfolio is permitted to diverge from that of the benchmark index may be limited by the client. Interest rate expectations strategies are commonly referred to as *duration strategies.*

A portfolio's duration may be altered in the cash market by swapping (or exchanging) bonds in the portfolio for other bonds that will achieve the target portfolio duration. Alternatively, a more efficient means for altering the duration of a bond portfolio is to use interest rate futures contracts.[13] Buying futures increases a portfolio's duration, while selling futures decreases it.

The key to this active strategy is, of course, an ability to forecast the direction of future interest rates. The academic literature does not support the view that interest rates can be forecasted so that risk-adjusted excess returns can be consistently realized. It is doubtful whether betting on future interest rates will provide a consistently superior return.

Yield Curve Strategies As we explained in Chapter 2, the yield curve for U.S. Treasury securities shows the relationship between maturity and yield. The shape of the yield curve changes over time. A *shift in the yield curve* refers to the relative change in the yield for each Treasury maturity. A *parallel shift in the yield curve* refers to a shift in which the change in the yield for all maturities is the same. A *nonparallel shift in the yield curve* means that the yield for every maturity does not change by the same number of basis points.

Top-down yield curve strategies involve positioning a portfolio to capitalize on expected changes in the shape of the Treasury yield curve. There are three yield curve strategies: (1) bullet strategies, (2) barbell strategies, and (3) ladder strategies. In a *bullet strategy*, the portfolio is constructed so that the maturities of the bonds in the portfolio are highly concentrated at one point on the yield curve. In a *barbell strategy*, the maturity of the bonds included in the portfolio is concentrated at two extreme maturities. Actually, in practice when managers refer to a barbell strategy it is relative to a bullet strategy. For example, a bullet strategy might be to create a portfolio with maturities concentrated around 10 years, while a corresponding barbell strategy might be a portfolio with 5-year and 20-year maturities. In a *ladder strategy* the portfolio is constructed to have approximately equal amounts of each maturity. So, for example, a portfolio might have equal amounts of bonds with one year to maturity, two years to maturity, and so on.

Each of these strategies will result in different performance when the yield curve shifts. The actual performance will depend on both the type of shift and the magnitude of the shift. Thus, no general statements can be made about the optimal yield curve strategy.

Inter- and Intrasector Allocation Strategies   A manager can allocate funds among the major bond sectors that is different from that the allocation in the index. This is referred to as an *intersector allocation strategy*. In an *intrasector allocation strategy*, the portfolio manager's allocation of funds within a sector differs from that of the index.

In making inter- and intrasector allocations, a portfolio manager is anticipating how spreads will change. Spreads reflect differences in credit risk, call risk, and liquidity risk.[14] When the spread for a particular sector or subsector is expected to decline or "narrow," a portfolio manager may decide to overweight that particular sector or subsector. The sector or subsector will be underweighted if the portfolio manager expects the spread to increase or "widen."

Credit spreads change because of expected changes in economic prospects. Credit spreads between Treasury and non-Treasury issues widen in a declining or contracting economy and narrow during economic expansion. The economic rationale is that in a declining or contracting economy, corporations experience a decline in revenue and cash flow, making it difficult for corporate issuers to service their contractual debt obligations. To induce investors to hold non-Treasury securities, the yield spread relative to Treasury securities must widen. The converse is that during economic expansion and brisk economic activity, revenue and cash flow pick up, increasing the likelihood that corporate issuers will have the capacity to service their contractual debt obligations. Yield spreads between Treasury and federal agency securities will vary depending on investor expectations about the prospects that an implicit government guarantee will be honored.

A portfolio manager can therefore use economic forecasts of the economy in developing forecasts of credit spreads. Also, some managers base forecasts on historical credit spreads. The underlying principle is that there is a "normal" credit spread relationship that exists. If the current credit spread in the market differs materially from that "normal" credit spread, then the portfolio manager should position the portfolio so as to benefit from a return to the "normal" credit spread. The assumption is that the "normal" credit spread is some type of average or mean value and that mean reversion will occur. If, in fact, there has been a structural shift in the marketplace, this may not occur as the normal spread may change.

A portfolio manager will also look at technical factors to assess relative value. For example, a manager may analyze the prospective supply and demand for new issues on spreads in individual sectors or issuers to determine whether they should be overweighted or underweighted. This commonly used tactical strategy is referred to as *primary market analysis.*

Individual Security Selection Strategies   Once the allocation to a sector or subsector has been made, the portfolio manager must decide on the specific issues to select. This is because a manager will typically not invest in all issues within a sector or subsector. Instead, depending on the dollar size of the portfolio, the manager will select a representative number of issues.

It is at this stage that a portfolio manager makes an intrasector allocation decision to the specific issues. The portfolio manager may believe that there are securities that are mispriced within a subsector and therefore will outperform other issues within the same sector over the investment horizon. There are several active strategies that portfolio managers pursue to identify mispriced securities. The most common strategy identifies an issue as undervalued because either (1) its yield is higher than that of comparably rated issues or (2) its yield is expected to decline (and price therefore rise) because credit analysis indicates that its rating will be upgraded.

Once a portfolio is constructed, a portfolio manager may undertake a swap that involves exchanging one bond for another bond that is similar in terms of coupon, maturity, and credit quality, but offers a higher yield. This is called a *substitution swap* and depends on a capital market imperfection. Such situations sometimes exist in the bond market owing to temporary market imbalances and the fragmented nature of the non-Treasury.[15]

10.2.7   Using Quantitative Methods for Portfolio Allocation

The portfolio allocation strategies we described so far in this section are often aided by quantitative approaches and software that enable portfolio managers to sort through alternative strategies quickly. For example, there are two methodologies used to construct a portfolio to replicate an index: the stratified sampling and the optimization approach. Both approaches assume that the performance of an individual bond depends on a number of systematic factors that affect the performance of all bonds and on a factor unique to the individual issue.[16] This last risk is diversifiable risk. The objective of the two approaches is to construct an indexed portfolio that eliminates this diversifiable risk.

Stratified Sampling Approach In the *stratified sampling approach* (or *cellular approach*) to indexing, the index is divided into cells representing the primary risk factors. The objective is then to select from all of the issues in the index one or more issues in each cell that can be used to represent that entire cell. The total dollar amount purchased of the issues from each cell will be based on the percentage of the index's total market value that the cell represents. For example, consider two factors: credit quality and duration. Imagine a table with rows that correspond to the different credit ratings[17] and columns that correspond to different ranges for durations. In effect, we have "buckets" in which we place all bonds under consideration depending on their credit quality and duration.

The number of cells that the indexer uses will depend on the dollar amount of the portfolio to be indexed. In indexing a portfolio of less than $50 million, for example, using a large number of cells would require purchasing odd lots of issues. This increases the cost of buying the issues to represent a cell, and hence increases the tracking error risk. However, reducing the number of cells to overcome this problem also increases tracking error risk, because the major risk factors of the indexed portfolio may differ materially from those of the index.

Optimization Approach In the optimization approach, the manager seeks to design an indexed portfolio that will match the cell breakdown just as described, but that will also satisfy other constraints, and optimize some objective. An objective might be to maximize convexity or to maximize expected total returns or to minimize tracking error.[18] Constraints other than matching the cell breakdown might include not purchasing more than a specified amount of one issuer or group of issuers within the same strategy.

Although on the surface the stratified sampling approach is more straightforward to use than the optimization approach, it is extremely difficult to implement the stratified sampling approach when large, diversified portfolios are taken as the benchmark. In this case, many cells are required, and the problem becomes complex. Also, because the handpicking of issues to match each cell is subjective, large tracking errors may result. Optimization modeling reduces the work for the manager, allowing for efficient analysis of large quantities of data.

10.3 LIABILITY-DRIVEN STRATEGIES

Thus far, the bond portfolio strategies discussed in this chapter have focused on managing funds relative to a benchmark that is a market index. In a liability-driven strategy, the goal is to manage funds to satisfy contractual liabilities. The two liability-driven strategies are immunization and cash flow matching. Insurance companies, sponsors of defined benefit pension plans, and other institutions with liabilities often take advantage of such strategies.

10.3.1 Immunization Strategy for a Single-Period Liability

Immunization is a hybrid strategy that has elements of both active and passive strategies. Classical immunization can be defined as the process by which a bond portfolio is created so that it has an assured return for a specific time horizon irrespective of interest rate changes. The following are the important characteristics:

1. A specified time horizon.
2. An assured rate of return during the holding period to a fixed horizon date.
3. Insulation from the effects of potential adverse interest rate changes on the portfolio value at the horizon date.

The fundamental mechanism underlying immunization is a portfolio structure that balances the change in the value of the portfolio at the end of the investment horizon with the return from the reinvestment of portfolio cash flows (coupon payments and maturing securities). That is, immunization requires offsetting interest rate risk and reinvestment risk. To accomplish this balancing act requires controlling duration and setting the present value of the cash flows from the bond portfolio to the present value of the liability. By setting the duration of the portfolio equal to the desired portfolio time horizon, the offsetting of positive and negative incremental return sources can under certain circumstances be assured. However, given the fact that duration is the tool that is used, the portfolio is only immunized if there is a parallel shift in the yield curve. If there is a change in interest rates that does not correspond to this shape-preserving shift, matching the duration to the investment horizon no longer assures immunization.

A Simple Example Let us see an example of how immunization works. Suppose we have a liability of $1,000,000 that must be paid five years from now. We would like to invest enough money today to meet this future obligation. Our investment universe consists of two bonds, B_1 and B_2, with face values of $100, maturities of 12 years and 5 years, and coupon rates of 6% and 5%, respectively. For simplicity, we will assume that the coupons are paid once per year (as opposed to semiannually). How much should we

EXHIBIT 10.2 Current yield curve, discount factors, cash flows from bonds 1 and 2, as well as present values of cash flows from the two bonds.

Year	Spot	df	B1	PV1	B2	PV2
1	3.64%	0.965	6	5.79	10	9.65
2	4.17%	0.922	6	5.53	10	9.22
3	4.70%	0.871	6	5.23	10	8.71
4	5.21%	0.816	6	4.90	10	8.16
5	5.45%	0.767	6	4.60	110	84.36
6	6.06%	0.703	6	4.22		
7	6.43%	0.646	6	3.88		
8	6.75%	0.593	6	3.56		
9	7.10%	0.539	6	3.24		
10	7.35%	0.492	6	2.95		
11	7.57%	0.448	6	2.69		
12	7.79%	0.406	106	43.09		
Price of bond today			B1	89.66	B2	120.10

invest in the two bonds so that the overall portfolio (bonds and liability) is immunized against changes in interest rates?

Exhibit 10.2 contains the current yield curve (column "Spot"), the discount factors computed from the yield curve (column "df"), the cash flows from bonds 1 and 2 (columns "B1" and "B2"), and the present values of the cash flows from the two bonds (columns "PV1" and "PV2"). (See also Excel workbook **Ch10-Immunization.xlsx**.) The current prices of the bonds are determined by summing up the present values of the cash flows for each bond. They are $89.66 and $120.10, respectively.

Now let us compute the durations of the bonds and the liabilities. As we explained in Chapter 2, duration can be interpreted as the change in the value of the bond per unit change in interest rates, and the formula can be stated as

$$D = \frac{B_- - B_+}{2 \cdot B_0 \cdot \Delta y}.$$

Exhibit 10.3 shows how the duration can be determined for bonds 1 and 2. We consider a shift in interest rates of $\Delta y = 25$ basis points,[19] and compute the new yield curves, present values, and bond prices if interest rates shift up or down by this amount. The notation used is as follows: df− and df+ are the discount factors under a negative shift and a positive shift of the yield curve, respectively, PV1− and PV1+ are the present values of the

EXHIBIT 10.3 Effect of shift of $\Delta y = 25$ basis points on bond prices.

df−	PV1−	PV2−	df+	PV1+	PV2+
0.967	5.80	9.67	0.963	5.78	9.63
0.926	5.56	9.26	0.917	5.50	9.17
0.878	5.27	8.78	0.865	5.19	8.65
0.824	4.94	8.24	0.808	4.85	8.08
0.776	4.66	85.37	0.758	4.55	83.37
0.713	4.28		0.693	4.16	
0.657	3.94		0.636	3.82	
0.604	3.63		0.582	3.49	
0.551	3.31		0.528	3.17	
0.504	3.02		0.481	2.88	
0.460	2.76		0.437	2.62	
0.418	44.31		0.395	41.91	
	91.46	121.32		87.91	118.90

cash flows for bond 1 under a negative shift and a positive shift of interest rates, and similarly, PV2− and PV2+ are the present values of the cash flows for bond 2 under a negative shift and a positive shift of interest rates. The bond prices are as follows: under a negative shift in interest rates, $B_1- =$ \$91.46 and $B_2- =$ \$121.32. Under a positive shift in interest rates, $B_1+ =$ \$87.91 and $B_2+ =$ \$118.90. This allows us to compute the durations for the two bonds. For example, for bond 1, we have

$$D_1 = \frac{91.46 - 87.91}{2 \cdot 89.66 \cdot 0.0025} = 7.91.$$

Similarly, the duration for bond 2 can be computed to be 4.02.

To compute the duration of the liability of \$1,000,000, we go through a similar procedure. The 5-year spot rate is 5.45%, so the present value of the liability is

$$\frac{1,000,000}{(1 + 0.0545)^5} = \$766,950.05.$$

Under a negative shift in interest rates of 25 basis points, the value of the liability becomes

$$\frac{1,000,000}{(1 + 0.0545 - 0.0025)^5} = \$776,106.46,$$

and under a positive shift in interest rates, it becomes \$757,922.96. Therefore, the duration of the liability is 4.74.

To immunize against interest rate changes, we look for the number of units of bonds (x_1 and x_2) to invest so that the present value of the cash flows from the bonds equals the present value of the liability and the duration of the portfolio of bonds matches the duration of the liability. How do we compute the duration of the portfolio of bonds? Recall from section 10.1.1 in this chapter that the duration of the portfolio is the weighted average of the durations of the individual bonds, where the weights are the weights of the bonds in the portfolio. In this case, the weights can be expressed as $x_1/(x_1 + x_2)$ and $x_2/(x_1 + x_2)$. (This is because $(x_1 + x_2)$ is the total amount invested.)

We need to solve the following system of equation, in which the unknowns are the number of units x_1 and x_2 to invest in bond 1 and bond 2, respectively:

$$B_1 \cdot x_1 + B_2 \cdot x_2 = PV(\text{Liability})$$
$$D_1 \cdot x_1/(x_1 + x_2) + D_2 \cdot x_1/(x_1 + x_2) = D(\text{Liability})$$

In order to make this a linear system of equations, we will multiply both sides of the second equation by $(x_1 + x_2)$. Hence, we want to find x_1 and x_2 that satisfy

$$B_1 \cdot x_1 + B_2 \cdot x_2 = PV(\text{Liability})$$
$$D_1 \cdot x_1 + D_2 \cdot x_1 = D(\text{Liability}) \cdot (x_1 + x_2)$$

This can be done with a simple linear optimization solver or a numerical procedure. (In the case of two bonds, it is easy to solve by hand, but in the case of larger portfolios it would require numerical implementation.) If we have an optimization solver, the decision variables will be the number of units to invest in bond 1 and bond 2, x_1 and x_2. We can minimize, for example, the expression on the left hand side of the first equation, subject to constraints that are represented by the two equations.[20] This will make sure that the two equations are satisfied. In our example, the optimal solution is to purchase 1,239.14 of bond 1 and 5,460.68 of bond 2.

Let us now verify that this investment will indeed cover the liability if there are parallel shifts in the yield curve. Exhibit 10.4 summarizes the information on the price of the bonds, the value of the liability, and the total portfolio value under a positive and a negative shift of 1% (100 basis points)

EXHIBIT 10.4 Immunization results.

	$\Delta y = 0$	$\Delta y = 100$ bp	$\Delta y = -100$ bp
Bond 1			
Units	1,239.14	1,239.14	1,239.14
Price	$89.66	$82.93	$97.15
Bond 2			
Units	5,460.68	5,460.68	5,460.68
Price	$120.10	$115.40	$125.07
Liability value	$766,950.05	$731,596.59	$804,373.54
Portfolio value (Bonds – Liability)	0	$1,324.19	−$1,048.30

in interest rates. We can see that the portfolio remains largely (although not perfectly) immunized against changes in interest rates.[21]

Further Issues How often should the portfolio be rebalanced to adjust its duration? On the one hand, more frequent rebalancing increases transaction costs, thereby reducing the likelihood of achieving the target return. On the other hand, less frequent rebalancing results in the portfolio's duration wandering from the target duration, which will also reduce the likelihood of achieving the target return. Thus a portfolio manager faces a trade-off: some transaction costs must be accepted to prevent the portfolio duration from wandering too far from its target, but some misalignment in the portfolio duration must be tolerated, or transaction costs will become prohibitively high.

In the actual process leading to the construction of an immunized portfolio, the selection of the investment universe is extremely important. Immunization theory assumes there will be no defaults and that securities will be responsive only to overall changes in interest rates. The lower the credit quality permitted in the portfolio, the greater the likelihood that these assumptions will not be met. Furthermore, securities with embedded options such as call features or mortgage-backed prepayments complicate and may even prevent the accurate estimation of cash flows and hence duration, which prevents immunization from achieving the desired effect. Finally, liquidity is a consideration for immunized portfolios because, as just noted, they must be rebalanced over time.

A natural extension of classical immunization theory is a technique for modifying the assumption of parallel shifts in the yield curve. One approach is a strategy that can handle any arbitrary interest rate change so that it

A. Portfolio A: High-risk immunized portfolio:

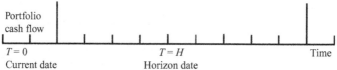

Portfolio
cash flow

$T = 0$ $T = H$ Time
Current date   Horizon date
Note: Portfolio duration matches horizon length. Portfolio's cash flow dispersed.

B. Portfolio B: Low-risk immunized portfolio:

Portfolio
cash flow

$T = 0$ $T = H$ Time
Current date   Horizon date
Note: Portfolio duration matches horizon length. Portfolio's cash flow
concentrated around horizon dates.

EXHIBIT 10.5   Immunization risk measure.
Source: Fabozzi (2009).

is not necessary to specify an alternative duration measure. The approach, developed by Fong and Vasicek (1984), establishes a measure of immunization risk against any arbitrary interest rate change. The immunization risk measure can then be minimized subject to the constraint that the duration of the portfolio is equal to the investment horizon, resulting in a portfolio with minimum exposure to any interest rate movements.

One way of minimizing immunization risk is shown in Exhibit 10.5. The spikes in the two panels of the exhibit represent actual portfolio cash flows. The taller spikes depict the actual cash flows generated by matured securities while the smaller spikes represent coupon payments. Both portfolio A and portfolio B are composed of two bonds with duration equal to the investment horizon. Portfolio A is, in effect, a barbell portfolio—a portfolio comprising short and long maturities and interim coupon payments. For portfolio B, the two bonds mature very close to the investment horizon and the coupon payments are nominal over the investment horizon, so portfolio B is a bullet portfolio. It is not difficult to see why the barbell portfolio should be riskier than the bullet portfolio. Assume that both portfolios have durations equal to the horizon length, so that both portfolios are immune to parallel rate changes. This immunity is attained as a consequence of balancing the effect of changes in reinvestment rates on payments received during the investment horizon against the effect of changes in market value of the portion of the portfolio still outstanding at the end of the investment horizon.

When interest rates change in an arbitrary nonparallel way, however, the effect on the two portfolios is very different. Suppose, for instance, that short rates decline while long rates go up. Both portfolios would realize a decline of the portfolio value at the end of the investment horizon below the target investment value, since they experience a capital loss in addition to lower reinvestment rates. The decline, however, would be substantially higher for the barbell portfolio for two reasons. First, the lower reinvestment rates are experienced on the barbell portfolio for longer time intervals than on the bullet portfolio, so that the opportunity loss is much greater. Second, the portion of the barbell portfolio still outstanding at the end of the investment horizon is much longer than that of the bullet portfolio, which means that the same rate increase would result in a much greater capital loss. Thus the bullet portfolio has less exposure to whatever the change in the interest rate structure may be than the barbell portfolio.

It should be clear from the foregoing discussion that immunization risk is the risk of reinvestment. The portfolio that has the least reinvestment risk will have the least immunization risk. When there is a high dispersion of cash flows around the horizon date, as in the barbell portfolio, the portfolio is exposed to higher reinvestment risk. However, when the cash flows are concentrated around the horizon date, as in the bullet portfolio, the portfolio is subject to minimum reinvestment risk.

10.3.2 Cash Flow Matching Strategy

The immunization strategy described in the previous section is used to immunize a portfolio created to satisfy a single liability in the future against adverse interest rate movements. However, it is more common to have multiple future liabilities. One example is the liability structure of pension funds. Another example is a life insurance annuity contract. It is possible to extend the principles of immunization to multiple future liabilities. However, it is more common in practice to use a *cash flow matching strategy*. This strategy is used to construct a portfolio that can fund a schedule of liabilities from portfolio return and asset value, with the portfolio's value diminishing to zero after payment of the last liability.

A cash flow matching strategy can be described intuitively as follows. A bond is selected with a maturity that matches the last liability. An amount of principal equal to the amount of the last liability is then invested in this bond. The remaining elements of the liability stream are then reduced by the coupon payments on this bond, and another bond is chosen for the next-to-last liability, adjusted for any coupon payments of the first bond selected. Going backward in time, this sequence is continued until all liabilities have been matched by payments on the securities selected for the portfolio.

However, optimization techniques are more effective for constructing a least-cost cash flow matching portfolio from an acceptable universe of bonds. We saw an example of a using optimization to design a cash flow matching strategy in section 5.3.2 of Chapter 5.

SUMMARY

- Most generally, bond portfolio management strategies can be classified in five categories: pure bond index matching, enhanced indexing/matching primary risk factors approach, enhanced indexing/minor risk factor mismatches, active management/larger risk factor mismatches, and active management/full-blown active.
- The difference between indexing and active management is the extent to which the portfolio can deviate from the primary risk factors associated with the index. The primary risk factors associated with an index are: (1) the duration of the index, (2) the present value distribution of the cash flows, (3) percent in sector and quality, (4) duration contribution of sector, (5) duration contribution of credit quality, (6) sector/coupon/maturity cell weights, and (7) issuer exposure control.
- Value added strategies seek to enhance return relative to an index and can be strategic or tactical. Strategic strategies include interest rate expectations strategies, yield curve strategies, and inter- and intrasector allocation strategies. Tactical strategies are short-term trading strategies that include strategies based on rich/cheap analysis, yield curve trading strategies, and return enhancing strategies employing derivatives (futures and options).
- Interest rate expectations strategies involve adjusting the duration of the portfolio relative to the index based on expected movements in interest rates. Top-down yield curve strategies involve positioning a portfolio to capitalize on expected changes in the shape of the Treasury yield curve by following either a bullet strategy, a barbell strategy, or a ladder strategy.
- An intersector allocation strategy involves a manager's allocation of funds among the major bond sectors. In making inter- and intrasector allocations, a manager is anticipating how spreads due to differences in credit risk, call risk, and liquidity risk will change.
- Immunization and cash flow matching are two liability-driven strategies whose goal is to make sure that the investor can meet a schedule of future liabilities.
- Classical immunization can be defined as the process by which a bond portfolio is created so that it has an assured return for a specific time

horizon irrespective of interest rate changes. It is accomplished by matching the present value of the liability as well as the duration of the liability. However, in practice immunization protects only against parallel changes in the yield curve.

■ A cash flow matching strategy is used to construct a portfolio that can fund a schedule of liabilities from portfolio return and asset value, with the portfolio's value diminishing to zero after payment of the last liability.

■ Optimization and simulation are valuable tools for bond portfolio risk management. Optimization is used in portfolio allocation under different measures of risk, such as tracking error relative to a benchmark, or CVaR. Simulation aids in estimating portfolio interest rate risk and portfolio credit risk by allowing the portfolio manager to understand the performance of the portfolio under different scenarios.

NOTES

1. See Chapter 2 for definitions of callable bonds, asset-backed, and mortgage-backed securities. We will discuss mortgage-backed securities in detail in Chapter 15.
2. We come back to the concept of option-adjusted duration in section 15.5.1 of Chapter 15.
3. See Chapter 2 for an introduction to credit ratings.
4. See Chapter 8.
5. See Chapter 2 for a definition of total return.
6. See section 3.11.1 of Chapter 3.
7. See, for example, Chapter 9 in Glasserman (2004).
8. MATLAB's Statistical Toolbox has built-in functions, such as `copularnd`, that allow for generating co-dependent random variables with a specific copula function, such as the *Gaussian* or *t*-copula.
9. See Chapter 2 for a definition of a yield curve.
10. See Chapter 2 for a definition of the total return of a bond.
11. Such securities are discussed in Chapter 15.
12. The concept of alpha is discussed in more detail in Chapter 11.
13. Futures contracts are derivatives. Financial derivatives are explained in Chapter 13.
14. Liquidity risk is the risk that issues will not be traded as quickly as anticipated. See Chapter 2 for definitions of credit risk and call risk.
15. Swaps are financial derivative contracts, which are discussed in Chapter 13.
16. This is referred to as a *factor model*. Factor models are discussed in detail in Chapter 11.
17. See Exhibit 2.1 in Chapter 2.

18. See section 9.3 in the previous chapter for a mathematical definition of tracking error.
19. This means that we change the interest rate for each maturity in the table by the amount Δy.
20. See the Solver dialog box in the file **Ch10-Immunization.xlsx**.
21. Try different investment amounts to see that the change in the portfolio value for a different number of units invested in the two bonds is worse. For example, a combination of 1,000 units of bond 1 and 5,639.21 units of bond 2 also results in a present value of $766,950.05, which offsets the present value of the liability. However, if interest rates shift by 100 basis points, the value of the overall portfolio is –$1,952.73 (in the case of a negative shift) and $2,094.94 (in the case of a positive shift), which is a larger discrepancy than in the case of the immunized portfolio found in this section.

Asset Pricing Models

Factor Models

The investment management industry dedicates a large part of its resources to forecasting future returns on securities. Quantitative finance practitioners use sophisticated mathematical models for calculating future returns. Some of these models represent relationships between the returns of different assets at any given point in time (cross-sectional relationships), and some analyze time-dependent components of the movements of asset prices.

This chapter focuses on basic asset pricing models that establish links between prices and returns and their lagged values or exogenous variables. The latter variables are referred to as *factors*. When a factor is a measure of risk, it is referred to as a *risk factor*. Predominantly, the justification of econometric models is empirical, that is, they are valid insofar as they fit empirical data. However, economic theory does offer some theoretical justification for factor models. The theoretical foundations of factor models stem from the idea that in a well-functioning capital market, investors should be rewarded for tolerating the risk that comes with investing in a security, and therefore the return on these securities should be higher than the return on a riskless security such as a Treasury bill. A part of the security's risk is shared by groups of other securities, while another part is unique to the specific security. Therefore, some of the risk of a security can be understood better by studying the underlying processes that determine how the economy behaves.

To identify the relevant factors, we would use regression analysis, or one of two econometric techniques, principal components analysis or factor analysis, both of which we will introduce briefly in this chapter. The factors identified with the latter two techniques, referred to as *statistical factors*, are not necessarily observable factors.

Our discussion begins with the classical factor models: the Capital Asset Pricing Model and the Arbitrage Pricing Theory. Next, we discuss practical issues in the estimation of factor models, and applications of factor models for portfolio performance, risk decomposition, and optimization.

This chapter does not directly deal with applications of simulation in finance, although, as we mentioned, it does discuss the importance of factor models in portfolio allocation decisions made using optimization (section 11.4.3 in this chapter). However, the concept of factor models is very important for more advanced asset pricing and risk estimation models, so it is useful to touch upon this subject. Our focus in this chapter is on applications in equities; however, factor models are widely used in fixed-income risk management as well. We illustrate one application in the Practice section on the companion web site.

11.1 THE CAPITAL ASSET PRICING MODEL

The first asset pricing model was derived independently by William Sharpe (1964), John Lintner (1965), and Jan Mossin (1966). They extended the microview of risk and return taken by Harry Markowitz (1952) in his statement of the individual investor's mean-variance problem to a statement about the entire economy. Their model holds if every investor optimizes his portfolio allocation by taking into consideration only the mean and the variance of his portfolio, subject to some additional assumptions, such as (1) investors are rational and risk-averse, (2) investors all invest for the same period of time, (3) there is a risk-free asset, (4) all investors can borrow or lend any amount at the risk-free rate, and (5) capital markets are perfectly competitive and frictionless.

It turns out that, given that security prices must clear in equilibrium, this assumed investor behavior implies something very specific about the returns of assets.[1] More precisely, the expected return $E(\tilde{r}_i)$ on any security i in the market should follow the equality

$$E(\tilde{r}_i) = r_f + \beta_i(E(\tilde{r}_M) - r_f).$$

Here r_f is the risk-free return (the return on a Treasury bill), r_M is the return on the market, and

$$\beta_i = \frac{\mathrm{Cov}(\tilde{r}_i, \tilde{r}_M)}{\mathrm{Var}(\tilde{r}_M)}.$$

The equation $E(\tilde{r}_i)$ is known as the *Capital Asset Pricing Model* (CAPM), and has had a significant impact on investment theory over the last five decades. The importance of Sharpe's contribution to finance theory and practice was recognized in 1990, when he was awarded the Nobel Memorial Prize in Economic Sciences together with Harry Markowitz and Merton Miller.

An alternative equivalent way of writing the equality is

$$E(\tilde{r}_i) - r_f = \beta_i(E(\tilde{r}_M) - r_f) + \varepsilon_i.$$

In words, this pricing model states that the excess return (i.e., return over the risk-free rate) on any security should be proportional to the excess market return. The coefficient β_i is known just as that: "beta." It can be interpreted as the sensitivity of the specific security's return to changes in the market return. For example, a beta of 1 means that the return of a security is perfectly correlated with the market return: for every point increase in excess market return, the excess return on the security should increase by one point. Beta is used as a measure of *systematic risk*; that is, risk that is exogenous to the particular security and is associated with the market itself. The remaining variability in the security's returns is *nonsystematic risk*; that is, risk that is specific to the security itself.

A security's beta can be estimated from a set of observed returns for the security and the market return using the following simple linear regression:[2]

$$r_{it} - r_{ft} = \alpha_i + \beta_i \cdot (r_{Mt} - r_{ft}) + e_{it}$$

where r_{it} is the observed return on security i for time t.

r_{ft} is the observed return on the risk-free asset for time t.

r_{Mt} is the observed return on the market portfolio for time t.

e_{it} is the error term for time t.

This equation (the equation of a line in the space determined by x coordinate $(r_M - r_f)$ and y coordinate $(r_i - r_f)$ describes the so-called *characteristic line*. The characteristic line can be expressed as

$$y_t = \alpha_i + \beta_i \cdot x_t + \varepsilon_{it}.$$

Note that, technically, the intercept term α_i should be statistically equivalent to 0 in order for this equation to be consistent with the CAPM. The intercept term has a specific interpretation in portfolio performance analysis, as will be explained in section 11.4.1.

To estimate the characteristic line for a security using regression analysis, we consider three time series of returns for (1) the security, (2) the market portfolio, and (3) the risk-free rate. Consider, for example, the monthly data on Oracle stock returns in the file **Ch11-Beta.xlsx**. For the market portfolio, we used the Standard & Poor's 500 (S&P 500) and for the risk-free rate we used the returns for the one-month Treasury bill rate. The estimate obtained for beta is 1.41. This means that if the market excess return is up by a point, we would expect the Oracle excess return to be up by 1.41 points on average. Clearly, the beta estimates will vary with the particular market index selected as well as with the sample period and the observations used (i.e., daily, weekly, monthly).

Some researchers and practitioners estimate a stock's beta by using returns rather than excess returns in the equation above. The estimated regression model is referred to as the *single-index market model*. This model was first suggested by Markowitz (1959) as a proxy measure of the covariance of a stock with an index so that the full mean-variance analysis need not be performed. While the approach was mentioned by Markowitz in a footnote in his book, it was Sharpe (1963) who investigated it further. It turns out that the betas estimated using the characteristic line and the single-index market model do not differ materially. In the Oracle example, the beta estimated with the single-index market model is 1.40—within a rounding difference of the beta estimated with the characteristic line. (See section 11.3.1 in for more detailed interpretation of the regression output and the Software Hints for instructions on how to run regression with Excel and MATLAB.)

The CAPM has come under much scrutiny over the past 50 years. Note that it can only be tested if the market portfolio can be identified, which is not easy. Is the market portfolio a domestic or an international portfolio? Does the market portfolio include, for example, real estate? In practical applications, these issues are not of as much concern because typically the candidates for the market portfolio are very highly correlated. One can use stock indices such as the Russell 3000, or composite indices. It comes as no surprise, however, that the stock beta estimates reported in different publications (Yahoo Finance, *Wall Street Journal*, etc.) may vary significantly.

It has been established also that the assumptions on which the CAPM is based do not hold in the real world. Namely, investor behavior is not influenced only by means and variances of returns, but also other parameters such as skewness and kurtosis. Empirically, it has been observed also that return distributions do not follow the distribution assumed by the CAPM. That is, real-world asset returns are not normally distributed. The ideas and the terminology introduced by the CAPM, however, continue to be widely used in investment practice today.

11.2 THE ARBITRAGE PRICING THEORY

The *Arbitrage Pricing Theory* (APT), developed by Stephen Ross (1976), starts from a different vantage point than the CAPM. Instead of making assumptions on investment behavior or asset return distributions, it assumes that there are a limited number of independent factors influencing returns. Namely, asset returns can be expressed as

$$\tilde{r}_i = E(\tilde{r}_i) + \beta_{i1} \tilde{f}_1 + \cdots \beta_{iK} \tilde{f}_K.$$

It turns out that the CAPM is a special case of the APT, in which there is only one factor—the market. However, the APT provides a more flexible and general framework that is more consistent with numerous studies on returns.

The derivation of the APT is based purely on arbitrage principles. We will explain the basics of arbitrage as a concept in detail in Chapter 13, and will not go through the formal derivation of the APT here. Instead, let us discuss several major advantages of the APT over the CAPM. First, the APT makes less restrictive assumptions about investor preferences toward risk and return than the CAPM. While the CAPM requires that investors consider trade-offs between risk and return solely on the basis of the expected returns and standard deviations of prospective investments, the APT simply requires that some bounds be placed on investors' utility functions.[3] Second, the APT is a "relative" pricing model, in the sense that it prices securities on the basis of the prices of other securities. By contrast, the CAPM is an "absolute" pricing model, in the sense that it relates returns on the securities to the fundamental source of risk inherent in the portfolio of total wealth. Finally, the APT does not rely on identifying the market portfolio, and does not require any assumptions about the distribution of asset returns except for the factor structure.

From a practical point of view, multifactor asset pricing models rather than single-factor models have long shown better promise. Regression-based tests seeking to dispute the CAPM have helped to identify factors that have been found to be statistically significant in explaining the variation in asset returns. Typically, these factors fall into one of three categories:

1. *External (economic) factors*, such as gross domestic product (GDP), consumer price index (CPI), unemployment rate, credit spreads on bonds, and the steepness of the yield curve.
2. *Fundamental factors (firm characteristics)*, such as the price-earnings ratio, the dividend-payout ratio, the earnings growth forecast, and financial leverage.[4]
3. *Extracted (statistical) factors*, such as the return on the market portfolio (computed as the compilation of returns on the individual securities) and the average of the returns of stocks in a particular industry (utilities, transportation, aerospace, etc.). Factors can be computed also through the methods of principal component analysis or factor analysis, as we will explain in section 11.3.

Proprietary multifactor models are widely used in industry. For example, Robert Jones (1998) of Goldman Sachs Asset Management reported factors found in the U.S. stock market for the period 1979 through 1996. He regressed monthly stock returns against "value," "momentum," and "risk" factors. The value factors included four ratios: book-market ratio, price-earnings ratio, sales-price ratio, and cash flow-price ratio. The three momentum factors included estimate revisions for earnings, revisions ratio, and price momentum. The first risk factor was the systematic risk or beta from the CAPM.[5] The second risk factor was the residual risk from the CAPM; this is the risk not explained by the CAPM. The third risk factor was an uncertainty estimate measure. The factors were beginning-of-month values that are properly lagged where necessary.[6] Jones calculated the average monthly regression coefficient and t-statistic for the series. All of the factors were found to be highly statistically significant. The conclusion from the regression results was that there are factors other than the CAPM beta that explain returns.

Some well-known factor models for the equity market are the models developed by Chen, Roll, and Ross (1986), Fama and French (1993, 1995, 1996, 1998), MSCI Barra, and Northfield Information Services. For example, an old version of MCSI Barra's factor model included 13 risk indices, such as volatility, momentum, size, and trading activity, and 55 industry groups, further classified into 13 sectors: basic materials, energy, consumer noncyclicals, consumer cyclicals, consumer services, industrials, utility, transport, health care, technology, telecommunications, commercial services, and financial services (Barra 1998). As an example, the energy sector comprises the following three industries: energy reserves and production, oil refining, and oil services. Given the risk factors, information about the exposure of every stock i to each risk factor k $(\beta_{i,k})$ is estimated using regression analysis.

11.3 BUILDING MULTIFACTOR MODELS IN PRACTICE

The APT provides a theoretical framework for asset pricing models that improve risk measurement and estimation by attributing it to multiple factors. Unfortunately, the APT does not explain *how* one may find these factors. Moreover, while these theoretical models are focused on estimating expected returns for long-term asset allocation, they are of little use in everyday trading. As we mentioned at the end of the previous section, practitioners usually employ sophisticated proprietary methods for return estimation. These methods are typically based on statistical techniques for identifying factors that drive returns and allow for establishing an advantage in asset allocation and trading by virtue of knowing something about how these underlying factors behave. By identifying the important factors that contribute to changes in security prices, portfolio managers can control portfolio risk more effectively.

There are two philosophically different approaches to identifying such factors. The first is to start by stating a hypothesis about which market factors influence returns, and then test whether the data confirm the hypothesis. The statistical technique used to test the hypothesis is *regression analysis*. The second approach is to "let the data speak for themselves." We start with data on security returns, and try to identify underlying factors by observing groups of securities that exhibit strong correlations in returns. The statistical methodology used to identify such factors is called *factor analysis*. While factor analysis helps to identify sources of risk common to groups of securities, it does not identify what these sources are.

Principal component analysis is also used in the context of empirical multifactor model building. It also attempts to identify factors that underlie asset return processes, but its general goal is to reduce the dimension of the representation, that is, to identify factors one by one in such a way that the first factor explains the largest percentage of the variability in the data; the second factor explains the second-largest percentage of the variability in the data, and so on. This enables the modeler to drop from consideration factors that contribute relatively little to the explanatory power of the model. The factors discovered by principal components analysis are also orthogonal to each other, that is, they are uncorrelated, which can be very useful for modeling purposes.

A comprehensive review of these approaches is beyond the scope of this book, but we provide some intuition and detail next.[7] Understanding how a security's risk can be attributed to different factors is important not only because it helps with the estimation of parameters of interest to portfolio managers. It also reduces substantially the computational burden of optimizing a portfolio and simulating possible states of the world in order to evaluate portfolio risk. We will come back to this point in section 11.4.3 of this chapter and Chapter 16.

11.3.1 Regression Analysis

In regression analysis, the modeler specifies the factors he thinks drive the covariation in asset returns, and the statistical analysis confirms or rejects this hypothesis. A regression equation assumes a linear relationship between the returns and the factors, that is, it assumes that the return on a particular stock i can be represented as

$$r_i = \alpha_i + \sum_{k=1}^{K} \beta_{ik} \cdot f_k + \varepsilon_i,$$

where α_i is the mean return, $f_1, \ldots, f_K$ are the K factors, β_{ik} are the coefficients in front of the factors, and ε_i is the residual error. In practice, the linearity assumption is not very restrictive because nonlinear relationships can be represented by transforming the data.

The factors f_k in this regression are the *explanatory variables* (also called *independent variables*). They help explain the variability in the *response variable* (also called *dependent variable*) r_i.

Exhibit 11.1 contains regression output obtained with Excel. Even though the output formats for different statistical packages differ, the information conveyed in them is standard, so we will use the Excel output in Exhibit 11.1 to discuss the most important terms.

The value for the coefficient beta in front of the explanatory variable (the S&P 500 excess return in our example) is 1.40556642 (cell B18). This value tells us the amount of change in the response variable when the explanatory variable increases by one unit. (In a regression with multiple explanatory variables, we would also have to hold the values of the other explanatory variables constant.) The value of the intercept alpha is -0.005062781 (cell B17). The intercept tells us the value of the response variable if the values for all explanatory variables are zero. If the regression coefficient beta is statistically different from 0, the explanatory variable to which the regression coefficient corresponds will be significant for explaining the response variable. To check whether the regression coefficient is statistically different from zero, we can check its *p-value* (cell E18) or the confidence interval associated with the coefficient (cells F18:G18). If the *p*-value is small

	A	B	C	D	E	F	G
1	SUMMARY OUTPUT		Regression using excess returns				
2							
3	*Regression Statistics*						
4	Multiple R	0.477748489					
5	R Square	0.228243619					
6	Adjusted R Square	0.214937474					
7	Standard Error	0.11258364					
8	Observations	60					
9							
10	ANOVA						
11		*df*	*SS*	*MS*	*F*	*Significance F*	
12	Regression	1	0.217418741	0.217419	17.15325	0.000113314	
13	Residual	58	0.735154402	0.012675			
14	Total	59	0.952573143				
15							
16		*Coefficients*	*Standard Error*	*t Stat*	*P-value*	*Lower 95%*	*Upper 95%*
17	Intercept	-0.005062781	0.014545779	-0.348058	0.729056	-0.034179322	0.024053759
18	S&P - Risk-free rate	1.40556642	0.339373689	4.141648	0.000113	0.726236179	2.084896661

EXHIBIT 11.1 Excel regression output for the beta estimation example in section 11.1.1.

(generally, less than 5% is considered small enough), then the beta coefficient is statistically different from zero. In this example, the p-value is 0.000113, so we can conclude that the S&P 500 excess return is a significant factor for forecasting the Oracle stock returns. The same conclusion can be reached by checking whether zero is contained in the confidence interval for the regression coefficient. In this case, the 95% confidence interval for beta is (0.726236179, 2.084896661). Zero is not contained in the interval; therefore, the beta coefficient is statistically different from zero, and the S&P 500 excess return is a significant factor for forecasting the Oracle stock returns.

There are several other statistics we should consider in evaluating the regression model. The p-value for the F-statistic (cell F12), which in Excel appears as "Significance F," tells us whether the regression model as a whole is statistically significant, i.e., whether the model explains a large part of the variability in asset returns. Since in our example the p-value is small, the regression model is significant.

Three measures of goodness of fit are reported as standard output for a regression. The coefficient of determination R^2 (which in Excel appears as "R square" in cell B5) tells us what percentage of the variability of the response variable is explained by the explanatory variable. The higher the number, ranging from 0% to 100%, the better it is. In this example, 22.82% of the variability in Oracle excess returns can be explained by the variability in the S&P 500 excess returns. The problem with R^2 is that as the number of explanatory variables (factors) increases, R^2 stays the same or continues to increase, even if the additional factors are not important. To control for that, in multiple regression models one typically uses the Adjusted R^2 (cell B6), which penalizes the model for having too many explanatory variables, rather than the R^2.

Another measure of goodness of fit is the *standard error* of the regression (cell B7), which equals the standard deviation of the regression residuals. The units of the standard error are the units of the residuals, which are also the units of the response variable. In our example, a standard error of 0.1126 tells us that the forecasts for the Oracle excess returns based on this regression model will be on average 0.1126 off from the real Oracle excess returns.

In order for the regression model to be valid, we need to check that three *residual assumptions* are satisfied:

- The residuals ε follow a normal distribution.
- The residuals ε exhibit *homoschedasticity*, that is, they have the same variability independently of the values of the response and the explanatory variables.
- The residuals ε are not autocorrelated, that is, they do not exhibit patterns with the order of the data in the data set.

Many statistical software packages produce graphs that allow for checking these assumptions as part of the standard regression output.

In regression models with multiple explanatory variables, we are also concerned about *multicollinearity*, which happens when the explanatory variables are highly correlated among themselves. This makes the estimates of the regression coefficients (the betas) meaningless because they can take on multiple values; inflates the value of the R^2 of the regression artificially, and leads to estimates of the p-values and other measures of the significance of the regression coefficients that cannot be trusted. To check for multicollinearity, we would examine the correlation matrix and other measures of codependence such as the *variance inflation factors* (VIFs), which are standard output in advanced statistical packages.

Finally, when we build factor models, there is a trade-off between finding a model with good explanatory power and *parsimony*, that is, limiting the number of factors that go into the model. On the one hand, we want to include all factors that are significant for explaining returns. On the other hand, including too many factors requires collecting a lot of data, and increases the risk of problems with the regression model, such as multicollinearity.

11.3.2 Factor Analysis

To illustrate the main idea behind factor analysis, let us begin with a simple nonfinance example. Suppose that we have the grades for 1,000 students in nine different subjects: literature, composition, Spanish, algebra, calculus, geometry, physics, biology, and chemistry. If we compute the pairwise correlations for grades in each subject, we would expect to find higher correlations between grades within the literature, composition, Spanish group than between grades in, say, literature and calculus. Suppose we observe that we have high correlations for grades in the literature, composition, Spanish group, high correlations for grades in the algebra, calculus, geometry group, and high correlations for grades in the physics, biology, chemistry group. There will still be some correlations between grades in different groups, but suppose that they are not nearly as high as the correlations within the groups. This may indicate that there are three factors that determine a student's performance in these subjects: a verbal aptitude, an aptitude for math, and an aptitude for science. A single factor does not necessarily determine a student's performance; otherwise all correlations would be 0 or 1. However, some factors will be weighted more than others for a particular student. Note, by the way, that these factors (the aptitudes for different subjects) are invisible. We can only observe the strength of the correlations within the groups and between them, and we need to provide interpretation for what the factors might be based on our intuition.

How does this example translate for financial applications? Suppose we have data on the returns of N stocks. You can think of the returns as the grades recorded for N different students. We compute the pairwise correlations between the different stock returns, and look for patterns. There may be a group of stocks for which the returns are highly correlated. All stocks in the group receive a large portion of their earnings from foreign operations, so we may conclude that exchange risk is one underlying factor. Another group of highly correlated stocks may have high debt-to-equity ratios, so we may conclude that the level of interest rates is another underlying factor. We proceed in the same way, and try to identify common factors from groups that exhibit high correlations.

There is a specific statistical technique for computing such underlying factors. Most advanced statistical packages have a function that can perform the calculations. Excel's statistical capabilities are unfortunately not as advanced, but MATLAB's Statistical Toolbox contains the function factoran, which allows a user to provide the data, specify the number of factors (which he can try to guess based on the preliminary analysis and intuition), and obtain the factor loadings. The *factor loadings* are the coefficients in front of the factors that determine how to compute the value of the observation (the grade or the stock return) from the hidden factors, and can be interpreted as the sensitivities of the stock returns to the different factors. A factor model equation in fact looks like the familiar regression equation; the difference is in the way the factors are computed. The output from running factor analysis with statistical software on our data set of stock returns will be a model

$$r_i = \alpha_i + \sum_{k=1}^{K} \beta_{ik} \cdot f_k + \varepsilon_i$$

or, in terms of the vector of returns for the assets in the portfolio,

$$\mathbf{r} = \alpha + \mathbf{B} \cdot \mathbf{f} + \varepsilon,$$

where α is the N-dimensional vector of mean returns, $\mathbf{f}$ is the K-dimensional vector of factors, $\mathbf{B}$ is the $K \times N$ matrix of factor loadings (the coefficients in front of every factor), and ε is the N-dimensional vector of residual errors.

The problem with the factor analysis procedure is that even if we have accounted for all the variability in the data and have identified the factors numerically, we may not be able to provide a good interpretation of their meaning. This makes factor analysis difficult to apply for risk management purposes.

11.3.3 Principal Components Analysis

Principal components analysis (PCA) is similar to factor analysis in the sense that the goal of the statistical procedure is to compute factors (*principal components*) out of a given set of data that explain the variability in the data. These factors are statistical, that is, they are not input by the user, but computed by software. However, the difference is that the main goal of PCA is to find *uncorrelated* factors in such a way that the first factor explains as much of the variability in the data as possible, the second factor explains as much of the remaining variability as possible, and so on. PCA is even less concerned with interpretation of the factors than factor analysis is, and this is a drawback in the sense that it is difficult to use the results from PCA for understanding portfolio risk. However, PCA models are helpful for modeling purposes[8] and can be used as a way to reduce the dimensionality of the data. Let us explain the latter point in more detail.

As mentioned earlier, each subsequent principal component explains a smaller portion of the variability in the original data. If we observe that a large percentage of the variability in the original data is explained by the first few components, we can drop the remaining components from consideration. For example, if we have data for the returns on 1,000 stocks and find that the first seven principal components explain 99% of the variability, we can drop the other principal components, and model only with seven variables (instead of the original 1,000). The representation of the data will in a sense be "inverse" to the original representation: each principal component will be expressed as a linear combination of the original data. For example, if we are given N stock returns $r_1, \ldots, r_N$, the principal components $x_1, \ldots, x_N$ will be given by

$$x_k = \sum_{i=1}^{N} \beta_{ik} \cdot r_i.$$

As with factor analysis, most advanced statistical packages have a function that can compute the principal components for a set of data. There is no such function in Excel; however, MATLAB's Statistical Toolbox contains the function `princomp`, which allows a user to provide the data and obtain useful output such as the coefficients in front of the original data, that is, β_{ik} in the equation above, the *scores* (i.e., the principal components themselves), and the percentage of the variability of the original data explained by each principal component.

11.4 APPLICATIONS OF FACTOR MODELS IN PORTFOLIO MANAGEMENT

In this section, we review several applications of factor models in portfolio management. The list of applications is by no means exhaustive. We discuss a classical portfolio performance measure, portfolio risk decomposition, and mean-variance optimization. Factor models are also widely used when pricing fixed-income securities and financial derivative contracts by Monte Carlo simulation.

11.4.1 Portfolio Performance Measurement

In evaluating the performance of a money manager, one must adjust for the risks accepted by the manager in generating return. Asset pricing models such as the CAPM or a multifactor model provide the expected return after adjusting for risk.

Various measures have been used to assess performance based on the excess return. One such measure is the *Jensen measure* (also called the *Jensen index*). In 1968, Michael Jensen used simple linear regression to analyze the performance of mutual fund managers. Basically, using time-series data for the return on the portfolio managed by the particular fund manager and the market index, Jensen estimated the same regression as the characteristic line explained in section 11.1. The intercept term, α_i, is interpreted as the unique return realized by the portfolio manager and is the estimated value of the Jensen measure. A statistically significant intercept term that is positive means that the portfolio manager outperformed the market; a negative value means that the portfolio manager underperformed the market. The Jensen measure is appropriate only when the portfolio is diversified. Hence, there are limitations in applying this measure to hedge funds, for example.

When Jensen proposed the model for measuring performance, he used the Greek letter alpha to represent the intercept term in the regression equation, as we did in section 11.1. Hence, the Jensen measure is also called the *Jensen alpha*. Consequently, the market sometimes refers to the "alpha" of a portfolio manager as a measure of performance. However, the concept of alpha used today in the investment industry is not the Jensen measure but rather the average excess return (also called *active return*) over a period of time. The *active return* is the difference between the return of a portfolio and the return of a benchmark index. Notice that unlike the Jensen measure or Jensen alpha, measuring performance by the average active return does not adjust for market risk.

11.4.2 Risk Decomposition in Equity Portfolios

As explained earlier in this chapter, the CAPM is not the typical asset pricing model used by professional money manager today. Rather, multifactor models are used. Money management firms will either develop proprietary multifactor models or use factor models provided by vendors such as MSCI Barra and Northfield Information Services. The multifactor models are used to evaluate exposure to different risk factors and to monitor performance.

The predicted return for a portfolio can be computed from the factor models for the returns on the individual assets in the portfolio. The exposure to a given risk factor of a portfolio is simply the weighted average of the exposure of each stock in the portfolio to that risk factor. For example, suppose a portfolio has 42 stocks. Suppose further that stocks 1 through 40 are equally weighted in the portfolio at 2.2%, stock 41 is 5% of the portfolio, and stock 42 is 7% of the portfolio. Then the exposure of the portfolio to risk factor k is

$$0.022 \cdot \beta_{1,k} + 0.022 \cdot \beta_{2,k} + \cdots + 0.022 \cdot \beta_{40,k} + 0.050 \cdot \beta_{41,k} + 0.007 \cdot \beta_{42,k}$$

This expression can then be added as a constraint in the portfolio construction process using an optimizer, as explained in section 9.2.4 of Chapter 9.

The nonfactor error term is measured in the same way as in the case of an individual stock. However, in a well diversified portfolio, the nonfactor error term will be considerably less for the portfolio than for the individual stocks in the portfolio.

Limiting the number of factors for portfolio risk management purposes has a number of advantages. First, an asset's sensitivity to a particular source of risk may be a lot more stable over time than its sensitivity to other securities in the portfolio. Second, having fewer sources of risk to estimate and control simplifies the portfolio management process significantly.

In addition to decomposing the total portfolio risk in a useful way for the purposes of portfolio allocation, multifactor risk models have the benefit of enabling managers and clients to decompose risk in order to assess the performance, both potential and actual, of a portfolio relative to factors or a benchmark. The idea is similar to the portfolio performance evaluation idea explained in section 11.4.1.

11.4.3 Efficient Mean-Variance Optimization

The real usefulness of a linear multifactor model lies in the ease with which the risk of a portfolio with a large number of assets can be estimated.

Consider a portfolio with N assets. As we explained in Chapter 7, risk is traditionally defined as the variance of the portfolio's returns. So, in this case, we need to find the covariance matrix of the N assets. That would require us to estimate N variances (one for each of the N assets) and $N \cdot (N-1)/2$ covariances. If we have a portfolio of 1,000 assets, this means we need to estimate 1,000 variances and 499,500 covariances. Adding the 1,000 estimates of expected returns (one for each asset), this is a total of 501,500 values to estimate, a very difficult undertaking.

Suppose, instead, that we use a three-factor model to represent asset returns. Then, we need to estimate (1) the three factor loadings (the beta coefficients) for each of the 1,000 assets (i.e., 3,000 values); (2) the six values of the factor variance-covariance matrix; and (3) the 1,000 residual variances (one for each asset). That is, in all, we need to estimate only 4,006 values. This represents a 99% reduction from the original number of 501,500 values, a huge improvement. Hence, with well-chosen factors, we can substantially reduce the work involved in estimating a portfolio's risk. From a statistical estimation point of view, factor covariance matrices also tend to be much more stable and reliable than asset covariance matrices.

Let us explain how the portfolio optimization would be done when asset returns are expressed through factors. Suppose that the vector of N asset returns $\mathbf{r}$ can be written as

$$\mathbf{r} = \alpha + \mathbf{B} \cdot \mathbf{f} + \varepsilon,$$

where α is the N-dimensional vector of mean returns, $\mathbf{f}$ is the K-dimensional vector of factors, $\mathbf{B}$ is the $K \times N$ matrix of factor loadings (the coefficients in front of every factor), and ε is the N-dimensional vector of residual errors.

If the portfolio weights invested in each asset are represented by the N-dimensional vector $\mathbf{w}$, it is easy to see that the expected excess portfolio return can be written as

$$\alpha' \cdot \mathbf{w},$$

the expected portfolio return can be written as

$$\alpha' \cdot \mathbf{w} + \mathbf{B} \cdot \mathbf{f} \cdot \mathbf{w},$$

where $\mathbf{f}$ is the vector of factor means, and the variance of the portfolio return can be written as

$$\mathbf{w}' \cdot (\mathbf{B}' \cdot \Sigma_f \cdot \mathbf{B} + \mathbf{D}) \cdot \mathbf{w},$$

where Σ_f is the factor covariance matrix, and $\mathbf{D}$ is the diagonal matrix (with zeros in all off-diagonal elements) containing the variance of the error terms.

These expressions for the mean and the variance of the portfolio return can be used directly in the mean-variance portfolio optimization problem introduced in Chapter 7.

11.4.4   Risk Decomposition in Bond Portfolios

In section 11.4.2 of this chapter, we explained that a factor risk model can be used in common stock portfolio management. Factor models are widely used in bond portfolio management as well. They allow a bond portfolio manager to assess the portfolio's risk and reconstruct or rebalance a portfolio if the risk exposures are unacceptable.

In particular, in many bond portfolio strategies, a factor model is used to identify the specific risks that contribute to the forward-looking tracking error relative to a benchmark, which is typically a market index.[9] All of the risks are quantified in terms of forward-looking tracking error as opposed to backward-looking tracking error or simple portfolio variance.[10]

In order to identify the specific risk factors, the tracking error is decomposed. We give an example of such decomposition based on Fabozzi (2009). The analysis begins with a decomposition of the risks into two general categories—systematic risk and nonsystematic risk (also referred to as *residual risk*).

Systematic risk can in turn be decomposed into two risks: term structure factor risk and nonterm structure factor risk. Term structure risk comprises the portfolio's exposure to changes in the general level of interest rates, measured in terms of exposure to (1) a parallel shift in the yield curve and (2) a nonparallel shift in the yield curve. A simple way to get a feel for the yield curve risk exposure of a portfolio relative to a benchmark is to look at the distribution of the present values of the cash flows for the portfolio and the benchmark index, and note the difference between the two distributions. A superior approach for assessing yield curve risk exposure is to determine the key rate durations of the portfolio and the benchmark. As we explained in section 2.6.7 of Chapter 2, key rate duration is the sensitivity of a portfolio's value to the change in a particular key spot rate. The specific maturities on the spot rate curve for which key rate durations are measured vary from vendor to vendor.

Nonterm structure systematic risk is the systematic risk that is not due to exposure to changes in interest rates. The risk factors that contribute to nonterm structure risk include quality risk, optionality risk, coupon risk, and MBS risk (sector, prepayment, and convexity risks). *Quality risk* refers to risk associated with the credit quality of the bond issues in the portfolio. *Optionality risk* has to do with embedded options that may exist in the bonds in the portfolio.[11] A change in interest rates, for example, may have an effect on the value of an embedded option, which in turn changes the value of the bond. The intuition behind the remaining risks will become clearer in Chapter 15.

Nonsystematic risk is divided into risks that are issuer-specific and components that are issue-specific. This risk is due to the fact that any portfolio has greater exposure to specific issues and issuers than the benchmark index. To understand this point, note that a portfolio typically has a lot fewer issues than a benchmark. Each issue may therefore make up a nontrivial fraction of the portfolio. Specifically, suppose that three corporate issuers individually represent more than 5% of the portfolio. If any of three issuers is downgraded, this would cause large losses in a, say, 80-bond portfolio, but it would not have a significant effect on the benchmark which could include more than 5,000 issues. Consequently, a large exposure to a specific corporate issuer represents a material mismatch between the exposure of the portfolio and the exposure of a benchmark index that must be taken into account in assessing a portfolio's risk relative to a benchmark index.

After constructing a factor model for the purposes of risk decomposition, the factor model is typically used to rebalance or restructure the portfolio. This is done using an optimizer. For example, a portfolio manager may want to rebalance the portfolio so as to minimize tracking error, or exposure to specific risk factors such as term structure risk.

SUMMARY

- The Capital Asset Pricing Model (CAPM) is an equilibrium model of asset prices that links the expected return on an asset or a portfolio to the expected return of the market.
- The Arbitrage Pricing Theory (APT) states that investors want to be compensated for the risk factors that systematically affect the return on a portfolio. The compensation in the APT is the sum of the products of each risk factor's systematic risk and the risk premium assigned to it by the financial market.
- In practice, the factors used in factor models can be external (economic), fundamental (firm characteristics), and extracted (statistical).
- Factor models can be constructed by using regression, factor analysis, or principal component analysis.
- Factor analysis is a statistical technique for identifying unobservable factors that drive correlations between observable quantities.
- Principal components analysis is a statistical technique for identifying uncorrelated factors that are linear combinations of the original data. The first principal component is constructed in such a way as to explain

the largest portion of the variability in the data, the second factor is constructed in such a way as to explain the largest portion of the remaining variability in the data, and the like.

- Factor models are used for portfolio performance evaluation, portfolio risk decomposition, and portfolio optimization.

SOFTWARE HINTS

Running a Regression with Excel

Let us use the data in the file **Ch11-Beta.xlsx**, worksheet **Data**. To run a regression, click on the **Data** tab, then on **Data Analysis**, and select **Regression** from the list of statistical functions in the dialog box. Enter the array of data in which the response variable (Y, in this case the Oracle excess stock returns) is recorded (F3:F63), then the array of data in which the explanatory variables are recorded, D3:D63 (in this case, there is only one, the S&P 500 excess return). The Regression dialog box is shown in Exhibit 11.2. Click OK, and you should obtain the output in Exhibit 11.1.

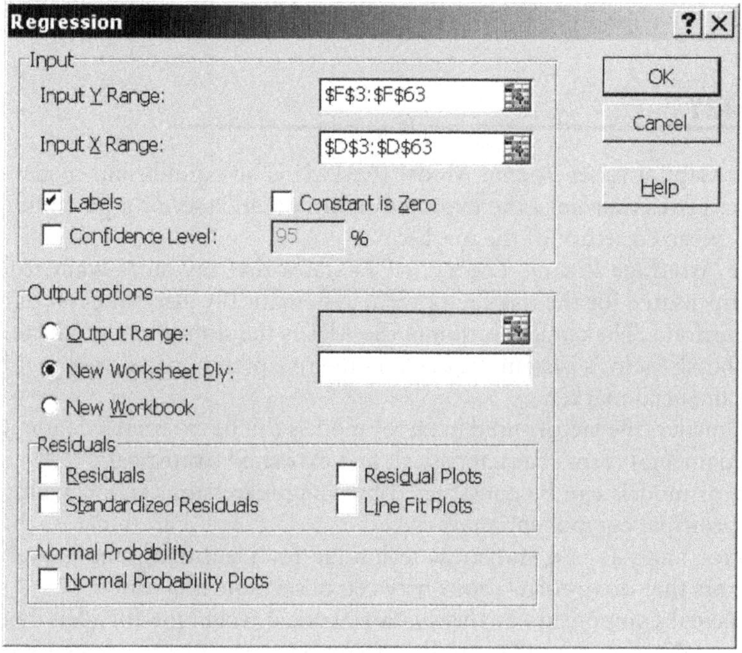

EXHIBIT 11.2   Excel regression dialog box for the Oracle example, file Ch11-Beta.xlsx.

Running a Regression with MATLAB

To run a regression in MATLAB, we use the `regress` function from the Statistics Toolbox. A note of caution when using the `regress` function: by default, MATLAB runs the regression with the intercept term set to 0. If we want MATLAB to estimate an intercept term, we need to take an extra step, and add a vector of ones to the array of explanatory variables. As an example, we can read in the data on the excess returns of the Oracle stock and the S&P 500, and run a regression to estimate the beta with the following code:

```
SP500ExcessRet = xlsread('Ch11-Beta.xlsx','Data','D4:D63');
OracleExcessRet = xlsread('Ch11-Beta.xlsx','Data','F4:F63');
beta = regress(OracleExcessRet,[ones(length(OracleExcessRet),
1), SP500ExcessRet])
```

This code returns a value of 1.41 for beta, which agrees with the Excel estimate. We can obtain additional information about the regression. For example, the command

```
[beta,betaint] = regress(OracleExcessRet,SP500ExcessRet)
```

will return not only the value for beta, but also a 95% confidence interval for beta (which turns out to be (0.7262, 2.0849). Since 0 is not contained within the confidence interval, we can conclude that the S&P 500 excess return is statistically significant for predicting the expected return on Oracle stock.

Further regression output can be obtained as well by adding more arguments in the function `regress`.

NOTES

1. For a full derivation, see, for example, Chapter 5 in Fabozzi, Kolm, Pachamanova, and Focardi (2007).
2. See section 11.3.1 for an overview of linear regression terminology.
3. See discussion of investor utility functions in section 7.5 of Chapter 7.
4. These characteristics are not technically "factors" in the sense of the APT, but they help reduce the variance of the error in the regression.
5. Jones used the Russell 1000 Index as a proxy for the market portfolio in the CAPM. This index includes large-cap stocks.
6. Lagging is required because certain financial information is reported with lag. For example, year-end income and balance sheet information for a given year is not reported until three months after the corporation's year end. When creating

a regression model for forecasting purposes, it is important to include only information that is available at the time the decision needs to be made. Thus, for example, we cannot use a regression equation to forecast returns at time t based on information that will become available at time $t + 1$.

7. For a more comprehensive overview and examples, see Rachev, Mittnik, Fabozzi, Focardi, and Jai (2006).

8. We will see an example in Chapter 16 in which PCA is used to create a more efficient simulation model for evaluating portfolio risk.

9. As we explained in section 9.3 of Chapter 9, the standard definition of tracking error is the variance of the deviations of the portfolio returns from the benchmark returns.

10. See Chapter 23, "Bond Portfolio Strategies," in Fabozzi (2009).

11. Embedded options were first mentioned in section 2.2.2 of Chapter 2; options and other financial derivative instruments are discussed in Chapter 13.

CHAPTER 12

Modeling Asset Price Dynamics

Our discussion so far has focused mostly on models that take a myopic view. For example, the CAPM and the APT consider events that happen one time period ahead, where the length of the time period is determined by the investor. In practice, asset prices are subject to ever-present uncertainty, and fluctuate continuously. Investors' decisions are updated dynamically. The volatility of asset prices is accounted for in market participants' views of the fair prices to pay for financial securities that depend on the realizations of continuing uncertainties. We therefore need to introduce new apparatus that can handle asset dynamics and volatility over time. The roots for the techniques described in this chapter are in physics and the other natural sciences. They were first applied in finance at the beginning of the twentieth century, and have represented the foundations of asset pricing ever since.

The dynamics of price processes in discrete time increments are typically described by two kinds of models: *trees* (such as *binomial trees*) and *random walks*. When the time increment used to model the asset price dynamics becomes infinitely small, we talk about *stochastic processes in continuous time*. We will discuss the special notation and terminology associated with stochastic processes later in this chapter; however, our focus in this book will be on interpretation and simulation of processes in discrete time.

This chapter will introduce the fundamentals of these models, and will provide examples for how they can be used in practice. Specifically, we will discuss arithmetic random walks, geometric random walks, mean reverting walks, and more complex combinations of walks.

Let us first introduce some definitions and notation. A financial *time series* is a sequence of observations of the values of a financial variable, such as an asset price (index level) or asset (index) returns, over time. Exhibit 12.1 shows an example of a time series, consisting of weekly observations of the S&P 500 price level over a period of five years (August 19, 2005 to August 19, 2009).

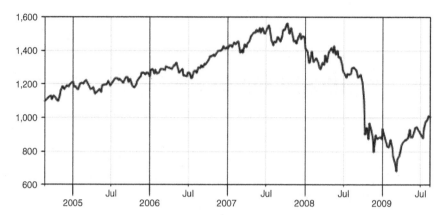

EXHIBIT 12.1 S&P 500 index level between August 19, 2005 and August 19, 2009.
Source: Dow Jones Factiva.

When we describe a time series, we talk about its drift and volatility. The term *drift* is used to indicate the direction of any observable trend in the time series. In the example in Exhibit 12.1, it appears that the time series has a positive drift up from August 2005 until about the middle of 2007, as the level of prices appears to have been generally increasing over that time period. From the middle of 2007 until the beginning of 2009, there is a negative drift. The volatility was smaller (the time series was less "squiggly") from August 2005 until about the middle of 2007, but increased dramatically between the middle of 2007 and the beginning of 2009. We are usually interested also in whether the volatility increases when the price level increases, decreases when the price level increases, or remains constant independently of the current price level. In this example, the volatility was lower when the price level was increasing, and was higher when the price level was decreasing. Finally, we talk about the *continuity* of the time series—is the time series smooth, or are there jumps whose magnitude appears to be large relative to the price movements the rest of the time? From August 2005 until about the middle of 2007, the time series is quite smooth. However, some dramatic drops in price levels can be observed between the middle of 2007 and the beginning of 2009—notably in the fall of 2008.

For the remainder of the chapter, we will use the following notation:

- S_t is the value of the underlying the variable (price, interest rate, index level, etc.) at time t;
- S_{t+1} is the value of the underlying variable (price, interest rate, etc.) at time $t + 1$;

- ω_t is a random error term observed at time t. (For the applications in this chapter, it will follow a normal distribution with mean equal to 0 and standard deviation equal to σ.)
- ε_t is a realization of a normal random variable with mean equal to 0 and standard deviation equal to 1 at time t. (We will use it in the context of modeling the random error term.)

12.1 BINOMIAL TREES

We introduced *binomial trees* (also called *binomial lattices*) earlier in the book, in the context of formulating dynamic programming problems in section 5.6.1 of Chapter 5. They provide a natural way to model the dynamics of a random process over time. The initial value of the security S_0 (at time 0) is known. The length of a time period, Δt, is specified before the tree is built.[1] The binomial tree model assumes that at the next time period, only two values are possible for the price, that is, the price may go up with probability p or down with probability $(1 - p)$. Usually, these values are represented as multiples of the price at the beginning of the period. The factor u is used for an up movement, and d is used for a down movement. For example, the two prices at the end of the first time period are $u \cdot S_0$ and $d \cdot S_0$. If the tree is recombining, there will be three possible prices at the end of the second time period: $u^2 \cdot S_0$, $u \cdot d \cdot S_0$, and $d^2 \cdot S_0$. Proceeding in a similar manner, we can build the tree in Exhibit 12.2.

The binomial tree model may appear simple because, given a current price, it only allows for two possibilities for the price at each time period. However, if the length of the time period is small, it is possible to represent a wide range of values for the price after only a few steps. To see this, notice that each step in the tree can be thought of as a Bernoulli trial[2]—it is a "success" with probability p, and a "failure" with probability $(1 - p)$. (The definition of success and failure here is arbitrary because an increase in price is not always desirable, but we define them in this way for the example's sake.) After n steps, each particular value for the price will be reached by realizing k successes and $(n - k)$ failures, where k is a number between 0 and n. The probability of reaching each value for the price after n steps will be[3]

$$P(k \text{ successes}) = \frac{n!}{k!(n - k)!} p^k (1 - p)^{n-k}$$

As Exhibit 3.5 in Chapter 3 illustrated, for large values of n, the shape of the binomial distribution becomes more and more symmetric, and looks like a continuum. In fact, it approximates the normal distribution.[4] One

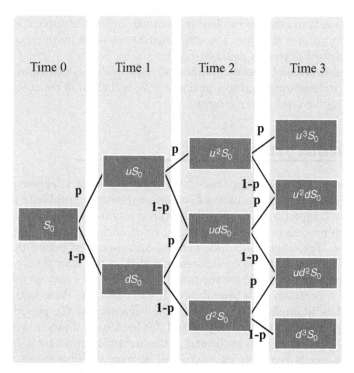

EXHIBIT 12.2   Example of a binomial tree.

can therefore represent a large range of values for the price as long as the number of time periods used in the binomial tree is large. Practitioners often use also trinomial trees, that is, trees with three branches emanating from each node, in order to obtain a better representation of the range of possible prices in the future.

12.2   ARITHMETIC RANDOM WALKS

Instead of assuming that at each step, the asset price can only move up or down by a certain multiple with a given probability, we could assume that the price moves by an amount that follows a normal distribution with mean μ and standard deviation σ. In other words, the price for each period is determined from the price of the previous period by the equation

$$S_{t+1} = S_t + \mu + \tilde{\omega}_t$$

where $\tilde{\omega}_t$ is a normal random variable with mean 0 and standard deviation σ. We also assume that the random variable $\tilde{\omega}_t$ describing the change in the price in one time period is independent of the random variables describing the change in the price in any other time period.[5] A sequence of independent and identically distributed (IID) random variables $\tilde{\omega}_0, \ldots, \tilde{\omega}_t, \ldots$ with zero mean and finite variance σ^2 is sometimes referred to as *white noise*.

The movement of the price expressed through the equation above is called an *arithmetic random walk with drift*. The drift term, μ, represents the average change in price over a single time period. Note that for every time period t, we can write the equation for the arithmetic random walk as

$$
\begin{aligned}
S_t &= S_{t-1} + \mu + \tilde{\omega}_{t-1} \\
&= (S_{t-2} + \mu + \tilde{\omega}_{t-2}) + \mu + \tilde{\omega}_{t-1} \\
&= (S_{t-3} + \mu + \tilde{\omega}_{t-2}) + 2 \cdot \mu + \tilde{\omega}_{t-1} + \tilde{\omega}_{t-2} \\
&= \cdots \\
&= S_0 + \mu \cdot t + \sum_{i=0}^{t-1} \tilde{\omega}_i
\end{aligned}
$$

Therefore, an arithmetic random walk can be thought of as a sum of two terms: a deterministic straight line $S_t = S_0 + \mu \cdot t$ and a sum of all past noise terms (see Exhibit 12.3).

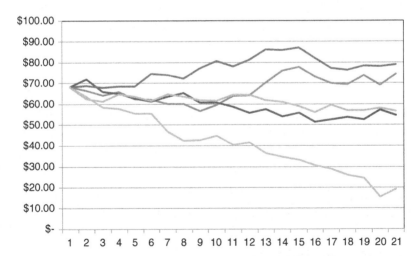

EXHIBIT 12.3 Five paths of an arithmetic random walk with $\mu = -0.1697$ and $\sigma = 3.1166$. See worksheet **ARW** in **Ch12-RandomWalks.xlsx**, or **RandomWalks.m** and **ARWPaths.m**.

12.2.1   Simulation

The equation for the arithmetic random walk can be expressed also as

$$S_{t+1} = S_t + \mu + \sigma \cdot \tilde{\varepsilon}_t,$$

where $\tilde{\varepsilon}_t$ is a standard normal random variable.[6]

This equation makes it easy to generate paths for the arithmetic random walk by simulation. All we need is a way of generating the normal random variables $\tilde{\varepsilon}_t$. We start with an initial price S_0, which is known. To generate the price at the next time period, S_1, we add μ to S_0, simulate a normal random variable from a standard normal distribution, multiply it by σ, and add it to $S_0 + \mu$. At the next step (time period 2), we use the price at time period 1 we already generated, S_1, add to it μ, simulate a new random variable from a standard normal distribution, multiply it by σ, and add it to $S_1 + \mu$. We proceed in the same way until we generate the desired number of steps of the random walk. For example, given a current price S:

- In Excel, the price for the next time period can be generated with the formula

$$S + \mu + \sigma^*\texttt{NORMINV(RAND(),0,1)}$$

- With @RISK, the price for the next time period can be generated with the formula

$$S + \mu + \sigma^*\texttt{RISKNORMAL(0,1)}$$

- In MATLAB, the price for the next time period can be generated with the formula[7]

$$S + \mu + \sigma^*\texttt{normrnd(0,1)}$$

(See this chapter's Software Hints and files **Ch12-RandomWalks.xlsx** and **ARWPaths.m** for implementation of an example.)

12.2.2   Parameter Estimation

In order to simulate paths of the arithmetic random walk, we need to have estimates of the parameters μ and σ. We need to assume that these parameters remain constant over the time period of estimation. Note that the equation for the arithmetic random walk can be written as

$$S_{t+1} - S_t = \mu + \sigma \cdot \tilde{\varepsilon}_t.$$

Given a historical series of T prices for an asset, we can therefore do the following to estimate μ and σ:

1. Compute the price changes $S_{t+1} - S_t$ for each time period t, $t = 0, \ldots, T - 1$.
2. Estimate the drift of the arithmetic random walk, μ, as the average of all the price changes.
3. Estimate the volatility of the arithmetic random walk, σ, as the standard deviation of all the price changes.

(See this chapter's Software Hints and files **Ch12-RandomWalks.xlsx** and **RandomWalks.m** for implementation of an example.)

An important point to keep in mind is the units in which the parameters are estimated. If we are given time series in monthly increments, then the estimates of μ and σ we will obtain through steps 1–3 will be for a monthly drift and monthly volatility. If we then need to simulate future paths for monthly observations, we can use the same μ and σ. However, if, for example, we need to simulate weekly observations, we will need to adjust μ and σ to account for the difference in the length of the time period. In general, the parameters should be stated as annual estimates. The annual estimates can then be adjusted for daily, weekly, monthly, as well as other increments.

12.2.3 Arithmetic Random Walk: Some Additional Facts

In general, if we use the arithmetic random walk model, any price in the future, S_t, can be expressed through the initial (known) price S_0 as

$$S_t = S_0 + \mu \cdot t + \sigma \sum_{i=0}^{t-1} \tilde{\varepsilon}_t.$$

The random variable corresponding to the sum of t independent normal random variables $\tilde{\varepsilon}_0, \ldots, \tilde{\varepsilon}_{t-1}$ is a normal random variable with mean equal to the sum of the means and standard deviation equal to the square root of the sum of variances. Since $\tilde{\varepsilon}_0, \ldots, \tilde{\varepsilon}_{t-1}$ are independent standard normal variables, their sum is a normal variable with mean 0 and standard deviation equal to

$$\underbrace{\sqrt{1 + \cdots + 1}}_{t \text{ times}} = \sqrt{t}.$$

Therefore, we can have a closed-form expression for computing the asset price at time t given the asset price at time 0:

$$S_t = S_0 + \mu \cdot t + \sigma \cdot \sqrt{t} \cdot \tilde{\varepsilon}$$

where $\tilde{\varepsilon}$ is a standard normal random variable.

Based on the discussion so far in this section, we can state the following observations about the arithmetic random walk:

- The arithmetic random walk has a constant drift μ and volatility.
- At every time period, the change in price is normally distributed, on average equal to μ, with a standard deviation of σ.
- The overall noise in an arithmetic random walk never decays. The price change over t time periods is distributed as a normal distribution with mean equal to $\mu \cdot t$ and standard deviation equal to $\sigma \sqrt{t}$. That is why in industry one often encounters the phrase "The uncertainty grows with the square root of time."
- Prices that follow an arithmetic random walk meander around a straight line $S_t = S_0 + \mu \cdot t$. They may depart from the line, and then cross it again.
- Because the distribution of future prices is normal, we can theoretically find the probability that the future price at any time will be within a given range.
- Because the distribution of future prices is normal, future prices can theoretically take infinitely large or infinitely small values. Thus, they can be negative, which is an undesirable consequence of using the model.

Asset prices, of course, cannot be negative. In practice, the probability of the price becoming negative can be made quite small as long as the drift and the volatility parameters are selected carefully. However, the possibility of generating negative prices with the arithmetic random walk model is real.

Another problem with the assumptions underlying the arithmetic random walk is that the change in the asset price is drawn from the same random probability distribution, independent of the current level of the prices. A more natural model is to assume that the parameters of the random probability distribution for the change in the asset price vary depending on the current price level. For example, a \$1 change in a stock price is more likely when the stock price is \$100 than when it is \$4. Empirical studies confirm that over time, asset prices tend to grow, and so do fluctuations. Only returns appear to remain stationary, that is, to follow the same probability distribution over time. A more realistic model for asset prices may therefore be that *returns* are an IID sequence. We describe such a model in the next section.

12.3 GEOMETRIC RANDOM WALKS

Consider the following model:

$$r_t = \mu + \sigma \cdot \tilde{\varepsilon}_t,$$

where $\tilde{\varepsilon}_0, \ldots, \tilde{\varepsilon}_t$ is a sequence of independent normal variables, and r_t, the return, is computed as[8]

$$r_t = \frac{S_{t+1} - S_t}{S_t}.$$

Returns are therefore normally distributed, and the return over each interval of length 1 has mean μ and standard deviation σ. How can we express future prices if returns are determined by the equations above?

Suppose we know the price at time t, S_t. The price at time $t + 1$ can be written as

$$
\begin{aligned}
S_{t+1} &= S_t \cdot \frac{S_{t+1}}{S_t} \\
&= S_t \cdot \left(\frac{S_t}{S_t} + \frac{S_{t+1} - S_t}{S_t} \right) \\
&= S_t \cdot \left(1 + \frac{S_{t+1} - S_t}{S_t} \right) \\
&= S_t \cdot (1 + \tilde{r}_t) \\
&= S_t + \mu \cdot S_t + \sigma \cdot S_t \cdot \tilde{\varepsilon}_t
\end{aligned}
$$

The equation is very similar to the equation for the arithmetic random walk, except that the price from the previous time period appears as a factor in all of the terms.

The equation for the geometric random walk makes it clear how paths for the geometric random walk can be generated. As in the case of the arithmetic random walk, all we need is a way of generating the normal random variables $\tilde{\varepsilon}_t$. We start with an initial price S_0, which is known. To generate the price at the next time period, S_1, we add $\mu \cdot S_0$ to S_0, simulate a normal random variable from a standard normal distribution, multiply it by σ and S_0, and add it to $S_0 + \mu \cdot S_0$. At the next step (time period 2), we use the price at time period 1 we already generated, S_1, add to it $\mu \cdot S_1$, simulate a new random variable from a standard normal distribution, multiply it by σ and S_1, and add it to $S_1 + \mu \cdot S_1$. We proceed in the same way until we generate the desired number of steps of the geometric random walk. Given a current price S:

- In Excel, the price for the next time period can be generated with the formula

$$S + \mu^*S + \sigma^*S^*\texttt{NORMINV(RAND(),0,1)}$$

- In @RISK, the price for the next time period can be generated with the formula

$$S + \mu^*S + \sigma^*S^*\texttt{RISKNORMAL(0,1)}$$

- In MATLAB, the price for the next time period can be generated with the formula[9]

$$S + \mu^*S + \sigma^*S^*\texttt{normrnd(0,1)}$$

Using similar logic to the derivation of the price equation earlier, we can express the price at any time t in terms of the known initial price S_0. Note that we can write the price at time t as

$$S_t = S_0 \cdot \frac{S_1}{S_0} \cdot \ldots \cdot \frac{S_{t-1}}{S_{t-2}} \cdot \frac{S_t}{S_{t-1}}.$$

Therefore,

$$S_t = S_0 \cdot (1 + \tilde{r}_0) \cdot \ldots \cdot (1 + \tilde{r}_{t-1}).$$

In the case of the arithmetic random walk, we determined that the price at any time period follows a normal distribution. That is, if we know the starting price S_0, then the price at any time period could be obtained by adding a sum of independent normal random variables to a constant term and S_0. The sum of independent normal random variables is a normal random variable itself. In the equation for the geometric random walk, each of the terms $(1 + \tilde{r}_0), \ldots, (1 + \tilde{r}_{t-1})$ is a normal random variable as well (it is the sum of a normal random variable and a constant). However, these terms are multiplied together. The product of normal random variables is not a normal random variable, which means that we cannot have a nice closed-form expression for computing the price S_t based on S_0.

To avoid this problem, let us consider the logarithm of prices.[10] If we take natural logarithms of both sides of the equation for S_t, we get

$$\ln(S_t) = \ln(S_0 \cdot (1 + \tilde{r}_0) \cdot \ldots \cdot (1 + \tilde{r}_{t-1}))$$
$$= \ln(S_0) + \ln(1 + \tilde{r}_0) + \cdots + \ln(1 + \tilde{r}_{t-1}).$$

Log returns are in fact differences of log prices. To see this, recall the definition of log return from Chapter 2:

$$\ln(1 + r_t) = \ln\left(1 + \frac{S_{t+1} - S_t}{S_t}\right)$$
$$= \ln\left(\frac{S_{t+1}}{S_t}\right)$$
$$= \ln(S_{t+1}) - \ln(S_t).$$

Now assume that log returns (not returns) are independent, and follow a normal distribution with mean μ and standard deviation σ:

$$\ln(1 + \tilde{r}_t) = \ln(S_{t+1}) - \ln(S_t) = \mu + \sigma \cdot \tilde{\varepsilon}_t$$

As a sum of independent normal variables, the expression

$$\ln(S_0) + \ln(1 + \tilde{r}_0) + \ldots + \ln(1 + \tilde{r}_{t-1})$$

is also normally distributed. This means that $\ln(S_t)$ is normally distributed, that is, S_t is a lognormal random variable.[11,12]

In fact, similarly to the case of an arithmetic random walk, we can compute a closed-form expression for the price S_t given S_0:

$$\ln(S_t) = \ln(S_0) + \left(\mu - \frac{1}{2} \cdot \sigma^2\right) \cdot t + \sigma \cdot \sqrt{t} \cdot \tilde{\varepsilon}$$

or, equivalently,

$$S_t = S_0 \cdot e^{(\mu - \frac{1}{2} \cdot \sigma^2) \cdot t + \sigma \cdot \sqrt{t} \cdot \tilde{\varepsilon}}$$

where $\tilde{\varepsilon}$ is a standard normal variable.

Notice that the only inconsistency with the formula for the arithmetic random walk is the presence of the extra term

$$\left(-\frac{1}{2} \cdot \sigma^2\right) \cdot t$$

in the drift term

$$\left(\mu - \frac{1}{2} \cdot \sigma^2\right) \cdot t.$$

Why is there an adjustment of one half of the variance in the expected drift? In general, if $\tilde{Y}$ is a normal random variable with mean μ and variance σ^2, then the random variable which is an exponential of the normal random variable $\tilde{Y}$, $\tilde{X} = e^{\tilde{Y}}$, has mean

$$E[\tilde{X}] = e^{\mu + \frac{1}{2} \cdot \sigma^2}.$$

At first, this seems unintuitive—why is the expected value of $\tilde{X}$ not

$$E[\tilde{X}] = e^{\mu}?$$

As we discussed in section 3.9 of Chapter 3, the expected value of a linear function of a random variable is a linear function of the expected value of the random variable. For example, if a is a constant, then

$$E[a \cdot \tilde{Y}] = a \cdot E[\tilde{Y}]$$

However, determining the expected value of a nonlinear function of a random variable (in particular, the exponential function, which is the function we are using here) is not as trivial. For example, there is a well-known relationship, the *Jensen inequality*, which states that the expected value of a convex function of a random variable is less than the value of the function at the expected value of the random variable.

In our example, $\tilde{X}$ is a lognormal random variable, so its probability distribution has the shape shown in Exhibit 3.15 in Chapter 3. The random variable $\tilde{X}$ cannot take values less than 0. Since its variance is related to the variance of the normal random variable $\tilde{Y}$, as the variance σ^2 of $\tilde{Y}$ increases, the distribution of $\tilde{X}$ will spread out in the upward direction. This means that the mean of the lognormal variable $\tilde{X}$ will increase not only as the mean of the normal variable $\tilde{Y}$, μ, increases, but also as $\tilde{Y}$'s variance, σ^2, increases. In the context of the geometric random walk, $\tilde{Y}$ represents the normally distributed log returns, and $\tilde{X}$ is in fact the factor by which the asset price from the previous period is multiplied to generate the asset price in the next time period. In order to make sure that the geometric random process grows exponentially at average rate μ, we need to subtract a term (that term turns out to be $\sigma^2/2$), which will correct the bias.

Specifically, suppose that we know the price at time t, S_t. We have

$$\ln(S_{t+1}) = \ln(S_t) + \ln(1 + \tilde{r}_t)$$

that is,

$$S_{t+1} = S_t \cdot e^{\ln(1+\tilde{r}_t)}$$

Note that we are explicitly assuming a *multiplicative model* for asset prices here—the price in the next time period is obtained by multiplying the price from the previous time period by a random factor. In the case of an arithmetic random walk in section 12.2, we had an *additive model*—a random shock was added to the asset price from the previous time period.

If the log-return $\log(1 + \tilde{r})$ is normally distributed with mean μ and standard deviation σ, then the expected value of

$$e^{\ln(1+\tilde{r})}$$

is

$$e^{\mu + \frac{1}{2} \cdot \sigma^2}.$$

and hence

$$E[S_{t+1}] = S_t \cdot e^{\mu + \frac{1}{2} \cdot \sigma^2}.$$

In order to make sure that the geometric random walk process grows exponentially at an average rate μ (rather than $(\mu + 0.5 \cdot \sigma^2)$), we need to subtract the term $0.5 \cdot \sigma^2$ when we generate the future price from this process. This argument can be extended to determining prices for more than one time period ahead.

We will understand better why this formula holds in section 12.6.

12.3.1 Simulation

It is easy to see that future prices can be simulated based on the initial price S_0. In general, for a current price of S:

- In Excel, the price t periods from now can be generated as

$$S^* \exp((\mu - 0.5^*\sigma\char`^2)^*t - \sigma^*\sqrt{t}^*\texttt{NORMINV(RAND(),0,1)})$$

- With @RISK, the price t periods from now can be generated with the formula

$$S^* \exp((\mu - 0.5^*\sigma\char`^2)^*t - \sigma^*\sqrt{t}^*\texttt{RISKNORMAL(0,1)})$$

- In MATLAB, the price t periods from now can be generated with the formula

$$S^* \exp((\mu - 0.5^*\sigma\char`^2)^*t - \sigma^*\sqrt{t}^*\texttt{normrnd(0,1)})$$

(See this chapter's Software Hints and files **Ch12-RandomWalks.xlsx** or **GRWPaths.m** for an example.)

One might wonder whether this approach for simulating realizations of an asset price following a geometric random walk is equivalent to the simulation approach mentioned earlier in this section, which is based on the discrete version of the equation for a random walk. The two approaches are different (for example, the approach based on the discrete version of the equation for the geometric random walk does not produce the expected lognormal price distribution), but it can be shown that the differences in the two simulation approaches tend to cancel over many steps.

12.3.2 Parameter Estimation

In order to simulate paths of the geometric random walk, we need to have estimates of the parameters μ and σ. The implicit assumption here, of course, is that these parameters remain constant over the time period of estimation.

(We will discuss how to incorporate considerations for changes in volatility in section 12.5.) Note that the equation for the geometric random walk can be written as

$$\ln(S_{t+1}) - \ln(S_t) = \ln(1 + \tilde{r}_t),$$

Equivalently,

$$\log\left(\frac{S_{t+1}}{S_t}\right) = \mu + \sigma \cdot \tilde{\varepsilon}_t.$$

Given a historical series of T prices for an asset, we can therefore do the following to estimate μ and σ:

1. Compute $\ln(S_{t+1} / S_t)$ for each time period t, $t = 0, \ldots, T - 1$.
2. Estimate the volatility of the geometric random walk, σ, as the standard deviation of all $\ln(S_{t+1} / S_t)$.
3. Estimate for the drift of the arithmetic random walk, μ, as the average of all $\ln(S_{t+1} / S_t)$, plus one half of the standard deviation squared.

Note that

$$\log\left(\frac{S_{t+1}}{S_t}\right) = \log\left(1 + \frac{S_{t+1} - S_t}{S_t}\right) = \log(1 + \tilde{r}_t)$$

Therefore, if we are given data on returns, rather than asset prices, we can compute $\ln(1 + \tilde{r}_t)$, and use it to replace $\ln(S_{t+1} / S_t)$ in steps 1–3 above. (See this chapter's Software Hints and files **Ch12-RandomWalks.xlsx** and **RandomWalks.m** for implementation of an example.)

12.3.3 Geometric Random Walk: Some Additional Facts

To summarize, the geometric random walk has several important characteristics:

- It is a multiplicative model, that is, the price at the next time period is a multiple of a random term and the price from the previous time period.
- It has a constant drift μ and volatility σ. At every time period, the *percentage change* in price is normally distributed, on average equal to μ, with a standard deviation of σ.

- The overall noise in a geometric random walk never decays. The *percentage price change* over t time periods is distributed as a normal distribution with mean equal to $\mu \cdot t$ and standard deviation equal to $\sigma \sqrt{t}$.
- The exact distribution of the future price knowing the initial price can be found. The price at time t is lognormally distributed with specific probability distribution parameters.
- Prices that follow a geometric random walk in continuous time never become negative.

The geometric random walk model is not perfect. However, its computational simplicity makes the geometric random walk and its variations the most widely used processes for modeling asset prices. The geometric random walk defined with log returns never becomes negative because future prices are always a multiple of the initial stock price and a positive term (see Exhibit 12.4). In addition, observed historical stock prices can actually be quite close to lognormal.

It is important to note that, actually, the assumption that log returns are normal is not required to justify the lognormal model for prices. If the

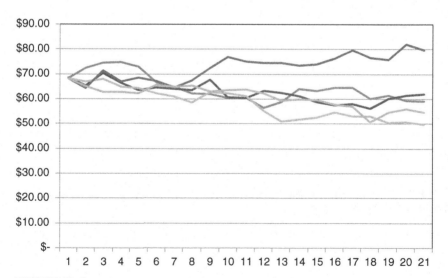

EXHIBIT 12.4 Five paths of a geometric random walk with $\mu = -0.0014$ and $\sigma = 0.0411$. Note that although the drift is slightly negative, it is still possible to generate paths that generally increase over time. See worksheet **GRW** in **Ch12-RandomWalks.xlsx**, or **RandomWalks.m** and **GRWPaths.m**.

distribution of log returns is nonnormal, but the log returns are IID with finite variance, the sum of the log returns is asymptotically normal.[13] Stated differently, the log return process is approximately normal if we consider changes over sufficiently long intervals of time.

Price processes, however, are not always geometric random walks, even asymptotically. A very important assumption for the geometric random walk is that price increments are independently distributed; if the time series exhibits autocorrelation, the geometric random walk is not a good representation. We will see some models that incorporate considerations for autocorrelation and other factors later in this chapter.

12.4 MEAN REVERSION

The geometric random walk provides the foundation for modeling the dynamics for asset prices of many different securities, including stock prices. However, in some cases it is not justified to assume that asset prices evolve with a particular drift, or can deviate arbitrarily far from some kind of a representative value. Interest rates, exchange rates, and the prices of some commodities are examples for which the geometric random walk does not provide a good representation over the long term. For example, if the price of copper becomes high, copper mines would increase production in order to maximize profits. This would increase the supply of copper in the market, therefore decreasing the price of copper back to some equilibrium level. Consumer demand plays a role as well—if the price of copper becomes too high, consumers may look for substitutes, which would reduce the price of copper back to its equilibrium level.

Exhibit 12.5 illustrates the behavior of the one-year Treasury bill yield from the beginning of January 1962 through the end of July 2009. It can be observed that, even though the variability of Treasury bill rates has changed over time, there is some kind of a long-term average level of interest rates to which they return after deviating up or down. This behavior is known as *mean reversion.*

The simplest mean reversion (MR) model is similar to an arithmetic random walk, but the means of the increments change depending on the current price level. The price dynamics are represented by the equation

$$S_{t+1} = S_t + \kappa \cdot (\mu - S_t) + \sigma \cdot \tilde{\varepsilon}_t,$$

where $\tilde{\varepsilon}_t$ is a standard normal random variable. The parameter κ is a nonnegative number that represents the *speed of adjustment* of the mean-reverting

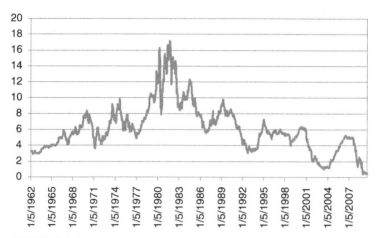

EXHIBIT 12.5   Weekly data on 1-Year Treasury Yield rates, January 5, 1962–July 31, 2009.

process—the larger its magnitude, the faster the process returns to its long-term mean. The parameter μ is the long-term mean of the process. When the current price S_t is lower than the long-term mean μ, the term $(\mu - S_t)$ is positive. Hence, on average there will be an upward adjustment to obtain the value of the price in the next time period, S_{t+1}. (We add a positive number, $\kappa \cdot (\mu - S_t)$, to the current price current price S_t.) By contrast, if the current price S_t is higher than the long-term mean μ, the term $(\mu - S_t)$ is negative. Hence, on average there will be a downward adjustment to obtain the value of the price in the next time period, S_{t+1}. (We add a negative number, $\kappa \cdot (\mu - S_t)$, to the current price current price S_t.) Thus, the mean-reverting process will behave in the way we desire—if the price becomes lower or higher than the long-term mean, it will be drawn back to the long-term mean.

In the case of the arithmetic and the geometric random walks, the volatility of the process increases over time. The volatility for one step of the mean-reverting process is σ^2; however, as the number of steps increases, the volatility peaks at

$$\frac{\sigma^2}{\kappa \cdot (2 - \kappa)}.$$

In continuous time, this basic mean-reversion process is called the *Ornstein-Uhlenbeck process* (see section 12.5). It is widely used when modeling interest rates and exchange rates in the context of computing bond

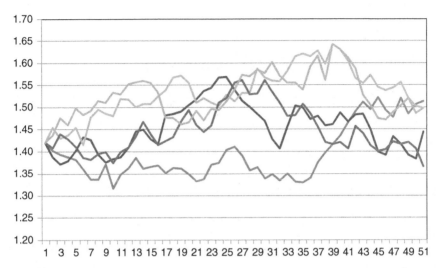

EXHIBIT 12.6 Five paths with 50 steps each of a mean reverting process with $\mu = 1.4404$, $\kappa = 0.0347$ and $\sigma = 0.0248$. See worksheet **MR** in **Ch12-RandomWalks.xlsx**, or **MRPaths.m**.

prices and prices of more complex fixed income securities. When used in the context of modeling interest rates, this simple mean-reversion process is also referred to as the *Vasicek model*.[14]

The mean-reversion process suffers from some of the disadvantages of the arithmetic random walk—for example, it can technically become negative. However, if the long-run mean is positive, and the speed of mean reversion is large relative to the volatility, the price will be pulled back to the mean quickly if it becomes negative. Exhibit 12.6 contains an example of five paths generated from a mean-reverting process.

12.4.1 Simulation

The formula for the mean-reverting process makes it clear how paths for the mean-reverting random walk can be generated with software. Given a current price S:

▪ In Excel, the price for the next time period can be generated with the formula

$$S + \kappa^*(\mu - S) + \sigma^*\texttt{NORMINV(RAND(),0,1)}$$

- With @RISK, the price for the next time period can be generated with the formula

$$S + \kappa^*(\mu - S) + \sigma^* \texttt{RISKNORMAL(0,1)}$$

- In MATLAB, the price for the next time period can be generated with the formula

$$S + \kappa^*(\mu - S) + \sigma^* \texttt{normrnd(0,1)}$$

12.4.2 Parameter Estimation

In order to simulate paths of the geometric random walk, we need to have estimates of the parameters κ, μ, and σ of the mean-reverting process. Again, we assume that these parameters remain constant over the time period of estimation. The equation for the mean-reverting process can be written as

$$S_{t+1} - S_t = \kappa \cdot (\mu - S_t) + \sigma \cdot \tilde{\varepsilon}_t$$

or, equivalently,

$$S_{t+1} - S_t = \kappa \cdot \mu - \kappa \cdot S_t + \sigma \cdot \tilde{\varepsilon}_t$$

This equation has the characteristics of a linear regression model, with the absolute price change $(S_{t+1} - S_t)$ as the response variable, and S_t as the explanatory variable. Given a historical series of T prices for an asset, we can therefore do the following to estimate κ, μ, and σ:

1. Compute the price changes $(S_{t+1} - S_t)$ for each time period t, $t = 0, \ldots, T-1$.
2. Run a linear regression with $(S_{t+1} - S_t)$ as the response variable and S_t as the explanatory variable. In Excel, click the **Data** tab, click **Data Analysis**, select **Regression** from the Analysis Tools. With MATLAB's Statistical Toolbox, use the `regress(Y,X)` function.[15]
3. Verify that the estimates from the linear regression model are valid:
   (a) Plot the values of S_t versus $(S_{t+1} - S_t)$. The points in the scatter plot should approximately vary around a straight line with no visible cyclical or other patterns.
   (b) The p-value for the coefficient in front of the explanatory variable S_t should be small, preferably less than 0.05.

4. An estimate for the speed of adjustment of the mean-reversion process, κ, can be obtained as the negative of the coefficient in front of S_t. Since the speed of adjustment cannot be a negative number, if the coefficient in front of S_t is positive, the regression model cannot be used for estimating the parameters of the mean reverting process.

5. An estimate for the long-term mean of the mean-reverting process, μ, can be obtained as the ratio of the intercept term estimated from the regression and the slope coefficient in front of S_t (if that slope coefficient is valid, that is, negative and with low p-value).

6. An estimate for the volatility of the mean-reverting process, σ, can be obtained as the standard error of the regression.[16]

(See this chapter's Software Hints and files **Ch12-RandomWalks.xlsx** and **RandomWalks.m** for implementation of an example.)

12.4.3 The Cox-Ingersoll-Ross Model for Interest Rates Dynamics

More advanced mean-reversion processes have been used to avoid the pitfalls of the simple mean-reversion process.

A commonly used model for interest rates, called the *Cox-Ingersoll-Ross* (CIR) *model*,[17] includes the square root of the current asset price as a factor in the random term of the mean reversion where we use r to denote the short-term interest rate in this section:

$$r_{t+1} = r_t + \kappa \cdot (\mu - r_t) + \sigma \cdot \sqrt{r_t} \cdot \tilde{\varepsilon}_t$$

The effect is that if the current interest rate is low, the variability of the process is relatively low, thus reducing the probability that the mean-reverting random walk will become negative. When the current interest rate is high, the variability of the process can afford to be higher without the risk that the interest rate will become negative. Future interest rates are easy to simulate with this model. Historically, the appeal of this model has been that a closed-form solution for the future interest rates knowing the current interest rate can be found. It turns out that

$$r_1 = r_0 + \frac{(1 - e^{-\kappa \cdot t}) \cdot \sigma^2}{2 \cdot \kappa} \cdot \tilde{\eta}$$

where $\tilde{\eta}$ has a chi-square distribution with $4 \cdot \kappa \cdot \mu/\sigma^2$ degrees of freedom and noncentrality parameter[18]

$$2 \cdot r_0 \cdot e^{-\kappa \cdot t} \cdot \frac{(1 - e^{-\kappa \cdot t}) \cdot \sigma^2}{2 \cdot \kappa}$$

It is worth noting that while the random processes described in previous sections are widely used for modeling stock and commodity prices, they cannot be directly applied to modeling bond prices. The prices of fixed income securities, such as bonds, evolve in a substantially more complex fashion than the evolution of stock or commodity prices described in this chapter. In some cases, such as in the case of the CIR model, there is a closed-form formula for bond prices based on the assumptions for the process followed by the short-term interest rate. This enables us to generate the entire yield curve,[19] and calculate the price of a fixed income security tied to these interest rates.

12.4.4 Geometric Mean Reversion

A more advanced mean-reversion models that bears some similarity to the geometric random walk is the geometric mean reversion (GMR) model[20]

$$S_{t+1} = S_t + \kappa \cdot (\mu - S_t) \cdot S_t + \sigma \cdot S_t \cdot \tilde{\varepsilon}_t$$

The intuition behind this model is similar to the intuition behind the discrete version of the geometric random walk—the variability of the process changes with the current level of the price, and we think of the change in price as a percentage change (roughly) rather than an absolute change. However, the GMR model allows for incorporating mean reversion. Exhibit 12.7 contains an example of five paths generated with a geometric mean-reversion model.

Even though it is difficult to estimate the future price analytically from this model, it is easy to simulate. As before, $\tilde{\varepsilon}_t$ is a standard normal random variable, which can be generated with standard commands in Excel, @RISK, or MATLAB. Given a current price S:

- In Excel, the price for the next time period can be generated with the formula

$$S + \kappa^*(\mu - S)^*S + \sigma^*S^*\text{NORMINV}(\text{RAND}(),0,1)$$

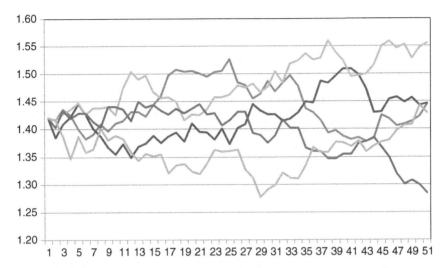

EXHIBIT 12.7 Five paths with 50 steps each of a geometric mean reverting process with $\mu = 1.4464$, $\kappa = 0.0253$, and $\sigma = 0.0177$. See worksheet **GMR** in **Ch12-RandomWalks.xlsx**, or **GMRPaths.m**.

- With @RISK, the price for the next time period can be generated with the formula

$$S + \kappa^*(\mu - S)^*S + \sigma^*S^*\texttt{RISKNORMAL(0,1)}$$

- In MATLAB, the price for the next time period can be generated with the formula

$$S + \kappa^*(\mu - S)^*S + \sigma^*S^*\texttt{normrnd(0,1)}$$

To estimate the parameters κ, μ, and σ to use in the simulation, we can use a series of T observations. Assume that the parameters of the geometric mean reversion remain constant during the time period of estimation.

Note that the equation for the geometric mean reversion can be written as

$$\frac{S_{t+1} - S_t}{S_t} = \kappa \cdot (\mu - S_t) + \sigma \cdot \tilde{\varepsilon}_t$$

or, equivalently, as

$$\frac{S_{t+1} - S_t}{S_t} = \kappa \cdot \mu - \kappa \cdot S_t + \sigma \cdot \tilde{\varepsilon}_t$$

Again, this equation bears characteristics of a linear regression model, with the percentage price change $(S_{t+1} - S_t)/S_t$ as the response variable, and S_t as the explanatory variable. Given a series of T asset prices, we can therefore do the following to estimate κ, μ, and σ:

1. Compute the percentage price changes $(S_{t+1} - S_t)/S_t$ for each time period t, $t = 0, \ldots, T{-}1$.
2. Run a linear regression with $(S_{t+1} - S_t)/S_t$ as the response variable and S_t as the explanatory variable. In Excel, click the **Data** tab, click **Data Analysis,** and then select **Regression** from the Analysis Tools. With MATLAB's Statistical Toolbox, use the `regress(Y,X)` function.
3. Verify that the estimates from the linear regression model are valid:
   (a) Plot the values of S_t versus $(S_{t+1} - S_t)/S_t$. The points in the scatter plot should approximately vary around a straight line with no visible cyclical or other patterns.
   (b) The p-value for the coefficient in front of the explanatory variable S_t should be small, preferably less than 0.05.
4. An estimate for the speed of adjustment of the mean-reverting process, κ, can be obtained as the negative of the coefficient in front of S_t. Since the speed of adjustment cannot be a negative number, if the coefficient in front of S_t is positive, the regression model cannot be used for estimating the parameters of the geometric mean-reverting process.
5. An estimate for the long-term mean of the mean-reverting process, μ, can be obtained as the ratio of the intercept term estimated from the regression and the slope coefficient in front of S_t (if that slope coefficient is valid, that is, negative and with low p-value).
6. An estimate for the volatility of the mean-reverting process, σ, can be obtained as the standard error of the regression.[21]

(See this chapter's Software Hints and files **Ch12-RandomWalks.xlsx** and **RandomWalks.m** for implementation of an example.)

12.5 ADVANCED RANDOM WALK MODELS

The models we described so far provide building blocks for representing the asset price dynamics. However, observed real-world asset price dynamics has features that cannot be incorporated in these basic models. For example, asset prices exhibit correlation—both with each other, and with themselves over time. Their volatility typically cannot be assumed constant. This section reviews several techniques for making asset price models more realistic depending on observed price behavior.

12.5.1 Correlated Random Walks

So far, we have discussed models for asset prices that assume that the dynamic processes for the prices of different assets evolve independently of each other. This is an unrealistic assumption—it is expected that market conditions and other factors will have an impact on the prices of groups of assets simultaneously. For example, it is likely that stock prices for companies in the oil industry will generally move together, as will stock prices for companies in the telecommunications industry.

The argument that asset prices are codependent has theoretical and empirical foundations as well. If asset prices were independent random walks, then large portfolios would be fully diversified, have no variability, and therefore be completely deterministic. Empirically, this is not the case. Even large aggregates of stock prices, such as the S&P 500, exhibit random behavior.

If we make the assumption that log returns are jointly normally distributed, then their dependencies can be represented through the covariance matrix (equivalently, through the correlation matrix).[22]

Let us give an example of how one can model two correlated stock prices assumed to follow geometric random walks. Suppose we are given two series of T observations each of observed asset prices for Stock 1 and Stock 2. We follow steps 1 and 2 from section 12.3.2 to estimate the drifts and the volatilities for the two processes. To estimate the correlation structure, we find the correlation between

$$\ln\left(\frac{S_{t+1}^{(1)}}{S_t^{(1)}}\right)$$

and

$$\ln\left(\frac{S_{t+1}^{(2)}}{S_t^{(2)}}\right)$$

where the indices (1) and (2) correspond to the stock number. In Excel, the correlation between two data series can be computed with the function

```
CORREL(Array1, Array2)
```

whereas in MATLAB, the correlation can be computed with the function

```
CORR([Array1 Array2])
```

for two vertical arrays Array1 and Array2.

This correlation can then be incorporated in the simulation. Excel cannot generate correlated normal random variables without special add-ins, but @RISK and MATLAB have functions for it. As explained in Chapter 4's Software Hints, to generate two correlated random variables in @RISK, use the formula

```
RISKCORRMAT(CorrMx, RowNumber, InstanceNumber)
```

where CorrMx   is the array in which the correlation matrix is
                    stored.

RowNumber   is the row number in the correlation matrix that
                    stores the correlations that correspond to that
                    stock.

InstanceNumber   basically refers to whether the random variables that are generated need to be correlated
                    across time periods. If we do not want them to
                    be correlated across time periods (only within
                    one time period), then we need to specify a different instance number for every time period
                    for which we generate a new price.

To generate the price for Stock 1 t periods from now, given a current price of S, use

```
S*exp((μ₁-0.5*σ₁^2)*t - σ₁*√t*RISKNORMAL(0,1,RISKCORRMAT
(CorrMx,1,t)))
```

To generate the price for Stock 2 t periods from now, given a current price of S, use

```
S*exp((μ₂-0.5*σ₂^2)*t - σ₂*√t*RISKNORMAL(0,1,RISKCORRMAT
(CorrMx,2,t)))
```

To generate two correlated normal random variables in MATLAB, use the formula

```
mvnrnd(muVec,CovMx,numObs)
```

where   muVec   is the vector of expected values.
         CovMx   is the covariance matrix.
         numObs   is the number of random observations we would like to
                  generate.

In the case of arithmetic or geometric random walk, we will need to simulate correlated standard normal random variables, so we will enter a vector of expected values of zero, a covariance matrix, and the number of steps we need to generate.

When we consider many different assets, the covariance matrix becomes very large, and cannot be estimated accurately. Instead, factor models[23] can be used to reduce the dimension of the covariance structure. Multivariate random walks are in fact *dynamic factor models* for asset prices. A multi-factor model for the return of asset *i* can be written in the following general form:

$$r_t^{(i)} = \mu^{(i)} + \sum_{k=1}^{K} \beta^{(i,k)} \cdot f_t^{(k)} + \varepsilon_t^{(i)}$$

where the K factors $f^{(k)}$ follow random walks, $\beta^{(i,k)}$ are the factor loadings, and $\varepsilon_t^{(i)}$ are normal random variables with zero mean.

It is important to note that the covariance matrix cannot capture correlations at lagged times (i.e., correlations of dynamic nature). Furthermore, the assumptions that log returns behave as multivariate normal variables is not always applicable—some assets exhibit dependency of nonlinear kind, which cannot be captured by the covariance or correlation matrix. Alternative tools for modeling covariability include *copula functions* and *transfer entropies*.[24]

12.5.2 Incorporating Jumps

Many of the dynamic asset price processes used in industry assume continuous sample paths, as was the case with the arithmetic, geometric, and the different mean-reverting random walks we considered earlier in this chapter. However, there is empirical evidence that the prices of many securities incorporate jumps. The prices of some commodities, such as electricity and oil, are notorious for exhibiting "spikes." The logarithm of a price process with jumps is not normally distributed, but is instead characterized by a high peak and heavy tails, which are more typical of market data than the normal distribution. Thus, more advanced models are needed to incorporate realistic price behavior.

A classical way to include jumps in models for asset price dynamics is to add a Poisson process to the process (geometric random walk or mean reversion) used to model the asset price. A Poisson process is a discrete process in which arrivals occur at random discrete points in time, and the times between arrivals are drawn from an exponential distribution with average time between arrivals equal to $1/\lambda$.[25] Recall from sections 3.7.1 and 3.7.2 of Chapter 3 that this means that the number of arrivals in a specific time interval follows a Poisson distribution with mean rate of arrival λ. The "jump" Poisson process is assumed to be independent of the underlying "smooth" random walk.

The Poisson process is typically used to figure out the times at which the jumps occur. The magnitude of the jumps itself could come from any distribution, although the lognormal distribution is often used for tractability.

Let us explain in more detail how one would model and simulate a geometric random walk with jumps. At every point in time, the process moves as a geometric random walk, and updates the price S_t to S_{t+1}. If a jump happens, the size of the jump is added to S_t as well to obtain S_{t+1}. In order to avoid confusion about whether or not we have included the jump in the calculation, let us denote the price right before we find out whether or not a jump has occurred $S_{t+1}^{(-)}$, and keep the total price for the next time period as S_{t+1}. We therefore have

$$S_{t+1}^{(-)} = S_t + \mu \cdot S_t + \sigma \cdot S_t \cdot \tilde{\varepsilon}_t$$

that is, $S_{t+1}^{(-)}$ is computed according to the normal geometric random walk rule. Now suppose that a jump of magnitude $\tilde{J}_t$ occurs between time t and time $t+1$. Let us express the jump magnitude as a percentage of the asset price, that is, let

$$S_{t+1} = S_{t+1}^{(-)} \cdot \tilde{J}_t$$

If we restrict the magnitude of the jumps $\tilde{J}_t$ to be nonnegative, we will make sure that the asset price itself does not become negative.

Let us now express the changes in price in terms of the jump size. Based on the relationship between S_{t+1}, $S_{t+1}^{(-)}$, and $\tilde{J}_t$, we can write

$$S_{t+1} - S_{t+1}^{(-)} = S_{t+1}^{(-)} \cdot (\tilde{J}_t - 1)$$

and, therefore,

$$S_{t+1}^{(-)} = S_{t+1} - S_{t+1}^{(-)} \cdot (\tilde{J}_t - 1)$$

Thus we can substitute this expression for $S_{t+1}^{(-)}$ and write the geometric random walk with jumps model as

$$S_{t+1} = S_t + \mu \cdot S_t + \sigma \cdot S_t \cdot \tilde{\varepsilon}_t + S_{t+1}^{(-)} \cdot (\tilde{J}_t - 1)$$

How would we simulate a path for the jump-geometric random walk process? Note that given the relationship between S_{t+1}, $S_{t+1}^{(-)}$, and $\tilde{J}_t$, we can write

$$\ln(S_{t+1}) = \ln(S_{t+1}^{(-)}) + \ln(\tilde{J}_t)$$

Since $S_{t+1}^{(-)}$ is the price resulting only from the geometric random walk at time t, we already know what $\ln(S_{t+1}^{(-)})$ is. Recall based on our discussion of the geometric random walk in section 12.3 that

$$\ln(S_{t+1}^{(-)}) = \ln(S_t) + (\mu - 0.5 \cdot \sigma^2) + \sigma \cdot \tilde{\varepsilon}_t$$

Therefore, the overall equation will be

$$\ln(S_{t+1}) = \ln(S_t) + (\mu - 0.5 \cdot \sigma^2) + \sigma \cdot \tilde{\varepsilon}_t + \sum_i \ln\left(J_t^{(i)}\right)$$

where $J_t^{(i)}$ are all the jumps that occur during the time period between t and $t+1$. This means that

$$S_{t+1} = S_t \cdot e^{\mu - 0.5 \cdot \sigma^2 + \sigma \cdot \tilde{\varepsilon}_t} \cdot \prod_i J_t^{(i)}$$

where the symbol $\prod$ denotes product. (If no jumps occurred between t and $t+1$, we set the product to 1.)

Hence, to simulate the price at time $t+1$, we need to simulate the following:

- A standard normal random variable $\tilde{\varepsilon}_t$, as in the case of a geometric random walk.
- How many jumps occur between t and $t+1$.
- The magnitude of each jump.

The exact simulation procedure is as follows:

1. Generate a standard normal random variable $\tilde{\varepsilon}_t$. With @RISK, this can be done with the command `RISKNORMAL(0,1)`. In MATLAB, use `normrnd(0,1)`.
2. Simulate the number of arrivals in the time period $(t, t + 1)$ by drawing a number from a Poisson distribution with arrival rate per unit period λ. In @RISK, use `RISKPOISSON(λ)`. In MATLAB, use `poissrnd(λ)`.
3. Suppose the number of arrivals generated in step 2 was K. For each arrival, generate a random number from the probability distribution that the jump size $\tilde{J}_t$ is assumed to follow. For example, if the jumps are assumed to come from a lognormal distribution with mean m and standard deviation s, then use the function `RISKLOGNORM(m,s)` in @RISK or the function `lognrnd(m,s)` in MATLAB to generate K random numbers $J_1, \ldots, J_K$ from that distribution.
4. Compute the sum of the natural logarithms of the random numbers generated in step 3, $\ln(J_1) + \cdots + \ln(J_K)$.
5. Compute the natural logarithm of the price at the next time period as

$$\ln(S_{t+1}) = \ln(S_t) + (\mu - 0.5 \cdot \sigma^2) + \sigma \cdot \varepsilon_t + \ln(J_1) + \cdots + \ln(J_K)$$

Note that we could compute S_{t+1} directly as well, as in the equation we showed earlier. However, if we are simulating a path for the random walk with jumps, we will need $\ln(S_{t+1})$, rather than S_{t+1}, for the calculation of the next step, so this equation is sufficient.

As Merton (1976) noted, if we assume that the jumps follow a lognormal distribution, then $\ln(\tilde{J}_t)$ is normal, and the simulation is even easier. See Glasserman (2004) for more advanced examples.

12.5.3 Stochastic Volatility

The models we considered so far all assumed that the volatility of the stochastic process remains constant over time. Empirical evidence suggests that the volatility changes over time, and more advanced models recognize that fact. Such models assume that the volatility parameter σ itself follows a random walk of some kind. Since there is some evidence that volatility tends to be mean-reverting, often different versions of mean-reversion models are used. For more details on stochastic volatility models and their simulation see, for example, Glasserman (2004) and Hull (2008).

12.6 STOCHASTIC PROCESSES

In this section, we provide an introduction to what is known as *stochastic calculus*. Our goal is not to achieve a working knowledge in the subject, but rather to provide context for some of the terminology and the formulas encountered in the literature on modeling asset prices with random walks.

So far, we discussed random walks for which every step is taken at a specific discrete point in time. When the time increments are very small, almost zero in length, the equation of a random walk describes a *stochastic process in continuous time*. In this context, the arithmetic random walk model is known as a *generalized Wiener process* or *Brownian motion* (BM). The geometric random walk is referred to as *Geometric Brownian Motion* (GBM), and the arithmetic mean-reverting walk is the Ornstein-Uhlenbeck process mentioned earlier.

Special notation is used to denote stochastic processes in continuous time. Increments are denoted by d or Δ. (For example, $(S_{t+1} - S_t)$ is denoted dS_t, meaning a change in S_t over an infinitely small interval.) The equations describing the process, however, have a very similar form to the equations we introduced earlier in this section:

$$dS_t = \mu\, dt + \sigma\, dW$$

Equations involving small changes ("differences") in variables are referred to as *differential equations*. In words, the equation above reads "The change in the price S_t over a small time period dt equals the average drift μ multiplied by the small time change plus a random term equal to the volatility σ multiplied by dW, where dW is the increment of a Wiener process." The Wiener process, or Brownian motion, is the fundamental building block for many of the classical asset price processes. A standard Wiener process $W(t)$ has the following properties:

- For any time $s < t$, the difference $W(t) - W(s)$ is a normal random variable with mean zero and variance $(t - s)$. It can be expressed as $\sqrt{t - s} \cdot \tilde{\varepsilon}$, where $\tilde{\varepsilon}$ is a standard normal random variable.[26]
- For any times $0 \leq t_1 < t_2 \leq t_3 < t_4$, the differences $(W(t_2) - W(t_1))$ and $(W(t_4) - W(t_3))$ (which are random variables) are independent.[27] Note that independent implies uncorrelated.
- The value of the Wiener process at the beginning is zero, $W(t_0) = 0$.

Using the new notation, the first two properties can be restated as

Property 1. The change dW during a small period of time dt is normally distributed with mean 0 and variance dt, and can be expressed as $\sqrt{dt} \cdot \tilde{\varepsilon}$.

Property 2. The values of dW for any two nonoverlapping time intervals are independent.

The arithmetic random walk can be obtained as a *generalized Wiener process*, which has the form

$$dS_t = a\,dt + b\,dW$$

The appeal of the generalized Wiener process is that we can find a closed-form expression for the price at any time period. Namely,

$$S_t = S_0 + a \cdot t + b \cdot W(t)$$

The generalized Wiener process is a special case of the more general class of *Ito processes*, in which both the drift term and the coefficient in front of the random term are allowed to be nonconstant. The equation for an Ito process is

$$dS_t = a(S, t)\,dt + b(S, t)\,dW$$

GBM and the Ornstein-Uhlenbeck process are both special cases of Ito processes.

In contrast to the generalized Wiener process, the equation for the Ito process does not allow us to write a general expression for the price at time t in closed form. However, an expression can be found for some special cases, such as GBM. We now show how this can be derived.

The main relevant result from stochastic calculus is the so-called *Ito Lemma*, which states the following. Suppose that a variable x follows an Ito process

$$dx_t = a(x, t)\,dt + b(x, t)\,dW$$

and let y be a function of x, that is,

$$y_t = f(x, t)$$

Then, y evolves according to the following differential equation:

$$dy = \left(\frac{\partial f}{\partial x} \cdot a + \frac{\partial f}{\partial t} + \frac{1}{2} \cdot \frac{\partial^2 f}{\partial x^2} \cdot b^2 \right) dt + \frac{\partial f}{\partial x} \cdot b \cdot dW$$

where the symbol ∂ is standard notation for the partial derivative of the function f with respect to the variable in the denominator. For example,

$$\frac{\partial f}{\partial t}$$

is the derivative of the function f with respect to t assuming that all terms in the expression for f that do not involve t are constant. Respectively, ∂^2 denotes the second derivative of the function f with respect to the variable in the denominator, that is, the derivative of the derivative.

This expression shows that a function of a variable that follows an Ito process also follows an Ito process.

A rigorous proof of Ito's Lemma is beyond the scope of this book, but let us provide some intuition. Let us see how we would go about computing the expression for y in Ito's Lemma.

In ordinary calculus, we could obtain an expression for a function of a variable in terms of that variable by writing the Taylor series extension:

$$dy = \frac{\partial f}{\partial x} \cdot dx + \frac{\partial f}{\partial t} \cdot dt + \frac{1}{2} \cdot \frac{\partial^2 f}{\partial x^2} \cdot dx^2 + \frac{1}{2} \cdot \frac{\partial^2 f}{\partial t^2} \cdot dt^2 + \frac{\partial^2 f}{\partial x \, \partial t} \cdot dx \, dt + \cdots$$

We will get rid of all terms of order dt^2 or higher, deeming them "too small." We need to expand the terms that contain dx, however, because they will contain terms of order dt. We have

$$dy = \frac{\partial f}{\partial x} \cdot (a(x, t) \, dt + b(x, t) \, dW) + \frac{\partial f}{\partial t} \cdot dt$$
$$+ \frac{1}{2} \cdot \frac{\partial^2 f}{\partial x^2} \cdot (a(x, t) \, dt + b(x, t) \, dW)^2$$

The last expression in parentheses, when expanded, becomes (dropping the arguments of a and b for notational convenience)

$$(a \, dt + b \, dW)^2 = a^2 (dt)^2 + b^2 (dW)^2 + 2ab \cdot dt \cdot dW$$
$$= b^2 \, dt$$

To obtain this expression, we dropped the first and the last term in the expanded expression because they are of order higher than dt. The middle term, $b^2(dW)^2$, in fact equals $b^2 \cdot dt$ as dt goes to 0. The latter is not an obvious fact, but it follows from the properties of the standard Wiener process. The intuition behind it is that the variance of $(dW)^2$ is of order dt^2, so we can ignore it and treat the expression as deterministic and equal to its expected value. The expected value of $(dW)^2$ is in fact dt.[28]

Substituting this expression back into the expression for dy, we obtain the expression in Ito's Lemma.

Using Ito's Lemma, let us derive the equation for the price at time t, S_t, that was the basis for the simulation method in section 12.3.1. Suppose that S_t follows the GBM

$$dS_t = (\mu \cdot S_t)\, dt + (\sigma \cdot S_t)\, dW$$

We will use Ito's Lemma to compute the equation for the process followed by the logarithm of the stock price. In other words, in the notation we used in the definition of Ito's Lemma, we have

$$y_t = f(x, t) = \ln S_t$$

We also have

$$a = \mu \cdot S \quad \text{and} \quad b = \sigma \cdot S$$

Finally, we have

$$\frac{\partial f}{\partial x} = \frac{\partial (\ln S)}{\partial S} = \frac{1}{S}$$

and

$$\frac{\partial^2 f}{\partial x^2} = \frac{\partial (1/S)}{\partial S} = -\frac{1}{S^2}$$

Plugging into the equation for y in Ito's Lemma, we obtain

$$d\ln S = \left(\frac{1}{S} \cdot a + 0 + \frac{1}{2} \cdot \left(-\frac{1}{S^2} \right) \cdot b^2 \right) dt + \frac{1}{S} \cdot b \cdot dW$$

$$= \left(\mu - \frac{1}{2} \cdot \sigma^2 \right) dt + \sigma \cdot dW$$

which is the equation we presented earlier. This explains also the presence of the

$$-\frac{1}{2} \cdot \sigma^2$$

term in the expression for the drift of the GBM.

As we will see in Chapters 13 and 14, some stochastic processes lead to closed-form formulas for the prices of the underlying securities and *financial derivatives* on those securities. When the pricing is instead done by simulation, we refer to the *discretization* of the underlying stochastic process, and talk about the *discretization error* which occurs because in practice it is computationally intractable (and in fact impossible) to simulate future prices at infinitely small time intervals. We need to resign to using time intervals of finite length, and the larger the length of the time intervals, the greater the divergence between the range of simulated prices and the prices we would expect based on the closed-form formula, that is, the larger the discretization error.

To illustrate the concept of discretization error, let us go back to the example of simulation of a geometric random walk in section 12.3. The real process for the price is described by the differential equation

$$dS_t = \mu S_t \, dt + \sigma S_t \, dW$$

To simulate paths for the price, we need to find an approximation for the terms dS_t, dt, and dW. The simplest scheme for doing that is the Euler scheme.[29] Then we would get

$$S_{t+\Delta t} - S_t = \mu \cdot S_t \cdot \Delta t + \sigma \cdot S_t \cdot \sqrt{\Delta t} \cdot \tilde{\varepsilon}_t$$

As we mentioned in section 12.3.2, however, the distribution of each $S_{t+\Delta t}$ we generate in this manner is normal, not lognormal. (This is because each $S_{t+\Delta t}$ is the sum of constants plus a normal random variable, $\tilde{\varepsilon}_t$.) If Δt is very small, this discretization error can be reduced and the distribution of the price after many steps will indeed approximate a lognormal distribution with the correct parameters. However, this is computationally intensive and time consuming. We can eliminate the discretization error altogether by using Ito's Lemma and the exact expression for the asset price we derived in this section:

$$S_t = S_0 \cdot e^{(\mu - \frac{1}{2} \cdot \sigma^2) \cdot t + \sigma \cdot \sqrt{t} \cdot \tilde{\varepsilon}}$$

However, such closed form results are not readily available for all stochastic processes. Thus, when simulating in practice we must tolerate some discretization error. With complicated stochastic differential equations, we can reduce the error by generating the whole path of the underlying variable (e.g., the stock price), even if we are only interested in what happens at the end of the time horizon. Such refined discretization schemes are widely used in practice.

SUMMARY

- Models of asset dynamics include trees (such as binomial trees) and random walks (such as arithmetic, geometric, and mean-reverting random walks). Such models are called discrete when the changes in the asset price are assumed to happen at discrete time increments. When the length of the time increment is assumed infinitely small, we refer to them as stochastic processes in continuous time.
- The arithmetic random walk is an additive model for asset prices—at every time period, the new price is determined by the price at the previous time period plus a deterministic drift term and a random shock that is distributed as a normal random variable with mean equal to zero and a standard deviation proportional to the square root of the length of the time period. The probability distribution of future asset prices conditional on a known current price is normal.
- The arithmetic random walk model is analytically tractable and convenient; however, it has some undesirable features such as a nonzero probability that the asset price will become negative.
- The geometric random walk is a multiplicative model for asset prices—at every time period, the new price is determined by the price at the previous time period multiplied by a deterministic drift term and a random shock that is distributed as a lognormal random variable. The volatility of the process grows with the square root of the elapsed amount of time. The probability distribution of future asset prices conditional on a known current price is lognormal.
- The geometric random walk is not only analytically tractable, but is more realistic than the arithmetic random walk because the asset price cannot become negative. It is widely used in practice, particularly for modeling stock prices.
- Mean reversion models assume that the asset price will meander, but will tend to return to a long-term mean at a speed called the speed of

adjustment. They are particularly useful for modeling prices of some commodities, interest rates and exchange rates.

- The codependence structure between the price processes for different assets can be incorporated directly (by computing the correlation between the random terms in their random walks), by using dynamic multifactor models, or by more advanced means such as copula functions and transfer entropies.

- A variety of more advanced random walk models are used to incorporate different assumptions, such as time-varying volatility and "spikes," or jumps, in the asset price. They are not as tractable analytically as the classical random walk models, but can easily be simulated.

- The Wiener process, a stochastic process in continuous time, is a basic building block for many of the stochastic processes used to model asset prices. The increments of a Wiener process are independent, normally distributed random variables with variance proportional to the length of the time period.

- An Ito process is a generalized Wiener process with drift and volatility terms that can be functions of the asset price and time.

- A main result in stochastic calculus is Ito's Lemma, which states that a variable that is a function of a variable that follows an Ito process follows an Ito process itself with specific drift and volatility terms.

SOFTWARE HINTS

@RISK

File **Ch12-RandomWalks.xlsx** contains examples of the estimation and simulation of four different types of random walks: arithmetic (worksheet **ARW**), geometric (worksheet **GRW**), mean reversion (worksheet **MR**), and geometric mean reversion (worksheet **GMR**).

Arithmetic random walk   Consider two years of historical data (104 observations) on Exxon Mobil weekly stock prices. The data are stored in cells B4:B107 in worksheet **ARW** (cells B26:C106 are hidden). A screenshot of the worksheet is provided in Exhibit 12.8.

To estimate the drift and the volatility of the arithmetic random walk, we first create a column (C), in which we compute the price changes $S_{t+1} - S_t$. For example, cell C5 contains the formula

=B5-B4

Arithmetic random walk

			Parameter estimation	
Exxon Mobil (XOM) stock prices			drift (mu)	0.1697
Date	Price (Close)	Price changes	volatility (sigma)	3.1166
24-Aug-07	$ 85.69			
31-Aug-07	$ 85.73	$ 0.04		
7-Sep-07	$ 85.75	$ 0.02		
14-Sep-07	$ 88.67	$ 2.92		
21-Sep-07	$ 92.31	$ 3.64		
28-Sep-07	$ 92.56	$ 0.25		
5-Oct-07	$ 91.36	$ (1.20)		
12-Oct-07	$ 93.48	$ 2.12		
19-Oct-07	$ 92.14	$ (1.34)		
26-Oct-07	$ 92.21	$ 0.07		
2-Nov-07	$ 87.93	$ (4.28)		
9-Nov-07	$ 86.85	$ (1.08)		
16-Nov-07	$ 85.10	$ (1.75)		
23-Nov-07	$ 88.29	$ 3.19		
30-Nov-07	$ 89.16	$ 0.87		
7-Dec-07	$ 91.50	$ 2.34		
14-Dec-07	$ 91.18	$ (0.32)		
21-Dec-07	$ 93.43	$ 2.25		
28-Dec-07	$ 95.00	$ 1.57		
4-Jan-08	$ 92.08	$ (2.92)		
11-Jan-08	$ 90.30	$ (1.78)		
18-Jan-08	$ 85.08	$ (5.22)		
107	$ 68.21	$ (1.26)		

Simulation

	Path 1	Path 2	Path 3	Path 4	Path 5
Initial price	$ 68.21	$ 68.21	$ 68.21	$ 68.21	$ 68.21
1	$ 70.18	$ 72.53	$ 70.14	$ 69.13	$ 65.54
2	$ 67.65	$ 71.78	$ 62.99	$ 70.68	$ 62.95
3	$ 66.50	$ 68.39	$ 63.52	$ 67.83	$ 58.35
4	$ 70.72	$ 70.20	$ 66.11	$ 70.61	$ 60.55
5	$ 69.74	$ 68.11	$ 63.76	$ 67.99	$ 57.75
6	$ 68.67	$ 71.29	$ 64.58	$ 68.09	$ 54.53
7	$ 69.36	$ 76.95	$ 56.82	$ 70.45	$ 56.90
8	$ 74.73	$ 78.61	$ 52.09	$ 71.70	$ 58.08
9	$ 79.96	$ 76.22	$ 50.05	$ 73.08	$ 56.88
10	$ 79.53	$ 76.50	$ 49.88	$ 75.54	$ 55.76
11	$ 73.63	$ 73.99	$ 47.88	$ 68.50	$ 52.44
12	$ 75.41	$ 72.69	$ 46.07	$ 68.94	$ 50.77
13	$ 73.86	$ 71.04	$ 48.48	$ 68.31	$ 45.93
14	$ 67.05	$ 71.64	$ 44.85	$ 85.03	$ 44.40
15	$ 58.31	$ 63.55	$ 46.68	$ 63.04	$ 43.90
16	$ 58.77	$ 67.18	$ 50.56	$ 57.03	$ 42.61
17	$ 57.23	$ 63.85	$ 53.73	$ 53.86	$ 41.77
18	$ 57.35	$ 73.37	$ 51.44	$ 53.25	$ 41.71
19	$ 58.21	$ 68.97	$ 56.07	$ 50.64	$ 40.36
20	$ 56.37	$ 66.45	$ 51.83	$ 50.05	$ 41.96

EXHIBIT 12.8 Worksheet ARW in spreadsheet Ch12-RandomWalks.xlsx.

The drift μ of the arithmetic random walk is computed in cell E2 with the formula

```
=AVERAGE(C5:C107)
```

The volatility σ of the arithmetic random walk is computed in cell E3 with the formula

```
=STDEV(C5:C107)
```

Note that these are estimates of the *weekly* drift and volatility of the Exxon Mobil stock price because we estimated them from weekly data. If we need to convert them to annual values, we should multiply the estimate of the weekly drift by 52 (the number of weeks in a year), and the estimate of the weekly volatility by $\sqrt{52}$.

In columns G through K, we simulate five paths for the arithmetic random walk. Since the simulation implementations are identical, let us focus on one of the columns, column G.

Cell G4 contains the starting price for the random walk (which is identical to the last price in our data set from cell B107). To simulate the price at the next step in cell G5, we use the equation for the arithmetic random walk from section 12.2.1. Cell G5 contains the formula

```
=G4+$E$2+$E$3*SQRT($F$5)*RiskNormal(0,1)
```

In words, we are adding the drift (from cell E2) to the current price, and adding a random term that involves the volatility (from cell E3) multiplied by the amount of time that expired during the first step (one unit of time is one week in this example, so we reference cell F5 and continue to reference it as we generate further values for the random walk).

The path for the arithmetic random walk is plotted in the figure next to columns G:K.

Geometric Random Walk   Consider two years of historical data (104 observations) on Exxon Mobil weekly stock prices. The data are stored in cells B4:B107 in worksheet **GRW** (cells B26:C106 are hidden). A screenshot of the worksheet is provided in Exhibit 12.9.

To estimate the drift and the volatility of the arithmetic random walk, we first create a column (C), in which we compute the natural logarithms of the price ratios (S_{t+1} / S_t). For example, cell C5 contains the formula

```
=LN(B5/B4)
```

	A	B	C	D	E	F	G	H	I	J	K
1	Geometric random walk.			**Parameter estimation**							
2	Exxon Mobil (XOM) stock prices			drift (mu)	-0.0014		**Simulation**				
3	Date	Price (Close)	Ln(S_t÷S_t-1)	volatility (sigma)	0.0411		Path 1	Path 2	Path 3	Path 4	Path 5
4	24-Aug-07	$ 85.69				Initial price	$ 68.21	$ 68.21	$ 68.21	$ 68.21	$ 68.21
5	31-Aug-07	$ 85.73	0.00			1	$ 68.21	$ 69.00	$ 65.00	$ 65.36	$ 67.01
6	7-Sep-07	$ 85.75	0.00			2	$ 67.75	$ 65.65	$ 68.34	$ 68.12	$ 72.28
7	14-Sep-07	$ 88.67	0.03			3	$ 66.67	$ 67.01	$ 68.92	$ 69.80	$ 70.67
8	21-Sep-07	$ 92.31	0.04			4	$ 68.86	$ 65.85	$ 72.36	$ 66.80	$ 64.90
9	28-Sep-07	$ 92.56	0.00			5	$ 71.92	$ 64.70	$ 73.80	$ 65.70	$ 62.42
10	5-Oct-07	$ 91.36	(0.01)			6	$ 71.17	$ 64.22	$ 77.13	$ 66.62	$ 58.57
11	12-Oct-07	$ 93.48	0.02			7	$ 73.59	$ 65.00	$ 75.39	$ 66.87	$ 57.36
12	19-Oct-07	$ 92.14	(0.01)			8	$ 70.50	$ 63.61	$ 75.95	$ 64.54	$ 58.51
13	26-Oct-07	$ 92.21	0.00			9	$ 73.20	$ 58.06	$ 82.09	$ 70.77	$ 57.99
14	2-Nov-07	$ 87.93	(0.05)			10	$ 70.85	$ 57.55	$ 86.58	$ 70.06	$ 61.54
15	9-Nov-07	$ 86.85	(0.01)			11	$ 73.24	$ 56.30	$ 88.01	$ 72.76	$ 62.15
16	16-Nov-07	$ 85.10	(0.02)			12	$ 76.00	$ 54.85	$ 89.14	$ 72.81	$ 59.75
17	23-Nov-07	$ 88.29	0.04			13	$ 73.62	$ 57.77	$ 90.84	$ 76.17	$ 60.09
18	30-Nov-07	$ 89.76	0.01			14	$ 75.10	$ 56.37	$ 87.36	$ 73.85	$ 54.87
19	7-Dec-07	$ 91.50	0.03			15	$ 80.87	$ 60.71	$ 79.85	$ 74.89	$ 55.63
20	14-Dec-07	$ 91.18	(0.00)			16	$ 80.35	$ 62.57	$ 82.83	$ 78.82	$ 58.01
21	21-Dec-07	$ 93.43	0.02			17	$ 75.84	$ 63.77	$ 86.23	$ 81.38	$ 59.61
22	28-Dec-07	$ 95.00	0.02			18	$ 75.11	$ 65.51	$ 82.73	$ 80.46	$ 57.89
23	4-Jan-08	$ 92.08	(0.03)			19	$ 81.16	$ 68.01	$ 81.72	$ 79.84	$ 60.63
24	11-Jan-08	$ 90.30	(0.02)			20	$ 78.66	$ 66.37	$ 78.25	$ 79.17	$ 62.49
25	18-Jan-08	$ 85.08	(0.06)								
107	14-Aug-09	$ 68.21	(0.02)								

EXHIBIT 12.9 Worksheet GRW in worksheet Ch12-RandomWalks.xlsx.

The volatility σ of the geometric random walk is computed in cell E3 with the formula

```
=STDEV(C5:C107)
```

The drift μ of the geometric random walk is computed in cell E2 with the formula

```
=AVERAGE(C5:C107)+0.5*E3^2
```

Again, these are estimates of the *weekly* drift and volatility of the Exxon Mobil stock price because we estimated them from weekly data. If we need to convert them to annual values, we should multiply the estimate of the weekly drift by 52 (the number of weeks in a year), and the estimate of the weekly volatility by $\sqrt{52}$.

In columns G through K, we simulate five paths for the geometric random walk. Since the simulation implementations are identical, let us focus on one of the columns, column G.

Cell G4 contains the starting price for the random walk (which is identical to the last price in our data set from cell B107). To simulate the price at the next step in cell G5, we use the equation for the geometric random walk from section 12.3.1. Cell G5 contains the formula

```
=G4*EXP(($E$2-0.5*$E$3^2)*$F$5+$E$3*SQRT($F$5)
*RiskNormal(0,1))
```

Again, the amount of time that expired during the first step is one week in this example, so we reference cell F5 and continue to reference it as we generate further values for the random walk.

The path for the arithmetic random walk is plotted in the figure next to columns G:K.

Mean Reversion Consider two years of historical data (104 observations) of the weekly USD/Euro exchange rate. The data are stored in cells B4:B107 in worksheet **MR** (cells B26:C106 are hidden). A screenshot of the worksheet is provided in Exhibit 12.10.

To estimate the drift and the volatility of the arithmetic random walk, we first create a column (C), in which we compute the rate changes $(S_{t+1} - S_t)$. In contrast to the arithmetic and geometric random walk, the matching of rate changes with current rates is important because we will need to

Mean reversion

US/Euro Exchange Rate

Parameter estimation

	drift [mu]	volatility [sigma]	speed [kappa]	
	1.4404	0.0248	0.0347	Initial price

Date	Close	Price changes
24-Aug-07	1.3679	
31-Aug-07	1.3629	-0.0051
7-Sep-07	1.3766	0.0038
14-Sep-07	1.3873	0.0107
21-Sep-07	1.4089	0.0206
28-Sep-07	1.4271	0.0082
5-Oct-07	1.4135	-0.0036
12-Oct-07	1.4178	0.0043
19-Oct-07	1.4304	0.0026
26-Oct-07	1.4396	0.0092
2-Nov-07	1.4507	0.0111
9-Nov-07	1.4674	0.0067
16-Nov-07	1.4557	-0.0017
23-Nov-07	1.4835	0.0078
30-Nov-07	1.4631	-0.0204
7-Dec-07	1.4655	0.0004
14-Dec-07	1.4417	-0.0238
21-Dec-07	1.4365	-0.0052
28-Dec-07	1.4475	0.0350
4-Jan-08	1.4743	0.0028
11-Jan-08	1.4775	0.0032
18-Jan-08	1.4609	-0.0066
14-Aug-09	1.4202	0.0061

Simulation

Initial price	Path 1	Path 2	Path 3	Path 4	Path 5
	1.42	1.42	1.42	1.42	1.42
1	1.43	1.40	1.42	1.46	1.41
2	1.41	1.42	1.42	1.40	1.40
3	1.43	1.41	1.45	1.40	1.35
4	1.43	1.40	1.49	1.42	1.37
5	1.42	1.38	1.46	1.41	1.41
6	1.38	1.33	1.47	1.41	1.39
7	1.36	1.39	1.47	1.39	1.41
8	1.37	1.38	1.46	1.42	1.41
9	1.34	1.33	1.42	1.43	1.41
10	1.36	1.30	1.42	1.43	1.40
11	1.40	1.32	1.42	1.42	1.44
12	1.39	1.33	1.46	1.41	1.44
13	1.36	1.37	1.46	1.39	1.41
14	1.41	1.39	1.43	1.35	1.40
15	1.44	1.40	1.44	1.35	1.38
16	1.42	1.43	1.45	1.32	1.40
17	1.41	1.39	1.45	1.35	1.43
18	1.46	1.42	1.48	1.37	1.45
19	1.46	1.46	1.44	1.39	1.43
20	1.43	1.42	1.47	1.39	1.44
21	1.44	1.38	1.48	1.37	1.48

EXHIBIT 12.10 Worksheet MR in worksheet Ch12-RandomWalks.xlsx.

run a regression on these observations. For example, cell C4 contains the formula

```
=B5-B4
```

and should be paired (in the same row) with cell B4, which contains the current rate.

We run a regression with cells C3:C106 (the rate changes) as the realizations of the response variable, and cells B3:B106 as the realizations of the explanatory variable (the current rate). In Excel, click the **Data** tab, click **Data Analysis**, select **Regression** from the Analysis Tools, and fill out the dialog box as shown in Exhibit 12.11.

The output of the regression is in worksheet **MR Regression**. (See a screenshot of the worksheet in Exhibit 12.12.) The important values are highlighted.

The volatility σ of the mean reverting walk is stored in cell E3 of worksheet **MR**, and equals the standard error of the regression (cell B7

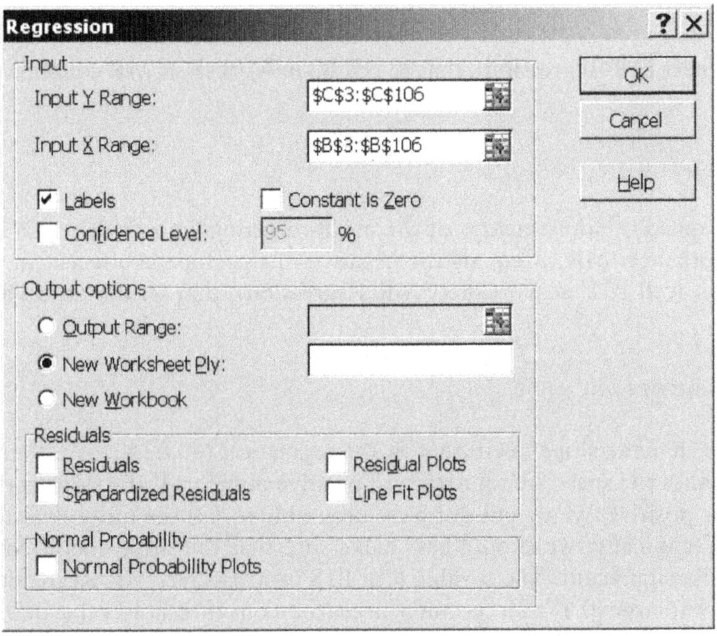

EXHIBIT 12.11   Excel regression dialog box.

	A	B	C	D	E	F	G
1	SUMMARY OUTPUT						
2							
3	*Regression Statistics*						
4	Multiple R	0.135223					
5	R Square	0.018285					
6	Adjusted R Square	0.008565					
7	Standard Error	0.024846					
8	Observations	103					
9							
10	ANOVA						
11		*df*	*SS*	*MS*	*F*	*Significance F*	
12	Regression	1	0.001161	0.001161	1.881203	0.17323684	
13	Residual	101	0.062349	0.000617			
14	Total	102	0.06351				
15							
16		*Coefficients*	*Standard Err*	*t Stat*	*P-value*	*Lower 95%*	*Upper 95%*
17	Intercept	0.050041	0.036197	1.382457	0.169881	-0.0217644	0.121846
18	Rate	-0.034742	0.02533	-1.371569	0.173237	-0.0849891	0.015506

EXHIBIT 12.12   Regression output for mean reversion model in worksheet
MR in the file Ch12-RandomWalks.xlsx.

in worksheet **MR Regression**), that is, cell E3 in worksheet **MR** contains the
formula

```
='MR Regression'!B7
```

The speed of adjustment κ of the mean reverting walk is stored in cell
E4 of worksheet **MR**. It equals the negative of the slope coefficient in the
regression (cell B18 in worksheet **MR Regression**), that is, the formula in
cell E4 is

```
=-'MR Regression'!B18
```

Note that the slope coefficient in the regression (-0.0347) is negative,
which makes the speed of adjustment a positive number. If the slope coefficient was positive, we would not have been able to use the mean reverting
model. Technically, we should also make sure that the slope coefficient is
statistically significant. The p-value (cell E18 in worksheet **MR Regression**)
is somewhat large (0.1732), certainly larger than our threshold value of 0.05
(see section 12.4.2). However, the thresholds are not always clear-cut, and
it is the judgment call of the modeler as to whether to proceed and use the
model anyway. For the sake of example, let us use these estimates.

The drift μ of the mean reverting walk is computed in cell E2 of worksheet **MR** with the formula

```
=-'MR Regression'!B17/'MR Regression'!B18
```

It is the ratio of the intercept term and the slope coefficient in the regression.

Again, these are estimates of the *weekly* drift, volatility, and speed of adjustment of the random walk followed by the USD/Euro exchange rate because we estimated them from weekly data. If we need to convert them to annual values, we should multiply the estimate of the weekly drift by 52 (the number of weeks in a year), and the estimate of the weekly volatility by $\sqrt{52}$.

In columns G through K of worksheet **MR**, we simulate five paths for the mean reverting walk. Since the simulation implementations are identical, let us focus on one of the columns, column G.

Cell G4 contains the starting rate for the random walk (which is identical to the last price in our data set from cell B107). To simulate the rate at the next step in cell G5, we use the equation for the mean reverting walk from section 12.4.1. Cell G5 contains the formula

```
=G4+$E$4*($E$2-G4)+$E$3*SQRT($F$5)*RiskNormal(0,1)
```

Again, the amount of time that expired during the first step is one week in this example, so we reference cell F5 and continue to reference it as we generate further values for the random walk.

The path for the mean-reverting walk is plotted in the figure next to columns G:K.

Geometric Mean Reversion Consider two years of historical data (104 observations) of the weekly USD/Euro exchange rate. The data are stored in cells B4:B107 in worksheet **GMR** (cells B26:C106 are hidden). A screenshot of the worksheet is provided in Exhibit 12.13.

To estimate the drift and the volatility of the arithmetic random walk, we first create a column (C), in which we compute the percentage rate changes $(S_{t+1} - S_t)/S_t$. As with the mean-reverting walk, the matching of rate changes with current rates is important because we will need to run a regression on these observations. For example, cell C4 contains the formula

```
= (B5-B4)/B4
```

and should be paired (in the same row) with cell B4, which contains the current rate.

Geometric mean reversion
USEuro Exchange Rate

Date	Rate	Percentage changes	Parameter estimation				Simulation				
			drift (mu)	volatility (sigma)	speed (kappa)		Path 1	Path 2	Path 3	Path 4	Path 5
			1.4464	0.0177	0.0753 Initial price						
24-Aug-07	1.3679	-0.0037				1	1.42	1.42	1.42	1.42	1.42
31-Aug-07	1.3628	0.0901				2	1.44	1.41	1.40	1.43	1.42
7-Sep-07	1.3706	0.0078				3	1.41	1.41	1.41	1.43	1.44
14-Sep-07	1.3873	0.0056				4	1.40	1.40	1.42	1.44	1.43
21-Sep-07	1.4089	0.0029				5	1.42	1.41	1.43	1.41	1.41
28-Sep-07	1.4227	-0.0095				6	1.41	1.41	1.43	1.41	1.43
5-Oct-07	1.4135	0.0030				7	1.42	1.42	1.46	1.40	1.43
12-Oct-07	1.4178	0.0098				8	1.40	1.42	1.46	1.41	1.43
19-Oct-07	1.4304	0.0064				9	1.36	1.43	1.46	1.40	1.41
26-Oct-07	1.4336	0.0077				10	1.36	1.42	1.48	1.40	1.45
2-Nov-07	1.4507	0.015				11	1.36	1.43	1.49	1.40	1.44
9-Nov-07	1.4674	-0.0012				12	1.36	1.43	1.47	1.42	1.46
16-Nov-07	1.4657	0.0121				13	1.34	1.45	1.47	1.44	1.44
23-Nov-07	1.4835	-0.0138				14	1.36	1.46	1.45	1.44	1.44
30-Nov-07	1.4631	0.0016				15	1.37	1.47	1.41	1.45	1.41
7-Dec-07	1.4655	-0.0062				16	1.36	1.49	1.37	1.46	1.42
14-Dec-07	1.4417	-0.0036				17	1.38	1.49	1.38	1.44	1.42
21-Dec-07	1.4385	0.0244				18	1.38	1.52	1.39	1.44	1.43
28-Dec-07	1.4775	0.0019				19	1.41	1.54	1.41	1.42	1.44
4-Jan-08	1.4743	0.0022				20	1.43	1.55	1.39	1.43	1.43
11-Jan-08	1.4775	-0.0112				21	1.44	1.53	1.40	1.45	1.44
18-Jan-08	1.4609	0.0042									
14-Aug-09	1.4302										

EXHIBIT 12.13 Worksheet GMR in worksheet Ch12-RandomWalks.xlsx.

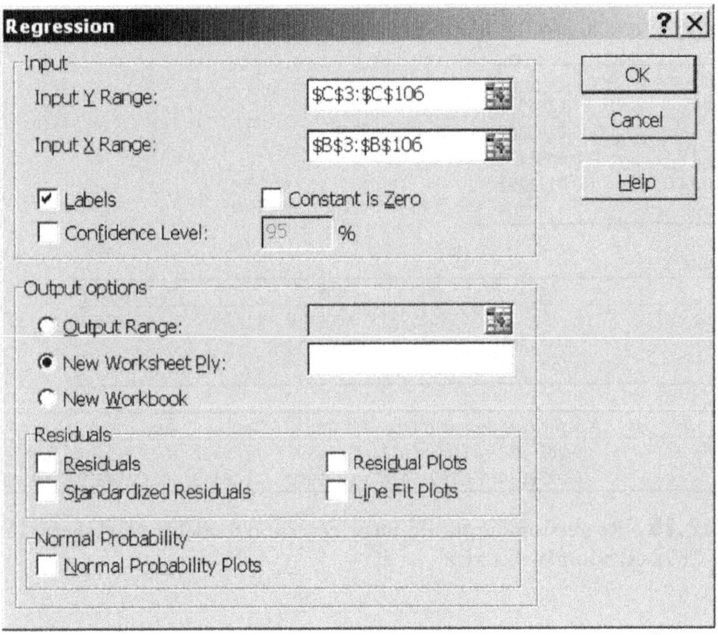

EXHIBIT 12.14 Excel regression dialog box.

We run a regression with cells C3:C106 (the percentage rate changes) as the realizations of the response variable, and cells B3:B106 as the realizations of the explanatory variable (the current rate). In Excel 2007, click the **Data** tab, **Data Analysis** in the Analysis group, select **Regression** from the Analysis tools and click **OK**. Fill out the dialog box as shown in Exhibit 12.14.

The output of the regression is in worksheet **GMR Regression**. (See a screenshot of the worksheet in Exhibit 12.15.) The important values are highlighted.

The volatility σ of the geometric mean reversion is stored in cell E3 of worksheet **GMR**, and equals the standard error of the regression (cell B7 in worksheet **GMR Regression**), that is, cell E3 in worksheet **GMR** contains the formula

```
='GMR Regression'!B7
```

The speed of adjustment κ of the geometric mean reversion is stored in cell E4 of worksheet **GMR**. It equals the negative of the slope coefficient in

	A	B	C	D	E	F	G
2							
3	*Regression Statistics*						
4	Multiple R	0.137972					
5	R Square	0.0190363					
6	Adjusted R Square	0.0093238					
7	Standard Error	0.0177251					
8	Observations	103					
9							
10	ANOVA						
11		*df*	*SS*	*MS*	*F*	*Significance F*	
12	Regression	1	0.000615783	0.000616	1.959974	0.164580421	
13	Residual	101	0.031732124	0.000314			
14	Total	102	0.032347908				
15							
16		*Coefficients*	*Standard Error*	*t Stat*	*P-value*	*Lower 95%*	*Upper 95%*
17	Intercept	0.0365913	0.02582317	1.416995	0.159562	-0.01463492	0.087818
18	Rate	-0.0252984	0.018070426	-1.399991	0.16458	-0.06114529	0.010548

EXHIBIT 12.15   Regression output for mean reversion model in worksheet **GMR** in the file **Ch12-RandomWalks.xlsx**.

the regression (cell B18 in worksheet **GMR Regression**), that is, the formula in cell E4 is

```
=-'GMR Regression'!B18
```

Note that the slope coefficient in the regression (–0.0253) is negative, which makes the speed of adjustment a positive number. If the slope coefficient was positive, we would not have been able to use the geometric mean reversion model. As in the case of mean reversion, technically, we should also make sure that the slope coefficient is statistically significant. The p-value (cell E18 in worksheet **GMR Regression**) is somewhat large (0.1646), certainly larger than our threshold value of 0.05. However, as in the case of mean reversion, the thresholds are not exactly clear-cut, and it is the judgment call of the modeler as to whether to proceed and use the model anyway. For the sake of example, let us use these estimates.

The drift μ of the geometric mean reversion is computed in cell E2 of worksheet **GMR** with the formula

```
=-'GMR Regression'!B17/'GMR Regression'!B18
```

In columns G through K of worksheet **GMR,** we simulate five paths for the mean reverting walk. Since the simulation implementations are identical, let us focus on one of the columns, column G.

Cell G4 contains the starting rate for the random walk (which is the same as the last price in our data set from cell B107). To simulate the rate at the next step in cell G5, we use the equation for the mean reverting walk from Chapter 12.4.3. Cell G5 contains the formula

```
=G4+$E$4*($E$2-G4)*G4+$E$3*SQRT($F$5)*RiskNormal(0,1))
```

Again, the amount of time that expired during the first step is one week in this example, so we reference cell F5 and continue to reference it as we generate further values for the random walk.

The path for the mean reverting walk is plotted in the figure next to columns G:K.

MATLAB

In this section, we will show how to generate paths for the arithmetic random walk (ARW), geometric random walk (GWR), mean reversion (MR), and geometric mean reversion (GMR). The implementation is summarized in the following files:

Files **ARWPaths.m, GRWPaths.m, MRPaths.m,** and **GMRPaths.m** contain functions that simulate and plot a given number of paths of the corresponding random walk. (Recall from Appendix C that functions in MATLAB need to be specified in separate files, and the name of the function should be the same as the name of the file.)

File **RandomWalks.m** contains a script that puts everything together—it reads in historical data on Exxon Mobil prices and on the US/Euro exchange rate, estimates the parameters for the different random walks, and calls the functions ARWPaths, GRWPaths, MRPaths, and GMRPaths to simulate possible paths.

First, we read in the data that is stored in the Excel file **Ch12-RandomWalks.xlsx.** To read in the Exxon Mobil stock price data we will use for the arithmetic and the geometric random walk and record the number of observations in the data set (numObsRW), we write the following commands:

```
ExxonPriceData = xlsread('Ch12-RandomWalks.xlsx','ARW',
'b4:b107');
[numObsRW,nn] = size(ExxonPriceData);
```

To read in the US/Euro exchange rate data we will use for the mean reversion and the geometric mean reversion and to record the number of observations (numObsMR) in the corresponding data set, we write the following commands:

```
USEuroRateData = xlsread('Ch12-RandomWalks.xlsx','MR',
'b4:b107');
[numObsMR,nn] = size(USEuroRateData);
```

Arithmetic and Geometric Random Walks To estimate the parameters of the arithmetic random walk, we first create a vector of price changes priceChangesARW, and find its mean muARW and standard deviation sigmaARW. We then use those parameters as arguments to the function ARWPaths to generate a number of paths (numPaths) specified by the user.

Similarly, to estimate the parameters of the geometric random walk, we first create a vector of natural logarithms of price ratios priceRatios-GRW, and find its mean muGRW and standard deviation sigmaGRW. We then use those parameters as arguments to the function GRWPaths to generate paths.

Mean Reversion and Geometric Mean Reversion To estimate the parameters of the mean reversion, we first create a vector of differences priceChangesMR. We then use the regress function in MATLAB to run a regression with priceChangesMR as the response variable and the original data as the explanatory variable. Recall that when using the regress function in MATLAB, if we want MATLAB to estimate an intercept term, we need to take an extra step, and add a vector of ones to the array of explanatory variables. At the end, the regression output is stored in a data structure that can be retrieved: the first element is a vector of coefficients b (intercept term and slopes), then output that is not of direct concern to us, and finally a vector of statistics (stats). The fourth element in the stats vector is the variance of error terms, which we can use to calculate the standard error of estimate. (The standard error of estimate is the square root of the variance of error terms, and is an estimate for the volatility parameter σ in the mean reversion equation.)

We use the parameters we find from the estimation step as arguments to the function MRPaths to generate paths.

Similarly to the case of mean reversion, to estimate the parameters of the geometric mean reversion, we first create a vector of percentage differences percentageChangesGMR. We then use the regress function in MATLAB to run a regression with `percentageChangesGMR` as the response variable and the original data as the explanatory variable.

We then use the parameters we find from the estimation step as arguments to the function `GMRPaths` to generate paths.

NOTES

1. In general, we use the symbol Δ to denote *difference*. The notation Δt therefore means time difference, that is, length of one time period.
2. See section 3.2 of Chapter 3.
3. See section 3.3 of Chapter 3.
4. See section 3.4 of Chapter 3.
5. This is known as *the Markov property*. It implies that past prices are irrelevant for forecasting the future, and only the current value of the price is relevant for predicting the price in the next time period.
6. To show this, we need to mention that every normal distribution can be expressed in terms of the standard normal distribution. Namely, if $\tilde{\varepsilon}$ is a standard normal variable with mean 0 and standard deviation 1, and $\tilde{x}$ is a normal random variable with mean μ and standard deviation σ, we have

$$\tilde{\varepsilon} = \frac{\tilde{x} - \mu}{\sigma} \text{(equivalently, } \tilde{x} = \sigma \cdot \tilde{\varepsilon} + \mu)$$

   This is a property unique to the normal distribution—no other family of probability distributions can be transformed in the same way. In the context of the equation for the arithmetic random walk, we have a normal random variable $\tilde{\omega}_t$ with mean 0 and standard deviation σ. It can be expressed through a standard normal variable $\tilde{\varepsilon}_t$ as $\sigma \cdot \tilde{\varepsilon} + 0$.
7. The function `normrnd` in MATLAB requires the Simulation Toolbox.
8. See Chapter 2.
9. The function `normrnd` in MATLAB requires the Simulation Toolbox.
10. See Chapter 2 for a definition of log returns. Unless otherwise specified, we use "logarithm" to refer to the natural logarithm, that is, the logarithm of base e. In many references, as well as software packages such as Excel, the abbreviation used for the natural logarithm is `ln`. In MATLAB, however, the function `log` is the default for natural logarithm.
11. See section 3.7.2 of Chapter 3. There we stated that if $\tilde{Y}$ is a normal random variable, then the random variable $\tilde{X} = e^{\tilde{Y}}$ is lognormal. In this case, $\log(S_t)$ is a normal random variable. Therefore, $e^{\ln(S_t)}$ (i.e., S_t) is lognormally distributed.
12. As a general matter, if the logarithm of a random variable is normally distributed, then the random variable itself follows a lognormal distribution. The lognormal distribution has a very convenient property, which is that products of independent lognormal random variables are themselves lognormal random

variables. This is another way to see that S_t is a lognormal random variable given S_0: it is a product of lognormal random variables, scaled by a constant (S_0):

$$S_t = (1 + \tilde{r}_{t-1}). \ldots .(1 + \tilde{r}_0) \cdot S_0$$

13. This is based on a version of the Central Limit Theorem (see section 3.11.1).
14. See Vasicek (1977).
15. Y is a standard notation for the response variable, and X is a standard notation for the array of explanatory variables data. See the instructions for running a regression in the Software Hints for Chapter 11.
16. The standard error of the regression measures the standard deviation of the points around the regression line.
17. See Cox, Ingersoll, and Ross (1985).
18. See section 3.7.2 of Chapter 3 for a definition of the chi-square random variable.
19. See Chapter 2 for a definition of yield and yield curve.
20. This is a special case of the mean reversion model $S_{t+1} = S_t + \kappa \cdot (\mu - S_t) \cdot S_t + \sigma \cdot S_t^{\gamma} \cdot \tilde{\varepsilon}_t$, where γ is a parameter selected in advance. The most commonly used model has $\gamma = 1$.
21. As we explained earlier, the standard error of the regression measures the average variability of the points around the line.
22. Recall from Chapter 3 that covariance and correlation are, in general, not equivalent with dependence of random variables. Covariance and correlation measure only the strength of linear dependence between two random variables. However, in the case of a multivariate normal distribution, covariance and correlation are sufficient to represent dependence.
23. See Chapter 11 for an introduction to factor models.
24. See, for example, Chapter 17 and Appendix B in Fabozzi, Focardi, and Kolm (2006).
25. See section 3.7.2 for a definition of an exponential distribution.
26. To show this, recall that if $\tilde{\varepsilon}$ is a standard normal variable with mean 0 and standard deviation 1, and $\tilde{x}$ is a normal random variable with mean μ and standard deviation σ, we have

$$\tilde{\varepsilon} = \frac{\tilde{x} - \mu}{\sigma} \text{ (equivalently, } \tilde{x} = \sigma \cdot \tilde{\varepsilon} + \mu)$$

In the context of Property 1 of the Wiener process, we have a normal random variable $(W(t) - W(s))$ with mean 0 and standard deviation $\sqrt{t-s}$. It can be expressed through a standard normal variable $\tilde{\varepsilon}$ as $\sqrt{t-s} \cdot \tilde{\varepsilon} + 0$.

27. These differences are the actual increments of the process at different points in time.
28. To see this, recall from the properties of the standard Wiener process that the difference between the values of the process between any two points in time is distributed as a normal random variable with mean 0 and variance equal to

the time difference itself. Therefore, dW (the difference over a very small time interval dt) is distributed as a normal random variable with mean 0 and variance dt, that is,

$$dW = \varepsilon \cdot \sqrt{dt}$$

where ε is a standard normal random variable. Finding the distribution of the squared difference $(dW)^2 = \varepsilon^2 \cdot dt$ is not as easy (it is no longer normal). However, we can say something about the mean and the variance of that distribution. The variance of a standard normal variable ε equals 1, and can be expressed as $E[\varepsilon^2] - (E[\varepsilon])^2$ (see section 3.6.2 in Chapter 3). Since $E[\varepsilon] = 0$, we must have $E[\varepsilon^2] = 1$. Therefore, the expected value of $(dW)^2 = E[\varepsilon^2] \cdot dt = 1 \cdot dt = dt$.

29. The Euler scheme replaces small terms with discrete differences.

Derivative Pricing and Use

CHAPTER 13

Introduction to Derivatives

Chapters 7 through 9 introduced the concept of risk management in the context of investment management. We saw that diversification was instrumental, and that a key statistical determinant of risk management policies was the ratio between the bulk of the risk and the risk of the tails of the probability distribution of portfolio returns.

Financial firms and insurance companies have taken the concept of risk management in three different directions: (1) by recognizing that the kind of risk is an important determinant of the risk-return trade-off; (2) by engineering contracts ("derivatives") able to transfer selected portions of risk; and (3) by trading these contracts. This part of the book focuses on item (2).

Derivative instruments, or simply derivatives, are contracts that derive their value from underlying financial securities such as stocks or bonds, market indices, interest rates, currencies, or commodities. There are many applications of financial derivatives, but the two main purposes of including them in an investor's portfolio are risk management (with hedging as a special case) and return enhancement (speculation). *Risk management* refers to investment strategies whose goal is to control risk, and hedging is a special case in which the goal is to eliminate risk. *Return enhancement* or *speculation* refer to investment strategies that bet on the direction in which the underlying uncertainties will be resolved, or attempt to take advantage of perceived discrepancies in pricing to make a profit. We discuss advanced portfolio strategies that involve derivatives in Chapter 16.

Derivatives are either traded on an exchange or in the *over-the-counter* (OTC) market. In other words, there are *exchange-traded derivatives* (also referred to as *listed derivatives*) and OTC *derivatives*. OTC derivatives offer portfolio managers customized solutions to deal with an investment strategy. Exchange-traded derivatives are standardized contracts, and thus may not provide the exact strategy the investment manager needs. However, exchange-traded derivatives are guaranteed by the exchange, whereas OTC derivatives are the obligation of a nonexchange entity that is the counterparty in the contract. Thus, the user of an OTC derivative is subject to the risk that the counterparty will not fulfill its contractual obligations. This is referred to as *credit risk* or *counterparty risk*.

This chapter introduces the basic types of derivatives and explains some standard principles for pricing these derivatives. A fundamental concept underlying the construction and trading of derivatives is the concept of arbitrage, so we discuss this concept in detail in this chapter. In the next chapter, we discuss pricing derivative contracts by simulation.

13.1 BASIC TYPES OF DERIVATIVES

There are three general classes of derivatives: (1) forwards and futures, (2) options, and (3) swaps. We review each class in this section.

13.1.1 Forwards and Futures

A *forward contract* is perhaps the simplest derivative. It is an agreement to buy or sell an asset at a specific time in the future for a specific price. Forward contracts are sold in the OTC market, that is, they are nonstandard and negotiated directly between a buyer and a seller. The buyer of a forward contract assumes a *long position* in the forward contract, and agrees to buy the underlying asset at the prespecified price and date in the future. The seller of a forward contract assumes a *short position* in the contract, and agrees to sell the underlying asset at the prespecified price and date in the future. The prespecified price (or "delivery price") in the future is called the *forward price*. When the underlying is a rate such as an interest rate or a foreign exchange rate, the prespecified rate is referred to as a *forward rate*.

Forward contracts on currencies and commodities such as oil are particularly popular. For example, an American company that needs to make a payment of €1 million in six months can eliminate its exchange rate risk by buying a forward contract from a bank with settlement date six months from now for €1 million that is, by assuming a long position in a forward contract on euros at a USD/Euro forward exchange rate. The bank that holds the short position in the forward contract will have to sell €1 million in six months at the USD/Euro forward exchange rate.

Let T be the time to delivery of the forward contract, K be the forward price at which the underlying asset will be traded at time T, and S_T be the cash market price of the underlying asset at T. It is easy to see that the final payoff from a long position in a forward contract is

$$S_T - K$$

This is because if the cash market price of the underlying asset S_T is higher than the forward price K, the holder of the long position will have made a positive profit by locking in the lower price through the contract. If, on the other hand, the cash market price of the underlying asset S_T is lower than the forward price K, the holder of the long position will realize a loss by locking in the higher price for the underlying. By similar reasoning, the final payoff from a short position in a forward contract will be

$$K - S_T$$

Futures are very similar to forwards, but they are standardized contracts traded on exchanges. Associated with every futures exchange is a clearinghouse, which performs several functions. One of these functions is to guarantee that the two parties to the transaction will perform. Because of the clearinghouse, one party need not worry about the financial strength and integrity of the party taking the opposite side of the contract. After initial execution of an order, the relationship between the two parties ends. The clearinghouse interposes itself as the buyer for every sale and as the seller for every purchase. Thus, the two parties are then free to liquidate their positions without involving the other party in the original contract, and without worry that the other party may default.

When a position is first taken in a futures contract, the investor must deposit a minimum dollar amount per contract as specified by the exchange. This amount, called *initial margin*, is required as a deposit for the contract. The initial margin may be in the form of an interest-bearing security such as a Treasury bill. The initial margin is placed in an account, and the amount in this account is referred to as the *investor's equity*. As the price of the futures contract fluctuates each trading day, the value of the investor's equity in the position changes.

At the end of each trading day, the exchange determines the *settlement price* for the futures contract. The settlement price is different from the closing price, which is the price of the security in the final trade of the day (whenever that trade occurred during the day). By contrast, the settlement price is that value which the exchange considers to be representative of trading at the end of the day. The exchange uses the settlement price to mark to market the investor's position, so that any gain or loss from the position is quickly reflected in the investor's equity account.

Given that futures contracts are marked to market at the end of each trading day, they are subject to interim cash flows because additional margin may be required in the case of adverse price movements or because cash may be withdrawn in the case of favorable price movements. In contrast, a forward contract may or may not be marked to market.[1] Thus, when a forward contract is marked to market, there are interim cash flows just as with a futures contract. When a forward contract is not marked to market, then there are no interim cash flows. Because there is no clearinghouse that guarantees the performance of a counterparty in a forward contract, the parties to a forward contract are exposed to *counterparty risk*. As we explained earlier, this is not the case for futures contracts. Once a futures contract is traded between two parties, the exchange itself (or the clearinghouse associated with the exchange) becomes the counterparty to the trade. That is, neither party to the trade need be concerned with the other party to the original trade. Rather both parties are exposed to the counterparty risk of the exchange.

However, by virtue of being standardized contracts, futures contracts may not meet the precise needs of investment managers. For example, most financial futures contracts have settlement dates in March, June, September, and December. Thus, if an investment manager needs to lock in the price for the underlying asset at dates that do not coincide with the standardized settlement dates, he needs to find a futures contract with terms that are closest to the terms he would like to have.

13.1.2 Options

An *option* is a contract in which the option seller grants the option buyer the right but not the obligation to enter into a transaction with the seller to either buy or sell an underlying asset at a specified price on or before a specified date. The specified price is called the *strike price* or *exercise price*, and the specified date is called the *expiration date* or the *maturity date*. The option seller grants this right in exchange for a certain amount of money called the *option premium* or *option price*.

The option seller is also known as the *option writer*, while the option buyer is known as the *option holder*. The asset that is the subject of the option is called the *underlying*. The underlying can be an individual stock, a stock index, a bond, an interest rate, an exchange rate, or even another derivative instrument such as a futures contract. The option writer can grant the option holder one of two rights. If the right is to purchase the underlying, the option is referred to as a *call option*. If the right is to sell the underlying, the option is referred to as a *put option*.

An option can also be categorized according to when it may be exercised by the buyer, that is, by its *exercise style*. A *European option* can only be exercised at the option's expiration date. An *American option*, in contrast, can be exercised any time on or before the expiration date. An option that can be exercised before the expiration date but only on specified dates is called a *Bermuda option* or an *Atlantic option*.

Complex option contracts are referred to as *exotic options* or *exotics*. Examples of exotic options include *Asian options*, which pay the difference between the strike price and the average price of the underlying over a prespecified period, and *barrier options*, whose payoff is determined by whether the price of the underlying reaches a certain barrier over the life of the option. There is, however, virtually no limit to the possibilities for designing nonstandard derivatives.

Options, like other financial instruments, may be traded either on an organized exchange or in the OTC market. An option that is traded on an exchange is referred to as a *listed option* or an *exchange-traded option*. An option traded in the OTC market is called an *OTC option* or a *dealer option*. The advantages of a listed option are as follows. First, the exercise price and expiration date of the contract are standardized, making them more liquid (that is, easier to trade prior to the expiration date). Second, as in the case of futures contracts, the direct link between buyer and seller is severed after the trade is executed because of the interchangeability of listed options. Finally, the transactions costs are lower for listed options than for OTC options.

The higher cost of an OTC option reflects the cost of customizing the option for an investor whose investment objectives are not satisfied by the standardized listed options. While an OTC option is less liquid than a listed option, this is typically not of concern to the user of such an option. The explosive growth in OTC options suggests that portfolio managers find that these products serve an important investment purpose.

Note that, unlike in a forward or a futures contract, one party to an option contract is not obligated to transact—specifically, the option buyer has the right but not the obligation to transact. The option writer does have that obligation. In the case of a forward or futures contract, both buyer and seller are obligated to transact. Of course, at the outset of the trade a forward or a futures buyer does not pay the seller to accept the obligation, while an option buyer pays the seller the option price. Consequently, the risk/reward characteristics of option contracts are also different from those of futures and forwards. In the case of a forward or a futures contract, the buyer of the contract realizes a dollar-for-dollar gain when the price of the futures contract increases and suffers a dollar-for-dollar loss when the price of the futures contract decreases. The opposite occurs for the seller of a forward or futures contract. Because of this relationship, forward and futures contracts are said to have a *linear payoff*.

Options do not provide this symmetric risk/reward relationship. The most that the buyer of an option can lose is the option price. While the buyer of an option retains all the potential benefits from a favorable price movement of the underlying, the gain is always reduced by the amount of the option price. The maximum profit that the writer may realize is the option price; this is offset against substantial downside risk. Because of this characteristic, options are said to have a *nonlinear payoff*.

The difference in the type of payoff between futures and options is very important because market participants can use futures to protect against symmetric risk and options to protect against asymmetric risk.[2]

Exhibit 13.1 shows the payoffs of different options graphically. For comparison, the payoffs from a long and a short position in a forward contract are shown as well, in Exhibit 13.1(A) and (B).

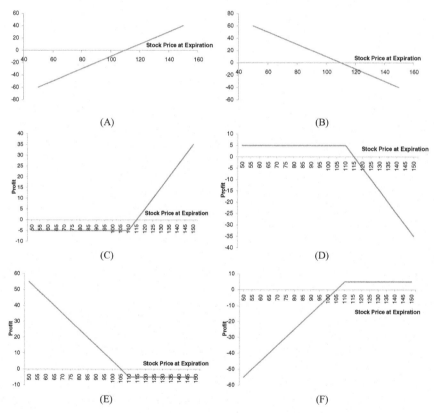

EXHIBIT 13.1 (A), (B): Payoffs of a long and a short position in a forward contract, respectively, at their expiration date. Forward price = $110. (C), (D), (E), (F): Payoffs of a call and a put option at their expiration date with assumed market price of $5.00 each. Strike price = $110.00; initial stock price = $100. (C) Long call; (D) Short call; (E) Long put; (F) Short put.

Let us explain how the payoff of the basic option contract is determined at the expiration date. We will denote the time to maturity of the option by T, the underlying asset's price at maturity by S_T, and the strike price by K.

Buying a European Call Option (Long a Call Option) A European call option gives the option holder the right to buy the underlying asset for a price K at maturity. If the market price S_T at the expiration date is lower than the strike price, the option holder will not exercise the option because it will be cheaper to buy the underlying in the market, that is, the payoff from the option will be zero, and the profit from holding the option will be $-C$, where C is the price of the call. If the market price S_T at expiration date is higher than the strike price, the option holder will exercise the option and the payoff will be $S_T - K$. Summarizing, the payoff from a European call option to the option holder is

$$\max\{S_T - K, 0\}$$

and the profit from the position is

$$\max\{S_T - K, 0\} - C$$

(See Exhibit 13.1(C).)

Selling a Call Option (Short a Call Option) A European call option obligates the option writer to buy the underlying asset for a price K at the expiration date if the option holder desires to buy it. Thus, the payoff and profit are exactly the mirror images of the payoff and profit of the call option holder. If the market price S_T at the expiration date is lower than the strike price, the option holder will not exercise the option because it will be cheaper to buy the underlying in the market. Therefore, the payoff from the option to the writer will be C, the call option price. If the market price S_T at the expiration date is higher than the strike price, the option holder will exercise the option, resulting in a payoff to the option writer will be $-(S_T - K)$ before considering the option price received. Summarizing, the payoff from a European call option to the option writer is

$$-\max\{S_T - K, 0\}$$

and the profit is

$$C - \max\{S_T - K, 0\}$$

(See Exhibit 13.1(D).)

Buying a Put Option (Long a Put Option)   A European put option gives the option holder the right to sell the underlying asset for a price K at the expiration date. If the market price S_T at the expiration date is higher than the strike price, the option holder will not exercise the option because it will be more profitable to sell the underlying in the market, that is, the payoff from the option will be zero, and the profit from holding the option will be $-P$, where P is the price paid for the put. If the market price S_T at the expiration date is lower than the strike price, the option holder will exercise the option, that is, the payoff will be $K - S_T$, before considering the cost of acquiring the option. Summarizing, the payoff from a European put option to the option holder is

$$\max\{K - S_T, 0\}$$

and the profit from the position is

$$\max\{K - S_T, 0\} - P$$

(See Exhibit 13.1(E).)

Selling a Put Option (Short a Put Option)   A European put option obligates the option writer to buy the underlying asset for a price K at the expiration date if the option holder desires to sell it. Thus, the payoff and profit of the put option writer are exactly the mirror images of the payoff and profit of the put option holder. If the market price S_T at the expiration date is higher than the strike price, the option holder will not exercise the option because it will be more profitable to sell the underlying in the market. Thus, the payoff from the option will be zero, and the profit from holding the option to the option writer will be P, where P is the price of the put. (When the market price S_T is higher than the strike price K for a European put option, we say that the option is *out-of-the-money*.) If the market price S_T at maturity is lower than the strike price, the option holder will exercise the option, that is, the payoff to the option writer will be $-(K - S_T)$. (When the market price S_T is lower than the strike price K for a European put option, we say that the option is *in-the-money*.) Summarizing, the payoff from a European put option to the option writer is

$$-\max\{K - S_T, 0\}$$

and the profit from the position is

$$P - \max\{K - S_T, 0\}$$

(See Exhibit 13.1(F).)

13.1.3 Swaps

Most generally, *swaps* are contractual agreements in which two counterparties agree to exchange returns on different assets over a prespecified period of time. There are numerous types of swaps, including equity swaps, interest rate swaps, and credit default swaps. We review some important types next.

Equity Swaps *Equity swaps* are contractual agreements between two counterparties which provide for the periodic exchange of cash flows over a specified time period. At least one of the two payments is linked to the performance of an equity index, a basket of stocks, or a single stock. In a standard or plain vanilla equity swap, one party agrees to pay the other the total return to an equity index in exchange for receiving either the total return of another asset or a fixed or floating interest rate. All payments are based on a notional amount and payments are made over a fixed time period.

Equity swap structures are very flexible, with maturities ranging from a few months to 10 years. The returns of virtually any asset can be swapped for another without incurring the transaction costs associated with trading in the cash market. Payments that are exchanged between the two parties can be denominated in any currency irrespective of the underlying equity asset and payments can be exchanged monthly, quarterly, annually, or at maturity. The equity asset can be any equity index or portfolio of stocks. An example of an equity swap is a one-year agreement in which one party agrees to pay the counterparty on a quarterly basis the total return on the S&P 500 index in exchange for receiving the London Interbank Exchange Rate (LIBOR) plus a specified spread. Both payments would be based on the notional amount of the contract. This type of equity swap is the economic equivalent of financing a long position in the S&P 500 index at a spread to LIBOR. The advantages of using the swap are no transaction costs, no sales or dividend withholding tax, and no tracking error or basis risk versus the index.[3]

The basic mechanics of equity swaps are the same regardless of the structure. However, the rules governing the exchange of payments may differ. For example, a U.S. investor who wants to diversify internationally can enter into an equity swap and, depending on the investor's investment objective, exchange payments in such a way that he is protected against currency fluctuations. If the investment objective is to reduce U.S. equity exposure and increase Japanese equity exposure, for example, an equity swap could be structured to exchange the total returns to the S&P 500 index for the total returns to the Nikkei 225 index. If, however, the investment objective is to gain access to the Japanese equity market, an equity swap can be structured to exchange LIBOR plus a spread for the total returns to the Nikkei 225 Index. The latter is an example of diversifying internationally and the cash flows can be denominated in either yen or dollars. The advantages of entering into an equity swap to obtain international diversification are that the investor exposure is devoid of tracking error, and the investor incurs no sales tax, custodial fees, withholding fees, or market impact cost associated with entering and exiting a market. This swap is the economic equivalent of being long the Nikkei 225 financed at a spread to LIBOR at a fixed exchange rate.

Interest Rate Swaps   Interest rate swaps are actually far more common than equity swaps. Different types of interest rate swaps exist, including plain vanilla (or generic) swaps, basis swaps, indexed-amortizing swaps, and callable swaps, to name a few.

In its most basic form, an interest rate swap is an agreement between two parties to exchange cash flows periodically. In a plain vanilla swap, one party pays a fixed rate of interest based on a notional amount in return for the receipt of a floating rate of interest based on the same notional amount from the counterparty. These cash flows are exchanged periodically for the life (also known as the *tenor*) of the swap. Typically, no principal is exchanged at the beginning or end of a swap.

The fixed rate on a swap is ordinarily set at a rate such that the net present value of the swap's cash flow is zero at the start of the swap contract. This type of swap is known as a *par swap*, and the fixed rate is called the *swap rate*. The difference between the swap rate and the yield on an equivalent-maturity Treasury is called the *swap spread*.

The floating rate on a swap is typically benchmarked off LIBOR or constant maturity Treasury (CMT) rate. In a plain vanilla swap, the floating rate is three-month LIBOR, which resets and pays quarterly.

Interest rate swaps can be callable or putable prior to the swap's maturity by one of the parties in the swap. They can also be part of popular interest rate options called *swaptions*. We will discuss swaptions in section 14.4.4 of the next chapter.

Credit Default Swaps   *Credit default swaps* are the simplest example of a credit derivative.[4] They are contracts in which one party (the *protection buyer*) pays a periodic premium to the counterparty (the *protection seller*) in exchange for protection against a prespecified credit event. That is, a credit default swap has a payout that is contingent upon the occurrence of a *credit event*. The documentation on credit default swaps provides a list of eight possible credit events: bankruptcy, credit event upon merger, cross acceleration, cross default, downgrade, failure to pay, repudiation/moratorium, and restructuring. *Bankruptcy* is defined as a variety of acts that are associated with bankruptcy or insolvency laws. *Failure to pay* results when a reference entity fails to make one or more required payments when due. When a reference entity breaches a covenant, it has defaulted on its obligation. When a default occurs, the obligation becomes due and payable prior to the original scheduled due date (had the reference entity not defaulted). This is referred to as an *obligation acceleration*. A reference entity may disaffirm or challenge the validity of its obligation. This is a credit event that is covered by *repudiation/moratorium*. A *restructuring* occurs when the terms of the obligation are altered so as to make the new terms less attractive to the debt holder than the original terms.

The settlement of the contract can be physical or through a cash valuation mechanism. With physical settlement, the protection buyer transfers the reference obligations, typically bonds or loans, to the protection seller. In return, the protection seller pays to the protection buyer a cash amount equal to 100% of the notional of the transaction. In the case of cash settlement, the protection seller pays to the protection buyer the difference between the notional amount of the transaction and a final value for the reference obligations. The final value is typically determined through a dealer poll. Cash settlement is less popular than physical settlement because of the wide bid-offer spread on the obligation once the reference credit is distressed.

Credit default swaps can be more complex—for example, they can be written on multiple reference obligations. In the latter case, they are referred to as *basket credit default swaps*. We will discuss credit default swaps further in the context of managing portfolio credit risk in Chapter 16.

13.2 IMPORTANT CONCEPTS FOR DERIVATIVE PRICING AND USE

In the rest of this chapter, we will review classical approaches to the valuation of some plain types of financial derivatives in order to introduce important pricing concepts and terminology. These classical methods will be contrasted with simulation methods for pricing classical and exotic derivatives in Chapter 14.

Two concepts that underlie all derivative pricing methods we will present are arbitrage and hedging. We explain their meaning next.

13.2.1 Arbitrage

Most generally, arbitrage is the opportunity to make "free money," that is, to realize a profit with no risk. Academic definitions are more technical, and generally refer to the opportunity to hold a portfolio of securities that can realize positive cash flows today or at some point in the future without realizing negative cash flows at any point in time. *Type A arbitrage* is associated with a situation in which an investor can make money immediately and never has to pay anything in the future. You can think of it as investing in a security that pays zero with certainty, but has a negative price today. *Type B arbitrage* is associated with a situation in which an investment has a nonpositive cost but a positive probability of yielding a positive payoff and no probability of yielding a negative payoff.

When an investor attempts to make money by taking advantage of a perceived arbitrage opportunity, he is said to have an *arbitrage strategy*. Originally, realizing arbitrage opportunities was all about access to the right information. Classic arbitrage involved buying a currency or a commodity in one market and selling it as close to simultaneously as possible in another market. Improved communications and increased competition have eroded meaningful profit opportunities in such traditional forms of arbitrage. Many traders, however, switched to *relative value arbitrage*, which involves watching for distortions in the price relationship between different commodities or currencies, or between them and financial derivative instruments whose payoff is based on them, using interest rates and other factors to estimate the appropriate relative values.

In this and the following chapters, we will often talk about *pricing a financial instrument by arbitrage*. A financial instrument can be either a security or a derivative. What this means is that we can construct a portfolio of other securities with observable prices that mimics the payoff of the financial instrument whose price we are trying to find. If such a *replicating portfolio* exists, then the price of the financial instrument should be equal to the cost of the replicating portfolio. If this is not the case, there will be an arbitrage opportunity. Namely, if the price of the replicating portfolio is higher than the price of the financial instrument, then investors will choose to short the replicating portfolio and buy the financial instrument (which will be cheaper relative to the replicating portfolio). This will realize an immediate positive cash flow with no future obligations, since the payoffs of the two securities will be the same. Inversely, if the price of the replicating portfolio is lower, then investors will choose to short the security and buy the replicating portfolio, again realizing riskless profit.

Typically, for pricing purposes, it is assumed that no arbitrage exists in the market, otherwise investors would have already taken advantage of the arbitrage opportunities and brought the prices of the securities involved into alignment. Obviously, this is an assumption that does not always hold in practice, and some investment managers focus explicitly on identifying and exploiting such arbitrage opportunities.

To illustrate the concept of arbitrage, let us consider a simple example. Exhibit 13.2 presents a strategy for taking advantage of a Type A arbitrage opportunity. The prices of five bonds are $102.36, $110.83, $96.94, $114.65, and $96.63. Their coupon payments at eight future dates are listed in columns underneath the prices. For example, Bond 1 has a principal value of $100, a 5% coupon rate paid semiannually, and a maturity of 2.5 years. It makes four coupon payments of $2.50, after which it pays the principal value and the last coupon payment.

Based on the output in Exhibit 13.2, consider the following portfolio:

Bond	Amount Invested
1	0
2	1,400.25
3	70.01
4	−14,927.40
5	14,999.51

The negative sign for the amount invested in Bond 4 means that this bond was shorted.

This portfolio provides a nonnegative cash flow at each coupon date ($0.00 at coupon payment dates 1, 2, 3, 4, 5, 7, and 8 and $140,025.33 at date 6), and a cash flow of $100,000 today. The cash flow today appears with a negative sign, but it is in fact a net inflow of cash generated by short selling Bond 4 (that is, borrowing it and selling it in the market) and buying the other bonds. The net cash flows at the future coupon dates consist of the positive cash flows from long bond positions and the negative cash flows for the short position in Bond 4.

To find the arbitrage strategy, we used linear programming, imposing the constraints that at each coupon payment date, the cash flow generated from coupons should be nonnegative, and we minimized the cash flow today. In this example, we arbitrarily imposed a limit of $100,000 on the cash flow today. If an arbitrage strategy exists in this situation, technically, we could make as much money as desired, since we can just invest multiples of the amounts invested here. (See this chapter's Software Hints and files **Ch13-Arbitrage.xlsx** and **Arbitrage.m** for an actual implementation.)

Of course, we ignored many issues in this example. We assumed that the bonds were infinitely divisible (that is, we could trade portions of actual issues).[5] We assumed that the bid and ask prices for the bonds were the same.[6] We also ignored transaction costs, issue size, and possible differences in the credit quality of these bonds that can account for the apparent

EXHIBIT 13.2 Five bonds that are priced in such a way that they allow for an arbitrage strategy.

	Bond 1	Bond 2	Bond 3	Bond 4	Bond 5	Cash flow today
Amounts	0.00	1,400.25	70.01	(14,927.40)	14,999.15	$(100,000.00)
Prices	$102.36	$ 110.83	$ 96.94	$ 114.65	$ 96.63	Total
$t=1$	$ 2.50	$ 5.00	$ 3.00	$ 4.00	$ 3.50	$ (0.00) $\geq$ 0
$t=2$	$ 2.50	$ 5.00	$ 3.00	$ 4.00	$ 3.50	$ (0.00) $\geq$ 0
$t=3$	$ 2.50	$ 5.00	$ 3.00	$ 4.00	$ 3.50	$ (0.00) $\geq$ 0
$t=4$	$ 2.50	$ 5.00	$ 3.00	$ 4.00	$ 3.50	$ (0.00) $\geq$ 0
$t=5$	$102.50	$ 5.00	$ 3.00	$ 4.00	$ 3.50	$ (0.00) $\geq$ 0
$t=6$	$ —	$ 105.00	$ 3.00	$ 4.00	$ 3.50	$ 140,025.33 $\geq$ 0
$t=7$	$ —	$ —	$103.00	$ 4.00	$ 3.50	$ (0.00) $\geq$ 0
$t=8$	$ —	$ —	$ —	$ 104.00	$103.50	$ (0.00) $\geq$ 0

discrepancy. These issues should be carefully considered before a strategy is actually implemented.

Sophisticated analytical models can be built to explore mispricing in baskets of assets or derivatives on multiple assets, and optimization modeling is a handy technique to help identify such opportunities. See Practice 13.2 on the companion web site for an example of using optimization to identify arbitrage opportunities in the currency markets; and see Cornuejols and Tutuncu (2007) for an example of using optimization to identify mispricing in options on the same stock with different strike prices.

A special kind of arbitrage strategies often used in practice are so-called *risk arbitrage strategies*, or *equity arbitrage strategies*. They are strategies that involve the simultaneous purchase of shares in one company and the short sale of shares in another. Such strategies are typically used in expectation of a pending announcement of a takeover by a company or a merger of two companies. By purchasing shares in the company that is expected to be taken over (with the anticipation that its market value will increase) and selling short shares in the acquiring company (with the anticipation that its market value will decrease), an investor hopes to gain from both sides of the trade.

Risk arbitrage strategies are not textbook arbitrage strategies because they do not guarantee riskless profit. The profit depends on a number of uncertain events. Simulation can be helpful for evaluating the risk of such strategies. By incorporating assumptions about the behavior of the stock prices and the likelihood that the deal goes through, an investor can obtain an estimate of the risk involved in betting on the deal.

13.2.2 Hedging

A *hedging strategy* is a trading or investment strategy that reduces risk. For example, consider an airline that will lose $1 million for every cent increase in the price of jet fuel, and gain $1 million for every cent decrease in the price of jet fuel. The airline sells tickets well in advance of the date of travel, and incurs the risk of fuel price increases. To reduce that risk, suppose that the airline buys futures on the price of jet fuel, which will guarantee that it can buy jet fuel at a particular price. If the price of jet fuel increases, the airline will lose money when it buys jet fuel but will make money on the futures because they will be more valuable.[7] So the airline will be able to offset its risk.

If there were jet fuel futures in the market with the appropriate settlement date, the airline may have been able to achieve a *perfect hedge*. A perfect hedging strategy eliminates risk completely. However, in practice, perfect hedge opportunities rarely exist. Even in cases in which one can find a counterparty to take the opposite side in a contract with the desired specifications, one incurs counterparty risk.

In the airline example, the airline would not be able to achieve a perfect hedge. Two important reasons are that, first, there are no futures on jet fuel, and second, futures contracts are traded in the market and have prespecified delivery dates that may not coincide with dates that are relevant to the airline. The airline could purchase futures on crude or heating oil with longer settlement dates than it needs. Generally, prices of jet fuel and oil go hand in hand, although they are not perfectly correlated. If the price of jet fuel goes up, the airline could sell the oil futures, which should go up in value as well, and make up for at least some of its losses. See Case 13.1 in the Practice section on the companion web site for an example of how simulation can be used to evaluate the risk of such a hedging strategy.

Who would take the opposite side in the futures contracts the airline buys? There are companies that risk incurring losses if the price of oil goes down. For example, an oil and gas company such as ExxonMobil would hedge its risk by selling futures on oil.

The hedging strategy we discussed involved a hedge that was constructed once, at the beginning. Hedging strategies can be also *dynamic*, that is, assets can be traded over the duration of time for which the hedge is needed. The celebrated Black-Scholes formula for pricing European options, which we will discuss later in this chapter, relies on such a hedging strategy to come up with the fair price of an option.

We will discuss more advanced portfolio hedging strategies in Chapter 16.

13.3 PRICING FORWARDS AND FUTURES

The classical models for pricing futures are in fact models for pricing forwards. Different adjustments can be made depending on the specific features of the contracts as well as the type of underlying asset. We will use the following notation:

- T is the time until the delivery date of the forward or futures contract (in years);
- S_0 is the cash price of the asset underlying the futures or forward contract at time 0 (today);
- F_0 is the price of the forward or futures contract at time 0 (today);
- r is the annual risk-free interest rate (with continuous compounding) for an investment maturing at the delivery date T.

The simplest forward contract is one written on an asset with no income, such as a zero-coupon bond or a stock that does not pay dividends. In this case, the forward price is given by

$$F_0 = S_0 \cdot e^{r \cdot T}$$

To see this, observe that if $F_0 > S_0 \cdot e^{r \cdot T}$, an investor can borrow S_0 at time 0 at the risk-free rate r, buy the asset, and take a short position in the forward contract. At time T, the investor can deliver the asset under the forward contract for a price of F_0, and repay the loan, which at that time is $S_0 \cdot e^{r \cdot T}$. The investor will realize a riskless positive profit $F_0 - S_0 \cdot e^{r \cdot T}$ at the settlement date, that is, there will be an arbitrage opportunity.

If the opposite holds, that is, $F_0 < S_0 \cdot e^{r \cdot T}$, an investor can take a long position in the forward contract and short the asset. By shorting the asset, the investor realizes a cash flow of S_0, which can then be invested at the risk-free rate of r for a time period T. At the delivery date, the investor can buy the asset for F_0 under the terms of the forward contract, and close out the short position in the asset. The profit realized at maturity is $S_0 \cdot e^{r \cdot T} - F_0$.

Even though we used shorting in this argument, the formula above holds also when shorting is not allowed.[8]

The formula can be generalized to include the case when the underlying asset provides an income of I during the life of the forward contract. A similar argument can be used to show that in that case, the fair forward price should be

$$F_0 = (S_0 - I) \cdot e^{r \cdot T}$$

If, instead, we know that the asset will pay a continuous dividend yield of q per annum, the formula is

$$F_0 = S_0 \cdot e^{(r-q) \cdot T}$$

These pricing formulas also apply to futures prices; however, in such cases they are only approximations. It can be shown that if the risk-free interest rate is constant during the life of the contract, and the same for all maturities, the price of a forward and a futures contract will be the same. However, when interest rates vary, which is the case in the real world, we no longer have such guarantees. For example, when interest rates increase and the price of the underlying asset is strongly positively correlated with the level of interest rates, futures prices tend to be higher than forward prices. This is because an investor who holds a long futures position gains due to the daily settlement procedure, which then allows the investor to invest the gains at a higher interest rate, whereas an investor holding a forward contract is not necessarily affected in the same way. There are also a number of factors that affect the theoretical prices of forward and futures contracts and the actual trading price, such as the interim cash flows, differences in borrowing and lending rates, taxes, transaction costs, and treatment of margins.[9] However, for futures and forward contracts with short times to delivery (up to several months), the price differences are often sufficiently small.

13.4 PRICING OPTIONS

Now let us look at the general principles of pricing options. The price of an option is made up of two components: the intrinsic value and the time premium over the intrinsic value.

The *intrinsic value* of an option is the maximum of zero and the value the option would have if exercised immediately. The intrinsic value for an American call option at any point in time t before its expiration, for example, is $\max\{S_t - K, 0\}$. When the intrinsic value of an option is positive, we say that the option is *in-the-money*. When the intrinsic value is 0, we say that the option is *out-of-the-money*.

The *time premium*, also called the *time value* of an option, is so named because of the possibility of future favorable movements in the underlying's price. It equals the amount by which the market price of the option exceeds its intrinsic value. For example, if the price of a call option with a strike price of $100 is $12 when the underlying's market price is $104, the time premium of this option is $8 ($12 minus its intrinsic value of $4). Had the underlying's market price been $95 instead of $104, then the time premium of this option would be the entire $12 because the option has no intrinsic value. All other things being equal, the time premium of an option will increase with the amount of time remaining to expiration. The time value of the option equals zero after the expiration date, or when it is optimal to exercise the option.

One can come up with bounds on the price of an option based on its intrinsic value and its time premium. It can be shown, for example, that the minimum price of an American call option at any point in time is its intrinsic value. However, for most practical purposes this is not enough. Traders and investors need a way to calculate the exact price of an option.

For a long time, practitioners did not know how to approach pricing options. It was not until the Black and Scholes option pricing model was introduced in 1973 that the tools for tackling problems of pricing options of all kinds became available. Among those tools were:

- *No-arbitrage pricing*. The idea that the only kind of pricing that can be stable is one that does not give rise to arbitrage opportunities.

■ *Perfect hedging.* The idea of creating a replicating portfolio that mimics that payoffs of the option to be priced in all states of the world.

■ *Ito's stochastic calculus.* A previously obscure tool for modeling random processes in physics that allowed for certain types of options to be priced exactly given assumptions about the random process followed by the price of underlying asset.

Basically, the idea behind deriving option pricing models is that if the payoff from owning, say, a call option can be replicated by (1) purchasing the underlying for the call option and (2) borrowing funds, then the price of the option will be (at most) the cost of creating the replicating strategy.

This section introduces the binomial method for pricing European and American equity options, as well as the Black-Scholes formula for European options. Chronologically, binomial methods appeared after the Black-Scholes model—they were suggested by Sharpe (1978), Cox, Ross, and Rubinstein (1979), and Rendleman and Bartter (1979). However, the binomial methods provide an intuitive introduction to the main ideas of option pricing, so we discuss the binomial tree method first.

13.4.1 Using Binomial Trees to Price European Options

Binomial trees are a very popular method for pricing both European and American options. In this section, we focus on European options. In section 13.4.3, we illustrate how the same concepts, together with the dynamic programming technique, can be applied for pricing American options.

A Simple One-Period Example   Suppose we would like to find the fair price of a European call option with strike price $K = \$52$ and time to maturity $T = 6$ months (0.5 years) on a stock whose current price is $50. Let us start simple. Suppose that at the end of $T = 0.5$ years the stock price can only be in one of two states: it can go up to $60, or it can go down to $42. The probability of the stock price going up is 60%. The probability of the stock price going down is 40%. The risk-free rate is 10%.

In what follows, we use the assumption that there is no arbitrage in the market to derive the price of the option. The main idea is the following. We set up a portfolio of the stock and the option in such a way that there is no uncertainty about the value of the portfolio at the end of six months. We then argue that, because there is no risk, the return the portfolio will earn should equal the risk-free rate (otherwise, there will be an arbitrage opportunity). This will enable us to work out the cost of setting up the portfolio and, therefore, the price of the option. Since there are two assets (the stock and the option) and only two possible outcomes (up or down),

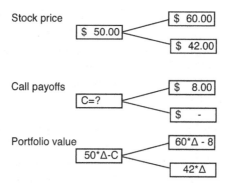

EXHIBIT 13.3 One-period binomial tree with values for the stock, payoffs for the call option, and the value of a portfolio consisting of a long position in Δ shares of stock and a short position in the option.

it is always possible to set up the riskless portfolio. While this is a simple argument, it can be extended to a more general setting in which there are infinitely many possible states for the stock price. This is the idea behind the Black-Scholes formula, which we will introduce in the next section.

Consider a portfolio that consists of a long position in Δ shares of stock and a short position in one call option. What is the value of Δ that makes the portfolio riskless?

If the stock price goes up from $50 to $60, the value of the shares is $60Δ, and the value of the call option is max{$60 – $52,0} = $8. Therefore, the total value of the portfolio is ($60Δ – $8).

If the stock price goes down from $50 to $42, then the value of the shares is $42Δ, and the value of the call option is max{$42 – $52,0} = $0. Therefore, the total value of the portfolio is $42Δ. This is illustrated in Exhibit 13.3.

In order for the portfolio to be riskless, its future value should be the same independently of the state of the world in which the stock price ends up. Therefore, we have the condition

$$\$60\Delta - \$8 = \$42\Delta$$

that is, Δ = $8/$18 = 0.4444. Therefore, a riskless portfolio would consist of a long position in 0.4444 shares of the stock, and a short position in 1 call option. The value of the portfolio is $60 · 0.4444 – $8 (or 42 · 0.4444) = $18.67 in both states of the world.

Since the portfolio is riskless, it must earn the risk-free rate of interest, 10%. Given that the portfolio value is $18.67 half a year from the current date, the present value of the portfolio can be calculated by discounting its future value, $18.67, by the risk-free rate. Therefore, the value of the portfolio today is

$$\$18.67 \cdot e^{-0.10 \cdot 0.5} = \$17.76$$

We know the value of the stock part of the portfolio today—it is the current price of the stock ($50) times the number of shares (0.44). Therefore, we can find the value of the call option (C) today. Namely, we have

$$\$50 \cdot 0.4444 \text{ (the value of the shares today)} - 1 \cdot C$$

$$= \$17.76 \text{ (the present value of the portfolio)},$$

or

$$C = \$4.46$$

By the way, notice that we never used the information about the probabilities of the stock price going up or down. In fact, all the information we needed about the stock was already incorporated into the values of the stock prices in the up and the down state. It turns out that there are different probabilities that are at play, and those are the probabilities that determine possible values for the stock price one period from now. We explain the intuition behind this fact next.

Risk-Neutral Probabilities Now let us generalize the method from the previous section. Suppose that the stock price today is S_0, and it can go up to uS_0 or down to dS_0 over a given period Δt. We would like to find the value f of an option written on the stock. Let the payoffs of the derivative in the up and the down state of the world be f_u and f_d, respectively.

We take a long position in Δ shares of stock and a short position in one call option. The portfolio values in the up and the down states are

$$(uS_0) \cdot \Delta - f_u \quad \text{and} \quad (dS_0) \cdot \Delta - f_d$$

respectively. The two portfolio values are the same when

$$(uS_0) \cdot \Delta - f_u = (dS_0) \cdot \Delta - f_d$$

that is, when

$$\Delta = \frac{f_u - f_d}{uS_0 - dS_0}$$

The above equation shows that Δ is actually the ratio of the change in the option price and the change in the stock price. We will come back to this observation in section 13.4.4.

The present value of the portfolio is

$$((uS_0) \cdot \Delta - f_u) \cdot e^{-r \cdot (\Delta t)}$$

The value of the portfolio today is also $(S_0 \cdot \Delta - f)$, therefore,

$$((uS_0) \cdot \Delta - f_u) \cdot e^{-r \cdot (\Delta t)} = (S_0 \cdot \Delta - f)$$

From here we deduce that the fair value of the option today is

$$f = S_0 \cdot \Delta - ((uS_0) \cdot \Delta - f_u) \cdot e^{-r \cdot (\Delta t)}$$

Substituting the value for Δ, we get

$$f = e^{-r \cdot (\Delta t)} \cdot (p \cdot f_u + (1 - p) \cdot f_d)$$

where

$$p = \frac{e^{r \cdot (\Delta t)} - d}{u - d}$$

The parameter p in the expression for the option price f can be viewed as a special probability. It is in fact called a *risk-neutral probability*. Note that if we use this new probability, the value of the option today equals the expected value of its future payoffs, f_u and f_d. In fact, this is the same probability that makes the value of the stock today equal to the expected value of its discounted future values when the discount rate is the risk-free rate. To see this, note that in our example in the previous section, we had

$$u = \$60/\$50 = 1.20$$

$$d = \$42/\$50 = 0.84$$

$$\Delta t = 0.5$$

$$f_u = \$8$$

$$f_d = \$0$$

$$p = \frac{e^{0.10 \cdot (0.5)} - 0.84}{1.20 - 0.84} = 0.5869$$

$$1 - p = 0.4131$$

The value of the call option today was[10]

$$C = e^{-0.10 \cdot 0.5} \cdot (0.5869 \cdot \$8 + (1 - 0.5869) \cdot \$0) = \$4.47$$

The expected value of the stock under this probability distribution today, assuming that the return on the stock is the risk-free rate, is

$$e^{-0.10 \cdot 0.5} \cdot (0.5869 \cdot \$60 + (1 - 0.5869) \cdot \$42) = \$50.00$$

which was indeed its current value.

Generalization to Multiple Periods The formula for the price of the option as an expected value of its discounted payoffs under a risk-neutral probability measure can be derived for multiple time periods. For example, if we have two time periods, we get

$$f = e^{-2r \cdot (\Delta t)} \left[p^2 \cdot f_{uu} + 2 \cdot p \cdot (1 - p) \cdot f_{ud} + (1 - p)^2 \cdot f_{dd} \right]$$

Note that the coefficients in front of the terms containing the probabilities p count how many ways there are to get to the particular end node in the tree. For example, there are two ways to get a payoff of f_{ud}: the stock price can go up first and then down (probability $p \cdot (1 - p)$), or down first and then up (probability $(1 - p) \cdot p$). So, the probability of getting a payoff of f_{ud} is $2 \cdot p \cdot (1 - p)$. To get f, the expected value of the option today, we take the weighted average of all possible future payoffs (with weights that are products of the risk-neutral probabilities), and discount it to the present.

Exhibit 13.4 shows the example of pricing the same call option as in the previous section, but over two time periods (rather than one). The parameters u, d, and p are slightly different—they are adjusted for the fact that each time period has a shorter length than the time period considered in the previous section. Now $u = 1.13$, $d = 0.88$, $p = 56.99\%$. We will explain their exact computation in section 13.4.2.

At time 0, we start with an initial stock price of $50. At time 1, we have two possible prices: $50 \cdot 1.19 = \$56.67$ and $50 \cdot 0.88 = \$44.12$. At the option's expiration date, we have three (instead of two) possible values for the underlying stock price: $64.22, $50.00, and $38.93.[11] You can imagine that as you continue to divide the time to maturity into smaller and smaller intervals, you will obtain a large number of possible stock prices at the expiration date, which will represent the possible states of the world better.

In Exhibit 13.4, we show the value of the option in the possible states of the world at time 0, 1, and 2. At time 2, we simply compute the payoffs of

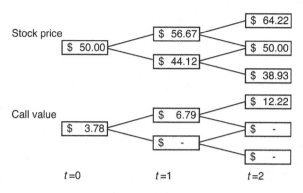

EXHIBIT 13.4   Pricing of a European call option using a two-period binomial tree.

the option. For example, the top payoff at time 2 is $12.22 = \max\{\$64.22 - \$52.00, 0\}$. We fill out the remaining two nodes at time 2 similarly. If we use the formula for the value of the option at the beginning of this section, we get the following value for the European call price:

$$C = e^{-0.10 \cdot 0.5} \cdot (0.5699^2 \cdot \$12.22 + 2 \cdot 0.5699 \cdot (1 - 0.5699) \cdot \$0$$
$$+ (1 - 0.5699)^2 \cdot \$0) = \$3.78$$

Basically, we weighted all final payoffs at time 2 by the probabilities of obtaining them, and discounted the weighted average to time 0. For example, the payoff of $12.22 was weighted by 0.5699^2 because in order to obtain it, the stock price needs to go up at time period 1, and then up again at time period 2.

Let us show how we would compute the option value at each time period. Although we do not need to do it in the case of European options, it is instructive for when we discuss American options in section 13.4.3.

The value of $6.79 obtained at time 1 in Exhibit 13.4 is the discounted expected payoff from the two nodes at time 2 that are reachable from the node at time 1:

$$\$6.79 = e^{-0.10 \cdot (0.5/2)} \cdot (0.5699 \cdot \$12.22 + (1 - 0.5699) \cdot \$0)$$

Note that the discount factor takes into consideration the fact that the time period is of length $T/2$. Similarly, we can compute the second possible value for the option at time 1. (It turns out that value is 0, since it is the expected value of two zero payoffs.)

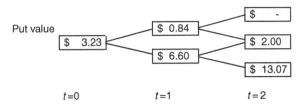

EXHIBIT 13.5 Pricing a European put option with a two-period binomial tree.

At time 0, we compute the discounted expected value of the option values at time 1, that is,

$$e^{-0.10 \cdot (0.5/2)} \cdot (0.5699 \cdot \$6.79 + (1 - 0.5699) \cdot \$0)$$

This gives us the price of the option, $3.78.

We can similarly compute the price of a put option on the same stock. The only thing we need to change is how we compute the option payoffs at time 2, which in turn changes the option values at time 0 and 1 (see Exhibit 13.5).

What if there are more time periods? Suppose there are n time periods, each of length Δt (that is, $\Delta t = T/n$, where T is the maturity of the option). Then,

$$f = e^{-n \cdot r \cdot (\Delta t)} \left[p^n \cdot f_n + \binom{n}{n-1} \cdot p^{n-1} \cdot (1-p) \cdot f_{n-1} + \cdots \right.$$
$$\left. + \binom{n}{1} \cdot p \cdot (1-p)^{n-1} \cdot f_1 + (1-p)^n \cdot f_0 \right]$$
$$= e^{-n \cdot r \cdot (\Delta t)} \left[\sum_{j=0}^{n} \binom{n}{j} \cdot p^j \cdot (1-p)^{n-j} \cdot f_j \right]$$

In the above formula, $f_j = \max(u^j d^{n-j} S_0 - K, 0)$ for a European call option, and $f_j = \max(K - u^j d^{n-j} S_0, 0)$ for a European put option ($j = 0, 1, \ldots, n$).[12]

As we mentioned earlier, even though we assume that the stock price can only take a discrete set of values, if we divide the time to maturity of the option T into many small time periods, there will be many possible values (end nodes) for the final stock price. This allows us to price the option quite accurately.

13.4.2 The Black-Scholes Formula for European Options

Instead of assuming that the future stock price can take only two values—uS_0 or dS_0—the Black-Scholes model assumes that the future stock price can take a continuous range of values with a specific probability distribution, the lognormal distribution. The Black-Scholes formulas for a European call (C) and put (P) option are as follows:

$$C = S_0 \cdot e^{-qT} \cdot \Phi(d_1) - K \cdot e^{-rT} \cdot \Phi(d_2)$$

and

$$P = K \cdot e^{-rT} \cdot \Phi(-d_2) - S_0 \cdot e^{-qT} \cdot \Phi(-d_1)$$

where

$$d_1 = \frac{\ln(S_0/K) + (r - q + \sigma^2/2) \cdot T}{\sigma \cdot \sqrt{T}}$$

$$d_2 = d_1 - \sigma \cdot \sqrt{T}$$

K is the strike price.

T is the time to maturity.

q is the percentage of stock value paid annually in dividends.

Φ denotes the cumulative probability density function for the normal distribution.[13]

To illustrate the Black-Scholes option pricing formula, assume the following values:

Current stock price $(S_0) = \$50$

Strike price $(K) = \$52$

Time remaining to expiration $(T) = 183$ days $= 0.5$ years (183 days/365, rounded)

Stock return volatility $(\sigma) = 0.25$ (25%)

Short-term risk-free interest rate $= 0.10$ (10%)

Plugging into the formula, we obtain

$$d_1 = \frac{\ln(50/52) + (0.10 - 0 + 0.25^2/2) \cdot 0.5}{0.25 \cdot \sqrt{0.5}} = 0.1502$$

$$d_2 = 0.1502 - 0.25 \cdot \sqrt{0.5} = -0.0268$$

$$\Phi(0.1502) = 0.5597$$

$$\Phi(-0.0268) = 0.4893$$

$$C = 50 \cdot 1 \cdot 0.5597 - 52 \cdot e^{-0.10 \cdot 0.5} \cdot 0.4893 = \$3.79$$

(See this chapter's Software Hints, worksheets **B-S** and **B-S VBA** in the file **Ch13-BlackScholes.xlsm**, and file **BSPrice.m** for an implementation of the formula.)

It is a good idea to check how sensitive the Black-Scholes price is to the values of different inputs. We have implemented that using Excel **Data Tables**[14] in worksheet **B-S** of file **Ch13-Pricing.xlsx**, and you can also easily create a script in MATLAB that computes the value of Black-Scholes call price for different values of one of the input parameters, such as time to expiration or volatility.

Prices of European call and put options with the parameters above, but using the Black-Scholes formula for different values of the time to maturity T and the volatility σ, are given in Exhibit 13.6.

EXHIBIT 13.6 Prices of European call and put options for different values of the time to maturity T and the volatility σ.

Time to Expiration (Years)	Call	Put		Volatility	Call	Put
0.5	$ 3.78	$3.24		10%	$ 1.69	$ 1.15
1.0	$ 6.44	$3.49		20%	$ 3.09	$ 2.54
1.5	$ 8.76	$3.51		30%	$ 4.48	$ 3.94
2.0	$10.86	$3.43		40%	$ 5.88	$ 5.33
2.5	$12.81	$3.31		50%	$ 7.26	$ 6.72
3.0	$14.63	$2.15		60%	$ 8.64	$ 8.10
3.5	$16.35	$2.99		70%	$10.10	$ 9.46
4.0	$17.97	$2.82		80%	$11.36	$10.82

It is easy to observe that both calls and puts become more valuable as the volatility of the process for the underlying price increases. Also, the call option becomes more valuable as the time to expiration increases.

While the Black-Scholes formula is still widely used in practice, it is not always well understood. It is important to realize that the formula only applies under very specific assumptions.

- *Assumption 1.* The option to be priced is a European option.

  The Black-Scholes model assumes that the call option is a European call option. It is not appropriate to use the Black-Scholes model (except as a part of approximation schemes) when derivatives with American features are priced. The binomial option pricing model, which we described in the previous section, can easily handle American call options.
- *Assumption 2.* The stock return volatility σ is constant over the life of the option and known with certainty.

  If the first part of the assumption does not hold, an option pricing model can be developed that allows the variance to change. The violation of the second part of the assumption, however, is more serious. Because the Black-Scholes model depends on the riskless hedge argument and, in turn, the stock return volatility must be known to construct the proper hedge, if the stock return volatility is uncertain, the hedge will not be riskless.
- *Assumption 3.* The risk-free rate r is constant over the life of the option, and is the same for borrowing and lending.

  The first part of the assumption is unrealistic because interest rates change daily. As we will show in section 14.1.1, the model can be made more realistic by using simulation. The second part of the assumption is unlikely to hold as well because in real-world financial markets borrowing rates are higher than lending rates. Realistically, the market price for a call option would be between the call prices derived from the Black-Scholes model using the two interest rates.
- *Assumption 4.* The stochastic process generating stock prices is a diffusion process.

  To derive an exact option pricing model, an assumption is needed about the way stock prices move. As we will show shortly, the Black-Scholes model is based on the assumption that stock prices follow a diffusion process (geometric random walk). In other words, the future stock price is assumed to be determined from the equation

$$S_T = S_0 e^{(r-q-\frac{1}{2}\sigma^2)\cdot T + \sigma\cdot\sqrt{T}\cdot\tilde{\varepsilon}}$$

where $\tilde{\varepsilon}$ is a standard normal random variable, $\tilde{\varepsilon} \sim \Phi(0,1)$. Recall that in a diffusion process, the stock price can take on any positive value, but it does not jump from one stock price to another, skipping over interim prices. The Black-Scholes formula does not apply when stock prices follow a jump process; that is, when prices are not continuous and smooth, but exhibit jumps. Merton (1973) and Cox and Ross (1979) have developed alternative option-pricing models assuming a jump process for the price of the underlying.

■ *Assumption 5.* There are no transaction costs and taxes.

The Black-Scholes model ignores taxes and transaction costs. The model can be modified to account for taxes, but the problem is that there is not just one tax rate. Transaction costs include both commissions and the bid-ask spreads for the stock and the option, as well as other costs associated with trading options.

Estimating the Parameters in the Black-Scholes Formula Most of the parameters in the Black-Scholes formula—the initial stock price, the time to maturity, the short-term risk-free interest rate—can be observed directly. The one parameter that needs to be estimated is the volatility of the underlying asset's price. Market participants determine this input into the Black-Scholes option pricing model in one of two ways: (1) by calculating the implied volatility from current option prices or (2) by calculating the standard deviation using historical daily stock returns.

Calculation of the *implied probability* relies on the fact that an option pricing model relates a given volatility estimate to a unique price for the option. If the option price is known, the same option pricing model can be used to determine the corresponding volatility. Therefore, the volatility to use in the pricing model for an option we seek to value can be *implied* from observed market prices for other options on the same stock. (See this chapter's Software Hints for the implementation of an example.)

In addition to its use as input in an option pricing model, implied volatility has other applications in strategies employing options. The most straightforward application is a comparison of implied volatility with the estimate of volatility using historical return data, which we will describe shortly. If an investor believes that the estimated volatility using historical data is a better estimate than implied volatility, then the two volatility estimates can be compared to assess whether an option is cheap or expensive. Specifically, if the estimate of volatility using historical data is higher than implied volatility, then the option is cheap; if it is less than implied volatility, then the option is expensive.

A further use for implied volatility is to compare put and call options on the same stock and with the same time to expiration. Implied volatility can also be used to compare options on the same underlying stock and time to expiration but with different strike prices. For example, suppose

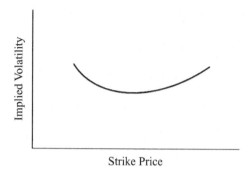

EXHIBIT 13.7 Volatility smile for
in-the-money call options.

that the implied volatility for a call option with a strike price of 90 is 8%
when a call option with a strike of 100 has an implied volatility of 12%.
Then, on a relative basis, the call option with a strike of 90 is cheaper
than the call option with a strike of 100. One fact to keep in mind for
latter application, however, is that a phenomenon called *volatility smile* is
often naturally observed in option markets. Namely, implied volatilities for
options on the same stock but with different strike prices exhibit a pattern
similar to the pattern in Exhibit 13.7. More specifically, options that are
at-the-money tend to have a lower implied volatility than options that are
out-of the-money or in-the-money. When trying to determine the "correct"
volatility to use for pricing a new option, practitioners often use a quick and
dirty approach: they interpolate between volatility values on the smile.[15]

The second method used to estimate stock return volatility is to calculate
the standard deviation of historical daily stock returns. Market practices
with respect to the number of trading days that are used to calculate the
daily standard deviation vary. The number of trading days can be as few as
10 or as many as 100. Since market participants are interested in annualized
volatility, the daily standard deviation is annualized as follows:

$$\text{Daily standard deviation} \cdot \sqrt{\text{Number of trading days in a year}}$$

Conventions about the number of trading days in a year to use vary as
well. Typically, either 250, 260, or 365 trading days are used. The first two
are used because they represent the number of actual trading days for certain
options. Given the different conventions about the number of trading days
of data to use for the estimation and the number of trading days in a year
to use for annualizing the estimated historical daily volatility, estimates of
historical volatility can vary significantly.

Whereas historical volatility estimates are backward-looking, implied volatility estimates are forward-looking, in the sense that the latter incorporate market participants' expectations about where the volatility will be. Generally, implied volatility estimates are preferred, but sometimes they are not easy to produce. Sometimes, a combination of historical and implied volatilities is used.

The Black-Scholes Option Pricing Formula and Geometric Random Walks

We will now show that the assumption that the underlying asset price follows a geometric random walk leads to the Black-Scholes formula. We will focus on deriving the formula for the price of a European call option. (The formula for the price of a European put option can be derived in a similar way.) Recall that the assumption that the stock price follows a geometric random walk means that the future stock price at time T is lognormally distributed (that is, that the log of the stock returns at time T is normally distributed).

The call value equals the discounted expected value of the call payoffs under the risk neutral probability distribution. We can write

$$C = e^{-rT} E[\max(S_T - K, 0)]$$

This expression can be rewritten as

$$C = e^{-rT} E[S_T | S_T > K] - e^{-rT} E[K | S_T > K]$$

As explained in Chapter 3, $E[. | .]$ denotes conditional expectation. For example, $E[S_T | S_T > K]$ is the expectation of the possible values for the future stock price conditional on the fact that the future stock price value is greater than the strike price K. (This is because we do not worry about the case when the stock price is less than the strike price; the payoff from the call option in the latter case is zero.)

As mentioned before, the fact that the log of the stock returns is normally distributed means that $S_T = S_0 e^{\tilde{\omega}_T}$, where $\tilde{\omega}_T$ is a normal random variable with mean $m = (r - q - 0.5 \cdot \sigma^2) \cdot T$ and standard deviation $s = \sigma \cdot \sqrt{T}$. (Note that we replaced μ, the drift of the geometric random walk for the stock price, with r, the risk-free rate. This is because we will be doing the computations in a risk-neutral world, where the rate of return for all assets is assumed to be the risk-free rate.)

Recalling the fact that an expectation is a weighted average, the expected value in the second term of the formula for the call price can be written as $K \cdot P(S_T > K)$, where "P" stands for "probability." Since $S_T = S_0 e^{\tilde{\omega}_T}$, the expectation can be written as

$$K \cdot P(S_0 e^{\tilde{\omega}_T} > K) = K \cdot P(\tilde{\omega}_T > \ln(K/S_0))$$

This expression implies that the option will be exercised only if the value of $\tilde{\omega}_T$ is greater than $\ln(K/S_0)$.

$\tilde{\omega}_T$ can be converted to a standard normal variable, $\tilde{\varepsilon}_T$, by subtracting its mean and dividing by its standard deviation.[16] Thus, the variable

$$\tilde{\varepsilon}_T = \frac{\tilde{\omega}_T - m}{s}$$

has a standard normal distribution. The cumulative normal distribution function, $\Phi(d)$, gives the probability in the left-hand tail of the distribution, that is, $P(\tilde{\varepsilon}_T < d)$. The expression $\Phi(-d)$ then gives the probability in the right-hand tail of the standard normal distribution. (Here we are using the fact that the normal distribution is symmetric.)

We can write

$$P(\tilde{\omega}_T > \ln(K/S_0)) = P\left(\tilde{\varepsilon}_T > \frac{\ln(K/S_0) - m}{s}\right)$$

$$= P\left(\tilde{\varepsilon} < -\frac{\ln(K/S_0) - m}{s}\right) = P\left(\tilde{\varepsilon} < \frac{-\ln(K/S_0) + m}{s}\right)$$

$$= P\left(\tilde{\varepsilon} < \frac{\ln(S_0/K) + (r - q - \frac{1}{2}\sigma^2)T}{\sigma\sqrt{T}}\right) = P(\tilde{\varepsilon} < d_2)$$

This is where the second term in the Black-Scholes call option pricing formula comes from. The first term can be derived similarly, but involves more complicated mathematical transformations, so we will omit it here.

Relationship between the Black-Scholes Option Pricing Formula and the Binomial Tree Pricing Model We showed in section 13.4.1 that

$$f = e^{-n \cdot r \cdot (\Delta t)} \cdot \left[\sum_{j=0}^{n} \binom{n}{j} \cdot p^j \cdot (1-p)^{n-j} \cdot f_j \right]$$

is the generalized expression for the price of a call or put option with the binomial tree model with n steps. Let us focus on the call option price. In that case,

$$f_j = \max(u^j d^{n-j} S_0 - K, 0)$$

We will show that as the number of time periods increases, the binomial option pricing formula and the Black-Scholes pricing formula produce the same option price.

We are not interested in states of the world in which the future stock price is less than the strike price (the option payoffs in those cases are zero), so we would like to eliminate them from consideration. Then, we would no longer have to deal with a clumsy formula of the kind max{.,0}, and can compute the expression for the option price in closed form. Let $a =$ minimum number of steps so that the payoff is nonnegative, that is, so that the option is in the money. We have

$$u^a d^{n-a} S_0 > K > u^{a-1} d^{n-(a-1)} S_0$$

Dividing both sides of the inequalities by $d^n S_0$, we have

$$\left(\frac{u}{d}\right)^a > \frac{K}{d^n S_0} > \left(\frac{u}{d}\right)^{a-1}$$

Taking natural logarithms of both sides, we get

$$a \cdot \ln\left(\frac{u}{d}\right) > \ln\left(\frac{K}{d^n S_0}\right) > (a-1) \cdot \ln\left(\frac{u}{d}\right)$$

This trick allows us to compute the value of a. Since

$$a > \frac{\ln\left(\frac{K}{d^n S_0}\right)}{\ln\left(\frac{u}{d}\right)} > (a-1)$$

it follows that

$$a = \left\lfloor \frac{\ln\left(\frac{K}{d^n S_0}\right)}{\ln\left(\frac{u}{d}\right)} \right\rfloor + 1$$

Here $\lfloor . \rfloor$ stands for "the largest integer less than or equal to the number inside the brackets."

Knowing a allows us to rewrite the call option pricing formula as

$$f = e^{-n \cdot r \cdot (\Delta t)} \cdot \left[\sum_{j=a}^{n} \binom{n}{j} \cdot p^j \cdot (1-p)^{n-j} \cdot (u^j d^{n-j} S_0 - K) \right]$$

which in turn can be written as

$$f = e^{-n \cdot r \cdot (\Delta t)} \cdot \left[\sum_{j=a}^{n} \binom{n}{j} \cdot p^j \cdot (1-p)^{n-j} \cdot u^j d^{n-j} S_0 \right.$$

$$\left. - \sum_{j=a}^{n} \binom{n}{j} \cdot p^j \cdot (1-p)^{n-j} \cdot K \right]$$

$$= \sum_{j=a}^{n} \binom{n}{j} \cdot \left(p \cdot u \cdot e^{-r \cdot (\Delta t)} \right)^j \cdot \left((1-p) \cdot d \cdot e^{-r \cdot (\Delta t)} \right)^{n-j} \cdot S_0$$

$$- \left[\sum_{j=a}^{n} \binom{n}{j} \cdot p^j \cdot (1-p)^{n-j} \right] \cdot K \cdot e^{-n \cdot r \cdot (\Delta t)}$$

$$= \sum_{j=a}^{n} \binom{n}{j} \cdot \left(p \cdot u \cdot e^{-r \cdot (\Delta t)} \right)^j \cdot \left(1 - p \cdot u \cdot e^{-r \cdot (\Delta t)} \right)^{n-j} \cdot S_0$$

$$- \left[\sum_{j=a}^{n} \binom{n}{j} \cdot p^j \cdot (1-p)^{n-j} \right] \cdot K \cdot e^{-n \cdot r \cdot (\Delta t)}$$

$$= S_0 \cdot \text{B}(n, a, \text{probability of success} = p \cdot u \cdot e^{-r(\Delta t)})$$

$$- K \cdot e^{-n \cdot r \cdot (\Delta t)} \cdot \text{B}(n, a, \text{probability of success} = p)$$

where B(.) stands for "1 minus the cumulative binomial probability distribution up to a."

As we illustrated in Exhibit 3.5 in section 3.4 of Chapter 3, as n becomes larger, the binomial distribution starts looking more symmetric, and approximates the normal distribution more and more closely. Therefore, for carefully selected parameters u and d, the formula derived with the binomial tree will approximate the call option price derived using the assumption of a geometric random walk (that is, the original Black-Scholes formula).

While it is reassuring to know that two popular different models for pricing European options lead to consistent estimates, one may ask why we need to work with binomial trees when the Black-Scholes expression provides such a nice closed-form formula. More complicated options and other derivatives (American options are one example) cannot be priced in closed form. So, trees are often used to come up with a set of possible values for the stock price, evaluate the possible payoffs for these types of options, and discount the payoffs to the present to obtain a fair price.

Matching Parameters   How can we make the parameters used in constructing a binomial tree consistent with the parameters used in the Black-Scholes model and at the same time, ensure that the tree will be recombining? One can derive specific formulas by so-called *moment matching*. The parameters in the binomial tree model are selected in such a way that the first and the second moment of the stock price (that is, its expected value and its variance) are the same in both models. For example, the expected stock price for the first time period on the tree is

$$(p \cdot u \cdot S_0 + (1 - p) \cdot d \cdot S_0)$$

where p and $(1 - p)$ are the risk-neutral probabilities. The expected stock price at the end of the first step if the stock price follows a geometric random walk (the assumption behind the Black-Scholes model) is

$$S_0 \cdot e^{\mu \cdot (\Delta t)}$$

(When pricing the actual option under the risk-neutral probability measure, the drift parameter μ will be replaced by the risk-free rate r.) These two expressions must be equal.

Similarly, we can come up with a condition that links the volatility in the binomial tree model and the Black-Scholes model. From these two conditions and the condition that the tree should be recombining, we can derive the following equivalency relationship:

$$u = e^{\sigma \cdot \sqrt{\Delta t}}$$

$$d = \frac{1}{u} = e^{-\sigma \cdot \sqrt{\Delta t}}$$

$$p = \frac{e^{r \cdot (\Delta t)} - d}{u - d}$$

Here, σ is the observed (implied or historical) volatility.

So, for instance, the example we gave to illustrate the Black-Scholes formula can be matched directly to the one-period and the two-period binomial trees we considered in section 13.4.1. That is also why the option prices computed with both the Black-Scholes and the binomial tree models turned out to be close. (The binomial tree with two periods gave us an estimate closer to the price of the Black-Scholes option than the single-period binomial tree. The more time periods we consider for the binomial tree, the closer the approximation will be.)

The Black-Scholes Formula and Bonds While the Black-Scholes formula is still widely used in the valuation of European options on equities, it is not as straightforward to apply it to the valuation of options on bonds. There are three assumptions underlying the Black-Scholes model that limit its use in pricing options on Treasury securities.

First, the probability distribution for the prices assumed by the Black-Scholes model permits some probability—no matter how small—that the price can take on any positive value. But in the case of a zero-coupon bond, for example, cannot take on a value above the maturity value. In the case of a coupon bond, we know that the price cannot exceed the sum of the coupon payments plus the maturity value. Thus, unlike stock prices, bond prices have a maximum value. So, any probability distribution for prices assumed by an option pricing model that permits bond prices to be higher than the maximum value could generate nonsensical option prices. The Black-Scholes model does allow bond prices to exceed the maximum bond value.

The second assumption of the Black-Scholes model is that the short-term interest rate is constant over the life of the option. Yet the price of a bond will change as interest rates change. A change in the short-term interest rate changes the rates along the yield curve. Therefore, to assume that the short-term rate will be constant is inappropriate for options where the underlying is a bond.

The third assumption is that the variance of prices is constant over the life of the option. However, as a bond moves closer to maturity, its price volatility declines. This is a fundamental mathematical property of fixed-rate coupon bonds. Therefore, the assumption that price variance is constant over the life of a bond option is inappropriate.

The most common type of bond options are options on Treasury futures. For such options, referred to as *futures options*, the option buyer has the right to establish a position in a bond futures contract (a long futures position if the case of a call futures option and a short futures position in the case of a put futures option). The model used for valuing bond futures options is the one developed by Black (1976). The Black model was initially developed for valuing European options on forward contracts. There are two problems with this model. First, the Black model does not overcome the problems just identified for the Black-Scholes model. Failing to recognize the yield curve means that there will not be a consistency between pricing Treasury futures and options on Treasury futures. Second, the Black model was developed for pricing European-exercise style options on futures contracts. Treasury futures options that are exchange traded, however, are American-exercise style options. The second problem can be overcome. The Black model was extended by Barone-Adesi and Whaley (1987) to American options on futures contracts. This is the model used by the exchange where Treasury futures options are traded, the Chicago Board of Trade, to settle the certain types of Treasury futures options. However, this model was also developed for equities and is subject to the first problem noted above. Despite its limitations, the Black model is a very popular model for pricing options on Treasury futures.

13.4.3 Pricing American Options with Binomial Trees

As we explained in section 13.1.2, American-exercise style options can be exercised at any time up to and including the expiration date. This makes pricing them more challenging because we need to model not only the possible probability distribution of underlying asset prices at the expiration date, but also the dynamics of the asset price between time 0 and the expiration date. In practice, the possible paths for the asset price between time 0 and the expiration date are discretized—that is, the option value is computed at a finite number of intermediate time periods. If the number of such time periods is large, the approximation is reasonable. In section 14.4.2, we will show how to use simulation to generate paths for the price of the underlying, and price the option using this information. Such methods have been developed relatively recently. The classical methods for pricing American options include binomial (or trinomial) trees and finite difference methods. In this section, we show the idea behind a traditional pricing method for American options: binomial trees. The main technique underlying the methodology is dynamic programming—that is, finding an optimal solution over multiple stages.[17]

To illustrate the approach, let us consider the same example as in section 13.4.1 when we discussed a two-period binomial tree for pricing a European call option. Instead of the call option, however, let us consider a put option with the same strike price. (The price of an American call option on a nondividend-paying stock is the same as the price of a European call option on the stock, so let us consider the put option in order to make the example more interesting.[18]) In Exhibit 13.8, we show the value of the American put option in the possible states of the world at time 0, 1, and 2. To compute the price of the option, we start at the last time period (that is, the expiration date), and work our way backwards.

Similarly to the case of the European option, at the last time period (time 2), we simply compute the payoffs of the option. For example, the top payoff at time 2 is $0 = \max\{\$52.00 - \$64.22, 0\}$. The idea is that if the option holder has not exercised the option before the expiration date, he will only exercise it if the intrinsic value of the option is greater than 0. In the latter case, the payoff to the option holder will be the discounted payoff of the intrinsic value.

Computing the values for the option at time 1 is not as straightforward as at time 2. At time 1, we need to determine whether to exercise the option or continue to hold it (that is, not exercise), and the payoff will depend on our decision. We will exercise if the intrinsic value of the option (that is, the immediate payoff from exercising the option) is greater than the expected value of continuing to hold it. Note that here we are dealing with

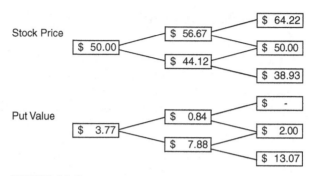

EXHIBIT 13.8 Pricing an American put option in a two-period binomial tree.

a relatively simple value function in a dynamic program: the value function is the maximum of the intrinsic value of the option, and the discounted expected payoff if we do not exercise.[19]

For example, the value of $0.84 obtained at the top node at time 1 in Exhibit 13.8 is the maximum of the discounted expected payoff from the two nodes at time 2 that are reachable from the node at time 1, and the intrinsic value of the option:

$$\$0.84 = \max\{\$52.00 - \$56.67, e^{-0.10 \cdot (0.5/2)} \cdot (0.5699 \cdot \$0.00$$
$$+ (1 - 0.5699) \cdot \$2.00)\}$$

Note that the discount factor takes into consideration the fact that the time period is of length $T/2$. It turns out that the intrinsic value of the option is negative, and less than the value of continuing to hold it, so the option holder would not choose to exercise the option at that node.

Similarly, we can compute the second possible value for the option at time 1. The computation is as follows

$$\$7.88 = \max\{\$52.00 - \$44.12, e^{-0.10 \cdot (0.5/2)} \cdot (0.5699 \cdot \$2.00$$
$$+ (1 - 0.5699) \cdot \$13.07)\}$$

In this case, it turns out that it is optimal to exercise the option. The intrinsic value is $7.88 (= $52.00 − $44.12), whereas the discounted expected payoff of continuing is

$$e^{-0.10 \cdot (0.5/2)} \cdot (0.5699 \cdot \$2.00 + (1 - 0.5699) \cdot \$13.07) = \$6.60$$

At time 0, we similarly compute the value of the option as

$$\max\{\$52.00 - \$50.00,\ e^{-0.10\cdot(0.5/2)}\cdot(0.5699\cdot\$0.84+(1-0.5699)\cdot\$7.88)\}$$

This gives us the price of the option, \$3.77. It is clear that it is not optimal to exercise at time 0—the intrinsic value of the option is \$2.00, whereas the value of continuing to hold it is \$3.77.

Exhibit 13.5 in section 13.4.1 shows that the price of the European put was \$3.23. The American put option on the same stock was more expensive—this is to be expected since the American option gives the option holder more flexibility than the European option.

The binomial tree technique for pricing American options can be extended to multiple periods. (See this chapter's Software Hints for MATLAB and VBA code for implementing the dynamic programming algorithm.) Moreover, the binomial tree model can be advanced to incorporate more than one underlying factor. However, as the number of factors grows, the dimension and the tractability of the tree become more and more problematic. For example, if we have two factors (e. g., suppose that the American option payoff depends on the performance of two stocks, rather than one), then at time 1, we have 4 nodes; at time 2, we have 9 nodes, and the number of nodes becomes larger and larger after that. Simulation techniques are useful in such applications. We will discuss one class of simulation techniques for pricing American options, regression-based methods, in section 14.4.2 of Chapter 14.

13.4.4 Measuring Sensitivities

In employing option strategies, an investor needs to know how sensitive the option price is to changes in any of the factors that determine it. Measures for the sensitivity of the option price with respect to the underlying factors are denoted by Greek letters, and are usually referred to as "the Greeks." Here, we discuss measures of the sensitivity of the option price with respect to the underlying stock, the time to expiration, and the volatility in the underlying stock price.

Delta   We have seen the importance of understanding the relationship between the option price and the price of the underlying stock in developing the option pricing model. Option traders and portfolio managers employing options to control the price risk of a portfolio need to know how the option position will change as the price of the underlying stock changes. The ratio of the change in the option price and the change in the price of the underlying is referred to as *delta* (Δ). On an intuitive level, Δ is the number of units of the stock we should hold for each option shorted in order to create a riskless hedge. (The selection of the notation Δ in section 13.4.1 was not by chance.) The option delta is formally defined as

$$\Delta = \frac{\partial f}{\partial S}$$

where f is the derivative price, and S is the price of the underlying.

Gamma   Oftentimes, it is of interest to estimate the rate of change of the option delta as the stock price changes. The ratio of the change in delta and the change in the underlying stock price is commonly referred to as *gamma* (Γ), and is formally defined as

$$\Gamma = \frac{\partial \Delta}{\partial S} = \frac{\partial^2 f}{\partial S^2}$$

Gamma can therefore be also viewed as the second derivative of the option price with respect to the price of the underlying.

Theta   All other factors remaining constant, the longer the time to expiration, the greater the option price. Because each day the option moves closer to the expiration date, the time to expiration decreases. The theta (Θ) of an option measures the change in the option price relative to the decrease in the time to expiration, or, equivalently, it is a measure of *time decay*. Formally, theta is defined as follows:

$$\Theta = \frac{\partial f}{\partial T}$$

Assuming that the price of the underlying stock does not change (which means that the intrinsic value of the option does not change), theta measures how quickly the time premium of the option changes as the option moves toward expiration. Theta is usually negative for an option (although there are exceptions) because as the time to maturity decreases, the option tends to become less valuable.

Buyers of options prefer a low theta so that the option price does not decline quickly as it moves toward the expiration date. An option writer, on the other hand, benefits from an option that has a high theta.

Vega   The option pricing models we considered so far assume that the volatility of the price of the underlying, σ, remains constant over time. In reality, this is not the case. The *vega* (V) of a derivative is the rate of change of the derivative value with respect to the volatility of the underlying stock price[20]

$$V = \frac{\partial f}{\partial \sigma}$$

If vega is high, the option value is very sensitive to small changes in the volatility of the underlying stock price.

13.5 PRICING SWAPS

As we explained in section 13.1.3, there is a wide variety of swaps. The main idea when pricing all of them, however, is that the fair value of a swap should be the difference between the present values of the expected cash flows exchanged between the two parties in the swap.

By far, the type of swaps most often used by asset managers and traders is interest rate swaps. Specifically, it is the generic interest rate swap (that is, swapping of fixed rate for floating rate interest rate payments). We discuss the pricing of a generic interest rate swap in detail in this section.

In a generic interest rate swap, the cash flows on the fixed component (that is, the fixed rate payments) are known at the inception of the swap. However, the future cash flows on the floating component are unknown since they depend on the future value of the reference rate. The future floating rates for purposes of valuing a swap are derived from forward rates that are embedded in the current yield curve.

By utilizing forward rates, a swap net cash flow can be derived throughout the life of a swap. The sum of these cash flows discounted at the corresponding forward rate for each time period is the current value of the swap. Mathematically, the value of a swap position is

$$\text{Swap value} = \sum_{t=1}^{T} PV(\text{Fixed cash flow}_t - \text{Floating cash flow}_t]$$

where $PV(x)$ denotes the present value of x, and t are the dates at which payments are made. The fair swap rate is the fixed rate that makes the swap value zero.

An alternative approach to pricing a generic interest rate swap is to view it as two simultaneous bond payments made by the two parties. Namely, think of the fixed rate payer as paying the notional amount to the floating rate payer at the termination date, and of the floating rate payer as paying the notional amount to the fixed rate payer at the termination date. This slight modification does not change the actual cash flows and value of the swap because the payments of the notional amounts cancel out at the termination date. However, it does help us imagine the stream of payments from the fixed rate payer as the value of a fixed coupon bond, and the stream of payments from the floating rate payer as the value of a floating rate bond.

Let the notional amounts be 100, and let v denote the premium (per annum) paid by the fixed rate payer. Assume that the payments happen at dates $1, 2, \ldots, T$, and that the time interval between payments is Δt. (The latter time interval is typically a quarter.)

At time 0, the value of the fixed rate bond is

$$100 \cdot v \cdot (\Delta t) \cdot \sum_{t=1}^{T} B(0, t) + 100 \cdot B(0, T)$$

where $B(0, t)$ denotes the value (at time 0) of a zero-coupon bond with a face value of 1 and maturity t. (This is because the collection of payments during the life of the swap can be thought of as a portfolio of zero-coupon bonds of face value 1 with time to maturities equal to the times of the swap payments.)

The value of the floating rate bond at time 0 is 100. To see this, note that the floating rate payer can replicate the value of the bond by investing 100 today at the current interest rate, and earning just enough interest to pay the first coupon on the floating rate bond to the fixed rate payer. Then, the floating rate payer can invest 100 again at the prevailing interest rates after the first swap payment, and earn enough interest to pay the second floating rate coupon, with 100 left over. Continuing in the same way, the floating rate payer can reinvest the 100 until the last time period, when he pays the 100 to the fixed rate payer. Therefore, the present value of the investment from the perspective of the floating rate payer is 100. From the perspective of the floating rate payer, the value of the swap today is the difference between the fixed rate payer's payments and his payments, that is,

$$100 \cdot v \cdot (\Delta t) \cdot \sum_{t=1}^{T} B(0, t) + 100 \cdot B(0, T) - 100$$

The fixed rate v that makes the value of the swap equal to zero at time 0 is the fair price of the swap at time 0. It is easy to see that the value of v should be

$$v = \frac{1 - B(0, T)}{(\Delta t) \cdot \sum_{t=1}^{T} B(0, t)}$$

The values of $B(0, t)$ can be determined from today's yield curve. (In practice, they are determined from the swap rate curve, which is a plot of swap rates against maturities in much the same manner as the bond yield curve.) They are in fact the discount factors that apply to different maturities.

SUMMARY

- Derivatives are contracts that derive their value from underlying financial securities, such as stocks, bonds, market indices, currencies, and commodities.
- There are three general classes of derivatives: (1) forwards and futures, (2) options, and (3) swaps.
- A forward contract is an agreement to buy or sell an asset at a specific time in the future for a specific price. Forward contracts are sold in the over-the-counter market, that is, they are nonstandard and are negotiated directly between a buyer and a seller.
- Futures are very similar to forwards, but they are standardized contracts traded on exchanges.
- An option is a contract in which the option seller grants the option buyer the right to enter into a transaction with the seller to either buy or sell an underlying asset at a specified price on or before a specified date. If the right is to purchase the underlying, the option is referred to as a call option. If the right is to sell the underlying, the option is referred to as a put option.
- An option can also be categorized according to when it may be exercised by the buyer. A European option can only be exercised at the option's expiration date. An American option can be exercised any time on or before the expiration date.
- More sophisticated option contracts are referred to as exotic options or exotics. Examples of exotic options include Asian options and barrier options.
- Options do not have a linear payoff, while futures and forwards do. The difference in the type of payoff between futures and options is important because market participants can use futures to protect against symmetric risk and options to protect against asymmetric risk.
- Swaps are contractual agreements in which two counterparties agree to exchange returns on different assets over a prespecified period of time.
- Arbitrage is the opportunity to make "free money," that is, to realize a profit with little or no risk of losing money in the future.
- A hedging strategy is a trading or investment strategy that reduces risk.

- The concept of no arbitrage and the idea of creating a replicating portfolio that mimics the payoff of a financial derivative provide the foundation for pricing complex financial instruments.
- Classical methods for pricing European options include binomial trees and the Black-Scholes formula. Those two methods result in similar estimates for appropriately chosen model parameters.
- The Black-Scholes formula holds under very specific conditions, and assumes that the price of the underlying asset follows a geometric random walk. It is not appropriate for use when pricing fixed income securities.
- Binomial and trinomial trees are widely used for pricing American options.
- Measures for the sensitivity of the option price with respect to underlying factors (such as the stock price, the time to maturity, and the volatility of the underlying) are denoted by Greek letters, and are usually referred to as Greeks. Such sensitivity measures include delta, gamma, theta, and vega.
- The value of a swap can be found by computing the difference between the discounted cash flows on the floating leg and the discounted cash flows on the fixed leg of the swap. The value of a swap can be also viewed as the difference between the value of a floating rate bond and a fixed rate bond.
- The fair swap rate is the fixed premium that makes the value of the swap zero.

SOFTWARE HINTS

Excel/VBA

Bond Arbitrage Using Optimization   Let us explain the bond arbitrage example implementation in section 13.2.1 of Chapter 13 in more detail. Exhibit 13.9 shows worksheet **Arbitrage** in the file **Ch13-Arbitrage.xlsx**.

Cells B4:F4 are changing cells for Solver—they store the optimal amounts to invest in each bond for the arbitrage strategy. Positive values indicate long positions, whereas negative values indicate short positions. Cell G7 is the target cell, and contains the objective function value. The formula in G7 is

```
=SUMPRODUCT(B7:F7,$B$4:$F$4)
```

This is the portfolio value at time 0. It equals the value of all short positions plus the value of all long positions. A negative value for cell G7

	A	B	C	D	E	F	G	H	I
1	Arbitrage								
2									
3	**Decision variables**	Bond 1	Bond 2	Bond 3	Bond 4	Bond 5			
4	amounts	0.00	1,400.25	70.01	(14,927.40)	14,999.51			
5									
6	**Objective function**								
7	cash flow today	$102.36	$110.83	$96.94	$114.65	$96.63	$ (100,000.00)		
8									
9	**Constraints**						Total		Required
10	*t* =1	$ 2.50	$ 5.00	$ 3.00	$ 4.00	$ 3.50	$ (0.00)	>=	0
11	*t* =2	$ 2.50	$ 5.00	$ 3.00	$ 4.00	$ 3.50	$ (0.00)	>=	0
12	*t* =3	$ 2.50	$ 5.00	$ 3.00	$ 4.00	$ 3.50	$ (0.00)	>=	0
13	*t* =4	$ 2.50	$ 5.00	$ 3.00	$ 4.00	$ 3.50	$ (0.00)	>=	0
14	*t* =5	$ 102.50	$ 5.00	$ 3.00	$ 4.00	$ 3.50	$ (0.00)	>=	0
15	*t* =6	$ -	$ 105.00	$ 3.00	$ 4.00	$ 3.50	$ 140,025.33	>=	0
16	*t* =7	$ -	$ -	$ 103.00	$ 4.00	$ 3.50	$ (0.00)	>=	0
17	*t* =8	$ -	$ -	$ -	$ 104.00	$ 103.50	$ (0.00)	>=	0
18	bound	1.00	1.00	1.00	1.00	1.00	$ (100,000.00)	>=	$ (100,000.00)

EXHIBIT 13.9 Worksheet **Arbitrage** in the file **Ch13-Arbitrage.xlsx**.

means a positive realized cash flow at time 0—this is because it indicates a higher amount in short positions than in long positions. The short positions generate a cash inflow at time 0 (after the bonds are borrowed, they are sold in the market). The long positions generate a cash outflow at time 0, when the bonds are purchased in the market.

Cells G10:G17 contain the left-hand side of the constraints on the cash flows at each future time period. These future cash flows consist of positive cash flows from coupon payments on the long positions, and negative cash flows from coupon payments on the short positions. For example, cell G10 contains the formula

```
=SUMPRODUCT(B10:F10,$B$4:$F$4)
```

If we are able to find a portfolio of bonds such that all future payments are nonnegative, but which has a negative value (that is, a positive cash flow) today, that would be an arbitrage opportunity. That is why, in the search of such an opportunity, we try to find the minimum cost portfolio (by minimizing the target cell G7) subject to the constraints that the cash flows are nonnegative at each future time period. If the optimal objective function value is positive, no such arbitrage opportunity exists.

The last row in the array of constraints, row 18, contains an artificially imposed bound just to make the problem well-behaved. We restrict the initial position not to be less than –$100,000, but it could have been any other amount consistent with our investment budget. The point is that if an arbitrage opportunity is available (that is, if all the constraints are satisfied and the optimal objective function value is negative), we may be able to

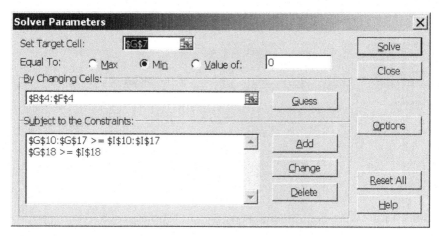

EXHIBIT 13.10 Solver dialog box for bond arbitrage problem, worksheet
Arbitrage in file **Ch13-Arbitrage.xlsx**.

drive the objective function value to negative infinity. Solver reports that as
an error and does not provide values for the changing cells. In order to figure
out the optimal investment strategy, it is a good idea to bound the value of
the objective function. If we have a larger or a smaller investment budget,
we can always change the right-hand side of the bound.

The Solver dialog box is shown in Exhibit 13.10. We also check the
Assume Linear Model option in Solver.

Implementing the Black-Scholes Formula with Excel   Worksheet B-S in
file **Ch13-BlackScholes.xlsm** contains a simple implementation in Excel
of the Black-Scholes option pricing formula for European calls and puts
(see Exhibit 13.11). Cells B3:B8, with self-explanatory descriptions, contain the inputs to the model, such as the strike price, the initial price,
the volatility, and the like. Cells B10:B13 contain other inputs for the
Black-Scholes formula. The parameter d_1 is computed in cell B10 with the
formula

```
=(LN(B3/B4)+(B6-B8+B7^2/2)*B5)/(B7*SQRT(B5))
```

The parameter d_2 is computed in cell B11 with the formula

```
=B10-B7*SQRT(B5)
```

	A	B	C	D	E	F	G	H	I	J	K	L	M
1	Black-Scholes option pricing formula						Time to expiration (years)				Volatility		
2							Call		Put			Call	Put
3	Initial price	$ 50.00						$ 3.79	$ 3.24			$ 3.79	$ 3.24
4	Strike price	$ 52.00					0.5	$ 3.78	$ 3.24		10%	$ 1.69	$ 1.15
5	Time to expiration	0.50					1.0	$ 6.44	$ 3.49		20%	$ 3.09	$ 2.54
6	Interest rate	10%					1.5	$ 8.76	$ 3.51		30%	$ 4.48	$ 3.94
7	Volatility	25%					2.0	$ 10.86	$ 3.43		40%	$ 5.88	$ 5.33
8	Dividend yield	0					2.5	$ 12.81	$ 3.31		50%	$ 7.26	$ 6.72
9							3.0	$ 14.63	$ 3.15		60%	$ 8.64	$ 8.10
10	d1	0.1502					3.5	$ 16.35	$ 2.99		70%	$ 10.01	$ 9.46
11	d2	-0.0268					4.0	$ 17.97	$ 2.82		80%	$ 11.36	$ 10.82
12	Φ(d1)	0.5597		Φ(-d1)	0.4403								
13	Φ(d2)	0.4893		Φ(-d2)	0.5107								
14													
15	Call price	$ 3.79		Put price	$ 3.24								

EXHIBIT 13.11 Calculation of call and put prices with the Black-Scholes formula in Excel.

The values for the cumulative normal distribution at d_1 and d_2, respectively, are computed in cells B12 and B13, respectively, with the formulas

```
=NORMDIST(B10,0,1,1)
```

(in cell B12) and

```
=NORMDIST(B11,0,1,1)
```

(in cell B13).

The Black-Scholes price for a European call option is computed in cell B15 with the formula

```
=B3*EXP(-B8*B5)*B12-B4*EXP(-B6*B5)*B13
```

The Black-Scholes formula for a European put option (cell E15) is implemented in a similar manner.

To determine the sensitivity of the option price with respect to different inputs, we create Excel data tables. Data tables allow one to enter a formula, point to an input in the formula, and ask Excel to create a table with the values of the formula for the different values of the prespecified input. For example, to create the data table in cells G3:I11 of worksheet **B-S**, take the following steps:

- Type the list of values you would like to substitute for the time to maturity of the option in a column (cells G4:G11).
- Type the formula you would like to have evaluated one cell above the top entry for time to maturity, and one column to the right (cell H3).

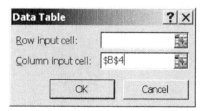

EXHIBIT 13.12 Data table dialog box.

In this case, we already have a cell (B15) with the exact formula for a European call, so we simply enter

```
=B15
```

in cell H3.

■ If there are additional formulas you would like to have evaluated based on changes in the same input (time to maturity), enter them in the same row in the columns to the right of the cell with the first formula. In this case, we wanted to evaluate also the price of a European put option, so we entered the formula for a European put option in cell I3. However, we could leave the data table with a single formula to be evaluated.

■ Select the range of cells with the changing input parameter to the left and the columns under the formulas that need to be evaluated (Cells G3:I11).

■ On the **Data** tab, in the Data Tools group, click **What-If Analysis**, and then click **Data Table**. You should see a window like the window in Exhibit 13.12. Since our data is in columns, enter the cell that contains the input to be changed (in this case, cell B4, which contains the time to expiration) under **Column input cell**. Click OK, and the data table will appear.

Implementing the Black-Scholes Formula with VBA The code for a call and a put option price (BSCallPrice and BSPutPrice) is provided in the file **Ch13-BlackScholes.xlsm**. For convenience, first we create a function dOne that computes the value of d_1 in the Black-Scholes formula.

Finding the Black-Scholes Implied Volatility with Excel Solver Worksheet B-S Implied Vol in the file **Ch13-BlackScholes.xlsm** illustrates how the implied volatility can be computed from an observed option price. (See a screenshot of the worksheet in Exhibit 13.13.) In the example in the previous

	A	B	C	D	E
1	Implied volatility for Black-Scholes option pricing formula				
2					
3	Initial price	$ 50.00			
4	Strike price	$ 52.00			
5	Time to expiration	0.50			
6	Interest rate	10%			
7	Volatility	35.00%			
8	Dividend yield	0			
9					
10	d1	0.1680			
11	d2	-0.0799			
12	Φ(d1)	0.5667		Φ(-d1)	0.4333
13	Φ(d2)	0.4682		Φ(-d2)	0.5318
14					
15	Call price (B-S)	$ 5.18		Put price (B-S)	$ 4.64
16	Observed call price	$ 5.18		Observed put price	

EXHIBIT 13.13 Worksheet B-S Implied Vol in the file Ch13-BlackScholes.xlsm.

section, we found that the price of a call option with the input parameters in Exhibit 13.13 should be $3.79. Now suppose that we have observed a market price of $5.18 for the option. What is the implied value of the volatility that will make the price of the option in the spreadsheet consistent with market prices?

We can use Excel's Solver to find that out. One of the options in Excel Solver is to find the value of a changing cell so that the target cell equals a specific value, instead of minimizing or maximizing, which is how we used Solver in previous applications. We fill out the Solver dialog box as shown in Exhibit 13.14. Namely, we set the target cell to be the cell that contains the Black-Scholes formula for the price of a European call option, and we ask Solver to set that cell's value to 4.20 by changing the cell that stores the value for the volatility (B7).

After clicking on **Solve**, Solver fills cells B15 and B17 with the best values it found. It turns out that the implied volatility in this case is 35.00%. You can use the same method to find the implied volatility from put prices. For practice, fill out columns D and E of the worksheet and change the inputs to Solver to find the implied volatility if the observed market put price is $3.63.

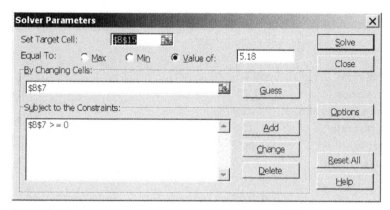

EXHIBIT 13.14   Solver dialog box for the implied volatility example.

Finding the Black-Scholes Implied Volatility with VBA   The file Ch13-BlackScholes.xlsm contains VBA code (the function BSImpliedVol) for computing the implied volatility with Excel VBA. This is a brute-force rather than an optimization approach, in which we start with a low and a high estimate for the volatility (0 and 1, respectively), and we tune it until we get an option price that is close to the observed market price and is within a certain tolerance band.

American Option Pricing with the Binomial Method   The VBA code saved as the function AmericanPutBin in a module in file Ch13-BinomialTrees.xlsm computes the price of an American put option using a binomial tree with numSteps time periods. We use two arrays—OptionValueCurrent and OptionValueNext—to store the option values at the current time period and one time period ahead. We resize the arrays periodically with the command ReDim so that they equal the number of nodes at the corresponding time period. At every step, we fill the OptionValueCurrent array with the current value of the option at each node as a maximum of the intrinsic value and the value of continuing, using the information about the current price (computed as initial price times a given number of up moves and a given number of down moves) and the expected payoffs from the next time period (stored in the array OptionValueNext). Once we have computed these values, the array OptionValueCurrent becomes OptionValueNext, and we proceed backwards in the same fashion, calculating the OptionValueCurrent array for the previous time period.

At the bottom of worksheet **American** in the file **Ch13-BinomialTrees.xlsm**, cell B33, we call the VBA function with the formula

```
=AmericanPutBin(B3,B4,B5,B6,B7,2)
```

(Here we used the input data for the two-period binomial tree on the same worksheet.) The value returned by the function is $3.77—the same price we computed manually from the tree in the spreadsheet.

MATLAB

Bond Arbitrage Using Optimization   The arbitrage example from section 13.2.1 can be repeated in MATLAB with the code provided in the file **Arbitrage.m**.

We use the function `linprog` because the optimization problem is linear. Note that since `linprog` assumes that the inequalities in the constraints are of the kind $Ax \leq b$, we create a matrix A that is the negative of the matrix of coupon cash flows, and a right-hand-side vector b that is the negative of the right-hand side in the Excel file.

Since MATLAB can find a solution to this problem, there is a potential arbitrage opportunity.

Implementing the Black-Scholes Formula   The function `BSPrice` in the file **BSPrice.m** computes the price of a call and a put option with the Black-Scholes formula.

Finding the Black-Scholes Implied Volatility   MATLAB's Financial Toolbox has a built-in function (`blsimpv`) for finding the implied volatility of the underlying stock price from the price of a given call (or put) option, assuming that the option price is derived from the Black-Scholes model.

The function can be implemented also without the Financial Toolbox. We can use a brute force approach, in which we start with a low and a high estimate for the volatility (0 and 1, respectively), and we tune it until we get an option price that is close to the observed market price and is within a certain tolerance band. Alternatively, if you have the Optimization Toolbox, you can use the `fzero` function in MATLAB to compute an estimate in a more optimal way.

The file **BSImpliedVol.m** implements the brute force approach.

American Option Pricing with the Binomial Method   The function available in the file **AmericanPutBin.m** computes the price of an American put option with the binomial tree method. We use two arrays—OptionValueCurrent and OptionValueNext—to store the option values at the current time period and one time period ahead. At every step, we fill the OptionValueCurrent array with the current value of the option at each node as a maximum of the intrinsic value and the value of continuing, using the information about the current price (computed as initial price times a given number of up moves and a given number of down moves) and the expected payoffs from the next time period (stored in the array OptionValueNext). Once we have computed these values, the array OptionValueCurrent becomes Option-ValueNext, and we proceed backwards in the same fashion, calculating the OptionValueCurrent array for the previous time period. Note that, in contrast to VBA, indices in arrays in MATLAB cannot be zero.

NOTES

1. When the counterparties are two high-credit-quality entities, the two parties may agree not to mark positions to market. However, if one or both of the parties are concerned with the counterparty risk of the other, then positions may be marked to market.
2. This statement will become clearer when we discuss risk management strategies with derivatives in Chapter 16.
3. We will explain basis risk in more detail in Chapter 16.
4. As the name implies, *credit derivatives* are contracts whose payoff depends on the credit worthiness of the underlying asset.
5. This issue can be fixed by restricting the amounts to be invested in the bonds to be integers. For computational issues with integer programming, see section 5.2.5 of Chapter 5.
6. See Practice 13.1 on the companion web site for an example in which the bid and ask prices are different.
7. Note that since we are talking about futures contracts, no physical delivery of jet fuel would actually take place. Instead, the futures contracts will be traded or settled in cash (at the delivery date).
8. See Hull (2008).
9. For more details, see Fabozzi (2009).
10. There is a one-cent difference with the previous estimate due to rounding error.
11. We have three final nodes because we built the binomial tree to be *recombining*. This keeps the dimension of the problem manageable. With a recombining tree, we have $t + 1$ nodes at time t. With a nonrecombining tree, we have 2^t nodes at time t. Thus, with a nonrecombining tree the number of nodes quickly becomes unmanageable.
12. As we saw in Chapter 3, the numbers $\binom{n}{k}$ (pronounced "n choose k") are the *binomial coefficients*. They count how many ways there are to choose k objects out of n. (In the particular context of option pricing, they count how many ways

there are to get k "up" moves of the stock price out of n possible moves.) These coefficients appear in the formula for the binomial probability distribution. (Recall from section 3.3 of Chapter 3 that the binomial distribution associates a probability with k successes out of n trials, and the probability is computed exactly in the same way as in the option pricing formula above.)

13. As explained previously in this book, the value for $\Phi(d)$ can be found with the formula =NORMDIST(d,0,1,1) in Excel, and normcdf(d,0,1) in MATLAB.

14. Data tables are a very useful tool in Excel. They allow one to reference a formula, and compute the values of the formula for different input values of one of the arguments in the formula. See this chapter's Software Hints for an implementation in the context of computing the price of a call and a put option with the Black-Scholes formula.

15. Note that if the Black-Scholes model truly applied to markets, the volatility smile phenomenon should not be observed. The fact that it exists implies that practitioners do not believe that the lognormal probability distribution for stock prices correctly represents extreme events. In the real world, extreme events (events that happen in the tails of the distribution) are more likely than the lognormal distribution would imply.

16. See section 3.4 of Chapter 3.

17. See sections 5.6 and 6.1 of Chapters 5 and 6, respectively, for an introduction to dynamic programming.

18. The price of an American call option in the two-period binomial tree example is computed in worksheet **American** in the file **Ch13-BinomialTrees.xlsm**. You can observe that the price of the American call is the same as the price of the European call. This is not a coincidence. The price of an American call option on a nondividend-paying stock is the same as the price of a European call option on the stock because it is never optimal to exercise early, that is, one would never take advantage of the early exercise feature of the American call option. There are a couple of reasons for this, one of which is the time value of money—from the perspective of the option holder, the later the strike price is paid out, the better. See Hull (2008) for a detailed explanation.

19. See section 6.1 of Chapter 6 for a definition and examples of value function in dynamic programming.

20. Even though *vega* is the term used in the context of option "Greeks," there is no actual letter vega in the Greek alphabet.

CHAPTER 14

Pricing Derivatives by Simulation

In Chapter 13, we introduced the main ideas behind the pricing of standard financial derivative instruments, or simply derivatives. We saw that the main assumption underlying derivative pricing schemes is the assumption that there is no arbitrage in the markets. When there is no arbitrage, the price of a derivative can be found as the expected value of its discounted payouts when the expected value is taken with respect to a transformation of the original probability distribution of outcomes, called the risk-neutral probability measure.

The same principles that guide the computation of the fair price of standard derivatives extend to the pricing of more complex derivatives. However, the difference is that nice closed-form formulas of the Black-Scholes type cannot necessarily be found for complex derivatives. Such derivatives must be priced with different numerical techniques, and simulation is one such tool.

We begin this chapter by showing how simulation can be used to price some of the simple derivatives we discussed in Chapter 13, such as European call options. Although simulation does not need to be applied in this context, techniques that make the simulation procedures more efficient can be demonstrated in a familiar setting, and benchmarked against a known final price. These examples help us illustrate more advanced simulation techniques, called variance reduction methods, whose goal is to make the simulation process as efficient as possible, and minimize the variance of the estimate. We review several such methods, including antithetic variables, stratified sampling, importance sampling, and control variates. We also review quasirandom (also called quasi–Monte Carlo) methods for simulation that use low discrepancy number sequences to obtain a good representation for the probability distribution being simulated. We then give examples of pricing more complex derivatives, such as barrier options and American options, by simulation, and discuss evaluating the sensitivity of derivative to changes in underlying parameters by crude and pathwise simulation methods.

14.1 COMPUTING OPTION PRICES WITH CRUDE MONTE CARLO SIMULATION

As we mentioned at the beginning of this chapter, the main idea behind computing prices of options (and other financial securities) by simulation is to generate a set of payoffs, and discount them to the present to find the expected value of all discounted payoffs under a probability distribution called the risk-neutral probability measure. The expected value of payoffs is the "fair" price of the derivative. Typically, when pricing financial derivatives, the prices of the underlying securities are assumed to follow specific kinds of random walks.[1] The most straightforward way to price a derivative is to create paths of realizations of the random walks for the derivative's underlying, compute the payoff along each path, discount to the present, and find the appropriate weighted average of the payoffs as an estimator for the expected value of the payoff. This is referred to as using *crude Monte Carlo*. It is not always the most efficient way to find a derivative's price, but it is tangible and easy to implement.

In this section, we give a couple of examples of how crude Monte Carlo can be used for pricing options. Smart ways to simulate the prices of options that exploit knowledge about the simulation process or the underlying distributions are discussed in section 14.2.

14.1.1 Pricing a European Call Option by Simulation

As we explained in section 13.4.2, a widely used formula for European options is the Black-Scholes formula.[2] It provides a closed-form expression for computing the price of the option. In section 13.4.2, we also showed that the underlying assumption used in the derivation of the Black-Scholes formula is that the underlying asset price follows a geometric Brownian motion.[3] The evolution of the asset price can then be described by the equation

$$dS_t = \mu S_t \, dt + \sigma S_t \, dW_t$$

where W_t is standard Brownian motion and μ and σ are the drift and the volatility of the process, respectively. For technical reasons (absence of arbitrage), when pricing an option, the drift μ is replaced by the risk-free rate r in the Black-Scholes formula.

Under the assumption for the random process followed by the asset price, the value of the asset price S_T at time T given the asset price S_t at time t can be computed as

$$S_T = S_t \, e^{(r - \frac{1}{2}\sigma^2)\cdot(T-t) + \sigma \cdot \sqrt{(T-t)}\cdot\tilde{\varepsilon}}$$

where $\tilde{\varepsilon}$ is a standard normal random variable.[4]

Hence, the option price obtained from the Black-Scholes formula can be approximated by simulation if a large number of values for the normal random variable $\tilde{\varepsilon}_t$ are generated. By creating scenarios for the stock price S_T at time T, we can compute the discounted payoffs of the option, and find the expected payoff. Suppose we generate N scenarios for $\tilde{\varepsilon}$: $\varepsilon^{(1)}, \ldots, \varepsilon^{(N)}$. Then the price of a European call option with strike price K will be

$$C_t = e^{-r\cdot(T-t)} \cdot \sum_{n=1}^{N} \frac{1}{N} \cdot \max\left\{ S_t \, e^{(r - \frac{1}{2}\sigma^2)\cdot(T-t) + \sigma \cdot \sqrt{(T-t)}\cdot\varepsilon^{(n)}} - K, 0 \right\}$$

The expression above is the expected value of the option payoffs, that is, the weighted average of the option payoffs. The "weight," or the probability of each scenario, is assumed to be $1/N$ since the scenarios are picked at random, and the frequency of their occurrence already incorporates the probability distribution of $\tilde{\varepsilon}$. (See this chapter's Software Hints, as well as files **Ch14-PricingBySimulation.xlsx, Ch14-OptionPricingVBA.xlsm,** and **EuropeanCall.m,** for an actual implementation of the simulation.)

It appears unnecessarily complicated to price the option this way, and indeed, in practice simulation is rarely used for this kind of simple problem. There are more complex derivatives and more sophisticated models for asset price behavior; in such cases, it can be simpler to generate scenarios and evaluate prices by simulation than to derive closed-form analytical formulas mathematically. For example, if the underlying asset follows a mean reversion process, the Black-Scholes formula will not work for a European call option, but simulation can help us evaluate the option price easily. In addition, in the case of portfolios and baskets of multiple assets, generating joint scenarios for multiple securities through simulation can help capture the otherwise complicated effect of interactions among different risk factors influencing the future value of the portfolio or derivatives.

Let us illustrate another advantage of simulating the price of a European call option rather than using the Black-Scholes formula. Recall that one of the assumptions in the Black-Scholes formula is that the interest rate r

remains constant during the life of the option, which is a limitation of the model. Simulation makes it easy to calibrate model parameters to observed market factors and to incorporate additional layers of modeling complexity. For example, suppose that at time 0 we observe a term structure[5] of zero-coupon bond prices $B(0, 1), \ldots, B(0, T)$ that is not necessarily consistent with a single interest rate r. In other words, we cannot find a short rate r such that

$$B(0, t) = e^{-r \cdot t}$$

for all intermediate time periods t. It would be difficult to correct for this in a closed-form formula such as the Black-Scholes formula. However, the correction can be easily implemented in the simulation: we only need to simulate future asset prices at each step as

$$S_{t+1} = S_t \cdot \frac{B(0, t)}{B(0, t + 1)} \cdot e^{-\frac{1}{2} \cdot \sigma^2 \cdot 1 + \sigma \cdot \sqrt{1} \cdot \tilde{\varepsilon}_t}$$

(See also Practice 14.3 on the companion web site for European call option pricing with simulation when interest rates are assumed to follow a mean reverting process.)

Similarly, if we have information about a collection of observed forward prices[6] $F(0, t), \ldots, F(0, T)$ on the underlying asset, we can obtain a more accurate representation of the possible scenarios in the simulation by using the formula

$$S_{t+1} = S_t \cdot \frac{F(0, t + 1)}{F(0, t)} \cdot e^{-\frac{1}{2} \cdot \sigma^2 \cdot 1 + \sigma \cdot \sqrt{1} \cdot \tilde{\varepsilon}_t}$$

The complexity of the simulation model can be increased further by incorporating random walk models for the volatility σ. The simulation technique therefore offers a great range of modeling capabilities. The need for such a technique will hopefully become more evident also in the Asian option pricing example in the next section.

14.1.2 Pricing an Asian Option by Simulation

As we mentioned in section 13.1.2, an Asian option is a contract whose value is determined by the average price of the underlying asset either continuously over the option's time to maturity or at a prespecified set of monitoring dates $t_1, \ldots, t_T$. In particular, the payoff of an Asian call option is

$$V_T = \max \left\{ S_{\text{average}} - K, 0 \right\}$$

The average is usually defined as the arithmetic average, that is, as

$$\frac{S_1 + \cdots + S_T}{T}$$

where T is the number of discrete time periods until the option's expiration date. The specific characteristics of an Asian option vary depending on how the average price is calculated (instead of the arithmetic average, it could be the geometric average[7]), whether there are early exercise features (in which case the average of the underlying asset price over the life of the option so far is calculated), and whether the option is a put or a call.

To find the value of an Asian option, we need information not only on the value of the asset at the expiration date (time T), but also on the possible paths the asset could take to reach its terminal value. This is referred to as *path dependency*, and is one of the situations in which simulation is particularly useful.

If the underlying asset price S is assumed to follow a geometric random walk, and if the average is computed as a geometric rather than arithmetic average, there are analytical formulas for pricing continuous Asian options.[8] However, there are no exact formulas in the case of an arithmetic average Asian call option with discrete monitoring dates or different assumptions on the process followed by the asset price.

Pricing the option is rather straightforward if we use crude Monte Carlo simulation. We simulate possible paths for the underlying asset price. Let $S_{t_i}(j)$ be the simulated asset price at time t_i, $i = 1, \ldots, T$, for path n, $n = 1, \ldots, N$. For example, if the underlying asset price S is assumed to follow a geometric random walk, then the asset price at time t_1 can be simulated given the asset price at time 0 as

$$S_{t_1} = S_0 e^{(r - \frac{1}{2}\sigma^2) \cdot (t_1 - 0) + \sigma \cdot \sqrt{(t_1 - 0)} \cdot \tilde{\varepsilon}_0}$$

where, as defined earlier, $\tilde{\varepsilon}_0$ is a random variable following a normal distribution with mean 0 and standard deviation 1 (the subscript "0" stands for the fact that this realization of $\tilde{\varepsilon}_0$ is for the time period $(0, t_1)$). Having generated a realization of S_{t_1}, we simulate a possible value for S_{t_2} by using the formula

$$S_{t_2} = S_{t_1} e^{(\mu - \frac{1}{2}\sigma^2) \cdot (t_2 - t_1) + \sigma \cdot \sqrt{(t_2 - t_1)} \cdot \tilde{\varepsilon}_1}$$

and generating a realization of the normal random variable $\tilde{\varepsilon}_1$. After repeating this T times, we have generated a path for the asset price. Averaging the (properly discounted) option payoff over N paths produces the fair price of the Asian option. (See this chapter's Software Hints and files **Ch14-PricingBySimulation.xlsx, Ch14-OptionPricingVBA.xlsm** and **ArithmeticAsianCall.m** for an implementation of an example.) There are more efficient ways to estimate the price of an arithmetic average Asian option. (We will discuss one such method in section 14.2.4.)

14.2 VARIANCE REDUCTION TECHNIQUES

As we explained in section 4.4 of Chapter 4, paradoxically, truly random numbers can be too random for practical purposes. Recall that the error in the average estimate obtained from "truly random" Monte Carlo simulation is proportional to $1/\sqrt{N}$, where N is the number of scenarios for the random variable (this fact would be approximately true for good pseudorandom number generators as well).[9] In order to make the estimate of a European call option price twice as accurate, for example, we would have to increase the number of generated scenarios for the underlying asset price four times. Much research has been dedicated in recent years to finding ways to reduce that error and to be computationally savvy when generating scenarios. Techniques for increasing the accuracy of the estimate from simulation are often referred to as *variance reduction methods* because their goal is to reduce the variability of the estimator. Stratified sampling, which we discussed in section 4.4.5, is one such method. In this section, we define and provide intuition for several variance reduction methods that are widely used in financial applications. There are numerous ways to achieve computational efficiency in specific situations, and we will not be able to review all here. For a detailed introduction to other advanced variance reduction techniques, see Glasserman (2004), Brandimarte (2006), and McLeish (2005).

14.2.1 Antithetic Variables

Simulating a random number is computationally expensive. One technique that is used to reduce the error in the average estimate in derivative pricing without increasing the number of simulated values is to incorporate the generated random number twice in computing the derivative payoff: once as the original simulated number, and another as its "antithetic" number.

For example, recall from our option pricing example in section 14.1 that the value of the stock price S_T at time T can be computed from the equation for a geometric random walk. In that expression, $\tilde{\varepsilon}$ is a random variable that follows a standard normal distribution. Suppose that N values for the normal random variable $\tilde{\varepsilon}$ are generated. With the antithetic variable method, the value of the derivative payoff in each of the N scenarios is computed as the average of two payoffs: one obtained by plugging in the simulated value for $\tilde{\varepsilon}$, and another obtained by plugging in the negative of the simulated value for $\tilde{\varepsilon}$. These N "adjusted" payoffs are otherwise treated in the same way as in the traditional simulation method described earlier in this chapter: at the end, the N payoffs are averaged and properly discounted to obtain the fair estimate of the derivative price. The difference is that this approach substantially reduces the standard error in the average estimate, while keeping the number of simulation trials at N.

The antithetic variable approach does not apply only to normal random variables. As explained in section 4.4.1 of Chapter 4, random number generation from an arbitrary probability distribution is often done by the inverse transform method, that is, a random number is generated in two stages. At the first stage, a uniform random number U between 0 and 1 is simulated. At the second stage, this random number is "inverted" to obtain a random number from the desired probability distribution. Thus, we can apply the antithetic technique at the first stage, and treat the randomly generated number U as two realizations: U and its "antithetic" number $1-U$. For example, if the number generated on the interval $[0,1]$ is 0.7, then the antithetic number is 0.3. Both of these numbers can then be "inverted" to obtain a pair of antithetic variables from a prespecified distribution such as the normal distribution.

It is important to realize, however, that antithetic sampling is not a cure-all. In some cases, the variance of the estimator of the expected price may actually increase if we use antithetic sampling. Basically, for the antithetic approach to work successfully, the payoffs generated with the antithetic variables must have a negative correlation. Specifically, the antithetic variables approach relies on generating two sets of N realizations each of a random variable simultaneously:

$$\varepsilon_1^{(1)}, \ldots, \varepsilon_1^{(N)}$$

and

$$\varepsilon_2^{(1)}, \ldots, \varepsilon_2^{(N)}$$

In the example of the European call option, we had $\varepsilon_2^{(n)} = -\varepsilon_1^{(n)}$, $n = 1, \ldots, N$, which was a cheap way to produce another realization of the random variable given a generated observation $\varepsilon_1^{(n)}$. The "vertical" dependencies between the sets of observations were perfectly negatively correlated, that is, each $\varepsilon_1^{(n)}$ was perfectly negatively correlated with $\varepsilon_2^{(n)} = -\varepsilon_1^{(n)}$, and that fortunately meant also that the resulting option payoffs ended up negatively correlated.

We produced a new sample of payoffs based on pairwise averages of the payoffs corresponding to each of the two samples of realizations for $\tilde{\varepsilon}$,

$$pf^{(1)} = \frac{pf_1^{(1)} + pf_2^{(1)}}{2}, \ldots, pf^{(N)} = \frac{pf_1^{(N)} + pf_2^{(N)}}{2}$$

Since the original observations for $\tilde{\varepsilon}$ were "horizontally" independent (we drew an independent and identically distributed [IID] sample $\varepsilon_1^{(1)}, \ldots, \varepsilon_1^{(N)}$), the pairwise averaged observations $pf^{(1)}, \ldots, pf^{(N)}$ are also IID. The variance of the average of the new sample of observations $pf^{(1)}, \ldots, pf^{(N)}$ is

$$\text{Var}(\overline{pf}) = \text{Var}\left(\frac{pf^{(1)} + \cdots + pf^{(N)}}{N}\right)$$

$$= \frac{1}{N^2} \cdot \left[N \cdot \text{Var}\left(pf^{(n)}\right)\right]$$

$$= \frac{1}{N} \cdot \text{Var}\left(\frac{pf_1^{(n)} + pf_2^{(n)}}{2}\right)$$

$$= \frac{1}{4N} \cdot \left(\text{Var}(pf_1^{(n)}) + \text{Var}(pf_2^{(n)}) + 2 \cdot \text{Covar}(pf_1^{(n)}, pf_2^{(n)})\right)$$

$$= \frac{1}{2N} \cdot \text{Var}(pf_1^{(n)}) + \frac{1}{2N} \cdot \text{Covar}(pf_1^{(n)}, pf_2^{(n)})$$

$$= \frac{1}{2N} \cdot \text{Var}(pf_1^{(n)}) + \frac{1}{2N} \cdot \underbrace{\sigma_{pf_1^{(n)}} \cdot \sigma_{pf_2^{(n)}}}_{\text{Var}(pf_1^{(n)})} \cdot \rho(pf_1^{(n)}, pf_2^{(n)})$$

$$= \frac{\text{Var}(pf_1^{(n)})}{2N} \cdot \left(1 + \rho(pf_1^{(n)}, pf_2^{(n)})\right)$$

If we did not generate N regular and N antithetic variables, but instead simply took a sample of $2 \cdot N$ IID random variables, the variance of the estimate of the average payoff would have been

$$\frac{\text{Var}(pf_1^{(n)})}{2N}$$

Thus, to reduce the variance of the average estimator $\text{Var}(\overline{pf})$, we would ideally want the correlation $\rho(pf_1^{(n)}, pf_2^{(n)})$ to be less than zero. This was true in the case of European option payoffs; however, there are some cases for which this will not happen:

■ *The payoffs are not monotonic functions of the random variables.* In the case of the European call option simulation, the formula for the payoff had the random variable $\tilde{\varepsilon}$ in the power of the exponential, and the exponential function is a monotonic function—it increases as its exponent increases. Imagine, however, a payoff function that increases and then decreases with the values of the random variable, so that U and $1-U$ generate the same value for the payoff. In this case, the antithetic variables method actually backfires, resulting in increased variance because the correlation between $pf_1^{(n)}$, $pf_2^{(n)}$ is 1. Therefore, the payoffs for some derivatives may not end up negatively correlated even if the antithetic variables based on the uniform random numbers U and $1-U$ are negatively correlated. An example of a payoff function that is nonmonotonic is that of a butterfly spread. (See Practice 14.4 on the companion web site.)

■ *The generated random variables and their antithetic variables are not negatively correlated.* We assumed that we would use the inverse transform method to generate the random numbers and the antithetic random numbers. However, as we mentioned in section 4.4.1, other simulation methods, such as the acceptance-rejection method and the Box-Muller method are used as well. The inverse transform method uses a monotonic function—the cumulative distribution function—to produce random variable realizations from different distributions based on the realization of the uniform random numbers U and $1-U$. With the acceptance-rejection method and the Box-Muller method, we no longer have the same guarantees.

14.2.2 Stratified Sampling

In section 4.4.5 of Chapter 4, we introduced stratified sampling as a technique that allows us to create a representative sample of the entire range of outcomes. Variations of stratified sampling are already incorporated in many random number generator software products, so it is not always necessary to implement the algorithm manually. For example, as we mentioned in section 4.4.5, an enhanced version of stratified sampling, Latin Hypercube Sampling, is the default option for simulation with @RISK.

Nevertheless, it is instructive to see a specific, relatively simple example of how stratified sampling would be implemented. We will price a European option with maturity T and a strike price K under the assumption that the asset price follows a geometric random walk.

When the underlying price follows a geometric random walk, we can simulate the price at maturity T using the equation

$$S_T = S_0 \, e^{(r - \frac{1}{2}\sigma^2) \cdot T + \sigma \cdot \sqrt{T} \cdot \tilde{\varepsilon}}$$

where $\tilde{\varepsilon}$ is a standard normal variable. Stratified sampling is applied for random numbers on the interval [0,1]. We generate the values for $\tilde{\varepsilon}$ by using the inverse transform method: first, generate N scenarios for realizations of a uniform random variable $\tilde{U}$ on the interval [0,1] and then use the inverse cumulative normal distribution function Φ^{-1} to get the values for $\tilde{\varepsilon}$.[10]

The scenarios $U_1, \ldots, U_N$ for the realizations of the uniform random variable $\tilde{U}$ will be generated in such a way that every realization falls in its own stratum n, $n = 1, \ldots, N$. To have N strata of equal probabilities, we divide the unit interval into N little intervals, each of length $1/N$. If we then consider the inverse cumulative normal distribution function,

$$\Phi^{-1}\left(\frac{n-1}{N} + \frac{U_n}{N}\right), \quad n = 1, \ldots, N$$

then we will have divided the standard normal distribution into N strata of equal probability. (Note that this does not mean that the corresponding intervals on the horizontal axis of the normal distribution will be of equal length, only that the area above them under the normal distribution PDF will be the same.) Thus, if we generate the N scenarios for $\tilde{\varepsilon}$ using the formula

$$S_T = S_0 \, e^{(r - \frac{1}{2}\sigma^2) \cdot T + \sigma \cdot \sqrt{T} \cdot \Phi^{-1}\left(\frac{n-1}{N} + \frac{U_n}{N}\right)}, \quad n = 1, \ldots, N$$

we will obtain a representative sample of values for the final asset price.[11] To compute the price of the option, we would then compute the pay-offs in all scenarios, discount them to the present, and find their average as usual:

$$C_0 = e^{-r \cdot T} \cdot \sum_{n=1}^{N} \frac{1}{N} \max\left\{ S_0 \, e^{(r - \frac{1}{2}\sigma^2) \cdot T + \sigma \cdot \sqrt{T} \cdot \Phi^{-1}\left(\frac{n-1}{N} + \frac{U_n}{N}\right)} - K, \, 0 \right\}$$

14.2.3 Importance Sampling

Importance sampling is an alternative to stratified sampling for dealing with rare events, or extreme observations, and for reducing the number of simulation trials necessary to achieve a particular level of accuracy. The method changes the underlying scenario probabilities so as to give more weight to important outcomes in the simulation. Such outcomes are generated with greater frequency than they otherwise would. At the end, the observations' weights are scaled back in the computation of the expression of interest, so that the estimation is correct.

There is no single recipe for how to construct good importance sampling methods. The specific construction depends on the underlying random process dynamics. Let us consider the example of pricing European call option in the Black-Scholes setting. In this setting, generating paths that are out-of-the-money is wasteful.[12] This is because only paths that are in-the-money count in the final computation of the option price—the contribution of out-of-the-money paths to the option price is zero. Although in practice one would not use importance sampling for pricing a European call option for which there is a closed-form formula, we use the European call example to provide some intuition about the idea behind the importance sampling method.

First, note that in-the-money paths will occur only if the asset price at the expiration date is greater than the strike price; that is, they will result from realizations of the standard normal random variable $\tilde{\varepsilon}$ such that

$$S_T = S_t \, e^{(r-\frac{1}{2}\sigma^2)\cdot(T-t)+\sigma\cdot\sqrt{(T-t)}\cdot\tilde{\varepsilon}} > K$$

From this inequality, we can derive that only normal random numbers higher than

$$\frac{\ln(K/S_t) - (r - \sigma^2/2) \cdot (T - t)}{\sigma \cdot \sqrt{T - t}}$$

will lead to in-the-money paths. Equivalently, this means that only random numbers between

$$\Phi\left(\frac{\ln(K/S_t) - (r - \sigma^2/2) \cdot (T - t)}{\sigma \cdot \sqrt{T - t}}\right)$$

and 1 on the unit interval [0,1], when "inverted" to obtain normal random numbers, will lead to in-the-money paths. ($\Phi(.)$ denotes the cumulative normal distribution, as before.) Thus, we only need to simulate random numbers in that range of the [0,1] interval. When computing the option price at the end, instead of weighing each payoff equally by multiplying it by $1/N$ as we would do in standard Monte Carlo sampling, we would multiply the sum of the payoffs obtained from the simulation by the probability that a particular random path would be in-the-money assuming truly random sampling, which is the standard Monte Carlo method. The latter probability is

$$1 - \Phi \left(\frac{\ln(K/S_t) - (r - \sigma^2/2) \cdot (T - t)}{\sigma \cdot \sqrt{T - t}} \right)$$

$$= \Phi \left(\frac{\ln(S_t/K) + (r - \sigma^2/2) \cdot (T - t)}{\sigma \cdot \sqrt{T - t}} \right)$$

The call option price is then

$$C_t = e^{-r(T-t)} \cdot \Phi \left(\frac{\ln(S_t/K) + (r - \sigma^2/2) \cdot (T - t)}{\sigma \cdot \sqrt{T - t}} \right)$$

$$\sum_{n=1}^{N} \max \left\{ S_t e^{(r - \frac{1}{2}\sigma^2) \cdot (T-t) + \sigma \cdot \sqrt{(T-t)} \cdot \varepsilon^{(n)}} - K, 0 \right\}$$

where $\varepsilon(1), \ldots, \varepsilon(N)$ are random numbers generated from the range of a normal distribution higher than

$$\frac{\ln(K/S_t) - (r - \sigma^2/2) \cdot (T - t)}{\sigma \cdot \sqrt{T - t}}$$

Now let us formalize the importance sampling approach.

When we attempt to find the expected value of the discounted payoffs from a derivative, we are in effect trying to evaluate an integral of a specific function over all values the random variable can take.[13] We evaluate that integral approximately—we generate the value of the function at multiple points, and we multiply those values by the probabilities that they happen. (With crude Monte Carlo simulation, each scenario we generate happens with the same probability, so we multiply the estimated value of the payoff function by one over the number of scenarios.)

The main idea of the importance sampling method is to introduce an *importance distribution* that rescales the original distribution and makes important scenarios more likely to appear. Suppose that the original integral we were trying to evaluate was

$$E[h(\mathbf{X})] = \int h(\mathbf{x}) \cdot f(\mathbf{x}) d\mathbf{x}$$

where $\mathbf{X}$ is a vector of random variables with joint probability density $f(\mathbf{x})$ and $h(\mathbf{X})$ is the discounted payoff function. If we can find another probability density function g such that $f(\mathbf{x}) = 0$ whenever $g(\mathbf{x}) = 0$, we have

$$
\begin{aligned}
E_f[h(\mathbf{X})] &= \int h(\mathbf{x}) \cdot f(\mathbf{x}) \, d\mathbf{x} \\
&= \int \frac{h(\mathbf{x}) \cdot f(\mathbf{x})}{g(\mathbf{x})} \cdot g(\mathbf{x}) \, d\mathbf{x} \\
&= \int h^*(\mathbf{x}) \cdot g(\mathbf{x}) d\mathbf{x} \\
&= E_g[h^*(\mathbf{X})]
\end{aligned}
$$

In other words, we can find the expected value of the payoff $h(\mathbf{X})$ with respect to the original probability density function $f(\mathbf{x})$ by finding the expected value of the modified payoff function

$$
h^*(\mathbf{x}) = \frac{h(\mathbf{x}) \cdot f(\mathbf{x})}{g(\mathbf{x})}
$$

with respect to the new probability density $g(\mathbf{x})$. The ratio

$$
\frac{f(\mathbf{x})}{g(\mathbf{x})}
$$

corrects the change in probability measure. It is called the likelihood ratio, but is also referred to as the Radon-Nikodym derivative in the context of stochastic calculus.

We see that on average, we will get the same answer by using importance sampling as when we use crude Monte Carlo sampling. How can we guarantee, however, that the function $g(\mathbf{x})$ we select will indeed reduce the variance of the estimator? Let us compute the variances of the two estimators $h(\mathbf{X})$ and $h^*(\mathbf{X})$. Using the equality[14]

$$
\operatorname{Var}(\tilde{X}) = \int\limits_{-\infty}^{\infty} x^2 \cdot f(x) \, dx - \left(\int\limits_{-\infty}^{\infty} x \cdot f(x) \, dx \right)^2
$$

we get

$$
\operatorname{Var}_f[h(\mathbf{X})] = \int h^2(\mathbf{x}) \cdot f(\mathbf{x}) \, d\mathbf{x} - \left(E_f[h(\mathbf{X})] \right)^2
$$

$$
\begin{aligned}
\operatorname{Var}_g[h^*(\mathbf{X})] &= \int h^2(\mathbf{x}) \cdot \frac{f^2(\mathbf{x})}{g^2(\mathbf{x})} \cdot g(\mathbf{x}) \, d\mathbf{x} - \left(E_g[h^*(\mathbf{X})] \right)^2 \\
&= \int h^2(\mathbf{x}) \cdot \frac{f(\mathbf{x})}{g(\mathbf{x})} \cdot f(\mathbf{x}) \, d\mathbf{x} - \left(E_f[h(\mathbf{X})] \right)^2
\end{aligned}
$$

The difference between the two variances is

$$\text{Var}_f[h(\mathbf{X})] - \text{Var}_g[h^*(\mathbf{X})] = \int h^2(\mathbf{x}) \cdot \left(1 - \frac{f(\mathbf{x})}{g(\mathbf{x})}\right) \cdot f(\mathbf{x}) \, d\mathbf{x}$$

Therefore, to ensure that the variance becomes smaller when we use important sampling, we should select $g(\mathbf{x})$ to be large (greater than $f(\mathbf{x})$) when the term $h^2(\mathbf{x}) \cdot f(\mathbf{x})$ is large, and $g(\mathbf{x})$ to be small (smaller than $f(\mathbf{x})$) when the term $h^2(\mathbf{x}) \cdot f(\mathbf{x})$ is small. In other words, we emphasize important observations.

How is this procedure applied in the case of the European call option? The discounted payoff function in the case of a European call option is

$$h(x) = e^{-rT} \cdot \max\{S_T - K, 0\}$$

We observed that important scenarios would be generated only if the simulated paths end up in-the-money, that is, above the strike price K. Suppose we decide to generate the values for the final price S_T from a probability distribution that is more likely to produce scenarios above the strike price K. Suppose further that instead of the original probability distribution f for the logarithm of the final asset price, which was normal with mean $(r - \sigma^2/2) \cdot T$ and variance $\sigma^2 \cdot T$, we consider a normal distribution with mean $\ln(K/S_0) - \sigma^2 \cdot T/2$ and the same variance, $\sigma^2 \cdot T$. In other words, in the notation used in this section,

$$f(x) = N(x, (r - \sigma^2/2) \cdot T, \sigma^2 \cdot T)$$

$$= \frac{1}{\sigma\sqrt{2\pi}} e^{-\frac{(x-(rT-\sigma^2 T/2))^2}{2(\sigma^2 T)}}$$

$$g(x) = N(x, \ln(K/S_0) - \sigma^2 \cdot T/2, \sigma^2 \cdot T)$$

$$= \frac{1}{\sigma\sqrt{2\pi}} e^{-\frac{(x-(\ln(K/S_0)-\sigma^2 T/2))^2}{2(\sigma^2 T)}}$$

The likelihood ratio is then simply the ratio of two normal density functions with different means. Therefore,

$$E_f[h(x)] = E_f\left[e^{-rT} \cdot \max\{S_T - K, 0\}\right]$$

$$= E_g\left[e^{-rT} \cdot \max\{S_T - K, 0\} \cdot \frac{f(x)}{g(x)}\right]$$

Hence, the estimator from the simulation is the average for all scenarios generated with the formula

$$
e^{-rT} \cdot \max \left\{ S_0 \cdot e^Z - K, 0 \right\} \cdot \frac{\frac{1}{\sigma \sqrt{2\pi}} \cdot e^{-\frac{(Z-(rT-\sigma^2 T/2))^2}{2(\sigma^2 T)}}}{\frac{1}{\sigma \sqrt{2\pi}} \cdot e^{-\frac{(Z-(\ln(K/S_0)-\sigma^2 T/2))^2}{2(\sigma^2 T)}}}
$$

where Z is simulated as a normal random variable with mean $\ln(K/S_0) - \sigma^2 \cdot T/2$ and variance $\sigma^2 \cdot T$. The paths generated in this manner will be less likely to produce payoffs that are zero.

As we mentioned at the beginning of this section, European call pricing with importance sampling was only a simple example in order to illustrate the main idea of importance sampling. More practical (albeit more technically challenging) applications can be found, for instance, in section 4.6 in Glasserman (2004). One such important application is importance sampling in the context of estimating value-at-risk. As we discussed in Chapter 8, the estimation of value-at-risk is very sensitive to the quality of sampled observations in the tail of the distribution of portfolio losses, but by definition observations in the tail of the distribution are very unlikely to happen during a simulation unless we generate an enormous number of scenarios. Importance sampling can be applied in this context, and the importance distribution is often selected to be a member of the exponential family of distributions, which increases the tilt in the right tail of the original distribution for specific values of its input parameters. See Chapter 4 in McLeish (2005) for a more detailed introduction to this application.

14.2.4 Control Variates

Like importance sampling, the *control variates method* uses knowledge about a function that is related somehow to the original function we are trying to estimate by simulation. Also, like importance sampling, the choice of function is subjective.

The main idea of the control variates method is to find the expected value of the discounted payoffs of a derivative for which no analytical formula is known by using knowledge about an expected value of a related variable that is known. Such a situation would arise, for example, if we are trying to price an Asian call option. Intuitively, the price of an Asian call option for which the payoff involves the arithmetic average of stock prices over the life of the option should be related to the price of an Asian call option for which the payoff involves the geometric average of stock prices over the life of the option. While there is no closed-form formula for the price of an Asian call option with arithmetic average, there is a closed-form formula for the price of an Asian call option with geometric average when the underlying asset follows a geometric random walk, so we can exploit this knowledge.

More generally, suppose that we would like to estimate the expected value of a random variable X, $E[X]$, and that there is another random variable Y with expected value $E[Y]$, which is somehow correlated to X. The variable Y is called the *control variate*. The estimator for X can be written as

$$X(b) = X - b \cdot (Y - E[Y])$$

where b is a parameter that must be specified. We employ the following procedure. We simulate N observations for the variable X, and along with those, compute N observations for the variable Y. Think of the observations $X_1, \ldots, X_N$ as the payoffs for the arithmetic average Asian call option, and of the observations $Y_1, \ldots, Y_N$ as the payoffs for the geometric average Asian call option. Both sets of payoffs are generated based on N sample paths for the underlying asset price S_t.

Now, instead of computing $E[X]$ directly as the average of $X_1, \ldots, X_N$, consider the average of $X_i(b)$ obtained as

$$\frac{1}{N} \cdot \sum_{i=1}^{N} (X_i - b \cdot (Y_i - E[Y])) = \overline{X} - b \cdot (\overline{Y} - E[Y])$$

where we use the standard notation $\overline{X}$ to denote the sample average, as opposed to the true expected value.[15] Again, note that we assume that $E[Y]$ is known. In the example of computing the arithmetic average Asian call option price, $E[Y]$ is the price of the geometric mean Asian call option.

It turns out that the optimal value for the constant b (the value that will minimize the variance of the estimator $X(b)$) is actually

$$b^* = \frac{Cov(X, Y)}{Var(Y)}$$

When we use this value of b, it can be shown that

$$\frac{Var(\overline{X} - b^* \cdot (\overline{Y} - E[Y]))}{Var(\overline{X})} = 1 - \rho^2(X, Y)$$

where ρ is the correlation coefficient between X and Y.

Therefore, the stronger the correlation between the variable of interest, X, and the control variate Y, the more significant the impact of using the control variable method for reducing the variance in the estimation of $E[X]$. Note, however, that whereas a correlation of 0.95 between X and Y results in a tenfold decrease in variance of the estimator for $E[X]$ $(1 - 0.95^2 = 0.0975$, which is approximately 1/10), a correlation of 0.70, which would be considered a strong correlation for all practical purposes, results in a twofold decrease in the variance of the estimator $(1 - 0.70^2 = 0.51$, which is approximately 1/2). Therefore, a rather strong correlation between the original variable and the control variate is needed in order to achieve a significant improvement. For example, using the geometric mean Asian option price as a control variate for the estimation of the arithmetic average Asian option price is a very successful approach, whereas using other quantities that are generally related to the Asian option payoff, such as the price of a European call option on the underlying asset, or the average of the asset prices realized with a geometric random walk, is not worth the additional computational effort.

We did not elaborate on how one may compute the actual estimate of the coefficient b. In practice, since we do not know $E[X]$ (we are trying to estimate it), it is unlikely that we will know the covariance between X and Y. The best we can do is estimate b. Typically, a preliminary simulation is run (with fewer trials than would be necessary to estimate the quantity of interest, $E[X]$, accurately), and the coefficient b is estimated as

$$\hat{b} = \frac{\displaystyle\sum_{i=1}^{N_p} (X_i - \overline{X}) \cdot (Y_i - \overline{Y})}{\displaystyle\sum_{i=1}^{N_p} (Y_i - \overline{Y})^2}$$

where N_p is the number of preliminary simulation trials.

To make the control variates method more intuitive, let us go through the Asian option pricing example in detail. We will take the following steps:

1. Compute the price of a geometric Asian call option, which will serve as our control variate.

   The price at time 0 of a geometric average Asian call option with time to maturity T and M intermediate evaluation steps of length Δt can be shown to be

   $$C_{A,G} = e^{-r \cdot T} \left(e^{a + \frac{1}{2} \cdot c} \cdot \Phi(x) - K \cdot \Phi(x - \sqrt{c}) \right)$$

where

$$\Delta t = \frac{T}{M}$$

$$v = r - q - \frac{1}{2} \cdot \sigma^2$$

$$a = \ln(S_0) + v \cdot (\Delta t) + \frac{1}{2} \cdot v \cdot (T - \Delta t)$$

$$c = \sigma^2 \cdot (\Delta t) + \sigma^2 \cdot (T - \Delta t) \cdot (2 \cdot M - 1)/(6 \cdot M)$$

$$x = \frac{a - \ln(K) + c}{\sqrt{b}}$$

2. Run a preliminary simulation to estimate the value of the coefficient b. Namely, we will simulate N_p paths for the underlying asset price, find the discounted payoffs for the geometric and the arithmetic Asian call along each path, compute their covariance, compute the variance of the discounted payoffs of the geometric Asian call, and use the formula $Cov(X, Y)/Var(Y)$ to estimate the value of b.

3. Simulate the number of paths for the price of the underlying stock we originally intended, and evaluate the payoffs for the geometric and the arithmetic Asian call along each path. For each of these paths, knowing the exact price for the geometric Asian call from Step 1, and a value for b from step 2, we can calculate an estimate for the arithmetic Asian call payoff as follows:

Estimate = Arithmetic Asian payoff $- b \ *$
(Geometric Asian payoff $-$ Exact geometric price)

4. The average of the estimates from step 3 over all the paths is the estimate of the arithmetic Asian call price with the control variates method.

(See this chapter's Software Hints and files **Ch14-OptionPricingVBA .xlsm** and **ArithmeticAsianCallCV.m** for an exact implementation.)

As we mentioned earlier, using the geometric Asian call price as a control variate is a very successful method for reducing the overall variance in computing the price of an arithmetic Asian call by simulation. Let us do a simple comparison of the estimation of the arithmetic Asian option price with and without control variates. Consider the example of an arithmetic

Asian call option with strike price $65, time to maturity 1 year, and monthly intermediate dates (that is, we will simulate a geometric random walk with 12 steps between time 0 and the maturity of the option). The annual risk-free rate is 10%. The volatility of the underlying stock is 40%; the initial stock price is $60. We will generate 100 paths for a geometric random walk for the underlying asset, and evaluate the price of the Asian option using crude Monte Carlo and the control variates method with 20 preliminary scenarios. The whole estimation will be repeated 30 times, and we will record the mean and the standard deviation of the 30 arithmetic Asian option prices generated with the crude Monte Carlo method and the 30 arithmetic Asian option prices generated with the control variates method. (See this chapter's Software Hints and files **Ch14-OptionPricingVBA.xlsm** and **ArithmeticAsianCallEstimationComparison.m** for the actual code.)

The results will vary from simulation to simulation, of course, but the order of magnitude of the difference between the variability of the prices obtained with the crude Monte Carlo and the control variates method remains the same. In our trial run, we obtained $5.40 for the mean price with the crude Monte Carlo method, and the variability of the 30 prices was 1.4046. With the control variates method, we obtained $5.02 for the mean price, and 0.0037 for the variability. The reduction in the variability of the estimate of the option price was approximately 380 times, and that happened with only 20 preliminary simulations to estimate the coefficient b in the control variates method!

14.3 QUASIRANDOM NUMBER SEQUENCES

In some sense, quasi–Monte Carlo methods fit in the section on variance reduction methods. You can think of them as an extreme version of stratification methods. As we explained in section 4.4.4 of Chapter 4, quasi–Monte Carlo methods rely on number theory to produce sequences of numbers that do not pretend to be random, but instead cover the unit interval in a uniform way, so that every part of the probability distribution is represented when simulating. Some quasi–Monte Carlo methods work better than others for pricing specific derivatives, but there is no comprehensive way to determine that in advance without testing. In this section, we review some of the most common types of quasi–Monte Carlo sequences used in derivative pricing, and give an example of how the actual implementation would work.

The exposition in this section is rather technical because quasirandom methods for pricing derivatives draw on concepts from calculus, statistics, and number theory. In fact, many of the techniques we will describe in this section are based on research in the most efficient ways to integrate a function. As we mentioned earlier in this chapter, integrals show up in derivative pricing because the expected value of a random variable can be expressed as a sum, or an integral.[16] In the context of derivative pricing, the random variable is the discounted payoff from the derivative. Under conditions of no arbitrage, the expected value of that random variable provides the derivative's fair value. Monte Carlo simulation has been a technique for numerical integration for a long time. The main idea is to simulate a representative set of points, and to evaluate the values of the function at the simulated points. As the concept of ever-more representative samples of points over which to evaluate the function has been pushed to the limit, the idea of low discrepancy sequences emerged. Such sequences must be evenly distributed in some sense, and cover the range [0,1] in a way that minimizes the discrepancies between the points.

We begin with the most fundamental sequence, the Van der Corput sequence. More advanced sequences, such as Halton and Faure, build on the Van der Corput sequence. There are three parameters that we will associate with a quasirandom sequence (some sequences may require more): N, the number of points from the sequence to generate; d, the dimension (that is, how many random variables are we generating at the same time), and b, the *base*, which we will explain in more detail next.

14.3.1 Van der Corput Sequence

In section 4.4.4 of Chapter 4, we showed an example of the Van der Corput sequence of base 2:

$$\frac{1}{2}, \frac{1}{4}, \frac{3}{4}, \frac{1}{8}, \frac{5}{8}, \frac{3}{8}, \frac{7}{8}, \cdots$$

Let us see how such a sequence would be generated.
Consider a sequence of natural numbers in base 10:[17]

$$1, 2, 3, 4, 5, 6, 7, 8, 9, 10, 11, 12, 13, \ldots$$

The same sequence in base 2 is

$$1, 10, 11, 100, 101, 110, 111, 1000, 1001, 1010, 1011, 1100, 1101, \ldots$$

Constructing the *Van der Corput sequence* in base b, involves two steps:

1. Express every natural number n in the sequence in base b, that is, as

$$(0.a_0(n) \quad a_1(n) \quad a_2(n) \quad a_3(n)\ldots a_m(n))_b = \sum_{k=0}^{m} a_k(n) \cdot b^{-(k+1)}$$

where $a_m(n),\ldots,a_0(n)$ are the digits in the representation of the number n in base b. For example, the number 13 in base 10, $(13)_{10}$, converted to base 2 is $(1101)_2$. In this case, $m = 3$ and $a_3(13) = 1$, $a_2(13) = 0$, $a_1(13) = 1$, $a_0(13) = 1$.

2. Reverse the digits and add a decimal point to obtain a number within the interval $[0,1]$ (we dropped the index n for notational convenience):

$$(0.a_0 a_1 a_2 a_3 \ldots a_m)_b = \sum_{k=0}^{m} a_k \cdot b^{-(k+1)}$$

For example, the digits of the number $(13)_{10} = (1101)_2$ get reversed to 1011, and then we transform that number to

$$1 \cdot 2^{-1} + 0 \cdot 2^{-2} + 0 \cdot 2^{-3} + 1 \cdot 2^{-4} = 11/16$$

Applying this method to the entire sequence, we obtain

$$\frac{1}{2}, \frac{1}{4}, \frac{3}{4}, \frac{1}{8}, \frac{5}{8}, \frac{3}{8}, \frac{7}{8}, \frac{1}{16}, \frac{9}{16}, \frac{5}{16}, \frac{13}{16}, \frac{3}{16}, \frac{11}{16} \cdots$$

As we mentioned in section 4.4.4 of Chapter 4, these values tend to fill the unit interval evenly. The larger the base, the greater the number of points needed to achieve uniform coverage of the interval. You can test this by using the Van der Corput sequence generating code in files **Ch14-OptionPricingVBA.xlsm** and **VanDerCorput.m**. (See also this chapter's Software Hints.)

14.3.2 Halton Sequence

The *Halton sequence* is basically the multivariate extension of the Van der Corput sequence. If we need to simulate multiple random variables (if there are d of them, we need to construct a sequence in dimension d), we choose d distinct prime numbers, $b_1,\ldots,b_d$ to serve as bases. (Usually, we select the smallest possible prime numbers.) For example, if we need to generate three random variables, $d = 3$. Suppose we select bases $b_1 = 2$, $b_2 = 3$, and $b_3 = 5$ (2, 3, and 5 are the smallest three prime numbers). We have three sequences:

Base 2:

$$\frac{1}{2}, \frac{1}{4}, \frac{3}{4}, \frac{1}{8}, \frac{5}{8}, \frac{3}{8}, \frac{7}{8}, \frac{1}{16}, \frac{9}{16}, \frac{5}{16}, \cdots$$

Base 3:

$$\frac{1}{3}, \frac{2}{3}, \frac{1}{9}, \frac{4}{9}, \frac{7}{9}, \frac{2}{9}, \frac{5}{9}, \frac{8}{9}, \frac{1}{27}, \frac{10}{27}, \cdots$$

Base 5:

$$\frac{1}{5}, \frac{2}{5}, \frac{3}{5}, \frac{4}{5}, \frac{1}{25}, \frac{6}{25}, \frac{11}{25}, \frac{16}{25}, \frac{21}{25}, \frac{2}{25}, \cdots$$

The points generated with the Halton sequence of dimension 3 will have three coordinates that correspond to the points with the same index in each Van der Corput sequence above, that is, the Halton sequence will be

$$\left(\frac{1}{2}, \frac{1}{3}, \frac{1}{5}\right), \left(\frac{1}{4}, \frac{2}{3}, \frac{2}{5}\right), \left(\frac{3}{4}, \frac{1}{9}, \frac{3}{5}\right), \cdots$$

(See this chapter's Software Hints and files **Ch14-OptionPricingVBA.xlsm** and **Halton.m** for an implementation of the algorithm with Visual Basic and MATLAB.)

14.3.3 Faure Sequence

As the dimension d of the Halton sequence grows large, the uniformity of covering the unit cube becomes worse and worse. This is because the increasing value for the base b makes the coverage more and more sparse. The *Faure sequence* attempts to rectify that by keeping the base the same independent of the number of dimensions. The value for the base needs to be at least as large as the number of dimensions d, and is usually selected to be the smallest prime number greater than or equal to d. For example, if d is 15, the Halton sequence uses the 15th prime number (which is 47) to generate the values of the sequence in its 15th dimension, whereas the Faure sequence uses the first prime number after 15 (which is 17). Thus, the components of the Faure sequence fill in the gaps faster than the components of the Halton sequence when the dimension d is large. (If $d = 1$, however, notice that the Van der Corput, Halton, and Faure sequences are equivalent.)

Instead of matching points with the same index in the individual Van der Corput sequences to create the coordinates of a point in d dimensions, the Faure sequence uses permutations of the indices for each of the coordinates. In fact, the coordinates of a Faure sequence are constructed by permuting segments of a single Van der Corput sequence. Recall that when generating a Van der Corput sequence, we expressed the nth point in the form

$$(a_m(n) \quad \ldots \quad a_3(n) \quad a_2(n) \quad a_1(n) \quad a_0(n))_b = \sum_{k=0}^{m} a_k(n) \cdot b^k$$

and those numbers were then transformed into

$$(0.a_0(n) \quad a_1(n) \quad a_2(n) \quad a_3(n) \quad \ldots a_m(n))_b = \sum_{k=0}^{m} a_k(n) \cdot b^{-(k+1)}$$

When generating the ith coordinate in a Faure sequence, the transformation uses different coefficients in front of $b^{-(k+1)}$ for every dimension. These coefficients (let us denote them $c_k^{(i)}(n)$) are related to the coefficients $a_k(n)$, but use only the last $(m - k + 1)$ values of the coefficients a. In particular, to generate the nth point in the ith coordinate in a Faure sequence, we use the expression

$$\sum_{k=0}^{m} c_k^{(i)}(n) \cdot b^{-(k+1)}$$

where the coefficients $c_k^{(i)}(n)$, $k = 0, \ldots, m$ are computed as

$$c_k^{(i)}(n) = \sum_{j=k}^{m} \binom{j}{k} \cdot (i-1)^{j-k} \cdot a_j(n) \quad \mod \quad b^{18}$$

As a consequence of these adjustments, the Faure sequence has better uniformity properties than the Halton sequence for moderately high dimensionality.

14.3.4 Sobol Sequence

The *Sobol sequence* is a yet more sophisticated quasirandom sequence that uses so-called *direction numbers* to generate the terms of the sequence. Similarly to the Faure sequence, it incorporates the idea of permuting the coordinates of the points generated by Van der Corput sequences in a clever way, but uses base 2 independently of the number of dimensions. Working in a small base has certain computational advantages.

The computation of the Sobol sequence is more technical than the computation of the Van der Corput, Halton, or Faure sequences, so we omit the details here and refer readers to Chapter 6 in McLeish (2005) or section 5.2.3 of Chapter 5 in Glasserman (2004) for a comprehensive introduction. Some software packages, and in particular MATLAB's Statistics Toolbox, have built-in capabilities for computing the elements of the Sobol sequence. (See the MATLAB section of this chapter's Software Hints.)

14.3.5 Illustrations

To illustrate how quasi–Monte Carlo methods can be used, let us implement a simple example. We know the exact value of a European call option when the underlying asset price is assumed to follow a geometric random walk—the value is given by the Black-Scholes formula (see Chapter 13). Let us compute the price of the European call option with crude Monte Carlo simulation and with quasi–Monte Carlo simulation, using the Halton and the Sobol sequences. Calculating the price of the European call option requires generating only one random variable—the normal random variable that represents the change in the underlying asset's price. Therefore, the quasirandom sequences have only one dimension. It follows that the Halton, Faure, and Van der Corput sequences will all give the same result.

To implement the algorithm, we generate the price of the underlying asset at maturity T as

$$S_T = S_t \, e^{(r - \frac{1}{2}\sigma^2) \cdot (T-t) + \sigma \cdot \sqrt{(T-t)} \cdot \tilde{\varepsilon}}$$

where $\tilde{\varepsilon}$ is a standard normal random variable.

When using the crude Monte Carlo method, $\tilde{\varepsilon}$ can be generated with the formula =NORMINV(rand()) in Excel, =RISKNORMAL(0,1) in @RISK, or normrnd(0,1) in MATLAB, as explained earlier in the book. We create N scenarios for $\tilde{\varepsilon}$, and average out the discounted payoffs over the scenarios.

When using quasi–Monte Carlo simulation, we generate N values from one of the low discrepancy sequences we discussed—Halton or Sobol, and use the norminv function in Excel or MATLAB to convert those values into values from a standard normal distribution. For example, to generate the number from the standard normal distribution that corresponds to the value 0.5 from the Halton sequence in one dimension, we will enter `norminv(0.5,0,1)` in both Excel and MATLAB. Repeating this for each of the N values in the quasirandom sequence, we obtain N scenarios for $\tilde{\varepsilon}$, which can be used to compute N asset prices at maturity. These N asset prices in turn can be used to compute the discounted payoffs of the option over all scenarios, and the discounted payoffs are then averaged out to compute the price of the option.

Exhibit 14.1 illustrates the performance of the crude Monte Carlo and a quasi–Monte Carlo method with the Halton sequences with base 2. We generated $1, 2, 3, \ldots, 100$ scenarios with each of the methods, and evaluated the option price in each case. The Black-Scholes price is also given on the

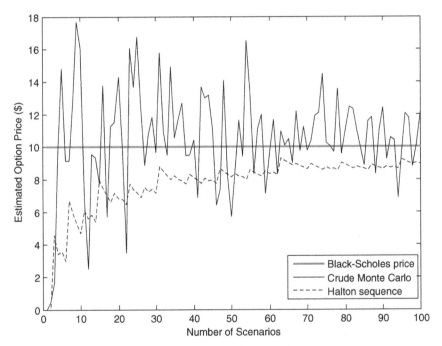

EXHIBIT 14.1 Comparison of performance of crude Monte Carlo and a quasi–Monte Carlo method (Halton sequence of base 2) for evaluating the price of a European call option. The initial stock price is assumed to be $60, the strike price is $65, the maturity of the option is 1 year, the volatility of the underlying stock is 0.4, and the risk-free rate is 10%. The true (Black-Scholes) price of the option is $10.02.

graph for reference. It can be observed that the crude Monte Carlo simulation method produces rather volatile estimates of the option price, especially for a small number of scenarios. The quasi–Monte Carlo method produces price estimates that tend to the real option price relatively monotonically.

(See files **Ch14-OptionPricingVBA.xlsm, EuropeanCallHalton.m, EuropeanCallSobol.m,** as well as this chapter's Software Hints for details on implementing the algorithms with Excel and MATLAB.)

Now let us think through a somewhat more complicated example. Suppose that we would like to price an Asian option by simulation. The time to maturity of the option is 1 year, and we would like to sample the price of the underlying asset monthly. This means that we want to generate N paths for the price of the underlying with 12 points each. Suppose also we would like to use a Halton sequence. How many dimensions should the Halton sequence have? Since we are sampling at 12 time instances, and at each time instance we are drawing a price for the underlying that is assumed to follow a specific (lognormal) probability distribution, we need to generate a Halton sequence of dimension 12, that is, we need to generate 12 Van der Corput sequences of length N. Note that each Van der Corput sequence (each dimension of the Halton sequence) is associated with a time instance, not with a path. The length of each Van der Corput sequence equals the number of scenarios we desire, which is N.

As we mentioned earlier, the advantages of using one versus another quasirandom sequence are not clear. There is a substantial amount of literature comparing the performance of different sequences, but the comparisons are typically for a small number of select applications. There is not strong evidence that if the dimension of the problem is small (e.g., less than 15), it makes a big difference whether we use the Halton, Faure, or Sobol sequence.

14.4 MORE SIMULATION APPLICATION EXAMPLES

While the features of derivatives are different, the main ideas behind using simulation to price them remain the same. This section contains several additional examples that illustrate the main ideas and show some further twists in the implementation.

14.4.1 Pricing a Barrier Option

There are many types of barrier options, but their common feature is that there is a trigger event that activates or cancels the option contract. For *knock-in options*, the option contract is activated if a barrier value is crossed by the underlying during the life of the option. For *knock-out options*, the option contract is canceled if the barrier value is crossed. When the barrier S_b is above the initial asset price S_0, the barrier option is an *up option*. When the barrier S_b is below the initial asset price S_0, the barrier option is a *down option*.

As an example, consider a down-and-out put option. This option contract becomes void if the asset price falls below the barrier S_b. Such an option provides a payoff to the option holder for relatively small drops in the asset price. It also protects the option writer from large risks, and so the option would be cheaper than a regular, or "vanilla" put option. From the point of view of the option holder, the down-and-out put option provides cheaper insurance than a vanilla put option, although the drawback is that the option holder will not be able to realize a large payoff if the price of the underlying drops substantially.

Let us now price a down-and-out put option with a strike price K and time to maturity T. In order to find its value, we need to keep track of whether the barrier has been crossed or not. We simulate paths for the underlying asset. Suppose that the underlying asset follows a geometric random walk. For every path we then have a variable, say crossed (in Excel, we can dedicate a cell) that stores the value 0 if the barrier has not been crossed, and 1 otherwise. When we compute the final payoffs, we set the payoff for a particular path to 0 if the value of the crossed variable for that path is 1, and we compute the payoff as $\max\{K - S_T, 0\}$, similarly to the payoff of a vanilla put option, when the value of the crossed variable for that path is 0. (See this chapter's Software Hints and files **Ch14-OptionPricingVBA.xlsm** and **DownAndOutPut.m** for the implementation of an example.)

14.4.2 Pricing an American Option

As mentioned in section 13.1.2 of Chapter 13, in contrast to European options, *American options* are contracts in which the option holder has the right to exercise the option *at any time* during the life of the option, rather than only at maturity.[19] The payoff of American options therefore depends on the time at which the option holder decides to exercise the option. Under certain conditions (no transaction costs, equal borrowing and lending costs), it can be shown that the price of an American call option should always be equal to the price of a European call option.[20] This, however, is not the case for American and European put options.

Until fairly recently, simulation was not considered a viable technique for pricing American options. The dynamic programming technique applied on binomial and trinomial trees, as illustrated in section 13.4.3 of Chapter 13, as well as finite difference methods[21] were the dominant techniques for pricing securities with early exercise features. However, binomial trees and finite difference methods become impractical when there are multiple stochastic factors that drive the price of the underlying security. Simulation, on the other hand, can handle multiple factors and their codependencies. In the last decade, various techniques for applying simulation to American option pricing have been suggested.[22] In this section, we present a simple example of a regression-based technique for approximating the price of an American option. Regression-based methods for approximating the value function in a dynamic program are a well-known *approximate dynamic programming technique* that has its roots in control theory.

Regression-based methods for pricing derivatives with American features have been suggested by Longstaff and Schwartz (2001) and Tsitsiklis and Van Roy (1999, 2001), among others. The main idea in these approaches is to generate possible scenarios for the future price by simulation, and use regression analysis to produce an approximate estimate of the dynamic programming value function.[23] This estimate is a function only of the time period, and not of the specific state (price). Based on that estimate, we decide whether to exercise early, or hold the option for another time period.

When pricing American options by simulation, as with pricing any other option by simulation, we discretize the time and possible space of outcomes; thus, we do not obtain a complete picture of the range of uncertainties that can occur. Furthermore, with regression-based methods for value function estimation, only an approximation of the state space is obtained in order to decide whether to exercise or not. The price estimate we obtain is in fact a lower bound on the true price of the American option.

A number of approaches have been suggested for producing an upper bound on the true price of the American option, but they are more technical than the exposition of this book, so we will not discuss them in detail. The simplest method is actually to assume that we have "perfect vision": that is, to compute the optimal strategy and payoff along each path we have simulated, and to find the expected value of the discounted payoffs along all simulated paths.[24] This upper bound on the option price is not particularly tight. More sophisticated approaches based on duality and resulting in tighter bounds have been suggested in Haugh and Kogan (2004) and Rogers (2002).

Let us now explain regression-based methods for estimating a lower bound on the price of the American option in more detail. For simplicity, assume that we have a vanilla American put option on a single stock. (The approach obviously applies to, and is more useful for, pricing of more complex securities with American features.) We generate N sample paths for the stock price $S^{(1)}, \ldots, S^{(N)}$. Each of these paths contains T observations of the stock price. If we used the dynamic programming approach to find the price of the American option (see section 13.4.3), we would proceed backwards from the last time period. At every time period, we would compare the intrinsic value of the option (that is, the value of exercising the option at that time) to the expected value of continuing. The latter is the quantity that is difficult to estimate because in practice we can have an infinite number of possible values for the stock price. Instead of evaluating that quantity precisely, we replace it with an estimate from a regression model. In the regression model, we use the conditional expectation of the value of continuing (based on the generated scenarios) as the response variable, and a collection of *basis functions* of the current stock price to create the explanatory variables. The simplest basis functions of the stock price S are $\varphi_0(S) = 1$, $\varphi_1(S) = S$ and $\varphi_2(S) = S^2$. It turns out, actually, that the choice of basis functions does not make a big difference in the end.[25]

At expiration, the value function in the dynamic program is

$$V_T(S_T(i)) = \max\{K - S_T(i), 0\}$$

for each sample path i, $i = 1, \ldots, N$.

At the second-to-last time period (time $T - 1$), we need to compare the value of exercising the option, or the intrinsic value

$$I_{T-1}(i) = \max\{K - S_{T-1}(i), 0\}$$

to the value of continuing,

$$E[e^{-r \cdot \Delta t} \cdot V_T(\tilde{S}_T)]$$

(Note that we have discounted the payoff at time T in order to compare both cash flows in time $[T - 1]$ dollars.)

We run a regression in which the values estimated from the last time period, $\max\{K - S_T(i), 0\}$, are the response variable (Y) values, and each generated scenario represents a data point. The regression equation is

$$e^{-r \cdot \Delta t} \cdot \max\{K - S_T(i), 0\}$$
$$= \beta_0 \cdot \varphi_0(S_{T-1}(i)) + \beta_1 \cdot \varphi_1(S_{T-1}(i)) + \beta_2 \cdot \varphi_2(S_{T-1}(i)),$$
$$i = 1, \ldots, N$$

or, for our choice of basis functions,

$$e^{-r \cdot \Delta t} \cdot \max\{K - S_T(i), 0\} = \beta_0 + \beta_1 \cdot S_{T-1}(i) + \beta_2 \cdot S_{T-1}^2(i), \quad i = 1, \ldots, N$$

After determining the regression coefficients β_0, β_1, and β_2, we have a way of approximating the value of continuing from every state for the stock price, i, $i = 1,\ldots,N$, at time $T - 1$. This approximate value can then be compared to the intrinsic value at that state to figure out whether to continue or not.

The procedure is repeated going backwards in time, including at time period 0.

To improve the speed of the calculations, we may want to run the regressions only for the subsets of paths at each time period for which the option is in the money because these are the only paths for which a decision needs to be made. For paths that are not in the money, it is clear that it is not optimal to exercise.

The best way to illustrate the approach is to show an example. We will use a simple example from Longstaff and Schwartz (2001). Consider a three-year American put option that can be exercised at the end of year 1, at the end of year 2, and at the end of year 3. The current stock price is $1, and the strike price is $1.10. The interest rate is 6% per annum. The discount factor for one time period is therefore $e^{-0.06 \cdot 1} = 0.9418$.

Suppose we have simulated eight paths for the price of the underlying stock. (In practice, we would simulate many more paths, but we want to keep the example tractable.) The values for the stock price in each of the paths are shown in Exhibit 14.2.

We begin at the last time period, $t = 3$. The cash flows at expiration are easy to compute (see Exhibit 14.3).

We next figure out which paths are in the money one period back (at time 2). There are five of them: paths 1, 3, 4, 6, and 7. For those paths, we compute the discounted values of the final cash flows, and use them as the response variable Y in a regression. (For example, the Y variable in the

EXHIBIT 14.2 Eight simulated paths for the price of the underlying stock.

Path	$t = 0$	$t = 1$	$t = 2$	$t = 3$
1	1.00	1.09	1.08	1.34
2	1.00	1.16	1.26	1.54
3	1.00	1.22	1.07	1.03
4	1.00	0.93	0.97	0.92
5	1.00	1.11	1.56	1.52
6	1.00	0.76	0.77	0.90
7	1.00	0.92	0.84	1.01
8	1.00	0.88	1.22	1.34

EXHIBIT 14.3 Cash flows at expiration.

Path	$t = 0$	$t = 1$	$t = 2$	$t = 3$
1	–	–	–	0.00
2	–	–	–	0.00
3	–	–	–	0.07
4	–	–	–	0.18
5	–	–	–	0.00
6	–	–	–	0.20
7	–	–	–	0.09
8	–	–	–	0.00

case of path 1 equals 0.00·0.9418.) The explanatory variables data in the regression are given by a constant, the stock price in the corresponding path at that time period, and the square of the stock price. Exhibit 14.4 contains the regression input data.

The estimated regression equation from the data in Exhibit 14.4 is

$$Y = -1.070 + 2.983 \cdot X - 1.813 \cdot X^2$$

Using this regression equation, we compute the estimates for the expected value of continuing at time $t = 2$.[26] For example, the approximate expected value of continuing at time 2 for path 1 is

$$-1.070 + 2.983 \cdot 1.08 - 1.813 \cdot 1.08^2 = 0.0369$$

EXHIBIT 14.4 Input data for the regression at time 2. Only paths 1, 3, 4, 6, and 7 are considered because they are in-the-money.

	Regression Data at Time 2			
Path	Y	Constant	X	X^2
1	0.00*0.9418	1.00	1.08	1.17
2	–	–	–	–
3	0.07*0.9418	1.00	1.07	1.14
4	0.18*0.9418	1.00	0.97	0.94
5	–	–	–	–
6	0.20*0.9418	1.00	0.77	0.59
7	0.09*0.9418	1.00	0.84	0.71
8	–	–	–	–

EXHIBIT 14.5 Value of continuing and exercising at time 2, optimal strategy at time 2, and cash flows for the eight simulated paths at time periods 2 and 3.

Path	Exercise	Continue	*Strategy?*	Cash Flow Matrix at Time 2		
				$t = 1$	$t = 2$	$t = 3$
1	0.02	0.0369	Continue	–	0.00	0.00
2	–	–	–	–	0.00	0.00
3	0.03	0.0461	Continue	–	0.00	0.07
4	0.13	0.1176	Exercise	–	0.13	0.00
5	–	–	–	–	0.00	0.00
6	0.33	0.1520	Exercise	–	0.33	0.00
7	0.26	0.1565	Exercise	–	0.26	0.00
8	–	–	–	–	0.00	0.00

(We used the simulated stock price at time 2 for path 1, $1.08.) We can now compare the intrinsic value of the option (the value of exercise at that time period) with the expected value of continuing. The value of exercise is given by $\max\{K - S_2(i), 0\}$, that is, by $1.10 - S_2(i)$ for the five paths of interest. The results are presented in Exhibit 14.5. Exhibit 14.5 also shows the cash flows at time periods 2 and 3 based on the optimal strategy computed so far and conditional on not exercising the option before time 2. Observe that if the option is exercised at time 2, the cash flow in the column for time 3 becomes 0. Once the option is exercised, there are no further cash flows because the option can be exercised only once. Note also that if the optimal strategy is to continue at time period 2, the cash flow is 0 (no immediate cash flow is realized), and the cash flow in time period 3 is determined independently based on whether it is optimal to exercise then or not. For example, for path 1, it is not optimal to exercise neither at time period 2, not at time period 3. In both cases, the cash flows are 0.

Now let us take a step back and consider time period 1. From the simulated data in Exhibit 14.2, there are again five paths where the option is in-the-money at time 1: 1, 4, 6, 7, and 8. For these paths, we create the regression data matrix in Exhibit 14.6. The values for the response variable Y are the discounted cash flows from time period 2. Note that we use the actual cash flows (computed in the second table in Exhibit 14.5), rather than the approximate expected values for Y computed for time period 2 (computed in the column with title Exercise in the first table in Exhibit 14.5). This is because there can be only one stopping (exercise) time per path.

EXHIBIT 14.6 Input data matrix for the regression at time 1.

Path	Y	Constant	X	X^2
		Regression Data at Time 3		
1	0.00*0.9418	1.00	1.09	1.19
2	–	–	–	–
3	–	–	–	–
4	0.13*0.9418	1.00	0.93	0.86
5	–	–	–	–
6	0.33*0.9418	1.00	0.76	0.58
7	0.26*0.9418	1.00	0.92	0.85
8	0.00*0.9418	1.00	0.88	0.77

The estimated regression equation from the data in Exhibit 14.6 is

$$Y = 2.038 - 3.335 \cdot X + 1.356 \cdot X^2$$

Again, using this regression equation, we compute the estimates for the expected value of continuing at time $t = 1$. For example, the approximate expected value of continuing at time 1 for path 1 is

$$2.038 - 3.335 \cdot 1.09 + 1.356 \cdot 1.09^2 = 0.0139$$

(We used the simulated stock price at time 1 for path 1, $1.09.) We can now compare the intrinsic value of the option with the expected value of continuing. The results are presented in Exhibit 14.7. Exhibit 14.7 also shows the cash flows at time periods 1, 2, and 3 based on the optimal strategy computed so far and conditional on not exercising the option before time 1.

The matrix of optimal stopping (exercise) times is given in Exhibit 14.8. For paths 4, 6, 7, and 8, it is optimal to exercise the option at time 1. For path 3, it is optimal to exercise at time 3.

Discounting all cash flows in the second table in Exhibit 14.7 with the appropriate discount factor and averaging over the eight sample paths, we obtain

$$(0.07 \cdot e^{-0.06 \cdot 3} + 0.17 \cdot e^{-0.06 \cdot 1} + 0.34 \cdot e^{-0.06 \cdot 1} + 0.18 \cdot e^{-0.06 \cdot 1}$$
$$+ 0.22 \cdot e^{-0.06 \cdot 1})/8 = 0.1144$$

This is the value of continuing at time 0. The intrinsic value of the option at time 0 is $1.10 - 1.00 = 0.10$, which is less than 0.1144. Therefore, 0.1144 is the fair value of the option.

EXHIBIT 14.7 Value of continuing and exercising at time 1, optimal strategy at time 1, and cash flows for the eight simulated paths at time periods 1, 2, and 3.

Path	Exercise	Continue	*Strategy?*	Cash Flow Matrix at Time 1		
				$t = 1$	$t = 2$	$t = 3$
1	0.01	0.0139	Continue	0.00	0.00	0.00
2	–	–	–	0.00	0.00	0.00
3	–	–	–	0.00	0.00	0.07
4	0.17	0.1092	Exercise	0.17	0.00	0.00
5	–	–	–	0.00	0.00	0.00
6	0.34	0.2866	Exercise	0.34	0.00	0.00
7	0.18	0.1175	Exercise	0.18	0.00	0.00
8	0.22	0.1533	Exercise	0.22	0.00	0.00

Files **Ch14-OptionPricingVBA.xlsm** and **AmericanPutLS.m** contain code for implementing the generalized algorithm with VBA and MATLAB, respectively. See this chapter's Software Hints for a detailed explanation of the code. You may also want to modify the inputs to the programs to test whether the results in the example presented in this section are correct and to check how American put price estimates obtained with regression-based methods compare with American put price estimates obtained with binomial trees, as explained in section 13.4.3 of the previous chapter.

As we mentioned at the beginning of this section, simulation-based methods for pricing derivatives with American features are most valuable in situations in which multiple factors drive the price of the underlying. Such situations often present themselves in fixed income markets, where modeling

EXHIBIT 14.8 Optimal exercise times. (One denotes optimal stopping time along each path.)

Path	$t = 0$	$t = 1$	$t = 2$	$t = 3$
1	0	0	0	0
2	0	0	0	0
3	0	0	0	1
4	0	1	0	0
5	0	0	0	0
6	0	1	0	0
7	0	1	0	0
8	0	1	0	0

basic building blocks like the yield curve can require specification of tens of factors. The pricing of a *swaption*—a widely used type of derivative in fixed income markets—is one such application described in Longstaff and Schwartz (2001). We discuss swaptions later in this section. For more examples, see Longstaff and Schwartz (2001) and Glasserman (2004).

14.4.3 Evaluating Greeks

Measuring price sensitivities is an important aspect of trading and risk management. In fact, while prices of securities can be observed in the market, and so new securities' prices can be calibrated, sensitivities are not directly observable, so one may argue that their estimation is even more important than pricing applications.

Simulation is a valuable tool for producing estimates for the various Greeks, but a few important issues that have to do with estimation bias and tractability need to be kept in mind. In order to illustrate these issues, let us discuss the estimation of the parameter (Δ) in the Black-Scholes setting.[27] We will use f to denote the price of the financial derivative in general, and C to denote the price of a call option in the Black-Scholes setting in this particular example.

By definition,

$$\Delta = \frac{df}{dS} = \lim_{\delta S \to 0} \frac{f(S + \delta S) - f(S)}{\delta S}$$

This is called a *forward-difference approximation* because we are using the difference between the current price and a price that is slightly higher than the current price. The formula above suggests a quick-and-dirty approach to estimating Δ: Simulate sample paths, and estimate Δ as the mean of the differences of the payoffs from an option with initial price equal to the current stock price and an option with initial price equal to the current stock price plus a "small" increment δS, divided by the increment δS.

This approach suffers from several problems. First, it is not very efficient. An immediate improvement that comes to mind is to use the same random numbers for computing the paths for both $f(S + \delta S)$ and $f(S)$.[28] This would reduce the variability of the estimate.

Second, in statistical terms, we are using a *biased estimator* for Δ. Recall that the fair prices of the financial derivatives can be viewed as the expected values of the discounted payoffs. We are interested in estimating

$$\lim_{\delta S \to 0} \frac{E[pf(S + \delta S)] - E[pf(S)]}{\delta S}$$

where pf is the discounted payoff. In fact, what we are estimating, however, is

$$E\left[\frac{pf(S+\delta S) - pf(S)}{\delta S}\right]$$

At first sight, the two expressions appear similar. However, in effect we are exchanging the order of the limit and the expectation. This is not generally allowed.

The quality of the estimator can be improved somewhat if we use central, rather than forward, differences. In other words, we should be computing

$$\frac{pf(S+\delta S) - pf(S-\delta S)}{2 \cdot \delta S}$$

The problem is that this involves many, many simulations. We need to repeat the same computations three times—once for $S + \delta S$, once for $S - \delta S$, and since we are typically also interested in pricing the option itself, once for S.

So-called pathwise derivative estimates provide a solution to many of the problems listed above. They differentiate each simulated outcome with respect to the parameter of interest, such as the underlying stock price, and produce unbiased estimates. The problem is that they use information about the simulated stochastic process to produce exact calculations, and can only be applied under specific circumstances. Fortunately, such estimators exist for many important options. The Black-Scholes delta, for example, can be determined in this way.

As we have noted several times, the price of a European call option in the Black-Scholes setting C equals the discounted payoff

$$e^{-r \cdot T} \cdot \max\{S_T - K, 0\}$$

where

$$S_T = S_0\, e^{(r-\frac{1}{2}\sigma^2)T + \sigma\sqrt{T}\cdot\bar{\varepsilon}}$$

Using the chain rule of differentiation, we get

$$\frac{dC}{dS_0} = \frac{dC}{dS_T} \cdot \frac{dS_T}{dS_0}$$

To evaluate the first factor in this product, we note that

$$\frac{d}{dS_T} \max\{S_T - K, 0\} = \begin{cases} 0, & S_T < K \\ 1, & S_T > K \end{cases}$$

There is no derivative at $S_T = K$, but we will ignore this because the assumption that S_T follows a continuous probability distribution means that the probability that S_T actually takes the value K is 0.[29] Therefore,

$$\frac{dC}{dS_T} = e^{-r \cdot T} \cdot 1\{S_T > K\}$$

where **1** (sometimes **I**) is standard notation for the indicator function. The indicator function equals 1 over the set specified in the brackets that follow, and 0 otherwise.

To evaluate the second factor, observe that S_T is a linear function of S_0. (S_T equals S_0 multiplied by a number.) Therefore,

$$\frac{dS_T}{dS_0} = \frac{S_T}{S_0}$$

Putting everything together, we have the following estimator:

$$\frac{dC}{dS_0} = e^{-r \cdot T} \cdot 1\{S_T > K\} \cdot \frac{S_T}{S_0}$$

The delta of the option is the average of these quantities computed over all simulated paths for the stock option price. The expression above shows that an estimate of Δ can be produced in the process of simulating the price at maturity S_T, which is very efficient. The code for implementing this approach, as well as the naïve approach described at the beginning of this section can be found in the Software Hints section for this chapter.

In the Black-Scholes setting, we had a closed-form formula for the option price, which is rarely the case with more complex derivatives. Interestingly, however, in some cases we may be able to obtain similarly convenient pathwise estimators of the Greeks even when there is no closed-form formula for the price of the financial derivative. As we discussed in section 14.1.2, there is no closed-form expression for the price of an arithmetic Asian option. However, there is a formula for computing the delta of such an option in closed form when the price of the underlying asset is assumed to follow a geometric random walk. It is

$$\frac{dC_A}{dS_0} = e^{-r \cdot T} \cdot I\{\bar{S} > K\} \cdot \frac{\bar{S}}{S_0} \quad 30$$

where $\bar{S}$ is the average price over the life of the option. The latter is a quantity that is easy to track during the simulation, so estimating the sensitivity of the option with respect to the initial price comes at virtually no additional computational cost.

14.4.4 Examples of Pricing Interest Rate Derivatives

In this section, we introduce briefly two popular interest rate derivatives: interest rate caps and swaptions, and we discuss how simulation can be useful in modeling their price.

Interest Rate Caps An interest rate cap is a portfolio of options that limits the interest paid on a floating rate note over a set of consecutive payment (reset) dates. Suppose that cap resets every three months. The interest rate paid for the first three months is the three-month LIBOR rate observed at time 0; the interest rate paid for the second three months is the three-month LIBOR observed at the first payment date (at three months), and so on. If the cap rate has been set to, say, 5%, and the three-month LIBOR at a particular date is greater, then only 5% (appropriately scaled for the time between payments) will be paid by the floating rate note, thus resulting in a positive payoff to the issuer of the floating rate note.

Each individual option is referred to as a *caplet*, and can be valued separately. The value of the cap is the sum of the values of the individual caplets. Let c be the cap rate, Δt be the time between reset dates, r_t be the interest rate for the period between reset dates t and $t + 1$, and the value of the principal be L. At time $t + 1$, the payoff to the floating rate issues is

$$L \cdot (\Delta t) \cdot \max\{r_t - c, 0\}$$

Thus, a caplet is a call option on the LIBOR rate observed at time t. (By convention, the payoff occurs at time $t + 1$.)

To price the caplet, we need to make an assumption about the movement of the interest rate r_t. There are a number of interest rate models that we can use, such as the Vasicek model, or the Cox-Ingersoll-Ross (CIR) model.[32] In some cases (e.g., if we assume that the interest rate follows a geometric random walk), we can derive a closed-form formula for the price of the caplet.[33] When this is not possible, we can value the option by simulation in much the same way in which we valued European options on stocks earlier in this chapter.

Swaptions Swaptions are a widely used type of interest rate derivative. There are two types of swaptions—a payer swaption and a receiver swaption. A *payer swaption* entitles the option buyer to enter into an interest rate swap in which the buyer of the option pays a fixed rate and receives a floating rate. In a *receiver swaption*, the buyer of the swaption has the right to enter into an interest-rate swap that requires paying a floating rate and receiving a fixed rate.

Consider a receiver swaption with notional of 1 that consists of an option (expiring at time T^o) to enter into a swap with payment dates $(T^o + 1)$, $(T^o + 2)$, ..., T^s. Following the notation and the discussion in section 13.5, we know that the value of the underlying swap at time T^o to the option holder is

$$v \cdot (\Delta t) \cdot \sum_{t=T^o+1}^{T^s} B(T^o, t) + 1 \cdot B(T^o, T^s) - 1$$

The holder of the option will exercise if this value is greater than 0, and let the option expire of the value is negative.

The value of the swap at time T^o can be written as

$$(\Delta t) \cdot \sum_{t=T^o+1}^{T^s} B(T^o, t) \cdot \max\{v - v(T^o + 1), 0\}$$

where $v(T^o+1)$ is the fair value of the swap rate for a swap starting at time T^o+1.[34] Hence, the swaption can be viewed as an option on the swap rate. In order to price a swaption, we therefore need to model the dynamics of the process followed by the swap rate.

Pricing a swaption becomes more complicated if the option to enter into a swap is American. As we mentioned at the end of section 4.2, regression-based methods for pricing American options can be very helpful in this situation. Longstaff and Schwartz (2001) describe one such application. They consider a receiver swaption such that the option holder has the right to enter into a swap in which the option holder receives fixed coupons and pays floating coupons on a semiannual cycle. The floating coupon paid at the end of the semiannual cycle is tied to the six-month rate determined at the beginning of the semiannual cycle. The time to maturity is 10 years, that is, there are 20 coupon payments. Since the underlying swap makes coupon payments at 20 different points in time, its value is sensitive to 20 different points along the yield curve. Longstaff and Schwartz (2001) consider each of these 20 points a separate but correlated factor, and model the joint dynamics of the 20 factors. These factors can be represented, for example, as the prices of zero-coupon bonds that mature at each of the 20 coupon payment dates. The simulation then consists of paths for which at each coupon date, the entire vector of zero-coupon bond prices is specified. The value of the underlying swap at that coupon date can be computed by discounting the remaining fixed coupon payments. The basis functions could consist of a constant, the first three powers of the value of the underlying swap, and all unmatured discount bond prices with final maturity dates up to and including the final maturity date of the swap, a total of 22 basis functions.

SUMMARY

- Crude Monte Carlo simulation methods involve most straightforward application of simulation for pricing derivatives: generating paths for the price of the underlying asset, and evaluating the average of the resulting discounted payoffs from the derivative. While not always the most efficient methods, they are intuitive and easy to apply.
- Various variance reduction methods exist to speed up the simulation and reduce the variance of the estimate. Such methods include using antithetic variables, stratified sampling, importance sampling, and control variates.
- The idea behind using antithetic variables is to generate one set of random numbers which can then be used twice in the estimation in a smart way. A set of "antithetic" numbers is created out of the originally generated set of random numbers, and paths for the underlying asset price are computed with both sets of random numbers. This information is then used in the calculation of the final derivative price. Since generating random numbers is computationally intensive, this method reduces both the computational time (by "reusing" already generated random numbers) and the variance of the estimate (by incorporating two sets of random numbers that are hopefully negatively correlated).
- Stratified sampling creates a representative sample of the entire range of outcomes by dividing the unit interval into pieces, called strata, and sampling within each stratum.

- Importance sampling changes the underlying scenario probabilities so as to give more weight to important outcomes in the simulation. Such outcomes are generated with greater frequency than they otherwise would. At the end, the observations' weights are scaled back in the computation of the expression of interest, so that the estimation is correct.
- The control variates method uses knowledge about a function that is related somehow to the original function we are trying to estimate by simulation. In the context of derivative pricing, the control variates method attempts to find the expected value of the discounted payoffs of a derivative for which no analytical formula is known by using knowledge about an expected value of a related variable that is known.
- Quasirandom, or quasi–Monte Carlo methods can be thought of as an extreme version of stratification methods. They rely on number theory to produce sequences of numbers (called low-discrepancy sequences) that do not pretend to be random, but instead cover the unit interval in a uniform way, so that every part of the probability distribution is represented when simulating.
- Widely used quasirandom sequences include the Van der Corput sequence, the Halton sequence, the Faure sequence, and the Sobol sequence. Some sequences work better than others for pricing specific derivatives, but there is no comprehensive way to determine that in advance without testing. For simulations in up to 15 dimensions (that is, simulations of up to 15 random variables at the same time), the choice of a quasirandom sequence does not make a big difference.
- Simulation is a flexible technique for determining the prices of complex derivatives for which no closed-form formulas exist. It can be used, for example, for pricing exotic options such as Asian and barrier options, pricing American options and interest rate derivatives, as well as evaluating sensitivities of derivative prices with respect to a variable of interest.

SOFTWARE HINTS

@RISK

The pricing of some of the simpler derivatives by simulation can be done directly in an Excel spreadsheet. We show here the examples of pricing a call option in the Black-Scholes setting and pricing an arithmetic Asian option when the price of the underlying asset is assumed to follow a geometric random walk. The more complicated algorithms explained in sections

	A	B	C	D	E
1	Black-Scholes option pricing formula (simulation)				
2					
3	Initial price	$ 50.00			
4	Strike price	$ 52.00			
5	Time to expiration	0.50			
6	Interest rate	10%			
7	Volatility	35%			
8	Dividend yield	0			
9					
10	Price at expiration	$ 59.88			
11	Discounted payoff (call)	$ 7.49			
12	Discounted payoff (put)	$ -			
13					
14					
15	Call price	$ 5.20		Put price	$ 4.64
16					

EXHIBIT 14.9 Worksheet B-S Sim in the file Ch14-PricingBySimulation.xlsx.

14.4.2 through 14.4.4 of this chapter are implemented using VBA in the next section.

Pricing a European Call Option Worksheet B-S Sim in the file Ch14-PricingBySimulation.xlsx contains a simple illustration of the assumptions underlying the Black-Scholes option pricing formula (see section 14.1.1). A snapshot of the spreadsheet is shown in Exhibit 14.9.

Cells B3:B8 contain the input data—initial price, strike price, time to expiration, interest rate, volatility, and dividend yield. In cell B10, we simulate the price of the underlying stock at expiration. It contains the formula

```
=B3*EXP((B6-0.5*B7^2)*B5+B7*SQRT(B5)*RiskNormal(0,1))
```

Cell B11 is an output cell for @RISK: it computes the discounted payoff for the call from the simulation of the stock price at maturity, and contains the formula

```
=RiskOutput("Discounted payoff (call)")+EXP(-B6*B5)*MAX(B10-
B4,0)
```

Similarly, cell B12 computes the discounted payoff for the put from the simulation of the stock price at maturity, and contains the formula

```
=RiskOutput("Discounted payoff (put)")+EXP(-B6*B5)*MAX(B4-
B10,0)
```

Cells B15 and E15 compute the fair price of the call (respectively, the put), and contain the formulas =RiskMean(B11) and =RiskMean(B12), respectively. The RiskMean command is a shortcut to recording the average realized in the simulation. Alternatively, we can simply look at the output from the simulation (output cells B11 and B12), and make a note of the realized mean.

Pricing an Asian Call Option Suppose now that we have an arithmetic Asian option with the parameters specified in cells B3:B8 in worksheet **Asian Sim** of the file **Ch14-PricingBySimulation.xlsx** (see Exhibit 14.10). The time to maturity is still 0.5 years, and we need to keep track of the average realized price of the option during the simulation. We simulate paths for the price of the underlying stock price. The larger the number of intermediate time periods, the better. For illustration purposes, we choose to record the value of the underlying price 12 times over the life of the option, that is, approximately every two weeks. The simulated values for the stock price are in cells F4:F15. For example, cell F4 contains the formula

```
=F3*EXP(($B$6-0.5*$B$7^2)*$B$5/12+$B$7*SQRT($B$5/12)
*RiskNormal(0,1))
```

	A	B	C	D	E	F	G	H	I	J
1	Arithmetic Asian option (simulation)									
2						Simulated stock price			Average realized stock price	
3	Initial price	$ 50.00				$ 50.00				
4	Strike price	$ 52.00			1	$ 48.43			$ 52.04	
5	Time to expiration	0.50			2	$ 53.27				
6	Interest rate	10%			3	$ 46.76				
7	Volatility	35%			4	$ 53.71				
8	Dividend yield	0			5	$ 53.10				
9					6	$ 59.10				
10	Discounted payoff (call)	$ 0.04			7	$ 54.54				
11	Discounted payoff (put)	$ -			8	$ 55.25				
12					9	$ 50.78				
13	Call price	$ 2.88			10	$ 49.78				
14	Put price	$ 3.39			11	$ 48.24				
15					12	$ 51.51				

EXHIBIT 14.10 Worksheet **Asian Sim** in the file Ch14-PricingBySimulation.xlsm.

Note that the time parameter in the above formula is $B$5/12 (i.e., 0.5/12) because we are simulating each of the 12 steps of the geometric random walk for the stock price between the initial time and maturity. The drift and the volatility parameter therefore get adjusted.

The average realized stock price over the 12 steps is recorded in cell H4, which contains the formula =AVERAGE(F4:F15). The discounted payoff for the call and the put are recorded in cells B10 and B11, respectively. For example, cell B10 contains the formula

```
=RiskOutput("Discounted payoff (call)")+EXP(-B6*B5)
*MAX(H4-B4,0)
```

Cells B13 and B14 compute the fair arithmetic Asian option price using the @RISK formula RiskMean.

Visual Basic

The VBA code for the different option pricing models presented in this section is in the file **Ch14-OptionPricingVBA.xlsm**. In many of these models, we generate the paths for the underlying assuming a geometric random walk. The code for generating geometric random walk paths in VBA is similar to the code for generating geometric random walk paths in MATLAB from the Software Hints section in Chapter 12. It can be found in the function GRWPaths in the file **Ch14-OptionPricingVBA.xlsm**. When the underlying stock pays a continuous dividend yield (denoted by q in the code), we use the same function GRWPaths to generate paths, but we pass the interest rate minus the dividend rate as an argument in place of r. (In other words, we reduce the growth rate by the amount of the continuous dividend.)

Pricing a European Call Option Using Crude Monte Carlo   The code for a function that returns the price of a European call option given a number of geometric random walk paths numPaths for the underlying is in the function EuropeanCall (see section 14.1.1).

Pricing an Asian Call Option with Crude Monte Carlo   The code for generating the Asian call option price with crude Monte Carlo is in the function ArithmeticAsianCall (see section 14.1.2).

Pricing a European Call Option with Antithetic Variables   The code for finding the value of a European call option is in the function EuropeanCallAntithetic. We create two arrays with payoffs, payoffsOrig (obtained with the originally generated random numbers stored in array randNumOrig), and payoffsAnt (obtained with the antithetic variables stored in array randNumAnt). The payoffs we consider for the pricing of the option are the averages of payoffsOrig and payoffsAnt (see section 14.2.1).

Pricing an Asian Call Option with the Control Variates Method

The code for finding the value of a geometric average Asian call option is in the function GeometricAsianCall (see section 14.2.4.)

To use the control variates method, we need to estimate the value of the coefficient b. The first part of the code does that—it runs N_p (numPrelim) preliminary trials, and uses the observations to estimate b. The second part of the code estimates the actual value of the arithmetic Asian call option with the control variates method. To simulate paths for the underlying stock, we assume that the stock follows a geometric random walk, and use the GRWPaths function.

The function uses the user-defined functions MeanSub and ProdSub, which find the sum and the product of a subarray. The code for the functions is provided earlier in the same module.

The code for comparing the performance of the simulation algorithm for evaluating the Asian option price with and without the control variates method is provided in the function ArithmeticAsianCallEstimation-Comparison.

Constructing a Van der Corput Quasirandom Sequence

The code for constructing N points from a Van der Corput sequence of base b is in the function VanDerCorput (see section 14.3.1).

The vector array vVec stores the values of the points in the sequence. For a given index (which varies from 1 to the total number of points to be calculated), the Do While loop creates the point in the Van der Corput sequence by effectively computing the representation of the index in base b, and then inverting that representation.

Constructing a Halton Quasirandom Sequence

The code in the Halton function generates the first K points from a Halton sequence of dimension d (see section 14.3.2). If we are given a dimension d, we need to generate d prime numbers. The function Primes finds all prime numbers up to a given number d. A well-known fact from number theory is that there are approximately $d/\ln(d)$ prime numbers that are less than or equal to d. The dth prime number should be approximately $d \cdot \ln(d)$. This is not an exact approximation—for some values of d, it will be quite accurate; for others, not. So, to make sure that we generate at least d prime numbers to use in the Halton function, we will take at least double the number. The rest of the

`Halton` function code calls the function for computing a Van der Corput sequence in each dimension.

Computing the Price of a European Call Option with the Halton Sequence

The function `EuropeanCallHalton` illustrates how to calculate the price of a European call option with the Halton sequences. (See section 14.3.5.) We use the function `Halton(N,d)`, which we introduced in the previous section.

Pricing a Down-and-Out Put Option with Crude Monte Carlo   The code for finding the value of a down-and-out put is in the function `DownAndOutPut`. (See section 14.4.1.)

In the code of the `DownAndOutPut` function, we check whether any of the elements in the `path` array generated as a geometric random walk path is less than or equal to the barrier S_b. If it is, then the value of the variable `crossedPaths` for that path will be 1; otherwise, it will be 0. If the barrier has been crossed on a particular path, we consider the payoff on that path; otherwise, the payoff is set to zero. We then take the average of the discounted payoffs along all paths.

Pricing an American Put Option with Regression Methods   The generalized code for computing the price of an American put option with least-squares (regression) methods is in the `AmericanPutLS` function. (See also section 14.4.2.)

There are several challenges of implementing this code in VBA compared to more advanced modeling languages like MATLAB. First, in contrast to MATLAB, one cannot pass function references as an input to a VBA function, so the three functions used to create the regression matrix were hard-coded in a separate function, `AmericanPutLSFn`.

Second, it is in general difficult to take advantage of other Excel add-ins from within VBA. In the American put option pricing example, we need to run a regression and estimate the regression coefficients. There are two ways to run regressions in Excel: through the Analysis ToolPak (under the **Data** tab) and through the `linest` function. Both of these options are problematic to use from within VBA. The regression function in the Analysis ToolPak requires writing data into the actual spreadsheet, which can be done from within a VBA script (starting with a `Sub`), but not from a function call (a script that starts with `Function`) such as our American option pricing function. The `linest` function behaves erratically when called with specific options (such as when we request that an intercept term is not included in the regression), and more frustratingly, it does not alert the user that the estimates are wrong, so it needs to be handled with care. While we provide working code below, we alert the reader that in order to work around the bug with the `linest` function, we need to assume that there will always be a constant term in the regression. This part of the code can be fixed when the `linest` function in Excel is fixed. While VBA can get the job done for small tasks, the American option pricing model with least squares requires complex enough calculations that illustrate the advantage of integrated modeling environments like MATLAB.

To test the `AmericanPutLS` function, you can enter the data for the eight generated paths from section 14.4.2, and verify that the option price is indeed $0.1144.

Evaluating a European Call Option Delta with Naïve Monte Carlo and a Pathwise Method   The function `EuropeanCallDeltaMC` contains the code for calculating the delta of a European call in the Black-Scholes setting with crude Monte Carlo, central differences, and blocking. (The same set of random numbers, `randomNumbers`, are used for computing both the call price with starting price $S_0 + \delta S_0$ and $S_0 - \delta S_0$.) See section 14.4.3 for a description of the method.

The function `EuropeanCallDeltaPW` contains the code for calculating the delta of a European call in the Black-Scholes setting with the pathwise method described in section 14.4.3.

MATLAB

Pricing a European Call Option Using Crude Monte Carlo   The code for a function that returns the price of a European call option given a number of geometric random walk paths `numPaths` for the underlying is in the function `EuropeanCall`. (See section 14.1.1 and file **EuropeanCall.m**.)

Pricing an Asian Call Option with Crude Monte Carlo   The code for generating the Asian call option price with crude Monte Carlo is in the function `ArithmeticAsianCall`. (See section 14.1.2. and file **ArithmeticAsianCall.m**.)

Pricing a European Call Option with Antithetic Variables   The code for finding the value of a European call option is in the function `EuropeanCallAntithetic`. We create two arrays with payoffs, `payoffsOrig` (obtained with the originally generated random numbers stored in array `randNumOrig`), and `payoffsAnt` (obtained with the antithetic variables stored in array `randNumAnt`). The payoffs we consider for the pricing of the option are the averages of `payoffsOrig` and `payoffsAnt`. See section 14.2.1 and file **EuropeanCallAntithetic.m**.

Pricing an Asian Call Option with the Control Variates Method The code for finding the value of a geometric average Asian call option is in the function GeometricAsianCall (see section 14.2.4 and file **GeometricAsianCall.m**).

To use the control variates method, we need to estimate the value of the coefficient b. The first part of the code below does that—it runs N_p preliminary trials, and uses the observations to estimate b. The second part of the code estimates the actual value of the arithmetic Asian call option with the control variates method. To simulate paths for the underlying stock, we assume that the stock follows a geometric random walk, and use the GRWPaths function we wrote in Chapter 12. The code is in file **ArithmeticAsianCallCV.m**.

The code for comparing the performance of the simulation algorithm for evaluating the Asian option price with and without the control variates method is provided in the file **ArithmeticAsianCallEstimationComparison.m**).[35]

Constructing a Van der Corput Quasirandom Sequence The code for constructing N points from a Van der Corput sequence of base b is provided in the function VanDerCorput (see section 14.3.1 and file **VanDerCorput.m**).

The vector array vVec stores the values of the points in the sequence. For a given index (which varies from 1 to the total number of points to be calculated), the while loop creates the point in the Van der Corput sequence by effectively computing the representation of the index in base b, and then inverting that representation.

Constructing a Halton Quasirandom Sequence MATLAB's Statistics Toolbox contains built-in syntax for computing the elements of a Halton sequence. The function haltonset(d) computes the sequence of dimension d, and the sequence can be retrieved with the command net. For example,

```
>> seq = haltonset(3); net(seq,5)
```

returns the first five elements of a Halton sequence of dimension 3.

Nevertheless, it is instructive to see a program that generates the first K points from a Halton sequence of dimension d (see section 14.3.2 and file **Halton.m**). If we are given a dimension d, we need to generate d prime numbers. In MATLAB, a function that generates all prime numbers less than or equal to d is primes (d). However, there is no function that returns d prime numbers. So, we need to approximate. A well-known fact from number theory is that there are approximately $d/\ln(d)$ prime numbers that are less than or equal to d. The dth prime number should be approximately $d/\ln(d)$. This is not an exact approximation—for some values of d, it will be quite accurate;

for others, not. So, to make sure that we generate at least d prime numbers, we double the number, and use the command `primes(2·d·max(1,log(d)))`. The rest of the code calls the function for computing a Van der Corput sequence in each dimension.

Constructing a Sobol Quasirandom Sequence MATLAB's Statistics Toolbox contains built-in syntax for computing the elements of a Sobol sequence (see section 14.3.4). The function `sobolset(d)` computes the sequence of dimension d, and the sequence can be retrieved with the command net. For example,

```
>> seq = sobolset(3); net(seq,5)
```

returns the first five elements of a Sobol sequence of dimension 3.

Computing the Price of a European Call Option with the Halton or the Sobol Sequence The following two functions illustrate how to calculate the price of a European call option with the Halton and the Sobol sequences (see section 14.3.5). In the case of the Halton sequence, we use the function `Halton(N,d)`, which we introduced earlier. In the case of the Sobol sequence, we use the function `sobolset` in MATLAB's Statistics Toolbox. Note that the Halton sequence implementation can also be done directly by using the function `haltonset` in MATLAB's Statistics Toolbox. We offer two different implementations for illustration purposes.

The code for pricing a European call option using a Halton sequence is in file **EuropeanCallHalton.m**.

In this function, we use a nice feature in MATLAB, which is that we can pass an array (`HaltonPoints`) into a formula (`initPrice*exp((r-q-0.5*sigma^2)*T + sigma*sqrt(T)*norminv(HaltonPoints))`), and MATLAB automatically creates an array with results (`assetPrices`). In other programming languages, we would need to implement this by creating a `for` loop.

The code for pricing a European call option using a Sobol sequence is in the file **EuropeanCallSobol.m**. Here we generate the Sobol sequence of dimension 1 and length $N+1$ with the commands

```
seq = sobolset(1);
SobolPoints = net(seq,numPaths+1);
```

and remove the first element, which is 0, with the command

```
SobolPoints = SobolPoints(2:numPaths+1);
```

It is common to drop some number of elements of quasirandom sequences, so that we can use directly scenarios that represent the unit interval well. As Exhibit 14.1 illustrated, it takes a certain "warming up" for the quasirandom sequence to begin producing stable and accurate estimates.

Pricing a Down-and-Out Put Option with Crude Monte Carlo The code for finding the value of a down-and-out put is in the function DownAndOutPut (see section 14.4.1 and file **DownAndOutPut.m**).

In the code of the DownAndOutPut function, we use the MATLAB function any. It returns one ("True") if the condition in the parentheses is satisfied, and 0 otherwise. In this example, it checks whether any of the elements in the path array generated as a geometric random walk path is less than or equal to the barrier S_b. If it is, then the expression path <= Sb is true, and value of the variable crossedPaths for that path will be 1; otherwise, it will be 0.

Pricing an American Put Option with Regression Methods File **American-PutLS.m** contains generalized code for computing the price of an American put option with least-squares (regression) methods (see also section 14.4.2).

Let us briefly explain the idea behind the algorithm, as well as some new MATLAB syntax.

We begin by computing the discount factors for every time period. We create a vector, discountFactors, which has as many elements as there are time periods. The first element in the vector contains the discount factor for one time period (it will be used to discount the cash flows for the second-to-last time period), the next element contains the discount factor for two time periods (it will be used to discount the cash flows for the third-to-last time period), and the like.

Next, we handle the basis functions that are passed as arguments to the function through the expression fhandles (function handles). Function handles are a way in MATLAB to call functions indirectly. In our case, we need a way to state the functions of the stock price that will be used in the regression as an argument of the function AmericanPutLS. This needs to be done symbolically. So, if the basis functions of the stock price are a constant, S, and S^2, the argument fhandles to the function AmericanPutLS will have the following form:

```
{@(x)ones(length(x),1),@(x)x,@(x)x.^2}
```

The interpretation is as follows: there are three functions, each of them is a function of a single variable (x), and when an argument is passed to the function handles (which is what the @ signs mean), the following operations will be performed:

1. The first function (called with fhandle{1}) will take the argument that is passed to it and will create a vector of ones of length equal to that argument.
2. The second function (called with fhandle{2}) will take the argument that is passed to it and return that argument.
3. The third function (called with fhandle{3}) will take the argument that is passed to it and return the square of that argument.

We use these function handles later, when we iterate through the data at each time period, and compute each column of the regression matrix by calling the corresponding basis function. To execute a function in the body of the program, we can use one of two methods. The first is to call the function handle directly with an argument. For example, the command

```
>fhandles{3}(5)
```

will return 25, which is the square of the argument 5. (fhandles{3} calls the third element of the structure of function handles, which is the function computing the square of a number.)

Alternatively, we can execute a function that is an element of the array fhandles by using the command feval. The command

```
>>feval(fhandles{3},5)
```

will produce the same result: 25. In the program, we evaluate the function for the array XData, which contains the values of the stock prices at a particular time period. By evaluating calling each element of the array fhandles on XData, we create the columns of the regression data matrix.

The parameter numBasisFns stores the number of basis functions we consider. (We use that parameter when we specify the number of columns of data in the regression matrix as well.)

We also have a vector cashFlows, which stores the intrinsic value (in the case of an American put option, this is the maximum of the strike price minus the current price and 0) along every path at a particular point in time. (We work backwards, so that the initial cashFlows vector is simply the intrinsic value of the option at the final time period, assuming the option has not been exercised until then. At the second-to-last period, we store the intrinsic value for those paths for which the intrinsic value is greater than the value of continuing (that is, the paths for which it is optimal to exercise the option at that time)). MATLAB's syntax is quite convenient—referencing only of the cash flows for which it is optimal to exercise the option is accomplished with the expression `cashFlows(exercisePaths)`.

The vector `inMoneyPathIndices` stores the indices of the paths which are in the money at the current time period (`iStep`). These are the sample paths that get used in the regression to determine a function (only of the current time period) that approximates the value of continuing. We run the regression with a response variable (`YData`) that contains the cash flows from the previous step, discounted properly. The explanatory variables (stored in the array `regressionMx`) are a constant, a vector of current prices, and a vector of current prices squared. To determine the regression coefficients, we use a new (very useful) syntax,

```
betaCoefficients = regressionMx\YData
```

This is sort of a "division" of two matrices—basically since

```
YData = betaCoefficients*regressionMx
```

this command is an efficient way to determine the regression coefficients. The same result can be obtained with the command

```
[betaCoefficients,nn,nn,nn,nn] = regress(YData,regressionMx)
```
[36]

but the latter command requires MATLAB's Statistics Toolbox.

At the end of the loop, we discount the cash flows from the last step in the `for` loop (the first time period since we are working backwards) to the present depending on when the option was exercised along a particular simulated path. If the option was never exercised, then the exercise time was never modified from its initial value (the last time period), and so use a discount factor for the entire duration of the option (the discount factor does not matter because if the option was not exercised, the payoff along that path will be zero anyway).

Finally, at time 0 we compare the intrinsic value of the option with the value of continuing (which is the mean of the discounted payoffs along all the sampled paths) to determine whether we should exercise the option at time 0. The maximum of the intrinsic value and the value of continuing equals the value of the option.

You can verify that the code works by testing the simple example described in section 14.4.2. Instead of generating paths for a stock price that follows a geometric random walk, enter the data for the eight simulated paths directly into the function, and print out intermediate results (or step through the function using the debugger) to see whether you obtain the cash flows, the exercise times, the regression equations, and the final option price described in the example.

Evaluating a European Call Option Delta with Naïve Monte Carlo and a Pathwise Method   File EuropeanCallDeltaMC.m contains the code for calculating the delta of a European call in the Black-Scholes setting with crude Monte Carlo, central differences, and blocking. (The same set of random numbers, `randomNumbers`, are used for computing both the call price with starting price $S_0 + \delta S_0$ and $S_0 - \delta S_0$.) See section 14.4.3 for a description of the method.

File **EuropeanCallDeltaPW.m** contains the code for calculating the delta of a European call in the Black-Scholes setting with the pathwise method described in section 14.4.3.

You can verify that the pathwise estimator method above produces much more accurate estimates for the option delta than the crude Monte Carlo method. To see this, compare the results from using the two functions in this section to the results obtained with MATLAB's built-in function `blsdelta`.[37]

NOTES

1. See Chapter 12 for an introduction to different types of random walks.
2. See Black and Scholes (1973).
3. See Chapter 12, Sections 3 and 6.
4. If the stock pays a continuously compounded dividend yield of q, then we use $(r - q - 0.5 \cdot \sigma 2)$ instead of $(r - 0.5 \cdot \sigma 2)$ as the drift term.
5. See Chapter 2 for a definition of term structure of interest rates.
6. See Chapter 13 for a definition of forward price.
7. Recall that the geometric average would be computed as $(S_1 \cdot \ldots \cdot S_T)^{1/T}$.
8. See the example in section 14.2.4.
9. See section 4.3 of Chapter 4 for a discussion of estimator efficiency and bias.
10. Recall that this function can be called with the command =NORMINV(`number, mean, standard deviation`) in Excel, or `norminv`(`number, mean, standard deviation`) in MATLAB. In the case of the standard normal distribution, mean = 0 and `standard deviation` = 1.
11. The formula for Φ^{-1} can be entered as =NORMINV(($(n-1+U_n)/N,0,1$) in Excel or `norminv`(($n-1+ U_n$)/$N,0,1$) in MATLAB. The subscripts are, of course, not entered: U_n represents the value for the nth simulated number from the uniform distribution.
12. See section 13.1.2 of Chapter 13 for a definition of in-the-money and out-of-the-money options.

13. See section 3.6.1 of Chapter 3 for the definition of expected value as an integral over all values the random variable can take.
14. See section 3.6.2 of Chapter 3.
15. See Chapter 3.
16. See section 3.6.1 of Chapter 3.
17. The base is essentially how many digits are used to express a number. The conventional way to work with numbers is in base 10—it derives from the fact that humans have 10 fingers, and the earliest counting systems were often based on that fact. We use 10 digits—0,1,2,3,4,5,6,7,8,9 to express every number in base 10. Nothing prevents us, however, from working with numbers in different bases. The idea is to express the number as a sum of powers of the base. For example, the number 13 in base 10 can be written as $13 = 1 \cdot 10^1 + 3 \cdot 10^0$. The same number, 13, in base 2 will contain only two digits—0 and 1—and will be expressed as 1101: $1 \cdot 2^3 + 1 \cdot 2^2 + 0 \cdot 2^1 + 1 \cdot 2^0$.
18. Here we have used several standard notations. The expression $a \bmod b$ returns the remainder of a after division with b, that is, the amount by which a exceeds the largest multiple of b that is less than a. The notation

$$\binom{j}{k}$$

(read "j choose k") returns a number that equals the number of ways in which k items can be selected out of j items. As we saw in the context of pricing options with binomial trees, it equals

$$\frac{j!}{k!(j-k)!}$$

if $j \geq k$, and 0 otherwise. As we explained earlier in the book, the expression $j!$ (read "j factorial") equals the product $1 \cdot 2 \cdot \ldots \cdot j$. If $j = 0$, $j! = 1$ by convention.
19. When the option holder has the right to exercise the option contract at specific preset dates, the options are referred to as Bermudan options or Mid-Atlantic options since their features are somewhere between European and American option features.
20. See, for example, Hull (2008).
21. See, for example, Brandimarte (2006).
22. For a nice overview, see Glasserman (2004).
23. Recall that the value function measures of the expected reward going forward from the current state. See the introduction to dynamic programming in section 6.1 in Chapter 6, and the introduction to American option pricing with binomial trees in Chapter 13.
24. Readers may wonder why we do not do this to estimate the value of the option to begin with. Note that assuming perfect vision means that you can anticipate what happens in the future when you make the decision of whether to exercise or not today. In practice, we do not have that knowledge, so it would be incorrect to assume that we can use the knowledge to compute the optimal price of the option.

25. See Longstaff and Schwartz (2001).
26. Typically, we would care about the validity of the regression equation, and pay attention to the significance of the regression coefficients as well as to multicollinearity issues (that is, whether the explanatory variables are correlated among themselves, which would produce poor estimates of the regression coefficients). However, in this application we use the regression equation for forecasting purposes, so we are concerned with the model as a whole, and not with the significance of the individual explanatory variables.
27. See section 13.4.4 of Chapter 13 for a definition of delta.
28. See section 4.2.3 of Chapter 4 for a justification for this approach.
29. See section 3.4 of Chapter 3.
30. See section 7.2 of Chapter 7 in Glasserman (2004).
31. See Chapter 2 for a definition of term structure.
32. See section 12.4.3.
33. See Hull (2008).
34. This can be derived with some simple algebra following the arguments in section 13.5; see also Appendix C in Glasserman (2004).
35. Make sure that you comment out the `figure` and `plot` command from the file **GRWPaths.m** before you run this code, so that you do not overwhelm the memory with thousands of figures for every generated geometric random walk path.
36. Recall that we used the command in the code for estimating random walk parameters in Chapter 12.
37. The MATLAB function `blsdelta` requires the Financial Toolbox.

CHAPTER 15

Structuring and Pricing Residential Mortgage-Backed Securities

Chapter 2 briefly introduced the different types of fixed income securities such as bonds, asset-backed securities (ABSs), and bank loans. This chapter deals with the valuation of specific types of ABSs, which is challenging both from a theoretical and from an implementation point of view: residential mortgage-backed securities. As shown in this chapter, simulation and dynamic programming are valuable tools for handling the structuring and pricing of this type of ABS.

We begin with a detailed account ABS types and important terminology. Then we proceed with defining concepts relevant for pricing these securities, such as prepayment models. We conclude with a discussion of how simulation and dynamic programming are applied in this context.

15.1 TYPES OF ASSET-BACKED SECURITIES

Asset-backed securities are debt instruments that are backed by a pool of loans or receivables. They are also referred to as *structured products*. The process for creating ABSs, referred to as *securitization*, is as follows. The owner of assets sells a pool of assets to a bankruptcy remote vehicle called a *special purpose entity* (SPE). The SPE obtains the proceeds to acquire the asset pool, referred to as the *collateral*, by issuing debt instruments. The cash flow of the asset pool is used to satisfy the obligations of the debt instruments issued by the SPE. The debt instruments issued by the SPE are generically referred to as asset-backed securities, asset-backed notes, asset-backed bonds, and asset-backed obligations.

ABSs issued in a single securitization can have different credit exposure. Based on the credit priority, securities are described as *senior notes* and *junior notes* (subordinate notes). In the prospectus for a securitization transaction, the securities are actually referred to as *certificates*: pass-through certificates or pay-through certificates. The distinction between these two types is the nature of the claim that the investor has on the cash flow generated by the asset pool. If the investor has a direct claim on all of the cash flows, and the certificate holder has a proportionate share of the collateral's cash flow, the term *pass-through certificate* (or *beneficial interest certificate*) is used. When there are rules to allocate the collateral's cash flow among different classes of investors, the asset-backed securities are referred to as *pay-through certificates*.

There is considerable variety of types of assets that have been securitized. Most generally, these assets can be classified as mortgage assets and non-mortgage assets. Securities backed by residential and commercial mortgage loans[1] are referred to as *residential mortgage-backed securities* (RMBSs) and *commercial mortgage-backed securities* (CMBSs), respectively. In turn, RMBSs can be further classified as *agency RMBSs* and *private-label* (or nonagency) *RMBSs*. Agency RMBSs are those issued by three government-related entities, and constitute by far the largest sector in the investment-grade bond market (more than 35%). Private-label RMBSs are issued by any other entity. Because of the credit risk associated with private-label RMBSs, they require credit enhancement to provide some form of credit protection against default on the pool of assets backing a transaction.

Credit enhancement mechanisms are typical in ABS transactions. In the case of agency RMBSs, the credit enhancement is either a government guarantee or the guarantee of a government-sponsored enterprise. Private-label RMBSs are further classified based on the credit quality of the mortgage loans in the pool: *prime loans* and *subprime loans*. Subprime loans are loans made to borrowers with impaired credit ratings, and RMBSs backed by them are referred to as *subprime RMBSs*. The market classifies prime loans as part of the nonagency RMBS market, while those backed by subprime loans are part of the ABS market.

In addition to mortgages, other traditional assets that have been securitized include credit card loans, auto loans, bonds (corporate and sovereign), and bank loans. Some examples of nontraditional assets include future music royalties that were securitized for recording artists David Bowie, James Brown, the Isley Brothers, and Rod Stewart.[2]

15.2 MORTGAGE-BACKED SECURITIES: IMPORTANT TERMINOLOGY

A mortgage is a loan secured by the collateral of some specified real estate property that obliges the borrower to make a predetermined series of payments. The mortgage gives the lender (mortgagee) the right, if the borrower (the mortgagor) defaults (i.e., fails to make the contractual payments), to foreclose on the loan and seize the property in order to ensure that the debt is paid off. The interest rate on the mortgage loan is called the *note rate*.

The fundamental unit in a mortgage-backed security (MBS) is the *pool*. At its lowest common denominator, mortgage-backed pools are aggregations of large numbers of mortgage loans with similar (but not identical) characteristics. Loans with common attributes such as note rate, term to maturity, credit quality, loan balance, and type of mortgage design are combined using a variety of legal mechanisms to create relatively fungible investment vehicles. With the creation of MBSs, mortgage loans are transformed from a heterogeneous group of disparate assets into sizeable and homogenous securities that trade in a liquid market.

The transformation of groups of mortgage loans with common attributes into MBS occurs using one of two mechanisms. Loans that meet the underwriting guidelines of three entities—Ginnie Mae, Fannie Mae, and Freddie Mac—are securitized as an agency pool. While Ginnie Mae (Government National Mortgage Association) is an agency of the U.S. government, carrying the full faith and credit of U.S. government, Fannie Mae and Freddie Mac are government-sponsored enterprises. Despite this distinction, MBSs issued by these three entities are referred to as *agency MBSs*. There are three types of agency MBSs: pass-through securities, stripped mortgage-backed securities, and collateralized mortgage obligations.

Loans that do not qualify for agency pools are securitized in nonagency or "private-label" transactions. These types of securities do not have an agency guaranty, and must therefore be issued under the registration entity or "shelf" of the issuer. Private-label deals share many features and structuring techniques with agency collateralized mortgage obligations that we will describe below. There are some important differences, however, due to the nature of the loans collateralizing the deal as well as legal and regulatory issues associated with the different shelves. One important distinction is that such deals must have some form of credit enhancement in order to create large amounts of investment-grade bonds. Another is that they may include assets other than mortgages. We discuss these differences later in this chapter.

As noted in the previous section, there is a special category of mortgage-related asset-backed securities called subprime MBSs. Such securities are riskier than those in prime deals, either because the loans in the pool are granted to borrowers with impaired credit (which greatly increases their expected defaults and losses), or because they are in an inferior lien position (which creates high-loss severities). As such, these loans are characterized by higher note rates than those in the prime sector, reflecting risk-based pricing on the part of the lenders.

15.2.1 Cash Flow Characteristics
of a Residential Mortgage Loan

Although a mortgagor may select from many types of mortgage loans, for the sake of simplicity we use the most common mortgage design: the level payment, fixed rate mortgage. The basic idea behind the design of the level payment, fixed rate mortgage, or simply *level payment mortgage*, is that the borrower pays interest and repays principal in equal installments over an agreed-upon period of time, called the *maturity* or *term* of the mortgage. At the end of the term, the loan has been fully amortized. For a level payment mortgage, each monthly mortgage payment is due on the first of each month and consists of:

- Interest of one-twelfth of the fixed annual note rate times the amount of the outstanding mortgage balance at the beginning of the previous month.
- A repayment of a portion of the outstanding mortgage balance (principal).

The difference between the monthly mortgage payment and the portion of the payment that represents interest equals the amount that is applied to reduce the outstanding mortgage balance. The monthly mortgage payment is designed so that after the last scheduled monthly payment of the loan is made, the amount of the outstanding mortgage balance is zero (i.e., the mortgage is fully repaid). Thus, the portion of the monthly mortgage payment applied to interest declines each month, and the portion applied to reducing the mortgage balance increases. The reason for this is that because the mortgage balance is reduced with each monthly mortgage payment, the interest on the mortgage balance declines. Since the monthly mortgage payment is fixed, an increasingly larger portion of the monthly payment is applied to reduce the principal in each subsequent month.

For the mortgagee, the cash flow from the mortgage loan is not the same as what the mortgagor pays. This is because of a servicing fee, which covers the collection of monthly payments and forwarding the proceeds to the owners of the loan, maintaining records, sending payment notices when payments are overdue, furnishing tax information for mortgagors, and so on. Therefore, the monthly cash flow from a mortgage loan can be divided into three parts:

1. The servicing fee.
2. The interest payment net of the servicing fee.
3. The scheduled principal payment (referred to as *amortization*).

15.2.2 Prepayments and Cash Flow Uncertainty

The most critical feature of the mortgages underlying a RMBS is that the mortgagor may pay off any portion of the mortgage balance prior to the scheduled due date. Payments made in excess of the scheduled principal repayment are called *prepayments*. Hence, the mortgagor holds a *prepayment option*.

Prepayments occur for a variety reasons. First, borrowers prepay the entire mortgage balance when they sell their home. Second, borrowers may be economically motivated to pay off the loan as market rates fall below the loan's note rate. This reason for prepaying a mortgage loan is referred to as *refinancing*. Third, in the case of borrowers who cannot meet their mortgage obligations, the property is repossessed and sold. The proceeds from the sale are used to pay off the mortgage loan. Finally, if property is destroyed by fire or if another insured catastrophe occurs, the insurance proceeds are used to pay off the mortgage loan.

The effect of prepayments is that the cash flow from a mortgage is not known with certainty—by this, we mean that the amount and the timing of the cash flows is uncertain. Consequently, ignoring defaults, the mortgagor knows that as long as the loan is outstanding, interest will be received and the principal will be repaid at the scheduled date each month. By the maturity date of the mortgage loan, the investor (mortgagee) would recover the amount lent. However, what the mortgagee does not know is for how long the mortgage loan will be outstanding, as well as the timing of the principal payments.

The embedded prepayment option benefits the mortgagor at the expense of the lender. For example, a borrower who takes out a mortgage at a 10% interest rate may choose to refinance if rates fall to 7%. This will lower the borrower's monthly payment; he will be paying 7% interest instead of 10%. However, the lender must now reinvest the returned principal at 7%, below the 10% rate he previously enjoyed.

The risk of receiving principal back at an inopportune time (i.e., in a lower-rate environment) is called *prepayment risk*. The prepayment risk associated with the individual mortgages passes through to the holder of a MBS, although this risk for a pool of mortgages can be divided up unequally depending on the MBS structure.

15.2.3 Prepayments and Prepayment Conventions

In the RMBS market, several conventions have been used as a benchmark for prepayment rates. Today the benchmarks used are the conditional prepayment rate and the Public Securities Association (PSA) prepayment benchmark.

The *conditional prepayment rate* (CPR) as a measure of the speed of prepayments assumes that some fraction of the remaining principal in the mortgage pool is prepaid each month for the remaining term of the collateral. The CPR used for a particular deal is based on the characteristics of the collateral (including its historical prepayment experience) and the current and expected future economic environment.

The CPR is an annual prepayment rate. To estimate monthly prepayments, the CPR must be converted into a monthly prepayment rate, commonly referred to as the *single-monthly mortality rate* (SMM). The following formula is used to determine the SMM for a given CPR:

$$SMM = 1 - [(1 - CPR)^{1/12}]$$

An SMM of w percent means that approximately w percent of the remaining mortgage balance at the beginning of the month, less the scheduled principal payment, will prepay that month. That is,

Prepayment for month t = $SMM \cdot$ (Beginning mortgage balance for month t − Scheduled principal payment for month t)

One problem with using the CPR is that it assumes a constant prepayment rate from the very outset of the origination of the loans. For example, it is not likely that prepayments will be larger in dollar amount shortly after loans are originated than later on after loans have seasoned. Yet using a constant CPR makes that assumption. For residential mortgage loans, the *PSA prepayment benchmark* deals with this problem.[3] The PSA prepayment benchmark is expressed as a monthly series of annual prepayment rates. The basic PSA benchmark model assumes that prepayment rates are low for newly originated loans, speed up as the mortgages become seasoned, and eventually reach a plateau and remain at that level. This is a phenomenon observed in reality. Usually, new mortgages tend to have lower prepayments because homeowners stay in the home for several years before moving. After several years, the expected turnover increases as people move to larger houses or new locations. The remaining homeowners will exhibit a steady pattern of prepayments for the years left.

The PSA standard benchmark assumes the following prepayment rates for 30-year residential mortgages loans:

- A CPR of 0.2% for the first month, increased by 0.2% per year per month for the next 29 months, at which point it reaches 6% per year.
- A 6% CPR per annum (0.5% per month) for the remaining years.

Mathematically, the monthly value for the CPR can be expressed as

$$CPR = (6\%) \cdot (t/30), \ t < 30$$

and

$$CPR = (6\%)/12, \ t > 30$$

where t is the number of months since the origination of the pool.

In other words, the prepayment rate is 0.2% (on an annual basis) for the first month, 0.4% for the second month, 0.6% for the third month, and so on until month 30, at which point it becomes fixed at 0.5% per month. All months above are counted with reference to origination of the pool.

This benchmark is referred to as 100% PSA. Slower or faster speeds are then referred to as some percentage of PSA. For example, 50% PSA means one-half the CPR of the PSA benchmark prepayment rate, and 165% PSA means 1.65 times the CPR of the PSA benchmark prepayment rate. A prepayment rate of 0% PSA means that no prepayments are assumed. See Exhibit 15.1 for calculated CPR and SMM for assumed 100% PSA prepayments and 165% PSA prepayments. (See also worksheet **CPR** in file **Ch15-Examples.xlsx**.)

The PSA benchmark is commonly referred to as a *prepayment model*, suggesting that it can be used to estimate prepayment. However, it is important to note that characterizing this market convention for prepayments as a prepayment model is wrong. We will discuss an actual prepayment models in section 15.4.1.

15.2.4 Prepayments and Path Dependency

A complicated aspect of prepayments is that they are a function of the entire history of interest rates during the life of the RMBS. For instance, an RMBS may experience significant refinancing when interest rates fall. Some borrowers will refinance quickly, but others may lag because they are less aware of the refinancing opportunity, or do not have sufficient credit worthiness to refinance. After the first wave of refinancing, the RMBS is backed by mortgages of borrowers that are less likely to refinance. This effect is called *burnout*. So, if interest rates go up and then come down again, the prepayments are expected to be much less than the first time rates dropped. The fact that prepayments depend on the path interest rates have taken up to a particular time is referred to as *path dependency*, and it makes pricing and structuring RMBSs much more challenging.

EXHIBIT 15.1 Monthly CPR and SMM at 100% PSA and 165% PSA for 32 months.

	100% PSA		165% PSA	
Month	CPR	SMM	CPR	SMM
1	0.02%	0.0167%	0.03%	0.0023%
2	0.03%	0.0333%	0.06%	0.0552%
3	0.05%	0.0500%	0.08%	0.0829%
4	0.07%	0.0667%	0.11%	0.1107%
5	0.08%	0.0833%	0.14%	0.1386%
6	0.10%	0.1000%	0.17%	0.1665%
7	0.12%	0.1167%	0.19%	0.1946%
8	0.13%	0.1333%	0.22%	0.2227%
9	0.15%	0.1500%	0.25%	0.2509%
10	0.17%	0.1667%	0.28%	0.2792%
11	0.18%	0.1833%	0.30%	0.3077%
12	0.20%	0.2000%	0.33%	0.3361%
13	0.22%	0.2167%	0.36%	0.3647%
14	0.23%	0.2333%	0.39%	0.3934%
15	0.25%	0.2500%	0.41%	0.4222%
16	0.27%	0.2667%	0.44%	0.4510%
17	0.28%	0.2833%	0.47%	0.4800%
18	0.30%	0.3000%	0.50%	0.5090%
19	0.32%	0.3167%	0.52%	0.5381%
20	0.33%	0.3333%	0.55%	0.5674%
21	0.35%	0.3500%	0.58%	0.5967%
22	0.37%	0.3667%	0.61%	0.6261%
23	0.38%	0.3833%	0.63%	0.6556%
24	0.40%	0.4000%	0.66%	0.6852%
25	0.42%	0.4167%	0.69%	0.7150%
26	0.43%	0.4333%	0.72%	0.7448%
27	0.45%	0.4500%	0.74%	0.7747%
28	0.47%	0.4667%	0.77%	0.8047%
29	0.48%	0.4833%	0.80%	0.8348%
30	0.50%	0.5000%	0.83%	0.8650%
31	0.50%	0.5000%	0.83%	0.8650%
32	0.50%	0.5000%	0.83%	0.8650%

15.3 TYPES OF RMBS STRUCTURES

As we mentioned in the previous section, there are three basic types of agency RMBS structures. They are pass-through RMBSs, stripped RMBSs, and collateralized mortgage obligations. There are also private-label RMBSs that share a lot of common characteristics with collateralized mortgage obligations. We explain the main ideas behind these structures in this section.

15.3.1 Agency Pass-Through RMBS

In a mortgage pass-through security, or simply a *pass-through*, the monthly cash flow from the pool of mortgage loans is distributed on a pro rata basis to the certificate holders. To illustrate the structure of a pass-through, we will look at the monthly cash flow for a hypothetical pass-through given a PSA assumption. We will assume the following for the underlying mortgages:

- Type: fixed rate, level payment mortgages
- Weighted average coupon (WAC) rate:[4] 6.0%
- Weighted average maturity (WAM):[5] 358 months
- Servicing fee: 0.5%
- Outstanding balance: $660 million

The pass-through security has a coupon rate of 5.5% (WAC of 6% minus the servicing fee of 0.5%).

This first step in structuring the pass-through requires a projection of the cash flow of the mortgage pool. The cash flow is decomposed into three components:

- Interest (based on WAC of 6% and pass-through rate of 5.5%).
- Regularly scheduled principal (i.e., amortization).
- Prepayments based on some prepayment assumption.

To generate the cash flow for the hypothetical pass-through security we will assume a prepayment speed of 165% PSA. The cash flow is shown in Exhibit 15.2. (See also worksheet **Pass-Through** in the file **Ch15-Examples.xlsx**.) Column 2 shows the outstanding mortgage balance at the beginning of the month (i.e., outstanding balance at the beginning of the previous month reduced by the total principal payment in the previous month). Column 3 gives the SMM for 165% PSA. The aggregate monthly mortgage payment is reported in column 4.[6] Notice that the total monthly mortgage payment declines over time, as prepayments reduce the mortgage balance outstanding.

Column 5 shows the monthly interest that is determined by multiplying the outstanding mortgage balance at the beginning of the month by the pass-through rate of 5.5% and dividing by 12. The regularly scheduled principal repayment (amortization), shown in column 6 is the difference between the total monthly mortgage payment (column 4) and the gross coupon interest for the month (6.0% multiplied by the outstanding mortgage balance at the beginning of the month, then divided by 12). The prepayment for the month is reported in column 7 and is found by using the equation we introduced in section 15.2.3. The sum of the regularly scheduled principal and the prepayment is the total principal payment, which is shown in column 8. The projected monthly cash flow is then the sum of the monthly interest plus the total principal payment as shown in the last column of Exhibit 15.2.

At 165% PSA, the average life for this pass-through security can be computed to be 8.54 years. The *average life* is a weighted average of the principal cash flows divided by the par value where the weight is the month when the projected principal is expected to be received.[7]

15.3.2 Agency Stripped MBS

A *stripped mortgage-backed security (stripped MBS)* is created by altering that distribution of principal and interest from a pro rata distribution to an unequal distribution.

In the most common type of stripped MBS, all of the interest is allocated to one class—the *interest-only* class, and all of the principal to the other class—the *principal-only class*.

Principal-Only Securities A *principal-only security*, also called a *PO* or a *principal-only mortgage strip*, is purchased at a substantial discount from par value. The return an investor realizes depends on the speed at which prepayments are made. The faster the prepayments, the higher the investor's return. For example, suppose that there is a mortgage pool consisting only of 30-year mortgages, with $400 million in principal, and that investors can purchase POs backed by this mortgage pool for $175 million. The dollar return on this investment will be $225 million. How quickly that dollar return is recovered by PO investors determines the actual return that will be realized. In the extreme case, if all homeowners in the underlying mortgage pool decide to prepay their mortgage loans immediately, PO investors will realize the $225 million immediately. At the other extreme, if all homeowners decide to remain in their homes for 30 years and make no prepayments, the $225 million will be spread out over 30 years, which would result in a lower return for PO investors.

Let us see how the price of the PO would be expected to change as mortgage rates in the market change. When mortgage rates decline below the note rate for the loans in the mortgage pool, prepayments are expected to speed up, accelerating payments to the PO holder. Thus, the cash flow of a PO improves (in the sense that principal repayments are received earlier).

EXHIBIT 15.2 Monthly cash flow for a $660 million pass-through security with a 5.5% pass-through rate, a WAC of 6.00%, and a WAM of 358 months, assuming 165% PSA. Note that rows 31–348 are hidden.

(1) Month	(2) Outstanding Balance	(3) SMM	(4) Mortgage Payment	(5) Net Interest	(6) Scheduled Principal	(7) Prepayments	(8) Total Principal	(9) Cash Flow
1	$660,000,000.00	0.0829%	$3,964,947.45	$3,025,000.00	$664,947.45	$546,435.32	$1,211,382.78	$4,236,382.78
2	$658,788,617.22	0.1107%	$3,961,661.43	$3,019,447.83	$667,718.35	$728,350.08	$1,396,068.43	$4,415,516.26
3	$657,392,548.80	0.1386%	$3,957,277.02	$3,013,049.18	$670,314.27	$909,894.82	$1,580,209.10	$4,593,258.28
4	$655,812,339.70	0.1665%	$3,951,794.17	$3,005,806.56	$672,732.48	$1,090,916.16	$1,763,648.64	$4,769,455.20
5	$654,048,691.06	0.1946%	$3,945,213.78	$2,997,723.17	$674,970.33	$1,271,260.68	$1,946,231.01	$4,943,954.17
6	$652,102,460.06	0.2227%	$3,937,537.63	$2,988,802.94	$677,025.33	$1,450,775.13	$2,127,800.46	$5,116,603.41
7	$649,974,659.59	0.2509%	$3,928,768.43	$2,979,050.52	$678,895.13	$1,629,306.69	$2,308,201.82	$5,287,252.34
8	$647,666,457.77	0.2792%	$3,918,909.79	$2,968,471.26	$680,577.51	$1,806,703.12	$2,487,280.62	$5,455,751.89
9	$645,179,177.15	0.3077%	$3,907,966.27	$2,957,071.23	$682,070.38	$1,982,813.03	$2,664,883.42	$5,621,954.64
10	$642,514,293.73	0.3361%	$3,895,943.30	$2,944,857.18	$683,371.83	$2,157,486.08	$2,840,857.92	$5,785,715.10
11	$639,673,435.82	0.3647%	$3,882,847.26	$2,931,836.58	$684,480.08	$2,330,573.19	$3,015,053.27	$5,946,889.86
12	$636,658,382.54	0.3934%	$3,868,685.42	$2,918,017.59	$685,393.51	$2,501,926.75	$3,187,320.26	$6,105,337.85
13	$633,471,062.28	0.4222%	$3,853,465.96	$2,903,409.04	$686,110.65	$2,671,400.85	$3,357,511.50	$6,260,920.54
14	$630,113,550.78	0.4510%	$3,837,197.95	$2,888,020.44	$686,630.19	$2,838,851.49	$3,525,481.68	$6,413,502.13
15	$626,588,069.10	0.4800%	$3,819,891.36	$2,871,861.98	$686,951.01	$3,004,136.77	$3,691,087.78	$6,562,949.76
16	$622,896,981.32	0.5090%	$3,801,557.03	$2,854,944.50	$687,072.12	$3,167,117.12	$3,854,189.24	$6,709,133.74
17	$619,042,792.08	0.5381%	$3,782,206.68	$2,837,279.46	$686,992.72	$3,327,655.50	$4,014,648.22	$6,851,927.68
18	$615,028,143.86	0.5674%	$3,761,852.90	$2,818,878.99	$686,712.18	$3,485,617.58	$4,172,329.76	$6,991,208.75
19	$610,855,814.10	0.5967%	$3,740,509.10	$2,799,755.81	$686,230.03	$3,640,871.98	$4,327,102.01	$7,126,857.83
20	$606,528,712.09	0.6261%	$3,718,189.54	$2,779,923.26	$685,545.98	$3,793,290.42	$4,478,836.40	$7,258,759.67

(Continued)

EXHIBIT 15.2 (Continued)

(1)	(2)	(3)	(4)	(5)	(6)	(7)	(8)	(9)
Month	Outstanding Balance	SMM	Mortgage Payment	Net Interest	Scheduled Principal	Prepayments	Total Principal	Cash Flow
21	$602,049,875.68	0.6556%	$3,694,909.30	$2,759,395.26	$684,659.93	$3,942,747.93	$4,627,407.86	$7,386,803.12
22	$597,422,467.83	0.6852%	$3,670,684.27	$2,738,186.31	$683,571.93	$4,089,123.02	$4,772,694.95	$7,510,881.26
23	$592,649,772.87	0.7150%	$3,645,531.09	$2,716,311.46	$682,282.22	$4,232,297.89	$4,914,580.11	$7,630,891.57
24	$587,735,192.76	0.7448%	$3,619,467.20	$2,693,786.30	$680,791.24	$4,372,158.55	$5,052,949.78	$7,746,736.08
25	$582,682,242.98	0.7747%	$3,592,510.78	$2,670,626.95	$679,099.57	$4,508,595.02	$5,187,694.59	$7,858,321.54
26	$577,494,548.39	0.8047%	$3,564,680.73	$2,646,850.01	$677,207.99	$4,641,501.51	$5,318,709.50	$7,965,559.51
27	$572,175,838.89	0.8348%	$3,535,996.66	$2,622,472.59	$675,117.46	$4,770,776.51	$5,445,893.98	$8,068,366.57
28	$566,729,944.91	0.8650%	$3,506,478.85	$2,597,512.25	$672,829.12	$4,896,323.00	$5,569,152.12	$8,166,664.37
29	$561,160,792.79	0.8650%	$3,476,148.25	$2,571,986.97	$670,344.28	$4,848,172.03	$5,518,516.31	$8,090,503.28
30	$555,642,276.48	0.8650%	$3,446,080.00	$2,546,693.77	$667,868.62	$4,800,458.97	$5,468,327.59	$8,015,021.35
...								
349	$2,098,411.25	0.8650%	$215,654.93	$9,617.72	$205,162.87	$16,376.36	$221,539.23	$231,156.95
350	$1,876,872.02	0.8650%	$213,789.54	$8,602.33	$204,405.18	$14,466.63	$218,871.81	$227,474.14
351	$1,658,000.21	0.8650%	$211,940.29	$7,599.17	$203,650.28	$12,579.94	$216,230.23	$223,829.40
352	$1,441,769.98	0.8650%	$210,107.03	$6,608.11	$202,898.18	$10,716.09	$213,614.26	$220,222.38
353	$1,228,155.72	0.8650%	$208,289.63	$5,629.05	$202,148.85	$8,874.83	$211,023.68	$216,652.73
354	$1,017,132.04	0.8650%	$206,487.95	$4,661.86	$201,402.29	$7,055.96	$208,458.25	$213,120.10
355	$808,673.79	0.8650%	$204,701.85	$3,706.42	$200,658.49	$5,259.26	$205,917.74	$209,624.16
356	$602,756.05	0.8650%	$202,931.21	$2,762.63	$199,917.43	$3,484.50	$203,401.93	$206,164.56
357	$399,354.11	0.8650%	$201,175.88	$1,830.37	$199,179.11	$1,731.49	$200,910.60	$202,740.97
358	$198,443.52	0.8650%	$199,435.73	$909.53	$198,443.52	$0.00	$198,443.52	$199,353.05

The cash flow will be discounted at a lower interest rate because the mortgage rate in the market has declined. The result is that the PO price will increase when mortgage rates decline. When mortgage rates rise above the note rate for the loans in the mortgage pool, prepayments are expected to slow down. The cash flow deteriorates (in the sense that it takes longer to recover principal repayments). Couple this with a higher discount rate, and the price of a PO will fall when mortgage rates rise.

Interest-Only Securities An *interest-only security*, also called an *IO* or an *interest-only mortgage strip*, has no par value. In contrast to the PO investor, the IO investor wants prepayments to be slow because the IO investor receives interest only on the amount of the principal outstanding. When prepayments are made, less dollar interest will be received as the outstanding principal declines. In fact, if prepayments are too fast, the IO investor may not recover the amount paid for the IO even if the IO is held to maturity.

Let us look at the expected price response of an IO to changes in mortgage rates. If mortgage rates decline below the note rate for the loans in the mortgage pool, prepayments are expected to accelerate. This would result in a deterioration of the expected cash flow for an IO. While the cash flow will be discounted at a lower rate, the net effect typically is a decline in the price of an IO. If mortgage rates rise above the note rate for the loans in the mortgage pool, the expected cash flow improves, but the cash flow is discounted at a higher interest rate. The net effect may be either a rise or fall for the IO's price.

Thus, we see an interesting characteristic of an IO: Its price tends to move in the same direction as the change in mortgage rates (1) when mortgage rates fall below the note rate for the loans in the mortgage pool and (2) for some range of mortgage rates above the note rate. Both POs and IOs exhibit substantial price volatility when mortgage rates change. The greater price volatility of the IO and PO compared to the pass-through from which they were created is because the combined price volatility of the IO and PO must be equal to the price volatility of the pass-through.

15.3.3 Agency Collateralized Mortgage Obligations

A *collateralized mortgage obligation* (CMO) is a security backed by a pool of mortgage pass-through securities. CMOs are structured so that there are several classes of bondholders—also called *tranches*—with varying average lives. The principal payments from the underlying pool of pass-through securities are used to retire the bonds on a priority basis as specified in the prospectus.

EXHIBIT 15.3 Example of a sequential-pay structure ("Structure 1").

Bond Class	Par Amount ($)	Coupon Rate (%)
A	$320,925,000.00	5.50%
B	$59,400,000.00	5.50%
C	$159,225,000.00	5.50%
D	$120,450,000.00	5.50%

Although we will not explain the wide range of bond classes or tranches created in a CMO structure, we will provide a few for the purposes of showing how they are structured and how they alter the investment characteristics compared to the mortgage pass-through securities from which they were created: *sequential-pay bonds, planned amortization class bonds,* and *support bonds.* For a more detailed description of the different types of CMO bond classes, see Fabozzi, Bhattacharya, and Berliner (2007).

Sequential-Pay Structures The simplest type of CMO structure is the *sequential-pay structure.* To illustrate this structure, we will use the $660 million, 5.5% pass-through security (which is comprised of residential mortgage loans that confirm to the underwriting standards of Ginnie Mae, Fannie Mae, and Freddie Mac) to create a simple structure. The structure is given in Exhibit 15.3, and we refer to this structure as "Structure 1."

In structuring an agency deal, there are only rules specified for the distribution of principal and interest. There are no rules for deals with defaults and delinquencies because payments are guaranteed by the issuer. In Structure 1 we will use the following rules:

- *Interest.* The monthly interest is distributed to each bond class on the basis of the amount of principal outstanding at the beginning of the month.
- *Principal.* All monthly principal (i.e., regularly scheduled principal and prepayments) is distributed first to bond class A until it is completely paid off. After bond class A has completely paid off its par amount, all monthly principal payments are made to bond class B until it is completely paid off. After bond class B has completely paid off its par amount, all monthly principal payments are made to bond class C until it has completely paid off its par amount. Finally, after bond C is completely paid off, all monthly principal payments are made to bond class D.

Based on these rules for the distribution of interest and principal, Exhibits 15.4 and 15.5 show the cash flows for each bond class assuming one

EXHIBIT 15.4 Monthly cash flows for selected months for Structure 1, classes A and B.

	A			B		
Month	Beginning Balance	Principal	Interest	Beginning Balance	Principal	Interest
1	$320,925,000.00	$1,211,382.78	$1,470,906.25	$59,400,000.00	$0.00	$272,250.00
2	$319,713,617.22	$1,396,068.43	$1,465,354.08	$59,400,000.00	$0.00	$272,250.00
3	$318,317,548.80	$1,580,209.10	$1,458,955.43	$59,400,000.00	$0.00	$272,250.00
4	$316,737,339.70	$1,763,648.64	$1,451,712.81	$59,400,000.00	$0.00	$272,250.00
5	$314,973,691.06	$1,946,231.01	$1,443,629.42	$59,400,000.00	$0.00	$272,250.00
6	$313,027,460.06	$2,127,800.46	$1,434,709.19	$59,400,000.00	$0.00	$272,250.00
7	$310,899,659.59	$2,308,201.82	$1,424,956.77	$59,400,000.00	$0.00	$272,250.00
8	$308,591,457.77	$2,487,280.62	$1,414,377.51	$59,400,000.00	$0.00	$272,250.00
9	$306,104,177.15	$2,664,883.42	$1,402,977.48	$59,400,000.00	$0.00	$272,250.00
10	$303,439,293.73	$2,840,857.92	$1,390,763.43	$59,400,000.00	$0.00	$272,250.00
11	$300,598,435.82	$3,015,053.27	$1,377,742.83	$59,400,000.00	$0.00	$272,250.00
12	$297,583,382.54	$3,187,320.26	$1,363,923.84	$59,400,000.00	$0.00	$272,250.00
⋮						
74	$17,687,935.97	$3,648,575.33	$81,069.71	$59,400,000.00	$0.00	$272,250.00
75	$14,039,360.63	$3,614,937.79	$64,347.07	$59,400,000.00	$0.00	$272,250.00

(*Continued*)

EXHIBIT 15.4 (*Continued*)

Month	A			B		
	Beginning Balance	Principal	Interest	Beginning Balance	Principal	Interest
76	$10,424,422.85	$3,581,598.87	$47,778.60	$59,400,000.00	$0.00	$272,250.00
77	$6,842,823.97	$3,548,555.98	$31,362.94	$59,400,000.00	$0.00	$272,250.00
78	$3,294,267.99	$3,294,267.99	$15,098.73	$59,400,000.00	$221,538.54	$272,250.00
79	$0.00	$0.00	$0.00	$59,178,461.46	$3,483,347.94	$271,234.62
80	$0.00	$0.00	$0.00	$55,695,113.52	$3,451,177.68	$255,269.27
81	$0.00	$0.00	$0.00	$52,243,935.84	$3,419,293.21	$239,451.37
82	$0.00	$0.00	$0.00	$48,824,642.63	$3,387,692.05	$223,779.61
83	$0.00	$0.00	$0.00	$45,436,950.58	$3,356,371.72	$208,252.69
84	$0.00	$0.00	$0.00	$42,080,578.86	$3,325,329.75	$192,869.32
85	$0.00	$0.00	$0.00	$38,755,249.12	$3,294,563.71	$177,628.23
95	$0.00	$0.00	$0.00	$7,149,733.68	$3,001,558.67	$32,769.61
96	$0.00	$0.00	$0.00	$4,148,175.01	$2,973,673.07	$19,012.47
97	$0.00	$0.00	$0.00	$1,174,501.93	$1,174,501.93	$5,383.13
98	$0.00	$0.00	$0.00	$0.00	$0.00	$0.00

EXHIBIT 15.5 Monthly cash flows for selected months for Structure 1, classes C and D.

Month	C Beginning Balance	C Principal	C Interest	D Beginning Balance	D Principal	D Interest
1	$159,225,000.00	$0.00	$729,781.25	$120,450,000.00	$0.00	$552,062.50
2	$159,225,000.00	$0.00	$729,781.25	$120,450,000.00	$0.00	$552,062.50
3	$159,225,000.00	$0.00	$729,781.25	$120,450,000.00	$0.00	$552,062.50
4	$159,225,000.00	$0.00	$729,781.25	$120,450,000.00	$0.00	$552,062.50
5	$159,225,000.00	$0.00	$729,781.25	$120,450,000.00	$0.00	$552,062.50
6	$159,225,000.00	$0.00	$729,781.25	$120,450,000.00	$0.00	$552,062.50
7	$159,225,000.00	$0.00	$729,781.25	$120,450,000.00	$0.00	$552,062.50
8	$159,225,000.00	$0.00	$729,781.25	$120,450,000.00	$0.00	$552,062.50
9	$159,225,000.00	$0.00	$729,781.25	$120,450,000.00	$0.00	$552,062.50
10	$159,225,000.00	$0.00	$729,781.25	$120,450,000.00	$0.00	$552,062.50
11	$159,225,000.00	$0.00	$729,781.25	$120,450,000.00	$0.00	$552,062.50
12	$159,225,000.00	$0.00	$729,781.25	$120,450,000.00	$0.00	$552,062.50
...						
95	$159,225,000.00	$0.00	$729,781.25	$120,450,000.00	$0.00	$552,062.50
96	$159,225,000.00	$0.00	$729,781.25	$120,450,000.00	$0.00	$552,062.50
97	$159,225,000.00	$1,771,533.84	$729,781.25	$120,450,000.00	$0.00	$552,062.50
98	$157,453,466.16	$2,918,644.62	$721,661.72	$120,450,000.00	$0.00	$552,062.50
99	$154,534,821.54	$2,891,497.43	$708,284.60	$120,450,000.00	$0.00	$552,062.50
100	$151,643,324.11	$2,864,592.09	$695,031.90	$120,450,000.00	$0.00	$552,062.50
101	$148,778,732.01	$2,837,926.47	$681,902.52	$120,450,000.00	$0.00	$552,062.50
102	$145,940,805.54	$2,811,498.48	$668,895.36	$120,450,000.00	$0.00	$552,062.50

(*Continued*)

EXHIBIT 15.5 (*Continued*)

Month	C Beginning Balance	C Principal	C Interest	D Beginning Balance	D Principal	D Interest
103	$143,129,307.06	$2,785,306.03	$656,009.32	$120,450,000.00	$0.00	$552,062.50
104	$140,344,001.04	$2,759,347.06	$643,243.34	$120,450,000.00	$0.00	$552,062.50
105	$137,584,653.98	$2,733,619.52	$630,596.33	$120,450,000.00	$0.00	$552,062.50
...						
171	$2,747,229.44	$1,458,601.26	$12,591.47	$120,450,000.00	$0.00	$552,062.50
172	$1,288,628.18	$1,288,628.18	$5,906.21	$120,450,000.00	$155,905.11	$552,062.50
173	$0.00	$0.00	$0.00	$120,294,094.89	$1,430,592.36	$551,347.93
174	$0.00	$0.00	$0.00	$118,863,502.53	$1,416,777.37	$544,791.05
175	$0.00	$0.00	$0.00	$117,446,725.16	$1,403,087.19	$538,297.49
176	$0.00	$0.00	$0.00	$116,043,637.98	$1,389,520.73	$531,866.67
177	$0.00	$0.00	$0.00	$114,654,117.25	$1,376,076.90	$525,498.04
178	$0.00	$0.00	$0.00	$113,278,040.36	$1,362,754.61	$519,191.02
179	$0.00	$0.00	$0.00	$111,915,285.74	$1,349,552.81	$512,945.06
180	$0.00	$0.00	$0.00	$110,565,732.93	$1,336,470.42	$506,759.61
...						
350	$0.00	$0.00	$0.00	$1,876,872.02	$218,871.81	$8,602.33
351	$0.00	$0.00	$0.00	$1,658,000.21	$216,230.23	$7,599.17
352	$0.00	$0.00	$0.00	$1,441,769.98	$213,614.26	$6,608.11
353	$0.00	$0.00	$0.00	$1,228,155.72	$211,023.68	$5,629.05
354	$0.00	$0.00	$0.00	$1,017,132.04	$208,458.25	$4,661.86
355	$0.00	$0.00	$0.00	$808,673.79	$205,917.74	$3,706.42
356	$0.00	$0.00	$0.00	$602,756.05	$203,401.93	$2,762.63
357	$0.00	$0.00	$0.00	$399,354.11	$200,910.60	$1,830.37
358	$0.00	$0.00	$0.00	$198,443.52	$198,443.52	$909.53

prepayment speed, 165% PSA. (See also worksheet **Sequential-Pay** in the file **Ch15-Examples.xlsx.**) Note that bond class A is fully paid off in month 78. In the same month, principal payments begin for bond class B, which is fully paid off in month 97. Bond class C starts receiving principal payments in month 97, and bond class D—in month 172.

Before explaining what has been accomplished in Structure 1, a few comments are in order. First, the total par value of the four bond classes in the structure is equal to $660 million, which is equal to the par value of the collateral (the pass-through security). Second, we have simplified the illustration by assuming that all bond classes have the same coupon rate. In actual deals, the coupon rate would be determined by prevailing market conditions (i.e., the yield curve) and would not necessarily be equal to each bond class. A condition that must be satisfied is that the total interest to be paid to all the bond classes in a month may not exceed the interest from the collateral; otherwise an interest shortfall will occur. Equivalently, the weighted average coupon rate for the bond classes in the structure may not exceed the coupon rate for the collateral (6% in our illustration). Finally, although the payment rules for the distribution of the principal payments are known, the exact amount of monthly principal is not. The monthly principal will depend on the principal cash flows generated by the collateral, which in turn depends on the actual payment rate of the collateral. Thus, in order to project monthly cash flows, a prepayment assumption must be made. We will discuss prepayment models in section 15.4.1.

Now let us look at Structure 1. To see what has been accomplished, a summary of the average life (in years) of the collateral and the four bond classes under a range of prepayment assumptions is shown in Exhibit 15.6.

Notice the substantial differences in the average life for the collateral depending on the speed of prepayment. Given this risk, the collateral in its original form is unappealing to institutional investors who have specific

EXHIBIT 15.6 Average life for the collateral and the different bond classes of the CMO depending on the assumptions about prepayment speed as a percentage of PSA.

Prepayment Speed	100%	125%	165%	250%	400%	500%
Collateral	11.22	10.04	8.54	6.42	4.45	3.72
Bond Class						
A	4.70	4.09	3.42	2.63	1.98	1.74
B	10.33	8.90	7.28	5.32	3.73	3.17
C	15.05	13.15	10.85	7.84	5.31	4.41
D	24.01	22.36	19.75	15.17	10.25	8.33

liability structures and are trying to match their liabilities with their assets. However, the average lives for the different bond classes tell a different story. They are both shorter and longer than the collateral, thereby attracting institutional investors who have a preference for an average life different from that of the collateral. For example, a depository institution interested in shorter-term paper would find bond class A more appealing than the collateral because within a reasonable range of prepayment speeds, bond class A's average life will be less than five years under slow prepayment speeds, while the collateral's average life can extend to a little more than 11 years. At the other end of the maturity preference spectrum, consider a defined benefit pension plan that is seeking longer-term investments. That institutional investor would prefer bond class D to the collateral. While bond class D has considerable variation in its average life, the average life does remain long on average. Notice, for example, that at the fastest prepayment speed shown in Exhibit 15.6 (500 PSA), the average life for the collateral can contract to 3.7 years, but for bond class D to only 8.3 years.

Consequently, we can see that the rules for distribution of principal among the bond classes in this structure have redistributed the prepayment risk of the collateral among the bond classes. As a result, an unattractive asset or collateral from the perspective of some investors can be used to create securities that better match the needs of those investors.

Planned Amortization Class Bonds and Support Bonds   There are investors who seek securities (bond classes) that have even greater protection against prepayment risk. Planned amortization class bond structures are designed with this goal in mind. The main idea is to create a bond class, *planned amortization class bond* (popularly referred to as a PAC), that has priority over all other bond classes in the structure with respect to receiving the scheduled principal repayment. The non-PAC bond classes in the structure are referred to as the *support bonds* or *companion bonds*. The support bonds accept the prepayment risk if actual prepayment speeds are faster or slower than so-called *structuring speeds* or *structuring bands*. Hence, unlike a sequential-pay structure, in which the bond classes are given some protection against fast prepayments or slow prepayments, but not both, PAC bonds offer protection against both fast and slow prepayments, thus minimizing the variability for the investor.

In practice, a typical structure may have more than one class of PAC bonds. That is, there may be a series of PAC bonds. The first PAC bond in the series has a priority over the others, the second PAC bond has a priority over the others (except the first PAC bond), and so on. Similarly, typically there are several classes of support bonds.

15.3.4 Private-Label RMBS

The private-label RMBS market encompasses a variety of product and structuring variations. Technically, any deal that is not securitized under an agency (i.e., Ginnie Mae) or GSE shelf (i.e., Freddie Mac or Fannie Mae) can be considered private label, as the issuing entity has no connection to the U.S. government (either explicit or implicit). Private-label RMBSs are further classified based on the credit quality of the mortgage loans in the pool: prime loans (for higher-quality loans) and subprime loans (for lower-quality loans with high default risk).

As we mentioned earlier, because of the lack of federal guarantee, private-label RMBS deals must have some form of credit enhancement in order to create large amounts of investment-grade bonds. Aside from the presence of credit enhancement, private-label deals share many features and structuring techniques with agency CMOs. There are some important differences, however, due to the nature of the loans collateralizing the deal as well as legal and regulatory issues associated with the different shelves. First, private-label deals can be structured such that derivatives, such as interest rate swaps, can be inserted into the structures as risk mitigators. The GSEs, by contrast, do not allow for inclusion of derivatives in deals. Second, the loans collateralizing private-label deals are generally assumed to prepay faster than those in agency pools. The convention in the agency market is to structure deals using a base-case prepayment speed consistent with median prepayment speeds reported by Bloomberg. Private-label deals, by contrast, are structured either to a market convention (i.e., PSA speeds ranging from 250% to 300%) or a predefined ramp (i.e., 6% to 18% CPR ramping over 12 months). The ramp is defined in the prospectus and it is typically called the *prospectus prepayment curve*, or PPC. (100% PPC is simply the base ramp defined at the time of pricing.) Finally, private-label deals typically have *cleanup calls*. These are inserted into deals to relieve the trustees from the burden of having to oversee deals with very small remaining balances. The calls are triggered when the current face of the deal and/or collateral group declines below a predetermined level.

Next, we briefly review the mechanisms involved in creating the internal credit enhancement typically utilized in private-label deals.

The first step in structuring the credit enhancement for a private-label deal is to split the face value of the loans into senior and subordinated interests. The senior bonds have higher priority with respect to both the receipt of interest and principal and the allocation of realized losses, and are generally created with enough subordination to be rated AAA by the credit rating agencies. In most cases, the subordinate interests are subdivided (or *tranched*) into a series of bonds that decline sequentially in priority. The

EXHIBIT 15.7 Subordination by percentage of deal size for a hypothetical $400 million deal with 3.5% initial subordination.

	Face Value	Percent of Deal
AAA	$386,000,000.00	96.50%
AA	$6,000,000.00	1.50%
A	$2,600,000.00	0.65%
BBB	$1,800,000.00	0.45%
BB	$1,200,000.00	0.30%
B	$1,200,000.00	0.30%
First loss (nonrated)	$1,200,000.00	0.30%
Total subordination	$400,000,000.00	3.50%

subordinate classes normally range from AA in rating to an unrated first-loss piece. These securities are often referenced as the *six-pack* since there are six broad rating grades generally issued by the rating agencies. In the investment-grade category, bonds range from AA to BBB; noninvestment grade ratings decline from BB to the unrated first-loss piece.[8] The ratings are assigned according to the amount of *credit support* (also referred to as *buffer*) behind each bond. The structure (or *splits*) of a hypothetical $400 million deal with 3.5% initial subordination is shown in Exhibits 15.7 and 15.8.

Internal credit enhancement requires two complimentary mechanisms. The cash flows for deals are allocated through the mechanism of a *waterfall*,

EXHIBIT 15.8 Tranche size measured by percentage of subordination for each rating level (i.e., credit support). Calculated by summing the deal percentages of all tranches junior in priority. As an example, if cumulative losses on the deal were 0.40%, the first loss and the rated B tranche would be fully exhausted, but tranches rated BB and above would not be affected.

	Face Value	Credit Support
AAA	$386,000,000.00	3.50%
AA	$6,000,000.00	2.00%
A	$2,600,000.00	1.35%
BBB	$1,800,000.00	0.90%
BB	$1,200,000.00	0.60%
B	$1,200,000.00	0.30%
First loss (nonrated)	$1,200,000.00	0.00%

which dictates the allocation of principal and interest payments to tranches with different degrees of seniority. The allocation of realized losses is governed by a separate prioritization schedule, with the subordinates typically being impacted in reverse order of priority.

While the original subordination levels are set at the time of issuance (or, more precisely, at the time the attributes of the deal's collateral are finalized), deals with internal credit enhancement are designed so that the amount of credit enhancement grows over time. Private-label structures generally use a so-called shifting interest mechanism, in which the subordinate classes (or subs) do not receive principal prepayments for a period of time after issuance, generally five years for fixed rate deals. After the lockout period expires, the subs begin to receive prepayments on an escalating basis. It is only after 10 years that the subs receive a pro rata allocation of prepayments. Locking out the subs means that as the collateral experiences prepayments, the face value of the subs grows in proportion relative to the senior classes. The senior classes receive all of the collateral prepayments during the lockout period and, for that reason, decline proportionately over time. Deals often have more than one collateral group securitized in the same transaction to minimize costs. Typically, the collateral groups have different characteristics that make them difficult to commingle. For example, a deal may have separate collateral groups comprised of 30- and 15-year loans. Depending on the collateral in question, the two groups can have separate subordination groups. Alternatively, one set of subs can serve as credit support for both groups, in a so-called Y-structure. This creates larger subordinate classes, which are generally more liquid.

15.4 PRICING RMBS BY SIMULATION

The pricing of RMBSs involves the estimation of the present value of the uncertain future cash flows, and presents a number of challenges. There are two building blocks to RMBS pricing models: an interest rate model, which determines the discount factor, and a prepayment model, which determines the behavior of the mortgagor. However, the two models do not exist independently of one another. Historical evidence clearly indicates that interest rates impact prepayments. Furthermore, not only the current interest rate, but also past interest rates matter for the amount of current prepayments. As we explained in section 15.2.4, this is often referred to as the *burnout effect*: a mortgage pool that has already experienced low interest rates will prepay less quickly than a pool that has always experienced high interest rates, even if the two pools currently face the same interest rates. This means that valuation of RMBSs is path-dependent; that is, it depends on the path taken by interest rates so far. Pricing models like binomial trees get out of hand very quickly in this context.[9]

Simulation is therefore the preferred and more practical method for pricing RMBSs. Yet given the complexity of RMBS structures, simulation is often too slow for practical purposes. More recently, variance-reduction techniques (especially quasirandom number sequences)[10] have been successfully applied to RMBS pricing.

In this section, we explain the main ideas behind RMBS pricing by simulation. We start with a discussion of interest and prepayment models used in RMBS pricing, and explain how the models are put together. We then discuss more recent developments, specifically how quasirandom Monte Carlo methods can be applied to RMBS pricing.

15.4.1 Prepayment Models

In section 15.2.3, we introduced a prepayment function convention. Prepayment models are a very important factor for accurate pricing of RMBSs, and there is a variety of proprietary models.

Traditionally, prepayment models have been based on econometrics—they often include macroeconomic factors, such as the health of the economy or the housing market activity, or identify a prepayment pattern as a function of specific characteristics of the individual mortgages in the pool. Three classical models are (1) the arctangent model from the Office of Thrift Supervision (OTS), (2) Schwarz and Torous's proportional hazard model (1989), and (3) Richard and Roll's modified Goldman Sachs model (1989). Other models (see, for example Kalotay, Yang, and Fabozzi 2004) take into consideration borrower intelligence and are based on option theory, under the assumption that the borrower acts optimally to maximize the value of the option to prepay the mortgage.

Technically, prepayment models should be based on option pricing theory. The fact that a homeowner can pay off the outstanding principal of a mortgage in full at any time and be freed from the obligations to make further payments means that the homeowner/borrower holds an American call option on an otherwise identical, nonprepayable mortgage. The strike of the option equals the principal amount of the outstanding loan, and changes after every payment. Similarly, we can think of the homeowner as the issuer of a callable bond—the homeowner sells the bond, receives the proceeds, and undertakes to make a set of scheduled payments.

When pricing callable bonds issued by governments, agencies, and corporations, we may be able to assume that the driving force behind prepayments is the level of interest rates. However, individuals do not always act rationally. Furthermore, residential mortgages are often prepaid for reasons independent of the level of interest rates—homeowners move, sell their home, and pay off the mortgage; or there are natural disasters, and the insurance policy covers the value of the home. Even if interest rates provide a strong incentive for homeowners to change the terms of their mortgages, homeowners vary greatly in financial sophistication. The cost to them to analyze the prepayment options and handle all the necessary paperwork may turn out to be too high. When they do refinance, there is still usually a noticeable delay, and valuation models from the financial markets do not reflect this properly.

As mentioned, most prepayment function models used in practice are based on statistical models. The concern with such approaches is that historical data, on which these models are based, may render the models outdated as economic conditions change. However, the theoretically superior approaches based on modeling the homeowner's decision process have not been too successful in practice, and have not gained widespread industry acceptance.

It is important to keep in mind also that in the case of nonagency RMBSs, prepayments can be involuntary. In other words, prepayments can arise because of a default by homeowners.[11] These defaults should be projected in modeling prepayments. Modeling defaults involves modeling the timing of defaults, as well as the severity of defaults (i.e., the recovery rate after the default). Both voluntary and involuntary prepayments are included in the calculation of the cash flow from the RMBS.

Next, we introduce two simple econometric prepayment models for agency RMBSs used in practice. Our goal is not to provide a comprehensive review of the subject, but to give the reader an idea of the kind of modeling that is involved in the pricing of RMBSs. For more details on prepayment models, see, for example, Fabozzi (2005).

Arctangent Model The arctangent model expresses the CPR at time t as a function of the weighted average coupon (WAC) and the 10-year rate at time t, $r_{10}(t)$:

$$CPR(t) = 0.2406 - 0.1389 \cdot \arctan\left(5.9518 \cdot \left(1.089 - \frac{WAC}{r_{10}(t)}\right)\right)$$

This kind of model is derived empirically based on the observed relationship between different factors and the prepayment rate.

Modified Goldman Sachs Model In the modified Goldman Sachs model,[12] the CPR is assumed to be a product of four factors: the refinancing incentive

RI, the month multiplier MM, the seasoning factor Age, and the burnout multiplier BM:

$$CPR(t) = RI(t) \cdot MM(t) \cdot \text{Age}(t) \cdot BM(t)$$

The refinancing incentive in this model is related to the ratio or the spread between the weighted average coupon rate and the interest rate. The idea is that if the interest rate is much lower than the weighted average coupon rate, there is a higher incentive for homeowners to refinance the mortgage, that is, RI is higher. RI can be expressed as

$$RI = a + b \cdot \arctan(c + d \cdot (WAC - r))$$

or

$$RI = a + b \cdot \arctan(c + d \cdot (WAC/r))$$

The relevant interest rate r can be, for example, the 10-year rate $r_{10}(t)$. The 10-year rate is often the one used as an approximation for the refinancing rate for new loans. Often a time lag is assumed to incorporate the observation that investors refinance after observing a fall in mortgage rates, that is, $r_{10}(t-1)$ is used. A specific function for RI used in practice is

$$RI(t) = 0.28 + 0.14 \cdot \arctan(-8.571 + 430 \cdot (WAC - r_{10}(t)))$$

The monthly multiplier MM is associated with the specific month of the year. It has been observed that prepayments peak during the summer-fall months, and bottom out in the winter. The month multipliers from the original Richard and Roll (1989) paper are as follows (starting with month $i = \text{January}$):

$$MM(i) = (0.94, 0.76, 0.74, 0.95, 0.98, 0.92, 0.98, 1.10, 1.18, 1.22, 1.23, 0.98)$$

The seasoning factor Age reflects the empirical observation that newer loans tend to prepay slower than old or "seasoned" loans. This factor usually follows the convention behind the standard PSA model (see section 15.2.3). A specific function used for Age is

$$\text{Age}(t) = \min\{1, \ t/30\}$$

Finally, as we explained earlier, the burnout multiplier reflects the empirical observation that prepayments tend to decrease over time, even when conditions for refinancing are favorable. The reason is that not all mort-gagors prepay in an identical fashion. Some refinance as soon as mortgage rates become lower than the rate they are paying; others wait until rates drop further; and others never prepay. The "fast" prepayers leave, and as the pool ages, only the "slow" ones stay behind. Richard and Roll (1989) use the following function for the burnout multiplier:

$$BM(t) = 0.3 + 0.7 \cdot \frac{MB(t)}{MB(0)}$$

where $MB(0)$ is the mortgage balance at the beginning, and $MB(t)$ is the mortgage balance at time t. In effect, Richard and Roll (1989) quantify the burnout by estimating how deep in-the-money the prepayment option is at time t. If it has been deep in-the-money, this suggests that all else being equal, the prepayments are smaller.

15.4.2 Interest Rate Models

There is a variety of interest rate models that can be used to generate scenar-ios for the term structure of interest rates. They can be most generally split into two categories: *equilibrium models*, and *no-arbitrage models*. Equilib-rium models, which include the Vasicek model and the CIR model, start with assumptions about economic variables and a process for the instantaneous (short) rate r.[13] They then derive the bond prices that the process for the short-term rate imply, and use those bond prices to construct the implied term structure. The disadvantage of equilibrium models is that they do not automatically fit today's term structure, so adjustments need to be made by selecting the parameters of the processes carefully to make sure that the pricing of securities using the term structure implied from these models does not create arbitrage opportunities.

The Vasicek model and the CIR model are one-factor models of the short-term interest rate because they include only one random variable. A popular two-factor model is the one proposed by Brennan and Schwartz (1979), in which the process for the short rate is assumed to revert to a long rate, which in turn follows a particular stochastic process itself. Another two-factor model assumes that the volatility in the process followed by the short-term interest rate itself follows a stochastic process.[14]

No-arbitrage models include the Ho-Lee model and the Hull-White model.[15] Those models are designed to be exactly consistent with today's term structure. Some equilibrium models can be converted to no-arbitrage models by making the assumption that the drift term in the process for the short rate depends on time. (Both the Ho-Lee and the Hull-White model do.) This allows to fit the parameters of the process to the shape of the term structure at time 0, and to incorporate that information for the process followed by the interest rate in the future as well.

How do we use the interest rate models for MBS pricing and risk evaluation purposes? The procedure is as follows. We use the realizations of the short-term interest rate to generate discount factors for different maturities. Usually, we need to generate long-term rates as well, such as the 10-year rate. Such long-term rates can be determined by computing zero-coupon bond prices. (For some interest rate models, this is easier to do than for others.) Namely, from those prices, we generate a yield curve. From this yield curve, we can estimate the long-term rates or forward rates.[16]

Let us give a specific example by using the Vasicek and the CIR models for the short rate. Recall from section 12.4 of Chapter 12 that the Vasicek model assumes that the short rate r follows the random walk

$$r_{t+1} = r_t + \kappa \cdot (\mu - r_t) + \sigma \cdot \tilde{\varepsilon}_t.$$

Similarly, recall from section 12.4.3 that the CIR model assumes that the short rate r follows the random walk

$$r_{t+1} = r_t + \kappa \cdot (\mu - r_t) + \sigma \cdot \sqrt{r_t} \cdot \tilde{\varepsilon}_t.$$

Under these assumptions, one can generate paths for the short-term rate and use them to compute discount factors. One can also derive a closed-form expression for the price (at any time t) of a zero-coupon bond with face value of $1 maturing at time T, $B(t, T)$, in terms of r_t. The details of the derivation are beyond the scope of this book, but the formulas turn out to be:

- In the Vasicek model,

$$B(t, T) = A(t, T) \cdot e^{-C(t,T) \cdot r_t}$$

where

$$C(t, T) = \frac{1 - e^{\kappa \cdot (T-t)}}{\kappa}$$

and

$$A(t, T) = e^{\frac{(C(t,T) - T + t) \cdot (\kappa^2 \mu - \sigma^2/2)}{\kappa^2} - \frac{\sigma^2 \cdot C(t,T)^2}{4 \kappa}}$$

- In the CIR model,

$$B(t, T) = A(t, T) \cdot e^{-C(t,T) \cdot r_t}$$

where

$$C(t, T) = \frac{2 \cdot \left(e^{\gamma \cdot (T-t)} - 1\right)}{(\gamma + \kappa) \cdot \left(e^{\gamma \cdot (T-t)} - 1\right) + 2 \cdot \gamma}$$

$$A(t, T) = \left(\frac{2 \cdot \gamma \cdot e^{(\gamma + \kappa) \cdot (T-t)/2}}{(\gamma + \kappa) \cdot \left(e^{\gamma \cdot (T-t)} - 1\right) + 2 \cdot \gamma}\right)^{2 \cdot \kappa \cdot \mu / \sigma^2}$$

and

$$\gamma = \sqrt{\kappa^2 + 2 \cdot \sigma^2}$$

Given a realization of r_t, we can plug it into the above formulas, and determine $B(t, T)$. $B(t, T)$ is the price of a zero-coupon bond with a face value of 1. Thus, we can interpret the value for $B(t, T)$ as the discount factor between t and T. We also have

$$B(t, T) = e^{-r_{(t,T)} \cdot (T-t)}$$

This allows us to compute the long-term interest rate applicable for the period (t, T) as[17]

$$r_{(t,T)} = -\ln(B(t, T))/(T - t)$$

Thus, we can build the term structure of interest rates. Forward rates can be computed from the term structure as well. In particular, we can compute the 10-year interest rate, $_{10}r_t$ in our notation from Chapter 2, at each point in time t, to use in prepayment models.

15.4.3 Putting It All Together

As we explained in the previous two sections, the pricing of an RMBS requires a prepayment model and an interest rate model. The price of the RMBS is the expected value of the future cash flows over all generated scenarios for the interest rates and the corresponding prepayments. The procedure is as follows:

1. Generate N scenarios for interest rate paths, where a "path" includes the short interest rate and the corresponding discount factors for 360 months ahead. Record also the corresponding values for a required long-term rate, such as the 10-year rate.

For each interest rate path n, $n = 1, \ldots, N$:

A. At each point in time (360 of them), calculate the expected prepayment using a particular prepayment function. For example, if we use the modified Goldman Sachs prepayment function, we will plug in the estimated 10-year rate r_{10} at each point in time for each interest rate path.

B. After calculating the prepayment rates, compute the cash flow $CF_n(t)$ from the mortgage pool for each time t along that interest rate path. This is a difficult step, as RMBS structures can be incredibly complex. For pass-through RMBS, we have a specific formula for $CF_n(t)$:[18]

$$CF_n(t) = MP_n(t) + PP_n(t) = TPP_n(t) + IP_n(t)$$
$$MP_n(t) = SP_n(t) + IP_n(t)$$
$$TPP_n(t) = SP_n(t) + PP_n(t)$$

where $MP_n(t)$ is the scheduled mortgage payment for month t.
        $TPP_n(t)$ is the total principal payment for month t.
        $IP_n(t)$ is the interest payment for month t.
        $SP_n(t)$ is the scheduled principal payment for month t.
        $PP_n(t)$ is the principal prepayment for month t.

These quantities are calculated as follows:

$$MP_n(t) = MB_n(t-1) \cdot \left(\frac{WAC/12}{1 - (1 + WAC/12)^{-WAM+t}} \right)$$
$$IP_n(t) = MB_n(t-1) \cdot (WAC/12)$$
$$PP_n(t) = SMM_n(t) \cdot (MB_n(t-1) - SP_n(t))$$
$$MB_n(t) = MB_n(t-1) - TPP_n(t)$$
$$SMM_n(t) = 1 - \sqrt[12]{1 - CPR_n(t)}$$

where $MP_n(t)$ is the principal mortgage balance of the RMBS at the end of month t.
        WAC is the weighted average coupon rate for the RMBS (weighted by the balance of each mortgage).
        WAM is the weighted average maturity for the RMBS (weighted by the balance of each mortgage).
        $SMM_n(t)$ is the single monthly mortality for month t, observed at the end of month t.
        $CPR_n(t)$ is the conditional prepayment rate for month t, observed at the end of month t.

2. Calculate the total cash flow over the entire interest rate path as a sum of the cash flows at each point in time, properly discounted with the discount factor for that interest rate path at that time plus an appropriate risk-adjusted spread K.
3. Calculate the average of the cash flows over the N interest rate paths.

It is clear from the above algorithm that once we know $CPR(t)$ for each time and each interest rate path, everything else can be calculated. $CPR(t)$ will, of course, be different depending on the prepayment model used.

This procedure is valid for pricing more complex types of RMBSs as well; we just need to be careful about estimating the cash flows $CF(t)$. For example, in a sequential-pay structure, we apply the procedure to estimate the cash flows for classes A, B, C, and so on separately. This determines the price for each class.

15.4.4 Further Analysis

In the process of evaluating the RMBS price by simulation, we obtain a variety of other information that can be useful.

Distribution of Path Values   The average of the cash flows obtained along the N simulated interest rate paths gives us the price of the RMBS. However, we also obtain the distribution of cash flows, that is, N points from the probability distribution of cash flow values. This allows us to observe the variability in the cash flows and to decide how much confidence we can have in the estimate of the RMBS price obtained from the simulation.

Average Life   In the process of simulating the price of an RMBS, we work with estimates of the average life of the RMBS along each interest rate path. This allows us to obtain the probability distribution of the average life, which is useful for risk management purposes.

Option-Adjusted Spread   Traders like to compute a quantity called the *option-adjusted spread* (OAS) that allows them to have an estimate of the spread of the yield of the RMBS over Treasuries when the optionality has been taken into account. The OAS is the spread above the risk-free rate that makes the price of the RMBS equal to the observed market price. In the Monte Carlo simulation, it is the spread that makes the average present value of the RMBS cash flows along all the interest rate paths equal to the observed market price.

15.4.5 Improving the Degree of Accuracy with Variance-Reduction Methods

In Chapter 4, we discussed the issue of how many trials are needed in a simulation. The short answer is that this is not known. However, we can decide if the number of paths we generated in the simulation resulted in an estimate of the quantity of interest with small variance (i.e., with sufficient accuracy), and increase the number of generated paths if the estimate is too variable.[19] A typical RMBS is priced using between 512 and 1,024 paths. However, this number can be brought down to as few as 128 or 64 paths by using variance reduction methods. The actual variance reduction methods used in practice are proprietary, but Akesson and Lehoczky (2000) describe the basics of how to apply quasi–Monte Carlo number sequences in the context of RMBS pricing.

To price an RMBS, we need to simulate 360 monthly observations for interest rates N times. Therefore, we are dealing with generating N random points in a 360-dimensional cube, that is, a 360-dimensional problem. Quasi–Monte Carlo methods (low discrepancy sequences) are appropriate in this situation because they can generate points that can cover the space a lot better than purely random points, thus necessitating fewer points to achieve the same degree of accuracy as random number generators. It is important to keep in mind, though, that not all low discrepancy sequences outperform traditional Monte Carlo simulation. The selection of the specific low discrepancy sequence to use must be accompanied by a lot of tests. Akesson and Lehoczky (2000) use the Sobol low discrepancy sequence, together with other simulation speed enhancements, such as principal components[20] and Brownian bridge[21] constructions for the interest rate paths. They note a substantial improvement in the speed of RMBS pricing algorithms.

15.5 USING SIMULATION TO ESTIMATE SENSITIVITY OF RMBS PRICES TO DIFFERENT FACTORS

Investors in RMBSs are exposed to many different types of risk, such as interest rate risk, credit risk, and model risk. The sensitivity of the RMBS price to these factors is typically evaluated by simulation. This section discusses risk assessment in more detail.

15.5.1 Interest Rate Risk

One of the main risks of RMBSs is interest rate risk. MBSs are fixed income securities and, as such, are very sensitive to shifts in yields. Similarly to simpler fixed income securities, RMBS prices fall when interest rates rise, and RMBS prices rise when interest rates fall. However, recall that RMBSs in effect have embedded options; that is, mortgage holders have the option to refinance if interest rates fall. This has an effect on the life of the RMBSs. Hence, classical measures of interest sensitivity such as Macaulay duration and modified duration do not work well in the case of RMBSs.

Furthermore, in the case of plain vanilla bonds (without embedded options) duration measures underestimate price gains and overestimate price losses. In the case of a noncallable bond, this estimation error is due to the positive convexity and favors the investor. However, the opposite is the case for RMBSs, which have prepayment risk. Duration overestimates price gains and underestimates price losses. This is due to negative convexity, and works against the investor. The more prepayment risk a security has, the worse the estimation error will be and, in turn, the more negative its convexity will be.

That is why in the case of RMBSs, an option-adjusted duration is used.[22] The *option-adjusted duration* is computed by assuming changes of equal amounts (usually, increments of 50 basis points to 100 basis points) up or down, and evaluating the new RMBS prices. The sensitivity of the RMBS price computed in this way is the option-adjusted duration.

Other measures of interest rate sensitivity that are sometimes quoted are the average life (also called *weighted average life*, or WAL), which is an average time to receive back principal on the underlying loans, and *weighted average maturity* (WAM), which is weighted average maturity of the underlying loans. These can be evaluated directly, without generating scenarios. However, they are less useful as measures of sensitivity to interest rates because they do not take into consideration the inherent optionality in RMBSs.

15.5.2 Credit Risk

The credit risk associated with one type of agency RMBSs, those issued by Ginnie Mae, is minimal—Ginnie Mae MBS can be basically treated as credit-risk-free securities because they are backed by an explicit federal guarantee. There is uncertainty as to the credit risk of securities issued by the two government sponsored enterprises—Fannie Mae and Freddie Mac. Although both have a line of credit with the Treasury, the credit line is not sufficient to meet all obligations. There is no explicit or implicit government guarantee in the case of nonagency RMBSs. Private-label RMBSs are rated by rating agencies in order to incorporate information about credit risk. Considerations for their credit risk are used when pricing such RMBSs by simulating the spread over the risk-free U.S. Treasury yield curve in addition to the U.S. Treasury yield curve itself.

15.5.3 Model Risk

Virtually all security pricing models are exposed to model risk. *Model risk* is the risk of using an incorrect model.[23] In the case of RMBSs, the assumptions in the prepayment model can make an enormous difference in the RMBS price estimate and risk evaluation. There is no way to fix this, but it is important to conduct sensitivity analysis and scenario analysis that can raise a flag if the RMBS price and risk estimates are very sensitive to assumptions in the model.

15.6 STRUCTURING RMBS DEALS USING DYNAMIC PROGRAMMING

So far, we have taken the RMBS structure as given, and discussed how to price it and evaluate its sensitivity with respect to different factors. We mentioned that the procedure for determining the value of the RMBS by simulation is the same for all types of RMBSs, but that estimating the cash flow along each interest rate path is challenging. The cash flow is found according to the principal repayment and interest distributions rules of the deal. In the case of CMOs, a structuring model is needed. In any analysis of CMOs, one of the major stumbling blocks is getting a good CMO structuring deal.

Dynamic programming and integer programming methods can be used to approach the problem of optimal structuring of a CMO. From the perspective of the CMO issuer, for example, the tranches could be designed in many different ways. The issuers make money on the difference between the interest collected by the mortgage holders whose mortgages are in the pool, and the interest paid out to investors who buy the RMBS. While the mortgage holders pay 10- and 30-year interest rates on the principal outstanding, some tranches in a CMO pay out two-, four-, six-, and eight-year rates plus a spread. A natural question that arises is if there is a way to design a CMO so that the profit to the issuer is the largest. How many tranches should there be? How large should the tranches be? What coupon rates can the issuer afford to pay to the RMBS investors?

Cornuejols and Tutuncu (2007) describe a dynamic programming algorithm for answering these questions for a sequential-pay MBS. We provide some discussion of their approach next. The problem formulation that is described is one of private-label CMOs, where credit quality is an issue.[24]

When structuring a CMO, several constraints need to be taken into consideration. First, we need to make sure that the payments over the life of the CMO can service the promised payments to the bond holders under different scenarios. Two extreme such scenarios include the case of full early prepayments and no early prepayments. Second, we need to estimate the average life of each tranche.[25] The price of the tranche will then be determined based on the rate of a Treasury bond with the same duration, and an appropriate spread which depends on the tranche's credit rating. Third, we need to calculate the required credit support, or buffer, for each tranche as a function of the average life of the tranche and rating. The required buffer is computed as

Average life of tranche · Expected default rate · Loss multiple

and the size of the buffer determines the credit rating that will be assigned to a tranche. The larger the buffer, the more collateral is "behind" the tranche. If the buffer of a particular tranche is large, the CMO will have to experience a lot of defaults before payments to that tranche are stopped. The last tranche in the CMO has no buffer.[26]

The *loss multiple* is a multiplier that is set by the rating agencies. For example, a tranche with AAA rating must have a buffer equal to six times the expected default rate, so its loss multiple is six.

Finally, the coupon paid out on each tranche is estimated based on the tranche's credit rating and rates on comparable securities. Spreads on corporate bonds with similar credit ratings typically provide a benchmark.

Suppose we would like to structure a CMO with four tranches. The objective is to maximize the profits from the issuance by choosing the size of each tranche. A dynamic programming algorithm can be developed to find the optimal sizes. As we mentioned in section 5.6.3 of Chapter 5, one of the most difficult problems in dynamic programming is identifying the states and the stages. In this case, the states are t, the indices of the months, and the stages are k, the number of tranches up to month t. This enumerates all possible tranches—there are t possible maturities for the tranches, and k possible starting dates for the tranche ($k \leq t$). Tranche (k, t) starts amortizing at the beginning of month k and ends at the end of month t.

Let T_{kt} be the present value of the payments on tranche (k, t). (T_{kt} can be computed exactly for every pair (k, t).) Let $f(k, t)$ denote the minimum present value of total payments to bondholders in months 1 through t when the CMO has k tranches up to year t. It is easy to see that $f(1, t) = T_{1t}$. (If there is only one tranche up to year t, then there is nothing to minimize—we know the present value of that tranche.) For larger values of k, the dynamic programming recursion can be written as follows:

$$f(k, t) = \min_{j=k-1,\dots t-1} \left\{ f(k-1, j) + T_{j+1,t} \right\}$$

For example, if $k = 2$ and $t = 5$, we compute $f(1, j) + T_{j+1,5}$ for each $j = 1, 2, 3, 4$, and take the minimum. Note that for $k = 4$, there is no need to compute the minimum of thousands of possible combinations of four tranches. We just need to use the value $f(3, j)$ found at the previous stage, and enumerate over the size of the fourth tranche.

In the example of an RMBS ("Structure 1") from section 15.3.3, we had $k = 4$ and $t = 358$. Suppose that we would like to find the optimal size of the four tranches. (Assume also that this is a nonagency CMO.) We would compute $f(4,358)$, which would give us the minimum cost for structuring the CMO with four tranches. To find out what the actual tranche sizes are, we need to backtrack from the last stage and identify how the minimum was achieved at each stage.

SUMMARY

- Securitization is used to create various structured products referred to as asset-backed securities.
- An asset-backed security is a debt instrument backed by a pool of loans or receivables. The cash flow from the pool of loans is used to satisfy the obligations of the debt instruments.
- MBSs are a type of asset-backed securities which are backed by pools of mortgages.
- An RMBS is an MBS backed by a pool of residential mortgage loans; a CMBS is backed by a pool of commercial mortgage loans.
- RMBSs can be agency RMBSs or private-label RMBSs. Agency RMBSs are backed by three government-related entities (Ginnie Mae, Fannie Mae, and Freddie Mac).
- There are three types of agency RMBSs: pass-through securities, stripped MBSs, and collateralized mortgage obligations (CMOs).
- In a mortgage pass-through security, the monthly cash flow from the pool of mortgage loans is distributed on a pro rata basis to the certificate holders.
- A stripped MBS is created by altering the distribution of principal and interest from a pro rata distribution to an unequal distribution. In the most common type of stripped MBS, all of the interest is allocated to one class—the interest-only class, and all of the principal to the other class—the principal-only class.
- An agency CMO is a security backed by a pool of mortgage pass-through securities. Agency CMOs are structured so that there are several classes of bonds (called tranches) with varying maturities. The principal payments from the underlying pool of pass-through securities are used to retire the bonds on a priority basis as specified in the prospectus.
- There are numerous types of agency CMO bonds, including sequential-pay bonds, PAC bonds, and support bonds.

- Private-label RMBSs are issued by any entity other than Ginnie Mae, Fannie Mae, or Freddie Mac. Because of the credit risk associated with private-label RMBSs, they require credit enhancements to provide different degrees of credit protection against defaults on the pool of assets backing a transaction.
- The uncertainty about the cash flow attributable to prepayments is called prepayment risk and is the major risk in agency RMBSs.
- The pricing of RMBSs involves the estimation of the present value of the uncertain future cash flows, and presents a number of challenges. There are two building blocks to RMBS pricing models: an interest rate model, which determines the discount factor, and a prepayment model, which determines the behavior of the mortgagor.
- Prepayments depend on interest rates. Moreover, they depend on the history of interest rates, which makes RMBSs path-dependent, and makes their pricing challenging. Simulation is the preferred method for handling path dependency.
- Traditionally, prepayment models have been based on econometrics—they often include macroeconomic factors, such as the health of the economy or the housing market activity, or identify a prepayment pattern as a function of specific characteristics of the individual mortgages in the pool. Other models are based on option theory, and assume that the borrower acts optimally to maximize the value of the option to prepay the mortgage. The latter models are more complex, and less widely used in practice.
- Estimating the price of a RMBS involves simulating a particular number of interest rate paths. Along each path, the expected prepayments are simulated at each point in time (each month), and the cash flows are evaluated. The cash flows along that interest rate path are then discounted using the simulated interest rates plus an appropriate spread. The average of the total cash flows over all interest rate paths is the price of the RMBS.
- Simulation is an effective way to price the RMBS, but it can be very slow because of the large dimension of the problem. Quasi–Monte Carlo methods have shown promise for reducing the necessary number of generated paths and the amount of computational time without sacrificing accuracy.
- As a by-product of estimating the price of a RMBS by simulation, we obtain other useful information, such as the distribution of RMBS values for different interest rate scenarios, and the distribution of the average life of the RMBS.
- Simulation is useful also for estimating the sensitivity of the price of the RMBS to different factors, such as interest rates, credit events, and model risk.

- Dynamic programming can be used to structure CMOs optimally so as to maximize the profit for the issuer while satisfying a number of constraints.

NOTES

1. *Residential mortgages* are loans to individual households. *Commercial mortgages* are loans on income-producing property, such as multifamily properties (i.e., apartment buildings), office buildings, industrial properties (including warehouses), shopping centers, hotels, and health care facilities (i.e., senior housing care facilities).
2. David Bowie's music rights were the first such securitization in 1997. The $55 million of securities issued were backed by the current and future revenues of Bowie's first 25 music albums (287 songs) recorded prior to 1990. These bonds, popularly referred to as "Bowie bonds," were purchased by Prudential Insurance Company and had a maturity of 10 years. When the bonds matured in 2007, the royalty rights reverted back to David Bowie.
3. The PSA and the CPR approaches are not mutually exclusive alternatives but are mostly used together—the PSA to explain the ramp-up of the expected CPR over the initial months of seasoning. Thereafter, the pool undergoes a constant CPR.
4. The weighted average coupon rate is obtained by weighting the mortgage rate of each mortgage loan in the pool by the amount of mortgage balance outstanding.
5. The weighted average maturity is obtained by weighting the remaining number of months to maturity for each mortgage loan in the pool by the amount of mortgage balance outstanding.
6. The aggregate mortgage payment is the payment that will amortize (i.e., reduce to 0) the outstanding loan, after accounting for interest and principal payments. The formula for computing the mortgage payment needed to bring the balance to zero after T years is

$$P \cdot \frac{I}{(1 - (1 + I))^T}$$

where P is the outstanding principal, and I is the interest rate (in decimal). In our example, we are working with months (rather than years). To compute the aggregate mortgage payment for the first month, for example, we use the formula

$$660,000,000 \cdot \frac{(0.06/12)}{(1 - (1 + (0.06/12)))^{358}}$$

7. In other words, the average life in years is obtained by multiplying the entries in column 8, Total Principal, by the corresponding entries in column 1, Month,

then dividing by the collateral ($660 million) and by 12 to convert the number to years instead of months.

8. See Chapter 2 for an introduction to credit ratings.
9. See section 14.9 in Luenberger (1998) for an example of how a binomial tree for the process followed by interest rates can be applied for pricing a simple RMBS. The example points out the difficulty of using binomial lattices, and the need to employ nonrecombining binomial trees. The dimension of the problem then quickly becomes computationally prohibitive.
10. See Chapter 14.
11. Recall that in the case of nonagency RMBS, the mortgages do not have federal guarantees.
12. The modified Goldman Sachs model was developed by Richard and Roll (1989) and modified by the OTS. Typically, the details of prepayment models by banks are proprietary. The Goldman Sachs model as formulated by Richard and Roll has probably changed dramatically over the past 20 or so years since the article appeared.
13. As we saw in section 12.4.3 of Chapter 12, the Vasicek and the CIR model assume that the short-term interest rate is mean-reverting.
14. See Longstaff and Schwartz (1992).
15. See Hull (2008).
16. See Chapter 2 for how to compute forward rates off the given term structure of interest rates.
17. We simply took logarithms of both sides of the equation.
18. See Chapter 19 in Fabozzi (1993).
19. Note that this criterion does not tell us how good the estimate is relative to the truth; only how good it is relative to the model we are using.
20. See Chapter 11.
21. A Brownian bridge construction is the generation of a sequence of values for a Brownian motion in a not necessarily sequential mode after generating the end points (the first point and the last point in the process) first. The remaining points are then filled out in different order depending on the variance reduction method or low discrepancy sequence used. See section 12.6 for a definition of Brownian motion, and Glasserman (2004) for more details on Brownian bridge construction.
22. See section 2.6.5 of Chapter 2 and Goldman Sachs Asset Management (2007).
23. Note that model risk is different from estimation error. The latter assumes that the model is correct, but the estimates of the inputs to the model are inaccurate.
24. See section 15.3.4.
25. See sections 15.3.1 and 15.3.2 for how to estimate the average life of a tranche.
26. See Exhibit 15.7.

CHAPTER 16

Using Derivatives in Portfolio Management

As mentioned in Chapter 13, there are many applications of financial derivatives, but the two main reasons for including them in an investor's portfolio are (1) risk management and (2) return enhancement. *Risk management* refers to strategies whose goal is to control risk with hedging as a special case. *Return enhancement* refers to investment strategies that seek to capitalize on the direction in which the underlying uncertainties will be resolved or take advantage of discrepancies in pricing to make profit. This is more popularly referred to as "taking a view" on some factor that is expected to drive returns. Prior to the existence of futures, for example, an investor who wanted to take a view on the direction of future stock prices had to buy or short individual stocks to do it. Now, one can buy futures on entire market indices, and the transaction costs of such strategies are a lot smaller than the transaction costs of individual stock purchases.

The decision of whether to use derivatives in portfolio construction is not unlike any other business decision—it requires careful analysis. Sanford and Borge (1993) suggested a process that investment managers go through before deciding whether to make derivatives a part of their portfolio. They outlined some necessary steps:

- Define the investment process in terms of risk management.
- Establish clear investment objectives and acceptable risk tolerance level.
- Create a set of boundary conditions for the level of risk.
- Assess the full range of possible outcomes from using derivatives.
- Assess the impact of using derivatives on the portfolio's risk profile.
- Establish monitoring protocol to measure risk.
- Develop an adjustment response mechanism.

This chapter provides some examples of equity and fixed income investment strategies with derivatives, and explains the use of simulation for evaluating the effect of including derivatives on the portfolio risk profile. The list of investment strategies involving derivatives provided here is by no means exhaustive—there is an infinite variety of possible uses of derivatives for risk management or return enhancement purposes.

16.1 USING DERIVATIVES IN EQUITY PORTFOLIO MANAGEMENT

Investors can use the listed options market to address a range of investment problems. In this section, we consider the use of calls, puts, and combinations in the context of the investment process, which could involve (1) risk management or (2) return enhancement. Recall from the discussion in section 13.1.2 of Chapter 13 that the distinction between options and futures is that the former have nonlinear payoffs that will fundamentally alter the risk profile of an existing portfolio. The following basic strategies can be used to establish a hedged position in an individual stock or a portfolio.

16.1.1 Risk Management Strategies

Risk management in the context of equity portfolio management focuses on price risk. Consequently, the strategies discussed in this section in some way address the risk of a price decline or a loss due to adverse price movement. Options can be used to create asymmetric risk exposures across all or part of the core equity portfolio. This allows the investor to hedge downside risk at a fixed cost with a specific limit to losses should the market turn down. The basic risk management objective is to create the optimal risk exposure and to achieve the target rate of return. Options can help accomplish this by reducing risk exposure. The various risk management strategies will also affect the expected rate of return on the position unless some form of inefficiency is involved. This may involve the current mix of risk and return or be the result of the use of options. Below we discuss two risk management strategies: protective put and collar.

Protective Put Strategies   *Protective put strategies* are valuable to portfolio managers who currently hold a long position in the underlying security or investors who desire upside exposure and downside protection by using put options. The motivation is to hedge some or all of the total risk. Index put options hedge mostly market risk, while equity put options hedge the total risk associated with a specific stock. This allows portfolio managers to use protective put strategies for separating tactical and strategic strategies. Consider, for example, a portfolio manager who is concerned about exogenous or nonfinancial events increasing the level of risk in the marketplace. Furthermore, assume the portfolio manager is satisfied with the core portfolio holdings and the strategic mix. Put options could be employed as a tactical risk reduction strategy designed to preserve capital and still maintain strategic targets for portfolio returns. Protective put strategies may not be suitable for all portfolio managers, but the value of protective put strategies is that they provide the investor with the ability to invest in volatile stocks with a degree of desired insurance and unlimited profit potential over the life of the strategy.

The protective put involves the purchase of a put option combined with a long stock position. This is the equivalent of a position in a call option on the stock combined with the purchase of risk-free bond. In fact, the combined position yields the call option payoff pattern described in section 13.1.2 of Chapter 13. The put option is comparable to an insurance policy written against the long stock position. The option price is the cost of the insurance premium and the amount the option is out-of-the-money is the deductible. Just as in the case of insurance, the deductible is inversely related to the insurance premium. The deductible is reduced as the strike price increases, which makes the put option more in-the-money or less out-of-the-money. A higher strike price causes the put price to increase and makes the insurance policy more expensive.

The profitability of the strategy from inception to termination can be expressed as follows:

$$\text{Profit} = N_s \cdot (S_T - S_t) + N_p \cdot (\max\{K - S_T, 0\} - P)$$

where N_s is the number of stocks.
N_p is the number of put options.
P is the price of the put.
S_t is the current stock price.
S_T is the stock price at maturity.
K is the strike price.

The profitability of the protective put strategy is the sum of the profit from the long stock position and the put option. If held to expiration, the minimum payout is the strike price (K) and the maximum is the stock price (S_T). If the stock price is below the strike price of the put option at expiration, the investor exercises the option and sells the stock to the option writer for K.

If we assume that the number of shares N_s is equal to N_p, the number of put options, then the loss would amount to

$$\text{Profit} = S_T - S_t + K - S_T - P = K - S_t - P$$

Notice that the price of the stock at the termination date does not enter into the profit equation.

For example, if the original stock price S_t was \$100, the strike price K was \$95, the closing stock price S_T was \$80, and the put price P was \$4, then the profit would equal

$$\text{Profit} = \$95 - \$100 - \$4 = -\$9$$

Without the protective put strategy, the manager would have realized a loss of \$20 (= \$100 – \$80).

If, on the other hand, the stock closed up \$20, then the profit would be

$$\text{Profit} = S_T - S_t - P = \$120 - \$100 - \$4 = \$16$$

The cost of the insurance is 4% in percentage terms, and manifests itself as a loss of upside potential. If we add transaction costs, the shortfall is increased slightly. The maximum loss, however, is the sum of the put premium and the difference between the strike price and the original stock price, which is the amount of the deductible. The problem arises when the portfolio manager is measured against a benchmark and the cost of what amounted to an unused insurance policy causes the portfolio to underperform the benchmark. Equity managers can use stock selection, market timing, and options to reduce the cost of insurance. The break-even stock price is given by the sum of the original stock price and the put price. In this example, the break-even stock price is \$104, which is the stock price necessary to recover the put premium. The put premium is never really recovered because of the performance lag. This lag falls in significance as the return increases.

A graphical depiction of a protective put strategy is provided in Exhibit 16.1. The figure shows the individual long stock and long put positions and the combined impact, which is essentially a long call option. The maximum loss is the put premium plus the out-of-the-money amount, which is the insurance premium plus the deductible.

Collar Strategies An alternative to a protective put is a *collar*. A collar strategy consists of a long stock, a long put, and a short call. By varying the strike prices, a range of trade-offs among downside protection, costs, and upside potential is possible.

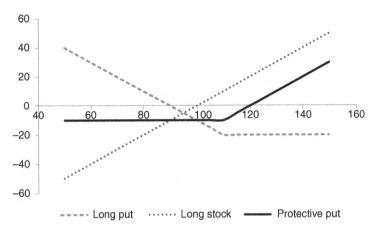

EXHIBIT 16.1   Example of a protective put strategy.

When the long put is completely financed by the short call position (i.e., the put premium is paid for by the proceeds from shorting the call), the strategy is referred to as a *zero-cost collar*.

Collars are designed for investors who currently hold a long equity position and want to achieve a level of risk reduction. The put exercise price establishes a floor and the call exercise price a ceiling. An example of the resulting payout pattern is shown in Exhibit 16.2. The graph includes the components of the strategy and the combined position. This particular example is a near zero-cost collar. In order to pay for the put option, a call option was written with a strike price of $110. Selling this call option pays for the put premium, but caps the upside to 10.23%. The floor completes the collar and limits downside losses to the out-of-the money amount of the put option. In order to provide full insurance, an at-the-money put option would cost slightly above 6%, which would be paid for by limiting upside potential returns to 5%. Portfolio managers can determine the appropriate trade-offs and protection consistent with their objectives.

The profit equation for a collar is simply the sum of a long stock position, a long put, and a short call:

$$\text{Profit} = N_s \cdot (S_T - S_t) + N_p \cdot (\max\{K_p - S_T, 0\} - P) \\ - N_c \cdot (\max\{S_T - K_c, 0\} - C)$$

where K_p and K_c are the strike prices of the put and the call, respectively, N_c is the number of calls, and C is the call premium.

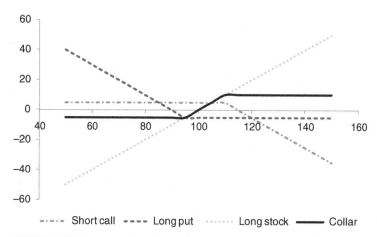

EXHIBIT 16.2   Example of a collar strategy.

16.1.2 Return Enhancement Strategies

Options can be used for return enhancement. Here we describe the most popular return enhance strategy: *covered call strategy*. Other return enhancement strategies include covered combination strategy and volatility valuation strategy.

We introduced covered call strategies in the last case in the practice section for Chapter 13. There are many variations of covered call strategies. If the portfolio manager owns the stock and writes a call on that stock, the strategy has been referred to as an *overwrite strategy*. If the strategy is implemented all at once (i.e., buy the stock and sell the call option), it is referred to as a *buy-write strategy*. The essence of the covered call is to trade price appreciation for income. The strategy is appropriate for slightly bullish investors who don't expect much out of the stock and want to produce additional income. These are investors who are willing either to limit upside appreciation for limited downside protection or to manage the costs of selling the underlying stock. The primary motive is to generate additional income from owning the stock.

Although the call premium provides some limited downside protection, the covered call is not an insurance strategy because it has significant downside risk. Consequently, investors should proceed with caution when considering a covered call strategy.

A covered call is less risky than buying the stock because the call premium lowers the break-even recovery price. The strategy behaves like a long stock position when the stock price is below the strike price. On the other

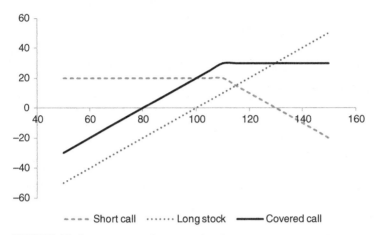

EXHIBIT 16.3 Example of a covered call strategy.

hand, the strategy is insensitive to stock prices above the strike price and is therefore capped on the upside. The maximum profit is given by the call premium and the out-the-money amount of the call option.

The payout pattern diagram is presented in Exhibit 16.3. It includes the long stock, short call, and covered call positions.

16.2 USING DERIVATIVES IN BOND PORTFOLIO MANAGEMENT

Derivatives are widely used in bond portfolio management for controlling different types of risk, such as interest rate and credit risk. We describe some applications next.

16.2.1 Controlling Interest Rate Risk

As we explained in Chapter 10, investment managers with strong expectations about the direction of the future course of interest rates will adjust the duration of their fixed income portfolios so as to capitalize on their expectations. It is easy to see that a money manager who expects rates to increase will shorten duration; a money manager who expects interest rates to decrease will lengthen duration.[1] While this can be achieved by altering the portfolio composition, using derivative contracts provides a quicker and less expensive means for changing the interest rate sensitivity, or duration, of a portfolio (on either a temporary or permanent basis).

Using Futures   A formula to approximate the number of futures contracts necessary to adjust the portfolio duration to some target duration is

$$\frac{\text{Target portfolio duration} - \text{Current portfolio duration}}{\text{Dollar duration of the futures contract}} \cdot \frac{\text{Market value of}}{\text{the portfolio}}$$

The dollar duration of the futures contract is the dollar price sensitivity of the futures contract to a change in interest rates.

Notice that if the asset manager wishes to increase the portfolio's current duration, the numerator of the formula is positive. This means that futures contracts will be purchased. That is, buying futures increases the duration of the portfolio. The opposite is true if the objective is to shorten the portfolio's current duration: The numerator of the formula is negative and this means that futures must be sold. Hence, selling futures contracts reduces the portfolio's duration.

Hedging is a special case of risk control where the target duration sought is zero. If cash and futures prices move together, any loss realized by the hedger from one position (whether cash or futures) will be offset by a profit on the other position. When the net profit or loss from the positions is exactly as anticipated, the hedge is referred to as a *perfect hedge*.

In bond portfolio management, typically the bond to be hedged is not identical to the bond underlying the futures contract and therefore there is *cross hedging*. This may result in substantial risk, referred to as *basis risk*.[2]

For example, suppose that on December 24, 2007, a bond portfolio manager wants to hedge a position in a Procter & Gamble (P&G) 5.55% of 3/5/2037 bond that he anticipates selling on March 31, 2008. The par value of the P&G bonds is $10 million. The portfolio manager decides that he will use the March 2008 Treasury bond futures to hedge the bond position, which he can settle on March 31, 2008. Because the portfolio manager is trying to protect against a decline in the value of the P&G bonds between December 24, 2007, and the anticipated sale date, he will short (sell) a number of March 2008 Treasury bond futures contracts. Because the bond to be hedged is a corporate bond and the hedging instrument is a Treasury bond futures contract, this is an example of a cross hedge.

Using Options   Interest rate options can be written on a fixed income security or an interest rate futures contract. The former options are called options on physicals and the latter are called futures options. The most liquid exchange-traded option on a fixed income security is an option on

Treasury bonds traded on the Chicago Board of Trade (CBOT). Options on interest rate futures have been far more popular than options on physicals. However, portfolio managers have made increasingly greater use of over-the-counter (OTC) options. Typically they are purchased by investors who want to hedge the risk associated with a specific security or index. Besides options on fixed income securities, there are OTC options on the shape of the yield curve or the yield spread between two securities.

Buying puts on Treasury futures options is one of the easiest ways to purchase protection against rising interest rates. The mechanics of this strategy involve more background in fixed income than we have given in this book.[3]

Using Swaps Hedging bonds with interest rates swaps is similar to hedging bonds with Treasury notes or futures contracts. To hedge a long position in a bond, an asset manager needs to establish a pay-fixed swap position since changes in the value of a swap are inversely related to changes in the value of the bond being hedged. In a pay-fixed swap position, which is analogous to a short-bond position, the asset manager pays a fixed rate to receive a floating rate. In designing a hedge using interest rate swaps, the maturity of the interest rate swap should match the maturity of the instrument that is used as the pricing reference for the security being hedged. This is analogous to hedging in the Treasury market.

For example, if a two-year corporate bond is priced relative to the two-year Treasury, the corporate bond's price changes as yield spreads change and as the yield on the two-year Treasury changes. The appropriate swap hedge for this corporate bond is a two-year swap since it is also priced relative to the two-year Treasury. A two-year swap's value changes as swap spreads change and as the two-year Treasury's yield changes. As a result of using a two-year swap to hedge the corporate bond, the interest rate risk of the two-year corporate bond that is attributable to movements in two-year Treasury yields can be mitigated. To the extent that the two-year corporate bond's yield spread is correlated to two-year swap spreads, spread risk also may be mitigated.

Usually, bonds are hedged in the cash market using Treasury securities or in the futures markets with Treasury futures. The Treasury market can provide effective and similar protection as interest rate swaps when hedging against interest rate risk. The advantage of the Treasury market is that it is a highly liquid market with very small bid/offer costs, especially in on-the-run maturities. It is also easy to enter into and liquidate Treasury positions quickly and efficiently. In contrast, interest rate swaps, although liquid, have higher bid/offer costs (typically one basis point in yield) and are more time consuming to enter and exit. Since swaps are customized contracts between two parties and are not exchange traded, they cannot be sold and actually have to be terminated, which is time consuming and can be less efficient. Alternatively, a swap position can be effectively terminated by entering into an opposite position in another interest rate swap; however, this strategy is not efficient. For short-term hedging purposes, Treasuries may be more desirable hedge instruments.

Many times in the hedging context, however, hedging in the Treasury market may be expensive if a Treasury security that is on "special" or if an off-the-run Treasury needs to be utilized in the hedge. Interest rate swaps can be cheaper alternatives in these cases.

Swaps have other advantages over Treasury securities. Swaps are off-balance-sheet instruments, unlike Treasury securities, and therefore should not affect the capital structure. In addition, to the extent that swap spreads are correlated with the spread of the security being hedged, an interest rate swap will provide some protection against spread risk, unlike both Treasury securities and Treasury futures contracts. Another advantage of an interest rate swap is that, because it is a structured agreement, call options and amortization can be embedded into a swap. This is particularly useful when hedging amortizing and callable securities.

The use of futures in the hedging context exposes the hedged portfolio to basis risk. Thus, when hedging a security that is priced relative to an on-the-run Treasury with a futures contract, there is the risk that movements in futures prices will not fully hedge price movements in the bond. An interest rate swap does not have the basis risk that is inherent in a futures contract since on-the-run swaps are priced relative to on-the-run Treasuries. From a basis risk standpoint, interest rate swaps are better hedging instruments than futures contracts.

16.2.2 Managing Credit Risk

Credit risk can be effectively managed by the purchase of credit derivatives. Consider, for example, a credit default swap (CDS). As we explained in Chapter 13, a CDS provides the buyer with insurance should a prespecified credit event, such as a default of the underlying, occur. This is in fact the most obvious way for an asset manager to use a CDS—to acquire credit protection for the holding of a credit name in the portfolio. The question is why doesn't the asset manager just sell the bonds? There are two reasons. First, the market for corporate bonds is not very liquid. The asset manager may find it beneficial to acquire protection rather than sell the bond when there is poor liquidity. Second, there may be a tax reason for doing so. For example, the asset manager may have to hold a corporate bond for, say, two months in order to benefit from a favorable capital gains treatment.

A CDS can be used to provide protection against credit risk during that two-month period.

If an asset manager wants to purchase the obligation of a corporate entity (i.e., gain long exposure), then the most obvious way to do so is to purchase the bond in the cash market. However, as just noted, because of the illiquidity of the corporate bond market, there may be better execution by transacting in the CDS market. More specifically, the selling of credit protection on a corporate entity provides long credit exposure to that entity. To understand why, consider what happens when an asset manager sells credit protection on a reference entity. The asset manager receives the swap premium and if there is no credit event, the swap premium is received over the life of the CDS contract. However, this is equivalent to buying the bond of the corporate entity. Instead of receiving coupon interest payments, the asset manager receives the swap premium payments. If there is a credit event, then the asset manager under the terms of the CDS must make a payment to the credit protection buyer. However, this is equivalent to a loss that would be realized if the bond was purchased. Hence, selling credit protection via a CDS is economically equivalent to a long position in the reference entity.

Suppose that an asset manager wants to short a corporate bond because it is believed that the corporation is going to experience a credit event that will cause a decline in the value of the bond. In the absence of a CDS, the asset manager would have to short the bonds in the cash market. However, it is extremely difficult to short corporate bonds. With a liquid CDS, it is easy effectively to short the bond of a corporate entity. Recall that shorting a bond involves making payments to another party, and then if the investor is correct and the bond's price declines, selling the bond at a higher price (i.e., realizing a gain). That is precisely what occurs when a CDS is purchased: the investor makes payments (the swap premium payments) and realizes a gain if a credit event occurs. Hence, buying credit protection via a CDS is equivalent to shorting.

Finally, for an asset manager seeking a leveraged position[4] in a corporate bond, this can be achieved by selling credit protection. As just noted, selling credit protection is equivalent to a long position in the reference entity. Moreover, as with other derivatives, CDS allows this to be done on a leveraged basis.

So far, we discussed the use of a single-name CDS—in other words, a CDS that involves a single bond issue. Alternatively, an investment manager can reduce or eliminate exposure to a whole index of underlying securities. Unlike a single-name CDS, the underlying for a credit default swap index (CDX) is a standardized basket of reference entities. There are standardized CDX compiled and managed by Dow Jones. For the corporate bond indices, there are separate indices for investment-grade corporate entities, the most actively traded being the North America Investment Grade Index (denoted by DJ.CDX.NA.IG). As the index name suggests, the reference entities in this index are those with an investment-grade rating. The index includes 125 corporate names in North America with each corporate name having an equal weight in the index (0.8%). The index is updated semiannually by Dow Jones.

The mechanics of a CDX are different from that of a single-name CDS. For both types of CDS, there is a swap premium that is paid periodically. If a credit event occurs, the swap premium payment ceases in the case of a single-name CDS and the contract is terminated. In contrast, for a CDX, the swap payment continues to be made by the credit protection buyer. However, the amount of the quarterly swap premium payment is reduced. This is because the notional amount is reduced as result of a credit event for a reference entity.

A CDX allows the management of exposure to a diversified portfolio of investment-grade corporate names. Thus, an asset manager seeking credit protection for the investment-grade corporate sector of a portfolio can obtain that protection by buying a CDX. This is the same as reducing credit exposure to that sector. A corporate manager seeking to increase exposure to the investment-grade corporate sector can do so by selling a CDX.

16.3 USING FUTURES TO IMPLEMENT AN ASSET ALLOCATION DECISION

As explained in Chapter 9, one of the major tasks in investment management is the allocation of funds among major asset classes. As the asset allocation of a client changes, it is necessary to shift funds among the asset classes. Funds can be shifted in one of two ways. The most obvious is by buying or selling the amount specified in the asset mix in the cash market, that is, purchasing or selling stocks and bonds in the portfolio. The costs associated with shifting funds in this manner are the transaction costs with respect to commissions, bid-ask spreads, and market impact. Moreover, there will be a disruption of the activities of the asset managers who are managing funds for each asset class. For example, a pension sponsor typically engages certain assets managers for managing equity funds, and different ones for managing bond funds. An asset allocation decision requiring the reallocation of funds will necessitate the withdrawal of funds from some asset managers and the placement of funds with others. If the shift is temporary, there will be a subsequent revision of the asset allocation, further disrupting the activities of the asset managers.

An alternative approach is to use the futures market to change an exposure to an asset class. As we explained earlier in this chapter, buying futures contracts increases exposure to the asset class underlying the futures contract, while selling futures contracts reduces it. For the major asset classes, equities and bonds, a client can use stock index futures and Treasury bond futures to alter the asset mix. The advantages of using financial futures contracts over transacting in the cash market for each asset class are (1) transaction costs are lower; (2) execution is faster in the futures market; (3) market impact costs are avoided or reduced because the asset manager has more time to buy and sell securities in the cash market; and (4) activities of the asset managers employed by the client are not disrupted. A strategy of using futures for asset allocation to avoid disrupting the activities of asset managers is sometimes referred to as an *overlay strategy*.

16.4 MEASURING PORTFOLIO RISK WHEN THE PORTFOLIO CONTAINS DERIVATIVES

We have introduced some important uses of derivatives for equity and bond portfolio management. While at an intuitive level the applications we described make sense, one may ask for more accurate estimates of the impact of including derivative securities on a portfolio risk profile.

Simulation is essential for measuring the portfolio risk in the presence of derivatives. Closed-form measures of risk that are widely used for equity portfolios, such as variance and standard deviation, can be especially misleading when the payoffs of the financial instruments in the portfolio are not symmetric, which is the case when there are derivatives. As an example, consider the distribution of a call option payoff at expiration and the distribution of the price of the underlying stock (Exhibit 16.4(B) and (A), respectively). The skewness in the distribution of the option payoffs is a lot more pronounced than the skewness in the distribution of the stock prices. In fact, the stock prices we generated came from a geometric random walk, so the distribution in Exhibit 16.4(A) is lognormal. If we worked in return space (rather than payoff space), we would have obtained a normal distribution—a perfect bell-shaped curve. Option payoffs do not follow such symmetric distributions. Using the expected value and the volatility of the probability distribution for an option payoff is not very informative (and can in fact be misleading), given how far the distribution is from normal.

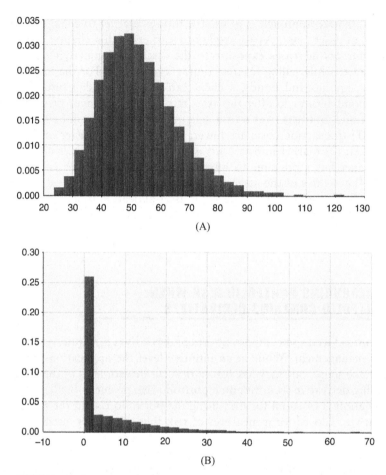

EXHIBIT 16.4 Probability distribution of (A) the price of a stock at expiration, and (B) the discounted payoff of a call option on the stock at expiration.

Estimating the risk of a portfolio by simulation is simple in concept. The following steps are implemented:

1. Generate N realizations of the vector whose elements are the changes in value for the M securities in the portfolio, ΔS.
2. For each of the N vectors (knowing the current portfolio weights), compute the resulting change in portfolio value.

3. Analyze different characteristics of the so-obtained future portfolio value probability distribution.

For example, if we would like to evaluate the value-at-risk (VaR), we can record the change in portfolio value $L = V(S,t) - V(S + \Delta S, t + \Delta t)$, which represents the loss realized in each of the N scenarios. We can then estimate the 95th percentile of the loss distribution by using the method described in Chapter 8. Alternatively, if we would like to compute the probability that the loss will be greater than a certain value x, we can compute the loss probability as the percentage of all losses over the value x, that is, as

$$\frac{1}{N} \cdot \sum_{i=1}^{N} 1\{L_i > x\}$$

where 1 is the indicator function, as introduced in section 14.4.3 of Chapter 14.

This is a theoretically sound algorithm for evaluating the probability distribution of portfolio changes. The problem arises in its actual implementation for large and complex portfolios, especially in step 2, the portfolio revaluation step. Generating every scenario in step 2 for a portfolio of thousands of securities requires running thousands of numerical algorithms, including additional simulations. This can be a very time consuming process. For example, suppose that we are trying to simulate N scenarios for each of M securities in the portfolio. The total number of scenarios for the portfolio value would be N^M. For a portfolio of 1,000 securities, each of which can be in one of 100 scenarios, we could have a total of $100^{1,000}$ scenarios—this is basically impossible to evaluate, even with today's advanced technology.

One technique that can help reduce the number of scenarios is to identify factors that drive the changes in portfolio value, and simulate scenarios for those factors. (Hopefully, there are a lot fewer of these factors than the number of securities in the portfolio.) We already encountered this idea in Chapter 11. Consider, for example, a bond portfolio of 100 bonds. To simulate the future value of the portfolio, we would use the current yield curve, the volatilities of the risk factors that drive the yield curve evolution process, and their correlation matrix. For instance, the yield curve could be described by 10 risk factors representing the following key rates: 6-month, 1-, 2-, 3-, 4-, 5-, 10-, 15-, 20-, and 30-year zero-coupon rates.

Jamshidian and Zhu (1997) suggested a method for further reducing the number of factors by using principal components analysis[5] and keeping only the first two to three components. For example, suppose that the 10 key rates in this example (assume they are the rates on zero-coupon bonds), $r_1, \ldots, r_{10}$, follow simple geometric random walks

$$r_{t+1}^{(i)} = r_t^{(i)} + \mu^{(i)} \cdot r_t^{(i)} + \sigma \cdot r_t^{(i)} \cdot \tilde{\varepsilon}_t^{(i)}, \, i = 1, \ldots, 10$$

These random walks are correlated with some correlation matrix $\mathbf{C}$ (i.e., the normal random variables $\tilde{\varepsilon}_t^{(i)}$ are correlated with a 10×10 correlation matrix $\mathbf{C}$). If we were to simulate realizations of these ten random walks, we would generate scenarios for the standard normal random variables $\tilde{\varepsilon}_t^{(i)}$ by drawing them from a multivariate normal distribution with correlation matrix $\mathbf{C}$, and computing the values of the key rates in each of the scenarios.

Instead, we run principal components on the data which we would normally use to estimate the drifts $\mu^{(i)}$, the volatilities $\sigma^{(i)}$, and the correlation matrix $\mathbf{C}$, and we obtain estimates for the loadings (i.e., the coefficients) $\beta_j^{(i)}$ in front of the principal components j.

Suppose we keep only the first three principal components, that is, $j = 1,2,3$. The random walk for each key rate i becomes

$$_{t+1}^{(i)} \approx r_t^{(i)} + \mu^{(i)} \cdot r_t^{(i)} + \sigma \cdot r_t^{(i)} \cdot \beta_1^{(i)} \cdot \tilde{z}_t^{(1)} + \sigma \cdot r_t^{(i)} \cdot \beta_2^{(i)} \cdot \tilde{z}_t^{(2)} + \sigma \cdot r_t^{(i)} \cdot \beta_3^{(i)} \cdot \tilde{z}_t^{(3)}$$

where $\tilde{z}_t^{(1)}, \tilde{z}_t^{(2)}, \tilde{z}_t^{(3)}$ are three uncorrelated standard normal random variables.

The dimension of the simulation is therefore reduced to three—we need to simulate three uncorrelated, rather than ten correlated standard normal random variables. Each simulation trial will produce values for $\tilde{z}_t^{(1)}, \tilde{z}_t^{(2)}, \tilde{z}_t^{(3)}$, which we would plug into the equations for $r_{t+1}^{(i)}$ to estimate the realizations for the future values for the key rates, which will then give us estimates for possible yield curves.

Suppose we generate 10,000 scenarios for possible yield curves. Each of the 10,000 scenarios will have an equal probability of occurring. All positions in the portfolio will then be evaluated in each of the 10,000 scenarios, and the distribution of the portfolio values will be stored. Still, the revaluation of the portfolio in 10,000 scenarios can be a daunting task. Furthermore, if the number of scenarios is not enough, we may still have difficulty obtaining a good representation of the tail of the distribution of portfolio values, which would skew the portfolio risk estimation results.

One technique used in practice is simply to run a historical simulation. Using historical scenarios allows for a compact representation of the data, and the portfolio evaluation process can be sped up significantly. Unfortunately, historical simulation suffers from many problems, as we discussed in Chapter 8. Forward-looking simulation is preferable, but ideally, it should be done with methods that reduce computational time. Such methods include (Glasserman 2004):

1. Reduce the time required for computing each scenario for the portfolio value by approximate portfolio revaluation.
2. Reduce the number of scenarios required to achieve a target precision by applying a variance reduction technique.[6]

We explain the intuition behind each of these approaches next.

16.4.1 Approximate Portfolio Revaluation

The approximate portfolio revaluation approach uses ideas similar to the ideas underlying American option pricing with regression methods, described in section 14.4.2 of Chapter 14. A fixed (relatively small) number of scenarios are generated, and the portfolio value is evaluated exactly in those scenarios. The next step is to fit a function to the portfolio values obtained in the scenarios using some kind of interpolation or nonlinear regression. If the fitted approximation is easy to evaluate, then it can be used in a simulation algorithm to generate more (approximate) scenarios for the portfolio value, and analyze the resulting probability distribution of portfolio values. The issue in this approach is how to select the appropriate function, and how to decide on the appropriate number of scenarios to generate for the initial valuation. While the former issue is difficult to address in a general way, the latter issue has been addressed in the literature.

Jamshidian and Zhu (1997) were among the first to propose this approach in combination with the principal components decomposition to reduce the number of factors for simulation we described earlier. In their model, each of the three principal components $\tilde{z}_t^{(1)}, \tilde{z}_t^{(2)}, \tilde{z}_t^{(3)}$ is allowed to take on one of a limited number of states, and the probability of being in that state is drawn from a special case of a multinomial probability distribution (a generalization of the binomial distribution in multiple dimensions). Recall that the binomial distribution assumes that there are n trials and two outcomes, success and failure, in each trial. The multinomial distribution considers n trials as well, but assumes that there are $(k + 1)$ possible categorical outcomes in each trial. If we assume that each of these states is equally likely, we have the following expression for the probability of the principal component being in state i:

$$P(i) = \left(\frac{1}{2}\right)^k \cdot \frac{k!}{i!(k-i)!}, \quad i = 0, \ldots, k$$

In our example, we could consider five states (outcomes) for a particular principal component: "no change" (middle state), "moderate up" and "moderate down" states, and "extreme up" and "extreme down" states. In this case, $k = 4$. Therefore, the probabilities of the first principal component being in each of these five states are

$$\frac{1}{16}, \frac{1}{4}, \frac{3}{8}, \frac{1}{4}, \frac{1}{16}$$

The middle state is more likely than the moderate states, which in turn are more likely than the extreme states. Given that the first principal component is more important than the second, and the second is more important than the third, we could consider more scenarios for the first component than for the second and the third. Jamshidian and Zhu suggest using seven scenarios (states) for the first component, five for the second, and three for the third. We can then define a yield curve scenario to be a set of states for each principal component, which amounts to a total of $7 \cdot 5 \cdot 3 = 105$ scenarios for the yield curve. The probability of the yield curve being in one of these 105 scenarios is given by the product of the multinomial probabilities for each state (since the states for the different principal components are independent). Moreover, we only need to do $(k_1 + 1) \cdot (k_2 + 1) \cdot (k_3 + 1)$ portfolio revaluations, where k_1, k_2, and k_3 are the number of states considered for principal component 1, 2, and 3, respectively.

Technically speaking, this is not exactly Monte Carlo simulation—we do not need to draw random numbers. However, it is a scenario simulation method in the sense that it involves evaluating portfolio performance over different scenarios, and it associates probabilities with the different scenarios. An attractive feature of the method is that we can generate scenarios that have very low probability of occurrence. Some of the scenarios in Jamshidian and Zhu's example of 105 scenarios for portfolio values have only 0.024% probability of occurring, which is useful in evaluating tail risk measures such as VaR.

Jamshidian and Zhu's scenario simulation method can also be extended to more complex portfolios such as multicurrency portfolios or portfolios with credit exposures. Of course, such complex situations require modeling with greater number of risk factors, and the dimension of the problem does increase. In a special case—when different types of risks can be assumed to be independent, the number of scenarios can be kept down. For example, we may assume that credit and market risks are independent, or that interest rates and exchange rates are independent. Not all of these assumptions are reasonable, and risk managers need to weigh considerations for realism versus considerations for speed when implementing the model.

Given the low computational burden, Jamshidian and Zhu's scenario simulation method is expected to perform well compared to other methods for portfolio revaluation. Jamshidian and Zhu's own computational studies indicate that. However, Abken (2000) tests the method on portfolios of multicurrency interest rate derivatives, and reports mixed results.

16.4.2 Variance Reduction Techniques

Glasserman, Heidelberger, and Shahabuddin (2000) suggested and studied the performance of different variance reduction techniques for improving simulation performance in the context of estimating the VaR of a portfolio. Most generally, their idea is to use a control variate method[7] that relies on already available information. Such information can include results of simulations of the portfolio's value in recent days under similar market conditions, or approximations to the portfolio value such as the linear delta approximation or the quadratic delta-gamma approximation, which we discuss next.

The *linear delta approximation* is basically an approximation to the portfolio value given a change of ΔS in the prices of the securities in the portfolio and assuming that the change in the portfolio value is proportional to the change in the prices of the securities. If the changes ΔS are multivariate normal, then the change in the value of the portfolio ΔV (and, hence the portfolio loss L) is also normally distributed. Specifically, if ΔS has multivariate normal distribution with mean 0 and covariance matrix Σ_S, then if we assume that the change in the portfolio value is proportional to the change ΔS, we can write

$$\Delta V = \delta' \cdot (\Delta S)$$

where δ is a vector of sensitivities. Then the loss L is normally distributed with mean 0 and variance $\sigma_L^2 = \delta' \cdot \Sigma_S \cdot \delta$, and the 95% VaR, for example, equals $\Phi^{-1}(0.95) = 1.65 \cdot \sigma_L$.[8]

The assumption that the portfolio value V is a linear function of S (which also implies that the change in the portfolio value is proportional to the change ΔS) may work if we are dealing with an equity portfolio in which S is the vector of stock prices. The change in stock prices could be evaluated using a factor model (as in Chapter 11), which is also a linear function in the underlying factors. However, a portfolio that contains derivatives has a nonlinear dependence on the prices of the underlying assets, and a bond portfolio depends nonlinearly on changes in interest rates.

A better approximation in this case so that some of the nonlinearity is captured (although not a perfect solution) may be the *delta-gamma approximation*, which in effect is a second-order approximation to the value of the portfolio, based on the Taylor series expansion:

$$\Delta V = \frac{\partial V}{\partial t} \cdot \Delta t + \delta \cdot \Delta S + \frac{1}{2} \cdot (\Delta S)' \cdot \Gamma \cdot \Delta S$$

where

$$\delta_i = \frac{\partial V}{\partial S_i}$$

and

$$\Gamma_{ij} = \frac{\partial^2 V}{\partial S_i \partial S_j}$$

are the first and second partial derivatives of V evaluated at (S_t, t).

Although the calculation of δ and Γ can be challenging, these coefficients, which represent sensitivities,[9] are often routinely calculated by individual trading desks, and are generally available.

We can use the delta-gamma approximation to the portfolio value as a control variate in the simulation to obtain an estimate for the actual portfolio value VaR. Glasserman, Heidelberger, and Shahabuddin (2000) report that the method reduces the variance of the estimate for the portfolio VaR obtained from the simulation by a factor of between 2 and 5.

Alternatively, improvement in the accuracy of estimation can be achieved if the delta-gamma approximation is used to guide the sampling of scenarios before computing portfolio losses, rather than to adjust the estimate after the scenarios are generated. This is done through importance sampling, another variance reduction technique introduced in section 14.2.3 of

Chapter 14. Finally, stratified sampling[10] on the values for the delta-gamma approximation can be applied in order to reduce the variance further. In other words, we find intervals of known (and perhaps equal) probability for the portfolio loss realized according to the delta-gamma approximation.

The actual details of the implementation are technical, but the underlying ideas are intuitive. In their computational experiments, Glasserman, Heidelberger, and Shahabuddin (2000) report that the most effective variance reduction method for estimating portfolio VaR was realized when using a combination of importance sampling and stratified sampling methods.

SUMMARY

- In equity portfolio management, derivatives are used for (1) risk management and (2) return enhancement.
- Two risk management strategies that focus on hedging downside risk at a fixed cost with a specific limit to losses are protective put and collar strategies.
- The protective put strategy involves the purchase of a put option combined with a long stock position. This is the equivalent of a position in a call option on the stock combined with the purchase of risk-free bond. Protective put strategies are valuable to portfolio managers who currently hold a long position in the underlying security or investors who desire upside exposure and downside protection.
- A collar strategy consists of a long stock, a long put, and a short call. By varying the strike prices, a range of trade-offs among downside protection, costs, and upside potential is possible. Collars are designed for investors who currently hold a long equity position and want to achieve a level of risk reduction.
- A covered call strategy is a return enhancement strategy. It involves selling a call while holding the underlying stock. The strategy is appropriate for slightly bullish investors who don't expect much out of the stock and want to produce additional income. The strategy behaves like a long stock position when the stock price is below the strike price, but is capped on the upside.
- Derivatives are widely used in bond portfolio management for controlling different types of risk, such as interest rate and credit risk.
- Futures, options, and swaps can all be used for managing portfolio interest rate risk.

- Credit risk can be effectively managed using credit default swaps.
- An investment manager can reduce credit exposure to a single bond issue by entering into a credit default swap, and paying a premium for protection against prespecified credit events. An investor seeking a leveraged position in a corporate bond can enter a credit default swap and sell credit protection.
- An investor can reduce credit exposure to an entire index of underlying securities by buying a credit default swap index.
- Futures can be used to change allocation of assets among classes with minimum disruption to activities of asset managers managing funds for each asset class.
- Simulation is essential for measuring the portfolio risk in the presence of derivatives. Closed-form measures of risk that are widely used in the case of equity portfolios, such as variance and standard deviation, can be very misleading when the payoffs of the securities in the portfolio are not symmetric, which is the case when there are derivatives.
- Revaluating the portfolio value for every simulation trial can be very time consuming. One technique that can help reduce the number of scenarios is to identify factors that drive the changes in portfolio value, and simulate scenarios for those factors.
- Methods to reduce the time for revaluation further include approximate portfolio revaluation and variance reduction techniques.

NOTES

1. See the immunization example in section 10.3.1 of Chapter 10, and check this fact by using the setup in file **Ch10-Immunization.xlsx**.
2. Specifically, basis risk is the risk that supposedly offsetting investments in a hedging strategy will not experience price changes in entirely opposite directions from each other. This imperfect correlation between the two investments adds risk to the position.
3. For more information, see Fabozzi (2009).
4. See section 2.3.1 of Chapter 2 for a definition of leveraged position.
5. As we explained in section 11.3.3 of Chapter 11, principal component analysis is a multivariate statistical technique that transforms a number of correlated variables (in this case, the factors driving the evolution of prices) into a smaller number of uncorrelated components. The first principal component accounts for as much of the variability in the data as possible, and each succeeding component accounts for as much of the remaining variability as possible.

6. See sections 14.2 and 14.3 of Chapter 14 for an introduction to variance reduction techniques.
7. See the introduction to the control variate method in section 14.2.4.
8. See section 8.2.2 of Chapter 8 for calculation of the VaR for normally distributed returns.
9. See section 13.4.4 of Chapter 13.
10. See section 14.2.2 for an introduction to stratified sampling.

Capital Budgeting
Decisions

Capital Budgeting under Uncertainty

Companies continually invest funds in assets, and these assets produce income and cash flows that the company may either reinvest in more assets or pay to the owners. The total amounts of assets a company owns, including both tangible and intangible assets, are its *capital*. These assets include physical (tangible) assets (such as land, buildings, equipment, and machinery), as well as assets that represent property rights (intangible assets), such as accounts receivable, securities, patents, and copyrights. When we refer to *capital investment*, we are referring to the company's investment in its assets, where the term "capital" also has come to mean the funds used to finance the company's assets and, in some contexts, refers to the sum of equity and interest-bearing debt.

Capital budgeting decisions involve the long-term commitment of a company's resources in capital investments. These decisions play a prominent role in determining whether a company will be successful. The commitment of funds to a particular capital project can be enormous and may be irreversible. Whereas some capital budgeting decisions are routine decisions that do not change the course or risk of a company, there are strategic capital budgeting decisions that either impact the company's future market position in its current product lines or permit it to expand into a new product line in the future.

The company's capital investment decision may be comprised of a number of distinct decisions, each referred to as a *project*. A capital project is a set of assets that are contingent on one another and are considered together. For example, suppose a company is considering the production of a new product. This capital project requires the company to acquire land, build facilities, and purchase production equipment. And this project may also require the company to increase its investment in its working capital—inventory, cash, or accounts receivable. *Working capital* is the collection of assets needed for day-to-day operations that support a company's long-term investments.

There are several techniques that are used to evaluate capital budgeting proposals. These include the payback and discounted payback techniques, net present value technique, profitability index technique, internal rate of return technique, and modified internal rate of return technique. While used in practice, some of these techniques are limited in their ability to help managers identify proposed capital projects that are profitable, and are not necessarily consistent with maximization of shareholder wealth. Moreover, where capital rationing exists, some techniques give conflicting rankings of the relative attractiveness of capital projects.

Evaluating whether a company should invest in a capital project requires an analysis of whether the project adds value to the company. What is essential in this analysis is an assessment of the project's risk. The risk analysis of a project is challenging because most capital projects are unique and a project's contribution to the company's risk is difficult to quantify. There are several tools available to help incorporate a project's risk into the decision. Monte Carlo simulation methods are one such tool that has grown in importance over the years.

This chapter reviews capital budgeting under uncertainty. It provides an overview of the classification of investment projects and tools for evaluating projects, such as net present value, profitability index, internal rate of return, and payback period. The chapter also contains specific instructions for evaluating project risk, such as creating an investment profile, estimating market risk, and estimating project stand-along risk using simulation. Section 17.3 of this chapter is a case study that incorporates every stage of the process.

17.1 CLASSIFYING INVESTMENT PROJECTS

There are different ways managers classify capital investment projects. One way of classifying projects is by project life, whether short term or long term. This is done because in the case of long-term projects, the time value of money plays an important role in evaluating long-term projects. Another ways of classifying projects is by their risk. The riskier the project's future cash flows, the greater the role of the cost of capital in decision-making. Still another way of classifying projects is by their dependence on other projects. The relationship between a project's cash flows and the cash flows of some other project of the company must be incorporated explicitly into the analysis since we want to analyze how a project affects the total cash flows of the company.

17.1.1 Classification According to Economic Life

An investment project generally provides benefits over a limited period of time, referred to as its economic life. The *economic life* or *useful life* of an asset is determined by:

- Physical deterioration.
- Obsolescence.
- The degree of competition in the market for a product.

The economic life is an estimate of the length of time that the asset will provide benefits to the company. After its useful life, the revenues generated by the asset tend to decline rapidly and its expenses tend to increase.

Typically, an investment requires an immediate expenditure and provides benefits in the form of cash flows received in the future. If benefits are received only within the current period—within one year of making the investment—we refer to the investment as a *short-term investment*. If these benefits are received beyond the current period, we refer to the investment as a *long-term investment* and refer to the expenditure as a *capital expenditure*.

An investment project may comprise one or more capital expenditures. For example, a new product may require investment in production equipment, a building, and transportation equipment.

Short-term investment decisions involve primarily investments in current assets: cash, marketable securities, accounts receivable, and inventory. The objective of investing in short-term assets is the same as long-term assets: maximizing owners' wealth. Nevertheless, we consider them separately for two practical reasons:

- Decisions about long-term assets are based on projections of cash flows far into the future and require us to consider the time value of money.
- Long-term assets do not figure into the daily operating needs of the company.

Decisions regarding short-term investments, or current assets, are concerned with day-to-day operations. A company needs some level of current assets to act as a cushion in case of unusually poor operating periods, when cash flows from operations are less than expected.

17.1.2 Classification According to Risk

Suppose you are faced with two investments, A and B, each promising a $10 million cash inflow 10 years from today. If A is riskier than B, what are they worth to you today? If you are risk averse, you would consider A less valuable than B because the chance of getting the $10 million in 10 years is less for A than for B. Therefore, valuing a project requires considering the risk associated with its future cash flows.

The investment's risk of return can be classified according to the nature of the project represented by the investment:

- *Replacement projects.* Investments in the replacement of existing equipment or facilities.
- *Expansion projects.* Investments in projects that broaden existing product lines and existing markets.
- *New products and markets.* Projects that involve introducing a new product or entering into a new market.
- *Mandated projects.* Projects required by government laws or agency rules.

Replacement projects include the maintenance of existing assets to continue the current level of operating activity. Projects that reduce costs, such as replacing old equipment or improving the efficiency, are also considered replacement projects. Evaluating replacement projects requires us to compare the value of the company with the replacement asset to the value of the company without that same replacement asset. What we are really doing in this comparison is looking at opportunity costs: what cash flows would have been if the company had stayed with the old asset.

There is little risk in the cash flows from replacement projects. The company is simply replacing equipment or buildings already operating and producing cash flows. And the company typically has experience in managing similar new equipment.

Expansion projects, when intended to enlarge a company's established product or market, also involve little risk. However, investment projects that involve introducing new products or entering into new markets are riskier because the company has little or no management experience in the new product or market.

A company is forced or coerced into its mandated projects. These are government-mandated projects typically found in "heavy" industries, such as utilities, transportation, and chemicals, all industries requiring a large portion of their assets in production activities. Government agencies, such as the Occupational Health and Safety Agency (OSHA) or the Environmental Protection Agency (EPA), may impose requirements that companies install specific equipment or alter their activities (such as how they dispose of waste).

We can further classify mandated projects into two types: *contingent* and *retroactive*. Suppose, as a steel manufacturer, we are required by law to include pollution control devices on all smoke stacks. If we are considering a new plant, this mandated equipment is really part of our new plant investment decision—the investment in pollution control equipment is contingent on our building the new plant. On the other hand, if a company is required by law to place pollution control devices on existing smoke stacks, the law is retroactive. A company does not have a choice. The company must invest in the equipment whether it increases the value of the company or not. In this case, the company has three choices: select from among possible equipment that satisfies the mandate, weigh the decision whether to halt production in the offending plant, or, if available, consider the purchase of pollution emissions allowances.

17.1.3 Classification According to Dependence on Other Projects

In addition to considering the future cash flows generated by a project, a company must consider how it affects the assets already in place—the results of previous project decisions—as well as other projects that may be undertaken. Projects can be classified according to the degree of dependence with other projects: independent projects, mutually exclusive projects, contingent projects, and complementary projects.

An *independent project* is one whose cash flows are not related to the cash flows of any other project. Accepting or rejecting an independent project does not affect the acceptance or rejection of other projects. Projects are *mutually exclusive* if the acceptance of one precludes the acceptance of other projects. For example, suppose a manufacturer is considering whether to replace its production facilities with more modern equipment. The company may solicit bids among the different manufacturers of this equipment. The decision consists of comparing two choices, either keeping its existing production facilities or replacing the facilities with the modern equipment of one manufacturer. Because the company cannot use more than one production facility, it must evaluate each bid and choose the most attractive one. The alternative production facilities are mutually exclusive projects: The company can accept only one bid.

Contingent projects are dependent on the acceptance of another project. Suppose a greeting card company develops a new character, Pippy, and is considering starting a line of Pippy cards. If Pippy catches on, the company will consider producing a line of Pippy T-shirts—but only if the Pippy character becomes popular. The T-shirt project is a contingent project.

Another form of dependence is found in *complementary projects*, where the investment in one enhances the cash flows of one or more other projects. Consider a manufacturer of personal computer equipment and software. If it develops new software that enhances the abilities of a computer mouse, the introduction of this new software may enhance its mouse sales as well.

17.2 INVESTMENT DECISIONS AND WEALTH MAXIMIZATION

The value of a company today is the present value of all of its future cash flows. These future cash flows come from assets that are already in place and from future investment opportunities. The value of the company today is therefore represented as

$$\sum_{t=1}^{\infty} \frac{CF_t}{(1+r)^t}$$

where CF_t is the cash flow obtained by the company in time period t, and r is the required rate of return.

A company's management makes decisions about which capital projects to undertake by evaluating their value to the company. This process is referred to as *capital budgeting*. The capital budgeting decision for a project requires analysis of (1) the project's future cash flows, (2) the degree of uncertainty associated with the project's future cash flows, and (3) the value of the project's future cash flows considering their uncertainty. The evaluation of *future cash flows* involves estimation of changes in operating cash flows (changes in revenues, expenses, and taxes) and changes in investment cash flows (cash flows from the acquisition and disposition of the project's assets). The *degree of risk* associated with obtaining these cash flows is typically incorporated in the project's cost of capital. The *cost of capital* is the cost of the funds for the company's investment in the project. The value of the project's future cash flows considering the risk is computed using disciplined methods such as net present value, profitability index, internal rate of return, modified internal rate of the return, payback period, and discounted payback period. In general, project value evaluation techniques should:

- Consider all future incremental cash flows from the project.
- Consider the time value of money.
- Consider the risk associated with future cash flows.
- Have an objective criterion by which to select a project.

Not all of the techniques listed above satisfy all these criteria. We will focus on the most popular methods for project value estimation: net present value, internal rate of return, profitability index, and payback period.

17.2.1 Cost of Capital, Required Rate of Return, and Discount Rate

As we mentioned earlier, the future cash flows of a project are discounted to the present using an interest rate that incorporates to some extent the degree of risk associated with these cash flows. At an intuitive level, the greater the risk associated with the cash flows, the higher the *discount rate* that should be used, which is equivalent to assigning a lower present value to these future cash flows. In the case of internal rate of return, the term used to describe this discount rate is the *hurdle rate*. The hurdle rate must be exceeded by the project's return.

This rate—whether the discount or the hurdle rate—is the opportunity cost of funds. For a corporation, the opportunity cost of funds reflects the cost of capital to be paid to suppliers of capital (the creditors and owners). The term cost of capital is used interchangeably with the term *required rate of return* (RRR). The RRR is the rate of return that suppliers of capital demand on their investment. Cost of capital and RRR are the same concepts, but from different perspectives—that of the company versus that of the investors.

The cost of capital impacts almost all methods for project valuation, and is therefore very important. We will review common methods for its estimation later in this chapter.

17.2.2 Net Present Value

The *net present value* (NPV) project valuation method considers the present value of all cash flows expected over the life of the project, and nets the positive and the negative expected cash flows. Specifically,

$$NPV = \text{Present value of future cash flows} - \text{Initial cash outlay}$$

All cash flows are discounted by a rate involving the estimated cost of capital, which we denote by r. This is to allow for "apples-to-apples" comparison, that is, to net cash flows in today's dollars.

We can write all cash flows in the equation above with their corresponding sign, using "plus" for inflows and "minus" for outflows. Assuming that the life of the project is N time periods, the NPV can then be computed as

$$NPV = \sum_{t=0}^{N} \frac{CF_t}{(1+r)^t}$$

Note that the calculation involves the cash flow at time 0, and since $(1+r)^0 = 1$, the initial cash flow is not actually discounted. Typically, the

EXHIBIT 17.1   Example of calculating NPV from a sequence of cash flows.

Year	Cash Flow	Discounted Cash Flow
0	−$1,500,000.00	−$1,500,000.00
1	$0.00	$0.00
2	$200,000.00	$165,289.26
3	$500,000.00	$375,657.40
4	$900,000.00	$614,712.11
5	$1,000,000.00	$620,921.32
	NPV =	$276,580.09

initial cash flow is an outlay, and therefore has a negative sign, but project specifications vary.

The decision rule is simple: If the NPV is greater than 0, then the value of the expected cash inflows is higher than the value of the expected cash outflows, and management should consider investing in the project. An example of an NPV calculation for Project X is presented in Exhibit 17.1.

Project X requires an investment of $1.5 million today, and returns $0, $200,000, $500,000, $900,000, and $1 million in years 1, 2, 3, 4, and 5 of the project. Assuming a 10% cost of capital, the NPV is[1]

$$NPV = -\frac{1,500,000}{(1+0.10)^0} + \frac{0}{(1+0.10)^1} + \frac{200,000}{(1+0.10)^2} + \frac{500,000}{(1+0.10)^3}$$
$$+ \frac{900,000}{(1+0.10)^4} + \frac{1,000,000}{(1+0.10)^5}$$
$$= \$276,580.09.$$

Since the NPV is positive, Project X is expected to contribute to the value of the company, and should be considered.

It is important to study the sensitivity of the NPV estimate to the assumption made about the cost of capital. Graphing the value of the NPV for different values for the cost of capital is referred to as the *investment profile*, or the *NPV profile*. Exhibit 17.2 illustrates the investment profile for Project X described above. The NPV of Project X is positive for values of the cost of capital of less than 14.84%, and negative for values of the cost of capital of more than 14.84%. As we will see in section 17.2.4, 14.84% is the internal rate of return (discussed below); that is, the discount rate at which the NPV is equal to zero.

Creating the investment profile is useful not only because it allows us to study the sensitivity of the project NPV to the assumption about the discount

Cost of Capital	NPV
10%	$276,580.09
11%	$214,229.38
12%	$154,722.03
13%	$97,901.21
14%	$43,620.18
15%	−$8,258.49
16%	−$57,863.58
18%	−$150,728.47
19%	−$194,207.88
20%	−$235,853.91

(A)

(B)

EXHIBIT 17.2   (A) Data table with the value of the NPV for Project X for values of the cost of capital between 10% and 20%. (B) NPV profile of Project X.

rate. It is also a tool for comparing the NPVs of two or more projects. By plotting the investment profiles of two projects on the same graph, we can visualize for what assumptions of the discount rate one is preferable to the other.

17.2.3 Profitability Index

The *profitability index* (PI) uses the same information as the NPV, but is stated in terms of an index. While the NPV is computed as

$$NPV = \text{Present value of future cash flows} - \text{Initial cash outlay}$$

the PI is computed as

$$PI = \frac{\text{Present value of future cash flows}}{\text{Initial cash outlay}}$$

Since the PI measures performance in terms of an index and not dollar amounts, it provides a measure of the benefit per dollar investment. Therefore, the PI translates the NPV into an indexed value, and has an advantage relative to NPV when ranking projects. This advantage may be a disadvantage, however, when the capital budget is limited (a situation referred to as *capital rationing*) and the actual dollar amounts for the different projects are of very different orders of magnitude. In this case, prioritizing projects based on their PI, rather than their NPV, will not necessarily result in the most profitable decision for the company.[2]

For Project X,

$$PI = \frac{\$1,776,580.09}{1,500,000} = 1.18.$$

Since the PI is greater than 1, this means that the investment produces more benefits than costs.

17.2.4 Internal Rate of Return

The *internal rate of return* (IRR) is the discount rate that makes the present value of all cash flows (positive and negative) equal to zero. In other words, the IRR solves the equation

$$0 = \sum_{t=0}^{N} \frac{CF_t}{(1 + IRR)^t}$$

Consider the projected cash flows for Project X from section 17.2.2. We want to find a value for IRR such that

$$0 = -\frac{1,500,000}{(1 + IRR)^0} + \frac{0}{(1 + IRR)^1} + \frac{200,000}{(1 + IRR)^2} + \frac{500,000}{(1 + IRR)^3}$$
$$+ \frac{900,000}{(1 + IRR)^4} + \frac{1,000,000}{(1 + IRR)^5}$$

It turns out that

$$0 = -\frac{1,500,000}{(1 + 0.1484)^0} + \frac{0}{(1 + 0.1484)^1} + \frac{200,000}{(1 + 0.1484)^2} + \frac{500,000}{(1 + 0.1484)^3}$$
$$+ \frac{900,000}{(1 + 0.1484)^4} + \frac{1,000,000}{(1 + 0.1484)^5}$$

Therefore, the IRR for Project X is 14.84%.[3]

The IRR is a yield—what is earned, on average, per year. To make a decision on whether to choose an investment, we compare the IRR of the project with the cost of capital. The decision rule for the IRR is to invest in a project if it provides a return greater than the cost of capital. The cost of capital, in the context of the IRR, is the hurdle rate—the minimum acceptable rate of return.

We need to be careful, however, when we use the IRR to distinguish between projects. The project with the highest IRR may not be the one with the best NPV.[4] The IRR and the NPV methods may suggest different decisions because of the assumption about what rate can be earned when reinvesting the cash flows. While we have not discussed this assumption, it is a property of any yield calculation, and the IRR is a yield calculation. To realize the computed yield, it is assumed that the cash flows are reinvested at the computed IRR. Thus we have:

- NPV assumes cash flows reinvested at the cost of capital.
- IRR assumes cash flows reinvested at the internal rate of return.

This reinvestment assumption may cause different decisions in choosing among projects when:

- The timing of the cash flows is different among the projects.
- There are scale differences (that is, very different cash flow amounts).
- The projects have different useful lives.

To understand the points above, note that a part of the return on a project is from the reinvestment of its future cash flows to the expected terminal date of the project. If Project Y's cash flows are received sooner than Project X's, there will be more return from the reinvestment of the future cash flows in the case of Project Y. The question is what is done by the company with the future cash flows from a project when they are received. We generally assume that when the company receives future cash flows, they are reinvested in other assets. If the best we can do is reinvest cash flows at the cost of capital, then we should evaluate projects on the basis of the NPV.

Another problem with the IRR becomes apparent if we note that the IRR is a percentage, not a dollar amount. Because of this, we cannot determine how to distribute the capital budget to maximize wealth because a project that produces the highest yield does not necessarily produce the greatest wealth.

Finally, the IRR suffers from a purely mathematical problem. It has to do with the uniqueness of the IRR estimate depending on the cash flow structure of the project (i.e., the pattern of positive and negative future cash flows).

Project X, the example we considered, was characterized by a negative cash flow at the beginning, followed by a sequence of positive future cash flows. Many projects have the same characteristics, but not all. Suppose, for example, that management is considering a project that uses environmentally

EXHIBIT 17.3 Example of a project with multiple IRRs.

Year	End of Year Cash Flow
0	−$1,000.00
1	$1,500.00
2	$1,500.00
3	−$2,100.00

sensitive chemicals. It may cost a great deal to dispose of them at the end of the project's life, and that will mean a negative cash flow at the end of the project.

The IRR for projects for which there is an initial negative cash flow followed by positive future cash flows has only one IRR. However, there could be multiple IRRs for projects for which negative and positive future cash flows happen in a different order. Consider, for example, a project with the cash flows in Exhibit 17.3.

What is this project's IRR? One possible solution is IRR = 7.21%, yet another possible solution is IRR = 62.97%. That is, both IRRs will make the present value of the cash flows equal to zero.

The NPV of these cash flows are shown in Exhibit 17.4 for discount rates from 0% to 70%. Remember that the IRR is the discount rate that causes the NPV to be zero. In terms of Exhibit 17.4, this means that the

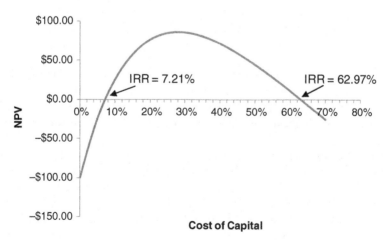

EXHIBIT 17.4 NPV of a project with multiple IRRs.

IRR is the discount rate where the NPV is zero, the point at which the NPV changes sign—from positive to negative or from negative to positive. In the case of this project, the NPV changes from negative to positive at 7.21%, and from positive to negative at 62.97%. Hence, the IRR needs to be applied with care.

17.2.5 Modified Internal Rate of Return

The NPV method assumes that future cash flows from a project are reinvested at the project's cost of capital, whereas the IRR method assumes that future cash flows are reinvested at the project's IRR. These assumptions are built into the mathematics of the methods, but they may not represent the actual opportunities of the company.

The *modified internal rate of return* (MIRR) method is an alternative that considers a specific reinvestment rate for cash inflows from a project. MIRR is a yield on an investment considering a specific interest rate on the reinvestment of funds.

To understand this reinvestment rate assumption better, consider Project X from section 17.2.2. The IRR is 14.84%. If each of the cash inflows from Project X is reinvested at 14.84%, the sum of these future cash flows will be \$2,995,815.12 at the end of year 5 (see Exhibit 17.5). For example, year 3's cash flow of \$200,000 is reinvested at 14.84% for three years (years 3, 4, and 5), so its future value is $\$200,000 \cdot (1 + 0.1484)^3 = \$302,889.52$.

The \$2,995,815.12 is referred to as the project's *terminal value*. The terminal value is how much the company has from an investment at the end of the project if all proceeds are reinvested at the assumed reinvestment rate. In our illustration, we assumed the reinvestment rate is the IRR. So what is

EXHIBIT 17.5 Concept of terminal value of a project.

Number of Periods Earning Return	Cash Flow	Future Value of Cash Flow Reinvested at 14.84%
5	−\$1,500,000.00	\$0.00
4	\$0.00	\$0.00
3	\$200,000.00	\$302,889.52
2	\$500,000.00	\$659,385.67
1	\$900,000.00	\$1,033,539.93
0	\$1,000,000.00	\$1,000,000.00
	Terminal value =	\$2,995,815.12

the return on this project? Using the terminal value as the future value and the investment outlay as the present value, we have

$$PV = \$1,500,000 \text{ (amount invested)}.$$

$$FV = \$2,995,815.12 \text{ (amount at the end)}.$$

$$N = 5 \text{ years (investment horizon)}.$$

$$r = \sqrt[4]{\frac{\$2,995,815.12}{\$1,500,000}} - 1 = 14.84\%.$$

The last procedure shows how to compute the MIRR for an investment in general. Given the project's initial investment, the terminal value of its future cash flows based on the assumed reinvestment rate, and the length of the investment horizon, we determine the implied return of the investment. The latter is the MIRR. The example above was a special case. The MIRR was the same as the IRR because we assumed that all cash flows from the project are reinvested at the IRR.

Note that the pattern of the project's future cash flows makes a difference. If a project's future cash flows are received mostly at the beginning of the project, the MIRR is more sensitive to the reinvestment rate because the future cash flows are invested at the reinvestment rate for longer time periods.

The decision rule for the MIRR is to invest in a project if it provides a return (MIRR) greater than the cost of capital. As in the case of IRR, the cost of capital is the hurdle rate. Clearly, all else being equal, a higher reinvestment rate makes a project more attractive in terms of its MIRR.

17.2.6 Payback Period and Discounted Payback Period

The *payback period* for a project is the time from the initial cash outlay to invest in it until the time when its future cash flows add up to the initial cash outlay. In other words, how long it takes to recover the initial cash outlay. The payback period is also referred to as the *payoff period* or the *capital recovery period*. If $10 million is invested today and the investment is expected to generate $5 million one year from today and $5 million two years from today, the payback period is two years—it takes two years to recoup the $10 million investment.

Let us calculate the payback period for Project X. We invest $1,500,000 at the beginning. By year 3, the entire $1,500,000 has not been paid back, but in year 4, we have not only recouped the $1,500,000, but in fact exceeded

EXHIBIT 17.6 Payback period for Project X.

Year	Cash Flow	Received Up to That Period
0	−$1,500,000.00	$0.00
1	$0.00	$0.00
2	$200,000.00	$200,000.00
3	$500,000.00	$700,000.00
4	$900,000.00	$1,600,000.00
5	$1,000,000.00	$2,600,000.00

the investment amount (we have $1,600,000) (see Exhibit 17.6). Therefore, the payback period for Project X is 4 years.

Payback period analysis is a type of "break-even" measure. It tends to provide a measure of the economic life of the investment in terms of its payback period. The more likely the economic life exceeds the payback period, the more attractive the investment. The economic life beyond the payback period is referred to as the *postpayback duration*. If the postpayback duration is zero, the investment is unattractive no matter how short the payback. This is because the sum of the future cash flows is no greater than the initial investment outlay. And since these future cash flows are really worth less today than in the future, a zero postpayback duration means that the present value of the future cash flows is less than the project's initial investment outlay.

A shorter payback period is better than a longer payback period, but it is not clear how short is good. The payback method should only be used as a coarse initial screen of investment projects—it can, however, be a useful indicator of some things. Because a dollar of cash flow in the early years is worth more than a dollar of cash flow in later years, the payback period method provides a crude, but simple measure of the liquidity of the investment. The payback period also offers some indication on the risk of the investment. In industries where equipment becomes obsolete rapidly or where there are very competitive conditions, investments with earlier payback are more valuable. This is because cash flows farther into the future are more uncertain and therefore have lower present value. In the computer industry, for example, the fierce competition and rapidly changing technology require investment in projects that have a payback of less than one year since there is no expectation of project benefits beyond one year.

The payback measure can be adjusted to account for the time value of the future cash flows. The resulting measure is called the *discounted payback period*. More precisely, the discounted payback period is the time needed to

EXHIBIT 17.7 Calculation of the discounted payback period for Project X.

Year	Cash Flow	Cash Flow Discounted to Year 0	Discounted Cash Flows Up to That Period
0	−$1,500,000.00	−$1,500,000.00	−$1,500,000.00
1	$0.00	$0.00	−$1,500,000.00
2	$200,000.00	$165,289.26	−$1,334,710.74
3	$500,000.00	$375,657.40	−$959,053.34
4	$900,000.00	$614,712.11	−$344,341.23
5	$1,000,000.00	$620,921.32	$276,580.09

pay back the original investment in terms of discounted future cash flows. In this technique, each cash flow is discounted back to the beginning of the investment at a rate that reflects both the time value of money and the perceived riskiness of the future cash flows.

Returning to Project X, suppose that the cost of capital is 10%. The first step in determining the discounted payback period is to discount each year's cash flow to the beginning of the investment (year 0) at the cost of capital. As Exhibit 17.7 illustrates, the accumulated future cash flows from the investment discounted to year 0 (the last column in the table) do not become positive until year 5. Therefore, the discounted payback period of Project X is 5 years.

17.2.7 Issues in Capital Budgeting

Not all discounted cash flows methods are appropriate in all circumstances. Care must be exercised when faced with mutually exclusive projects, scale differences, different project lives, and capital rationing.

Scale Differences Scale differences between projects—that is, differences in the amount of the initial investment—can lead to conflicting investment decisions among the discounted cash flow techniques. Consider two projects, Project Bigger and Project Smaller, each with a cost of capital of 5% per year with the cash flows in Exhibit 17.8. Applying the discounted cash flow techniques to each project, we obtain the estimates in Exhibit 17.9.

If there is no limit to the capital budget—that is, there is no capital rationing—then both projects are acceptable, value-increasing projects as indicated by all four techniques. However, if the projects are mutually exclusive projects or there is a limit to the capital budget, then the four methods provide differing accept-reject decisions.

EXHIBIT 17.8 Cash flows for Projects Bigger and Smaller.

Year	Project Bigger	Project Smaller
0	−$4,000.00	−$2,000.00
1	$1,250.00	$650.00
2	$1,250.00	$650.00
3	$1,250.00	$650.00
4	$1,250.00	$650.00

If Project Bigger and Project Smaller are mutually exclusive projects and if the company goes strictly by the PI, IRR, or MIRR criteria, management would choose Project Smaller. But is this the better project? Project Bigger provides more value—$432.44 versus $304.87. The techniques that ignore the scale of the investment—PI, IRR, and MIRR—may lead to an incorrect decision.

If the company is subject to capital rationing—say a limit of $5,000—and the two projects are independent projects, the company can only choose one project—spend $4,000 or $2,000, but not $6,000. Applying the PI, IRR, or MIRR criteria, the company would choose Project Smaller. But is this the better project? According to the NPV criterion, the dollar contribution of Project Smaller is worse. Again, the techniques that ignore the scale of the investment—PI, IRR, and MIRR—lead to an incorrect decision.

Unequal Lives If projects have unequal lives, the comparison strictly on the basis of the techniques discussed in this chapter may lead to an incorrect decision, whether choosing among mutually exclusive projects or independent projects when there is capital rationing. Consider the projects whose cash flows are provided in Exhibit 17.10. Project AA has a life of five years, Project BB a life of 10 years, and Project CC a life of 15 years. Projects AA and CC have a cost of capital of 4% and Project BB has a cost of capital of 5%.[5]

EXHIBIT 17.9 NPV, IRR, MIRR, and PI for Projects Bigger and Smaller.

Method	Project Bigger	Project Smaller
NFV	$432.44	$304.87
IRR	9.56%	11.39%
MIRR	7.73%	8.79%
PI	1.11	1.15

EXHIBIT 17.10 Projects AA, BB, and CC.

Year	AA	BB	CC
0	−$1,000.00	−$1,000.00	−$1,000.00
1	$260.00	$160.00	$120.00
2	$260.00	$160.00	$120.00
3	$260.00	$160.00	$120.00
4	$260.00	$160.00	$120.00
5	$260.00	$160.00	$120.00
6		$160.00	$120.00
7		$160.00	$120.00
8		$160.00	$120.00
9		$160.00	$120.00
10		$160.00	$120.00
11			$120.00
12			$120.00
13			$120.00
14			$120.00
15			$120.00

Applying the four discounted cash flow techniques without considering their different lives suggests that Project CC provides the most value added; Project CC produces the higher IRR benefit per $1 invested (see Exhibit 17.11).

However, comparing these projects without any adjustment for the different lives ignores the fact that at the completion of the shorter projects, there is reinvestment necessary that is not reflected in the straightforward application of the techniques. In other words, this is an "apples to oranges" comparison if an adjustment is not made. One alternative is to find the common denominator life for the projects. In the case of projects AA, BB, and CC, this would be 30 years. This requires then looking at Project AA

EXHIBIT 17.11 NPV, IRR, MIRR, and PI for Projects AA, BB, and CC.

Method	AA	BB	CC
NPV	$157.47	$235.48	$334.21
IRR	9.43%	9.61%	8.44%
MIRR	7.09%	7.24%	6.02%
PI	1.16	1.24	1.33

as reinvested in the same project five more times, resulting in a "life" for analysis of 30 years.

The common denominator approach may be cumbersome when there are many projects. An alternative is to use the *equivalent annual annuity method*.[6] This method requires two steps:

1. Calculate the annual annuity that is equivalent to the NPV of the project, considering the discount rate and the original life of the project. In the case of Project AA, the annuity amount is $35.37.[7]
2. Calculate the present value of this annuity if received ad infinitum. In the case of Project AA, this is $35.37/0.04 = $884.32. This allows for comparing the projects assuming an infinite life (which is the same for each of them, so we can compare "apples to apples").

The second step is only necessary if the comparison involves projects with different costs of capital. If the costs of capital are the same for the projects, the ranking of the projects in Step 1 is identical to that of Step 2. The values in perpetuity for the three projects are given in Exhibit 17.12. After adjusting for the different lives, the conclusion is that Project AA provides the most value added of the three projects.

17.2.8 Capital Budgeting in Practice

Among the project evaluation methods, NPV is the only one that is consistent and maximizes owner wealth under the most general circumstances. According to surveys and anecdotal evidence, it is also the most widely used in practice. Observations from recent surveys also indicate:

- Techniques that use discounted cash flows are preferred over techniques that fail to take into consideration the time value of money.
- There is an increased use of the NPV method.

EXHIBIT 17.12 Value in perpetuity for Projects AA, BB, and CC, with different lives.

	AA	BB	CC
Equivalent annual annuity	$35.37	$30.50	$30.06
Value in perpetuity	$884.32	$609.91	$751.47

- Management uses more than one technique to evaluate the same projects, with a discounted cash flow techniques used as a primary method and payback period used as a secondary method.
- The most commonly used technique is the NPV method, though the IRR method is still widely used.

The mechanics of calculating the measures in this chapter given (1) the initial cash outlay, (2) the future cash flow, and (3) the required return (or hurdle rate) are not complicated. The most complex activity of the capital budgeting procedure in practice is actually estimating cash flows. How can such cash flows be estimated, especially in situations like the introduction of a new technology, which may have not only an impact on the company's future cash flows, but also on the company's domestic and global competitive positioning? Even when cash flows can be estimated reliably, these cash flows must be discounted at an assumed discount rate. Estimating this discount rate is a problem in itself. Given the number of assumptions made in estimating various inputs to the model, Monte Carlo simulation emerges as an even more important tool to evaluate the risk in the decisions made by using these models. We will discuss Monte Carlo simulation applications in sections 17.4.3 through 17.4.5.

Finally, in addition to the possible inaccuracies associated with estimating future cash flows or the discount rate associated with investment projects, there is the potential problem of ignoring the real options that are present in projects. A *real option* associated with an investment project has value arising from the option the company possesses, for example, to defer investment in the project, abandon the project, or expand the project. It may be the case, for example, that a new technology that provides a comparative or competitive advantage is unique, patented technology. If this is the case, the company may have a real option to defer investment, which enhances the value of the project beyond the value attributed simply to discounted cash flows. (Real options are discussed in detail in Chapter 18.)

17.3 EVALUATING PROJECT RISK

The capital budgeting decisions require analyzing a proposed project's future cash flows, the risk associated with its future cash flows, and the value of the future cash flows. When looking at the available investment opportunities, management must determine the project or set of projects that is expected to add the most value to the company. This requires evaluating how each project's benefits compare with its costs. The projects that are expected to increase owners' wealth the most are the best ones. In weighing a project's benefits and its costs, the costs include both the cash flow necessary to make the investment (the initial investment outlay) and the opportunity costs of not using the cash tied up in this investment.

The benefits are the future cash flows generated by the investment. But nothing in the future is certain, so there is risk associated with the future cash flows. Therefore, for an evaluation of any investment to be meaningful, management must represent how much risk there is that its cash flows will differ from what is expected in terms of both the amount and the timing of the cash flows.

The risk associated with the cash flow estimates arises from different sources, depending on the type of investment being considered, as well as the circumstances and the industry in which the company is operating. A project's risk may be attributable to many sources, including:

- *Economic conditions.* Will consumers be spending or saving? Will the economy be in a recession? Will the government stimulate spending? What will be the rate of inflation?
- *Market conditions.* Is the market competitive? How long does it take competitors to enter into the market? Are there any barriers, such as patents or trademarks, that will keep competitors away? Is there sufficient supply of raw materials and labor? How much will raw materials and labor cost in the future?
- *Interest rates.* What will be the cost of raising capital in future years?
- *Taxes.* What will tax rates be? Will Congress alter the tax system?
- *International conditions.* Will the exchange rate between different countries' currencies where the company transacts change? Are the governments of the countries in which the company does business stable?

Risk is typically incorporated in one of two ways (1) discount future cash flows using a higher discount rate, the greater the cash flow's risk and (2) require a higher hurdle rate on a project, the greater the cash flow's risk. As we explained earlier in this chapter, the required rate of return is also called the cost of capital. An additional layer of risk can be incorporated by using Monte Carlo simulation to generate scenarios for the factors driving the future cash flows. These approaches for incorporating risk are the focus of section 17.3.2.

It is important to realize that a company typically has a portfolio of projects, and so management needs to estimate not only the stand-alone risk of the project, but also how the addition of the project to the company's portfolio of assets changes the risk of the company's portfolio. Taking this one step further, if the company's owners hold diversified investments—a safe assumption to make for all large corporations—it is the project's market risk that is relevant to the company's decision making because investors would require compensation for market risk, the risk they cannot diversify away.

Even though market risk is generally the most important risk to analyze, stand-alone risk should not be ignored, especially when making decisions for a small, closely held company, whose owners do not hold well-diversified portfolios. Stand-alone risk is usually easier to measure than market risk, and can be gauged by evaluating the project's future cash flows using statistical measures, sensitivity analysis, and simulation.

17.3.1   Measuring a Project's Market Risk

When an investor is trying to evaluate the risk of an investment in a share of stock, he can look at that stock's returns and the returns of the entire market over some time period as a way of measuring the stock's market risk. While this is not a perfect measurement, it provides an estimate of the sensitivity of the particular stock's returns to changes in the returns of the market. Things are more complicated when one tries to evaluate the market risk of a new project. A manager can do the next best thing: He can estimate the market risk of the stock of another company whose only line of business is the same as the project's risk. If he could find such a company, he could estimate its stock's market risk and use that as a first step in estimating the project's market risk.

As we explained in Chapter 11, the Greek letter β (beta) is used to denote a measure of the market risk—the sensitivity of an asset's returns to changes in the returns of the market. To distinguish the beta of an asset from the beta we used for a company's stock, the asset's beta is denoted by β_{asset} and the beta of a company's stock by β_{equity}. If a company has no debt, the market risk of its common stock is the same as the market risk of its assets. However, it is rarely the case that a company has no debt in its capital structure, so we must consider the effect of financial leverage on a company's equity beta.

Financial leverage is the use of debt obligations that require fixed contractual payments to finance a company's assets.[8] The greater the use of debt obligations, the more financial leverage there is, and the greater the risk associated with cash flows to owners. This is because creditors have seniority and receive a fixed amount (interest and principal), so a greater portion of the market risk of the equity is born by the owners as opposed to the creditors. In fact, the following equality holds:

$$\beta_{asset} = \beta_{debt} \cdot \text{Proportion of assets financed with debt}$$
$$+ \beta_{equity} \cdot \text{Proportion of assets financed with equity}$$

or, equivalently,

$$\beta_{asset} = \beta_{debt} \cdot w_{debt} + \beta_{equity} \cdot w_{equity}$$

Since interest on debt is deducted to arrive at taxable income, the claim that creditors have on the company's assets does not cost the company the full amount, but rather the after-tax claim, so the burden of debt financing is actually less. Let D denote the market value of debt,[9] E denote the market value of equity, and τ be the marginal tax rate. The relationship between the asset beta and the equity beta can be written as

$$\beta_{asset} = \beta_{debt}\frac{(1-\tau)D}{(1-\tau)D+E} + \beta_{equity}\frac{E}{(1-\tau)D+E}$$

If β_{debt} is assumed equal to 0, that is, if debt is assumed not to be subject to market risk, we have

$$\beta_{asset} = \beta_{equity}\frac{1}{\left(1+(1-\tau)\dfrac{D}{E}\right)}$$

This means that an asset's beta is related to the company's equity beta, with adjustments for financial leverage. If a company does not use debt, $\beta_{equity} = \beta_{asset}$, and if the company does use debt, $\beta_{equity} > \beta_{asset}$. Therefore, a β_{equity} may be translated into a β_{asset} by removing the influence of the company's financial risk from β_{equity}. To accomplish this, the following must be known:

- The company's marginal tax rate.
- The amount of the company's debt financing in market value terms.
- The amount of the company's equity financing in market value terms.

The process of translating an equity beta into an asset beta is referred to as *unlevering* because the effects of financial leverage are removed from the equity beta, β_{equity}, to arrive at a beta for the company's assets, β_{asset}. This beta therefore is an estimate of the market risk of a company's assets.

The insights in this section can be used to compute the cost of capital, the discount rate to use in evaluating risky future cash flows. As we explained in section 17.2.1, the cost of capital is the cost of funds from the providers of capital, creditors, and owners. This cost is the return required by these suppliers of capital. The greater the risk of a project, the greater the return required and, hence, the greater the cost of capital.

The project's cost of capital is comprised of two parts:

■ The return if the project were risk-free, which provides compensation for the time value of money.
■ The compensation for risk.

The compensation for the time value of money includes compensation for any anticipated inflation. The risk-free rate of interest, such as the yield on a long-term U.S. Treasury bond, is typically used to represent the time value of money. The compensation for risk is the extra return required because the project's future cash flows are uncertain. The greater the project's market risk, the greater the return investors should require.

Computing the Cost of Capital Based on the CAPM   A commonly used method for estimating a project's cost of capital is to use the return formula from the capital asset pricing model (CAPM).[10] This requires first specifying the premium for bearing the average amount of risk for the market as a whole and then, using a measure of market risk, fine tuning this to reflect the market risk of the project. The market risk premium for the market as a whole is the difference between the average expected market return, r_M, and the expected risk-free rate of interest, r_f.[11] If a company buys an asset whose market risk is the same as that of the market as a whole, the company expects a return of $r_M - r_f$ to compensate investors for market risk.

Adjusting the market risk premium for the market risk of the particular project requires multiplying the market risk premium by that project's asset beta, β_{asset}:

$$\text{Compensation for market risk} = \beta_{asset} \cdot (r_M - r_f)$$

This is the extra return necessary to compensate for the project's market risk. The asset beta fine-tunes the risk premium for the market as a whole to reflect the market risk of the particular project. If we then add the risk-free interest rate, we arrive at the cost of capital:

$$\text{Cost of capital} = r_f + \beta_{asset} \cdot (r_M - r_f)$$

Suppose the expected risk-free rate of interest is 4% and the expected return on the market as a whole is 10%. If $\beta_{asset} = 2$, this means that if there is a 1% change in the market risk premium, a 2% change (in the same direction) in the return on the project is expected. In this case, the cost of capital is 16%:

$$\text{Cost of capital} = 0.04 + 2 \cdot (0.10 - 0.04) = 0.16$$

or 16%. If, instead, $\beta_{\text{asset}} = 0.75$, the cost of capital is 8.5%:

$$\text{Cost of capital} = 0.04 + 0.75 \cdot (0.06) = 0.085$$

or 8.5%.

The calculation of the cost of capital takes advantage of the information in the asset beta. The application is not always straightforward, however. There are many instances in which a company invests in assets with differing risks. Using the company's asset beta would be inappropriate for evaluating the risk of a single project because the asset beta reflects the market risk of all of the company's assets and this may not be the same risk as for the project being evaluated. One approach to handle this situation is to estimate the cost of capital of a company that has a single line of business that is similar to the project under consideration. A company with a single line of business is referred to as a *pure-play company*. Selecting the company or companies that have a single line of business, where this line of business is similar to the project's, helps in estimating the market risk of a project.

One method of estimating the pure-play company's equity beta is regressing the returns on the pure-play company's stock and the returns on the market. Once the pure-play company's equity beta is calculated, management unlevers it by adjusting it for the financial leverage of the pure-play company.

Because many U.S. corporations whose stock's returns are readily available have more than one line of business, finding an appropriate pure-play company may be difficult. Care must be taken to identify those that have lines of business similar to the project's. Estimating a pure-play asset beta is useful in many other applications, including valuing divisions or segments of a business and valuing small businesses.

Adjusting the Company's Cost of Capital It is often the case that management is not able to estimate the project's market risk, not even the expected risk-free rate. Another way to estimate the cost of capital for a project without estimating the risk premium directly is to use the company's *weighted average cost of capital* (WACC) as a starting point. The WACC is the company's marginal cost of raising one more dollar of capital—the cost of raising one more dollar in the context of all the company's projects considered altogether, not just the project being evaluated.

The WACC is computed as follows:

$$r_{WACC} = \frac{(1 - \tau) \cdot r_D \cdot D + r_E \cdot E}{D + E}$$

where, as before D is the market value of debt, E is the market value of equity, and τ is the marginal tax rate. r_D and r_E are the cost of debt and cost of equity, respectively. r_D can be computed by considering the yields of the outstanding company bonds, weighted appropriately by the percentage they represent of the total company debt. r_E is simply $r_f + \beta_{equity} \cdot (r_M - r_f)$.

The WACC of the company can be adjusted to suit the perceived risk of the project:

- If a new project being considered is riskier than the average project of the company, the cost of capital of the new project is greater than the WACC.
- If the new project is less risky, its cost of capital is less than the WACC.
- If the new project is as risky as the average project of the company, the new project's cost of capital is equal to the WACC.

However, altering the company's cost of capital to reflect a project's cost of capital requires judgment. How much do we adjust it? If the project is riskier than the typical project, do we add 2%? 4%? 10%? There is no prescription here. It depends on the judgment and experience of the decision maker. But this is where the measures of a project's stand-alone risk can be used to help form that judgment.

17.3.2 Measuring a Project's Stand-Alone Risk

A project's stand-alone risk can be evaluated by performing sensitivity analysis. For example, we can create data tables in Excel to study the dependence of the project outcomes to slight changes in the forecasts of different variables in the model. A step further is to conduct scenario analysis, in which scenarios are explicitly created for the factors that impact the future cash flows. Conducting a scenario analysis is an important part of the process of assessing a project's total risk because different realizations of uncertain variables (such as sales forecasts, acquired market share, and cannibalization with other projects) can substantially change the decision of whether or not to undertake a project. While specific scenario analysis has many strong points, it is often useful to elevate the level of analysis to considering multiple scenarios at the same time. Monte Carlo simulation is the tool for analyzing the joint effects of changes in uncertain variables.

The risk associated with the future cash flows can be expressed statistically in terms of measures such as the range, the standard deviation, and the coefficient of variation.[12] Given the probability distributions of the project's future cash flows, these statistical tools can be applied to evaluate a project's risk.

The management arrives at these probability distributions based on research, judgment, and experience—for example, sensitivity analysis or simulation analysis using past experience of similar projects, if available, to get an idea of a project's possible future cash flows and their uncertainty can be used. Estimates of cash flows are based on assumptions about the economy, competitors, consumer tastes and preferences, construction costs, and taxes, among a host of other possible assumptions.

17.3.3 Assessment of Project Risk in Practice

Most U.S. companies consider risk in some manner in evaluating investment projects. But considering risk is usually a subjective analysis as opposed to the more objective results obtainable with simulation or sensitivity analysis.

Surveys indicate that companies that use discounted cash flow techniques, such as net present value and internal rate of return methods, tend to use a risk-adjusted cost of capital, but generally use the company's weighted average cost of capital as a benchmark.[13] But a significant portion of companies use a single cost of capital for all projects, which can be problematic.

The company's cost of capital reflects the company's average risk project. What happens when this cost of capital is applied in discounted cash flow techniques, such as the net present value or the internal rate of return, to all projects? This will result in the company's:

- Rejecting profitable projects (which would have increased owners' wealth) that have risk below the risk of the average risk project because the company has discounted the project's future cash flows too much.
- Accepting unprofitable projects whose risk is above the risk of the average project because the company did not discount the project's future cash flows enough.

Companies that use a risk-adjusted discount rate usually do so by classifying projects into risk classes by the type of project. For example, a company with a cost of capital of 10% may use a 14% cost of capital for new products and a much lower rate of 8% for replacement projects. Given a set of costs of capital, management need only figure out what class a project belongs to and then apply the rate assigned to that class.

Companies may also make adjustments in the cost of capital for factors other than the type of project. For example, companies investing in projects in foreign countries will sometimes make an adjustment for the additional risk of the foreign project, such as exchange rate risk, inflation risk, and political risk.

There are tools available to assist the decision maker in measuring and evaluating project risk. But much of what is actually done in practice is subjective. Judgment, with a large dose of experience, is used more often than scientific means of incorporating risk. Is this bad? Well, the scientific approaches to measurement and evaluation of risk depend, in part, on subjective assessments of risk, the probability distributions of future cash flows, and judgments about market risk. So, it is possible that by-passing the more technical analyses in favor of completely subjective assessment of risk may result in cost-of-capital estimates that better reflect the project's risk. But then again, it may not. The proof may be in the pudding, but it is difficult to assess the "proof" because it can never be determined how well a company may have done had it used more technical techniques.

17.4 CASE STUDY

In order to illustrate the classical financial concepts behind project valuation and the richer perspective that simulation provides, let us discuss the real-life-based case study of AirMax Shoes, Inc.[14]

AirMax Shoes, Inc. is considering introducing a new basketball shoe, "Rapid Bounce." The shoe would be endorsed by the most valuable NBA player for the previous year. However, the company has done a poor job of anticipating consumer preferences in the basketball shoe market in recent years. Its market share had decreased from 21.6% to about 16% of the $18 billion athletic shoe industry. Moreover, the overall trend in the industry is away from basketball shoes.

Another proposal under consideration is to launch an AirMax hiking shoe called "Persistence." The hiking sector is one of the fastest growing areas of the footwear industry—and one that AirMax has not yet entered. AirMax only has the resources to undertake the "Rapid Bounce" or "Persistence" projects, but not both. There are a number of uncertainties associated with both projects. The question is which project to choose.

The project lives for both projects are three years, and the federal plus state marginal tax rate for AirMax is 40%. Specific characteristics of the two projects are as follows:

Rapid Bounce

Revenues
- The athletic shoe market is projected to be $18.3 billion during year 1 and to continue growing at a rate of 3% per year. The market share projections for AirMax's "Rapid Bounce" are: year 1: 1.80%; year 2: 2.00%; year 3: 1.70%.

Costs
- Sales of Rapid Bounce are expected to reduce sales of other AirMax basketball sneakers. Specifically, AirMax's other sneaker sales are expected to decrease by $170 million during each year of the project. We will assume that these lost sales have the same margins as Rapid Bounce.
- In order to produce the shoe, AirMax will need to build a factory in New Delhi, India. This will require an immediate outlay of $100 million, which will be depreciated on a 20-year straight-line basis.[15] (In other words, the depreciation amounts for each of the three years of the project life will be $100/20 = $5 million per year.)
- AirMax must also immediately purchase equipment costing $15 million. Freight and installation of the equipment will cost $5 million. The equipment and freight/installation costs will be depreciated on a five-year straight-line basis. (In other words, the depreciation amounts for each of the three years of the project life will be $20/5 = $4 million per year.)
- Variable costs of producing the shoe are expected to be 31% of the shoe's sales.
- Selling, general, and administrative expenses are expected to be $7 million per year for the project.
- AirMax would pay its celebrity endorser $10 million dollars annually for three years.
- Other advertising and promotion costs are expected to be $20 million per year.
- In order to manufacture Rapid Bounce, two of AirMax's working capital accounts (the inventory balance and the accounts payable) are expected to increase immediately. The net change in the working capital for the duration of the project will be –$45 million. These balances will be maintained until the final year of the project, at which time they will be recovered.

Persistence

Revenues

- The hiking and walking segment of the athletic shoe market is projected to reach $350 million during year 1 and is growing at a rate of 15% per year. The segment market share projections for "Persistence" are: year 1: 12%; year 2: 13%; year 3: 16%.

Costs

- AirMax will be able to use an idle section of one of its factories to produce the hiking shoe.
- AirMax must purchase manufacturing equipment costing $9 million. The equipment will be depreciated on a 3-year straight-line basis, with annual depreciation amounts for the three years equal to $3 million. The cash outlay will be today, in year 0, and depreciation will start in year 1.
- Variable costs of producing the shoe are expected to be 17% of the shoe's sales.
- General and administrative expenses for Persistence will be 20% of revenues per year.
- The product will not have a celebrity endorser, and advertising and promotion costs are expected to be $3 million per year, beginning in year 1.
- The net change in the working capital for the duration of the project will be –$15 million. The balances will be maintained until the final year of the project, at which time they will be recovered.
- In order to begin immediate production of Persistence, the design technology and manufacturing specifications for a simple hiking shoe will be purchased from an outside source for $50 million before taxes. It is assumed this outlay takes place immediately and will be expensed immediately for tax purposes.

This information is entered into a worksheet (see Exhibits 17.13 and 17.14 and file **Ch17-AirMax.xlsx**), and the NPV and IRR for the two projects are computed. In order to do the computation, we need to estimate the cost of capital. Once the base case worksheet models for the two projects are created by using our estimate of market risk, we incorporate stand-alone risk by modeling a number of the input parameters as uncertain variables. For example, the forecasts for the market share of the two products are estimates, and so is the amount of cannibalization that project Rapid Bounce will cause on other AirMax basketball shoes.

			"Rapid Bounce" Projected Project Cash Flow Statements ($ millions)			
Rapid Bounce						
Assumptions ($ millions)			Year 0	Year 1	Year 2	Year 3
Length of project (years):	3	Revenues		$329.40	$376.98	$360.65
Athletic footwear market:	$18,300.00	Cannibalization (Erosion of existing sales)		-$170.00	-$170.00	-$170.00
Growth of market:	3.00%	Net revenues (after erosion)		$159.40	$206.98	$190.65
Market share (year 1):	1.80%	Variable costs		-$49.41	-$64.16	-$59.10
Market share (year 2):	2.00%	S G & A expenses		-$7.00	-$7.00	-$7.00
Market share (year 3):	1.70%	Endorsement		-$10.00	-$10.00	
Factory expansion:	$100.00	Advertising & promotion		-$20.00	-$20.00	-$20.00
Equipment:	$15.00	Factory depreciation		-$5.00	-$5.00	-$5.00
Freight and installation:	$5.00	Equipment depreciation		-$4.00	-$4.00	-$4.00
Variable costs as a % of sales:	31.00%	EBIT (Earnings before interest and taxes)		$63.99	$96.82	$95.55
Cannibalization per year:	$170.00	Taxes		-$25.59	-$38.73	-$38.22
SG&A expenses:	$7.00	EBIAT		$38.39	$58.09	$57.33
Endorsement:	$10.00	Plus depreciation of factory		$5.00	$5.00	$5.00
Other advertising & promotion:	$20.00	Plus depreciation of equipment		$4.00	$4.00	$4.00
Net change in working capital	-$45.00	Change in NWC	-$45.00	$0.00	$0.00	$45.00
Tax rate:	40.00%	New factory	-$100.00			
		Equipment, freight & installation	-$20.00			
		Project net cash flows	**-$165.00**	**$47.39**	**$67.09**	**$111.33**
		Analysis of project				
		Assumed cost of capital:	10.51%			
		Net Present Value:	$15.31			
		IRR:	15.04%			

EXHIBIT 17.13 Rapid Bounce's NPV and IRR calculation.

Persistence

Assumptions ($ millions)			"Persistence" Projected Project Cash Flow Statements ($ millions)				
				Year 0	Year 1	Year 2	Year 3
Length of project (years):	3		Revenues		$42.00	$52.33	$74.06
Hiking & walking market:	$350.00		Variable costs		-$7.14	-$8.90	-$12.59
Growth of market:	15.00%		G & A expenses		-$8.40	-$10.47	-$14.81
Market share (year 1):	12.00%		Advertising & promotion		-$3.00	-$3.00	-$3.00
Market share (year 2):	13.00%		Equipment depreciation		-$3.00	-$3.00	-$3.00
Market share (year 3):	16.00%		Technology purchase	-$50.00	$0.00	$0.00	$0.00
Purchase of technology:	$50.00		EBIT (Earnings before interest and taxes)	-$50.00	$20.46	$26.96	$40.66
Equipment:	$9.00		Taxes	$20.00	-$8.18	-$10.79	-$16.26
Variable costs as a % of sales:	17.00%		EBIAT	-$30.00	$12.28	$16.18	$24.39
Percentage increase in VC/year	0.0%		Plus depreciation of equipment	$0.00	$3.00	$3.00	$3.00
AirMax other hiking sales:	$0.00		Change in NWC	-$15.00	$0.00	$0.00	$15.00
Growth in other hiking sales:	0%		Equipment, freight & installation	-$9.00	$0.00	$0.00	$0.00
Cannibalization % of sales:	0%		**Project net cash flows**	**-$54.00**	**$15.28**	**$19.18**	**$42.39**
SG&A Expenses (% of sales):	20%						
Other advertising & promotion:	$3.00		**Analysis of project**				
Net change in working capital	-$15.00		Assumed cost of capital:	13.00%			
Tax rate:	40.00%		Net Present Value:	$3.92			
			IRR:	16.55%			

EXHIBIT 17.14 Persistence's NPV and IRR calculation.

17.4.1 Computing the Cost of Capital

First, let us show how we would evaluate the cost of capital for the two projects. We will use the company WACC as a starting point. In order to compute it, we need the values of the risk-free rate r_f, the company beta, the excess return on the market, the yields to maturity for AirMax's outstanding debt, and the market value weights of debt and equity for AirMax. We will assume the following:

1. The risk-free rate r_f is 5%. This input should be the yield on Treasury securities with approximately the same maturity as the life of the project.
2. The market risk premium $(r_M - r_f)$ is 6.2%. This is the approximate historical excess return on the market. We cannot observe the market risk premium relevant for evaluating this project, but we make the assumption that investors will demand a premium that its consistent with historically observed values.
3. The company beta β is 1.08. This was estimated using data on past company stock returns and the returns on the Russell 3000, a broad market index (see worksheet **Beta Data** in the file **Ch17-AirMax.xlsx**).
4. The cost of equity is therefore

$$r_e = r_f + \beta \cdot (r_M - r_f) = 0.05 + 1.08 \cdot 0.062 = 0.11696 = 11.70\%$$

5. AirMax's current stock price is $36.42, and there are 59.7 million shares outstanding. Therefore, the market value of AirMax's equity is $E = \$36.42 \cdot (59.7 \text{ million}) = \$2,174.27$ million.
6. Suppose AirMax has two bond issues, short-term debt with yield to maturity 2.72% and long-term debt with yield to maturity 7.05%. The price per unit for the short-term debt is $1,078.53, and there are 101,408 units in the market. The price per unit of the long-term debt is $1,032.50, and there are 250,000 units in the market. The total market value of short-term debt is therefore ($1,078.53 101,408) = $109.37 million, and the total market value of long-term debt is ($1,032.50 250,000) = $258.13 million.
7. Based on 6., the total market value for debt is $D = \$109.37 + \$258.13 = \$367.5$ million. Of those, 29.8% are short-term debt, and 70.2% are long-term debt.
8. The cost of debt is therefore

$$r_D = (2.72\%) \cdot (29.8\%) + (7.05\%) \cdot (70.2\%) = 0.057597 = 5.76\%$$

9. The after-tax cost of debt is

$$(1 - \tau) \cdot r_D = (1 - 0.40) \cdot 5.76\% = 3.46\%$$

10. Based on 5. and 7., the total market value for debt plus equity (D + E) is $367.5 + \$2,174.27 = \$2541.77$ million. The weight of debt is 14.5% of the total, and the weight of the equity is 85.5% of the total.

11. Based on 4., 9., and 10., the WACC is

$$
\begin{aligned}
r_{WACC} &= \frac{(1-\tau) \cdot r_D \cdot D + r_E \cdot E}{D+E} \\
&= (1-\tau) \cdot r_D \cdot \frac{D}{D+E} + r_E \cdot \frac{E}{D+E} \\
&= (3.46\%) \cdot (14.5\%) + (11.70\%) \cdot (85.5\%) \\
&= 10.51\%
\end{aligned}
$$

Rapid Bounce is a project that is similar to the company's existing projects, so we will assume that it carries the same magnitude of risk and its cash flows can be discounted using the WACC as the discount rate (i.e., we will use a discount rate of 10.51%). The Persistence project, on the other hand, is outside AirMax's current line of business, so we may deem it more risky and use a higher discount rate than WACC, say 13%.

With these discount rates, the NPV for Rapid Bounce is $15.31 million, and the IRR is 15.04%. The NPV for Persistence is $3.92 million, and the IRR is 16.55%.

If we use the IRR as a criterion, we would pick Persistence. But here we have an example of capital rationing and two projects with differences of scale. NPV is the more appropriate criterion to use. Based on the NPV, we would pick Rapid Bounce.

17.4.2 Computing the NPV Profiles

The next step is to analyze how sensitive the solution is to the assumptions made about the discount rates to use in the case of each project. Exhibit 17.15 shows the NPV profiles for the two projects. We can observe that the NPV for Rapid Bounce is higher than the NPV for Persistence for low values of cost of capital, including the current assumed values. At about cost of capital of 14.5%, the two NPVs become equal, and then eventually both become negative, with the NPV for Rapid Bounce decreasing faster than the NPV for Persistence. Clearly, deciding which project to pick is very sensitive to small changes in the current estimates of the cost of capital for the two projects, so we may want additional information to make the final decision. Note that so far, we have incorporated only considerations for market risk in the analysis of the two projects. The next step is to include the stand-alone risks as well by running a Monte Carlo simulation.

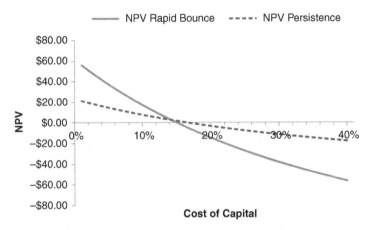

NPV Rapid Bounce ⸺ NPV Persistence ⸺

EXHIBIT 17.15 NPV profiles for Rapid Bounce and Persistence.

17.4.3 Running a Simulation to Estimate Project Stand-Alone Risk

Let us list some sources of uncertainty for the two projects, and how we could model them with probability distributions. See Exhibits 17.16 and 17.17 for a graphical representation of the different probability distributions used in the simulation. If you are using @RISK, see also worksheet **Simulation** in the file **Ch17-AirMax.xlsx**.

Rapid Bounce

1. The projected market size ($18.3 billion) for the athletic shoe market in Year 1 is an estimate. We will assume that $18.3 billion is the expected value of the market size, but that the actual value for the market size will follow a normal distribution that is on average $18,300 million, and has a standard deviation of $1,100 million. (We explain how we came up with these numbers later.) This distribution assumes that deviations above and below the expected market size of 18,300 are equally likely, and that the average deviation from the estimate will be $1,100 million. See Exhibit 17.16(A).[16]
2. The growth of the athletic footwear market was assumed to be 3% per year. Let us assume instead that it follows a general beta distribution with parameters $\alpha = 5.5$, $\beta = 4$, minimum $= -0.08$, and maximum $= 0.11$. This results in a mean value for growth of 3%; however, it also allows us to input an anticipated range for the market growth (between -8% and 11%), and express general optimism about the growth of the

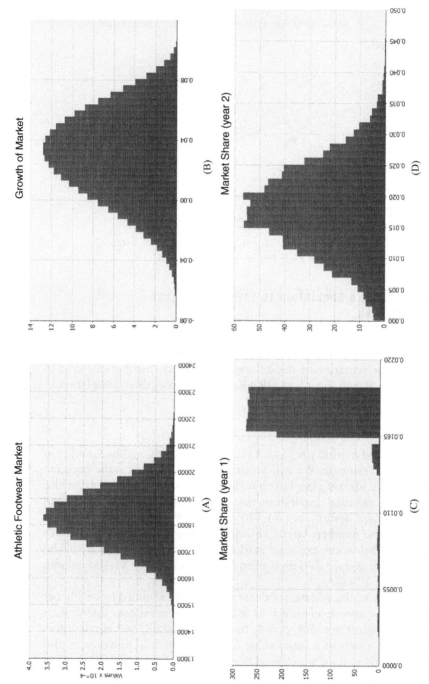

EXHIBIT 17.16 Probability distributions used in the simulation of the NPV of Rapid Bounce. (A) Size of athletic shoe market; (B) Growth of the athletic shoe market; (C) Market share in year 1; (D) Market share in year 2.

market. (The latter is because the probability distribution is left-skewed, which means that most of the mass is to the right side of the mean, and higher values for the actual market growth will be more likely to happen in the simulation.) See Exhibit 17.16(B).

3. One of the important items with the Rapid Bounce project is the reliance on the celebrity endorser's reputation for advertising the new basketball shoe. His image would have a significant impact on the market share AirMax will be able to achieve in the first year. AirMax could consider three possible scenarios: with 95% probability, there will be a very positive perception of the NBA player, and AirMax's market share in the first year will be between 1.65% and 2.00%. With 3% probability, the NBA player's name will not generate the expected buzz, and AirMax's market share in the first year will be between 1.40% and 1.60%. Finally, there is a 2% chance that the NBA player will have a negative image, and AirMax's market share in the first year will be between 0.20% and 0.40%.[17] See Exhibit 17.16(C).

4. We assume that the market shares in years 2 and 3 depend on the market share established in year 1 with some probability of deviating from the previous year's market share. The market share for year 2 will follow a normal distribution, truncated at 0, with mean equal to the realized market share in year 1, and a standard deviation of 0.7%. The market share for year 3 will follow a normal distribution, truncated at 0, with mean equal to the realized market share in year 2, and a standard deviation of 0.7%.[18] See Exhibit 17.16(D).

5. The estimate for the amount of cannibalization (erosion of sales of current basketball shoe models) is very rough, and it makes sense to generate multiple scenarios for this assumption. We assume that the actual amount of sales erosion is normally distributed with mean equal to $170 million, and a standard deviation of $20 million.

Persistence

1. The projected market size ($350 million) for the athletic shoe market in year 1 is an estimate. We assume that $350 million is the expected value of the market size, but that the actual value for the market size follows a normal distribution that is on average $350 million, and has a standard deviation of $10 million. See Exhibit 17.17(A).[19]

2. The growth of the hiking and walking shoe market was assumed to be 15% per year. Let us assume instead that it follows a general beta distribution with parameters $\alpha = 2.6$, $\beta = 1.9$, minimum $= 0.08$, and maximum $= 0.20$. This results in a mean value for growth of approximately 15%; however, it also allows us to input an anticipated range for the market growth (between 8% and 11%), and express general

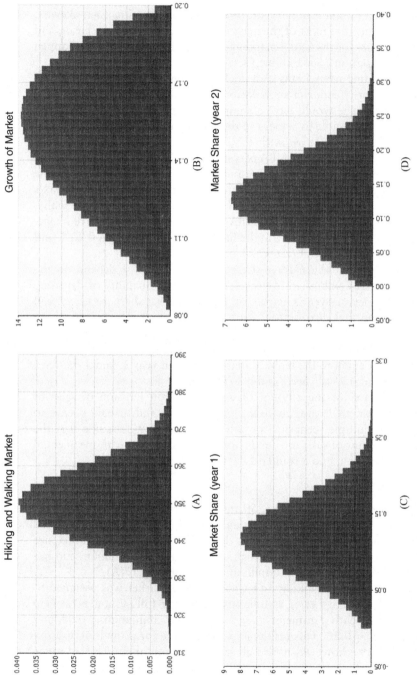

EXHIBIT 17.17 Probability distributions used in the simulation of the NPV of Persistence. (A) Size of hiking and walking shoe market; (B) Growth of the hiking and walking shoe market; (C) Market share in year 1; (D) Market share in year 2.

optimism about the growth of the market. (As in item 2 for Rapid Bounce, the latter is because the probability distribution is left-skewed, which means that most of the mass is to the right side of the mean, and higher values for the actual market growth will be more likely to happen in the simulation.) See Exhibit 17.17(B).

3. We assume that the AirMax market shares for years 1, 2, and 3 are, as forecasted, 12%, 13%, and 16% on average. The actual market share for each year will follow normal distributions with standard deviations of 5%, 6%, and 7%, respectively. We need to truncate these normal distributions at 0 because the standard deviations are large relative to the means, and there is a large probability that a negative number will be generated for market share in the simulation. When we truncate the normal distribution at 0, however, its mass shifts to the right, and its mean increases. In order to preserve means of 12%, 13%, and 16% for the actual simulated numbers, we draw random numbers with truncated normal distributions with means of 11.88%, 12.75%, and 15.78%.

4. We also assume that the market shares in the three years are positively correlated: with correlation of 0.8 for years 1 and 2 and years 2 and 3, and with correlation of 0.4 for years 1 and 3.[20]

We can, of course, incorporate further assumptions. For example, we may assume that variable costs are uncertain with a particular probability distribution. The assumptions we have modeled so far, however, are sufficient for illustration of the main ideas.

If we plug in the expected values for all assumed probability distributions into the worksheet, we will get NPV and IRR estimates for Rapid Bounce and Persistence that are very close to the estimates we obtained in the last section. However, analyzing the probability distributions of the NPVs tells a different story. The distributions for the NPVs for Rapid Bounce and Persistence, as well as relevant statistical summaries from the simulation, are presented in Exhibit 17.18.

We can observe that while the NPV for Rapid Bounce is higher on average than the NPV for Persistence ($12.68 versus $3.90 million), its variability is also higher (standard deviation of $111.04 million versus $18.42 million), higher standard deviation as a percentage of the mean (the coefficient of variation is $8.76 million versus $4.72 million), and lower fifth percentile of –$160.74 million versus –$26.01 million). The NPV for Rapid Bounce also has a slightly lower probability of being positive (53.11% versus 57.32% for the NPV of Persistence). Hence, in terms of risk, Persistence appears to be the more attractive project.

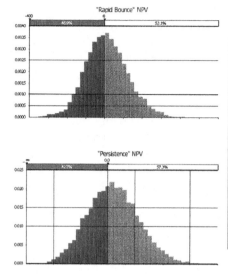

	"Rapid Bounce" NPV	"Persistence" NPV
Minimum	−$353.12	−$44.88
Maximum	$539.69	$78.75
Mean	$12.68	$3.90
Standard deviation	$111.04	$18.42
Coefficient of variation	$8.76	$4.72
Skewness	0.1840	0.1692
Kurtosis	3.1529	2.8641
Mode	$12.03	−$0.49
5% Percentile	−$160.74	−$26.01
50% Percentile	$8.33	$3.55
95% Percentile	$205.64	$35.09
Prob. NPV >=0	53.11%	57.32%

EXHIBIT 17.18 Simulation output: Distribution for the NPV of Rapid Bounce; Distribution for the NPV of Persistence; Statistical summary.

Additional useful information can be obtained if we compare the NPVs on a scenario-by-scenario basis. As discussed in section 4.2.3 of Chapter 4, this can be accomplished by creating an additional output variable in the worksheet that measures the difference between the two NPVs, and analyzing its simulated distribution. The results are presented in Exhibit 17.19.

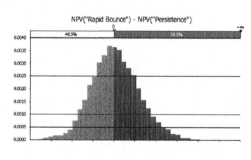

	NPV("RapidBounce")−NPV("Persistence")
Minimum	−$383.47
Maximum	$551.78
Mean	$8.78
Standard deviation	$112.58
Coefficient of variation	$12.83
Skewness	0.1813
Kurtosis	$3.15
Mode	−$13.50
5% Perc	−$167.18
50% Perc	−$9.42
95% Perc	$202.21

EXHIBIT 17.19 Simulation output for the difference between the NPV of Rapid Bounce and the NPV of Persistence.

It can be seen that the NPV of Rapid Bounce was higher than the NPV of Persistence in about 51.5% of the generated scenarios, and by about $8.78 million on average. So, on a scenario-by-scenario basis, Rapid Bounce appears to be the more attractive project.

It is difficult to decide which one of the two options to choose. The answer will depend on management's priorities. However, the information obtained by running a simulation adds to the information obtained from the financial analysis at the first step of the project evaluation process and this helps management make a more informed decision.

17.4.4 Determining the Inputs to the Simulation

In the last section, we explained how one can incorporate uncertainty about the inputs in the model, and interpret the results from the simulation. How can one come up with the parameters used to construct the different probability distributions?

The first question to ask ourselves is whether the probability distribution representing an estimate should be symmetric or skewed. A symmetric distribution would assume that deviations above and below the estimated value are equally likely. A skewed distribution would enable us to impart some subjective judgment. Recall the probability distributions we used to model the growth of the athletic footwear and the hiking and walking shoe markets. A right-skewed distribution would have more of its probability mass to the right of the mean, and most simulation trials will result in outcomes that are below the mean. A left-skewed distribution would have more of its probability mass to the left of the mean, and most simulation trials will generate outcomes that are above the mean.

The second question to ask is whether the actual values are clustered around the estimate, or could be far from the estimate. For example, both the normal distribution and the uniform distribution are symmetric, but the uniform distribution assumes that the values can be anywhere on the specified range with the same probability, while the normal distribution incorporates the assumption that the values are likely to be close to the mean—the closer to the mean they are, the more likely they will be generated during the simulation.

Important variables that have a big impact on the bottom line, such as sales or market share, are often forecast by analysts with a lot of experience in the industry. Simulation can be used to combine forecasts from multiple analysts by figuring out the average estimate and the variability in these estimates.

Finally, statistical techniques can be used to derive estimates from historical data. For example, our estimate of $18.3 billion for the size of the athletic footwear market was derived by recording the market size for the 20 years prior to the present time, running a regression to determine if there is a trend, and using the regression to forecast the next point, as well as the variability in the estimate. The data and the regression output can be found in worksheet **Market Size Data** of the file **Ch17-AirMax.xlsx**, and are shown in Exhibit 17.20.

The response variable in the regression is the market size, and the explanatory variable is the year. The regression equation can be recovered from the regression output. We have

$$\text{Market size (\$ billions)} = 11.68 + 0.32 \cdot \text{Year}$$

Therefore, to make a forecast for next year (year 21), we plug in 21 for Year:

$$\text{Market size forecast (\$ billions)} = \$11.68 + \$0.32 \cdot 21 = \$18.30$$

This is the point estimate. The standard error of the regression ($1.0792 billion, or approximately $1080 million) tells us how far the actual point will be from this estimate on average. This is why we plugged in 18,300 as the mean, and $1,100 (a slightly more conservative estimate) as the standard deviation for the normal distribution we used to model the market size for athletic footwear in year 1.

Estimating inputs to the simulation reliably adds an additional step to the simulation process, and may require a lot of time and resources. Some software packages focused specifically on simulation, such as @RISK, contain tools that allow the modeler to decide whether achieving an additional degree of accuracy in the estimate of given simulation inputs is worth the extra time. In particular, @RISK can create *tornado graphs*, graphs that list the simulation input variables that impact the variability in the simulation output variable in order of importance. Exhibit 17.21 contains the tornado graphs for the NPVs of Rapid Bounce and Persistence.

There are several types of tornado graphs, including regression coefficient graphs, correlation graphs, and regression-mapped values graphs. A user of @RISK can toggle between the different types of graphs.[21] We choose to show regression-mapped values tornado graphs in Exhibit 17.21 because the interpretation is quite intuitive. The length of the bar that corresponds to a specific simulation input variable is the amount of change in the output variable that will result from a change in the input variable equal to one standard deviation change. In other words, when the input changes by +1 standard deviation, the output will change by the value on the horizontal axis associated with the length of the bar. For example, Exhibit 17.21(A)

Year	Market Size ($ billions)
1	11.44
2	11.72
3	13.85
4	13.68
5	12.23
6	12.01
7	13.92
8	13.25
9	15.61
10	14.64
11	16.11
12	15.07
13	17.16
14	16.37
15	17.82
16	18.08
17	17.65
18	16.12
19	15.87
20	17.21

SUMMARY OUTPUT

Regression Statistics

Multiple R	0.871153984
R-square	0.758909264
Adjusted R-square	0.745515334
Standard Error	1.079220811
Observations	20

ANOVA

	df	SS	MS	F	Significance F
Regression	1	65.99369721	65.9937	56.66069	5.77E-07
Residual	18	20.96491608	1.164718		
Total	19	86.95861329			

	Coefficients	Standard Error	t-stat	P-value	Lower 95%	Upper 95%
Intercept	11.68333317	0.501332015	23.30458	6.77E-15	10.63007	12.73659
Year	0.315021654	0.041850388	7.527329	5.77E-07	0.227097	0.402946

EXHIBIT 17.20 Data for determining the size of the athletic footwear market.

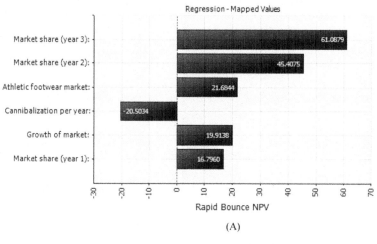

(A)

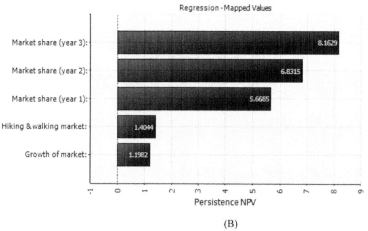

(B)

EXHIBIT 17.21 Sensitivity of (A) Rapid Bounce NPV and (B) Persistence NPV to different factors.

tells us that the most significant variable for the variability in the NPV of Rapid Bounce is the market share in year 3. A change of +1 standard deviation in the market share from year 3 will increase the NPV of Rapid Bounce by $61.088 million. The fourth most-influential input variable is the amount of cannibalization of sales in a year. A change of +1 standard deviation in the amount of cannibalization will decrease the NPV of Rapid Bounce by $20.503 million. These estimates will vary from simulation to simulation—they are obtained by running a regression on the generated simulation inputs and outputs.

Tornado graphs showing regression coefficients and correlation coefficients contain similar information. In the regression coefficients tornado graph, the length of the bar shown for input variable shows the number of standard deviation the NPV will change if the input variable changes by one standard deviation. In the correlation coefficients tornado graph, the length of the bar shows the strength of the correlation between the changes in the input variable and the NPV.

In this example, the conclusion is that it is most important to make sure that the estimates of the market shares in year 3 and year 2, as well as the size of the market, are accurate. Those input distributions are responsible for the majority of the variability in the estimate of the NPV.

17.5 MANAGING PORTFOLIOS OF PROJECTS

Capital budgeting shares many aspects of financial investment management. Although investment projects at companies have traditionally been evaluated on a single-project basis, there are many arguments for using tools from the management of financial investments in the corporate finance context. Projects are often linked to one another, and subject to common risk factors. They can be characterized by their risk-return profiles. The theory of optimal portfolio management and operations research tools such as optimization can and should be applied in this area, although few companies actually do.

This area of research is known as *project portfolio management* (PPM). Most known PPM methods and tools are based on subjective weighted scoring methods, not quantitatively rigorous methods with roots in modern portfolio theory or operations research. The field has traditionally been tied to information technology projects at companies, and has only recently begun to attract attention as an important area of study. It is easy to understand how the problem of optimal project management can be related to the problem of optimal investment management. The important thing is to define project outcomes and risks in terms of easily quantifiable, statistically meaningful metrics.

SUMMARY

- One of the most important functions in financial management is the evaluation of capital expenditures. Decisions involving capital expenditures are known as capital budgeting decisions.

- Unlike working capital decisions, capital budgeting decisions commit funds for a time period longer than one year and may have an impact of a company's strategic position within its industry.
- The capital budgeting process encompasses the initial investment screening and selection through the post-completion audit of the project. Classifying capital projects along different dimensions (that is, economic life, risk, and dependence on other projects) is necessary because these characteristics of the projects affect the analysis of the projects.
- The six most commonly used techniques for evaluating capital budgeting proposals are net present value, profitability index, internal rate of return, modified internal rate of return, payback period, and discounted payback period.
- The net present value method and the profitability index are preferred methods because they consider all the project's cash flows, involve discounting (which considers the time value of money and risk), and are useful in cases in which projects are mutually exclusive.
- The net present value method produces an amount that is the expected value added from investing in a project. That is, the net present value is an estimate of the value added from an investment project.
- The profitability index translates the NPV into an indexed value, and can be useful in ranking projects.
- The internal rate of return is the yield on the investment. It is the discount rate that causes the net present value to be equal to zero. The internal rate of return is hazardous to use when selecting among mutually exclusive projects or when there is a limit on capital spending.
- The modified internal rate of return is a yield on the investment, assuming that cash inflows are reinvested at some rate other than the internal rate of return. This method overcomes the problems associated with unrealistic reinvestment rate assumptions inherent in the internal rate of return method. However, this method is hazardous to use when selecting among mutually exclusive projects or when there is a limit on capital spending.
- The payback period and the discounted payback period methods provide a measure of the time it takes to recover the initial investment in a project. Both of these methods have limitations in that they fail to consider all cash flows from a project.
- When there are scale differences among projects, the net present value should be used.
- When evaluating projects that have different economics lives, the different lives must be taken into account before selecting projects based on one of the six methods described in this chapter.

- Evaluating capital projects requires assessing the risk associated with the future cash flows. This risk may be measured in terms of the market risk or the stand-alone risk.
- Market risk is typically incorporated into decision making by using a cost of capital that reflects the project's risk in relation to the company's capital structure and the portfolio of projects it holds.
- The stand-alone risk of a project can be estimated using statistics and simulation techniques.
- Simulation can be used to determine the distributions of possible outcomes for different metrics of a project's promise, and to compare outcomes from different projects on a scenario-by-scenario basis.

SOFTWARE HINTS

@RISK

This section explains how the simulation in the AirMax case was run. Of course, we start by filling out a static worksheet model in which all dependencies between the different variables are incorporated through Excel formulas. For the rest of this section, we will be referring to worksheet **Simulation** in the file **Ch17-AirMax.xlsx**.

Creating the Simulation Inputs   The simulation inputs are created by simply clicking on the **Define Distribution** in the Model group under the @RISK tab, and entering the appropriate distribution. Given the assumptions in the model, we have the following entries for simulation input distributions (see Exhibit 17.22):

The two more complex modeling issues are:

1. How to model the scenarios for the market share in year 1 in the case of Rapid Bounce, and
2. How to create the correlated variables for the market shares in different years in the case of Persistence.

To accomplish 1. we create an array in cells A27:D30 (see Exhibit 17.23). It contains the scenario number (cells A28:30), the lower and upper bounds of the intervals from which the random number for the market share will be drawn in each scenario (cells B28:B30), and the probability with which each scenario occurs (cells D28:D30). Cell B31 contains a formula (`RiskDiscrete(A28:A30,D28:D30)`) that makes sure that a random

EXHIBIT 17.22 Simulation input distributions.

Variable	Cell Reference	@RISK/Excel Formula
Rapid Bounce		
Size of athletic footwear market	B4	RiskNormal(18300,1100)
Growth of market	B5	RiskBetaGeneral(5.5,4,-0.08,0.11)
Random scenario for market share in year 1	B31	RiskDiscrete(A28:A30,D28:D30)
Market share for year 1	B6	RiskUniform(VLOOKUP(B31,A28:C30,2), VLOOKUP(B31,A28:C30,3))
Market share for year 2	B7	RiskNormal(B6,0.007,RiskTruncate(0,))
Market share for year 3	B8	RiskNormal(B7,0.007,RiskTruncate(0,))
Cannibalization per year	B13	RiskNormal(170,20)
Persistence		
Size of hiking and walking market	K4	RiskNormal(350,10)
Growth of market	K5	RiskBetaGeneral(2.6,1.9,0.08,0.2)
Market share in year 1	K6	RiskNormal(0.1188,0.05, RiskTruncate(0,), RiskCorrmat(PMktShareCorrelations,1))
Market share in year 2	K7	RiskNormal(0.1275,0.06, RiskTruncate(0,), RiskCorrmat(PMktShareCorrelations,2))
Market share in year 3	K8	RiskNormal(0.1578,0.07, RiskTruncate(0,), RiskCorrmat(PMktShareCorrelations,3))

number (1, 2, or 3) is drawn from the scenarios in cells A28:30 with the probabilities assigned in cells D28:D30. To generate the actual market share in year 1 in cell B6, we use VLOOKUP[22] to look up the upper and lower bound for the interval corresponding to the random scenario drawn in cell B31. The formula

```
RiskUniform(VLOOKUP(B31,A28:C30,2),VLOOKUP(B31,A28:C30,3))
```

	A	B	C	D
26				
27	Market share scenarios for year 1	Lower bound	Upper bound	Probability
28	1	1.65%	2.00%	95%
29	2	1.40%	1.60%	3%
30	3	0.20%	0.40%	2%
31	Random scenario drawn	1		
32				

EXHIBIT 17.23 Array for modeling the market scenarios for Rapid Bounce for year 1.

draws a random number between the lower bound for the range (found in the second column of the array A28:C30 with the formula VLOOKUP(B31,A28:C30,2)) and the upper bound for the range (found in the third column of the array A28:C30 with the formula VLOOKUP(B31,A28:C30,3)).

To accomplish 2. select the three cells corresponding to the market shares in years 1, 2, and 3 and right-click on them, then select **@RISK** and click **Define Correlations** (see Exhibit 17.24.) This opens the @RISK Define Correlations dialog box (see Exhibit 17.25), which we can use to specify a

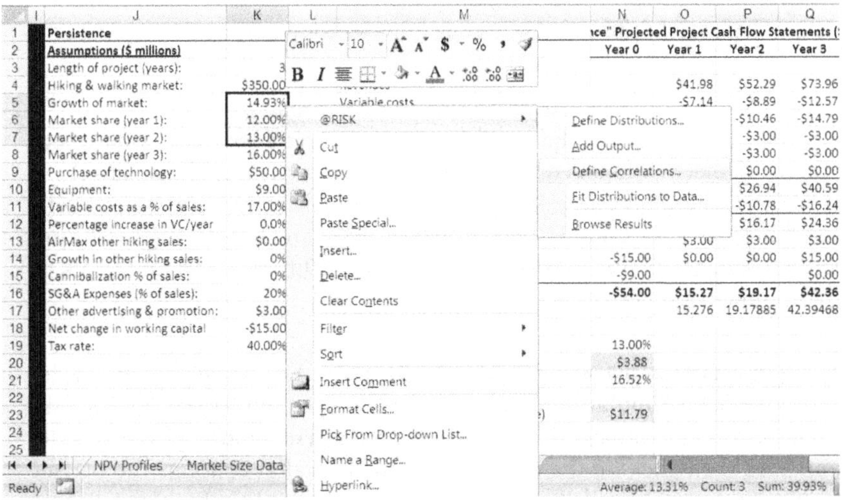

EXHIBIT 17.24 Defining correlations for market shares in years 1, 2, and 3 for Persistence.

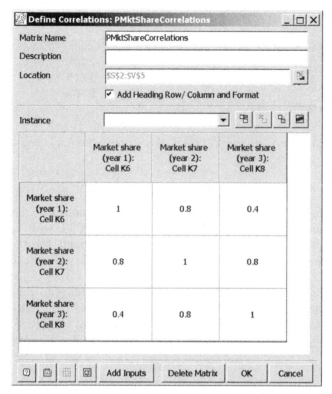

EXHIBIT 17.25   @RISK Define Correlations dialog box.

correlation matrix and name it. The matrix then can be saved somewhere on the worksheet. (We saved it in cells S2:V5 in worksheet **Simulation**.)

We then need to make sure to specify which cells were output cells by clicking the **Add Output** button. These cells are E24 (NPV for Rapid Bounce), N20 (NPV for Persistence), and N23 (Difference in the NPVs of Rapid Bounce and Persistence).

Running the Simulation and Formatting Output   The simulation is run by clicking the **Start Simulation** in the Simulation group under the @RISK tab. The output can be obtained by clicking the **Browse Results** in the Results group, and then clicking the cell in the worksheet that contains the output variable of interest. Detailed statistics and output directly in Excel worksheet format can be obtained by clicking the **Excel Reports** in the Tools group under the @RISK tab, and selecting the simulation data of interest.

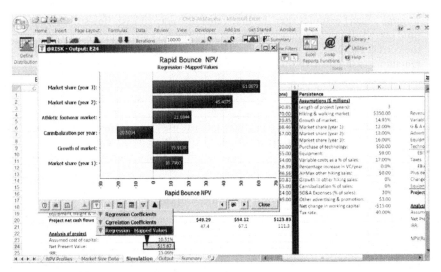

EXHIBIT 17.26 Creating a tornado graph.

Creating Tornado Graphs Tornado graphs are created by clicking on the tornado button in the graph for the output variable (see Exhibit 17.26). As explained in Appendix B on the companion web site, such a graph appears automatically at the end of a simulation run if you click on an output or input cell. Alternatively, it can be called by clicking on the **Browse Results** button in the Results group in the @RISK tab after a simulation.

MATLAB

MATLAB is not as well-suited for performing a simple simulation directly off a worksheet as @RISK, but the whole model for NPV and IRR calculation for the two projects can be implemented in a MATLAB script, scenarios can be generated for the different input variables, and the output variable distributions saved and evaluated. The important thing is to represent correctly the relationships between the different variables in the base case model.

NOTES

1. MS Excel and MATLAB's Financial Toolbox have commands for computing NPV. Excel's command is =NPV(Discount rate, Array of cash

flows). Excel assumes that the first value in Array of cash flows occurs one time period from now, and it discounts it to the present. Therefore, to obtain the correct estimate, we need to add the cash flow at time 0 to the NPV for the remaining cash flows. In this particular example, we would enter

```
-1500000 + NPV(0.10,0,200000,500000,900000,1000000)
```

In MATLAB, the appropriate function to use is pvvar(CashFlows, DiscountRate). In contrast to Excel, MATLAB assumes that the first cash flow happens at time 0, and does not discount it. To calculate the NPV in our example, we would enter

```
pvvar([-1500000,0,200000,500000,900000,1000000],0.10)
```

2. We will see an example of this situation in section 17.2.7.
3. In Excel, the IRR can be computed with the formula =IRR(Array of cash flows, initial guess), where initial guess is an optional argument, and specifies the starting point from which the numerical algorithm tries to determine the value of the IRR. It is best if initial guess is a point close to the actual IRR. In the case of Project X, we used the investment profile to determine an approximate starting point of 14.5%. In MATLAB, the Financial Toolbox contains the function irr(CashFlow), which can be used to compute the IRR for a stream of cash flows at equal time periods, or xirr(CashFlows, CashFlowDates), which can be used to compute the IRR for a stream of cash flows at unequal time periods.
4. It may or may not—and that is the problem. It is possible to make a value-maximizing decision by using the IRR method, but it is also possible to make a decision that is not value-maximizing by using the IRR method.
5. We will explain the concept of cost of capital and its estimation in more detail in sections 17.3.1 and 17.3.3 in this chapter. For now, it is important to know that different projects for the same company may have different costs of capital depending on the riskiness of the projects. A company with a large portfolio of projects has an "averaged-out" cost of capital that can be estimated from the information available from capital markets, but estimating the cost of capital for individual projects requires additional care.
6. An annuity is an income payable in equal installments at specific intervals for a period of length N. The present value of an annuity is

$$PV = \sum_{i=1}^{N} \frac{A}{(1+r)^i}$$

where r is the interest rate per period. It can be shown that

$$PV = \frac{A}{r} - \frac{A}{r \cdot (1+r)^N} = \frac{A}{r} \cdot \left[1 - \frac{1}{(1+r)^N}\right]$$

and from there it follows that the equal installments each period should be

$$A = \frac{r \cdot (1 + r)^N \cdot PV}{(1 + r)^N - 1}$$

If the annuity is paid for an infinite number of periods (i.e., N is infinity), its present value is

$$PV = \frac{A}{r}$$

7. Based on the equation for A in endnote 6, we have $PV = \$157.47$, $r = 4\%$, $N = 5$, and, therefore, $A = \$35.37$.
8. See also section 2.3 of Chapter 2.
9. It is sometimes difficult to value the market value of debt. Generally, we would take all outstanding bond issues for the company, and multiply the number of units issued by their market price. In some cases, we may substitute the book value.
10. See section 11.1 of Chapter 11 for an introduction to the CAPM.
11. See section 11.1 of Chapter 11.
12. See section 3.6 of Chapter 3.
13. See, for example, the survey by Graham and Harvey (2002).
14. All names and references in this case are fictional, and the situation is simplified on purpose so as to illustrate the main points of this chapter. This case study is based on the case *Reebok International: Strategic Asset Allocation* by Mark Potter, Babson College, 1998. We thank Professor Potter for allowing us to create a version of the case for this example. We also thank Professors Kathleen Hevert and Richard Bliss, Babson College, for providing some of the data and ideas for the simulation application.
15. Under the *straight-line depreciation method*, annual depreciation equals a constant proportion of the initial investment (less salvage value, which here we assume to be 0). In general, including salvage value in the calculations is done for financial reporting purposes. Here, we are concerned with the cash flow impact of taxes. For tax purposes, it is not necessary for firms to include salvage value.
16. Note that the assumption that the market size follows a normal distribution technically does not preclude the possibility that in the process of the simulation, negative numbers for market size would be simulated. (This is because the normal distribution stretches from negative infinity to positive infinity.) In this particular case, we do not need to worry much about this issue because the distance between 18,300 and 0 is approximately 17 standard deviations (where the standard deviation is 1,100). Outcomes that are more than 6 standard deviations from the mean have a miniscule probability of occurring.
17. This kind of assumption—where a range for possible values needs to be selected randomly before the number within that range is selected randomly—is a little

bit more difficult to model than what we have seen so far. The trick is to create a random variable that corresponds to the scenario number drawn (in this case, there are three possible scenarios—one for each range of values) and then base the random number generation on the outcome of this random variable. If we use @RISK in Excel, we can create a cell dedicated to storing the random scenario drawn (cell B31 in worksheet **Simulation**), and then use VLOOKUP to reference that cell and the range of values to which the scenario corresponds when simulating market share in the first year (cell B6).

18. Here, we truncate the normal distribution at 0 because we have a nontrivial probability of generating a negative number for the market share during the simulation if we do not. If the standard deviation is 0.7%, then 0 is approximately two to three standard deviations from the mean of the distribution, and even though the probability of generating a negative number is still small (less than 2.5%), the event is not as unlikely to happen as it was in the case of the projected market size.

19. Similarly to the projected market size for Rapid Bounce, here we are not concerned about truncating the normal distribution so that 0 is the minimum value we can generate. The standard deviation is small relative to the mean value of the normal distribution.

20. See worksheet **Simulation** in the file **Ch17-AirMax.xlsx** and Chapter 4's Software Hints for instructions on how to simulate correlated random variables.

21. See this chapter's Software Hints.

22. Recall that VLOOKUP(Value, Array, ColumnNumber) tries to find Value in the first column of Array, and returns the entry in the same row and in column ColumnNumber.

CHAPTER 18

Real Options

The capital budgeting tools presented in Chapter 17 are widely used and represent the fundamentals of the so-called *discounted cash flow* (DCF) analysis framework for evaluating investment decisions. However, an explicit assumption underlying the DCF framework is that once the decision is made at the beginning, future stages of the project happen as planned. In reality, companies are constantly reevaluating their strategies and modifying their decisions. If cash flows are better than expected, the project may be expanded. If cash flows are worse than expected, the project may be abandoned. Management may decide to postpone the project by a year hoping for better market conditions, or change the input mix in response to changes in the prices of raw materials.

What all of these situations have in common is that the company has *options*—an option to change its course of action in the future, an option to acquire an asset in the future, or an option to delay the project. These options enhance a project's investment value because management has the right, but not the obligation, to take actions in the future. In each case, management can do that because it will have access to information not available at the time of the original decision.

Options in the corporate finance context are referred to as *real options*. In contrast to *financial options*, in which the underlying is a financial instrument or financial index, the underlying in the case of real options is a physical asset. The importance of including real options in financial valuation can be appreciated by realizing that virtually no research-and-development (R&D) project would be undertaken according to the net present value (NPV) criterion (the overall cash flows would be negative), were it not for the option to exploit potential results from the research with follow-up investments. We will see some examples in this chapter.

Pharmaceutical companies embraced real options as a tool early on. This is not surprising because they face such situations all the time. Beginning with a small number of chemical components with the potential to induce the necessary reaction in the human body to cope with a particular illness, only about 1 in 15 eventually shows enough potential to become an actual drug. The drug then needs to undergo a number of stages of clinical tests to achieve Federal Drug Administration (FDA) approval: preclinical testing involving animals, testing on healthy humans to evaluate side effects, and testing on human subjects with the actual illness. The life of such projects is often in the 12- to 15-year range. When the traditional NPV of such projects is evaluated at the beginning, it is often negative, given the small probability that a drug will make it through the process. However, what the traditional NPV does not take into consideration is the fact that at any stage, the company can drop a project that does not appear promising. The company therefore does not need to incur all subsequent costs in the process. Instead of thinking of such projects as a series of cash flows, it is more correct to think of them as a series of options on options. For example, the investment in the study of the chemical components can be thought of as the purchase of an option to develop the drug, the development of the drug can be thought of as the purchase of an option to do preclinical testing, and so forth.

While real options analysis has become a standard tool for many companies' capital budgeting decisions, there are also many that have tried and abandoned the approach. A 2001 "Management Tools and Techniques" survey by Bain & Company of 451 senior executives who had tried the real options approach found that a third of them had given up using it in the same year (Copeland and Tufano 2004). Real option valuation is indeed a challenging undertaking. We will obtain a better intuition about this fact as we discuss examples in this chapter, but most generally, the difficulty stems from the fact that fundamental option pricing formulas from the securities markets, such as the Black-Scholes formula,[1] do not apply exactly to situations in which the underlying securities are not liquid and traded in markets in which no arbitrage can be assumed. Nevertheless, there is widespread recognition of the fact that the insights one can obtain from real options analysis are valuable. Given the fact that financial derivative pricing formulas do not apply easily in the real options framework, however, sensitivity analysis and simulation become even more important tools in this context.

This chapter covers some basic types of real options, such as options to expand, abandon, and wait. The variety of real option types is even greater than the variety of financial options, so we cannot easily cover even all basic types of real options. We focus on a few fundamental applications in order to illustrate the advantages of simulation and dynamic programming techniques for real options valuation. For a recent treatment of the subject and more examples, see also Moore (2008), Finnerty (2008), and Mun (2006).

18.1 TYPES OF REAL OPTIONS

Real options can most generally be divided into the following types:

- Option to expand
- Option to abandon
- Option to delay
- Option to choose
- Option to switch
- Option for sequential investments

Let us consider some examples:

- *Option to expand or abandon.* When considering an acquisition, management thinks not only about the cash flows that are generated from the operations of the company to be acquired, but also about the strategic advantages that come with the deal. Suppose that the company to be acquired owns the intellectual property on a new technology, but it needs development funding. If the new technology is highly successful, buying the company and investing capital into development will provide the acquiring company the option to expand into further profitable areas. If the new technology is not successful, the acquiring company will have the option to abandon the project at some point in the development phase, and perhaps sell off any remaining tangible assets of the acquired company.
- *Option to delay.* Consider an American company that needs to forecast demand for equipment it produces months in advance, so that it can have sufficient time to order the parts, assemble them, and ship them to its customers in Europe. Management could consider the project of building assembly plants in Europe, so that it can do assembly there and reduce the risks associated with its forecasts. While building assembly plants in Europe will incur costs, an evaluation of the overall costs and benefits of the project the company should include the value of the option that building these plants will give the company—the option to delay making the decision on how much equipment to produce until demand is known better. In other words, the cost of acquiring an option to delay production is the cost of building the assembly plants in Europe, and the benefits from holding the option are the savings associated with not having to forecast demand too far in advance.
- *Option to choose.* Consider a company like Boeing that has a huge amount of development costs and many years of development for its

product. The company can only produce a limited number of models at a time, and cannot afford to be wrong about the type of aircraft it should be building. Such a company benefits from creating an option to choose by investing in several promising projects at the same time and running them in parallel, with the goal of eliminating all but one at the end. This way, the company can evaluate the merits and the drawbacks of each version of the product as more information becomes available over time, and learn from product prototypes even if they do not become the model it produces in the end. The cost of the option to choose is the development cost of the parallel projects, and the benefit is the hedge this strategy provides against choosing the wrong direction at the beginning.

- *Option to switch.* Consider a company in the oil and gas industry. The management of such a company may consider a project to invest in making its refineries more flexible with respect to output. Outputs include heating oil, diesel, or different kinds of fuel. This project will give the company the option to switch its output to one that is more profitable depending on prevailing market prices.

  Similarly, a company may vary its input mix in order to minimize the impact of market prices of raw materials on its operations. For example, a company may hold an inventory of excess raw materials (thus increasing inventory costs), or maintain excess contractual obligations with multiple vendors for similar materials in different parts of the world, so that it can switch vendors when a particular raw material becomes relatively expensive in that part of the world.

- *Option for sequential investments.* The pharmaceutical company that invests in the research and development (R&D) of a new drug is an example of a company that creates options for sequential investment. At each stage of the project, the company's management has the option to wait, abandon, or expand into subsequent stages. Thus, an R&D project that may appear unprofitable according to the NPV criterion could in fact be profitable because the options to defer costs and proceed only if the current stage is promising create additional value for the project.

18.2   REAL OPTIONS AND FINANCIAL OPTIONS

There are many similarities between real options and financial options. For example, the profile of a typical option to expand looks very much like the profile of a long position in a classical financial call option.[2] Specifically, it is often the case that a company pays a setup cost for the option to acquire a larger project, or expand, in the future. This setup cost is equivalent to paying the premium on a call option—the option to purchase an asset at a predetermined (strike) price in the future. The estimated current value of this future expansion project is today's "stock price" in the classical option pricing framework. Over time, the value of the project may change depending on market conditions and the company's strategy. In the future, management may choose to expand if the immediate cost of doing so (paying the "strike price") is lower than the value of the project at the future date. Note that the company will not have the obligation to expand, and will expand only of the conditions are favorable. The maximum loss incurred by the company would be the value of the premium of the call option.

Similarly, the profile of a typical option to abandon looks very much like the profile of a long position in a classical financial put option.[3] Namely, a company may invest money into a project today (which is equivalent to paying the premium on a put option). If in the future the estimated benefit of continuing the project (equivalent to the future "stock price") is less than the estimated cost of continuing with the project (equivalent to the "strike price"), then the company's management can exercise the option to abandon the project. Again, the maximum loss the company can incur is the value of the premium for acquiring the option.

Sequential investment decisions such as R&D are best understood as compound options, that is, options on options. Other types of real options have their own interpretations, as we will see later in this chapter. The takeaway from this discussion is that, given the many parallels between real options and financial options, we should be able to tap into the large amount of research on pricing financial options to value investment projects as well. In fact, the Black-Scholes option pricing formula[4] and binomial trees are widely used for real option valuation.

However, it is important to keep in mind that there are limitations in applying financial option pricing methods for valuing real options. These limitations include:

- The underlying asset for a financial option is a publicly traded asset, and its market value is observable. The underlying asset for a real option is typically a physical asset, such as a plant or a resource deposit, and its value is not readily available. Real options are therefore inherently proprietary in nature, with no market comparables.
- Financial options typically have short maturities. Real options have multiyear durations.
- Financial options have clearly spelled out exercise features. This is not the case for real options, where there is flexibility with respect to the timing and nature of exercise of the option, and therefore additional assumptions must be made for the purposes of valuing the real option.

- The value of financial options cannot be manipulated by the trader because the prices of financial options are driven by the value of the underlying, which in turn is determined by exogenous market forces. In contrast, the value of strategic real options can be changed by timing, management actions, and flexibility.
- As we explained in Chapter 13, a fundamental principle underlying financial option pricing is the assumption that no arbitrage exists in the markets. This condition allowed us to price financial options as the expected values (under risk-neutral probabilities) of their future payoffs at the risk-free rate. Given the fact that the underlying asset is not traded in the case of real options, the no-arbitrage condition does not hold exactly, so it is not clear if the same principle can be applied. It is applied in practice for lack of a better method, but one needs to exercise caution in interpreting the results.
- Given our discussion in the previous item, there is no easy way to determine the rate appropriate for discounting the cash flows from real options. The conclusion that we should use the risk-free rate when discounting cash flows from financial options came from the assumption of no-arbitrage. This principle does not quite hold in the case of real options. We will discuss this issue further in section 18.7.1.

Some real options are directly valued by adjusting financial option pricing methods. Others require more creative modeling. Since the focus of this book is on applications of simulation and optimization in finance, we will give examples mainly of real options that allow for pricing using simulation or optimization (dynamic programming) techniques. For further examples, see, for instance, Mun (2006).

18.3 NEW VIEW OF NPV

As the concept of real options became widespread, some economists began referring to the traditional NPV as the *neoclassical NPV*.[5] In other words, NPV is the value of a project assuming there is no flexibility and no optionality. If we add the present value of all options inherent in the project to NPV, we obtain NPV*—the total value of the project, including options. We may think of NPV* as a "postmodern" NPV. The decision rule for evaluating project that we associate with NPV* is the same as the decision rule we associate with NPV—if NPV* is greater than 0, we should accept the project; otherwise we should reject it. Similarly, if we are considering several projects and there is capital rationing, the project with the highest

NPV* should be selected. The only difference is that NPV* reflects project potential more fully than NPV.

Is the traditional NPV bad? Not necessarily. As with any model, NPV is good as long as the underlying assumptions hold. And, as we will see in this chapter, the valuation of the options embedded in projects can be challenging and not very accurate. Hence, it is valuable to have an estimate of the traditional NPV. If it is negative, we could interpret the amount it takes to make it zero as the minimum amount at which we should value the flexibility in order to make the project worthwhile. The NPV method still provides the framework within which to evaluate the overall profitability of the project.

Let us consider a simple example to illustrate this point. Management is evaluating the opportunity to invest in an R&D project for a new product. The life of the project is four years, and the costs are $1.2 million per year. After the end of the R&D project (in year 5), the management can spend an additional $10 million to launch the product, and the expected NPV of the cash flows from that point on (in year 5 dollars) is $21 million. Assume that the risk-free rate is 5% per year and that the discount rate is 14%. (For consistency, assume that both are continuously compounded.) Should the company invest in the R&D project?

Exhibit 18.1 contains a snapshot of worksheet **Classical NPV** of the file **Ch18-ExpansionAbandonOptions.xlsx,** in which the classical NPV is computed. The costs for each year are listed in cells B7:F7. The revenue of $21 million (in year 5 dollars) is shown in cell F8. To compute the NPV, we discount the costs and the revenues to the present by multiplying each cash flow by $e^{-r \cdot t}$, where r is the applicable discount rate, and t is the time period in which the cash flow happens. Since the costs are certain cash flows (we will definitely spend them), and the revenues are uncertain cash flows, we use the risk-free interest rate of 5% to discount the costs, and the discount rate of 14% to discount the revenues.[6] The discounted costs and revenues are shown in cells B10:F11. For example, the discounted value of the revenues in year 5 is $e^{-0.14 \cdot 5} \cdot (\$21) = \$10.43$ million, and the discounted value of the costs in year 5 is $e^{-0.05 \cdot 5} \cdot (\$10) = \$7.79$ million.

The sum of all discounted cash flows results in an NPV of –$1.6 million. Since the NPV is negative, the company should technically not invest in the R&D project. However, this valuation omits a very important detail. The NPV is computed with the information we have currently. The revenues in year 5 are a rough estimate. That estimate can change a lot during the four years of R&D. For example, the R&D stage may not result in a viable product. If the projected value of future revenues falls, the company may decide, at the end of the R&D project, that it is not worthwhile to spend the additional $10 million to launch the product. Additionally, the company

	A	B	C	D	E	F
1	R&D project					
2						
3	Risk-free rate	5.00%				
4	Discount rate	14.00%				
5						
6	Time (yrs)	1	2	3	4	5
7	Costs ($m)	$1.20	$1.20	$1.20	$1.20	$10.00
8	Revenues ($m)					$21.00
9						
10	PV Costs ($m)	$1.14	$1.09	$1.03	$0.98	$7.79
11	PV Revenues ($m)	$0.00	$0.00	$0.00	$0.00	$10.43
12	PV Cash flows ($m)	-$1.14	-$1.09	-$1.03	-$0.98	$2.64
13						
14	NPV	-$1.60				

EXHIBIT 18.1 Calculation of classical NPV.

may have the option to abandon the project while it is still in development in years 1 through 4.

The NPV that takes into consideration this flexibility, NPV*, can be computed. It will be higher than the NPV. If NPV* is greater than 0, this is an argument for investing in the R&D project. We will discuss the valuation method in section 18.4.

18.4 OPTION TO EXPAND

Let us consider again the example in the previous section. Suppose that after the company invests in R&D for four years, management has the option to proceed with the next stage (product launch) at a cost of $10 million, or not proceed. How much is this option worth?

In order to estimate the value of this option, we need to make some assumptions on how the estimated value of future revenues from the product will change between today and year 5. Suppose that the company estimates, based on experience with similar products in the past, that there is a 10% chance that the R&D project will result in a viable product, and bring in a revenue of $210 million (in year 5 dollars), but that there is a 90% chance that the R&D project will be a failure, and will not bring in any revenue. It is not difficult to see that the expected value of the future revenue is $(10\%) \cdot (\$210) + (90\%) \cdot (\$0) = \$21$ million, as in the example in the previous section.

However, note that if the R&D part of the project is a failure, the company does not have to spend $10 million to launch the product. In this case, the company would realize nothing in future revenues.

We can think of the $10 million as the strike price of a European call option, and the future revenue estimate in year 5 as the price of the underlying. Management will only exercise the option if the price of the underlying is higher than the strike price. There are only two possible states of the world in the future, and the discounted payoff of the option is

$$e^{-0.05\cdot 5} \cdot (0.10 \cdot \max\{\$210 - \$10, \ \$0\} + 0.90 \cdot \max\{\$0 - \$10, \ \$0\})$$
$$= \$15.58 \text{ million.}^7$$

The value of the option is very high because there the volatility of the future cash flows is high.[8]

The present value of the remaining cash flows for the project (the costs incurred in years 1–4) equals

$$\$1.2 \cdot e^{-0.05\cdot 4} + \$1.2 \cdot e^{-0.05\cdot 4} + \$1.2 \cdot e^{-0.05\cdot 4} + \$1.2 \cdot e^{-0.05\cdot 4} = \$4.24$$

Therefore, the NPV taking into consideration optionality, NPV*, equals

$$\$15.58 - \$4.24 = \$11.34 \text{ million}$$

Since NPV* is positive, the project should be considered for funding.

The example we gave was very simple—we assumed that the project value in the future can be either $210 million or zero with certain probabilities. We could assume a more complex process for the random variable that is the value of the project between time 0 and time 5. For example, we can assume that it follows a geometric random walk. If this is the case, we can value the real option by using the Black-Scholes formula for European call options. Suppose the volatility of the process is 35%. (We will talk more about estimating volatility in section 18.7.2.) The strike price is $10 million. What about the initial price? For the initial price, we use the present value of the project discounted at the cost of capital (14%), that is, $10.43. The risk-free rate is assumed to be 5%, as before. According to the Black-Scholes formula, the value of the real option is $4.27 million. (See Exhibit 18.2 and worksheet **Expansion B-S Price** in the file **Ch18-ExpansionAbandonOptions.xlsx**.) Based on this estimate, it is worthwhile to invest in the R&D project, but only barely—NPV* equals $4.27 – $4.24 (the present value of the costs in years 1–4) = $0.03 million.

	A	B	C
1	R&D project with option to expand		
2			
3	Initial price	$10.43	
4	Strike price	$10.00	
5	Time to expiration	5	
6	Interest rate	5.00%	
7	Volatility	35%	
8	Dividend yield	0	
9			
10	d1	0.7643	
11	d2	-0.0183	
12	Φ(d1)	0.7777	
13	Φ(d2)	0.4927	
14			
15	Call price	$ 4.27	
16			

EXHIBIT 18.2 Valuation of the option to expand using the Black-Scholes formula for European call options.

It is very important to conduct sensitivity analysis and determine how influenced the option price is by our assumption about the volatility of the project. Exhibit 18.3 contains a data table with the price of the real option for different values for the volatility. We can see that the option price estimates for NPV* around the current value for volatility (35%) are very unstable—they go from positive to negative with a small change in the volatility parameter. Therefore, the fact that NPV* is positive is not by itself a reason to undertake the project.

Finally, recall from Chapter 13 that we can use simulation to price the call option. The advantage of using simulation is that we can assume different processes for the price of the underlying (in this case, the value of the project). If we assume that the underlying follows a geometric random walk with volatility 35%, we should obtain the same estimate for the price of the option (or very close) as the estimate we obtained with the Black-Scholes formula. To implement the simulation, we treat the present value of the project, $10.43 million (obtained as $21 million discounted at a rate equal to the cost of capital, i.e., 14%) as the initial price of the underlying. We then simulate the price of the underlying five years from now using

EXHIBIT 18.3 Sensitivity of the value of the expansion option to the volatility estimate.

Volatility	Option Price ($m)	NPV* ($m)
10%	$2.73	−$1.51
15%	$2.96	−$1.28
20%	$3.26	−$0.98
25%	$3.58	−$0.66
30%	$3.93	−$0.31
35%	$4.27	$0.03
40%	$4.62	$0.38
45%	$4.96	$0.72
50%	$5.30	$1.06
55%	$5.63	$1.39
60%	$5.94	$1.70
65%	$6.25	$2.01
70%	$6.55	$2.31
75%	$6.83	$2.59
80%	$7.11	$2.87

the formula for the geometric random walk. We computed the drift of the geometric random walk as the risk-free rate of 5% minus one half of the volatility squared, but the value of the drift may need to be adjusted. (See section 18.7.) In some situations, it may be more appropriate to assume a mean-reverting process or a specific probability distribution for the value of the project in five years.

18.5   OPTION TO ABANDON

Let us consider a slightly different example of a development project in order to illustrate how a real option to abandon the current course of action translates into owning a put option, and increases the value of a project. Consider a pharmaceutical company (Company A) that owns a patent and is trying to develop a drug based on that patent. The patent has 10 years remaining, and so the life of the project is 10 years. Company A is spending $50 million in year 0 to build a new research facility for the drug development project, and $2.5 per year in years 1 and 2. The development is expected to end at the end of year 2, and the drug is expected to generate $8 million per year from year 3 onwards. At the end of year 2, Company A has the option to reevaluate its investment. It has entered into a contract

	A	B	C	D	E	F	G	H	I	J	K	L
1	Development project											
2												
3	Risk-free rate	5.00%										
4	Discount rate	10.00%										
5												
6	Time (yrs)	0	1	2	3	4	5	6	7	8	9	10
7	Costs ($m)	$50.00	$2.50	$2.50	$0.00	$0.00	$0.00	$0.00	$0.00	$0.00	$0.00	$0.00
8	Revenues ($m)	$0.00	$0.00	$0.00	$8.00	$8.00	$8.00	$8.00	$8.00	$8.00	$8.00	$8.00
9												
10	PV Costs ($m)	$50.00	$2.26	$2.05	$0.00	$0.00	$0.00	$0.00	$0.00	$0.00	$0.00	$0.00
11	PV Revenues ($m)	$0.00	$0.00	$0.00	$5.93	$5.36	$4.85	$4.39	$3.97	$3.59	$3.25	$2.94
12	PV Cash flows ($m)	-$50.00	-$2.26	-$2.05	$5.93	$5.36	$4.85	$4.39	$3.97	$3.59	$3.25	$2.94
13												
14	NPV	-$20.01										

EXHIBIT 18.4   Classical NPV of drug development project (worksheet **Abandon** in the file **Ch18-ExpansionAbandonOptions.xlsx**).

with another pharmaceutical company (Company B) that lets Company A sell its intellectual property and research facility to Company B in year 3 for a salvage value of $70 million if the development process is not going as well as planned. What is this option worth?

Exhibit 18.4 illustrates the different cash flows and the NPV of the project without considering optionality. Both costs and revenues are discounted at the cost of capital, 10%. The NPV of the project is −$20.01 million.

At the end of year 2, Company A can sell the project for a salvage value of $70 million. The present value of all revenues in year 3 and onward is the sum of the values in cells E11:L11, which is $34.29 million. Thus, Company A owns a put option to sell an asset with initial value of $34.29 million for $70 million two years from now. We can use the Black-Scholes put option pricing formula to value this option (see Exhibit 18.5). The value obtained from the formula is $30.21 million.

Therefore, it is worthwhile to invest in the drug development project. We can obtain a similar estimate by simulating the value of the future cash flows at the end of year 2 (assuming that the total value follows a geometric random walk).

18.6   MORE REAL OPTIONS EXAMPLES

The real option examples we considered in sections 18.4 and 18.5 were very basic. Most real life projects are more complicated, and the Black-Scholes formula is not as useful. In this section, to give a flavor of the variety of real option models, we discuss an example of a timing option that takes

	A	B
1	Project with option to abandon	
2		
3	Initial price	$34.29
4	Strike price	$70.00
5	Time to expiration	2
6	Interest rate	5.00%
7	Volatility	35%
8	Dividend yield	0
9		
10	d1	-0.9920
11	d2	-1.4870
12	Φ(-d1)	0.8394
13	Φ(-d2)	0.9315
14		
15	Put price	$ 30.21
16		

EXHIBIT 18.5 Valuation of the option to abandon the development project with the Black-Scholes put option pricing formula (worksheet **Abandon B-S Price** in the file **Ch18-ExpansionAbandonOptions.xlsx**).

advantage of simulation to value a project, as well as examples of projects that are of a multiperiod nature. Binomial trees[9] can be applied in the latter context because they allow for greater flexibility in modeling the continuous nature of adjustments in investment decisions. Dynamic programming is then used to determine the optimal strategy given some assumptions about the way the underlying process behaves.

18.6.1 Project to Abandon or Expand

Let us consider a variation on the project described in section 18.4. Suppose that, as before, the company's management has the option to invest $10 million in the project in year 5, or not invest. However, suppose also that management has the additional flexibility of abandoning the project in any of years 1 through 4 if it is not satisfied with the direction of the project.

We therefore have two implicit options to value: (1) a European call option with a maturity of five years, as before and (2) an American put option with a maturity of four years. To value them together, we create a binomial tree for the process followed by the estimated value of the revenues starting in year 5.

As explained in section 18.4, the present value of the estimated cash flows of the project (discounted at the cost of capital, 14%) is \$10.43 million. We assume that the volatility of the project (σ) is 35% and the risk-free rate (r) is 5%, and construct a recombining binomial tree in which the value of the project each year is expected to go up or down by certain multipliers (u and d) with certain probabilities (p and $1 - p$). These parameters can be found from our assumptions about the volatility of the process and the time increment.[10] We have:

$r = 0.05.$

$\Delta t = 1$ year.

$\sigma = 0.35.$

Discount factor for each time period $df = e^{-r \cdot \Delta t} = 0.9512.$

$u = e^{\sigma \cdot \sqrt{\Delta t}} = e^{0.35 \cdot \sqrt{1}} = 1.42.$

$d = e^{-\sigma \cdot \sqrt{\Delta t}} = e^{-0.35 \cdot \sqrt{1}} = 0.70.$

$p = \dfrac{e^{r \cdot (\Delta t)} - d}{u - d} = 48.52\%.$

The binomial tree with the values of the project for years 1 through 5 is shown in Exhibit 18.6.

	A	B	C	D	E	F	G
9	Project value						
10	time period	0	1	2	3	4	5
11	0	\$10.43	\$14.80	\$21.00	\$29.80	\$42.29	\$60.01
12	1		\$7.35	\$10.43	\$14.80	\$21.00	\$29.80
13	2			\$5.18	\$7.35	\$10.43	\$14.80
14	3				\$3.65	\$5.18	\$7.35
15	4					\$2.57	\$3.65
16	5						\$1.81

EXHIBIT 18.6 Binomial tree for the process followed by the value of future revenues (worksheet **Expansion and Abandon** in the file Ch18-ExpansionAbandonOptions.xlsx).

	A	B	C	D	E	F	G
27	Value with						
28	abandonment	0	1	2	3	4	5
29	0	$1.57	$3.41	$9.28	$18.41	$31.58	$50.01
30	1		$0.00	$0.67	$4.04	$10.29	$19.80
31	2			$0.00	$0.00	$1.01	$4.80
32	3				$0.00	$0.00	$0.00
33	4					$0.00	$0.00
34	5						$0.00
35							

EXHIBIT 18.7 Valuation of the real option to expand in year 5 or abandon in years 1–4 (worksheet **Expansion and Abandon** in the file Ch18-ExpansionAbandonOptions.xlsx).

The value of the project with the option to abandon at any time between 1 and 4 or expand at time 5 can be computed by using dynamic programming. The results are presented in Exhibit 18.7.

We start at the last time period, year 5. The value at each node can be computed as the maximum of the difference between the project value at that node (Exhibit 18.6) and the "strike price" of $10 million to expand. For example, in cell G29, we compute the maximum of ($60.01 – $10) million and 0, which is $50.01 million. In cell G32, we compute the maximum of ($7.35 – $10) million and 0, which is 0.

At the previous step (year 4), we have the option to abandon the project if the expected value of continuing is less than the value of abandoning, which carries a value of 0. The expected value of continuing is the cost of $1.2 million plus the discounted value of the expected payoffs in the next time period. For example, in cell F30, we compute

$$\max\left\{0, \; -\$1.2 + 0.9512 \cdot (0.4852 \cdot \$50.01 + (1 - 0.4852) \cdot \$19.80\right\}$$

which equals $31.58 million. At this node, it is optimal to continue. We proceed backwards through the tree until we reach time 0. At that time, the value of the node is simply

$$0.9512 \cdot (0.4852 \cdot \$3.41 + (1 - 0.4852) \cdot \$0 = \$1.57 \text{ million}$$

If we did not have the option to abandon the project during years 1 through 4, the value of the project would have been $0.13 million (see

	A	B	C	D	E	F	G
18	Value without						
19	abandonment	0	1	2	3	4	5
20		0	$0.13	$3.09	$9.28	$18.41	$31.58	$50.01
21		1		-$2.64	$0.02	$4.04	$10.29	$19.80
22		2			-$2.96	-$1.32	$1.01	$4.80
23		3				-$2.34	-$1.20	$0.00
24		4					-$1.20	$0.00
25		5						$0.00
26								

EXHIBIT 18.8 Valuation of the real option to expand without the option to abandon (worksheet **Expansion and Abandon** in the file Ch18-ExpansionAbandonOptions.xlsx).

Exhibit 18.8 and worksheet **Expansion and Abandon** in the file **Ch18-ExpansionAbandonOptions.xlsx**). This is because instead of computing the maximum value of continuing or abandoning at each node, we would have been forced to continue. Having the option to abandon increases the value of the project.

18.6.2 Valuing an Option to Wait

There is a wide variety of situations in which real option models apply, and oftentimes there is a lot of flexibility as to how management can model its choices. In this section, we present a simulation model for estimating the value of the choice to wait or execute today. See Moore (2008) for a more general principle for valuing timing options over multiple periods that involves the profitability index.[11]

We use a classical example introduced in Titman (1985).[12] Suppose we are considering buying a parcel of land that has been zoned for multifamily housing. The size of the lot is such that we can use it either for a two-story building, or for a three-story building. Each building can have three units per floor. A two-story building will therefore have six apartments, whereas a three-story building will have nine apartments. Taller buildings are more expensive because of additional foundation and elevator costs. It will cost $80,000 to build a unit in a six-unit building, and $90,000 to build a unit in a nine-unit building. The current market value of each unit is $100,000.

We also have the option to time the development. We can either build the building this year (as soon as we buy the land), or wait until next year. The question is, how much should we be willing to pay for the land, and what is the optimal policy?

If we build this year, the optimal strategy is easy to calculate. The six-unit building will bring in profit of

$$6 \cdot (\$100,000 - \$80,000) = \$120,000$$

The nine-unit building will bring in profit of

$$9 \cdot (\$100,000 - \$90,000) = \$90,000$$

Therefore, we should build the six-unit building, and we should be willing to pay up to \$120,000 for the land.

If we wait until next year, the market price of a unit is likely to change. For simplicity, however, we assume that the building costs will stay the same. In order to estimate whether it makes sense to wait, we need to make assumptions on the process followed by the market price of the unit. Suppose that apartment prices follow a geometric random walk. Next year, they are expected to be 5% higher on average, but the volatility in real estate prices has been about 35%. Suppose also that the risk-free rate is 3% per year.

To value the *option* to build and sell the units, we assume that the market price of the unit grows at the risk-free rate. We can compute the market price of a unit next year with the formula

$$S_1 = (\$100,000) \cdot e^{(0.03 - \frac{1}{2} \cdot 0.35^2 + 0.35 \cdot \tilde{\varepsilon})}$$

where $\tilde{\varepsilon}$ is a standard normal random variable. We will build as many units as are optimal in a year, that is, the number of units that results in the maximum profit given the market price of a unit in a year. In fact, if the market price of a unit is such that we would realize a loss by building any number of units, we can choose to not build for a profit of 0.

We also need to discount the profit in year 1 in order to value the real option and to make sure that we have a fair comparison with the profit in year 1. We have the following expression for the discounted profit if we wait a year:

$$e^{-0.03 \cdot 1} \cdot \max \left\{ 6 \cdot (S_1 - 80,000), 9 \cdot (S_1 - 90,000), 0 \right\}$$

After simulating 10,000 paths for the market price of a unit in a year, we obtain the output in Exhibit 18.9.[13] Therefore, the value of waiting to develop for a year is approximately \$193,094.49. This number is higher than the profit that would be obtained by developing immediately (\$120,000), and is in fact the estimate we should use to determine how much we should

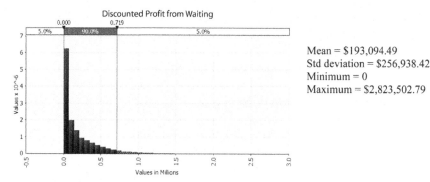

EXHIBIT 18.9 Simulation output for the discounted profit from waiting to develop the land for a year.

be willing to pay for the land. Having the flexibility to wait increases the value of the project.

18.6.3 Valuing a Multiperiod Real Estate Project

Many projects require modeling the price of a commodity or the level of an index. Such variables determine the cash flows of the project, and change with market conditions. Examples include multistage oil field development (Smit 1997), in which the profitability of operations is determined by the market price of oil, and gold mine exploitation,[14] which depends on the price of gold (Luenberger 1998 and Winston 2000). Let us consider a real estate example related to the example in section 18.6.2, but over multiple years. The underlying variable is an index of property values. A real estate developer is considering investing in land that can be used for condominium development. The life of the project is 10 years. Every year, the developer can build and sell up to three condominiums. The cost of a single condominium is $250,000, and the current selling price for a single condominium is $350,000. How much should the developer be willing to pay for the land? Note that the developer has the option not to build condominiums in any particular year in which the cost of building them is greater than the market value at which they can be sold.

We have the following additional information. The value of the real estate index in year 0 is 1893, and past data indicate an annual drift of 10.30% and a volatility of 5.90%. Building costs have been increasing at a relatively constant rate of 5.53% per year. We assume that the market price for the condominiums is perfectly correlated with the price of the real estate index.

	A	B	C	D	E	F	G	H	I	J	K	L
9	Index value											
10	time period	0	1	2	3	4	5	6	7	8	9	10
11	0	1893.00	2008.05	2130.09	2259.54	2396.87	2542.54	2697.06	2860.98	3034.85	3219.30	3414.95
12	1		1784.54	1893.00	2008.05	2130.09	2259.54	2396.87	2542.54	2697.06	2860.98	3034.85
13	2			1682.30	1784.54	1893.00	2008.05	2130.09	2259.54	2396.87	2542.54	2697.06
14	3				1585.92	1682.30	1784.54	1893.00	2008.05	2130.09	2259.54	2396.87
15	4					1495.05	1585.92	1682.30	1784.54	1893.00	2008.05	2130.09
16	5						1409.40	1495.05	1585.92	1682.30	1784.54	1893.00
17	6							1328.65	1409.40	1495.05	1585.92	1682.30
18	7								1252.53	1328.65	1409.40	1495.05
19	8									1180.77	1252.53	1328.65
20	9										1113.12	1180.77
21	10											1049.34

EXHIBIT 18.10 Binomial tree for the process followed by the real estate index.

Based on this information, we can create a binomial tree for the process followed by the index level over the next 10 years:

$r = 0.03.$

$\Delta t = 1$ year.

$\sigma = 0.059.$

Discount factor for each time period $df = e^{-r \cdot \Delta t} = 0.9704.$

$u = e^{\sigma \cdot \sqrt{\Delta t}} = e^{0.059 \cdot \sqrt{1}} = 1.06.$

$d = e^{-\sigma \cdot \sqrt{\Delta t}} = e^{-0.059 \cdot \sqrt{1}} = 0.94.$

$p = \dfrac{e^{r \cdot (\Delta t)} - d}{u - d} = 74.32\%.$

The tree for the index levels is shown in Exhibit 18.10. The corresponding tree for the revenues from selling three condos per year, as well as the costs of building three condos per year, are shown in Exhibit 18.11.[15]

	A	B	C	D	E	F	G	H	I	J	K	L
24	Condo revenues	0	1	2	3	4	5	6	7	8	9	10
25	0	1125.00	1193.37	1265.90	1342.83	1424.45	1511.02	1602.85	1700.26	1803.60	1913.21	2029.49
26	1		1060.55	1125.00	1193.37	1265.90	1342.83	1424.45	1511.02	1602.85	1700.26	1803.60
27	2			999.78	1060.55	1125.00	1193.37	1265.90	1342.83	1424.45	1511.02	1602.85
28	3				942.50	999.78	1060.55	1125.00	1193.37	1265.90	1342.83	1424.45
29	4					888.50	942.50	999.78	1060.55	1125.00	1193.37	1265.90
30	5						837.60	888.50	942.50	999.78	1060.55	1125.00
31	6							789.61	837.60	888.50	942.50	999.78
32	7								744.37	789.61	837.60	888.50
33	8									701.72	744.37	789.61
34	9										661.52	701.72
35	10											623.62
36												
37	Costs	0	1	2	3	4	5	6	7	8	9	10
38		$0.00	$792.64	$837.71	$885.34	$935.68	$988.88	$1,045.11	$1,104.53	$1,167.33	$1,233.70	$1,303.85

EXHIBIT 18.11 Binomial tree for the revenues and costs associated with building and selling three condos per year.

We are now ready to compute the value of the option to develop the land (see Exhibit 18.12). At every node, except at time 0, the developer will build three condos only if the price of building them exceeds the cost of building them in that particular year (based on the data in Exhibit 18.11). For example, at the first node in year 10 (cell L42), the value of the project is the maximum of the revenues minus the costs, or 0:

$$\max\{\$2029.49 - \$1303.85, 0\} = \$725.64$$

For the second node in year 10 (cell L43), we have

$$\max\{\$1803.60 - \$1303.85, 0\} = \$499.75$$

Going backwards through the tree, at each node we record the reward from being at that node,[16] which is the maximum of the profit the developer can achieve at that node and 0, as well as the discounted expected value of the profit from that node on. For example, at the first node in year 9 (cell K42), we have

$$\max\{\$1,913.21 - \$1,233.70, 0\} + 0.9704 \cdot (0.7432 \cdot \$725.64$$
$$+ (1 - 0.7432) \cdot 499.75) = \$1,327.41$$

The value of the land with the flexibility to develop or not develop in any particular year (cell B42) is $2,652.83 thousand (i.e., $2,652,830). The developer should be willing to pay up to this amount for the land.

It is useful to do some sensitivity analysis to figure out if this estimate is very sensitive to assumptions we have made about different input parameters. For example, a data table can be created that references the estimated value of the project, and computes it based on different estimates of the

	A	B	C	D	E	F	G	H	I	J	K	L
40	Value of option											
41	to develop	0	1	2	3	4	5	6	7	8	9	10
42	0	$2,652.83	$3,055.18	$3,047.77	$2,998.27	$2,898.69	$2,740.37	$2,514.13	$2,210.22	$1,818.31	$1,327.41	$725.64
43	1		$1,803.05	$1,830.98	$1,834.30	$1,806.32	$1,739.38	$1,624.98	$1,453.82	$1,216.07	$901.52	$499.75
44	2			$861.07	$885.72	$896.82	$889.20	$856.48	$790.88	$683.21	$523.02	$299.00
45	3				$241.52	$255.62	$265.55	$268.82	$261.95	$240.02	$196.12	$120.60
46	4					$0.00	$0.00	$0.00	$0.00	$0.00	$0.00	$0.00
47	5						$0.00	$0.00	$0.00	$0.00	$0.00	$0.00
48	6							$0.00	$0.00	$0.00	$0.00	$0.00
49	7								$0.00	$0.00	$0.00	$0.00
50	8									$0.00	$0.00	$0.00
51	9										$0.00	$0.00
52	10											$0.00

EXHIBIT 18.12 Value of the project with flexibility to develop or not develop each year.

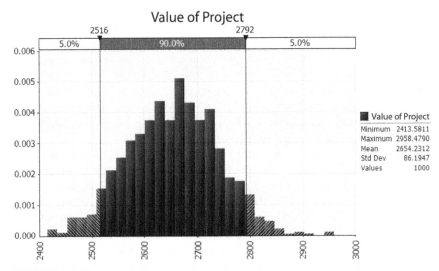

EXHIBIT 18.13 Variability in project value as the cost estimate varies.

volatility in the process for the property value index level. Finally, additional simulation and scenario analysis can be done. For example, so far, we assumed that costs every year are growing at a constant rate. It is possible, however, that there is some variability in our estimate. We can use simulation to determine the effect of the variability in costs on the variability in the estimated value of the project. For example, suppose that our estimate of the costs in each year has a standard deviation of 3.40% of the current value. (This is consistent with historical observed volatility in the building cost index.) What is the resulting variability in the estimated project value?

Exhibit 18.13 shows the distribution of possible project values for 1,000 generated scenarios for the costs over 10 years.[17] We can see that 90% of the time, the project value can be expected to be between $2,516,000 and $2,792,000.

18.7 ESTIMATION OF INPUTS FOR REAL OPTION VALUATION MODELS

An overview of real option valuation is not complete without a discussion of how important parameters, such as the discount rate and the volatility, are estimated.

18.7.1 Discount Rate

As explained in Chapter 17, the discount rate commonly used for computing the classical NPV is the WACC. (As we mentioned earlier in this chapter, however, different cash flows in a project can be discounted using different discount rates, depending on their perceived risk.) Determining a good estimate of the WACC for calculating "pure" NPV with no optionality can itself be problematic because it is based on evaluating the risk of similar projects, and many of these projects have their own options.

Finding the appropriate discount rate for the purposes of real option valuation has its own issues. As we mentioned in section 18.2, financial options are priced by discounting the cash flows from the options at the risk-free rate. This is not quite the appropriate rate to use in pricing real options, however, because the concept of no-arbitrage and the idea of a risk-neutral world do not exactly apply in this context. If we use the risk-free rate to discount the cash flows relevant for the valuation for the real option, we may end up with an overly optimistic estimate of the real option value. Several adjustments are made in practice:

1. An artificially inflated discount rate is applied to cash flows impacting the real option value, so that the real option value is reduced. This method can be very subjective, and difficult to apply. A theoretically justified approach for inflating the discount rate is discussed next, but it can only be applied in circumstances in which we have historical data on the process followed by the underlying asset for the real option and a strongly correlated traded asset.
2. It can be shown[18] that under certain assumptions, the appropriate risk-adjusted rate to use so that options are priced correctly even if we cannot talk about a risk-neutral world is

$$\mu - \lambda \cdot \sigma$$

where μ and σ are the drift and the volatility of the process followed by the underlying, respectively, and is λ the market price of risk. In other words, if we assume that the rate of growth of the underlying asset is $\mu - \lambda \cdot \sigma$ (which equals the asset's rate of growth μ adjusted downward by $\lambda \cdot \sigma$), and then discount the cash flows at the risk-free rate, we can price the real option correctly.

The *market price of risk* is related to the excess return of a traded asset over the risk-free rate r_{rf}; in other words,

$$\mu - r_{rf} = \lambda \cdot \sigma$$

If we have historical data on a traded asset and a nontraded variable (e.g., company sales), we can do the following to estimate the market price of risk for company sales:

A. Estimate the coefficient of correlation ρ between the returns on the traded asset and the percentage changes in the nontraded variable.

B. Estimate the volatility of returns of the market, σ_M. (This is usually done by estimating the volatility of a broad stock market index.)

C. Estimate the expected return on the market, r_M.

D. Find the short-term risk-free rate, r_{rf}.

E. Compute the market price of risk of the nontraded variable as

$$\lambda = \frac{\rho}{\sigma_M} \cdot (r_M - r_{rf})$$

3. Sometimes, to adjust the value of the real option downward, the price of the real option is reduced by the price of a put option.[19] The idea is that since the underlying asset in the real option is not tradable, it cannot be sold to realize its assumed value for the purposes of valuation. This inflexibility decreases the value of the real option. The maturity of the put option is typically assumed to be lower than the maturity of the real option in order to reflect the time period over which tradability is an important factor, and the strike price is set at the asset value to reflect the ability to sell the asset at its estimated price at a moment's notice.

Often in practice, however, none of these approaches are taken. A simple adjustment is to use the WACC reduced by the risk-free rate as a discount rate for the purposes of valuing the real options in the project. The exact valuation is not of as big importance when comparing multiple projects, as long as we use the same methodology to value each project. In this chapter, for simplicity, we used the risk-free rate for discounting. However, it is important to understand the underlying problems with this assumption.

18.7.2 Volatility

The volatility σ we have been using in real option valuation is the annualized standard deviation of the continuously compounded rate of the return on the underlying asset. As we discussed in section 13.6.2 of Chapter 13, the volatility in financial options can be estimated from observed market prices of financial derivatives. But where do we get such an estimate for the volatility of company projects? One possibility is to use data on the volatility of the company's stock prices (where the volatility is estimated either from historical returns, or from market prices of options on the company's stock), but this volatility is "levered" volatility, that is, it incorporates information about the company's debt-to-equity ratio D/E. Before using it for project valuation purposes, we need to "delever" it. If σ_L is the implied volatility estimated from the company's stock price, we can estimate the "unlevered" volatility σ_U from the following relationship:

$$\sigma_L = (1 + D/E) \cdot \sigma_U$$

What about an estimate for the volatility of a company that is not publicly traded? We can attempt to estimate it by estimating the volatility for similar companies that are publicly traded, but needless to say, this method introduces a lot of subjectivity and inaccuracy into the process.

What about the volatility of nontraded variables that determine the value of projects, such as company sales or the value of a research facility? There is not a good solution. The best approach in general is to use sensitivity analysis to evaluate whether the recommended course of action is sensitive to the current estimate of the volatility. As Moore (2008) said, ". . . real options analysis is hardly an arena for an obsession with precision. Precision can be pushed only so far."

SUMMARY

- Evaluation of capital investment decisions is a dynamic process. Companies typically have the option to change their initial course of action. Options in context of capital investment decisions are referred to as real options (as opposed to financial options).
- Real options enhance investment value because the company has the right, but not the obligation, to take actions in the future. The company can do that because in the future, it will have access to information not available at the time of the original decision.
- Most generally, real options fall into the following categories: option to expand, option to abandon, option to delay, option to choose, option to switch, option for sequential investments.
- There are many similarities between real options and financial options. However, it is also important to keep in mind that models for pricing financial options cannot be automatically translated into models for real option valuation because the assumptions made for pricing financial options do not hold for real options.
- A typical option to expand looks very much like a long position in a classical financial call option. The company has the right, but not the

obligation, to buy an asset in the future if the future estimate of the value of that asset is more than the cost of acquiring it at that time.

- A typical option to abandon looks very much like a long position in a classical financial put option. The company has the right, but not the obligation, to abandon a project (get rid of an asset) if the estimated benefit of continuing the project in the future is less than the estimated cost of continuing with the project.
- Given the similarity between real options and financial options, the Black-Scholes formula and binomial trees are often applied for real option valuation.
- The inputs to real option valuation models, such as volatility and the correct discount rate to use, are difficult to estimate. Sensitivity analysis and simulation are even more important in the real options valuation context.

SOFTWARE HINTS

The tools for valuing real options are similar to the tools for valuing financial options, so we omit specific details about the implementation of the models in this section. For instructions on building binomial trees and evaluating the Black-Scholes formula with Excel and MATLAB, see Chapter 13's Software Hints.

NOTES

1. See section 13.4.2 of Chapter 13.
2. See Chapter 13 and Exhibit 13.1(C).
3. See Chapter 13 and Exhibit 13.1(E).
4. See Chapter 13.
5. See, for example, Dixit and Pindyck (1994).
6. This is a commonly used method in practice. More risky cash flows are discounted at a higher discount rate.
7. Here we used the risk-free rate to discount the cash flows from the option. The issue of what discount rate to use is complex, and we will come back to it in section 18.7.1.
8. Recall from Chapter 13 that the price of a call option increases with the volatility of the process followed by the underlying asset.
9. See section 13.4.1 of Chapter 13.
10. See section 13.4.2 of Chapter 13.
11. See section 17.2.3 of Chapter 17 for a definition of the profitability index.
12. See also Shockley (2007) and Winston (2000).

13. See file **Ch18-OptionToWait.xlsx**.
14. See also Practice 18.1 on the companion web site.
15. See section 13.4.1 of Chapter 13 for explanation of how to build binomial trees, and file **Ch18-RealEstateOption.xlsx** for an implementation of this particular binomial tree.
16. See section 6.1 of Chapter 6.
17. Note that this calculation involves recomputing the binomial tree to determine the value of the option for each scenario for the costs (i.e., in this case, computing 1000 binomial trees).
18. See Hull (2008).
19. See Mun (2006).

References

Abken, P. 2000. An empirical evaluation of value at risk by scenario simulation. *Journal of Derivatives* 7 (4): 12–29.

Adcock, C., and N. Meade. 1994. A simple algorithm to incorporate transaction costs in quadratic optimization. *European Journal of Operational Research* 79 (1): 85–94.

Akesson, F., and J. P. Lehoczky. 2000. Path generation for quasi-monte carlo simulation of mortgage-backed securities. *Management Science* 46 (9): 1171–1187.

Anderson, F., H. Mausser, D. Rosen, and S. Uryasev. 2001. Credit risk optimization with conditional value-at-risk criteria. *Mathematical Programming B* 89: 273–291.

Apelfeld, R., G. B. Fowler, and J. P. Gordon. 1996. Tax-aware equity investing. *Journal of Portfolio Management* 22 (2): 18–28.

Artzner, P., F. Delbaen, J.-M. Eber, and D. Heath. 1999. Coherent measures of risk. *Mathematical Finance* 9 (November): 203–228.

Barra. 1998. *Risk model handbook united states equity: Version 3*. Berkeley, CA: Barra.

Bazaraa, M., H. Sharali, and C. Shetty. 1993. *Nonlinear programming: Theory and algorithms*. New York: John Wiley & Sons.

Beasley, J. D., and S. G. Springer. 1977. The percentage points of the normal distribution. *Applied Statistics* 26: 118–121.

Bellman, R. 1957. *Dynamic programming*. Princeton, NJ: Princeton University Press.

Ben-Tal, A., T. Margalit, and A. Nemirovski. 2000. Robust modeling of multi-stage portfolio problems. In *High-Performance Optimization*, edited by H. Frenk, K. Roos, T. Terlaky, and S. Zhang, pp. 303–328. Dordrecht: Kluwer.

Bertsekas, D. 1995. *Dynamic programming and optimal control*, vols. 1 and 2. Belmont, MA: Athena Scientific.

Bertsimas, D., C. Darnell, and R. Soucy. 1999. Portfolio construction through mixed-integer programming at Grantham, Mayo, Van Otterloo and Company. *Interfaces* 29 (1): 49–66.

Bertsimas, D., and D. Pachamanova. 2008. Robust multiperiod portfolio management with transaction costs. *Computers and Operations Research*, special issue of *Applications of Operations Research in Finance* 35 (1): 3–17.

Bertsimas, D., and J. Tsitsiklis. 1997. *Introduction to linear optimization*. Belmont, MA: Athena Scientific.

Birge, J. 1985. Decomposition and partitioning methods for multistage stochastic linear programs. *Operations Research* 33: 989–1007.

Black, F. 1972. Capital market equilibrium with restricted borrowings. *Journal of Business* 45 (3): 444–455.

Black, F., and R. Litterman. 1992. Global portfolio optimization. *Financial Analysts Journal* 48 (5): 28–43.

Black, F., and M. Scholes. 1973. The pricing of options and corporate liabilities. *Journal of Political Economy* 81 (3): 637–654.

Bogentoft, E., H. E. Romeijn, and S. Uryasev. 2001. Asset/liability management for pension funds using CVaR constraints. *Journal of Risk Finance* (Fall): 57–71.

Box, G. E. P., and M. E. Muller. 1958. A note on the generation of random normal deviates. *Annals of Mathematical Statistics* 29: 610–611.

Boyle, P. 1977. Options: A Monte Carlo approach. *Journal of Financial Economics* 4 (3): 323–338.

Boyle, P., M. Broadie, and P. Glasserman. 1997. Monte Carlo methods for security pricing. *Journal of Economic Dynamics & Control* 21: 1267–1321.

Brandimarte, P. 2006. *Numerical methods in finance and economics.* 2nd ed. Hoboken, NJ: John Wiley & Sons.

Brennan, M. J., and E. S. Schwartz. 1979. A continuous time approach to pricing bonds. *Journal of Banking and Finance* 3 (July): 133–155.

Campbell, J. Y., M. L. Lettau, B. G. Malkiel, and Y. Xu. 2001. Have individual stocks become more volatile? An empirical exploration of idiosyncratic risk. *Journal of Finance* 56 (1): 1–43.

Canuel, D., and C. Melchreit. 1998. Total return Analysis in CMO portfolio management. In *Advances in the valuation and management of mortgage-backed securities,* edited by F. Fabozzi, pp. 41–58. Hoboken, NJ: John Wiley & Sons.

Carino, D., and W. Ziemba. 1998. Formulation of the Russell-Yasuda Kasai financial planning model. *Operations Research* 46 (4): 433–449.

Ceria, S., and R. Stubbs. 2006. Incorporating estimation errors into portfolio selection: Robust portfolio construction. *Journal of Asset Management* 7 (2): 109–127.

Chen, N., R. Roll, and S. A. Ross. 1986. Economic forces and the stock market. *Journal of Business* 59 (July): 383–403.

Chen, X., M. Sim, and P. Sun. 2007. A robust optimization perspective on stochastic programming. *Operations Research* 55 (6): 1058–1107.

Chewlow, L., and C. Strickland. 1998. *Implementing derivatives models.* Chichester: John Wiley & Sons.

Chryssikou, E. 1998. Multiperiod portfolio optimization in the presence of transaction costs. Ph.D. thesis, MIT.

Consigli, G., and M. A. H. Dempster. 1998. Dynamic stochastic programming for asset-liability management. *Annals of Operations Research* 81: 131–161.

Constantinides, G. 1983. Capital market equilibrium with personal taxes. *Econometrica* 51: 611–636.

Copeland, T., and P. Tufano. 2004. A real world way to manage real options. *Harvard Business Review* 82 (3): 90–99.

Cox, J. C., J. E. Ingersoll, and S. A. Ross. 1985. A theory of the term structure of interest rates. *Econometrica* 53: 385–407.

Cox, J. C., S. A. Ross, and M. Rubinstein. 1979. Option pricing: A simplified approach. *Journal of Financial Economics* 7 (3): 229–263.

Cremers, J. H., M. Kritzman, and S. Page. 2003. Portfolio formation with higher moments and plausible utility. Revere Street Working Papers, November 22.

———. 2005. Optimal hedge fund allocations: Do higher moments matter? *Journal of Portfolio Management* 31 (3): 70–81.

Dammon, R. M., and C. S. Spatt. 1996. The optimal trading and pricing of securities with asymmetric capital gains taxes and transaction costs. *Review of Financial Studies* 9 (3): 921–952.

Dammon, R. M., C. S. Spatt, and H. H. Zhang. 2001. Optimal consumption and investment with capital gains taxes. *Review of Financial Studies* 14 (3): 583–617.

———. 2004. Optimal asset location and allocation with taxable and tax-deferred investing. *Journal of Finance* 59 (3): 999–1037.

Danielsson, J., and J.-P. Zigrand. 2001. What happens when you regulate risk? Evidence from a simple general equilibrium model. Memo, London School of Economics.

DiBartolomeo, D. 2000. Recent advances in management of taxable portfolios. Paper, Northfield Information Services.

Disatnik, D. and S. Benninga. 2007. Shrinking the covariance matrix—simpler is better. *Journal of Portfolio Management* 33 (4): 56–63.

Dixit, A. K., and R. S. Pindyck. 1994. *Investment under uncertainty*. Princeton, NJ: Princeton University Press.

Duffie, D., and N. Garleanu. 2001. Risk and valuation of collateralized debt obligations. *Financial Analysts Journal* 57 (1): 41–59.

Evans, J., and D. Olson. 2002. *Introduction to simulation and risk analysis*, 2nd ed. Upper Saddle River, NJ: Prentice Hall.

Evans, J. L., and S. H. Archer. 1968. Diversification and the reduction of dispersion: An empirical analysis. *Journal of Finance* 23 (5): 761–767.

Evans, M., N. Hastings, and B. Peacock. 2000. *Statistical distributions*, 3rd ed. New York: John Wiley & Sons.

Fabozzi, F. J. 1993. *Fixed income mathematics*, New York: McGraw-Hill.

———. (ed.). 2005. *The handbook of mortgage-backed securities*, 6th ed. New York: McGraw-Hill.

———. 2007. *Fixed income analysis*, 2nd ed. Hoboken, NJ: John Wiley & Sons.

———. 2009. *Institutional investment management*. Hoboken, NJ: John Wiley & Sons.

Fabozzi, F. J., A. K. Bhattacharya, and W. S. Berliner. 2007. *Mortgage-backed securities: Products, structuring, and analytical techniques*. Hoboken, NJ: John Wiley & Sons.

Fabozzi, F. J., S. Focardi, and P. Kolm. 2006. *Financial modeling of the equity market*. Hoboken, NJ: John Wiley & Sons.

Fabozzi, F. J., P. Kolm, D. Pachamanova, and S. Focardi. 2007. *Robust portfolio optimization and management*. Hoboken, NJ: John Wiley & Sons.

Fama, E. F. 1965. Portfolio analysis in a stable Paretian market. *Management Science* 11 (3): 404–419.

————. 1970. Efficient capital markets: A review of theory and empirical work. *Journal of Finance* 25 (2): 383–417.

Fama, E. F., and K. French. 1993. Common risk factors in the returns on stocks and bonds. *Journal of Financial Economics* 33: 3–56.

————. 1995. Size and book-to-market factors in earnings and returns. *Journal of Finance* 50: 131–155.

————. 1996. Multifactor explanations of asset pricing anomalies. *Journal of Finance* 51: 55–84.

————. 1998. Value versus growth: The international evidence. *Journal of Finance* 53: 1975–1999.

Faure, H. 1982. Discrépence de suites associées á un systéme de numération (en Simension s). *Acta Arithmetica* 41: 337–351.

Finnerty, J. D. 2008. Real options. Chapter 69 in *Handbook of Finance*, edited by F. Fabozzi, pp. 2:697–2:714. Hoboken, NJ: John Wiley & Sons.

Fishburn, P. 1977. Mean-risk analysis with risk associated with below-target returns. *American Economic Review* 67 (2): 116–126.

Fishman, G. 2006. *A first course in Monte Carlo*. Stamford: CT: Thomson Learning.

Fong, H. G., and O. A. Vasicek. 1984. A risk minimizing strategy for portfolio immunization. *Journal of Finance* 30: 1541–1546.

Fragniere, E., and J. Gondzio. 2005. Stochastic programming from modeling languages. Chapter 7 in *Applications of stochastic programming*, edited by S. Wallace and W. Ziemba, pp. 95–114. Philadelphia, PA: MPS-SIAM Series on Optimization.

Freund, R. 2004. Lecture notes in nonlinear optimization. Unpublished manuscript, MIT Open CourseWare, http://ocw.mit.edu/OcwWeb/Sloan-School-of-Management/15–084JSpring2004/LectureNotes/index.htm.

Glasserman, P. 2004. *Monte Carlo methods in financial engineering*. New York: Springer.

Glasserman, P., P. Heidelberger, and P. Shahabuddin. 2000. Variance reduction techniques for estimating value-at-risk. *Management Science* 46 (10): 1349–1364.

Goldfarb, D., and G. Iyengar. 2003. Robust portfolio selection problems. *Mathematics of Operations Research* 28 (1): 1–38.

Goldman Sachs Asset Management. 2007. *Introduction to mortgage-backed securities and other securitized assets*.

Gordon, M. 1962. *The investment, financing, and valuation of the corporation*. Homewood, IL: Irwin.

Graham, J., and C. R. Harvey. 2002. How do CFOs make capital budgeting and capital structure decisions? *Journal of Applied Corporate Finance* 15 (1): 8–23.

Gulpinar, N., B. Rustem, and R. Settergren. 2004. Simulation and optimization approaches to scenario tree generation. *Journal of Economic Dynamics and Control* 28: 1291–1315.

Halton, J. 1960. On the efficiency of certain quasi-random sequences of points in evaluating multi-dimensional integrals. *Numerische Mathematik* 2: 84–90.

Hammersley, J. 1960. Monte Carlo methods for solving multivariable problems. *Annals of the New York Academy of Sciences* 86: 844–874.

Haug, E. 2007. *The complete guide to option pricing formulas*, 2nd ed. New York: McGraw-Hill.

Haugh, M., and L. Kogan. 2004. Pricing American options: A duality approach. *Operations Research* 52 (2): 258–270.

Hertz, D. B. 1964. Risk analysis in capital investment. *Harvard Business Review* 42 (1): 95–106.

Hillier, R. S., and J. Eckstein. 1993. Stochastic dedication: Designing fixed income portfolios using massively parallel Benders decomposition. *Management Science* 39 (11): 1422–1438.

Ho, Thomas S. Y. 1999. Key rate duration: A measure of interest rate risk exposure. In *Interest Rate risk measurement and management*, edited by S. Nawalkha and D. R. Chambers. New York, NY: Institutional Investors.

Hoppe, R. 1998. VaR and the unreal world. *Risk* (July): 45–50.

Huang, C., and R. Litzenberger. 1988. *Foundations for financial economics*. Englewood Cliffs, NJ: Prentice Hall.

Hull, J. 2008. *Options, futures and other derivatives*, 7th ed. Upper Saddle River, NJ: Prentice Hall.

Ingersoll, J., Jr. 1987. *Theory of financial decision making*. Savage, MD: Rowman and Littlefield.

Jamshidian, F., and Y. Zhu. 1997. Scenario simulation: Theory and methodology. *Finance and Stochastics* 1: 43–67.

———. 2006. Scenario simulation model for fixed income portfolio risk management. In *Advanced bond portfolio management*, edited by F. J. Fabozzi, L. Martellini, and P. Priaulet, pp. 291–310. Hoboken, NJ: John Wiley & Sons.

Jean, W. H. 1971. The extension of portfolio analysis to three or more parameters. *Journal of Financial and Quantitative Analysis* 6 (1): 505–515.

Jones, R. C. 1998. The active versus passive debate: perspectives on an active quant. Chapter 3 in *Active Equity Portfolio Management*, edited by F. J. Fabozzi. New York: John Wiley & Sons.

Jorion, P. 1986. Bayes-Stein estimator for portfolio analysis. *Journal of Financial and Quantitative Analysis* 21 (3): 279–292.

———. 1992. Portfolio optimization in practice. *Financial Analysts Journal* 48 (1): 68–74.

Kahneman, D., and A. Tversky. 1979. Prospect theory: An analysis of decision under risk. *Econometrica* 47 (2): 263–290.

Kalotay, A., D. Yang, and F. J. Fabozzi. 2004. An option-theoretic prepayment model for mortgages and mortgage-backed securities. *International Journal of Theoretical and Applied Finance* 7 (December): 949–978.

Kalvelagen, E. 2003. Benders decomposition for stochastic programming with GAMS. Paper, 17 January. http://www.amsterdamoptimization.com/pdf/stochbenders.pdf.

Khodadadi, A., R. Tutuncu, and P. Zangari. 2006. Optimization and Quantitative Investment Management. *Journal of Asset Management* 7 (2): 83–92.

Konno, H., and H. Yamazaki. 1991. Mean-absolute deviation portfolio optimization model and its applications to the Tokyo stock market. *Management Science* 37 (5): 519–531.

Ledoit, O., and M. Wolf. 2003. Improved estimation of the covariance matrix of stock returns with an application to portfolio selection. *Journal of Empirical Finance* 10 (5): 603–621.

Lee, J.-H., D. Stefek, and A. Zhelenyak. 2006. Robust portfolio optimization—A closer look. Report, *MSCI Barra Research Insights*, June.

Levy, H. 1992. Stochastic dominance and expected utility: survey and analysis. *Management Science* 38 (4): 555–593.

Levy, H., and Y. Kroll. 1978. Ordering uncertain options with borrowing and lending. *Journal of Finance* 33 (2): 553–574.

Levy, H., and H. M. Markowitz. 1979. Approximating expected utility by a function of mean and variance. *American Economic Review* 69 (3): 308–317.

Lintner, J. 1965. The valuation of risk assets and the selection of risky investments in stock portfolio and capital budgets. *Review of Economics and Statistics* 47 (1): 13–37.

Lobo, M. S., M. Fazel, and S. Boyd. 2007. Portfolio optimization with linear and fixed transaction costs. *Annals of Operations Research* 152 (1): 376–394.

Longstaff, F. A., and E. S. Schwartz. 1992. Interest rate volatility and the term structure: A two-factor general equilibrium model. *Journal of Finance* 47 (4): 1259–1282.

———. 2001. Valuing American options by simulation: A simple least-squares approach. *Review of Financial Studies* 14: 113–147.

Maginn, J. L., and D. L. Tuttle (eds.). 1990. *Managing investment portfolios: A dynamic process*, 2nd ed. New York: Warren, Gorham & Lamont.

Malkiel, B. G. 2002. How much diversification is enough? *Proceedings of the AIMR seminar: The Future of the Equity Portfolio Construction* (March): 26–27.

Mandelbrot, B. B. 1963. The variation of certain speculative prices. *Journal of Business* 26: 394–419.

Markowitz, H. 1952. Portfolio selection. *Journal of Finance* 7: 77–91.

———. 1959. *Portfolio selection: Efficient diversification of investments.* New York: John Wiley & Sons.

McLeish, D. 2005. *Monte Carlo simulation and finance.* Hoboken, NJ: John Wiley & Sons.

Merton, R. C. 1976. Option pricing when underlying stock returns are discontinuous. *Journal of Finance* 29: 449–470.

———. 1995. *Continuous-time finance*, rev. ed. Cambridge, MA: Blackwell.

Michaud, R. O. 1998. *Efficient asset management: A practical guide to stock portfolio optimization and asset allocation.* Oxford: Oxford University Press.

Mitchell, J. E., and S. Braun. 2004. Rebalancing an investment portfolio in the presence of convex transaction costs. Technical report, Department of Mathematical Sciences, Rensselaer Polytechnic Institute.

Moore, W. T. 2008. Real options and modern capital investment decisions. Chapter 70 in *Handbook of finance*, edited by F. Fabozzi, pp. 2:715–2:726. Hoboken, NJ: John Wiley & Sons.

Moro, B. 1995. The Full Monte. *Risk* 8 (February): 57–58.

Mossin, J. 1966. Equilibrium in a Capital Asset Market. *Econometrica* 34 (4): 768–783.

Mulvey, J., R. Rush, J. Mitchell, and T. Willemain. 2000. Stratified filtered sampling in stochastic optimization. *Journal of Applied Mathematics and Decision Sciences* 4 (1): 17–38.

Mulvey, J., R. Vanderbei, and S. Zenios. 1995. Robust optimization of large-scale systems. *Operations Research* 43 (2): 264–281.

Natarajan, K., D. Pachamanova, and M. Sim. 2008. Incorporating asymmetric distributional information in robust value-at-risk optimization. *Management Science* 54 (3): 573–585.

Nemhauser, G., and L. Wolsey. 1999. *Integer and combinatorial optimization*. New York: John Wiley & Sons.

Nocera, J. 2009. Risk mismanagement. *New York Times*, January 4.

O'Cinneide, C., B. Scherer, and X. Xu. 2006. Pooling trades in a quantitative investment process. *Journal of Portfolio Management* 32 (4): 33–43.

O'Harrow, R., Jr., and J. Gerth. 2009. Geithner pressed but fell short. *Washington Post*, April 3.

Overbye, D. 2009. They tried to outsmart Wall Street. *New York Times*, March 10.

Peterson, P., and F. Fabozzi. 2002. Traditional fundamental analysis III: Earnings analysis, cash analysis, dividends, and dividend discount models. Chapter 11 in *The theory and practice of investment management*, edited by F. J. Fabozzi and H. M. Markowitz. Hoboken, NJ: John Wiley & Sons.

Pogue, G. 1970. An extension of the Markowitz portfolio selection model to include variable transactions costs, short sales, leverage policies, and taxes. *Journal of Finance* 25 (5): 1005–1027.

Rachev, S. T., S. Mittnik, F. J. Fabozzi, S. M. Focardi, and T. Jai. 2006. *Financial econometrics: From basics to advanced modeling techniques*. Hoboken, NJ: John Wiley & Sons.

Rendleman, R., and B. Bartter. 1979. Two-state option pricing. *Journal of Finance* 34: 1093–1110.

Richard, S., and R. Roll. 1989. Prepayment and the valuation of mortgage-backed securities. *Journal of Portfolio Management* 15: 73–82.

Rockafellar, R. T., and S. Uryasev. 2000. Optimization of conditional value-at-risk. *Journal of Risk* 3: 21–41.

Rockafellar, R. T., and S. Uryasev. 2002. Conditional value-at-risk for general loss distributions. *Journal of Banking and Finance* 26: 1443–1471.

Rogers, L. C. G. 2002. Monte Carlo valuation of American options. *Mathematical Finance* 12: 271–286.

Roman, S. 2002. *Writing Excel macros with VBA*, 2nd ed. Sebastopol, CA: O'Reilly Media, Inc.

Ross, S. A. 1976. The arbitrage theory of capital asset pricing. *Journal of Economic Theory* 16 (December): 343–362.

Roy, A. 1952. Safety-first and the holding of assets. *Econometrica* 20 (3): 431–449.

Ruszczynski, A., and A. Shapiro. 2003. *Stochastic programming, handbook in operations research and management science.* Amsterdam: Elsevier Science.

Sanford, C., and D. Borge. 1993. The Risk Management Revolution. Paper, October. http://www.libs.uga.edu/hargrett/manuscrip/sanford/charles.html.

Scherer, B. 2002. Portfolio resampling: Review and critique. *Financial Analysts Journal* 58 (6): 98–109.

Schreiner, J. 1980. Portfolio revision: A turnover-constrained approach. *Financial Management* 9 (1): 67–75.

Schwartz, E., and W. Torous. 1989. Prepayment and the valuation of mortgage-backed securities. *Journal of Finance* 44: 375–392.

Sharpe, W. F. 1963. A simplified model for portfolio analysis. *Management Science* 9 (January): 277–293.

———. 1964. Capital asset prices. *Journal of Finance* 19 (3): 425–442.

———. 1978. *Investments.* Englewood Cliffs, NJ: Prentice-Hall.

———. 1994. The Sharpe ratio. *Journal of Portfolio Management* 21 (1): 49–58.

Shokley, R. L., Jr. 2007. *An applied course in real options valuation.* Mason, OH: Thomson South-Western.

Siegel, L. 2003. *Benchmarks and investment management,* Charlottesville, VA: Research Foundation of AIMR.

Smit, H. T. J. 1997. Investment analysis of offshore concessions in the Netherlands. *Financial Management* 26 (Summer): 5–17.

Sobol, I. 1967. The distribution of points in a cube and the approximate evaluation of integrals. *USSR Computational Mathematics and Mathematical Physics* 7 (4): 86–112.

Spearman, C. 1904. General intelligence, objectively determined and measured. *American Journal of Psychology* 15: 201–293.

Stein, D. M. 1998. Measuring and evaluating portfolio performance after taxes. *Journal of Portfolio Management* 24 (2): 117–124.

Stubbs, R., and P. Vance. 2005. Computing return estimation error matrices for robust optimization. Report, Axioma.

Taleb, N. 1997a. The World According to Nassim Taleb. *Derivatives Strategy* 2 (December–January): 37–40.

———. 1997b. Against VaR. *Derivatives Strategy* 2 (April): 21–26.

———. 2007. *The black swan: The impact of the highly improbable.* New York: Random House.

Titman, S. 1985. Urban land prices under uncertainty. *American Economic Review* 75 (3): 505–513.

Tobin, J. 1958. Liquidity preference as a behavior towards risk. *Review of Economic Studies* 67 (February): 65–86.

Tsitsiklis, J., and B. Van Roy. 1999. Optimal stopping of markov processes: Hilbert space theory, approximation algorithms, and an application to pricing high-dimensional financial derivatives. *IEEE Transactions on Automatic Control* 44: 1840–1851.

———. 2001. Regression methods for pricing complex American-style options. *IEEE Transactions on Neural Networks* 12: 694–703.

Vasicek, O. 1977. An equilibrium characterisation of the term structure. *Journal of Financial Economics* 5: 177–188.

Volpert, V. E. 1997. Managing indexed and enhanced indexed bond portfolios. In *Managing fixed income portfolios*, edited by F. J. Fabozzi, pp. 191–211. New York: John Wiley & Sons.

Walkenbach, J. 2004. *Excel 2003 power programming with VBA*. Hoboken, NJ: John Wiley & Sons.

Wallace, S., and W. Ziemba. 2005. *Applications of stochastic programming*. Philadelphia, PA: MPS-SIAM Series on Optimization.

Williams, J. 1938. *The theory of investment value*. Cambridge, MA: Harvard University Press.

Winston, W. 2000. *Financial models using simulation and optimization*, vols. 1 and 2. Newfield, NY: Palisade Corporation.

Yu, L., X. Ji, and S. Wang. 2003. Stochastic programming models in financial optimization: A survey. Paper, http://en.scientificcommons.org/42910402.

Zenios, S., and P. Kang. 1993. Mean-absolute deviation portfolio optimization for mortgage-backed securities. *Annals of Operations Research* 45: 433–450.

Ziemba, W. T. 2003. *The stochastic programming approach to asset, liability, and wealth management*. Charlottesville, VA: CFA Institute.

Ziemba, W. T., and J. M. Mulvey (eds.). 1998. *Worldwide asset and liability modeling*. Cambridge: Cambridge University Press.

Index

CPSIA information can be obtained at www.ICGtesting.com
Printed in the USA
BVOW08*0105230714

360125BV00001B/1/P

9 780470 371893